This Is Who We Were:
In The 1950s

This Is Who We Were:
In The 1950s

Based on material from Grey House Publishing's
Working American Series by Scott Derks

Grey House
Publishing

PUBLISHER:	Leslie Mackenzie
EDITORIAL DIRECTOR:	Laura Mars
ASSOCIATE EDITOR:	Diana Delgado
PRODUCTION MANAGER:	Kristen Thatcher
MARKETING DIRECTOR:	Jessica Moody
COMPOSITION:	David Garoogian

Grey House Publishing, Inc.
4919 Route 22
Amenia, NY 12501
518.789.8700
FAX 845.373.6390
www.greyhouse.com
e-mail: books @greyhouse.com

While every effort has been made to ensure the reliability of the information presented in this publication, Grey House Publishing neither guarantees the accuracy of the data contained herein nor assumes any responsibility for errors, omissions or discrepancies. Grey House accepts no payment for listing; inclusion in the publication of any organization, agency, institution, publication, service or individual does not imply endorsement of the editors or publisher.

Errors brought to the attention of the publisher and verified to the satisfaction of the publisher will be corrected in future editions.

Publisher's Cataloging-In-Publication Data
(Prepared by The Donohue Group, Inc.)

Derks, Scott.
    This is who we were : in the 1950s / by Scott Derks. — [1st ed.]

    443 p. : ill., maps ; cm.

    Includes bibliographical references and index.
    ISBN: 978-1-61925-179-3

    1. United States—Economic conditions—1945- 2. United States-Social conditions—1945- 3. United States—Civilization—1945- 4. United States—History—1945-1953. 5. United States—History—1953-1961. 6. Nineteen fifties. I. Title.

HC106.5 .D47 2013
330.973

TABLE OF CONTENTS

Section One: Profiles

This section contains 34 profiles of individuals and families living and working in the 1950s. It examines their lives at home, at work, and in their neighborhoods. Based upon historic materials, personal interviews, and diaries, the profiles give a sense of what it was like to live in the years 1950 to 1959.

Section Two: Historical Snapshots

This section includes lists of important "firsts" for America, from technical advances and political events to new products and top selling books. Combining serious American history with fun facts, these snapshots present, in chronological categories, an easy-to-read overview of what happened in the 1950s.

Section Three: Economy of the Times

This section looks at a wide range of economic data, including food, clothing, transportation, housing and other selected prices, with reprints of actual advertisements for products and services of the time. It includes figures for the following categories, plus a valuable year-by-year listing of the value of a dollar.

Section Four: All Around Us—What We Saw, Wrote, Read & Listened To

This section includes reprints of newspaper and magazine articles, speeches, and others items designed to help readers focus on what was on the minds of Americans in the 1950s. These printed pieces show how popular opinion was formed, and how American life was affected.

Section Five: Census Data

This section includes state-by-state comparative tables and a U.S. Census study that summarizes demographic trends 1990–2000.

ESSAY ON THE 1950s

America the Great

As the 1950s began, optimism was everywhere, and there was much to be optimistic about. The average American enjoyed an income 15 times greater than that of the average foreigner. The vast majority of families considered themselves middle class, many were enjoying the benefits of health insurance for the first time, and everyone knew someone who owned a television set.

The consequences of WW II included industries infused with energy and confidence, plans for interstate highways, hydroelectric dams to power America, and many new national brands. America was manufacturing half the world's products, 57 percent of the steel, 43 percent of the electricity, and 62 percent of the oil. The economies of Europe and Asia lay in ruins, while America's industrial and agricultural structure were untouched and primed to supply the goods needed by a war-weary world.

In 1954, the Dow Jones Industrial Average regained enough strength to top the highs achieved before the stock market crash of 1929, and the war years' high employment and optimism spurred the longest sustained period of peacetime prosperity in the nation's history. A decade of full employment and pent-up desire produced demands for all types of consumer goods, and businesses of all sizes and specialties prospered.

This economic prosperity also ushered in conservative politics and social conformity. Tidy lawns, "proper" suburban homes, and buttoned-down sexual attitudes were "in" in the 1950s. A virtual revival of Victorian respectability and domesticity reigned, resulting in a drop in divorce rates and female college attendance, and a rise in birth rates and the sale of Bibles. Corporate America promoted the benefits of respectable men in gray flannel suits whose wives remained at home to tend house, enjoy ladies clubs, and raise children. It's interesting to note that the decade also witnessed lots of a newly marketed product known as tranquilizers, whose sales were astounding.

The average wage earner benefited more from the booming industrial system than at any time in American history. The 40-hour work week became standard in manufacturing. In offices many workers were becoming accustomed to a 35-hour week. Health benefits for workers became more common and paid vacations were standard in most industries. In 1950, 25 percent of American wives worked outside the home and by 1959, the number had risen to 40 percent. Communications technology, expanding roads, and inexpensive airline tickets meant that people and commerce were no longer prisoners of distance. It wasn't all rosy, however; in the midst of this prosperity, up to one-third of the population lived below the government's poverty level.

Let's Get Specific

In addition to profiling regular working folks from all classes, backgrounds and regions, some families profiled in this edition tell their story about life in the 1950s based on a specific environment. A number of families speak from the following reference points, offering another, more specific, slice of 1950 America.

Immigration: During this time Congress established the modern-day U.S. immigration system which included a quota system that imposed limits on a per-country basis and a preference system that gave priority to family members and people with special skills. This was followed by the Refugee Relief Acts of 1953 and 1954 that authorized the admission of another 200,000 refugees from war-torn Europe and escapees from Communist-dominated countries. During the next 40 years of the Cold War, America would remain preoccupied with immigrants and refugees from Communist regimes.

Sports: At the beginning of the 1950s, the most significant sports in America were major league baseball and collegiate football. By the end of the decade the National Football League was a major force, the National Basketball Association was stable and attracting rabid fans, and the Professional Golf Association was inspiring weekend golfers to join "Arnie's Army" on the golf course. Athletics was viewed as an effective counterweight to the threat of godless communism for a nation in the midst of a Cold War. Participation in Little League Baseball, Pop Warner football, and Biddy Basketball rose dramatically for boys. Girls suffered, however, from the newfound belief that they could not directly benefit from sports participation.

Music: America's music reflected the country's newfound prosperity and sense of place. Jazz became cool, symphony orchestras bloomed in major cities, and by the mid-50s, songs by Elvis Presley, Fats Domino, and Little Richard were broadcast into homes, car radios and juke boxes across America. At the same time, television was altering the definition of celebrity.

Education: Much of American's energy was focused on the potential of its children. Education reform at the elementary, high school and college levels was intensely debated. Dozens of television programs geared toward children were created and toys to expand the child's mind were in vogue.

The Cold War between the United States and the Soviet Union spawned demands for more science and math. The expanding role of the federal government was also felt after the Supreme Court ruled to desegregate schools "with all possible speed." Americans debated the need for a mandatory one-year universal service for all youth, while educators once again proposed that the nation's superior students receive a more demanding curriculum—overtly allowing schools to be a social sorting machine focused on meeting the employment needs of American corporations.

At War: As World War II drew to a close, America pushed East to free Europe from Nazi rule, while the Soviet Union advanced West. The geographic point at which the U.S. and the U.S.S.R. met in Berlin was to have a profound effect on Europe for over four decades. The Soviet Union claimed the east side of Berlin, and eventually built the Berlin Wall, while closing off most of Eastern Europe behind an imaginary "Iron Curtain."

The far-reaching consequence of this "remapping" of the globe between Soviet Russia and the West—between communism and capitalism—was the Cold War. Government policies were rewritten according to the difference in philosophy between the U.S. and the U.S.S.R. and, it seemed, no conflict could occur anywhere in the world without involving either of these two superpowers in some way. Americans became obsessed with the threat of the atomic bomb, the need for building fallout shelters, and the weeding out of suspected communists.

One final note: Although *This Is Who We Were: In The 1950s* includes profiles that take the reader deep into the specifics of the topics outlined above, there are also stories of working, middle and upper class families, as well as of the kid next door, all told in their own words. From the telephone company lineman in 1950 to the young women who led her hospital coworkers in a labor strike, this "history from the bottom up" approach makes for interesting—and memorable—reading.

INTRODUCTION

This Is Who We Were: In The 1950s is an offspring of our 13-volume *Working Americans* series, which was devoted, volume by volume, to Americans by class, occupation, or social cause. This new edition is devoted to one decade—the 1950s.

It represents all classes, dozens of occupations, and all regions of the country. This comprehensive look at the decade in America when optimism was high and confidence strong, presents American history through the eyes and ears of everyday Americans, not the words of historians or politicians.

This Is Who We Were: In The 1950s presents 34 family profiles—their life at home, at work, and in their community—with lots of photos and images of the time. The stories are told through the eyes and ears of everyday Americans, some struggling and some successful.

Together with the profiles, the sections outlined below present a complete picture of what it was like to live in America in the 1950s, from the immigrant just learning the ropes, to a physician whose family lived a comfortable middle class life in Southern comfort to the heiress to a family fortune.

Section One: Profiles

Each of 34 profiles in Section One begins with a brief introduction that anchors the text to the decade. Then, each profile is arranged in three categories: Life at Home; Life at Work; Life in the Community. The detailed Table of Contents that precedes this Introduction give specifics about jobs and geographic region.

Section Two: Historical Snapshots

Section Two is made up of three long, bulleted lists—and what significant lists they are! In chronological order—Early 1950s, Mid 1950s and Late 1950s—these include an amazing range of firsts and turning points in American history, from the debut of the *Peanuts* comic strip to the Vietnam War's first American casualties.

Section Three: Economy of the Times

One of the most interesting things about researching an earlier time is learning how much things cost and what people earned. This section offers this information in spades. Each of three categories—Consumer Expenditures, Annual Income of Selected Jobs, and Selected Prices—offers actual figures from three years—1953, 1955, and 1958—for easy comparison and study.

Also included is a *Value of a Dollar Index* that compares the burying power of $1.00 in 2010 to the buying power of $1.00 in every year prior, back to 1860, helping to put the economic data in *This Is Who We Were: In The 1950s* into context.

Section Four: All Around Us

There is no better way to put your finger on the pulse of a country than to read its magazines and newspapers. This section offers 33 original pieces—articles, book excerpts and speeches—that influenced Americans who lived in the 1950s.

Section Five: Census Data

This section includes two elements, both invaluable in helping to define the times in which the families in Section One lived:

- 16 State-by-State comparative tables that rank data from the 1950, 1960, and 2010 census. Topics include: Population, Education, Housing, Home Value, and Rent.

- Demographic Trends in the 20th Century—a study by the U.S. Census of four topics: Population, Age, Race, and Housing, chock full of charts, graphs and maps.

This Is Who We Were: In The 1950s ends with a comprehensive Bibliography, arranged by topic, and a detailed Index.

Phone Company Veteran

The Duncans lived in St. Louis, Missouri in 1950. Ed was 50 years old and worked as a lineman for the telephone company. After 30 years, he made $3,880 a year and was at the top of his pay scale. His wife Gina never worked outside the home, putting her energy first into raising their two children and then into enjoying their grandchildren, a common lifestyle for married women in the 1950s.

Life at Home

- The Duncans purchased a five-room home in their neighborhood near the airport to control the rapidly rising cost of housing rent.
- Following the war, housing demands rose quickly as soldiers took advantage of the GI Bill to buy homes, attend college, and start families.
- The neighborhood was a mix of young couples with small children and older couples who lived in the area for 30 years.
- The family's overall cost of housing, including taxes, life insurance, and household expenses rose 10 percent since 1947.
- The Duncan's food costs included two meals outside the home per month, costing approximately $25.00; often this included a night out with their grandchildren, who lived nearby.
- Their two daughters both graduated from high school and married men who fought in World War II; one son-in-law obtained some college training under the GI Bill before going to work at a glass factory.
- Under the GI Bill, the Veteran's Administration paid $500.00 a year toward all tuition and books, plus a monthly subsistence allowance of $85.00 a month.
- Ed and his family had an automobile and two radios, but no television or air-conditioning.
- The grandchildren had a Mr. Potato Head to play with at grandmother's house; Mr. Potato Head, an overnight success, proved the power of television, becoming the first toy ever advertised on TV.
- The grandchildren wanted grandmother to redo her kitchen in pink—the in color at the time, from prize fighter Sugar Ray Robinson's 1950 Cadillac to the sports coats worn by young men.
- The Duncan didn't have a telephone until the 1940s, even though Ed worked for the telephone company; in many working class families, an automobile was considered more important than a phone.

Gina Duncan's grandchildren lived nearby and visited often.

Eloise book

Dr. Seuss book

Tonka pickup truck

Erector Set

Mr. Potato Head

The Duncans loved watching the St. Louis Cardinals.

- Ed and Gina followed the local professional baseball team, the St. Louis Cardinals and their favorite player was Stan Musial.
- They couldn't afford season tickets, but went to the ballgame at least a half-dozen times each year; many summer nights were spent on the porch listening to the St. Louis Cardinal's games on the radio.
- Gina was a great letter writer and often corresponded with friends who moved from St. Louis, paying $0.03 postage for a first class letter.
- Both Ed and Gina voted for Harry Truman in 1948, proud that a "man from Missouri" was in the White House.

Life at Work: The Telephone Company

- In the early days of telephone, telephone poles had eight to 10 cross arms, all holding open telephone wires in an attempt to keep the wires untangled during St. Louis's frequent storms.
- Telephone linemen were considered a hardy lot, working through emergencies and bad weather to restore service.
- Ed, like most linemen, was physically strong, capable of climbing the pole with nothing supporting him but the spurs of the climbing irons dug into the pole and the strength of his arms grasping the pole.
- Once in the desired position on the pole, he hung on with one arm, unhooked the safety strap from the belt, threw it around the pole, and rehooked it into the ring on the belt—a task that required considerable strength and coordination.
- Climbing tall poles at night in a snowstorm often led to injury, and typically linemen found it difficult to obtain life insurance unless they lied about their occupation.
- Ed's job included maintenance such as replacing broken glass insulators on the poles, repairing broken wire, and splicing cables.
- After 30 years on the job, Ed helped train young men on the poles, often climbing poles himself to demonstrate his skills.
- Ed's benefits included a two-week, paid vacation, and eight paid holidays a year.
- For the past three years he also received a Christmas cash bonus.
- St. Louis started moving away from open lines in the late 1940s, and more telephone lines were buried underground.

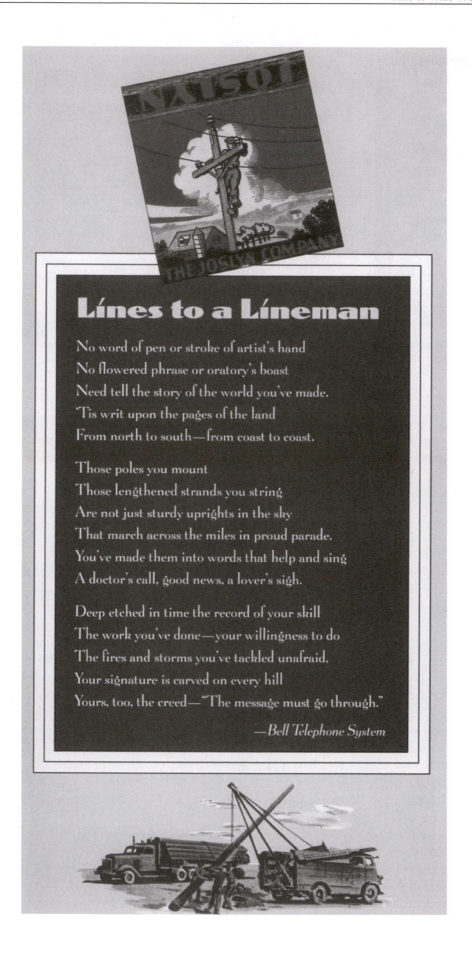

Lines to a Lineman

No word of pen or stroke of artist's hand
No flowered phrase or oratory's boast
Need tell the story of the world you've made.
'Tis writ upon the pages of the land
From north to south—from coast to coast.

Those poles you mount
Those lengthened strands you string
Are not just sturdy uprights in the sky
That march across the miles in proud parade.
You've made them into words that help and sing
A doctor's call, good news, a lover's sigh.

Deep etched in time the record of your skill
The work you've done—your willingness to do
The fires and storms you've tackled unafraid.
Your signature is carved on every hill
Yours, too, the creed—"The message must go through."

—*Bell Telephone System*

Life in the Community: St. Louis, Missouri

- When Ed was born in 1900, the population of St. Louis was 575,238; 50 years later, the population of the city was 856,796, with 1.5 million in the metro area.
- The 1904 World's Fair opened in St. Louis.
- St. Louis was struggling with growth and corruption at the turn of the century and earned the title of America's worst-governed city.
- In 1916 "Negro segregation ordinances" were passed by heavy majority of the electorate.
- In 1923 the school board of St. Louis added a pig and a cow to the municipal zoo because so many children had never seen either animal.
- In 1925 the pride of the city, the St. Louis Cardinals, was in the World Series.
- In 1931 the mayor ordered construction of a municipal auditorium to provide unemployment relief.
- In 1937 the deepening industrial smoke crisis sparked a smoke abatement crusade, resulting in the banning of cheap, impure coal in the city, often brought in from nearby southern Illinois.
- In 1950 St. Louis was one of the 10 largest cities in America, boasting "strategic location, its favorable transportation facilities, the character and diversification of its industries, and its wholesale and retail trade."

St. Louis was located on the Mississippi River.

The Telephone and Telephone Industry

- Shortly after Alexander Graham Bell created the first "dual" lecture in 1877 using telephone lines, St. Louis, Chicago, San Francisco, Albany, and Philadelphia all opened central telephone exchanges; the leasing fee for a phone that year was $100.00.
- Initially the phone company owned all phones and "rented only to persons of good breeding and refinement," an early advertisement reminded customers.
- The yellow pages arrived in 1883 when a printer in Cheyenne, Wyoming, ran out of white paper and used the nearest ream of paper, which happened to be yellow; the customers loved it and the phone book evolved.

- Between 1880 and 1893 the number of telephones in the United States grew from 60,000 (1 per 1,000 people) to about 260,000 (1 per 250 people).
- In 1891 the New York and New Jersey Telephone Company served 7,322 commercial customers, including 937 physicians and hospitals, 401 drug stores, 363 liquor stores, 315 livery stables, 162 metalworking plants, 146 lawyers, 126 contractors, 100 printing shops, and only 1,422 residences - mostly the homes of doctors or business owners.
- By 1900, when Alexander Graham Bell's original patent expired, 6,000 new independent telephone companies sprang up nationwide, with several established in St. Louis, offering a 10-party line to customers for $21.50 a year.
- The working class often shared phones with neighbors or used telephones at the local drug stores, as most did not have telephone service in their homes.
- The invention was not universally loved; many businessmen were hesitant to replace the telegraph with the telephone because they valued having a written record.
- Teddy Roosevelt disliked the telephone and used it only in extreme emergencies; Woodrow Wilson hated it and instructed the operators not to ring him; Herbert Hoover was the first president to have a telephone on his desk.
- Dwight Eisenhower was so accustomed to phone service from military and White House operators that he did not know how to use a dial phone when he left the White House in 1960.
- From the turn of the century to 1925 the numbers of telephones and automobiles in America were about even; after 1925 automobiles took a commanding lead.

- By 1930, 60 percent of American families had automobiles, 41 percent had telephones; a connection from one phone to another took six seconds; nationally 36 percent of Bell subscribers shared a two-party line, while 27 percent shared a four-party line.
- Henry Dreyfuss designed the 300 Desk Set Series phone in 1937; the 10 finger holes were clearly marked with letters in red and numbers in black, and the phone itself was available only in black.
- When the 500 series arrived in 1949, it was "the very model of post-war modernity: low-slung and accessible, it hugged the table like a Studebaker hugged the road. Its cord was coiled, its volume adjustable, its classic body an engineering feat."
- In 1954 consumers still could not buy their own telephones, but were able to choose the color from a limited range.

Post-War America

- In 1950 the United States was completing its transition to a peacetime economy.
- The wealth of America was leveling—by 1950 the percentage of total personal income held by the top five percent stood at 21.4 percent vs. in 1930 when the top five percent held 30 percent.
- Military spending was pumping millions into the economy; 10 percent of all goods and consumer services in the United States (about half of the federal budget) went to the armed forces.
- Births rose sharply after the war, reaching 3.6 million in 1950 and 4.3 million in 1960.
- Slightly better than half of all non-farm homes were owned in 1950.
- A worker in 1950, working a 40-hour week, was considered three times more productive than his grandfather in 1910, working a 72-hour week.
- In 1950, 74 percent of 16-year-olds were in school, up from 43 percent 40 years earlier.

- Unlike early in the century, when working class families sent their teenage children to work in factories, most teenage children remained in school in the early 1950s, when finishing high school was a sign of joining the middle class.
- Wives in the labor force increased dramatically since the war, and many became accustomed to working, and did not wish to return to full-time homemaking.

Clarence Day, Life with Father, 1948:
The Impact of the Telephone...

Mother agreed with Father-she didn't like telephones either. She distrusted machines of all kinds; they weren't human, they popped or exploded and made her nervous. She never knew what they might do to her. And the telephone seemed to her, and many other people, especially dangerous. They were afraid that if they stood near one in a thunderstorm they might get hit by lightning. Even if there wasn't any storm, the electric wiring might give them a shock. When they saw a telephone in some hotel or office, they stood away from it or picked it up gingerly. It was a freak way to use electricity, and mother wouldn't even touch the queer toy. Besides, she said, she had to see the face of any person she talked to. She didn't want to be answered by a voice coming out of a box on the way.

The Use and Care of Pole Climbing Equipment: A Field Manual

It is hazardous to stand at the foot of a pole while a lineman is working above, ascending or descending. Warn all persons, especially children, to keep away for the following reasons:

1. He may drop tools

2. He may dislodge splinters and chips

3. A lineman's gaff may cut off

A second lineman, preparing to ascend, should always wait until the first has reached the working position and placed his safety strap. In descending, one lineman should remain in his work area until the other has reached the ground. If possible on poles which are wet or on which there is snow or ice, climb with the gaffs engaging the slippery side of the pole in order that the hands may engage the drier side and reduce the hazard of slipping.

Pins, crossarm braces, insulators, and hardware other than pole straps do not furnish a safe support as they may pull loose or break. The gloved hands may be cut on such devices that may be rough or broken. Do not use this equipment for support by the hands or for attachment of the safety strap.

She snatched up the shirt and looked at each new button. There was a fleck of lipstick on every thread

But, Genie, they say you should be a little bit jealous . . . . It keeps you on your toes . . .

Perfect Wife?

ON THE hot stone terrace outside her cool stone house, Genie Bingham sat cross-legged on a yellow chaise, one finger pressed into her cheek, and smiled. The musical sounds of dishes being washed by somebody else came from the kitchen, but that was not why she smiled. Her legs were a beautiful copper although it was only July, but that was not why she smiled.

Medium pretty, medium tall, she had been a medium-good student in school with a B average, but she had just this minute received a score of one hundred in a quiz entitled "How Good a Wife Are You?" And so she smiled to herself with delight and satisfaction.

To be sure, she had awarded herself the score—but with meticulous honesty. She had just finished adding it and she was amazed. Now she turned to the front of the magazine to check the questions and make sure she had been absolutely fair.

Some of the questions had required no hesitation, those on grooming, cooking and getting along with her in-laws. Did she nag? Frequent requests for that shelf over the kitchen stove could not be considered nagging. She had needed that shelf ever [continued on page 41]

BY NAOMI HINTZE ILLUSTRATOR: CLYDE ROSS

Former Slave and Proud Matriarch

Born as a slave on a plantation in South Carolina, Ida Davis was the proud matriarch or four generations. She lived for over 70 years in the same cabin she and her husband built when they were married. Despite her strong desire for her children to get the best education possible, Ida wasn't sure how she felt about integration in the schools, a concept beginning to take hold in 1951.

Life at Home

- Ida Davis was old, but not exactly sure of her age, so she told her friends she was 88.
- Born as a slave on the Davis Plantation in Pine Tree Bluff, South Carolina, Ida lived on the same property, in only two houses, her entire life.
- The first was the wood cabin in which she was born. She lived there until she was 16, when she married Columbus Davis, known as Boy-Boy.
- They built a cabin together on the Davis Plantation, where she lived ever since.
- Neither house had running water or an indoor bathroom.
- Electricity arrived in 1940, thanks to the rural electrical cooperatives that brought service to the farm regions of the state.
- Ida and Boy-Boy had 14 children, 10 of whom lived to adulthood.
- Over time, eight of their children moved away—one to New York, three to Baltimore, two to Columbia, SC and two to Sumter, SC.
- One child moved to the nearby town of Summerton, while the oldest child, known as Junior, sharecropped with his daddy in Pine Tree Bluff.

- Today, Ida has 56 grandchildren and more great- and great-great-grand children than nearly anyone can count, except for Ida.
- She meticulously created a set of scrapbooks, dedicating a page or two for each great grandchild using pictures, locks of hair and other memorabilia to honor every birth.
- Her favorite leisure activity, after churchgoing, is to look at her "sweet memory" books, or listen while her children read her letters or the newspaper clippings stored in the books.
- Born during the Civil War, Ida never learned to read or write; times were hard and schools few for the former slave children of the Reconstruction South, when Ida was a girl.
- Following a lifelong habit, Ida listened hard and remembered well when the Bible, letters and articles were read aloud.

Ida Davis was the matriarch of several generations.

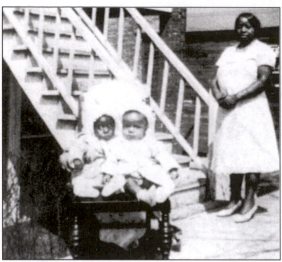

Ida's family visited her often.

- Ida placed great stock in the belief that education is the key to lifting the Negro out of poverty.
- She was proud that all of her children stayed in school until at least the eighth grade; two even graduated high school, as have many of the grandchildren.
- Many of the grandchildren, who were raised in the North, returned to Summerton to raise their children and live near the family matriarch.
- Ida was particularly focused on the progress of the great-grandchildren who were drafted into the newly racially integrated army to fight in Korea.
- She was almost beside herself with joy that one of the great-grands was accepted at the new law school for Negroes in nearby Orangeburg, SC.
- Having one of the family on the verge of becoming a lawyer ranked alongside the moment her grandson Zebulon became a minister, or when the first of several granddaughters became teachers.
- Most of the family up North had jobs in industry, a couple worked as domestics, two sons in Baltimore owned a grocery together, and one son was a porter on the railroad.
- Though she never considered herself an activist, Ida was always been keenly interested in seeing that the members of her community had opportunity and education.

Life at Work: Midwife

- Ida Davis was trained by her aunt as a midwife, and for more than 60 years she cared for most of the black babies and many of the white ones born in her part of the county.
- Her family insisted she "retire" on her eightieth birthday.
- The family offered to build her a brick home with electricity, running water and a septic system, but she figured that the little unpainted frame house where she spent the last 72 years had too many happy memories to move away from.
- The house started out with a large main room and a small bedroom, and two other bedrooms were added over time, one for the boys and one for the girls.
- The living room was neatly wallpapered with the covers of *Life* magazine, a project of many years in which Boy-Boy took great pride.
- One of the former bedrooms was where she made quilts, and was filled with cloth scraps that family members brought whenever they visited.
- All the descendants came to expect a Mama Ida quilt on their sixteenth birthday.
- She said that she was too old to sew anymore and will stop soon, but her family knew that when she stopped, her last breath would be near.
- She went to the Mt. Hebron Methodist Church where her grandboy Zeb preached.
- He often complained, only half in jest, that she knew the Bible better than he did, even though she couldn't read.
- Years of careful listening made an impression.
- When Ida was in her forties, she was so active in the church, the congregation asked her to represent them at a church convention in Little Rock, Arkansas.
- She traveled by train and was quite proud of going, but never accepted another call by the church to travel that far again.
- The unfamiliar places and names were just too hard to comprehend without knowing how to read.

- Her illiteracy also prevented her from voting, although she knew of many neighbors who could read, but were prevented from voting by draconian "literacy" and poll taxes.
- In her part of the state, it cost $2.00 to vote in a local or national election.

- Just a couple of years before, South Carolina's governor, Strom Thurmond, ran for president on the States' Rights ticket, promising to preserve segregation.
- Still, things were are better now than they were earlier in the century when the Ku Klux Klan ran rampant.
- During those days, one of her sons-in-law was lynched. The newspaper ran a picture of the lynch mob with his body and the photographer tried to sell prints of the lynching for $2.00 plus postage.
- No one was ever punished, and no trial ever held.
- Over the years, many of her family members were threatened and harassed by the Klan and less formal groups.
- By and large, however, white people treated Ida well over the years, especially the women whose babies she delivered.
- Five years ago, after her husband Boy-Boy died, the Davises, the white family still in possession of the plantation, paid his medical bills.
- She kept a garden beside her house, although the grandchildren and great grandchildren did most of the work.
- Depending on the season, she grew corn, okra, tomatoes, cucumbers, collards, mustard and turnip greens, lima beans, field peas and peanuts.
- When peanuts were in season, Ida had a kettle of them boiling in the yard whenever large numbers of young guests were expected.
- Ida was known countywide for her boiled peanuts.
- Until electricity came to the area, vegetables had to be used quickly.
- Since electricity, they were stored in the refrigerators and freezers of nearby relatives in the area, which helped feed the family in winter, when food was scarce.
- Fall was Ida's favorite time of year.
- During September, October and often November, she sat in a chair Boy-Boy made for her, located just outside the door of her home, and smoked her hand-carved pipe.
- It made her feel close to Boy-Boy and the life they had together.
- She liked to sit and look at pictures, and her favorite was of her and Boy-Boy pretending to drive Mr. Davis's car.
- The porch chair was also a great place to watch for the old Ford truck that belonged to her grandgirl Lucasta's husband Tom.
- They regularly brought Ida a meal that included steaming greens and cornbread, along with a mess of children who demanded Ida's loving attention.

Ida and Boy Boy liked pretending to drive Mr. Davis's car.

Life in the Community: Summerton, South Carolina

- The Summerton community was in an uproar when the school district refused to buy a school bus to transport black kids to their school.

- Every school morning, the whites' school bus rolled past black children walking several miles to the colored, segregated school.
- Nationally, a movement was started to integrate the schools, Ida's children told her.
- The National Association for the Advancement of Colored People (NAACP) was determined to fight the issue in the courts.
- Ida was not sure how she felt about this.
- She knew she wanted her family to receive the best education, but she also believed that the Lord made the races different for a reason.
- When school integration talk started, one local gas station and store posted signs reading, "No Nigger or Negro allowed inside building."

Talk of school integration encouraged racism.

- Another sign read, "Negros not wanted in the North or South. Send them back to Africa where God Almighty put them to begin with. That is their home."
- With the backing of the NAACP, 20 parents of black schoolchildren filed a lawsuit on May 16, 1950—*Briggs v. Elliott*—challenging the unequal treatment of their children.

GI-Bill Navy Enlistee

Under the slogan "Where the Fleet Goes, We've Been," Edwin Sherman Webber from California became a navy crewman in 1951, fresh out of high school. Anti-Communist sentiment was strong in American and Edwin was proud to fight the Communists in Korea aboard a minesweeper, a tiny wooden shop critical to the naval assault.

Life at Home

- When Ed Webber learned he was going into the navy, his head was filled with dynamic destroyers and elegant, super ship carriers, not being assigned to a minesweeper in Korea.
- In fact, when he finished high school in Salinas, California, he wasn't even sure where Korea was, but hoped that going into the navy would impress his girlfriend Jane.
- Ed grew up in a small house in a new development outside Salinas that was flooded with kids to play with.
- In Ed's junior year in high school, his father, who worked on road construction, was made foreman of a large grading crew.
- Ed's father was a smart, proud man who understood math and how to make a crew work hard, but he could barely read; his mother was a part-time beautician.
- Ed's parents were determined that all five children finish high school, because they believed that working class kids who were educated could be rich one day.
- Starting in the ninth grade, Ed worked afternoons and summers at a neighborhood grocery.

Edwin Webber grew up in a middle class neighborhood.

- Enlisting in the navy was his ticket to the GI Bill and college.
- Ed failed his first physical due to being underweight and having high blood pressure.
- The doctor told him: "Go home, eat a lot of bananas, drink lots of milk and take some tranquilizers."
- He did as he was told, and was accepted on the second try.

Life at Work: Minesweeper

- Minesweeping was not what Ed had been promised upon enlisting, but that's what he got.
- Although it was dangerous and not a desired assignment, it did earn Ed a regular paycheck.
- During training, Ed found out just how dangerous—no amphibious landing is undertaken until the minesweepers found and disarmed all the mines in the area.
- Upon completion of his final training course, he took a short leave and married Jane before he shipped out to the Far East.

War, Sea, Death for the *Magpie*, *Time*, October 16, 1950

Before she became a minesweeper, the *USS Magpie* worked in the California fishing fleet as a dragger, or purse seiner, and she was known as the *City of San Pedro*. In 1936 the navy bought her and 20 sister boats, gave them each a three-inch gun, gear to catch something more deadly than tuna, and names from the birds, such as Bunting, Cross-bill, Crow, Puffin and Heath Hen. They all had wooden hulls so thin that a dummy torpedo dropped in practice from a plane once sank one. Still, the *Magpie* and her sisters, not without casualties, served in World War II, sweeping up enemy mines off Palau, Okinawa, the Philippines and Normandy.

Last week, while clearing the waters off the east Korean shore, the *Magpie's* wooden hull bumped a floating mine. The explosion sent her to the bottom, with her crew, including her commander, Lieut. Warren Roy Person; only 12 survivors were picked up.

The *Magpie* was the third U.S. warship hit by floating mines off Korea…In Washington, Chief of Naval Operations Admiral Forrest P. Sherman said the mines were Russian-made, "only recently from the warehouse," probably set adrift in Korean rivers. More than 65 have been swept up so far. They are illegal under The Hague Convention of 1907, which forbids unmoored mines. Russia, however, had never signed the convention.

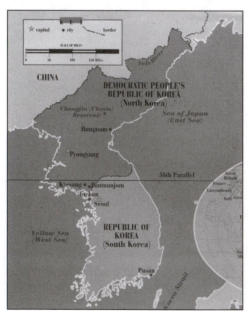

- Their honeymoon was too short, and Ed's voyage from San Diego to Japan was too quick.
- In Japan, introductions were succinct—the *Yellowhammer*, a 136-foot wooden-hull vessel, was now home.
- Before serving as a minesweeper in the Philippines during the darkest days of World War II, the *Yellowhammer* was a tuna boat in California.
- Commanded by a reserve lieutenant who was called into active service for the Korean conflict, she carried a crew of 29 men and four officers.
- Ed lived for letters from his new bride, but those from his little brother, Cotten, were a godsend.
- Cotten told Ed how he was crowned the red-hot cinnamon jawbreaker king after he kept one in his mouth almost 20 minutes.
- Cotten was also assembling the world's largest bottle-cap collection by hanging around the gas station where folks buy lots of drinks.

- Despite having dozens of rare caps, he was still missing a Vernor's ginger ale cap, because few people would drink the gingery drink.
- The *Yellowhammer's* assignment, with the Korean conflict well under way, was patrolling the east coast of the Korean peninsula.
- On small missions, she operated alone, but on larger jobs the *Yellowhammer* was part of a flotilla of minesweepers acting in concert to clear the waters before the destroyers arrive.
- In the larger operations, several of the vessels swept the water for mines using steel wires extending from the beams.
- The wires were stretched out and kept submerged with steel "kites."
- Every 250 feet, the wires had cutters capable of severing the mooring cables of contact mines, causing them to float to the surface.
- One vessel acted as the "destruct," following the sweepers to detonate or destroy the mines using rifle or machine-gun fire.
- The one or two remaining vessels had "dunning" duty, marking the cleared area with buoys.

Ed's brother, Cotton, wrote to Ed about his bottle cap collection.

- The majority of the mines used by the North Koreans were contact mines, but Ed was also trained to recognize Russian-made magnetic mines which sat at the bottom of a body of water and were set off by the magnetic field of a passing ship.
- These mines were swept by streaming two large cables from the stern of the sweeper that created a magnetic field capable of detonating the mine.
- Unfortunately for the sweepers, the Russian magnetic mines could be calibrated to detonate only after several ships had passed over, to ensure an explosion takes place in the middle of a convoy.
- This forced minesweepers to work a section of water numerous times to make sure all the mines were been found.
- On the *Yellowhammer*, the entire mine-related work, including sweeping, marking of the buoys and destruction of floating mines, were part of Ed's duty.
- Every member of a minesweeper knew the grim statistics—minesweepers comprise two percent of naval personnel, but 20 percent of naval deaths.
- In Korea, Ed experienced some long, tense days, often clearing mines for 24 to 36 hours at a stretch, especially if a major amphibious landing was planned.

The U.S. Navy's Korean War: Dull, Dirty, and They Die, Too
Newsweek, January 12, 1953

Shortly after sunrise one morning last week, a small wooden ship flying the U.S. flag slipped quietly into Wonsan Harbor. At her bow, on the lookout for mines, stood a seaman wearing a steel helmet, a flak vest, and a life jacket. Other seamen in helmets, flak vests and life jackets stood by her guns. This day, as every day the weather permits, the 136-foot *U.S.S. Waxbill* was on a dull, yet dangerous mission. We were sweeping the channel into Wonsan so that other and bigger United Nations ships could enter it safely to shell the Communist installations there.

ROK Marines, under the command of U.S. Marines, hold eight of the islands in Wonsan Harbor but the Communists have many more. The hills ringing the harbor are pock-marked with caves, and every cave hides a gun. The men aboard the *Waxbill* made no bones about it: This was not their idea of a full life. There was always the chance of running into a mine before they spotted it. And every now and then, whenever the Communists felt they could spare the ammunition, they liked to use the *Waxbill* for

target practice. They had done so only the day before, bracketing her with gunfire. One shell had fallen in her wake, another off her port bow, and another off her starboard bow. She has been able to escape only by cutting loose her minesweeping gear and laying a smokescreen. This particular morning, in hopes that the Communists again would open up, two U.S. destroyers were hovering outside the harbor. If the Communists did fire, they would reveal their positions, and the destroyers could then get to work on them. It didn't make the *Waxbill's* crew any less nervous to know that they were being used as decoys....

On the bridge, the *Waxbill's* youthful skipper, Lieutenant Thomas R. Allen of Sioux City, Iowa, peered through his glasses at the Communist caves. "A ship as small as this one is pretty hard

to hit," observed Lt. Allen. "However, if the Communists keep trying long enough, they are obviously bound to, eventually."

The morning wore on and nothing happened, but still the men couldn't relax. Those Communist guns were too close. And then, a few minutes before noon, the plotter, Chief Quartermaster Angelo John Zanoni of Walsenburg, Colorado, told Lt. Allen: "Sir, we've covered the channel." The lieutenant gave the order to leave the harbor. Smiles broke out all over the ship. A youngster joked: "Man, we'll never earn our combat pay if the Reds don't cooperate more." A seaman gets $45 extra if his ship is under fire on six days of the month. "Listen, stupid," said Hospital Corpsman Ivan Bently Owen of Senath, Missouri, "I'd be willing to pay Uncle Sam $45 a month if he'd just get me out of here."

Korean War Calendar

- August 10, 1945: U.S. officials select the 38th parallel as the dividing line across Korea. Americans accept the Japanese surrender south of the 38th parallel; the Soviets will receive the surrender north of the line
- August 15, 1945: As Japan surrenders, Korean leaders prepare an interim government, forming the Committee for the Preparation of Korean Independence
- September 5, 1945: American troops arrive in South Korea to establish a U.S. military government
- October 1945: Exiled Korean leader Syngman Rhee arrives in Seoul
- September 1947: The United States passes the matter of Korea to the United Nations
- May 1948: Members of the United Nations' Temporary Commission on Korea arrive to supervise elections; the North Koreans refuse to allow them north of the 38th parallel
- May 10, 1948: The Republic of Korea's first National Assembly is elected without participation of the North

War dominated life in Korea.

- August 15, 1948: Rhee is inaugurated as president of the Republic of Korea, representing South Korea
- December 1948: The Soviet Union withdraws its troops from North Korea
- 1949: Guerilla resistance to the rule of Rhee rages in the southern provinces of the Republic of Korea
- October 1949: Mao Zedong establishes the People's Republic of China after driving Chinese Nationalist leader Chiang Kai-shek and his forces to the island of Taiwan
- December 1949: The United States withdraws from Korea
- June 25, 1950: Ninety thousand North Korean People's Army troops cross the 38th parallel, attacking the Republic of Korea's Army at five key locations
- June 26, 1950: The UN Security Council condemns North Korea's armed attack
- June 27, 1950: Seoul falls to the North Koreans
- June 30, 1950: President Truman authorizes General Douglas MacArthur to use ground forces; a naval blockade of North Korea is approved
- July 5, 1950: A small U.S. unit of 406 men is shattered by the North Koreans at Osan
- July 10, 1950: The UN Security Council creates a unified Korean command under MacArthur
- July 14-16, 1950: North Koreans crush two regiments of the 24th Division at the Kum River
- July 19, 1950: The city of Taejon falls to North Korea
- August 1950: The People's Republic of China begins to move troops into Manchuria; UN forces retreat to the Pusan perimeter
- August 17, 1950: U.S. Marines strike the North Koreans at the Naktong Bulge, scattering them
- September 15, 1950: MacArthur leads a successful amphibious assault on the port city of Inchon
- September 24, 1950: China protests the strafing of sites in Manchuria by U.S. aircraft
- September 27, 1950: UN troops recapture Seoul
- September 30, 1950: Republic of Korea forces cross the 38th parallel, followed by UN troops
- October 14, 1950: Communist Chinese forces, numbering 180,000, move from Manchuria into North Korea
- October 20, 1950: UN forces capture the North Korean capital of Pyongyang and continue toward the Chinese border

- October 26, 1950: Chinese Communist troops attack UN forces
- November 25, 1950: The Chinese aggressively attack the 8th Army
- November 27, 1950: The Chinese strike at seven different fronts near the Choson Reservoir; the 8th Army begins withdrawal
- December 3, 1950: MacArthur orders a withdrawal of all UN forces to the 38th parallel
- January 1, 1951: The Chinese launch their third offensive, pushing UN forces 50 miles south of the 38th parallel
- January 4, 1951: Seoul is recaptured by Communist forces
- March 14, 1951: Seoul returns to UN control
- April 11, 1951: MacArthur is relieved of command; General Matthew Ridgway is named commander of the UN forces
- April 21, 1951: UN forces successfully battle Chinese and North Koreans

- June 1951: Chinese and UN forces dig in across from each other at the crater known as the Punchbowl
- July 10, 1951: The first armistice meeting convenes
- July 16, 1951: Korean officials declare their unwillingness to accept cease-fire while Korea remains divided
- August 1951: Communists call off the armistice talks, claiming UN aircraft are bombing neutral zones
- September 13-26, 1951: The battle at Heartbreak Ridge results in many deaths on both sides, but little territory is exchanged
- November 23, 1951: During armistice negotiations, a demilitarized zone stretching two kilometers on each side of the 38th parallel is established
- January 1952: Armistice talks enter a long stalemate over the issue of repatriating prisoners of war who do not wish to return to their country
- May 1952: Mark W. Clark replaces General Matthew B. Ridgway as commander of the Far East Force and the UN Command
- March 5, 1953: Soviet Premier Joseph Stalin dies and is replaced by Georgy M. Malenkov, who quickly expresses the Soviet Union's desire for peace in Asia
- April-May 1953: The first exchanges of Korean War POWs begin with the transfer of sick and wounded prisoners
- June 18, 1953: As truce negotiations near completion, South Korean President Syngman Rhee secretly orders the release of about 25,000 North Korean POWs who do not wish to be repatriated, effectively sabotaging the armistice agreements
- July 11, 1953: With promises of enormous economic aid and the continued security role of U.S. troops in South Korea, Rhee agrees not to obstruct the armistice
- July 27, 1953: The armistice agreement is signed by both sides

Men of the Minesweepers: Where the Fleet Goes, We've Been!
Charlotte Knight, *Collier's*, November 10, 1951

It was a grim morning and an even grimmer mission. Cold, driving rain stung our faces and beat hard on the decks of our plucky little minesweeper, the *Osprey*, as we left Korea's "unswept" channel in the Yellow Sea. We were on the hunt for the most insidious weapon UN forces have encountered in 17 months of the Korean war: the magnetic underwater mine. Like most minesweep missions in this war, this was another urgent, top-priority, sweep-it-right-now assignment.

Minesweepers left port knowing the dangers they faced.

Intelligence sources, evaluated as reliable, had produced information that Communist forces had laid several magnetic mines in the channel of Chawol-to, one of the approaches to the vital UN supply port of Inchon. The *Osprey* and two of her sister sweepers, the *Swallow* and the *Waxbill*, had been suddenly diverted from their major sweeping operation off Wonsan on the east coast and ordered to steam full-speed for the Yellow Sea to take care of the situation. It was up to them to locate and explode the dreaded mines-or be able to assure our high command that the mines had become inactive and were therefore no longer a threat to UN warships.

A few mines, stealthily laid at night by innocent-appearing sampans and fishing junks could put an immediate and very likely disastrous end to our naval operations in the vicinity, unless we first took appropriate means to counter them. Of these methods, that of physically sweeping a given area clear of all types of mines still is, after almost half a century of coping with the mine as an offensive weapon, the most effective countermeasure.

It is hazardous work-as navy casualty figures offer somber proof-but danger is the *Osprey's* business and her crew takes it in stride…

Not that anybody on the *Osprey* had any doubts about what could happen. For these are the sobering statistics to date: 17 of our ships have been hit by Communist mines since the start of the Korean war; the deadliness of the weapon can be attested to by the fact that 12 of these vessels sank, and one of them, the destroyer *Walke*, suffered severe damage and 26 of her crew killed in the navy's worst single disaster in Korean waters. Six of the ships sunk were UN minesweepers; four were American. The *Magpie*, the first U.S. Navy sweeper lost, went down a year ago, with 21 of her small crew of four officers and 29 men missing in action.

Since then (although those who man the sweepers comprise less than two percent of naval personnel in the Far East), more than 20 percent of all naval dead or missing have been minesweeping people.

No Push-Button Gadgets for This Job

"Until we can come up with a classy, remote-control, push-button sweeper, looks like we'll have to keep on doing it the hard way," said one of the *Osprey's* officers as the little ship rocked and rolled on our way toward Chawol-to, past the stately *Los Angeles*, the *Eldorado* and some of the other great gray warships. Our 136-foot wooden craft suddenly seemed absurdly small. As though he read my thoughts, Lieutenant David A. Beadling of Prospect Park, Pennsylvania, the *Osprey's* executive officer, sprang to her defense. "Yeah, I know. I suppose we do look pretty silly alongside those steel jobs." (I was shortly to discover that to all minesweep personnel, everything from a small destroyer to a battleship falls under the simple classification "steel job.")

"I suppose they have a right to think they're pretty important-they're the only ones you read about; and nobody ever heard about the *Osprey*.

But you ought to see 'em run for cover the minute they smell a minefield. Yes, sir," reflected Beadling, with what appeared to be some satisfaction, "there's nothing like a few mines strewn about to cut the big boys down to size."

"Don't forget our motto," prompted Lieutenant Gordon Shoolman of Rochester, New York, " 'Where the Fleet Goes, We've Been!'"

Plenty of time for resting,
Plenty of time for bull sessions,
Plenty of ocean.

Navy crewmen lived in cramped quarters aboard ship.

"It may become apparent after a while that we don't quite consider ourselves part of the regular navy-or maybe it's vice versa," continued Beadling, known aboard the *Osprey* only as "the Beadle"…

Like any group of proud people whose jobs are specialized, dangerous, virtually unpublicized, and frequently unrecognized even in their own service, the minesweep personnel are inclined to be a bit hypersensitive. Slights and rebuffs are apt to be long-remembered…

"Mines are easy to mass-produce. Why, any toy factory or typewriter plant could turn 'em out in quantity and at very low cost. It's damned frightening."

The commander's words were reminiscent of those of the late Admiral Forrest P. Sherman in his testimony before a congressional committee shortly before his death. When the committee chairman pointed out that the several hundred mines the U.S. Navy had swept in

A deactivated minefield in the South Pacific.

Korean waters must have made serious inroads in the Communist mine supply, Admiral Sherman said: "Well, sir, I would like to be that optimistic, but I'm afraid they can probably be manufactured at a rate just as fast as our recovery of them."

The enemy has laid thousands of mines around the coasts of Korea, of which we have so far swept less than half, despite continuous dawn-to-dark operations. Ninety-eight mines were "cut" recently in one day, just off Wonsan alone.

"The whole idea gets grisly after a bit," said Commander Shouldice. "Some mines weigh as little as 750 pounds. So, a few coolies can pick one up and walk off with it. They can put four of them on a fishing boat with no strain at all. Or they can suspend a magnetic mine underneath an ordinary sampan by putting a few lines (which look like fishing lines, of course) over the side and conceal it that way. When they get the boat in position, they merely cut the lines and drop the mines."…

With few exceptions, all the mines swept have been the common, moored "contact" mines-mammoth spheres with protruding "horns" which detonate the explosive charge when they come in contact with a ship.

To date, the best method of sweeping these moored mines is for a vessel to tow from her stern two Oropesa or "O"-type sweeps: These are steel wires stretched out from the port and starboard beams by steel "kites" or "otters" which are designed to submerge the sweep wires at the required depth and keep them there; they are attached to Oropesa floats, torpedo-shaped affairs known in minesweep parlance as "pigs." These floating "pigs" stream out at an angle from the ship and keep taut the kite lines, along which are arranged, about 250 feet apart, a series of cutters capable of severing the mooring lines holding the mines in position.

When these lines have been cut, the buoyancy chamber within the submerged contact mine brings it to the surface, where it bobs about until destroyed by minesweep crews, usually by rifle fire. (It isn't necessary to hit the horns or explode the mine; filling the buoyancy chamber with rifle holes is sufficient to send the mine to the bottom, where it stays.)

"We kept on getting orders: 'Sweep this area instantly!'" said one of the mine people, "when sometimes we wouldn't even know if the beaches were in friendly hands. We're small so that we can maneuver close to shore, but we're also slow. We'd ask the brass; 'What if the shore batteries start firing?' 'Very simple,' they'd say, 'Duck 'em. Take evasive action.' At eight knots? Good grief!"

Sweeping up enemy mines is unpleasant enough even when the beaches are "ours." Add to this the ever-present fire from enemy shore batteries and you have Wonsan-exactly as it has been for the better part of a whole year, except for the comparatively short time when UN forces held that important North Korean port. Neither Dusty nor anyone else in the mine force here is likely to forget those first sweeps…

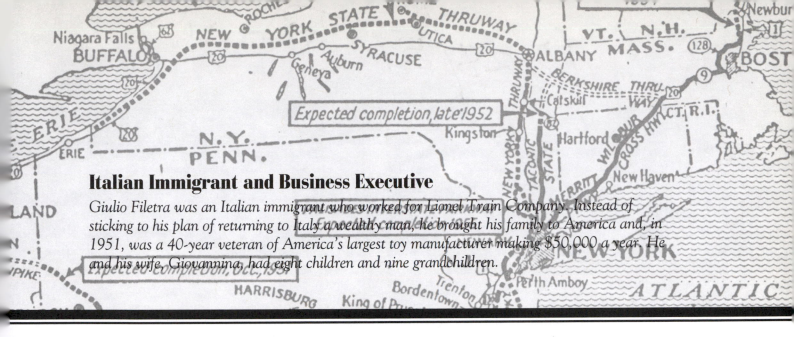

Italian Immigrant and Business Executive

Giulio Filetra was an Italian immigrant who worked for Lionel Train Company. Instead of sticking to his plan of returning to Italy a wealthy man, he brought his family to America and, in 1951, was a 40-year veteran of America's largest toy manufacturer making $50,000 a year. He and his wife, Giovannina, had eight children and nine grandchildren.

Life at Home

- Born in Italy, Giulio Filetra emigrated to America at the turn of the century, leaving his family behind, planning to return home a wealthy man.
- Instead, he found America to his liking and brought his wife and two children to New Jersey.
- Trained as an engineer, Giulio found employment at the Lionel Train Company, which was just emerging as a major player in the production of toys.
- He became wealthy through company stock, bonuses and patents, and was the number two man to Joshua Lionel Cowen, with the power to make or break an idea.
- He ruled with an iron hand at work, confident in his every decision, but at home, his giggling grandchildren, wife, and children could talk "Papa" into almost anything.
- Even though the home office was in New York City, the manufacturing facilities were in New Jersey, and the Filetra family lived in Livingston.
- To the amazement of his neighbors, his home had a small outdoor waterfall and pond, beside which Giovannina enjoyed sitting in the late afternoons.
- The house's music room on the second floor, originally designed as a ballroom, was covered with train tracks, scenery and prototypes, where a Lionel production engineer spent one day a week maintaining the tracks and implementing new ideas.
- At night, Giulio used the elaborate setup to think through problems encountered during the day.
- With his blessing and financial support, their oldest grandson, Joseph, attended the exclusive Hotchkiss School in Lakeville, Connecticut, headed by George Van Santvoord.
- For decades, the school prided itself on the development of character in its broadest sense, and Van Santvoord felt that both the Talmud and the Koran had something to say about character.
- Sunday services ranged from the traditional Church of England services to lectures by a rabbi or priest.

Giulio Filetra brought his family to America.

The Filetra's home included a model train room and an outdoor waterfall.

- Giulio agreed with the school's philosophy that it was more important to know why a war was fought than to memorize the actual dates it occurred.
- On the subject of morality, Van Santvoord taught, "One way to decide whether an act is moral or immoral is to ask yourself what the world would be like if everybody did it."
- The Duke, as Van Santvoord was called, emphasized one rule, "Be a gentleman," and even offered prizes for the most tastefully decorated dormitory rooms.

Life at Work: Toy Company Executive

- The biggest toy manufacturer in the world, Lionel Train Company experienced phenomenal growth since the Second World War ended.
- Its signature toy, a train set, was considered one of the "must-have" Christmas gifts for boys.
- The company sold nearly three million toy engines and freight cars in 1951, and sales were more than $28 million.
- Lionel's ability to manufacture engines that produce real smoke captured the imagination of America's men and boys, along with realistic knuckle couplers, radio wave transmitters that control individual cars and a detailed model of the Pennsylvania Railroad's 20-wheel steam turbine locomotive.
- To attract a wider market, Lionel trains emphasized realism and Giulio, always exacting in his standards of design and manufacture, loved getting the details right.
- Giulio's management control extended to the life style of his managers, and he frowned on those who drove cars more expensive than a Ford.
- He also discouraged managers from buying summer homes at the seashore, not wanting them too far removed from the workers.
- Small and explosive, he often pitted his managers against each other, believing that competition would produce better ideas and inventions, but it also fostered infighting and tension.
- Giulio believed that dynamic tension improved the creative process; "If everyone agrees with everyone," he liked to say, "nothing moves forward."
- The company hired New York Yankee baseball player and Lionel train fan Joe DiMaggio as its spokesman, paying him $125,000 to appear on 13 episodes of the

Giulio's grandson attended Hotchkiss School in Connecticut.

Joe DiMaggio was a spokesman for the Lionel Train Company.

Lionel Club House television program broadcast on Saturday afternoons.

- With experience from building war materials, Lionel created parts in plastic without harming quality, with more surface detail and at a lower cost than metal.
- Lightweight plastic cars also allowed an engine to pull a longer train—a must for many train families.
- Children pored over the company's catalogs, which featured fathers and sons, dreaming of building the ultimate city through which to drive their smoking, puffing train.
- Many soldiers returning home from war aboard a passenger train speculated about how to bond with the children they'd left behind.
- The wide use of trains to transport troops and move supplies during the war triggered a new familiarity and romance with train travel in America.

Collector's Guide to American Toy Trains, by Susan and Al Bagdale: Lionel's catalog was probably the most influential of all the sales devices used to promote toy trains. Children waited eagerly for its appearance each year, and it did much more than provide a list of trains and accessories. The child's imagination could go wild as he plotted his role as chief engineer of his very own railroad. Each and every decision was something to agonize over and dream about to make sure the best choices were made whether children were spending their allowances, their paper route money, or were choosing Christmas or birthday gifts.

- Only the Sears, Roebuck catalog was more widely read than the annual Lionel Train Company book.
- In addition to trains, the company manufactured a wide variety of accessories such as cattle cars and corrals.
- A vibrating platform allowed the cattle to move from the cattle car into the corral and back into the car using small feelers on the bottom of the plastic cows' hooves.

Life in the Community: Livingston, New Jersey

- Teenagers looked forward to Halloween when they painted the broad display windows of the area merchants.
- Merchants supplied the brushes and watercolor paint, and offered a $250 prize to the young artists who produced the best work.
- To lure customers, many New Jersey-based stores engaged in "price wars" on items that included electric mixers, toasters, summer suits and typewriters.
- Livingston and the surrounding communities wrestled with the need to eliminate unfair trade practices in the servicing of television sets, and considered an ordinance requiring a city license for all elevision repairmen.
- The local newspaper reported that nationwide, in the first week of June, 87 new cases of polio were discovered compared with 78 the previous week.

- In Newark, key campaign issues included failure to enact a law making bingo legal for charitable and church purposes and inequalities in the New Jersey Turnpike toll rates.
- A network of superhighways was taking shape, promising to link New England, New York, New Jersey and Pennsylvania.

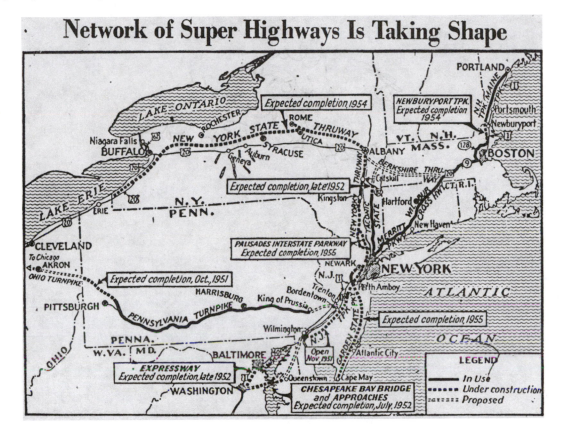

Network of Super Highways Is Taking Shape

Cowen in Profile, by Robert Lewis Taylor,
The New Yorker, December 13, 1951

Joshua Lionel Cowen, a small, bustling, choleric man of 67, is perhaps he country's most progressive and farsighted railroader. A magnate of exceptional and refreshing immodesty, he considers his contributions to the industry at least as impressive as those of the run-of-the-mill pioneers like James J. Hill and E.H. Harriman, and he feels that Robert R. Young (president of New York Central), although shooting in the right direction, is still pretty much an upstart. Cowen is Chairman of the Board of the Lionel Lines, some of whose terminals are separated by as much as 30 feet…At times he has served—together with important officials of other railroads, like the Pennsylvania and the Baltimore and Ohio—on the boards of large corporations, and he gives up-to-date methods a clamorous endorsement.

"Look alive!" he once shouted at the meeting of the board of an insurance company. "Keep moving. Never stand still. You stand still and you're moving backward. It's the same in everything. If you're a railroader," he added, directing a somewhat bilious glance toward a couple of railroad members on the board, "you need to keep your tracks in shape, put out new engine and car models, work up other modern equipment—in short, step out of the 1890s…"

The chairman of many corporation boards try to maintain a certain detachment from routine operations; Cowen, who is crazy about toy electric trains, even after 47 years, cannot take them or leave them alone. Separated from his plant for very long, he gets jumpy and tense.

…Cowen is short, standing just over five feet five, and has a ruddy complexion and gray hair. For his years, he appears uncommonly youthful. Some of his friends think he looks like ex-Governor Lehman, but other authorities have described him as resembling an anxious cherub. Cowen's harassed expression can be traced to his longstanding suspicion that the A.C. Gilbert Company, his only major business competitor, is trying to make good trains, too. Although the Lionel Company is by far the largest of the toy train manufacturers and has symbolized the industry for two generations, Cowen regards anybody's appearance in the field as rash and highly presumptuous.

…He has always felt that the children of America were looking over his shoulder as he worked. Furthermore, he has, he thinks, the viewpoint of a child himself, and he thus keeps a detached but automatic check on his progress. This picture of Cowen looking over his own shoulder while seated at his desk provides the best explanation of Lionel's somewhat exalted niche in the toy train world. Any sacrifice of excellence for expediency would tax his conscience severely, and might even age him out of his juvenile viewpoint.

- Military hospitals used fancy train layouts as occupational therapy for disturbed veterans, finding that playing with trains helped them both relax and learn to make decisions in cooperation with others.
- An elaborate Lionel train layout was sent to the Berlin World Youth Festival, at the request of West Berlin mayor Dr. Ernst Reuter, who wanted an exhibit that would extol the American way of life.

Giulio took pride in the details of the model trains and their surroundings.

Olympic Hurdler

Following in the footsteps of his hero, Jesse Owens, Harrison Dillard won four Olympic gold medals in 1952. Both athletes were African American, grew up in the same tough Cleveland neighborhood, went to the same high school, and were coached by the same man. Just like Jesse Owens, Harrison worked hard to overcome racism in America to pursue his dream.

Life at Home

- At age 13, Harrison Dillard gathered with his family around the radio to listen to the 1936 Summer Olympic Games broadcast from Berlin.
- He was most interested in track and field and the African American superstar, Jesse Owens, especially since he and Owens attended the same high school, East Tech.
- Owens was a local hero in Harrison's hometown of Cleveland, Ohio, and adored in the black community for his amazing achievements in sports.
- As Owens wowed the Berlin audience and the world press, he shattered the ideal promoted by Adolph Hitler in Germany, which was that the Germans would dominate and that African Americans were inferior.
- Owens spoiled this plan by winning four gold medals: 100 meter sprint; long jump; 200 meter sprint; and 4X100 meter relay.
- After he attended a parade in Cleveland honoring Jesse Owens, Harrison vowed to work harder at becoming faster and stronger.
- Summers meant more to Harrison than fun, ice cream and fireworks.
- In baseball, he showed his speed and athleticism by constantly stealing bases.
- In track, Harrison got serious about hurdling, a skill he began practicing at 8 years old using springs from car seats taken from abandoned vehicles.
- Rising at five am, Harrison ran through the quiet streets of his poor Cleveland neighborhood, encouraged by knowing that Jesse Owens had overcome this tough environment.
- He knew that black athletes—even the great Jesse Owens—had to work harder to succeed.
- Jim Crow, state and local racial segregation laws enacted between 1876 and 1965, was still alive and well in many parts of America.
- After a post-Olympic New York ticker-tape parade in his honor, Jesse Owens had to ride the freight elevator to attend his own reception at the Waldorf-Astoria.
- Harrison felt blessed to work with Charles Riley, Jesse's old coach.
- In high school, hurdles became his specialty, and he won 82 consecutive events.

Harrison Dillard emulated his hero, Jesse Owens.

Harrison and Jesse Owens ran in the same Cleveland neighborhood.

- He started Baldwin-Wallace College in Beretha, Ohio, and was drafted two years later, serving in the military until 1946.
- In 1948, despite not qualifying for the hurdles in the Olympics, he was chosen as a member of the 1948 USA Olympic relay team, which captured a gold.
- Harrison kept training, hoping to quality for the hurdle event in the 1952 games in Helsinki, Finland.
- At 5'10" and 152 pounds, he was considered frail for the Olympics, and was nick named "Bones."

Life at Work: Olympic Athlete

- As the 1952 Olympics in Helsinki approached, Harrison Dillard was determined to erase the memory of failing to qualify for the hurdles in the 1948 Olympics.
- His hard work paid off, and he qualified for the hurdle event.
- Helsinki beat out Los Angeles, Philadelphia, Detroit, Minneapolis, Amsterdam and Chicago for the opportunity to host the games.
- The Finns were very hospitable, and lived up to their motto, "You First."
- Some thought so highly of Finland that there was support to make Helsinki the Olympic destination for all time.
- In all, 5,678 athletes, representing 69 nations, were on hand to participate in 43 events in 19 sports.
- Quivering with anticipation, Harrison lined up, waiting for the starter pistol to fire.
- At the sound of the shot, he came up out of his position and raced down the track.
- He leaped over the hurdles ahead of everyone and managed the 110 meters of the race with grace and fortitude.
- Bones crossed the finish line to win the gold, with vociferous cries from the Helsinki crowd.
- The race was a sweep for the U.S., with Jack Davis and Arthur Barnard winning the silver and the bronze, respectively.
- The usually reserved Harrison leaped with joy and exclaimed, "Good things come to those who wait!"
- His Olympics were not over, for he still had the 4X100 meter relay.
- The Soviet team was considered a fierce competitor, but Harrison was confident, having been a part of the 1948 gold medal winning team.
- Harrison was running the second leg of the relay, and took the baton in his left hand from Dean Smith, who carried it in his right.
- Harrison was behind both USSR's Levan Kalyeyev and Hungary's Geza Varasdi.
- He overtook them easily, hearing only the quick, padded slap of his feet on the track and the beating of his heart within his chest.

Harrison felt a rush when he closed in for the gold.

- He breathed deeply as he rounded the track, made the transfer of the baton to Lindy Remigino's right hand, and watched his teammate run ahead of the crowd.
- As his teammate crossed the finish line to win the gold, white and black American athletes hugged and celebrated together.
- Harrison had become the first man ever to win Olympic gold medals in both the sprints and the high hurdles.

Life in Olympic Community: Helsinki, Finland

- Helsinki, Finland, was originally awarded the 1940 Olympic Games, but due to World War II, the games were canceled and Helsinki was awarded the 1952 games.
- Germany and Japan, both denied participation in the 1948 games as aggressor nations, were permitted to compete in 1952.
- Much controversy revolved around the USSR, which emerged after World War II as an American foe in the Cold War.
- The media and politicians were obsessed with the potential controversy, wondering what the reaction of the athletes might be in this atmosphere.
- Harrison wasn't worried.
- Having participated in the 1948 games, he knew athletes were not about politics or even ethnicity.
- As an African American athlete, Harrison learned in 1948 that most of the athletes put aside race and worked as a team and a community.
- Athletes from the USSR invited other Olympians to a pre-games party, serving caviar and other fine foods.
- Harrison and his fellow Americans were not interested in Capitalists versus Communists, just being the best athletes they could be.
- The new Russian team felt the same.
- The games brought out goodwill and sportsmanship among the athletes, and Harrison was glad to rise above the political intrigue.
- Not only did Germany, Japan, and the USSR create headlines, but also, for the first time ever, Israel was represented.

Olympics Timeline

1892: Baron Pierre de Fredi called for a rebirth of the Olympic Games, saying, "It is clear that the telegraph, the railways, the telephone, passionate scientific research, the congresses and exhibitions have done more for peace than any diplomatic convention. Well, I hope athleticism will do even more."

1896: The first games were held in Athens, Greece, with 14 nations participating in nine sports with 245 athletes (all male). Every winner received a silver medal and an olive branch.

1900: In Paris, women competed in four of the 20 sports, including lawn tennis, in which the ladies played wearing hats and long dresses.

1904: The Olympics were held outside of Europe, as St. Louis, Missouri, hosted the games; the low point came when an exposition was mounted to show the inferiority of African Americans and Native Americans.

For the first time, gold, silver, and bronze medals were awarded to the top three contestants.

1912: New technologies included electronic timing devices, photo finishes, and loudspeakers.

1916: No Olympic Games were held, as Berlin, the city awarded the site, was at war.

1920: The oldest medal winner in Olympic history was Sweden's 72-year-old Oscar Swahn, who won the gold in the double shot running deer event.

1924: The Olympic motto, "Citius, Altius, Fortius" (Swifter, Higher, Stronger), was introduced as France became the first nation to host the games twice.

1932: In order to finance their visit to Los Angeles, Brazilians traveled with a cargo of coffee that was sold along the way.

American Peter Mehringer won the gold medal in freestyle wrestling, having learned the sport through a correspondence course.

The Olympics made a profit for the first time, nearly $1 million.

1936: The Berlin Games, intended to be a showcase for Hitler's ideal man, were overshadowed by African American athletes led by Jesse Owens.

1940, 1944: The games were suspended due to World War II.

1948: The Olympics were televised for the first time.

The first political defection occurred when Marie Provaznikova refused to return to Czechoslovakia.

1952: Bill Havens, who declined an Olympic invitation in 1924 for rowing because of his wife being pregnant with their first son, watched his son, Frank, win the gold medal in singles canoeing.

Records Held by Harrison Dillard

World Record: 120 yd. hurdles-13.60 (April 17, 1948-)

Olympic Record: 100 m-10.30 (July 31, 1948-)

Championships:
1948 Olympics: 100 m-10.30 (First)
1948 Olympics: 400 m relay (First)
1952 Olympics: 110 m hurdles-13.70 (First)
1952 Olympics: 400 m relay (First)
1947 AAU: 60 yd. hurdles (First)
1948 AAU: 60 yd. hurdles (First)
1949 AAU: 60 yd. hurdles (First)
1950 AAU: 60 yd. hurdles (First)
1951 AAU: 60 yd. hurdles (First)
1952 AAU: 60 yd. hurdles (First)

Korean War Hero

Robert Hope's plans of his own chicken farm was put on hold when his ROTC unit from Clemson College was called to help defend South Korea against North Korea's attack. With the 1953 signing of a Korean War armistice only days away, Robert led a counter attack up Pork Chop Hill in Korea. Despite being wounded three times, he kept his command and was awarded the Silver Star.

Life at Home

- News of the invasion of Korea in June 1950 arrived while Robert Hope was attending an eight-week summer camp for infantry platoon leaders in Fort Benning, Georgia.
- While a student at Clemson College in South Carolina, Robert assumed that military exercise was simply the completion of his ROTC obligation.
- Suddenly, he was training for battle as America was at war with North Korea, the first hot conflict of the Cold War.
- It was hard for Robert to understand why America was willing to fight over land in a place like Korea.
- At the end of World War II and the defeat of the Japanese, North Korea was assigned to the communists, and South Korea to the United States.
- Now, with no warning, the North Korean Army crossed the 38th parallel (official dividing line) and attacked South Korea.
- In the fall, Robert was at Clemson completing his degree in chicken husbandry, cheering on his beloved Clemson Tigers and dreaming of establishing his own chicken farm.
- In March, he was back at Fort Benning with his entire ROTC unit from college, planning to go to war.

Robert Hope was called into action while at college.

> As we were moving through the field, we started to receive some fire from the Chinese. But, you know, I was tired and cold, just plain miserable, I didn't care. You can get that way.
> **—Sergeant Joseph DeMarco, B Company, 1st Battalion, 7th Marines**

The Korean War Casualty Totals

United Nations Forces:
United States: 36,913 dead, 103,248 wounded, 8,142 missing
South Korea: 58,127 dead, 175,743 wounded, 166,297 missing
Other Nations: 3,194 dead, 11,297 wounded, 2,769 missing

Communist Forces:
North Korea: 214,899 dead, 303,685 wounded, 101,680 missing
China: 401,401 dead, 486,995 wounded, 21,211 missing

Civilians:
An estimated 2 to 2.6 million dead, wounded and missing

- In July, Robert and his classmates were assigned to duty at Fort Jackson, South Carolina, where he was assigned as a trial lawyer in the judge advocate's office.
- Most of his cases involved soldiers who had gone AWOL—absent without leave—resulting in court marshal.
- Robert quickly became aware that, in the military, a soldier was assumed guilty before he was tried.
- Robert knew little about the court system and less about trying people, but he did know that his desk job kept him from getting up at 4 a.m. for duty on the rifle range.
- The onset of war upset not only his establishment of a poultry business, but also his marriage plans.
- He and his girlfriend Sadie decided to marry before he was shipped overseas so that she would be financially provided for if he was killed in action.
- His last month stateside was spent in a small apartment off-base with Sadie, dreaming of life after his tour ended.

U.S. Donates Huge Rice, Ration Supply to Korean People,
Stars and Stripes, Korean Edition, July 30, 1953

The first distribution of 10,000 tons of food donated by President Dwight D. Eisenhower in appreciation of the valiant courage and fighting ability of the Korean people was made to the citizens of Pusan today.

More than 600 tons of rice and C-rations were trucked to the eight docks of Pusan…The gift, not part of any present aid or relief program, was withdrawn from military stocks.

Broken down it will mean one C-ration, or eight cans of meat, and five hops of rice to every five people.

- When his orders arrived to report overseas, he realized that his court training at Jackson had prepared him poorly for the job ahead as an infantry platoon leader.
- He was shipped out of San Francisco aboard the *U.S.S. Black,* which had been brought out of mothballs for the Korean conflict.
- The trip from the U.S. to Yokohama took 16 days, and Robert's job as a second lieutenant was to guard the hole, where enlisted soldiers were housed during the long boat ride.
- The bunks were stacked four or five layers deep, and if one soldier became seasick, a dozen men could be affected.

Robert left San Francisco aboard the U.S.S. Black.

Life at Work: U.S. Army Officer

- When Robert arrived in Japan, he was assigned to the 17th Infantry, 7th Division, which defended the hills in Korea.
- On April 17, 1953, with rumors of an armistice in the air, the *U.S.S. Black* arrived at the harbor in Inchon—a city that experienced at least three major battles since the fighting began.
- People debated over whether General Douglas MacArthur should have been allowed to invade China—the source of many communist troops—and end the war quickly.
- Opinion was sharply divided about President Harry Truman's decision to remove MacArthur.
- In the harbor, Robert experienced his first taste of war, as a steady stream of helicopters flew the wounded to a Swiss hospital ship—two litters per chopper.
- Rumors circulated that the 7th Division was in Korea to replace the wounded he had seen that day.
- On the troop transport train, he was assigned guard duty to prevent frightened men from jumping off the train.
- None did, but he was still relieved when the journey ended.
- Equally disturbing was the sight of hordes of Korean children begging for food along the rail line.
- Giving a small amount of food set off riots, but giving no food resulted in children throwing rocks through the train windows.
- Robert's first duty was "graves registration" for the dead that were shipped in by the truckload for processing.
- Robert learned that the slot on each end of a dog tag was designed to be inserted between the teeth of the dead.
- When Robert arrived at his outpost, he discovered that the rumors were true: Every officer in Easy Company had been wounded, and warm bodies—even untrained Clemson men—were desperately needed as platoon leaders.
- When Robert was asked to take over the company, he was terrified, not only because he was untrained to lead a platoon, but also because he had not used live ammunition in nine months.
- Despite their fear, he and his troops prepared, with rumors of a truce on their minds.
- Generally, the weather was pleasant, between 75 and 80 degrees during the day and 45 to 50 at night.
- The biggest problem was the dust turning to mud when it rained.
- A letter written from the East Coast took six to seven days to reach Easy Company in Korea, and any word from home was a gift.
- Even with the obvious buildup toward a major battle, Robert continued to think about home.

- He wrote to his mother and wife of the 20,000 chickens his farm would boast next year, and he pledged all of his monthly pay to make it happen.
- Following 10 tough days in the field with little sleep, his biggest worry was a $300 bill to repair the roof of the farmhouse.
- He wrote when he could, using light from a gasoline lantern, but with constant patrols and fighting in the area, it was difficult to fit into his schedule.
- During a skirmish in mid-May, he lost three soldiers in battle.
- Much time was spent protecting his men, keeping back the Chinese troops, or trying to capture them.
- With both sides eager for intelligence, his company tried anything to get an enemy prisoner so they could obtain advance warning of battle plans.

- On one occasion, they even dropped a dummy from a low-flying plane to lure the Chinese from their hiding places in order to capture them.
- To coax deserters, American planes dropped thousands of brochures urging the soldiers to put down their weapons and return home.

The Buffalo Brigade aided Korean orphans.

- By June, Robert lost nine men in battle and respected the toughness of the Ethiopian soldiers assigned to a regiment attached to the 7th.
- He was less trusting of the South Korean soldiers, who seemed to switch sides on a whim.
- During an April night patrol on Pork Chop Hill, Robert saw the Chinese preparing to attack, and immediately called for a flash fire all around the perimeter.
- Quickly, the artillery responded with direct hits on the massed Chinese troops.
- By the light of the explosions, Robert watched as gaps were blown in the Chinese lines by the artillery assault, and later learned that the Chinese lost 1,400 men that day.
- Like most soldiers on the front, he kept close track of his points: 36 points gets a man home.
- Every frontline soldier earns four points a month, while a clerk away from the action earns only two points a month.

The wounded were all loaded down and the 'copters gone. The dead would go down in the morning with the gook train, silent slumps being carried down the hill to the battalion and the morgue. You didn't waste chopper space on the dead.

—James Brady, *The Coldest War: A Memoir of Korea*

Buffalo Bugle, May 28, 1953

It was a mere coincidence, but to PFC Dale Erickson, a machine gunner in "A" Company, 17th Infantry "Buffalo" Regiment, is sent a happy birthday. Erickson was 21 the twelfth of May. It was his first birthday overseas, and he hadn't received a scrap of mail in more than a week. He was feeling "pretty low," until the company mailman made his rounds. Addressed to this mother's young Buffalo were a birthday cake, six congratulatory cards and five letters. Although the chocolate cake was smashed to a one-inch mound of crumbs, Erickson and the rest of his squad still agreed it was "number one."

The U.S. delivered food and clothing to innocent civilians.

- By early July, when the peace talks had resumed, no one wanted to be the soldier who died on the day the treaty was signed.
- When the Chinese forces took the elevated positions on Pork Chop Hill, Robert's regiment was called out on a counterattack.
- It was clear that the Chinese held a superior strategic position against the outnumbered American forces, and casualties mounted quickly, including Easy Company's commander.
- Robert immediately assumed control, and after securing his men in the trenches, began planning a way to attack, even though his hand was wounded.
- Screaming at the top of his lungs, he led an attack on the enemy position where small grenades, known as potato smashers, were being tossed down 10 at a time.
- He then called on the mortars to fire from a distant hill and provide cover while the wounded were collected.
- Dozens of men were on the ground with no unoccupied trenches available for cover, and though Robert was wounded a second time in the leg and buttocks, he kept command as the fighting intensified.
- The next morning, orders arrived to send two men out on a scouting mission to pinpoint the Chinese positions, but both were killed almost instantly after leaving cover.
- Against orders, Robert did not send anymore.
- On July 10, while attempting to remove the wounded, Robert was hit for the third time with shrapnel, and ordered off Pork Chop Hill for treatment at the command post.
- A week later he was back with his unit.
- After word of his injury spread, more than a dozen friends and relatives wrote letters, ragging him about being injured in the buttocks.

Life in the Community: Pork Chop Hill, Korea

- To provide entertainment for the troops early in his tour, Robert made a volleyball court and organized a tournament.
- His other recreation was shooting pheasant and deer, which was a special treat for his company.
- A month after he and over 100 men were wounded or killed in the battle on Pork Chop Hill, he was pleased that base camp was moved 20 miles back to a location only 20 miles from Seoul.
- At the new location, Robert planned to keep the men occupied with sports: horseshoes, volleyball, softball, basketball, touch football and boxing.
- Trips around South Korea included visits with American POWs recently released by the Chinese.

- He organized a search of Pork Chop Hill to find his company's missing, about 130 men who were still unaccounted for.
- The plan was for both Americans and Chinese to visit the battleground in search of their missing and presumed dead soldiers.

> The son-of-a-bitch isn't going to resign on me! I want him fired.
>
> —*President Harry Truman in dismissing General Douglas MacArthur as commander of United Nations forces in Korea, 1951*

Award of the Silver Star for Gallantry in Action, 1953

First Lieutenant Robert M. Hope, 02004641, Infantry, United States Army, a member of Company E, 17th Infantry, distinguished himself by gallantry in action near Sokkogae, Korea. During the period 8 July 1953 to 10 July 1953, when his company commander was wounded during an attack against a strategic enemy-held outpost, Lieutenant Hope grasped the reins of command, maintained control, and led a well-coordinated attack. Lieutenant Hope was wounded on three separate occasions, but although suffering from his wounds and disregarding his own personal safety, inspiring his men by a show of valiant courage above that expected in the normal line of duty. On one occasion, Lieutenant Hope led a group of men up the hillside to annihilate a contingent of enemy soldiers who were rolling grenades down the slope of the hill on friendly positions. Through the singular courage of Lieutenant Hope, a breach in the numerically superior enemy line was effected, enabling the friendly attacking force to consolidate their positions and stave off the relentless enemy attacks. The gallantry displayed by Lieutenant Hope reflects great credit on himself and is in keeping with the highest traditions of the military service.

Letters from Lt. Robert M. Hope to his mother Edna Hope:

April 10, 1953: Well, here I am in Korea—The Land of the Morning Calm. It doesn't show me much. Nothing but hills. We landed at Inchon about 2:30. I got a deal on the train. I was on the staff. Our car had a train commander, executive officer, and I was mess officer. We had the only car with heat, lights, etc. We had 17 cars. Got eight or 10 windows broken out. The Korean kids will throw rocks at the train if they don't get any food. Rock-throwing is a great sport over here…

April 17, 1953: I've been tempted to buy a camera. The only way you can appreciate the country is to see this place…I'm getting along okay with my razor; however, cold water doesn't make for the best shaving. No bathing facilities close by. Oh, I could use my electric razor if I wanted to use the power in the staff officer's tent. This is quite different from what I expected. The thing you have to watch here is the Koreans stealing everything you have. They won't hurt you, but just want to steal and they are professional, I've been told. All that we have around here are attached to the company. The staff officers have a Korean (Christian) preacher for their houseboy. Reads his Bible every chance he gets.

April 29, 1953: My platoon is shaping up pretty good. We are full strength now and I have a wonderful platoon sergeant. We had a big feed tonight. Had the CO (Commanding Officer) and CO's brother for supper. I was right in with the wheels. Our CO is tops. Both he and his brother are West Pointers. Pay Day tomorrow so I spent my first money tonight. Bought a box of cigars, candy, etc. I get toothpaste, cig, chewing gum in rations so no sweat there. My platoon is on guard tonight so I had better close and check on them.

May 17, 1953: I'm all by my lonesome tonight. All the other officers went to Division CP tonight to a movie. Had the guard for tonight so couldn't go. Went to church today. A Hall boy from Hickory (SC) preached… I hear the other officers coming in now— we all played canasta last night. Me and my partner won, of course. We had two bad accidents in the company yesterday—three boys got hit with one machine gun bullet. The weapon has been hit with shrapnel and wouldn't operate. Two boys were fooling with it—one pulled the trigger and it discharged hitting three men outside working…How is your garden coming along? I would sure like to have some of those radishes. We are getting fine chow. Haven't had to eat too many "C" rations. Best close and go check my guard—5 o'clock comes pretty early. Don't worry about me, I'm fine.

Robert was awarded the Silver Star.

June 4, 1953: I talked with Stoney (a friend from home) this afternoon for the first time in 12 days. He has himself a deal now—managing the regimental baseball team. He is trying to get me back there to play ball for him. A few catches stand in the way. First, they only allow one officer to play and that is Stoney. We don't have any extra officers in the company to take my place. If they want me bad enough those things can be arranged. Just keep my fingers crossed I guess. I would duplicate Daddy's feat in World War I if a peace was signed and I got to play ball.

June 7, 1953: I got to church today. Didn't get to go last Sunday. I go every chance I get. War really makes a lot of new believers, not that I wasn't a firm believer before but it just helps out. I'm kinda looking for some kind of truce by and by. I'm kinda disgusted with all these postponements. I hope something is done before long. I'm fine and know I'm happy as long as I can play ball. I don't have much of a team but we may develop. I got several Puerto Ricans and they can't understand English. I have to take an interpreter along to get things across to them. All pretty good ball players.

June 10, 1953: Have just been listening to the news. I just don't know what to think. I still predict there will be a truce by the 20th. Everyone is mad at [South Korean President Syngman] Rhee. I think they will come across—wish they would do it and get it over with… I shouldn't have to serve my full time if an agreement is reached.

June 19, 1953: Peace talks are disgusting. We don't even bother to listen to the news anymore. My prediction has fallen through, I guess. I predicted a cease-fire would be in effect by 20 June.

July 10, 1953: Just a note for now. I want to get a jump ahead of the Red Cross and Dept. of Army—I have been slightly wounded. I have about 15 small pieces of steel in my thigh, my hand and buttocks. None of them went deep and all are in fleshier parts. You may get a telegram from Dept. of Army saying I regret to inform you that your son has been wounded in action. I expect you will get one but I want you to disregard it because I'm fine. It is no more than small grains of sand under the skin. Yes, it was the Pork Chop deal. Don't believe that's my favorite place anymore. We went up about 3:15 p.m. on the 8th and I came off this morning. The remaining men are coming off this afternoon. The CO got hit right at first so I had charge of the company. We suffered some pretty heavy losses. We have five officers wounded and about 25-30 men left out of the 189 we took on the hill with us. Most of them are just wounded.

July 13, 1953: Just a note this morning to tell you I am fine. I will begin where I left my last letter. I came to the hospital and they cleaned my hand and leg. I had to rest for two hours. They then put me to sleep to cut the pieces out. I didn't know a thing for four hours. I was on the table about one and a half hours. I woke up in the officers' ward. The thing they do when they cut is to open the wound and allow it to drain. Four days later (tomorrow for me) they sew them up. I don't have but three or four openings. I'm able to get around pretty good. The bandage on my hand is so big it is hard to write. The thing is I don't want you to worry about me. I will be back to duty in about another week. I have a job ahead of me when I get back. See, I was the only officer left and I was right in all the action from beginning to end, so I'm the only one that knows what every man did—award and decorations, etc. I just thank God I'm here. I've never seen anything like it. Where's that truce?

Family Life in the Military

Jeffrey Connor was a captain the Air Force, assigned to the Strategic Air Command. Upon returning from the Korean War in 1953, he and his family were stationed in Wichita, Kansas. They were used to moving around, having lived five different places in the past three years. What they could depend on was Jeffrey's $2,800 annual salary and military housing.

Life at Home

- In many ways, it doesn't matter where they lived, all Air Force bases looked alike.
- The Connor family was moved by the military five times in the past three years.
- Jeffrey's wife, Karen, insisted on hanging all the pictures they own on the first day to help create a home environment in an ever-changing world.
- The new house, provided for by the government, reminded Karen of mill village housing in the South—1,200 square feet with three small bedrooms, a living room, dining room, and kitchen.
- In Wichita, Kansas, there was lots of sunshine, wind, and bugs.
- Even though they were always conservative with their money, Jeffrey bought the "new, easy, miracle way to rid their home of flies and bugs, Bug-Kil" to reduce the insect population.
- The couple had an 18-month-old son, Michael, and a five-year-old daughter, Sally.
- Sally liked base school, and her teacher allowed her to read all the "Sally" parts of the Dick and Jane Reader because that was her first name.
- The school sponsored a Dress Up Day for Dogs and Sally took her English Bulldog to school wearing her dad's pajamas.
- On windy Kansas days Sally walked home from school backwards to keep the wind and sand from stinging her face.
- Her mother made her and Michael take naps every afternoon, thinking that keeping children indoors during the heat of the day reduced their chances of catching infantile polio.
- Every military base where they lived had a movie theater and a bowling alley, and Jeffery and Karen bowled weekly.
- Jeffrey played catch with his daughter for one half-hour each day he was home, and read regularly to Michael.
- Karen played bridge twice a month with other military, mostly pilot, wives.
- Because their husbands talked little about their assignments, the bridge games helped the wives understand their husbands' duties.

Jeffrey Connor was an Air Force Captain.

- For people like Karen, who moved constantly, the military was her only family.
- Because Scrabble was the rage, some bridge clubs experimented with one table of Scrabble, but Karen thought it was a dumb idea.
- The children knew that if the phone rang in the middle of the night, their dad got dressed, took his pistol from the top of the closet, and went out to wait for the carpool to the fight line.
- Karen slept poorly when he was away and compulsively cleaned the house until he returned.
- Even though money was a constant worry, she kept a full pantry at all times so she could entertain guests or feed her husband's crew if they returned home from an assignment sooner than expected.

Jeffrey's wife adapted to military base housing.

The Connor children were well adjusted.

- She could put a meal on the table in 30 minutes, and especially enjoyed preparing the Asian foods she experienced in Hawaii early in their marriage.
- A mild-mannered man by nature, Jeff enjoyed the structure of the military and believed the Air Force was good to him and his family.
- Karen saw her mother in South Carolina on odd years, and on even years the family drove to Michigan to see Jeffrey's parents.
- A native of Zeeland, Michigan, Jeffrey joined the army on his eighteenth birthday in January 1942.
- With the war raging, and older men in the community asking why he wasn't already in the military, he didn't want anyone to think he was a slackard.
- Although only a high school graduate, he was selected for officer candidate's school in the newly forming Army Air Corps.
- He was sent to Winthrop College in Rock Hill, South Carolina, which was exclusively for women before the war.
- Under the military's assignment system, the training at Winthrop included all candidates whose names started with "C" and while at Winthrop, he met Karen.
- After one year of training, he transferred to pilot school and later to communications and electronics school.
- After 11 years in the military he considered staying until 20 years to take advantage of the excellent military retirement.

Life at Work: U.S. Air Force Captain

- Jeffrey returned from Korea, where he flew the new B-29 and was stationed at McConnell Air Force Base assigned to the Strategic Air Command piloting the new B-47s.
- Although heavier than the B-29, the B-47's size was disguised by slender lines and the novelty of a fighter-type cockpit.
- A B-47 crew included a pilot, co-pilot, and navigator hidden in the nose of the plane.
- Its shoulder-mounted wings were razor thin, swept back at a startling angle of 35 degrees.
- Korea was Jeff's third overseas assignment.
- His first was to Wheeler Field, Hawaii, in 1946, where the military was still rebuilding the war-torn territory.

Jeffrey was always ready to leave quickly.

The Strategic Air Command flew worldwide to deliver bombs.

- The second was in support of the Berlin Airlift in 1948 to supply a city of two million people with everything needed for survival by air.
- In late 1950, he was in Korea, supporting the newly declared war against North Korea.
- North Korea, divided from South Korea following World War II, was controlled by Red China, and attacked the Republic of Korea in June 1950.
- Captain Connor flew B-29s in support of the United States while United Nations forces rushed to the area; the bombers struck industrial targets and occasionally flew in support of ground troops.

- The Air Force played a critical role in Korea, demonstrating America's ability to use superior technology to attack an invading force.
- One of Jeff's missions was to hit North Korea's giant hydroelectric plants, knocking out 90 percent of the country's electric power.
- A second wave of pilots struck the Toksan and Chasan irrigation dams, flooding important road and rail communications.
- Of the 839 Korean MIG fighters shot down over Korea, 792 were brought down by American F-86 Sabrejets.
- As a member of the Strategic Air Command (SAC), Jeff was required to be in full combat uniform while on duty.
- More than 40 SAC bases in the United States were able to launch their planes in minutes and SAC was considered the greatest deterrent to Soviet aggression.
- Once deployed, Jeff and his fellow pilots flew nonstop around the world to deliver bombs, often not knowing where until after they left the ground.

F-86 Sabre Jet
designed and built by
NORTH AMERICAN AVIATION, INC.
NORTH AMERICAN HAS BUILT MORE AIRPLANES THAN ANY OTHER COMPANY IN THE WORLD

Life in the Community: Wichita, Kansas

- Kansas was called as the plainest of the Plains states, a quip the Connors agreed with.
- Outside McConnell Air Force Base, the countryside appeared to be little more than an endless ocean of grains and grasses.
- Kansas was America's one wheat producer, and also the aircraft capital of the world, with Wichita producing nearly 60 percent of all the airplanes made in the United States, including Beechcraft, Cessna, and Lear.
- The Mid-Continent Airport, a major international port of call, was nearly completed.
- Kansas was also one of the windiest inland areas in the nation, and Karen, although used to 100 degree days, had difficulty with the cold and windy winters.

Kansas was called the plainest of the plain states.

Jewish Immigrants from Poland

The Rochman family—David, Judy, their children and Judy's parents—immigrated to America from their home in Poland. In 1954, David made $3,100 a year in a men's clothing store. He and his family slowly acclimated to American life, but discrimination against Jews, like not being allowed to stay at certain hotels, and was never far away.

Life at Home

- The Rochmans were forced out of their home in Poland in 1941 and after two years of petitions, were granted asylum in the United States.
- They arrived in Bangor, Maine in 1943, where friends already lived and work was available.
- David and Judy knew some English and their children learned quickly, but Judy's parents yearned for Poland and adopted few American customs.
- The Jewish Community and Hebrew School were the center of the family's life, especially for Judy's parents.
- Programs at the Community Center included lectures, classes, and cultural and social programs.
- The Rochmans had an automobile, although only David drove.
- The Rochmans regularly went to the movies, especially if sales were good at David's job.
- They purchased a small black and white television set and a phonograph turntable for the children.
- The Rochman family got the daily newspaper, including Sunday, delivered to the house for $2.20 per month.
- The children liked to read, so David brought home popular magazines when he could afford them, including *The Saturday Evening Post, Good Housekeeping,* and *McCall's.*
- Despite having a car, the Rochmans rarely went on long trips not only due to the expense, but also because many hotels in Maine did not permit Jewish customers.
- When they traveled, they usually stayed with friends to prevent being refused service.
- The children attended cheders, or Hebrew schools, which maintained the old custom of giving a child a taste of honey when he is beginning to learn to symbolize the sweetness of study.
- The American Council for Judaism officially opposed schools like cheders that "take children out of the general American environment and train them to lead segregated lives."

The Rochmans immigrated from Poland to Bangor, Maine.

Life at Work: Clothing Store Salesman

- David sold men's clothing in a store on Bangor's Main Street owned by a Jewish immigrant whose parents came to the city before the First World War.
- Although David lived in the United States for 11 years, he was still insecure about his manners.
- Using his hands too much or saying "oy vey" brought disapproving looks from the owner.
- Bangor Jews did not like to attract attention, and prided themselves on being different from New York or Boston Jews.

Judy and her children adapted to life in America.

- The clothing store catered to many of the city's professionals who made seasonal buys, and reduced price sales were rarely held.
- David was paid on commission, so his pay varied from week to week.
- Most men wore a suit and hat to all public functions, including church, and Bangor's Dow Field brought to the store military officers who were eager to "look sharp."
- The base closed in 1948 but reopened in 1950 at the start of the Korean War, and 4,500 people, including nearly 2,000 civilians, worked there.
- A new wool topcoat of a hard finished fabric sold in David's store for $45.25, and a two-piece man's suit of new wool with tailoring cost $62.00.
- Men's Oxford shoes sold for $13.30, while a typical shoe repair cost $3.00.
- David sometimes worried that new department stores would take his customers through sophisticated advertising.

Life in the Community: Bangor, Maine

- Bangor was known for its timbering and its wealth, with five shipyards in the city carrying wood to Cuba and lumber to South America.
- Bangor businessmen controlled 6,000 square miles of forest track, a territory as large as the states of Connecticut and Rhode Island combined.
- Most of Bangor's Jewish immigrants were pushed out of Russia and Russia-dominated Poland by violence and poverty where they could not own land, were excluded from state schools, and could not be employed in numerous trades.
- Almost all of the Jews who settled in Bangor came from small communities and lived in cramped, wooden houses with dirt floors, on unlit, unpaved streets surrounded by farms and forests.
- By 1915 most Orthodox Jews in Bangor, seeking to adapt, shed most of the Orthodox insignia of skullcaps worn by men, and wigs worn by women.

Bangor was known for its prosperous lumber industry.

- By 1945, the Jews of the city learned that the Russian and Polish villages where Bangor's Jewish immigrants had once lived were now devoid of Jewish life, their histories irretrievably lost to the Nazi campaign against the Jews.
- By 1951 the majority of Bangor's 1,200 Jews lived in middle and upper class areas, although they remained a self-contained group.
- A census taken by the Jewish Community Council in 1951 showed that Jews owned or

Jews began immigrating to Bangor early in the 20ᵗʰ century.

worked in over 200 shoe, clothing, and dry goods stores; more than 300 were self-employed; and 51 were professionals.

- By 1954 only a few families attending Bangor's three synagogues were strictly observant and one of the city's two kosher butcher shops sold non-kosher meat on the side; the other gave up selling kosher food to become the largest meat market in Bangor.
- In 1954 the Jewish community established a funeral chapel so that funeral services no longer need to be held in private homes.
- Guided by a master plan drawn up in 1951, Bangor began to transition its downtown from the once-bustling docks to roads that could handle cars and trucks.
- Efforts were under way to stop the dumping of sewage directly into the Kenduskeag Stream and the Penobscot River, which also served as the city's drinking water source.
- The women of Bangor, in a daily ritual of sociability, went downtown to shop, carefully dressed in suits or dresses, gloves, and hats.

The Jews in America

- In 1820 approximately 5,000 Jews lived in America; by 1850 the number had grown to 50,000, and by 1880 the number was 10 times larger.
- Although Jews, particularly from Germany, had come to America earlier, after 1880 Jewish immigration became a flood tide.
- More than two million Jews arrived in the United States over three decades, most from eastern Europe where three-quarters of the world's 7.7 million Jews were living.
- In Russia and the Austro-Hungarian empire, the growth of large-scale agriculture squeezed out Jewish middlemen as it destroyed the independent peasantry.
- In some countries savage discrimination and severe restrictions on the jobs they might hold forced them to emigrate.
- By the turn of the century, 700,000 arrived on the shores of the United States; one-quarter were illiterate, many had few skills and almost all were impoverished.
- Often the husband went to America first and by cautious living, he saved enough to fetch his children and wife from the old country.
- The average immigrant arrived in New York with only $20.00 to his or her name.
- The ocean voyage, which cost $34.00 in steerage class, was difficult for all immigrants, but particularly Orthodox Jews, whose religious diet required that they subsist on herring, black bread, and tea—all of which they brought on board with them.
- Upon arrival, according to survey in 1890, 60 percent of the immigrant Jews worked in the needle trades in New York City, typically using primitive machines to sew together cut goods provided by the manufacturer.
- Life in the sweatshops on the Lower East Side was difficult but provided unskilled immigrants with immediate employment opportunities and the chance to earn a weekly wage of $5.00.
- On the Lower East Side, where most of the Jewish families lived, rent was about $10.00 a month, milk was $0.04 a quart, bread was $0.02 a pound, herring was a penny, and a kitchen table could be bought for $1.00.

- Within the tenements, only one room in each four-room apartment received direct air and sunlight; all the families on each floor shared a toilet in the hall.
- Despite the highest population density in the city, the predominantly Jewish Tenth Ward had one of the lowest death rates; this was attributed to the strenuous personal cleanliness of the Jews.
- Tuberculosis, the white plague, did abound however, and it was why many Jews left the city for farms or other smaller cities such as Bangor to seek their fortune.
- Alcohol use among Jewish immigrants was limited; instead sales of seltzer or soda water to Jewish workers were so high it became known as "worker's champagne."

The Lower East Side of Manhattan was home to many Jewish immigrants.

- Despite their poverty, Jewish families were healthy and mothers considered their children woefully underweight unless they were well-cushioned with fat.
- The economic transition of the Jews took place quickly; thanks to an emphasis on education, many began entering white collar and professional jobs.
- Composer Irving Berlin, born in Russia and brought to America as a small child, electrified America with his songs including "Alexander's Ragtime Band" and "Annie Get Your Gun."
- Following the First World War and the Russian Revolution of 1917, America closed its doors to immigration.
- In 1917 Congress passed a literacy requirement, over President Wilson's veto, to restrict the flow of immigrants; the 1924 Johnson Bill provided that only two percent of each nationality group be admitted each year, based on the 1890 census; the immigration from southern and eastern Europe virtually stopped.
- Between the wars discrimination was practiced against Jews in housing and employment; many companies made no secret of the fact that they did not hire Jews.
- Certain neighborhoods were restricted to Jews; universities adopted a quota system that limited the number of Jewish students to a certain percentage.
- With Hitler's rise to power in Germany, many Jews, including the Rochmans, fled to America to avoid the concentration camps.
- The Nazi "ethnic cleansing" campaign resulted in six million Jews being killed or exterminated in Nazi death camps.
- Under the Displaced Persons Act, thousands of Jews were admitted to the U.S. after the war.

Mothers Against Comic Books

Ann O'Conner found it difficult to raise her son, Jonathan, alone after her husband was killed in World War II, and Ann's mother often watched Jonathan while Ann worked as a waitress at a local diner. Ann's constant worry escalated when her son's grades began to slip in 1954, which she was convinced was due to his obsession with horror comic books.

Life at Home

- Ann O'Conner of the Bronx, New York, was obsessed with providing better life for her and her teenaged son, Jonathan.
- She planned for him to attend college, and she would not allow comic books to get in the way, no matter how much he protested.
- She read in a national magazine the scientific evidence that proved how excessive comic book reading was directly linked to juvenile delinquency.
- Jonathan's father had died in World War II without ever meeting his son and namesake.
- Ann and Jonathan had dated for two years before hastily getting married only weeks before his deployment to Europe.
- After his death, Ann raised her son with the help of her parents, Karl and Mary Pagel, in their tiny apartment.
- Mary often watched Jonathan while Ann worked as a waitress at a local diner.
- The Bronx was full of activity and the restaurants were often busy, but Ann's tips rarely provided enough money to raise a child with college in his future.
- No one in her family had graduated from high school, much less college—her father worked in the shipyards of New York and her mother stayed at home to raise children.
- Ann and her family were practicing Catholics and attended church in the Bronx at Blessed Sacrament on Sundays and holy days.
- The most treasured items in the home were the family Bible and a crucifix Karl brought from Germany when he emigrated in 1913.
- Ann loved to hold the Bible, but because it was in Latin, she could only read the most familiar phrases.
- At Blessed Sacrament Elementary School, Jonathan was an exceptional student.

Ann O'Connor fought against violent comic books.

Jonathan was a grade A student when he entered high school.

- One of the nuns informed Ann about the opportunities at Regis High School in the Upper East Side of Manhattan, a tuition-free high school founded in 1914 by the Society of Jesus, also known as the Jesuits.
- The high school accepted eighth-grade Catholic boys with an "A" average regardless of their family income.
- After lots of tutoring and hard work, Jonathan was accepted into Regis High School.
- In the spring of his sophomore year in 1954, however, Jonathan's grades began to slip, and one of his teachers, who noticed that Jonathan enjoyed reading Batman and Superman comic books, was sure the books were influencing his academics.
- The detrimental effects of comic books were in the news, which reported that the U.S. Senate judiciary subcommittee was holding hearings on the role of comic books in the rise of juvenile delinquency.
- Reports from educational experts warned that the publications, especially those that emphasized crime fighting and horror, were having criminal effects on children.
- The comic book industry scoffed at the claims that mere comic books could turn children into "little monsters."
- Ann's worst suspicions were reaffirmed in May when she read in *Reader's Digest,* an excerpt from a book entitled *Seduction of the Innocent* by Dr. Fredric Wertham, whose studies indicated that comic books contributed to delinquency in children through the picture stories of sex and violence.
- According to Dr. Wertham's research, juvenile delinquency had increased about 20 percent since 1947.
- The books also illustrated "foreign-looking" people as villains, which belied American efforts to persuade the world that race hatred was not a staple of American life.
- The article disturbed Ann, who feared that these books may corrupt her son and jeopardize his future.
- As a result, she banned comics from her home, over Jonathan's protests.
- When she discovered he was reading comic books at friends' houses, she knew she had to organize.

Life at Work: Anti-Comic Book Advocate

- Ann voiced her concerns to the mothers in the neighborhood and then to the women of the church.
- She explained that comic books led to burglary, violence, gangs, and eventually drugs, and proposed that everyone ban comic books from their homes.
- Ann also managed to convince the women to clean up the neighborhood by protesting the sale of comic books.
- The owner of a corner newsstand told the women that he had to buy the horror comics to acquire the better-selling comic books and family magazines.
- This was known as "tie-in sales" and helped sell the lesser-quality comics and magazines.
- Many of the comic book companies and distributors required the vendors to accept the delivered bundles, regardless of content.

- Ann purchased a couple of the comic books and personally examined what her son was reading.
- She was shocked that for $0.10 her son could see the horrible drawings found in books with titles such as Tomb of Horror, and advertisements for knives and air rifles.
- Ann took her concerns to several more newsstands in her neighborhood, but most of the workers thought she was crazy and said they could not do anything about the deliveries.
- Frustrated by the excuses, she, along with her friends and neighbors, wrote letters to their congressmen, local newsstand owners and the Newsdealers Association.

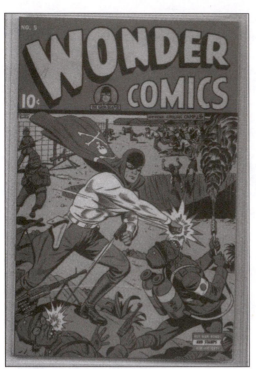

- Ann's mother Mary stayed out of the protest, not wanting to draw attention to herself or cause any trouble.
- Some of Ann's neighbors were active in women's clubs in New York which also protested the sale of violent comic books.
- Jonathan thought his mother went overboard, creating too much commotion over grades and reading Batman.
- That summer, Ann's efforts were rewarded with a small victory—Newsdealers Association of Greater New York would refuse to handle "lewd, horror or indecent magazines that may fall into the hands of juveniles."
- Later in June, the Kable News Company, a distributor of comics, said that reformers were going too far and were attempting to "destroy the imagination of American kids," and that if all the comics were removed from New York, there would be "more juvenile delinquency."
- Horror and crime comics were million-dollar business.
- During the Senate subcommittee hearings, reformers attacked many of the distributors, the comic book companies and their supporters for influencing delinquency.
- They said that comic book covers showing human heads boiling in vats were in poor taste and that books showing methods in crime were irresistible to juveniles.
- Ann O'Conner thought that greed was the motivating factor for these comics, and that federal legislation was needed to prevent the spread of indecency to children.
- One of the publishers of the horror comics, William Gaines of the Entertaining Comic Group, told the subcommittee that juvenile delinquency "is a product of the real environment in which the child lives, and not of the fiction he reads."
- By July, New York State law went into effect banning "tie-in" sales of magazines to newsdealers and New Jersey and Idaho passed similar measures.

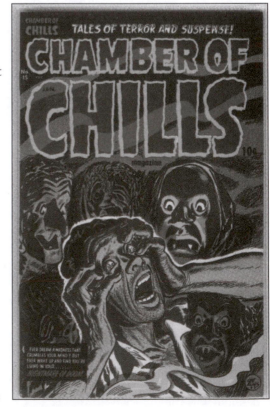

Life in the Community: Bronx, New York

- The U.S. Senate hearings, in addition to creating much national and international attention, got big play in the O'Conner household.
- The family read a news story about Canadian courts linking two homicides by teenaged killers to the reading of crime comics, and another report about British Prime Minster Winston Churchill reading a handful of horror comics to weigh the need for a possible ban.
- After the U.S. Senate hearings, legislators indicated that it would not be likely that federal law would ban

tie-in sales of horror comics packaged with family magazines.

- Congressmen hoped to see more local action and public pressure, and senators pressured the comic book industry to enforce a code of good taste.
- Ann and her friends did not believe that the industry code would do any good.
- During a July annual meeting, the General Federation of Women's Clubs declared a campaign against juvenile delinquency.
- The Federation compiled a list of current objectionable comics and sent them to all the other clubs so that they could protest.
- The Federation listed 36 comics "very objectionable," 122 "objectionable" and 158 as "on objections."
- Ann tried to acquire this list but was not a member of any women's organization, so she continued to communicate with her state and local representatives on the issue.
- Included in her letters were lists of the comics that she thought should be banned from newsstands, such as *True Crime, Two-Fisted Tales* and *Crypt of Terror.*
- Nationwide, women were campaigning to stop the objectionable materials.
- New York even held a special Joint Legislative Committee one weekend to discuss legislation barring the "glamorizing of brutality and sadism in publications" available to minors.
- Representatives from Governor Thomas Dewey's office also attended the meeting.
- After the committee meetings, Ann received a letter from her state senator thanking her for her interest in this important issue and telling her that he was working to find a solution.
- Ann's mother Mary was proud of her daughter's hard work and recognition by an important statesmen.
- Mary wanted to frame the letter but Ann's father insisted that it was only a form letter drafted by the senator's staff.
- Regardless, the letter reinforced that Ann's efforts were part of the greater good of society, especially the youth, and they were a step in protecting her son and the children of other families.
- In September, the comics industry formed a new self-regulatory group and planned to develop a code to protect the children from questionable content.
- The organization, called the Comic Magazine Association of America, was formed with 90 percent participation of the comic industry.
- The industry selected New York City Magistrate Charles F. Murphy as the official "censor" of the organization.
- The Comic Magazine Association gave Magistrate Murphy a $100,000 budget and a two-year contract to develop and enforce a comic book code.
- Upon his appointment, Murphy received numerous letters from legislators and citizens throughout the nation.
- Ann sent Murphy a letter every week with a list of books that should be banned and examples of comic issues that contained poor content.
- The Comic Magazine Association developed its code by the end of 1954, after which a vast majority of the crime and horror comics disappeared from the newsstands.
- Ann saw what had occurred over the past several months as a victory for women.
- During an afternoon discussion with a group of her friends over coffee, the topic turned to another issue that might lead to juvenile delinquency: the influence of television.

Charles Murphy was the censor of the Comic Book Association.

Not So Horrible, Commentary,
The New York Times, September 19, 1954

In New York last April, a Senate judiciary subcommittee on juvenile delinquency held hearings for two days on crime and horror comics. The sociologist and experts could not agree. Some held that only those children already "disturbed" mentally and emotionally were harmed by horror comics. Others argued that they were harmful primarily to normal children, and did not greatly affect morbid children already "wrapped in their own fantasies…"

Last Wednesday, the newly formed Comics Magazine Association of America announced that it had appointed an official censor—New York Magistrate Charles F. Murphy, who has been active in combating juvenile delinquency. Mr. Murphy said he had accepted the job on condition that member publishers take crime and horror comics off the list. Two days before Mr. Murphy's appointment, Mr. Gaines called a press conference to announce that he was substituting a "clean, clean line" since that "seems to be what the American parents want."

Real Curb Sought for Delinquency, Erik H. Erikson Deplores
Tendency to Make Comics and TV 'Scapegoats,'
Murray Illson, *The New York Times*, October 3, 1954

There is too much "scapegoating" on the subject of juvenile delinquency and not enough careful search for the real causes, an authority on adolescent psychology said today. Erik H. Erikson, senior staff member of the Austen Riggs Center here, asserted that there was an unfortunate and increasing tendency to blame without adequate evidence such media as comic books, television, movies and all the graphic representations of violence. He declared that these could not be dismissed as harmless, but the evidence as to the precise role they played in the world of atom bombs and total war had not been gathered…

"When people get worked up," Mr. Erikson said, "they often look for something or someone to blame. That makes them feel better but it doesn't mean they have found the cause.

"They fool themselves into believing they have an immediate cure, with no evidence whatever that it will work now or has worked in the past, because usually this 'remedy' is an old one that never really worked. This misleads everybody and helps to retard responsible efforts to solve the problem."

Druggists to Curb Comics,
The New York Times, October 1, 1954

Drugstore members of the Upstate Pharmaceutical Council will not handle comic books detrimental to youthful minds, it was announced today by the council at its annual meeting.…Members of the council unanimously approved the campaign by the New York State Pharmaceutical Association…

The New York Times, October 14, 1954

The American Legion Auxiliary announced today a nation-wide "Operation Book-swap" to give children a chance to trade crime and horror comics for good books.

The Standards of the Comic Code Authority
as Originally Adopted

(Excerpts)

General Standards (EDITORIAL MATTER)

1. Crimes shall never be presented in such a way as to create sympathy for the criminal, to promote distrust of the forces of law and justice, or to inspire others with a desire to imitate criminals.

2. No comics shall explicitly present the unique details and methods of a crime.

3. Policemen, judges, government officials and respected institutions shall never be presented in such a way as to create disrespect for established authority.

4. If crime is depicted it shall be as a sordid and unpleasant activity.

5. Criminals shall not be presented so as to be rendered glamorous or to occupy a position which creates a desire for emulation.

6. In every instance good shall triumph over evil and the criminal punished for his misdeeds.

7. Scenes of excessive violence shall be prohibited. Scenes of brutal torture, excessive and unnecessary knife and gun play, physical agony, gory and gruesome crime shall be eliminated.

8. No unique or unusual methods of concealing weapons shall be shown.

9. Instances of law enforcement officers dying as a result of a criminal's activities should be discouraged.

10. The crime of kidnapping shall never be portrayed in any detail, nor shall any profit accrue to the abductor or kidnapper. The criminal or the kidnapper must be punished in every case.

11. The letter of the word "crime" on a comics magazine cover shall never be appreciably greater in dimension than the other words contained in the title. The word "crime" shall never appear alone on a cover.

12. Restraint in the use of the word "crime" in titles or subtitles shall be exercised.

General Standards (GRAPHIC MATTER)

1. No comic magazine shall use the word horror or terror in its title.

2. All scenes of horror, excessive bloodshed, gory or gruesome crimes, depravity, lust, sadism, masochism shall not be permitted.

3. All lurid, unsavory, gruesome illustrations shall be eliminated.

4. Inclusion of stories dealing with evil shall be used or shall be published only where the intent is to illustrate a moral issue and in no case shall evil be presented alluringly nor so as to injure the sensibilities of the reader.

5. Scenes dealing with, or instruments associated with walking dead, torture, vampires and vampirism, ghouls, cannibalism and werewolfism are prohibited.

Dialogue

1. Profanity, obscenity, smut, vulgarity, or words or symbols which have acquired undesirable meanings are forbidden.

2. Special precautions to avoid references to physical afflictions or deformities shall be taken.

3. Although slang and colloquialisms are acceptable, excessive use should be discouraged and wherever possible good grammar shall be employed.

Marriage and Sex

1. Divorce shall not be treated humorously nor represented as desirable.

2. Illicit sex relations are neither to be hinted at nor portrayed. Violent love scenes as well as sexual abnormalities are unacceptable.

3. Respect for parents, the moral code, and for honorable behavior shall be fostered. A sympathetic understanding of the problems of love is not a license for morbid distortion.

4. The treatment of love-romance stories shall emphasize the value of the home and the sanctity of marriage.

5. Passion or romantic interest shall never be treated in such a way as to stimulate the lower and baser emotions.

6. Seduction and rape shall never be shown or suggested.

7. Sex perversion or any inference to same is strictly forbidden.

No Harm in Horror, Comics Issuer Says, Peter Kihss, *The New York Times*, April 22, 1954

A comic-book publisher, who boasted he was the first in the country to publish "horror comics," told a Senate subcommittee yesterday that he believed no healthy, normal child ever had been "ruined" by a comic book. A child's personality is set before he reaches reading age, the publisher contended.

William Gaines, president of the Entertaining Comics Group, which prints two million comic books a month with a gross sale of $80,000 and a net profit of $4,000, said that he opposed any censorship and recognized only a limit of "good taste."

He was asked by Senator Estes Kefauver, Democrat of Tennessee, if he considered in "good taste" the cover of his Shock SuspenStories, which depicted an axe-wielding man holding aloft the severed head of a blond women. Mr. Gaines replied: "Yes, I do—for the cover of a horror comic. I think it would be in bad taste if he were holding the head a little higher so the neck would show with the blood dripping from it."

"You've got blood dripping from the mouth," Senator Kefauver pointed out, softly....

Seduction of the Innocent, Fredric Wertham, M.D., Rinehart & Co., New York, 1954

In 1946 crime comics represented only about one-tenth of all comic books. By 1949 crime comics had increased to one-half the total output, and by 1953 formed the vast majority. The so-called "good" comics—sports, animal stories, Disney comics—today make up no more than one-fifth of the whole...

One comic book bears the legend, "We hope that within these pages the youth of America will learn to know crime for what it really is: a dead-end road of fools and tears." Inside, a criminal terrorizes a farm family, makes advances to the farmer's wife, beats the farmer, kidnaps the little boy as a hostage. "I'll knock yer teeth out!!" he snarls as he beats the child. In the end the criminal evades the law by shooting himself, like a hero. The story has 97 pictures of the criminal winning, and only for his violent end-a ratio of 97 parts of "crime" to one of "does not pay"...

Lurid advertisements, interspersed among the comics, are veritable invitations to delinquency. Pictures of air pistols, a "genuine .22 rifle" accompany sequences showing how the guns may be used to threaten people. An ad for a switchblade knife shows how to hold it, "with your thumb on the button." Another, for a telescope, points out that you can look into "neighbors' homes," and the illustration shows a half-nude girl. Still others offer secret creams for girls with small busts, and patent medicines to develop "virility"…

Many comic books describe how to set fires, by methods too various to enumerate. In some stories fire-setting is related just as a detail; in other stories such as "The Arson Racket" the lesson is more systematic. There are other sidelights, like how to break windows so you cannot be found out; all this highlighted by the philosophy of the character who says: "From now on—I'm making dough the easy way—with a gun! Only SAPS work!" That lesson, incidentally, is true of crime comics as a whole: glamour for crime, contempt for work…

Father of FM Radio

Edwin Howard Armstrong grasped the intricacies of electronics that many scientists could not. While at Columbia University, he made several discoveries that caused others to resent the young inventor. In 1954, he had FM radio figured out, but the constant battle for patents for his work got the better of his finances, his marriage and eventually his life.

Life at Home

- When Edwin Howard Armstrong jumped from the thirteenth-floor window of River House in New York City in 1954, his thoughts were not on a lifetime of innovation, but on the patent disputes that haunted his work.
- The architect of FM and the three basic circuits upon which rested the whole of modern radio communications lost the will to fight.
- Born in New York City in 1890, he was the son of John Armstrong, U.S. representative to the Oxford University Press.
- In his comfortable, literary household, Edwin grew up absorbing stories about inventors Watt, Volta, Hertz, Tesla, Marconi, and his hero, Michael Faraday.
- At nine years old, he came down with rheumatic fever that kept him out of school for two years and left him with a lifelong tic in his shoulder and jaw.
- A serious child, he soon caught up with his classmates and displayed a fascination for Marconi's inventions.
- When Edwin enrolled in electrical engineering at Columbia University in 1909, he knew all there was to know about wireless devices, and commuted to school on his red Indian motorcycle.
- As an undergrad, he made his first great discovery, regeneration, and ignited his first patent fight.
- At that time, inventor Lee De Forest's audion tube, the first triode vacuum tube, had been around for several years, but was not well understood.
- Edwin discovered that the voltage gain of a triode amplifier could be dramatically increased by using positive feedback—by feeding some of the amplifier output back into the input.

Edwin Armstrong invented FM radio.

Inventor Lee De Forest resented young Edwin's progress.

- Given enough feedback, the amplifier became a stable and powerful oscillator, perfect for driving radio transmitters.
- Supplied a little less feedback, the amplifier became a more sensitive radio receiver than anything else at the time.
- Titled a "wireless receiving system," and later as "regenerative radio," the invention improved the amplification of radio signals.
- Edwin sold his red motorcycle in 1913 to finance the patent fees.
- After De Forest heard of Edwin's work, he immediately directed his own research into regenerative techniques and quickly filed patents on variants of the technique.
- Then he started attacking Edwin's patents.
- De Forest, infuriated that such a young man used his own tubes better than he had, was determined to control their use.
- De Forest was backed up by American Telephone & Telegraph (AT&T), which stood to receive enormous financial gains if it could control a fundamental circuit of radio.
- The patent fight lasted 14 years, cost over $1 million, and was presented to the Supreme Court several times.
- De Forest's evidence of priority was a 1912 note in a lab book that a particular circuit emitted a howl when tuned a certain way.
- Eventually, De Forest and AT&T won in a widely criticized verdict, leaving Edwin bitter.
- Edwin's second invention came while he was still in his twenties, serving as an Army Signal Corps Major in World War I in France.
- The super heterodyne was a subtle and elegant technique for improving reception and tuning at the same time.
- Manufacturers had found it difficult to build an amplifier that would work at high frequencies, and at the same time construct a tuning filter than could select a narrow band of frequencies.
- The filter must tune in to one station and reject all others, but then be capable of tuning in to other stations.
- It was far easier to build a tunable oscillator, Edwin decided.
- Edwin's early inventions, vital to the new radio industry, brought him almost instant wealth and a professorship at Columbia.
- After World War I ended, Westinghouse Electric and Manufacturing Company paid him $530,000 over 10 years for his first two patents.
- In 1922, he sold a less important invention, the super regenerative circuit, to Radio Corporation of America (RCA) for $200,000 and 60,000 shares of RCA stock.
- At age 32, the now wealthy inventor went to Europe and came home with a Hispano-Suiza sports car to impress his girlfriend.
- Edwin and Marion were married in 1923, and on their honeymoon in Palm Beach, he carried along the first portable radio ever built—a present created for the occasion.
- Like his hero Faraday, whose discoveries founded the electrical industry, Ed was an original non-mathematical thinker in electric magnetic waves.

- Too many discoveries, he believed, had been put off by math calculations that said they were impossible and thus were never attempted.
- His forte was the acute analysis of ambiguous physical phenomena, and he relished debating accepted theories about the laws of nature.
- In his career, Edwin never became an employee, but was paid $1.00 a year as a faculty member at Columbia, since his patents paid him much more than the university could.
- He never taught classes, he never incorporated, and he did all his work with only a few assistants, some of whom went on to do significant work of their own.

Edwin's inventions brought him wealth, and a new car to impress his girlfriend.

Life at Work: Inventor of FM Radio

- The 14-year patent fight with Lee De Forest and AT&T left Edwin Armstrong exhausted and humiliated.
- When the courts turned against Edwin and the newspapers referred to him as "that discredited inventor" in 1934, he resolved to get even.
- Edwin was in his early forties, past the creative prime for most engineers, when he came up with his greatest invention of all, frequency modulation (FM).
- At the time, amplitude modulation (AM) dominated radio broadcasts, based on the idea that the strength of a radio signal was proportional to the strength of the audio signal being transmitted.
- Unfortunately, the natural world was full of similarly modulated signals, often heard as static.
- In FM, the frequency of the main signal varied instead of its amplitude.
- Detailed mathematical analyses in the 1920s showed that a narrow-band FM signal would always sound worse than an AM signal of the same power.
- Edwin's insight was that an FM signal didn't have to have a narrow range of frequencies, but could vary over a wide range, and have a far better signal-to-noise ratio.
- By relying on experimentation and physical reasoning, Edwin got beyond the equations.
- He offered the FM patents only for licensing, not for sale, as he was determined to control the quality of FM.
- To Edwin's way of thinking, AM was producing inferior sound because of its fundamental technology and the overcrowding of radio stations in limited frequencies transmitted to inferior receivers.
- He showed the innovation to RCA, but they had made vast investments in AM radio and were not interested in a competitive change.
- All of their transmitters and the millions of radios they sold used AM, and the investment had not depreciated.
- The industry giant informed Edwin that the public was not interested in high fidelity, and moreover, with television just on the horizon, FM had arrived too late.
- RCA said that consumers didn't care what the music sounded like from their radios, and they just wanted to get it as cheaply as possible.
- Edwin never forgot their insult, and licensed FM to smaller companies, including in the package a transmitter, antennas, and receivers, and set up pilot broadcasting services in New York and New England in 1939.
- The world was mesmerized by the quality of the music.
- RCA immediately struck back by petitioning the Federal Communications Commission to give FM's frequency assignments to upstart television, but this was rejected.

The military used Edwin's inventions in World War II.

- RCA next offered Edwin $1 million for his patents, but no subsequent royalties, and he refused.
- If every other licensee paid royalties, RCA could, too.
- When America's priorities shifted with the start of World War II, FM was extensively used for military purposes.
- Edwin allowed the military to use his patents royalty-free, and mobile FM communications proved to save thousands of lives across Europe and the Pacific.
- When the Germans and Japanese were defeated, Edwin still had corporations like RCA and Columbia Broadcasting System (CBS) as powerful foes.
- In 1945, RCA and a bloc of other radio companies successfully lobbied the FCC to move the FM band from 44-50 MHz to 88-108 MHz, which made obsolete all the transmitters and receivers that had been built.
- The FCC also voted to severely limit FM's broadcasting power, and disallow radio relays from central stations to mountaintop antennas.
- FM broadcasting was crippled by the decisions and AM continued to have a regulatory advantage.
- Edwin redesigned and reworked his invention at the higher frequencies, and by 1948 he was ready to move forward, even though his patents only had two years left until their expiration.
- RCA had been building FM receivers using his patents for the previous eight years without paying him, so he brought a patent infringement suit against them in 1949.
- At the trial, Edwin was called to be the first witness, and RCA's lawyers kept him on the witness stand for an entire year with questions.
- Another two years were consumed while RCA laid out the research it had done on FM in the 1930s, including the claim that RCA had invented FM all by itself without any help from Edwin, causing him to lose his ability to compromise or settle.
- By 1953, Edwin's licenses and patents had all expired.
- His crushing legal bills and research expenses brought him to near bankruptcy, and a bitter argument with his wife, Marion, on Thanksgiving day caused her to leave him.
- On January 31, 1954, he wrote a two-page letter to her and left it on his apartment desk. He dressed neatly in an overcoat, hat, scarf and gloves, and walked out a thirteenth-story window.
- He hit a third-story overhang, so his body wasn't discovered until the next day.
- Marion continued his suits and, unlike her husband, was willing to compromise.
- She settled with RCA for over $1 million, then went after other companies like Sylvania and CBS that had also infringed on his patents.

Life in the Community: New York City

- Modern New York City , with its five boroughs, was created in 1898 with the consolidation of the cities of New York, including Manhattan, the Bronx, Brooklyn, and the largely rural areas of Queens and Staten Island.
- The consolidation precipitated greater physical connections among the boroughs and facilitated the building of the New York City subway.
- The Williamsburg Bridge in 1903 and the Manhattan Bridge in 1909 further connected Manhattan to the rapidly expanding bedroom community in Brooklyn.

Marian Anderson was the first black singer hired by the Metropolitan Opera.

- Grand Central Terminal opened as the world's largest train station on February 1, 1913.
- New York City was the main point of embarkation for U.S. troops traveling to Europe during World War I.
- The 1920 Census showed Brooklyn for the first time overtaking Manhattan as the most populous borough, just as the Immigration Act of 1924 severely limited further immigrants from Southern and Eastern Europe.
- Instead, New York experienced growth as a result of the Great Migration of African-Americans from the South, resulting in a flowering of African-American culture in the Harlem Renaissance.
- Tin Pan Alley developed towards Broadway, and the first modern musical, Jerome Kern's Show Boat opened in 1927 as the theater district moved north of 42nd Street.
- New York City became known for its skyscrapers that transformed the skyline, epitomized by the dueling spires of the Chrysler Building and the Empire State Building, which was called the Empty State Building during the Great Depression.
- New York, long a city of immigrants, became a culturally international city with the influx of intellectual, musical and artistic European refugees that started in the late 1930s.
- The 1939 New York World's Fair marked the 150th anniversary of George Washington's inauguration in Federal Hall and carried the theme "Building the World of Tomorrow," until the outbreak of World War II in Europe, when the focus shifted to "For Peace and Freedom."
- For the duration of the war, the Port of New York handled 25 percent of the nation's trade.
- With 75,000 workers, the Navy Yard was the world's largest shipyard.
- The only major world city unscathed by the war, New York emerged as the leading world city, with Wall Street contributing to America's ascendancy and, in 1951, with the United Nations relocating from its first headquarters in Flushing Meadows Park, Queens, to the East Side of Manhattan.
- Marian Anderson became the first black singer hired by the Metropolitan Opera.
- The Broadway show Fanny opened at the Majestic Theater for 888 performances.
- Gian Carlo Menotti's opera Saint of Bleecker Street premiered.
- Joseph Papp founded the outdoor New York Shakespeare Festival.
- Opera singer Edith Mason performs on the first radio program of operas.

Edith Mason was the first opera singer to perform on the radio.

Cultural Events in New York City: 1954

The Caine Mutiny by Herman Wouk premiered.

After 1,928 performances, South Pacific closed at Majestic Theater.

The musical The Pajama Game opened on Broadway for 1,063 performances.

The King and I closed at St. James Theater after 1,246 performances.

Bill Haley & the Comets recorded "Rock Around the Clock" at Pythian Temple.

The Boy Friend opened at the Royale Theater for 483 performances.

Yale Scholar from Jackson Hole

Walter Perry was born and raised in Jackson Hole, Wyoming and enjoyed life in the mountains—climbing, skiing, hunting, fishing—and varsity football. Recruited by Yale in 1954 as part of a diversification program, Walter adapted to the Ivy League school on the East Coast without sacrificing what he learned in the natural habitat of his West Coast home.

Life at Home

- Growing up as the son of a federal park ranger had its advantages, one of which was the opportunity to hunt elk.
- Each fall, a herd of elk comprising about 16,000 to 20,000 head drifted down from the high summer range in the Yellowstone-Teton National Forest area to winter in the lower Jackson Hole Valley.
- Add to elk hunting mountain climbing, snow skiing, varsity football, high school's valedictorian, and a full scholarship to college, and you saw what a nice life Walter Perry had.
- During his senior year, Walter was asked to assist one of the world's finest mountain climbers in preparing to scale the cliff-hunt towers of the Middle Teton.
- Walter helped arrange for transportation, located the campsites and participated in the hike, only completing the first half of the climb before turning back—so he could play in his high school football game.
- As the starting right end, he found football fun, but hardly something around which a serious man would build his life.
- He also found the community's obsession with beating local rivals amusing and annoying.
- His goal was to attend college and learn the range of his skills.
- "Your own potential is the greatest burden God gives any person," his father told him over and over again.
- Until he received a personal call from a Yale recruiter offering him a scholarship, he had never considered leaving the area.
- His father called it a sign of things to come, encouraging him to take the challenge, but his mother was less sure.
- Not only was Walter the first in his family to attend college, but this invitation included a full scholarship to one of the nation's most prestigious schools.

Walter Perry received a full scholarship to Yale University.

65

Walter thought football fun, but not serious.

- Walter's initial excitement soon mingled with the fear of making a mistake and embarrassing his family and the community.
- He felt the same thing before his first elk hunt at age 12, his father reminded him, yet Walter made a kill on his first day with his first shot, and hasn't backed away from a challenge since.
- One of his father's duties in Jackson Hole was to monitor the activities of the beavers, whose dams can filter the mountain water and settle the silt, ensuring pure, clean stream water, while at the same time be destructive to the environment.
- Early on, Walter was taught to "think twice and act once" so he could discover which actions were helpful or harmful, and that "Not everything is what it seems."
- He also learned that clocks were invented by man, not by nature, and time was a sorry way to measure anything, including the length of time a conversation should last or that a hunting trip will require.
- Walter also recognized the downside of his region's informal way.

Walter and his friends enjoyed Jackson Hole.

- More than once he and his father made the long drive into town for a necessary tractor part, only to find a sign on Simpson's Hardware Store, reading: "Closed, gone elk hunting. Back Thursday."
- Growing up, he had plenty of "pets" around his cabin home: coyotes, ground squirrels, chipmunks, magpies, ravens, horned owls, sparrow hawks, prairie falcons, Canadian geese, trout and white-footed mice.
- The coyote his father found abandoned as a pup lived near the house, coming and going like the family dog.
- The environment around Jackson Hole also taught him to read danger signals.
- A moose will give warning of its intent to attack by lifting the hair along the back of its neck and spine, then stick out its tongue.
- He found that the signs of danger were harder to read in the East at Yale.

Life at School

- Walter was recruited by Yale as part of a program to diversify the Ivy League school.
- He had never been east of the Mississippi River before, never even seen pictures of the campus, and was still unsure of the correct spelling of "Connecticut."
- His first days were intimidating, as though he arrived in a strange country where everyone spoke a foreign language.
- The specially recruited diversity students, whose fathers and grandfathers had not attended Yale and who had no pedigree, quickly formed their own informal "Public High School Rube Society," where they could make fun of themselves and those around them.
- The ratio of private school graduates to those of public schools is 61:34 in favor of private schools.

Having fun in a sports jacket was difficult for Walter.

Walter was part of Yale's "rube society."

- Walter quickly discovered that the Eastern boarding-school students have their own way of dressing, talking and socializing.
- Walter and his "rube society" friends make great sport of imitating the legacy students who often possessed long links to Yale and lots of blueblood money.
- Yet, the bluebloods set a tone on campus that was cool, understated and confident, causing Walter to think of himself as a slobbering puppy dog beside these men of class.

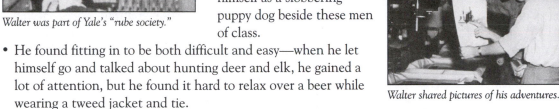

Walter shared pictures of his adventures.

- He found fitting in to be both difficult and easy—when he let himself go and talked about hunting deer and elk, he gained a lot of attention, but he found it hard to relax over a beer while wearing a tweed jacket and tie.

At the Roots of Ivy,
Newsweek, November 15, 1954

At Yale, Dr. Whitney Griswold informed his undergraduate-school faculty with some asperity that he has not relented on changes recommended to them a year ago. At that time, the report of a committee headed by the university's president suggested the abolition of regular courses for freshmen and sophomores. As a man who feels that the flaws in the present American system have forced colleges into "doing the high schools' job for them," Dr. Griswold thought improvement could be obtained if students were allowed to work semi-independently for two years, attending lectures only when they wished and participating once a week in a discussion group in "areas of concentration." Such freedom might snatch the student from a fate wherein, as the Griswold committee's report put it, he "first loses his interest in and then his respect for the education he's getting." At the end of two years, moreover, the student would have to pass a series of comprehensive tests to stay in school.

Privately, some Yale professors thought such changes would have catastrophic effects. Although they were urged to make the report their "chief academic activity," during the next year, few departments made concrete recommendations. Two weeks ago, Dr. Griswold, head of the university since 1950, made it clear that he still expects action.

- Dunkin' Donuts were the rage, shipped in weekly from Quincy, Massachusetts, by the father of a Yale sophomore—the sugary donuts seemed close to heaven after a long day of arcane English literature.
- Less popular among his classmates was Walter's love of Spam, which his family ate a lot of during World War II.
- When homesick, he resorted to eating Spam, even though his roommate gagged at the mere suggestion of a Spam sandwich.
- Movies, when time can be found, were crucial to his existence, especially anything by Alfred Hitchcock.
- Outside his window, he saw his fellow students endlessly tossing empty pie tins from the Frisbee Baking Company.
- Others played catch using the new Pluto Platter, shaped the same way as the pie tins but made of plastic.
- Although dozens of games of toss took place every day, Walter couldn't imagine this fad ever catching on anywhere else—especially out West.
- Across America, colleges debated philosophical issues of academic freedom, such as whether or not a communist should be allowed to teach.

- Academically, Yale was one of the great strongholds of liberal arts education and Walter and his roommates joked that its curriculum was not intended to train anyone to do anything, but instead to be somebody.
- About 630 undergraduate courses were offered at the school, one quarter of them consisting of small discussion groups and seminars in which students were encouraged to participate.
- An educational experiment under way when Walter attended Yale was called Directed Studies, whereby students took special courses in broad fields of learning for their first two years, along with an integrating philosophy class.
- Yale aimed its Directed Studies program at 50 extremely precocious 16-year-olds, all lifted out of high schools and preparatory schools, and supported by a Ford Foundation grant, to prove that four years of high school are two years too many.
- In addition, Yale established a Scholar of the House program in which 13 seniors take no classes, dropped in on an occasional class suggested by their advisor, and worked on lengthy projects in the fields of creative writing, literary criticism, philosophy, mathematics, international relations, city planning, art history, social history, political science and archaeology.

End of a Tradition,
Time, April 6, 1953

In every Yale man's life, there has been one traumatic experience that other people do not have. It is Tap Day—he tense afternoon in May when members of the junior class gather to await the whack on the back that will send 90 of them to the six great Senior societies. William Howard Taft had sweated it out (he went to Skull and Bones); so had his son Robert (Bones), and Robert's political adversary, Dean Acheson (Scroll and Key). Even that fictional stalwart, Dink Stover (Bones), had trembled at the thought of Tap Day; "The morning was interminable, a horror. They did not even joke about the approaching ordeal. No one was so sure of election that the possible rejection of some chum cast its gloom over the day." But the Dink Stovers who went to Yale after World War II seemed unable to take Tap Day too seriously. Many found it humiliating for the hundreds of juniors rejected; some found the etiquette of the societies ludicrous (in theory, a member hearing his society's name mentioned among outsiders was supposed to leave the room). Finally last week, Yales' Senior societies quietly came to a decision. After 75 years, Tap Day was abolished. Just how the societies will elect members from now on no one yet knew. Said the Yale Daily News: "Tap Day was not a great evil…but as a tangible symbol it has drawn most of the anti-society criticism…What remains is for the Societies to justify their existence."

- Walter loved the Yale library, and considered it a festival to walk among 2.8 million volumes.
- He calculated that the library back home was one half of one floor of this 16-story tower.

Yale celebrated its 250 anniversary in 1951.

- Vacuum tubes, elevators and machinery ran throughout the imposing, crowded building and permeated the stacks with a faint humming sound.
- It was considered one of the great research libraries in the world and included a Gutenberg Bible, the manuscripts of Gertrude Stein and the Kanjur, an ancient, 99-volume collection of sacred Buddhist writings.
- In 1947, Yale purchased the first book printed in the American colonies, the *Bay Psalm Book,* for $151,000.

Life in the Community: New Haven, Connecticut and Jackson Hole, Wyoming

- Having recently celebrated the 250th anniversary of its founding in 1701, Yale had a firm grip on tradition.
- Scattered around Connecticut, the school was pulled together in New Haven in 1716, thanks to the financial windfall of Elihu Yale, a rich London merchant who gave £562 to the fledgling "collegiate school."
- Following the establishment of a separate science department and autonomous schools of divinity, medicine and law, Yale became a university in 1887.
- This legacy is further reinforced by the occasional presence on campus of Old Blues, as loyal members of the alumni are called.
- Often they are introduced by their professional titles such as president, chairman of the board or Honorable.
- The school had 4,300 students, up from its traditional 3,800.
- The university was well-known for its graduate school programs, where Paul Hindemith is on the faculty of the Music School, Robert Penn Warren in the Drama School and Filmer S.C. Northrop in the Law School.
- Yale underwent considerable new construction to meet the needs of the modern era. Its clean, modern buildings were in sharp contrast to those in Walter's home town of Jackson Hole, where travelers looked west to the jagged granite skyline of the Teton Range, its tallest summit, clawing the sky at an elevation of nearly 14,000 feet.
- The first white man—a mountain man and trapper named John Colter—set foot in Jackson Hole around 1807.
- In 1829 Capt. William Sublette named the valley for his trapper partner, David E. Jackson, the term "hole" coming from a Western expression for an enclosed mountain valley.
- French-Canadian trappers gave the Tetons their name, dubbing three towering summits the "Trois Tetons" for their fancied resemblance to a woman's breasts.
- In 1897 the Teton National Forest was created, in 1912 Congress set aside land in the valley for a National Elk Refuge and established Grand Teton National Park in 1929.
- Congress in 1950 extended the boundaries of Grand Teton National Park to include privately owned land and larger areas formerly in Jackson Hole National Monument.
- This more than tripled the size of the park to over 310,000 acres, with about one-sixth of the new acreage consisting of former private holdings bought by John D. Rockefeller, Jr. and presented to the American people.
- Tourism was king in the Hole, and focused on mountain climbing and hiking in the summer and skiing in the winder.

The Yale Man, by John Knowles,
Holiday, May 1953

My classmates [in 1946] were busily rehearsing for their careers in a rich variety of other activities, such as the Political Union, which features a three-party system, treacherous parliamentary maneuvering and guest speakers of national renown. Others were trying out for team managerships or the widely traveled glee clubs, or the hoary *Literary Magazine,* where budding writers can consort with the shadows of Sinclair Lewis, Philip Barry, Steven Vincent Benét and other famous alumni. For those less intensely competitive there is an orchestra, a dramatic association, a band, a film-producing club, a debating team, an aviation club, and many other groups.

Meanwhile, like a good Stover (junior grade), I was moving through the labyrinth of Yale society life, in which the first stage is Mory's. As a freshman I was fascinated by this little white Colonial house with its name elegantly inscribed on a brass plate on the door, with its Whiffenproofs and the dear old Temple Bar. Mory's seemed to be the real Yale.

Two friends who were members submitted my name. In due course, I was permitted to pay 18 dollars for a lifetime membership. Inside Mory's I found a crowded little restaurant, the walls almost completely hidden by the pictures of Yale teams, crew oars hanging from the ceiling, the tables everywhere scarred with initials. The food was sometimes mediocre, sometimes awful, always expensive, and the waiters certainly the surliest in New England. The Temple Bar is just another name for Mory's. It is true that the Whiffenproofs sing there Monday nights, waxing loud and careless as they drink their way through a large silver urn, the exotic Green Cup, with its highly secret ingredients of champagne, brandy and crème de menthe. But it wasn't as I had pictured it.

Mory's launches the undergraduate into the social swim at Yale, and the secret societies are presumed to decide, at the end of his junior year, whether he is a winner. To the innocent, uninformed and impressionable freshman, the secret societies are like enormous icebergs glimpsed through the fog, and pondered over because of their immense unknowable beneath the surface.

Six of these icebergs float majestically upon the scene at Yale, cold, seemingly lifeless. Their headquarters are forbidding, windowless sepulchers. Skull and Bones occupies an ominous, rust-colored Egyptian pile. Wolf's Head is pure suburban Gothic. I remember, during my first week at Yale, walking past Book and Snake, a small white temple of purest classical Greek, and it seemed entirely useless, an extravagant ornament.

Inexorably, the societies glide into the student's life. The myths about "Bones" usually come first. If you say "Skull and Bones" in the presence of a member he will leave immediately. Three years later we badgered one of them with these words and he only looked embarrassed. "If you get into 'Bones' you're sure of an income of $10,000 a year." Yale is run by 'Bones' men." And new students may be subject to sudden startling encounters, such as the Thursday night I was strolling along a campus walk when out of the obscurity a phalanx of Wolf's Head lock-stepped past, stone-faced.

Family Doctor

Conrad Davis was 45 in 1955. As a successful doctor in a gracious Southern city, he loved his work and was devoted to his wife and four children. The family enjoyed all that his $29,000 annual salary afforded, including living in one of Charleston's most historic homes, and belonging to the most important social clubs in the city.

Life at Home

- Dr. Davis has spent his entire life in Charleston, except for a stint at schools in Atlanta, New Jersey, and New York City for his residency.
- He graduated from the College of Charleston and the Medical College of South Carolina, located in Charleston, in 1935.
- He served his internships at Grady Hospital in Atlanta and at Burlington County Hospital in New Jersey.
- He met his wife, Sylvia, in New York and they married in 1939 when he was associated with the Home for Incurables in New York City.
- Their home in Charleston was built in 1722, and believed to be the oldest single house in the city.
- Purchased for $14,100 at an executor's sale in 1943, the lot was 39 feet wide by 220 feet long.
- The three-story brick house had handsome marble quoins on either side, a shaped brick cornice, and a tile roof.
- It exemplified the floor plan peculiar to the city's houses, which were one room wide, and it was built sideways on the lot, with its length running perpendicular to the front property line and its side, or gabled end, facing the street.
- The second floor included the formal living room for entertaining, and the bedrooms were on the third floor.
- Sylvia's mother, who lived with the family, spent much of her time seeing friends or crocheting; Conrad's mother also crocheted and was making a tablecloth for each of her seven grandchildren.
- Conrad's roots ran deeply into the state; his ancestor was an Episcopal priest who helped start Trinity Church in Columbia, South Carolina, in 1814.
- The family attended St. Philip's Episcopal Church, which was completed in 1838 to replace the building destroyed by fire in 1835.

Dr. Conrad Davis, his wife, and their fourth child.

The Davis' home was built in 1722.

- The Davis family was part of the most important social clubs in the city, including the exclusive St. Cecilia Society and the Yacht Club.
- The annual St. Cecilia Society Ball, a card dance, was much anticipated, and Conrad and Sylvia traditionally exchanged dance partners with friends they knew for many years.
- In his free time, Conrad headed to the nearby waters of the Atlantic Ocean or the creeks of Wadmalaw Island.
- Charleston was seven miles from the open ocean; the channel is 40 feet deep at low water and 47 feet deep at high tide.
- While fishing off the old ferry wharf, he hauled in a 25 pound sea bream, a fish more common to Florida than to Charleston.
- Conrad purchased a 40-foot, ocean-going boat for fishing and travelling the intercoastal waterway.
- The boat was large enough for two couples to sleep aboard on long trips—if the mosquitoes stayed away.
- When at home, he indulged his passion for genealogy, and constructed elaborate charts of the lineage of his relatives and friends and often wrote dozens of letters to track down the most obscure details.
- Sylvia was five years younger than Conrad, and their four children ranged from newborn to 12 years.
- The family just purchased its first television set; the boys loved Westerns, while their six-year-old sister preferred Disney cartoons.

Dr. Davis caught a 25 lb bass.

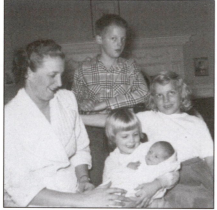
Their four children were newborn to 12 years.

- The two middle children took piano lessons, and the oldest boy, Brian, hunted and fished with his dad.
- On Thanksgiving, Brian took part in a deer-drive at Middleton Plantation, a tradition dating back to Colonial days in which deer were driven by dogs and handlers toward the hunters.
- With four children, Sylvia often felt stressed with carpooling the children, managing the house, and attending social functions with her gregarious husband.
- She ended her term as president of the Junior League, which established a speech correction school in the city.

Life at Work: Family Doctor

- Dr. Davis started work early most days, leaving the house by seven and beginning surgery at the hospital by 8 a.m.; a full schedule of patients at his downtown office started at 10 a.m.
- He drove a 1953 Oldsmobile to the hospital across town and then returned downtown for appointments at his office on Bull Street a dozen or so blocks from his home.
- He returned home at 2 p.m. for a midday meal—the main meal of the day—of rice, fresh vegetables and, frequently, shrimp or fish often purchased from the "shrimp man," who pushed a cart filled with fresh shrimp through the downtown neighborhoods each morning.

Dr. and Mrs. Davis entertained in the formal living room.

- The children ran out of the house when they heard him holler, "Shrimp man, shrimp man," collected the shrimp in a rice steamer or pot, and paid him on the spot.
- The family dinner, prepared by the family cook, often included okra and tomatoes.
- The cook traveled each morning from her home on one of the barrier islands surrounding Charleston, a trip that took 30 minutes each way.
- Following the meal, Conrad napped for 30 minutes in his upstairs bedroom, then saw patients for the remainder of the afternoon.
- Following work, he socialized at the Yacht Club before going home.
- He also was a member of a poker club that met every two weeks in one of the members' homes.

Vaccines, Salk and Otherwise
Worcester Massachusetts Medical News, May 1955

There are a lot of long-buried doctors, scientists, and intellects whirling in their graves at this moment as they hear of the mass acceptance of polio vaccination. The opposition of the people to all mass vaccinations in the past is reminiscent of the attacks of the anti-vivisection groups today. Where are the anti-polio-vaccination groups? Has the masterful publicity associated with the Salk vaccine driven them into their fanatic holes?

However much we deplore publicity, we must doff our hats and expose our crew cuts or scalps in admiration for a publicity stunt that outdid the unveiling of the Model A Ford. It did many things: It aroused the country. It made us forget what a small percentage of the money collected by the March of Dimes was unnecessary to effect this wonderful result. It made us overlook the high administrative expense prevalent for years in the March of Dimes. It made us forget that this was the last step in many steps to this perfection. It reminded us that a lot of money and a lot of brilliance exhibited by Jonas Salk proved the value of the anti-polio vaccine several years before it would ultimately be proved…

We must keep our feet off the ground and on our desks. The ground trembles with great noises and appropriations. Some of us in many specialties are swelling our chests and making plans. Give Salk his due and his glory and get our feet off this trembling ground. Treat this disease with what is available to us in our usual manner just as we do with typhoid and smallpox: with as little fanfare.

Let us not contribute to the hysteria of discovery. Let the publicists, like the lay executives of all fundraising organization, have their today; but let us try to control their tomorrow.

We have read in our own Medical Library the writing of our predecessors about preceding vaccines and their efforts to have them accepted. It is a much different story today. Theirs were voices crying for converts and advocates. The historians will find us crying for restraints and orderliness.

- The city had a long history of medical excellence; the Medical Society of South Carolina was founded in 1789, and in 1824, the state's first medical school was opened, attended in the 1830s by James Marion Sims, the father of American gynecology.
- By 1840, the Medical College opened a College Hospital for "furnishing instruction at the bedside of the sick" for medical students; it became one of the first teaching hospitals in America.
- The South Carolina Training School for Nurses was established in 1883 and by 1894, women were first admitted to train at the Medical College, the same year a College of Pharmacy was permanently added to the school.
- The cost of care for the city's indigent ill was shifted from the city to the Medical College of South Carolina, which through federal grants enjoyed tremendous growth.
- Statewide physicians attempted to organize the Salk vaccine program to eradicate polio, trying to determine who will provide the shots, who will pay, and how the administration will be handled.
- The president of the Medical University of South Carolina, Dr. Kenneth Lynch, was a pioneer in the investigation of industrial dust diseases and his 91 papers and two books helped reduce health hazards in industry.
- Since 1946, when the Hospital Survey and Construction Program was begun, 2,500 hospitals and health facilities have been approved for federal aid in construction nationwide, with 1,700 completed so far.
- Despite new construction, the nation's hospitals were short 800,000 beds, including those who served the general populations, as well as facilities for mental, tuberculosis, and chronic care.
- Dr. Davis joined with the Medical Association to defeat two pieces of legislation in South Carolina; one bill could lead to "socialized medicine" and the second would help "rid the state of the Naturopathic cult."
- Ninety percent, or 1,134, of the practicing physicians in the state, were participating members of the Blue Cross-Blue Shield insurance program provided by the Medical Association, and Dr. Davis served on the Committee on Medical and Hospital Insurance Contracts.

Life in the Community: Charleston, South Carolina

- Charleston was founded in 1670 by 93 passengers arriving aboard the ship Carolina and by the 18th century, it was a principal city of British North America.
- Charleston boosted tourism, and revived the Azalea Festival, which had been dormant for several years.
- Dr. Davis worked with the city council to approve a new traffic plan that created more one-way streets, and he encouraged the city to make further efforts to identify streets and house numbers "to facilitate finding patients."
- Charleston was a city of contrasts, with the nation's great architectural treasures next to the poorest areas in the nation.
- *The Charleston News and Courier*, owned by an associate of Dr. Davis, was vehemently opposed to the integration of the schools and in favor of the purging of unqualified black voters from the polls.
- As pressure for integration grew, the *News and Courier* excoriated the NAACP and its liberal friends who perpetuated the "utterly false contention that Southern colored people have not been well treated," maintaining,

Charleston is known for its decorative iron gates.

rather, that Southern Negroes have been "generously treated since they were brought to North America out of savagery and slavery in Africa."

- With racial tensions high, attacking the NAACP in the South was politically analogous to assaulting the Communist Party in the rest of the nation.
- When the U.S. Supreme Court made its unanimous ruling in *Brown v. the Board of Education of Topeka, Kansas,* calling for the end of "separate but equal" segregated schools, the *News and Courier* assailed the decision: "It can be carried out only by an army, dispatched into South Carolina from the outside."
- Other revolutionary winds blew in Charleston, as inexpensive and efficient window air-conditioning units came on the market, and Charleston's first television station, WCSC-TV, broadcast its first program.
- The state's economy was dominated by the textile industry, as 69 percent of all industrial wage earners, were in the textile business.

Key Events in Charleston

1901: The South Carolina Interstate and West Indian Exposition opened and the "world's fair" drew 375,000 visitors during its six-month run.

1902: President Theodore Roosevelt toured Fortt Sumter and the site of the new 1,189-acre Navy Yard.

1905: The Gibbes Museum of Art opened on Meeting Street.

1920: Concern for the destruction of historical buildings inspired the forming of the Society for Preservation of Old Dwelling Houses, later renamed the Preservation Society.

1929: The first Cooper River Bridge opened, spanning 2.7 miles, the fifth longest bridge in the world at that time, calling for a .50 toll to defray the $6 million construction cost.

1931: Dorothy Legge purchased 99 and 101 East Bay, beginning the restoration of the area known as Rainbow Row.

1931: Charleston adopted the first Historical Zoning Ordinance in the United States.

1935: The American folk opera *Porgy and Bess* opened in Boston and New York; George Gershwin spent three months in the city gathering material, launching songs such as "Summertime," "I Got Plenty of Nuttin," and "It Ain't Necessarily So."

1947: Charlestonians established the Historic Charleston Foundation to help preserve the city's architectural heritage, which instituted a "Festival of Houses" tour of private homes to raise money.

Problems of Prepaid Sickness Insurance, J. Decherd Guess, M.D., Medical Director, South Carolina Hospital Service and Medical Care Plans, Greenville, South Carolina, *Journal of the South Carolina Medical Association*

The basic problems of prepaid sickness insurance arise from unnecessary and wasteful utilization of hospital facilities by insured persons. This statement applies to both Blue Cross and Blue Shield nonprofit insurance plans and commercial insurance carriers. Already over-utilization has forced costs of sickness insurance up so high that such insurance is out of reach of at least 25 percent of American families. That is bad, but what is even worse is that, in spite of successive rate increases and some restrictions in benefits, most Blue Cross and some Blue Shield plans are experiencing financial difficulties. It is said that some commercial companies are compensating for losses from sickness insurance contracts by profits from life insurance coverage.

These commercial companies are able to restrict their losses to a considerable extent by the device of providing only cash indemnities with definite patient limitations.

The basic and unique principle of Blue Cross is to insure against all necessary hospital costs of covered illnesses. Insofar as it deviates from the principle, it approaches the type of coverage offered by commercial companies. Blue Shield attempts to provide similar service benefits to low-and medium-income groups, and in that way to take care of the doctor's entire bill. Perhaps the fear of the unpredictability of the amount of the costs of illness is greater than the fear of illness expense itself. When a Blue Cross member knows that he, by simply presenting his identification card, can be admitted to a member hospital without making an advance payment and with no expectation of a bill for extras, he enjoys a marvelous peace of mind which has therapeutic value. There is no fear of embarrassment of insolvency. . . By a method of trial and error . . .restrictions for eligibility for membership in Blue Cross have been reduced, so that almost anyone not already sick and under 65 years of age may join a Blue Cross plan.

Coincidental with this broadening of eligibility for Blue Cross membership, the spiral of increasing hospital costs began. There soon followed the building of many new hospitals. With all hospital charges covered by Blue Cross, it became both more convenient and cheaper to be sick in hospital than at home. It became also more worthwhile to join a plan in contemplation of operations and other illness, and to demand either that the doctor fake the history or for the patient to change doctors. Utilization began to climb and is still climbing.

There have arisen several other factors tending to increase hospital utilization. Doctors, busy as they are, more scientific in their approach to diagnosis, and more impatient for results, prefer hospital patients rather than home patients. They advise hospitalization for minor illness.

Furthermore, once the patient is in the hospital, it is so easy to order x-ray examinations, repeated laboratory examinations, EKGs, BMRs, etc., that such examinations are ordered frequently without very well-thought-through indications. Furthermore, because of half-knowledge gotten from parlor conversations, patients are asking for these tests—especially when they have insurance.

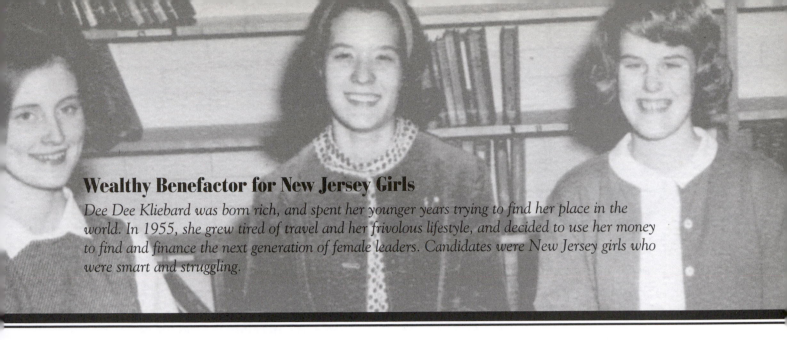

Wealthy Benefactor for New Jersey Girls

Dee Dee Kliebard was born rich, and spent her younger years trying to find her place in the world. In 1955, she grew tired of travel and her frivolous lifestyle, and decided to use her money to find and finance the next generation of female leaders. Candidates were New Jersey girls who were smart and struggling.

Life at Home

- Her real name was Jesse Elaine Torrey Kliebard, but everyone called her Dee-Dee.
- Through the years the origin of her nickname had changed dozens of times, depending on Dee-Dee's mood and the circumstances at hand.
- Sometimes she said that her first words were "Dee-Dee" instead of "dada"; after her mother died, she claimed Dee-Dee was her mother's middle name; when she became old enough to date, she "confessed" that it was based on the new method of measuring brassiere cup size; after her father died when she was 35, she claimed "darling daughter" evolved into Dee Dee.
- When Dee-Dee reached the age of 45, she took stock of her life.
- She was rich—that much was clear.
- Her mother's carefully invested ketchup fortune combined with her architect father's real estate holdings made her one of the wealthiest women in New Jersey.
- She was married once—for 31 days—"which was not enough time to use up a whole bar of soap."
- Her ex-husband loved her money and other women, a combination that failed to stir Dee Dee's passion.
- Her time at Sweet Briar College lasted longer—three semesters—where she acquired a taste for Kentucky bourbon, tall men with Southern accents, and the rousing music played at country honky-tonks.
- Her activities got her expelled and, after several years of touring Europe, learning to fly a plane, and a near-death experience, Dee-Dee had an epiphany.
- She realized that she was simply a custodian of the money sitting in her accounts, and the world was full of causes waiting to be rescued by her wealth.

Dee-Dee Kliebard created a college scholarship fund for girls.

Headmaster of Sweet Briar College, left.

- Dee Dee decided to help young women get an education, from a high school diploma to an opportunity to attend college.
- In the postwar 1950s, a high school education was not enough; college was vital for American world leadership.
- Dee-Dee believed that women should be included in the educational bonanza underway thanks to the thousands of men being educated through the G.I. Bill.
- She wanted to find and finance the next generation of female leaders, by providing a four-year scholarship to the college of their choice.
- Women, who were almost universally enrolled in two-year teachers' colleges, were expected to resign their teaching jobs when they married.
- The number of students from the working classes who could raise the tuition was usually kept in check by living expenses during school.

Life at Work

- The idea of creating a scholarship program for talented New Jersey girls was so exciting that Dee-Dee could not sleep at night.
- At first, she hired a team of educators and charity professionals to help her select the first crop of recipients from Trenton, New Jersey.
- They talked in theories and coded messages, and thought it best to keep Dee Dee out of the decision process.
- Undaunted, Dee-Dee ordered books and met with experts to decide the goals of education: to get a job, to create better citizens, to establish a foundation for lifetime learning, to find a mate, or to develop a business network.
- Should education stick to the basics? Should the curriculum be broad and wide? Should students be divided by potential or class or IQ?
- The first 10 girls were selected without Dee-Dee's input, and most of them couldn't pronounce her last name, let alone understand her aspirations for them.

Most women in college came from wealthy families.

Dee-Dee's scholarship recipients were smart high school girls.

- They did, however, fully understand how to behave during a formal tea, and fully expected to attend an Ivy League school.
- Dee-Dee quickly fired everyone in sight, explaining that they had not listened to her at all.
- Her scholarships were about opportunity for those who were struggling, not the perpetuation of the ruling, wealthy class.
- Dee-Dee wondered how many potential recipients were being hidden by the current system, believing they were not college bound because they couldn't afford more education.
- The second time around, Dee-Dee hired three teachers and one principal, invited them to her home for a week of training, and then directed them to find 25 girls capable of changing the world, without divulging where the money came from.

- After seven months, she was presented with the candidates, each of whom were driven with their parents to Dee-Dee's home for a personal interview.
- Dee-Dee was terrified that she would not know what to ask, but found the process pleasing and the high school seniors enchanting.
- Two of the girls had given up on going to college even before they entered high school, three others had marginal grades, and six had not started applying to schools.
- What they had in common was spunk and a teacher, coach or principal who spotted potential hidden from the rest of the world.
- Of the 25 candidates, one girl bragged that she had a trust fund and didn't need anyone else's money, while another confessed that she was pregnant and not planning to attend college for a while.
- The remaining 23 were chosen for full scholarships.
- Dee-Dee decided that future classes would also contain 23 winners, and that each year she would stage a reunion of "her girls" to celebrate their successes.
- Nineteen of the 23 college students returned to receive their second year's tuition and scholarship money.

WASHINGTON AT THE BATTLE OF TRENTON.

The Battle of Trenton was George Washington's first military victory.

Life in the Community: Trenton, New Jersey
- The first New Jersey settlement, which would become Trenton, was established in 1679 by Quakers, who were being persecuted in England at this time; North America provided the perfect opportunity to exercise their religious freedom.
- By 1719, the town adopted the name "Trent-towne," after William Trent, one of its leading landholders who purchased much of the surrounding land.

- During the Revolutionary War, the city was the site of the Battle of Trenton, George Washington's first military victory.
- After the war, Trenton was briefly the national capital in November and December of 1784.
- Trenton became the state capital in 1790, but prior to that year the Legislature often met here.
- Growth was rapid throughout the nineteenth century as Europeans came to work in the city's pottery and wire rope mills.
- Trenton was a major industrial center in the late nineteenth and early twentieth centuries, earning the slogan "Trenton Makes, The World Takes" for its role in the manufacture of rubber, wire rope, ceramics and cigars.

Annual Cost of University of Pennsylvania Undergraduate Schools

1900: College and the Wharton School
Tuition: $150
Room and Board: $185 minimum, $250 maximum
Text-books: $10

1930: College, School of Engineering & Applied Science (SEAS) and the Wharton School
Tuition: $400, which included the General Fee
Room and Board: $520
Clothing and Miscellaneous: $260
Text-books: $35

1955: College, College of Liberal Arts for Women, School of Engineering and Applied Science (SEAS), the Wharton School, the School of Nursing, and the School of Allied Medical Professions (SAMP)
Tuition: $800
General Fee: $135
Room and Board: $835
Text-books: $50

French Fry Entrepreneur

Jack Simplot quit school at 14, and wheeled and dealed his way through life until he won a potato sorter with the flip of a coin. He exploited the humble spud, which he fed to hungry World War II soldiers, dehydrated for instant mashed during the golden age of food processing, and, in 1955, froze during the up and coming fast food industry.

Life at Home

- John Richard "Jack" Simplot's success was built on potatoes.
- Jack and the humble spud were linked from the moment a flip of a coin in 1928 won him an electric potato sorter, to WW II, when his company became the largest shipper of potatoes in America, to the first commercial French fry.
- The $254 electric potato sorter speeded up work enough that Jack's Declo, Idaho, neighbors eagerly sought its services.
- One electric portable sorter led to four, one potato shed to 33, and an empire was born.
- Born on January 4, 1909, to Charles and Dorothy Simplot on an Iowa homestead, Jack was one of six children.
- He was still in diapers when the family moved to Declo, where his father built a log cabin and cleared land with a team of horses.
- Like most farm children, Jack got up at five am and milked the cows before walking to school, only to run home to do more chores in the afternoon.
- It was an unsentimental life.
- When young Jack lost a fingertip in an accident and a doctor admonished his parents for not bringing it to be reattached, they told him the chickens had eaten it.
- At 14, when his father refused to let him attend a basketball game, Jack left home, quit school and moved to Declo's Enyeart Hotel.
- With money he made raising orphaned lambs, he purchased interest-bearing scrips at $0.50 on the dollar from teachers living at the hotel and used it as collateral to buy 600 hogs at $1.00 a head, a rifle, and a pick-up truck.
- He used the rifle to shoot wild horses and, after stripping the hides for future sale at $2.00 each, he mixed their meat with potatoes cooked on sagebrush-fueled flames and fed it to his hogs.
- Jack sold the fattened pigs the next summer for $12.50 each during a nationwide pork shortage, and made more than $7,800 profit.

Jack Simplot made frozen French Fries a commercial success.

Jack sold pigs at a profit.

- With the money he bought farm machinery and six horses and became a farmer.
- For three years, he leased 120 acres to grow potatoes, beans and hay, then sold the horses and machinery but kept growing potatoes.
- Idaho's altitude, warm days, cool nights, light volcanic soil and abundance of irrigation made it an ideal setting for growing Russet Burbank potatoes.
- He bought an electric potato sorter with a partner, but won full ownership with the flip of a coin, and expanded to all phases of the potato industry.

A potato sorter started Jack's good fortune.

- Determined to create a regional reputation for the best potatoes, Jack decided that cull potatoes as seed stock weren't good enough, and bought certified seed by the carloads, furnish it to the growers.
- "I told 'em, 'You keep the sprouts off that damn stuff somehow or 'nother, keep 'em cool, turn 'em over, and plant 'em on the tenth of June. If you do, you'll raise yourself some good seed.'"
- In 1931, he married Ruby Rosevear whom he had met on a blind date and proposed to in his Model A Ford.

Jack's wife, Ruby, loved the simple life.

- She was quiet and introverted, and wanted a simple life.
- Nine years after Ruby and Jack married, he owned 30,000 acres of farm and ranch land and was shipping 10,000 boxcars of potatoes a year.
- While other Idahoans took their families to the mountains on vacation, Jack took his to Grand View, where the company farmed and fed up to 150,000 head of cattle.

Life at Work: Food Industry Entrepreneur

- World War II presented a special opportunity to Jack Simplot: hungry soldiers who could be fed with dehydrated and fresh potatoes.
- Already wealthy by 1941 due to a prune drying machine he bought in Southern California that he used to dry onions in Idaho, Jack understood opportunity.
- Before the war, he had used the prune drying machine to create dehydrated products for onion powder and onion flakes, netting him $600,000 the first year.
- With an order for 500,000 pounds of dried onions, he needed a plant to process them.
- He wanted to build the manufacturing facility at Parma, Idaho, but the owner of the property sicced his dogs on Jack, and he settled on Caldwell, Idaho, instead.
- The Caldwell plant, equipped with the world's largest food dehydrator, was key to his becoming the largest supplier of potatoes to the military during World War II.
- Under contract to the federal government during World War II, Jack shipped 33 million pounds of dehydrated potatoes to the U.S. Armed Forces from 1942 through 1945.
- By 1945, more than 50 million pounds of spuds were being used by the military and, of 156 companies supplying dried food, Simplot had one-third of the action.

Potato, left to right: dehydrated, natural, sliced.

- When war shipments started in 1942, Jack employed 100 workers in his Caldwell plant; by 1944, he had 1,200 employees and the largest dehydrating plant in the world.
- The potato waste from the dehydration plant encouraged Jack to build a 2,000-hog feedlot next door.
- When wartime shortages made it difficult to buy fertilizer, Jack built a manufacturing plant in Pocatello, Idaho, and produced his own.
- That kind of ingenuity continued during the early 1950s as the Simplot Company created and marketed the world's first commercially viable frozen French fries.
- In 1945, a chemist at the Simplot lab in Caldwell asked Jack to give him a freeze box so that he could practice freezing vegetables.
- "Hell," Jack told him, "you freeze spuds and they will go to mush."
- But he bought the guy a 10-foot box anyway and after a few months, Jack was tasting hot French fries that had been previously frozen.
- "I ate some and said, 'My God, good product.'"
- Within six months, he had bought a 10,000-ton cold storage facility and a 60-ton-per-day ice manufacturing plant.
- They also made potato granules, which became instant mashed potatoes, prime for this golden age of food processing.
- After World War II, millions of Americans bought refrigerators which, for the first time, included a freezer.
- Within a few years, one marvelous innovation after another promised to simplify the lives of American housewives: frozen orange juice, frozen TV dinners, Cheez Whiz, Jell-O salads, and Miracle Whip.
- Depression-era scarcity gave way to a cornucopia of new foods, as ad campaigns made space-age processed foods appear more attractive than fresh.
- Restaurants even featured frozen dinners on their menus.
- Jack began selling frozen French fries in 1953 just as the budding fast food industry was searching for its identity and a practical menu.
- French fries could be eaten without a fork and they tasted great—especially when cooked in beef tallow.
- For the emerging fast food industry, frozen French fries offered uniformity and reduced labor costs, and quickly became the most profitable item on the menu.
- Jack's company held all the relevant patents, and sales that began slowly in 1953, skyrocketed.
- By 1955, the year the company incorporated all of its operations under the name "J.R. Simplot Co.," annual French fry production exceeded 10 million pounds.
- A medium-size 5.3-ounce potato with the skin provided vitamin C, potassium, vitamin B6, and its fiber content equaled many whole grain foods.

Life in the Community: The State of Idaho

- In the early 1860s, when the U.S. Congress was considering a new territory in the Rocky Mountains, eccentric lobbyist George M. Willing suggested the name "Idaho," claiming it was derived from the Shoshone language meaning "the sun comes from the mountains" or "gem of the mountains."
- Willing later claimed that he had made up the name himself.

Shoshone Falls, Snake River, Idaho.

- Idaho, as part of the Oregon Country, was claimed by both the United States and Great Britain until the United States gained undisputed jurisdiction in 1846.
- Idaho achieved statehood in 1890 when its population was 88,000
- Its economy was primarily supported by metal mining, shifted towards agriculture and lumbering.
- Sixty percent of Idaho's land was held by the National Forest Service or the Bureau of Land Management, and boasted a perfect climate for growing potatoes.
- The landscape was home to some of the largest unspoiled natural areas in the United States, and the 2.3 million-acre River of No Return Wilderness Area is the largest contiguous region of protected wilderness in the continental United States.

Lumber was important to Idaho's economy.

- Potatoes were planted in Idaho as early as 1838 and by 1900, the state's production exceeded a million bushels.
- Prior to 1910, the crops were stored in barns or root cellars, but by the 1920s, potato cellars came into use.
- U.S. potato production increased steadily so that by 1955, two-thirds of the potato crop came from Idaho, Washington, Oregon, Colorado, and Maine.
- In the 1950s, the growth of the French fry industry led to a focus on developing different varieties of potatoes.

Potato Growing and Dehydration

- Potatoes were domesticated in Peru between 3000 BC and 2000 BC.
- In the Altiplano, potatoes provided the principal energy source for the Inca Empire, its predecessors, and its Spanish successor.
- Processing potatoes for storage has a long history, and the Incas used climate to produce the first dehydrated potatoes.
- Their method entailed an overnight freezing and thawing cycle plus low humidity, and the ice crystals that formed forced openings in the cell tissue, allowing liquid to escape.
- The cycle was repeated several times to lower the moisture content, and then the marble-sized potatoes were dried for storage.
- The Incas called it chuño, and it was a staple used by soldiers.

Potato cellars kept potatos long after they've been harvested.

- Potatoes were known for their abundant yield with little more effort than growing in a cool climate, moist enough for the plants to gather sufficient water from the soil to form the starchy tubers.
- There are about 5,000 potato varieties worldwide, 3,000 of them found in the Andes alone, mainly Peru, Bolivia, Ecuador, Chile and Colombia.
- Europeans first used potatoes for provisioning ships in the sixteenth century.
- By the eighteenth century, the potato had become the major food source in a large part of Europe.

- Introduced to Europe by Spain in 1536, the potato was subsequently conveyed by European mariners to territories and ports throughout the world.
- Throughout Europe, the most important new food in the nineteenth century was the potato, which had three major advantages over other foods for the consumer: its lower rate of spoilage, its ability to easily satisfy hunger, and its low cost.
- By 1845, the potato crop occupied one-third of Irish arable land and potatoes comprised about 10 percent of the caloric intake of Europeans.
- In England, the potato promoted economic development by underpinning the Industrial Revolution in the nineteenth century.
- It served as a cheap source of calories and nutrients that was easy for urban workers to cultivate on small backyard plots.
- Potatoes became popular in the north of England, where coal was readily available, so a potato-driven population boom provided ample workers for the new factories.
- In Ireland, the expansion of potato cultivation was due entirely to the landless laborers, renting tiny plots from predominantly English landowners, who were interested only in raising cattle or in producing grain for market.
- A single acre of potatoes and the milk of a single cow was enough to feed a whole Irish family a monotonous but nutritionally adequate diet for a healthy, vigorous, and desperately poor rural population.
- Often, even poor families grew enough extra potatoes to feed a pig that they could sell for cash.
- In 1845, a plant disease known as late blight spread rapidly through the poorer communities of western Ireland, resulting in the Great Irish Potato Famine.
- Two drawbacks to the potato was that it was bulky and it had a short shelf life in comparison to grains.
- Potato flour was prepared in 1786, and experiments were conducted to find processes for drying potatoes.
- Potato chips—first called Saratoga chips—appeared in the middle of the nineteenth century and they were first prepared in the home, accompanied by some small-scale commercial production.
- Major commercial applications had to await improved peeling and frying techniques.
- Potato chip production did not become a big business until after World War II.
- Increased consumer demand for convenience foods prompted a renewed search for ways of extending the shelf life of potatoes, with emphasis on developing instant mashed potatoes.
- Ultimately, two processes emerged for producing dehydrated mashed potatoes: granules and flakes.
- Fixing on a quick-drying process using a single-drum drier was a major breakthrough following research focused on the appearance and flavor of the reconstituted flakes.
- Idaho's Russet Burbank potatoes were used commercially in making dehydrated mashed potatoes because of their high solid content necessary to obtain good texture when reconstituted.

Dehydrated Potatoes Get Government Praise, *The Greeley Tribune* (Colorado), June 24, 1943:
Quality of dehydrated potatoes being turned out at the plant of Dehydrated Food Products Company of Colorado has been praised by government inspectors who have inspected the product and accepted delivery on about half a carload of the dehydrated product, according to Orville Ruler, general manager of the company....The plant is now employing about 150 people; 100 more women workers are needed. The plant operates three eight-hour shifts. Shifts are from 4 p.m. to midnight, from midnight to 8 a.m., and from 8 a.m. to 4 p.m. Workers are on a shift for a month and then transferred to another shift. Basic wages $0.40 an hour, and time and a half for overtime over 40 hours. Most workers get about 42 hours a week, Ruler said.

Jack Simplot Builds It!
The Salt Lake Tribune, January 16, 1949

Simplot is a magic name in intermountain West. In towns up and down Idaho's Snake River Valley are signs reading "J. R. Simplot Co.," signs of a new empire founded on the agricultural economy of the Gem State and its contiguous territory.

J. R. Simplot is the guiding genius of this empire, which reaches into Utah with the acquisition of the wartime Kalnite plant at Salt Lake City, now being converted to produce phosphate fertilizer to augment the supply pouring from his Pocatello plant.

Jack Simplot's interests are wide, but his chief holdings are concerned with agriculture. Besides his string of warehouses which make him Idaho's biggest shipper of potatoes and fresh vegetables, and his Pocatello and Salt Lake plants, he operates the world's largest dehydrating

The U.S. government praised dehydrated potatos.

plant, a string of Snake River Valley farms, hog ranches, a box factory, a real estate firm, an insurance firm, hotels. He is a director of the Idaho Power Company and has interests in gold, silver and lead mines.

Just turning 40, Jack Simplot is a multimillionaire of boundless energy and acute business acumen. He left school at the age of 14, and at 16 was farming on his own. At 20, he became a produce dealer when he shipped his first car of potatoes. During the Depression years, he acquired 18 warehouses and shipped as high as 8,000 boxcars of potatoes annually to 41 states. He bought more farms and raised onions, among other things. It was while inspecting an onion dehydrating plant in California that the idea for dehydrating potatoes was born. He constructed his own plant in Caldwell, equipped with six drying kilns. This was increased to 30 kilns during the war years and employed 1,200 workers. It produced some 65 percent of the Army's dehydrated potato consumption.

It was to supply his own farms with commercial fertilizer that got Simplot in the super phosphate manufacturing business, but the outside demand was so immediate and so great that the Pocatello plant has been under constant expansion since it began operating in December of 1944. Much of its output has gone to Japan and other Pacific Islands.

The organization Simplot has built, and is continuing to build, has a great deal to do with the success of his enterprises. His executives are young men all with that Simplot enthusiasm for the job at hand, no matter what it is. There are, as one of his aides remarked, no "old fogies" running the Simplot machinery, no institutional taboos to retard initiative. His executive force is, in the main, pretty free to make individual decisions and exercise sound judgment in matters of their own bailiwicks. This has built an intense loyalty for the "boss" throughout the entire organization.

Las Vegas Casino Operator

Eddie Curran spent years operating in the shadow of the law as a gangster in Detroit. Twice divorced with grown children, he moved to Las Vegas, where he used his related experience to make more than $400,000 in 1955 running a, telling his visiting son the secret of his success—"If you wanna get rich, make little people feel like big people."

Life at Home

- Eddie Curran lived in an apartment on the top floor of his Las Vegas Strip resort and, although smaller than his home in Detroit, it had everything, including room service.
- Notoriously a poor sleeper, the 24-hour nature of the hotel gambling business suited him well, simply going downstairs to watch showgirls and watch over his business when he couldn't sleep.
- After years of operating in the shadow of the law, Curran enjoyed operating a "legit" business in Las Vegas, which he opened in 1949.
- When Jack, his son from his first marriage, came to visit, Eddie showed him that Las Vegas' future was as a resort city, not just a gambling center.
- Eddie and a fellow resort owner talked about building a golf course near the Desert Inn with an entrance on Paradise Road, the street just east of the Strip, so that other casinos could benefit from it as well.
- Most of the other resort owners hated the idea, because they wanted visitors to gamble in their casinos, not play golf, but Eddie believed Las Vegas needed more variety to attract more tourists and families.
- He told Jack repeatedly, "If you wanna get rich, make little people feel like big people."
- Although five additional resorts were being discussed for the Strip, 60-year-old Eddie did not fear competition, only not being respected.
- His resort featured landscaped lawns and gardens, an elegant waterfall, a pool, health club, horse stables and shops.
- Not wanting tax trouble, he took great pains to include all of his income.

Eddie Curran operated a successful Las Vegas casino.

Life at Work: Casino Operator

- The Las Vegas scene lived on connections, a world where everyone knew everyone else, and who buttered whose bread.
- When the newspaper announced that new owners of a Strip hotel were "Miami Hotelmen," it meant the owners enjoyed the confidence of Miami-based mobster Meyer Lansky, who coordinated a substantial part of the mob investment on the Strip.
- Curran was closely tied to mob money in Detroit and Cleveland.
- He believed that Las Vegas must expand its image and offer entertainment beyond gambling if it was to have a long and prosperous future.

Curran got rich by making "little people feel like big people."

- A stickler for professionalism, he recruited to run his resort experienced hotelmen who learned the ins-and-outs of running a casino from some of Curran's business partners in Detroit.
- The Las Vegas Strip began taking shape in 1941 when Californian Thomas Hull opened a resort, not hotel, featuring expansive gardens, a large swimming pool and a rustic-looking casino and restaurant.
- He located his El Rancho beyond the city limits in an area called the Strip to escape an onerous city tax burden.
- In 1942, The Last Frontier opened a mile south of El Rancho, and the Strip began, but gambling was still a localized, small-time activity.
- In 1944, the county's Liquor and Licensing Board approved 244 gaming applications, mostly from the owners of bars, cafés, liquor stores, markets and other small businesses requesting slot machines.
- When mobster Bugsy Siegel took over the building of the Flamingo Hotel, he envisioned a national gambling constituency that was married to a deep access to capital.
- The Flamingo was the brainchild of Billy Wilkerson, who wanted to retreat from the sawdust-covered floors and cowboy motifs that had dominated Las Vegas, and transform the city into the Beverly Hills of the desert.
- The Flamingo Hotel was planned as an elegant resort that would appeal to a fashionable crowd, partnering with Bugsy Siegel for necessary capital.
- When the Flamingo opened in 1946, it quickly became the place to be, where black-chip

Law Vegas was born with a cowboy image.

($100-chip) gamblers flocked to enjoy its 105 lavish air conditioned rooms, spectacular three-story waterfall and tuxedo-clad staff.
- The Desert Inn opened in 1950, the Sands in 1952 and the Riviera in 1955.
- Within hours of Siegel's murder in 1947, Moe Sedway, Morris Rosen and Gus Greenbaum entered the Flamingo's lobby to announce they were taking over, their reputation making Las Vegas' image as a center of sin even uglier.
- The city's image, however, improved through top-flight entertainment talent including Nat King Cole, Pearl Bailey, Dean Martin, Jerry Lewis and Lena Horne.

- For Noel Coward's opening-night show, Frank Sinatra chartered a private plane to fly in Judy Garland, the Bogarts and the Nivens, who joined Zsa Zsa Gabor and Joan Fontaine.
- Coward was pleased by the reception of the stars, but also by his ability to amuse ordinary audiences who flocked to his shows from Kansas, Nebraska, Utah and Illinois.

Life in the Community: Las Vegas, Nevada

- The largest city in the only state in the nation that permited casino gambling, Las Vegas developed a reputation as a town designed and built to accommodate the pleasures of high rollers.
- Located in the scorching desert of southern Nevada with little industry and less water, Las Vegas nonetheless lured millions seeking excitement.
- The city's rise from the desert floor was marked by many from the day that mobster Benjamin "Bugsy" Siegel arrived in 1945 and began transforming Las Vegas into a national center for gambling, which, minus competing industries, rapidly became the culture of the city during the past decade.
- Tourists relished the "bad boy" image of a city built around gambling and openly funded by the underworld.
- It was an image promoted by U.S. Senator Estes Kefauver's investigation into organized crime, resulting in the televised interrogation of many of Eddie Curran's associates.
- Senator Kefauver's investigation showed that thousands of phone calls were routinely made to relay bets to all parts of the country, violating the laws of the other states, by out-of-state bookies who wished to lay off money in Las Vegas for their own benefit or for that of syndicate members.
- The state legislature promptly drew up new rules which forbade the horse parlors to have more than one phone installed.
- Also, as a result of the national investigation, the Nevada Gaming Control Board was created to administer the gaming industry of the state, principally in Las Vegas.

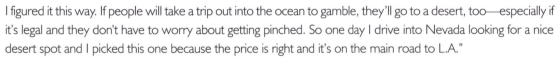

> I figured it this way. If people will take a trip out into the ocean to gamble, they'll go to a desert, too—especially if it's legal and they don't have to worry about getting pinched. So one day I drive into Nevada looking for a nice desert spot and I picked this one because the price is right and it's on the main road to L.A."
>
> —*Bugsy Siegel, 1946*

- The Gaming Board ruled that every stockholder of a gaming establishment had to be licensed by the Board, virtually eliminating corporate ownership of casinos, designed to ensure that "undesirable elements" would not operate casinos.
- The ruling effectively eliminated publicly held companies from investing in gambling, making the city even more dependent on underworld capital and the Teamsters pension funds for its growth.
- The Kefauver Committee created a wave of national reforms, but as other localities elected administrations pledging to wipe out illegal gambling, more capital flowed to Nevada, and Las Vegas in particular.

Las Vegas residents lived a quiet, all-American life.

- Its formula was simple, city leaders say—Las Vegas offered a time-out from daily life for people who, though respectable back home, can come here and cut loose, indulging in pleasures they could acquire at home only with the risk of embarrassment, stigma or even arrest.
- For most residents, the Strip and local life were separate—tourists reveled in the gambling and showgirls, while locals prided themselves on the quality of the Little League, Girls Scouts and high attendance levels at churches and synagogues.
- Clergymen found that the need to expand their buildings conflicted with the source of new capital; as one Methodist minister said, "There is no way a church in Las Vegas can avoid benefiting from gambling. We are here building a new church that will cost $220,000. We already have $40,000. Thirty thousand came from a man who owns the property on which the Golden Nugget gambling hall is situated. Without this income he could not give this amount of money; therefore, it derives from gambling. What can I do about it? I'll tell you. Nothing"
- Many of the locals lived in the never-never land of all-night gambling, working as dealers, croupiers, pit bosses, shills, change girls or cocktail waitresses.
- Generally, cocktail waitresses made up to $15,000 a year; an ordinary dealer took home $100 to $150 a week, doubling his take during the busy holiday seasons when tips are more frequent.
- The pit boss, who supervised a group of dealers, averaged $50 for an eight-hour shift, and even the lowly shill, the come-on guy who used the house's money, made a decent wage averaging up to $10 a day.
- Many lived well on unreported tip income, saving on income taxes.

Entertainment Tourism, Devil's Bargains, by Hal Rothman

Disneyland reached for the public in the same manner as did Las Vegas. Disneyland and its followers placed the visitor at the center of the story in a manner eerily reflective of Las Vegas; they promised complete experience, as did Las Vegas…In this way, Las Vegas and Disneyland shared enormous parallels. Founded in 1954, Disneyland became the epitome of entertainment tourism at a time when Las Vegas could not compete in the mainstream marketplace. Disneyland offered the same sort of refraction of experience as did Las Vegas, but through a lens focused directly on the heart of the baby boom generation. Disneyland offered a form of cultural and heritage tourism—some say indoctrination—along with its scripted entertainment. Like Santa Fe and Aspen, Disneyland created an identity; it became static and immutable in a way that Las Vegas could not afford to be. Disneyland invented faster rides. Las Vegas reinvented itself time and again.

- However, of Nevada's 17 counties, only two, Washoe, where Reno is located, and Clark, in which Vegas thrived, benefited from gambling.
- Vegas, at the southern tip of the state, was considered a sort of "economic plumb-bob" that represented a rich potential—like having a wealthy relative who might do you some good one day.
- When the other 15 counties, which did not have widespread gambling, began talking about a state gaming tax hike, 50 Nevada assemblymen and state senators were invited to the Strip by Vegas owners.
- There the gamblers explained their position over fine food and free floor shows; one senator stayed on for a month, studying the situation.

- When the proposed tax bill reached the senate, it died, failing even to come up for a vote.
- The other key element in the Las Vegas economy was nuclear research, and the U.S. Atomic Energy Commission conducted its first above-ground nuclear test in southern Nevada, at the proving grounds of Nellis Air Base.
- When the white puffball rose in the sky in January 1951, gamblers rushed out of the casinos to watch the desert sky glow in the light of an artificial sun.
- The nuclear test brought more business and prestige to the town, as soon, swimsuits and wedding cakes were fashioned after a mushroom cloud, hairdressers designed "atomic hairdos" and restaurants served "atom burgers."

Dealers made $100 - $150 a week.

Tourism in Nevada

- In the 1890s, recreational tourism was largely defined as a pursuit of the wealthy, who could afford to hire private train cars for hunting trips into the wilderness, often supported by elegant hunting lodges operated by the rich for the rich.
- Even the development of the ski industry and the emergence of pre-World War I resorts such as Sun Valley in Idaho or Aspen, Colorado, in the years after the war were largely elite activities.
- Only 10,000 Americans called themselves avid skiers in 1935 and most of those lived in the East.
- By 1945, more than 200,000 people had experienced the joys of skiing and were searching for more slopes to conquer.
- As the infrastructure that supported travel developed and roads stretched across the horizon of the American West, tourist camps and motor courts arose to meet the needs of the traveling middle class.
- The independence offered by the private automobile democratized travel and the industry of tourism, which boomed after the Second World War.
- The growth in population and employment opportunities in the post-World War II era, as well as technological innovations such as air travel and air conditioning, further fueled a highly mobile population, determined to see all of America.
- During the war, the population of the West grew substantially, attracted by new, war-related industries from shipbuilding to steel production, but rationing on goods and travel restricted Americans' ability to spend the money they earned from these industrial jobs.

- The end of the war changed all that; as early as 1945, millions of returning soldiers on their way home took side trips to the great icons of the American West—the Grand Canyon, Grand Teton and Yellowstone—traveling mostly by car.
- After World War II, a solid symbol of middle-class status was automobile ownership, which, coupled with the expanded popularity in the late 1940s of two-week annual vacations, made national park campsites more available.

- An affluent, mobile America was determined to be entertained during its leisure time allotment, and out of this desire came another form of entertainment, the packaging of unreality in places like Disneyland theme park.

Gambling—How It Is Run,
by Ed Reid

While gambling jobs are rewarding moneywise, the boredom that sets in comes from doing the same thing day in and day out. Dullest of all is the work of the shill. His shift consists of nothing more than putting down and picking up silver dollars with absolutely no interest in whether he wins or loses, since he can do neither.

The sole concern of the pit boss is to see that no one, customer or dealer, cheats anyone else. Once in a great while he gets a chance to capture a laugh, as in the case of Sherlock Feldman, colorful pit boss at the Sands Hotel. During an exciting roll of the dice, with frenetic tourists jumping up and down and whooping (which is usually what happens when the visitors start winning from the house), one portly gentleman with false dentures yelled a little too loudly. His teeth popped out and landed on the green felt of the dice table.

Quick as a flash, the agile mind of Sherlock acted. He whipped his hand to his mouth, pulled out his own false teeth and plopped them down on the table beside those of the astonished tourist. "You're faded," he yelled as everyone screamed with laughter that did not stop for a week as the story circulated around Vegas…

Cheaters are heartily disliked, whether they be dealers or players, and they are given scant shrift when caught. However, in one case, another rich story gained circulation after a cheater was caught in the act. He had approached a crap table with a pair of loaded dice and every intention of putting them in play. He put his money down and called for the croupier or stickman to pass him the house dice. The idea was to substitute the loaded dice for the ones given him by the casino.

This he tried to do as he shook the dice in his closed fist and yelled that baby needed a new pair of shoes. He threw the crooked dice on the table, confident that he had made the switch unnoticed. To his and everyone's vast astonishment three dice rolled out on the table, each one a five.

The stickman's eyes widened, then calmly he reached out his curved wand and flipped two of the dice back to the cheater. 'Okay, Bub, your point is 15; let's see you roll it!' he said as the player turned green."

- Thanks to television and its many "westerns," the romance of the West was ignited nationwide.
- Most of the tourism was clustered between Memorial Day in late May and Labor Day in early September, when children were not in school.
- Tourism was especially welcomed in communities where industrial changes or played-out mines had left workers idle; most tourism employment requires no special skills, save a willingness to be gracious and attentive.

From Sugar Plantation to New York City

Annette Martinez left Puerto Rico like her brothers and sister, to find work in America as machines replaced plantation workers. As American citizens, they had a love/hate relationship with the United States, where they could work and live legally, but where they were considered second class citizens by many in 1956.

Life at Home

- Annette Martinez was born in 1930 in Salinas, a small agricultural community on the southern coast of Puerto Rico, known for its sugar production; Annette's family made their living on the sugar plantations.
- Beginning in the 1940s, many sugar plantations were replaced by large foreign-owned industrial factories, a change that meant a higher standard of living for some, but fewer plantation jobs for others.
- As a result of the decreasing agricultural jobs, many members of Annette's family began thinking about leaving Puerto Rico to find work.
- Emigrating to the United States was the natural first choice because Puerto Ricans had American citizenship and could work legally.
- During World War II, many American labor recruiters came to the island in search of cheap labor to replace the workers lost to the military draft.
- This was how Annette's two older brothers became the first of her family to emigrate, being recruited by an American businessman to work in a toy factory in Baltimore, Maryland, in 1945.
- In 1946, Annette's older sister Glenda left to work as a domestic servant for a wealthy family in Philadelphia.
- Although Annette wanted to follow her siblings, she didn't trust the American recruiters, and hoped that her brothers or sister could find her work in America.
- In 1953, during a trip to San Juan to visit her cousins, 23-year-old Annette met an American family, the Santos, there on vacation.

Annette Martinez left Puerto Rico when she was 23.

Sugar plantations employed many in Puerto Rico.

- Mr. Santos offered her a job working in his hotel in New York City.
- Annette trusted him because he had not come to Puerto Rico specifically to recruit workers, and was soon on a plane to New York.
- Annette was terrified to fly, but was encouraged by her sister, who told her about the views from the airplane window and the food service.
- The flight took six and a half hours and cost $44.00.
- Annette paid for the trip with money she had saved since she was 14, plus $20.00 her grandmother gave her before she died.
- With the help of Mr. Santos, Annette rented a room in one of the poorest sections of Manhattan, known as Spanish Harlem, which was largely made up of Puerto Ricans and immigrants from other Spanish-speaking countries.
- She shared the apartment with two other Puerto Rican women.
- Annette had little money to live on, after sending most of her paycheck home to help support her family in Puerto Rico.
- Many Puerto Rican customs and traditions were preserved in New York, and she was not as homesick as she had feared she would be.
- She found many familiar foods that she had eaten at home, such as rice and beans, pork, and beef.
- Once in a while, Annette went out on the weekends dancing with her friends.
- In 1954, she met Wilfredo Rivera at a dancehall.
- Willy rolled cigars in his father's shop and, after a short courtship, they were married.
- Her brothers and sister were not able to travel to New York for the wedding and Annette felt terribly sad that she had no family to share the happy day.
- After the wedding, Annette moved in with Willy and his family in the South Bronx.
- Their first son, Carlos, was born in 1955.
- Wilfredo's mother took care of the baby so that Annette could continue working.
- Annette continued to send money to her family in Puerto Rico every week.
- Though living with her husband's family was inexpensive and convenient, both Annette and Willy longed for their own home.
- They both saved what was left of their paychecks after living expenses and family obligations.
- Home ownership was considered important in Puerto Rican culture.
- Annette was content with her life, but missed her family.
- She was not able to take time off from work to visit her brothers in Baltimore or her sister in Philadelphia and although she wrote to her parents in Puerto Rico often, she knew she would never see them again.

Machines and foreign owners reduced plantation jobs.

Life at Work: Domestic to Garment Worker

- Annette worked as a room maid at the Santos's large hotel—La Calienda Casa.
- After four months, a neighbor told Annette about a job as a sewing machine operator in a garment factory in downtown Manhattan.
- Working in the garment factory seemed like a good idea because the factory workers were almost entirely Puerto Ricans, and the factory job was also unionized.
- This was important because Puerto Rican workers were unfamiliar with American work practices, unable to speak English, and couldn't argue on their own behalf.
- The factory job paid more than her job at La Calienda Casa, a result of the collective bargaining agreements of the union.
- She made $0.75 per hour and sent $12.00 to $15.00 a week to Puerto Rico.
- Once she started saving for her own house, she sent a bit less, but still had to contribute to her husband's household.
- Despite the advantages, operating a sewing machine was very grueling work.
- The hours were long and Annette had to sit at her sewing machine for eight-hour stretches with only a few brief breaks.
- The factory was overcrowded with workers; the building was often too hot during the summer and too cold in the winter.
- Once, Annette fainted from heat exhaustion.
- To supplement her factory work, Annette often mended clothes at home to make extra money.
- She was grateful that her mother-in-law was able to help care for Carlos, allowing her to devote more hours to work.
- Her dream of being able to move out of the Riveras' house was always on her mind.

Life in the Community: New York City

- Annette was part of the group of Puerto Ricans who came to New York during the "Great Migration" of the 1940s and 1950s.
- They were needed to help replenish the workforce, as many of the city's more affluent residents relocated to the suburbs.
- New York City Mayor Robert F. Wagner, Jr. was in favor of Puerto Ricans settling in the city and encouraged businesses to recruit Puerto Rican workers.
- The part of the Bronx where Annette and Willy lived was predominantly Puerto Rican but more middle class than the impoverished Spanish Harlem section.
- Their neighborhood was full of Puerto Rican families, shops and businesses.
- Annette did grocery shopping at a nearby Bodega where the owners spoke only Spanish.
- She found many of the foods, including fish and produce, that she used to buy in Puerto Rico.
- Before the birth of their son, Annette and Willy would often go dancing at the same dancehall where they had first met.

Annette's parents and brother.

95

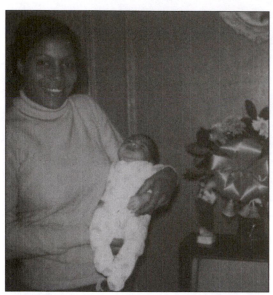

While Annette worked, her mother-in-law watched her son, Carlos.

- They enjoyed the music of popular Puerto Rican artists Pedro Flores and Cuarteto Victoria.
- The couple were practicing Catholics and tried to attend mass as much as possible, despite their busy work schedules.
- Annette considered herself very lucky to have a wonderful husband, a healthy son, and that her new family lived in a relatively safe neighborhood.
- Tensions sometimes ran high between Puerto Ricans and the city's other ethnic immigrant groups.
- Many resented Annette because she, like most Puerto Ricans, already had American citizenship even before arriving in the United States.
- Annette often asked herself who she was: Puerto Rican or American?
- Despite her citizenship, she was often viewed as an outsider by many of the city's longtime residents.
- Annette and Willy's family often felt pulled in opposite directions, welcomed by businesses looking for cheap labor, but shunned by residents afraid that their neighborhoods were being taken over by 'Ricans.
- Annette sometimes felt other young mothers thought their babies superior to her son, and secretly wondered if Carlos would ever be accepted as American.
- Willy's parents tried to strictly preserve the culture and traditions of Puerto Rico, while Annette felt it important to integrate into American life, causing hard feelings in the Rivera household.
- Another dividing issue among Puerto Ricans was language.
- Annette spoke English as a result of the government-mandated use of English in public schools when she was growing up in Puerto Rico.
- Many Puerto Ricans, including Willy's parents, were from the rural parts of the island and didn't have the same exposure to English.
- They struggled with the language when they came to New York, adding to their reluctance to shed their Puerto Rican traditions.
- Due to the large number of non-English-speaking immigrants, the city created services to assist the Spanish-speaking population.
- New schools, and social and civic services were established and funded by all the city's taxpayers.
- This angered longtime residents who thought that everyone should be forced to speak English, a conflict that was not new.
- Ever since Puerto Rico was ceded to the United States following the Spanish-American War of 1898, Americans struggled with what to do with a colony that was largely non-white and entirely Spanish-speaking.
- Though not fully independent, Puerto Ricans could receive many benefits from their association with America, including social benefits such as food stamps.

Puerto Rican Immigration Timeline

1493: On his second voyage, Christopher Columbus discovered the Virgin Islands and Puerto Rico.

1509: Ponce de Leon was appointed governor of Puerto Rico.

1580: Imported European diseases virtually wiped out the native Indians of Puerto Rico.

1868: The Fourteenth Amendment to the United States Constitution was adopted which declared that all people of Hispanic origin born in the United States would be U.S. citizens.

A Puerto Rican decree freed all children born of slaves.

Puerto Rican insurrectionists, fighting for independence, were defeated by the Spanish.

1870: The Spanish government freed all the slaves it owned in Cuba and Puerto Rico.

1873: All slavery was abolished in Puerto Rico.

1875: The U.S. Supreme Court ruled that the power to regulate immigration was held solely by the federal government.

1892: Revolutionary organizations focused on independence were created in both Cuba and Puerto Rico.

1897: Spain granted Puerto Rico and Cuba autonomy and home rule.

1898: Following the Spanish-American War, Spain signed the Treaty of Paris, transferring Cuba, Puerto Rico and the Philippines to the United States.

The Foraker Act established a civilian government in Puerto Rico under U.S. dominance that allowed the Islanders to elect their own House of Representatives but did not permit Puerto Rico a vote in Washington.

1917: The Jones Act was passed extending U.S. citizenship to all Puerto Ricans and created two Puerto Rican houses of legislature, elected by male suffrage. English was declared the official language of Puerto Rico. Congress passed the Immigration Act of 1917, imposing a literacy requirement on all immigrants.

1921: Limits on the number of immigrants allowed in the United States in a single year were imposed for the first time in the country's history.

1926: Puerto Ricans in Harlem were attacked by non-Hispanics fearful of the growing Puerto Rican population in New York.

1930: United States interests controlled 44 percent of the cultivated land in Puerto Rico.

U.S. capitalists controlled 60 percent of the banks and public services and all the maritime lines in Puerto Rico.

1933: The Roosevelt administration reversed the policy of English as the official language of Puerto Rico.

1934: During the early years of the Depression, 20 percent of all Puerto Ricans living in the United States returned to the island.

1940: An independent union was formed as the major labor organization in Puerto Rico.

1941: The Fair Employment Practices Act was passed, designed to eliminate discrimination in employment.

1944: Operation Bootstrap, initiated by the Puerto Rican government to meet labor demands in World War II, stimulated a major wave of immigration to the United States.

1946: The first Puerto Rican Governor, Jesus T. Pinero, was appointed by President Harry Truman.

1947: Approximately 20 airlines provided air service between San Juan, Puerto Rico, and New York.

1950: The United States Congress upgraded Puerto Rico's political status from protectorate to commonwealth.

1954: The U.S. Supreme Court ruled in *Hernandez v. Texas* that Hispanic Americans and all other racial groups had equal protection under the Fourteenth Amendment to the Constitution.

Puerto Rico Adds 50 Industries, *The New York Times,* January 3, 1950

SAN JUAN, P.R.—"Operation Bootstrap"—Puerto Rico's program initiated under Gov. Luis Munoz Marin to free this island from dependence on its sugar industry—is now showing results.

At Carolina, a few miles from here, Beacon Textiles is completing a $1.5 million plant that will start operations late in February. Near Bayamon, a short distance to the west, private capital from the States is putting up a $500,000 rayon mill, to be finished and equipped late in the spring. Meanwhile, the last machines are being installed in the big Textron mill at Ponce, on the south coast, and the first cloth has been run off in test production there, in preparation for regular operations early in March.

At Vega Baga, in north central Puerto Rico, Crane China's factory, which cost $1.5 million, now employs nearly 500 workers and will use 200 more when the training program is completed and full production of 25,000 dozen pieces weekly is reached.

At Guayanilla, near Ponce, a site has been chosen and preliminary details ironed out for the construction of an oil refinery that may represent an investment of nearly $20 million of private capital from the mainland.

Nearly a dozen new plants are in various stages of construction as the insular government presses its drive to industrialize this semitropical home of 2.2 million traditionally poor people.

Although there are some misgivings on the part of the operators of the sugar plants and plantations, who fear that in time the new factories will lure away too many of their workers, all admit that a new era has dawned in the midst of backward agricultural terrain.

Water power and better highways, new hotel and club facilities have come to the island as a part of the new dispensation. Most of the plants started under Government auspices to show what could be done there are working at capacity. The Government's cement plant is turning out one million barrels of cement a year, and finding a ready market for it in new housing, roads, business and factory construction.

The shoe factory at Ponce, after reaching a production of about 1,800 pairs daily to help supply a big part of the island's demand for $14 million worth of shoes a year, has been sold by the Puerto Rico Industrial Development Company to the Joyce interests of California as the first step in getting official industries into private hands.

Three bids are being considered by the development company for the Puerto Rico Clay Products plant, near here, and several offers are being weighed for the cement plant. The glass-bottle plant has made its first shipments to Central American countries. Only the paper-board plant has been listed as a failure.

The 50 new industries now operating or soon to start will give employment to about 8,000 persons, and will have an annual payroll of more than $8 million. Their output ranges from fur coats, jewelry and buttons to optical instruments and radio and television sets. The 25,000-spindle plant of Textile, perhaps the first of several planned by this company in Puerto Rico, will have a capacity of more than 10 million yards of "cotton print cloth gray goods" annually.

Environmentalist in Utah

Tom Baldwin was a geology professor dedicated to protecting the country's pristine western land. He was an integral part of the six-year fight against the building of Echo Park Dam in Dinosaur National Monument Park. In 1956 President Eisenhower signed a presidential order prohibiting dams in any part of the national park system.

Life at Home

- Tom Baldwin fell in love for the first time when he was nine years old, with the huge rock formations in his native Wyoming.
- As he got older, he explored on horseback the geologic mosaic laid before him in Utah, Colorado and Wyoming—a veritable showcase of geologic history, replete with ancient petroglyphs on the canyon walls.
- He cherished the writing of Western naturalist John Muir, who campaigned for the preservation of natural places.
- As early as 1908, Muir wrote an article entitled "A High Price to Pay for Water" for *Century* magazine concerning plans by the City of San Francisco to use portions of Yosemite National Park for its water supply.
- Tom, a loner with a scientific bent, surprised those who knew him by getting his Ph.D. so that he could teach in high school and college.
- Few had ever heard him say more than a few words at a time unless the subject was rocks, and fewer still could envision this confirmed bachelor lecturing for an entire class period.
- At 42, Tom had been working at a small college in Utah for six years when he was confronted by the possibility of a dam forever changing the landscape of Yampa Canyon.
- Utah had experienced astonishing economic growth since the beginning of World War II, which spurred demand for cheap electricity to support the burgeoning industrial infrastructure of a region desperate to grow prosperous.
- Damming the rivers was on the wish list of every aspiring politician.
- Since the late 1930s, economic forces had targeted the Colorado River as an unexploited resource capable of saving dozens of drought-ridden farm communities in New Mexico, Utah, Colorado and Wyoming.
- Especially in economically depressed areas, the construction of dams to regulate water, irrigate dry lands, attract tourists and generate

Tom Baldwin was a geology professor and environmental advocate.

Tom built his house on a rock ledge.

electricity—like the TVA miracle in Appalachia or the Hoover Dam in Nevada—was viewed as an obvious solution.

- The history of Western development revolved around the construction of railroads in advance of population and constructing dams to fuel twentieth-century Western growth was a logical next step.
- But not for Tom, who had grown up loving the scenic beauty of the Western lands.
- With the help of two friends, he constructed his own home on a rock ledge in a style that emphasized the landscape, not the house.

- Every day he was reminded of his Western heritage by a gallery of framed pictures, including one featuring his grandmother and her sisters standing outside a primitive prairie hut they had built.
- So when he told the Wilderness Society that he was willing to assist in preserving the natural beauty of Dinosaur National Monument, he was fully committed, never dreaming that the fight would last six years and serve to unify conservation groups across the nation.

Tom's grandmother and aunts lived in a primitive hut.

Life at Work: Environmental Advocate

- Tom Baldwin first became aware of the Echo Park Dam controversy at Dinosaur National Monument in 1950 shortly after a friend in the Department of the Interior told him about a clash with the Bureau of Reclamation.
- Echo Park Dam, planned for the Green River to generate power and create a recreational lake, would have flooded the Echo Park Valley inside Dinosaur National Monument on the Utah-Colorado border.
- The Department of the Interior was looking to protect the integrity of the national parks, while the Bureau of Reclamation wanted to develop America economically by using the country's resources, including parts of the parks system.
- The water and power vote of the West insisted that a prosperous America demanded that its natural resources not be locked away, but fully exploited.
- Some argued that few were able to visit Echo Park in Dinosaur National Monument because of poor roads and swift water; the greater good would be served with hydroelectricity and a glittering, manmade lake.
- At first, Tom was unsure of how to best participate in a project this big.
- He tried lecturing in Utah and Colorado about the beauty of the sacred place, but few were interested in protecting something they had never seen.
- To counter this problem, he started taking colored slides of the sheer cliffs and dazzling landscapes of Echo Park.
- This sparked interest, but not passion; after each talk his all-volunteer army of budding conservationists would express enthusiasm, and then go about their lives.
- After three years of crusading, Tom figured he needed another tactic; "I seem to be shoveling the same snow over and over again," he told friends.
- This was especially true of the issue of whether the dam at Echo Park would damage the ancient bone fossils for which Dinosaur National Monument was named.
- *Time* magazine derisively called opponents of Echo Park Dam "professional nature lovers."

Tom's photos illustrated the dazzling landscapes.

- Tom even asked himself whether a remote and virtually unknown national monument with a misleading name was the place to mount a preservation battle.
- Clearly, the canyons of the Green and Yampa Rivers—tributaries of the Colorado River—possessed undeniable beauty, but Dinosaur National Monument hardly had the kind of name recognition of Yellowstone.
- But when Western big business branded the preservation effort "Eastern elitism" populated by "armchair birdwatchers," Tom knew that as a native of Wyoming, he had a job to do.
- "I can stay in the saddle a little longer," he told himself.
- In the summer of 1953, he found the answer.
- While acting as a rafting guide on the Yampa River in hopes of exposing more people to this special place, he met a family determined to capture their vacation trip with an 8-mm film camera.
- The children giggled and waved a lot, the pictures occasionally went totally out of focus, but the breathtaking images captured by the $200 Wollensak 53 handheld camera were unmistakable.
- The Wollensak was capable of wide angle, normal and telephoto shots that made it possible to record the vastness of the canyons without losing the intimacy of a trek down the rivers, all on one reel.
- Within months, Tom became an expert cameraman and even purchased the equipment needed to splice the film, remove blurry sections and then set the trip to music with a portable phonograph he purchased.
- A film about the beauty of Echo Park came at the right time.
- Hesitation was in the air.
- The total cost of placing multiple dams on the tributaries to the Colorado River had diminished the Eisenhower Administration's desire to create new deficits, especially in the wake of the expensive Korean War.
- Besides, conservation had been able to call into question for the first time the economic justifications used by the Bureau of Reclamation.
- Additionally, the post-World War II generation had fallen in love with recreational traveling.
- This expansive, adventuresome spirit included the exploration of remote places and the kayaking of rivers in collapsible boats known as folboats.
- As the public relations battle raged from the hallowed halls of Washington to the echoing canyons of Utah, the conservationists developed their main approaches.
- First was the need to promote the beauty of Echo Park and the canyons of Dinosaur National Monument.

Rafting tours on the Colorado River were popular..

- Pictures, films, magazine articles and rafting tours formed the core of this strategy.
- Second was the forging of partnerships between conservationists and other political forces opposed to all or some of the damming of the Colorado River.
- This produced unlikely allies such as the U.S. Army Corps of Engineers, California businesses that feared that their use of the Colorado could be compromised, and Midwestern politicians who did not want the agricultural competition that the new dams could produce.
- The coalition then made conservationists vulnerable to attacks by the *Denver Post* as selling out to California water interests.
- Tom's colleagues questioned his motives and loyalties.
- He responded to his critics by reminding them that the development of the Colorado River was a national issue.
- "The expense of Colorado dam development will be borne by the American taxpayer and its beauty will be lost to all Americans no matter where they currently live."
- And he carefully noted who his friends were when the chips were down.
- But as the campaign moved into its fifth year, Tom came to appreciate the power of numbers.
- When the Wilderness Society was able to calculate the taxpayers' cost of the Colorado River projects, conservationists and critics alike had a field day.
- The cost of producing hydroelectricity was higher than standard, while the bill for irrigated land topped $124,000 per acre.
- For months, the cost-benefit analysis for water, power, beauty, birds and preservation was endlessly debated in Congress by committees and subcommittees.
- Along the way, the leaders of the Echo Park campaign picked up the support of Senators Hubert Humphrey and John Kennedy, who both spoke against the project.
- Several times, Tom was asked to speak in Washington, but he always declined.
- He was convinced his Western accent would be laughed at back East; he knew his place and it was west of the Mississippi River.

- On the day President Eisenhower signed a presidential order prohibiting dams in any part of the national park system, Tom was alone hiking well-known paths in Dinosaur National Monument.

Life in the Community: Dinosaur National Monument, Utah and Colorado

- In prehistoric times, the canyons of Dinosaur National Monument were inhabited by the Fremont people and later by the Ute.
- Few Europeans settled in the rocky cliff, but the discovery of dinosaur bones attracted considerable attention from archeologists and museums, particularly the Carnegie.
- On the strength of those discoveries, Dinosaur National Monument was created in 1915 with a caveat that included the possibility of dams and power plants within the preserve.
- Despite ambitious plans, most of the roads and the scale of the envisioned dinosaur museum were never realized.
- By 1950, the Echo Park Dam appeared a foregone conclusion to many.
- Among the monument's supporters was Frederick Law Olmsted, Jr., the nation's foremost landscape architect, who warned that the loss of "scenic and inspirational values obtainable by the public" at the monument would be "catastrophically great."
- Olmsted urged the Department of the Interior to choose an alternative site, but his pleas were ignored.
- That's when grassroots conservation groups joined the fight and refused to back down.
- In July 1950, an article by Bernard DeVoto informed over four million *Harper's* readers of the potential impact of a dam at Echo Park.
- DeVoto pleaded his case around the question of public ownership.

Hikers enjoyed Dinosaur National Monument.

- Soon, others joined the fight.
- Californians protested that their water was being diverted.
- Easterners declared themselves unwilling to pay taxes for Western water projects.
- Then, in 1952, David Brower became president of the Sierra Club and made the preservation of Dinosaur his personal crusade.
- River trips were promoted, scenic films were created and lectures given nationally.
- Brower then asked New York publisher Alfred A. Knopf to publish *This Is Dinosaur*, a collection of essays by notable wilderness advocates intended to show what would be lost through the damming of Echo Park.
- Each member of Congress was sent a copy of the book, with a special brochure about the monument sewn into the binding.
- The battle for Dinosaur National Monument was even featured in the 1954 movie, *The Long, Long Trailer*, starring Lucille Ball and Desi Arnaz, when Lucy declared her favorite souvenir to be a very, very large rock from Dinosaur National Monument.
- Western opposition, Eastern protests, a coalition of conservation groups and too high a cost eventually doomed the dam.
- In November 1955, Secretary of the Interior Douglas McKay announced that Echo Park would be removed from the Upper Colorado River project.
- In March, both Houses approved three water storage sites—Flaming Gorge, Utah; Glen Canyon in Northern Arizona; and Navajo, New Mexico—but excluded Echo Park.
- The Park Service quickly took advantage of Dinosaur's national fame to push for a visitor center.
- The Park Service chose to construct a monumental modernist building that demonstrated its commitment to the "protection and use" of Dinosaur National Monument.

Dinosaur National Monument Timeline

1909: Paleontologist Earl Douglass discovered an amazing deposit of fossilized dinosaur bones in the remote and arid northeastern corner of Utah that yielded many museum-quality full skeletons.

1915: Based on the discoveries, President Woodrow Wilson proclaimed Dinosaur a national monument encompassing 80 acres.

1924: Paleontologist Earl Douglass envisioned a museum exhibit and visitor center to house the discoveries.

Congress defeated a bill designed to properly display the discoveries at Dinosaur National Monument.

1925: Further excavation was halted until the bones could be properly protected after most of the site had been explored by the Carnegie Museum and others.

1930: The American Museum of Natural History in New York bargained with the Park Service for rights to fossilized remains in exchange for developing a public exhibit.

1936: Using state and federal relief project labor, a temporary structure for the paleontologists that served as a museum was constructed.

1937: Preliminary designs for a museum were produced through the collaboration of the American Museum of Natural History and the Park Service.

1938: The Dinosaur National Monument was enlarged from 80 acres to 325 square miles, bringing attention and financial support to the area.

1944: The Park Service produced two alternatives for museums in the Quarry area.

1951: Plans were approved for a utilitarian structure resembling a warehouse or farm building.

1956: The Park Service announced that $615,000 would be allocated for improvements at Dinosaur, including roads, a new $275,000 visitor center, employee housing, and water and sewer facilities.

This Is Dinosaur, by Devereux Butcher, *National Parks Magazine,* **October-December, 1950:**
Dinosaur National Monument, in the writer's opinion, is second to no other area of the national park and monument system in its magnificence of scenic grandeur, and its unique scenery is duplicated nowhere else in the system.

The West's Most Fabulous Highway, Claire Noall,
Deseret News Magazine, Salt Lake City, Utah, June 10, 1951

A million dollars for 30 miles of highway to reach a town of 217 people sounds fantastic, not just in regard to the money spent or the emancipation of the last packhorse-mail-route town in the United States, but in beauty.

Boulder would still be isolated in winter were it not for the amazing highway. In summer the town can be reached from Wayne County (on the north) via a narrow precipitous dirt road over Boulder Mountain. Between Escalante (30 miles southwest) and Boulder lies the romantic Hell's Backbone dirt road. But the Boulder Mountain road reaches an altitude of nearly 11,000 feet. Hell's Backbone strikes out at about 9,000. Both are closed in winter. Calf Creek, the most gloriously beautiful of the three, remains open all winter.

Prior to 1935, the way into Boulder from Escalante was by packhorse or mule back, over the Death Hollow trail if you took the shortcut. If you wanted to play safe, you might take the much longer but easier trail over the backbone. In winter, however, it was mighty cold in Hell and the Death Hollow trail was the best bet, though one's mule might slide off the narrow path down a rocky descent towards the infernal pit.

The Calf Creek turnpike has banished the use of both pack trails as a necessity. Hand-built by the CCC [Civilian Conservation Corps] boys, it has made the drive between Escalante and Boulder one of the most spectacularly beautiful in the whole United States. Yet how few people are aware of this treat in scenic novelties!

Race Car Driver

Bobby Epperson was a stock car racer who was used to making up the rules. In 1956, determined to make his mark on the NASCAR circuit, he dropped his "finish first or not at all" attitude, and managed to take advice from his fellow drivers, control his temper and finish most races with his car intact.

Life at Home

- Bobby Epperson was known for his shy manner, hard drinking and aggressive driving.
- Some people claimed that Bobby managed to be part of more racing wrecks and acquire more fines than any driver in stock car history.
- Orphaned at 13, he was raised by his eight brothers and sisters, none of whom had any success in making him go to school.
- Instead, he developed his racing style and didn't care what people said about him.
- The family earned a living by growing cotton and corn on 12 acres of worn-out land that their father had left them along the Catawba River near Charlotte, North Carolina.
- Bobby's first job away from the farm was delivering blocks of ice, then he worked for two years in a sawmill.
- Proceeds from stacking lumber financed his first pair of shoes at 16 years of age.
- Bobby drifted from job to job, including working in a pool hall and cotton mill, until he discovered a small dirt track in Hickory, North Carolina.
- There, he talked his way into the driver's seat of a hobby stock car one Saturday night.
- He lasted only two laps before flipping the car, but he was hooked.
- On dirt tracks, his power sliding technique, sending his car whipping around corners to line up perfectly for a fast run down the straightaway, was a work of art.
- Many of the tracks were so primitive that the cars literally bounced along the surfaces, moving from one rut to the next.

Bobby Epperson started racing cars at 16-years-old.

Few rules and a rough track made for exciting races.

- Drivers were a mix of devil-may-care adventurers eager to run unbridled behind a powerful engine and accomplished winning drivers hoping to improve their record.
- For Bobby, the strategy at the start of a 100-lapper on a sweltering hot Carolinas summer Saturday night was simple: just smash the pedal to the floor and go.
- As one competitor said, "Driving the cars was like having two mad bulls with one set of harnesses on them and you didn't know where they were going."
- Because of the clouds of dust kicked up on the dirt track, Bobby often could not see where he was driving.
- Sometimes he would pick a landmark—like a parked car—at a point on the track to know when to turn.
- Bobby loved to drive fast and loved having an excuse to do it.
- Driving was as unpredictable as the competition.
- One driver used a plow line for a seat belt, another drove with vice grips for a steering wheel, and another borrowed tires from spectators' cars when he ran out of spares.
- After the races, "extracurricular activities" often ensued if the drivers disputed the winner or his methods.
- "I've seen 26 drivers fighting in the infield at Greenwood (SC) one time, and 24 of them didn't know what they're fighting for," one driver said. "You kind of made up the rules as you went."
- In 1955 Bobby acquired a regular ride driving a 1934 Ford coupe in the sportsman division.
- His pay jumped from $0.75 an hour to $125 a week—based on his keeping one-third of his earnings on the track.
- On Thursday nights he raced in Columbia SC, Fridays in Cowpens SC, Saturdays in Gaffney SC, and Sundays in Harris NC.
- Off the track, he worked as a well driller and lived a hard life.

Life at Work: Race Car Driver

- As the 1956 season got underway, Bobby Epperson was determined to make his mark in NASCAR.
- Driver Lee Petty had shown that the series championship could be won through steady consistency that emphasized finishing the race even if he didn't win.
- Tim Flock, who had won 18 races in 1955 driving for millionaire businessman Carl Kiekhaefer, was rolling in money.
- At the same time, Bobby had finished seven races, wrecked nine cars and earned fines totaling $1,780 for aggressive driving.
- Clearly Bobby's method was not producing the kind of income he wanted.
- That year, a total of 56 races were planned, up from 41 just five years earlier.

Large crowds turned out to watch drivers cross the finish line.

- In just six years the Grand National racing schedule had migrated from 17 dirt track races and one asphalt-covered track event to a 1956 lineup that featured an almost equal number of dirt and unpaved tracks.
- Bobby needed a new plan to fit into the NASCAR mold if he was to win the big money and keep racing.
- A decade earlier, mechanic William France Sr., who lived in Daytona Beach FL had promoted the notion that people would pay to watch unmodified "stock" cars—like the ones they drove every day—race against each other.
- In 1947, France decided that racing needed a formal sanctioning organization, standardized rules, a regular schedule and an organized championship.
- On December 14, 1947, France began talks with other influential racers and promoters at the Ebony Bar at the Streamline Hotel in Daytona Beach.
- This resulted in the National Association for Stock Car Auto Racing (NASCAR), which was officially founded on February 21, 1948, with the help of several other drivers.
- NASCAR's first points system was written on a barroom napkin.
- The sanctioning body hosted their first event at Daytona Beach that year, when Red Byron beat Marshall Teague in the Modified Division Race.
- The first NASCAR "Strictly Stock" race was held at Charlotte Speedway on June 19, 1949.
- The cars raced with virtually no modifications to the factory models.

Large teams spent money on uniformed outfits and design.

- In 1950, this division was renamed "Grand National."
- Most races were on half-mile to one-mile oval tracks.
- Bobby deeply resented the fact that NASCAR had so quickly become a big business game.
- Carl Kiekhaefer's team approach was producing consistent wins, but even the fans booed when the big money won.
- Bobby was wise enough to hold his temper so some of the winnings would come his way.
- It happened in a year that pitted Chevrolets and Fords against each other in nearly every race.
- The two car giants collectively had spent better than $6 million to win NASCAR stock car races and sell their products to the motoring public.
- Despite their spending sprees, Kiekhaefer's Chryslers and Dodges still cleaned house, compiling an amazing 16-race winning streak during the early summer.
- NASCAR Grand National season opener at Hickory NC Speedway was marred by a hotel fire that killed a race official the night before the race.

- Bobby had finished out of the money on the familiar track—but he finished with his car intact and was eligible to race another day.
- His fellow drivers knew Bobby and his famous temper well, and had collected a pool betting on how long Bobby could hold his tongue, not wreck his car or avoid a fine.
- During the second race at West Palm Beach, Bobby was running ninth and trading paint with another driver when a tire blew, forcing Bobby to spin into the infield.
- No money, but no wrecks.
- Joe Weatherly and Jim Reed, the first two finishers in the 100-mile race, were both disqualified for technical violations, so Herb Thomas was declared the official winner.
- Bobby was distressed.
- He was driving well, minding his manners, and still running at the back of the pack.
- At Daytona he even finished behind black driver Charlie Scott, who finished in 19th place.
- At least he finished, unlike both Dodge entries, which turned turtle—flipped over—early in the race, eliminating both.
- Then something amazing happened.
- Tim Flock, the winner in Hickory, Daytona Beach and North Wilkesboro, astonished the racing world by quitting the championship Kiekhaefer Chrysler team.
- Finally, a break for Bobby, with no more Flock-Kiekhaefer to compete against.
- Short of money and tired of driving politely, Bobby decided to bet all his cards on the 100-mile race in Concord—a track he knew well.
- If he didn't finish in the money, he would not have enough cash to race in Merced, California, next on the list.
- On the 14th lap of the 100-miler, Bobby made a move to join the top 10 drivers.
- On lap 17, he locked bumpers with another driver, causing both cars to slide sideways down the track, resulting in a six-car pileup and blown tires.
- Bobby limped the car back to the pits and climbed out to smoke a cigarette while his crew threw on replacement tires.
- He then roared back onto the track still hearing the curses of his fellow drivers.
- At lap 77 he pulled into the pits for gas, only to learn he was going to be fined and suspended for causing the wreck.
- "Now or never," was Bobby's reply. "Let's see if they will suspend the winner."
- And he roared out of the pits.
- At lap 90 he was third, with his car handling well and his mind clear.
- Bobby was challenging for the lead in the far turn when he ran over metal from an earlier wreck.
- His tire blew immediately and the wall was his next stop, causing the Ford to flip twice.
- When he woke up in the hospital he was greeted by the news that he had not been suspended after all.
- Only later did they tell him that the car was a total loss and he would not be racing for a while.
- "Next time I'll try a Chevy," he said and fell back to sleep.

Life in the Community: Charlotte, North Carolina
- Agriculture attracted the first settlers to the Catawba River region near Charlotte, North Carolina.
- The first industry in the area was a rifle factory, started by two men from Lancaster, Pennsylvania.
- By 1786, the community of almost 300 had a flour and saw mill, a rifle factory, merchants, tailors, weavers, and blacksmiths.
- With the invention of the cotton gin by Eli Whitney in 1793, Charlotte became a ginning center, paving the way for its textile industry.
- Charlotte was lifted from its plantation economy by the discovery of gold in 1799, igniting America's first gold rush.

Bobby liked racing stock cars on familiar tracks.

- Production was so heavy that President Andrew Jackson authorized the establishment in Charlotte of a U.S. Mint branch, which was completed in 1837.
- The mint attracted banks to Charlotte, the first of which opened in 1834.
- Growth was also stimulated by the railroad in 1854, turning Charlotte into a transportation hub.
- By 1877, the Carolina Central Railroad stretched from Charlotte to Wilmington, and later expanded from Richmond, Virginia, to Atlanta, Georgia.
- This further fueled the expansion of the textile industry, leading to the creation of department stores, including Belks.
- In 1882, D.A. Tompkins designed and built over 100 cotton mills.
- By 1903, over half of the nation's textile production was located within a 100-mile radius of Charlotte.
- The banking industry developed around the time of the gold rush, and provided capital for new development in the entire Piedmont region.
- The Federal Reserve opened in Charlotte in 1927, bringing prestige and more growth.
- The first NASCAR stock race was held at Charlotte Speedway in 1949; the cars were "strictly stock," with no modifications from the factory.

Racing Timeline

Early 1900s: Stock car racing got its start during Prohibition, with moonshine runners attempting to flee federal tax agents.

December 14, 1947: During a meeting at the Streamline Hotel in Daytona Beach, "Big Bill" France Sr. and a group of ex moonshiners, gas station owners and local racing boys began talks that led to the forming of the National Association for Stock Car Auto Racing (NASCAR).

February 15, 1948: The first NASCAR race was run at the Daytona Beach Road Course.

February 21, 1948: NASCAR was incorporated.

June 19, 1949: In the NASCAR race run at Charlotte, North Carolina, Jim Roper won in a Lincoln.

September 4, 1950: The Southern 500, NASCAR's first 500-mile race, was held at Darlington Raceway.

1950: "Strictly Stock" series took the name of Grand National.

1951: Jim Flock became the first driver to qualify quicker than 100 mph, driving a Lincoln at the Daytona Beach Road Course.

1953: NASCAR applied the rules by the book and withdrew points to several drivers who had not filled in the inscription form in time.

June 13, 1954: NASCAR's first road race, the International 100, was held at Linden Airport in New Jersey.

There's Money in Old Cars, *Auto Sport Review,* April 1952

The only man in America who treats old cars as casually as cards in a filing cabinet is Barney Pollard of Detroit. In the northwestern factory area of Detroit, Mr. Pollard has shed after shed chockfull of valuable autos, so full, in fact, he can't tell you how many autos he owns.

He's not kidding, either. One old-car bug who ventured into this labyrinth of steel emerged after a few hours, drooling about hundreds and hundreds of priceless cars, makes he had never seen before. No one else, though, will venture into Pollard's sheds. Before stacking his cars like cards, Pollard de-rusts the steel portions, rubs linseed oil into the wood and

Neatsfoot oil into the leather upholstery. The net result is a greasy jungle no one dares to enter.

Not all of Pollard's cars are stacked up; he usually has several dozen waiting to go into storage at any one time. Just a brief survey is enough to convince anyone that the Pollard collection makes H. Ford looked like an amateur. Of the more than 2,000 makes of automobiles that were made in the US., Pollard has a model of almost every make.

He began collecting, seriously, back in 1939, when he took an old Cadillac as final payment on a long overdue debt. Today, he pursues his hobby with fanatical devotion, covering 400 miles a day when on "hunting expeditions." He scours the Midwestern countryside from the rolling hills of the Ohio River Valley northward into Canada. He has searched as far west as Kansas and, exploring the east, found an old Autocrat on Staten Island, New York.

Into barns, garages, homes, Pollard snoops everywhere. He considers small-town mechanics his best source of tips. Normally, Pollard operates a cinder's business in Detroit, which permits him to pursue this rather expensive hobby. "I don't spend more than 15 minutes with anyone talking about cars. If I can't find out in that length of time whether he wants to sell, I leave him." In some cases, says Pollard, he has waited several years for a "yes" or "no" answer from a car owner.

An old-time auto man, Pollard once worked for Chalmers, then tested (during World War I) Liberty aircraft engines while working for Packard, but has been his own boss since 1918. Detroit is apathetic about old cars, though, says Pollard. "All big cities are poor places in which to find old cars," says Pollard. "Detroit, the world's auto capital, is poorest of them all."

How much does he pay, Pollard won't say, and he has his reasons. "Owners are apt to ask any kind of price, because they've heard so much talk of big prices. Chevrolet and Dodge once

gave a new car in trade for an old one, and thus created a lasting impression that old car owners eventually will get an even-Stephen trade-in."

Name your favorite 1907 White Steamer, 1910 Cadillac, 1904 Olds, 1917 Renault Cabriolet, 1910 Stoddard-Dayton, 1911 Flanders 20, 1915 Krit, 1908 Poss truck, Dusenberry, Revere, Grant, Oliver, Pollard's got 'em all!

I had a moonshine car and we started fixing it on Monday to go to race at Darlington (South Carolina). We went down Tuesday and qualified and won the race. I drove the car back home. We took the headlights out and put beefed-up tires on it. There weren't a lot of major changes because what we would do in a car race was about what you'd do to run moonshine, anyway.

—Racing pioneer Junior Johnson

Single Mother Teaches in Florida

Mary Cronin was from Queens, New York, and a divorced, single mother in 1956. Finding it difficult to live and teach in New York City, she picked up her son and moved to Miami where her teaching style was better suited to the military air force base where she rekindled her passion for her chosen career.

Life at Home

- Thirty-one-year-old Mary Cronin grew up convinced that she was an ugly duckling with no chance of ever becoming a swan.
- Fairy tales, she frequently reminded herself, did not happen in Queens, New York.
- The product of a college-educated father and a bright mother—who dropped out of school to be married—Mary loved learning.
- Being smart is the next best thing to being pretty, she told herself.
- While still in high school, Mary decided that teaching could be a satisfying career.
- Her first serious opportunity to teach came when she was a junior in high school in New York City.
- Her chemistry teacher called her aside to explain that his 15-year-old son who had cerebral palsy couldn't attend school.
- He offered her an after-school job of teaching his son to read.
- Mary had no idea how to teach reading, but accepted the challenge, especially since the pay of $2.50 per week seemed an enormous sum.
- For their first, very awkward meeting, she brought a wide range of books, but her new pupil rejected them all, asking for a poem.
- Mary's student fully understood many words, but because of his limited experience, was unable to visualize the meanings of certain words like "dive" for a tavern, or to imagine New York's Fifty-second Street.
- So, instead of just describing the appearance of New York's Fifty-second Street, she also described the smells and tastes of the place.
- She felt for the first time in her life that she had done something truly powerful and positive for another person.

Queens native Mary Cronin flourished as a teacher in Florida.

- Wanting to teach, she concluded, was like wanting to have children or write a novel or think through a math problem that others couldn't solve.
- Her dream of being an elementary school teacher never diminished, but while in college at Radcliffe, Mary watched with fascination and confusion the debate raging about women and college.
- The year she graduated, 1943, was the first year that Radcliffe students could attend classes at Harvard.
- At the same time, Harvard Medical School was engaged in an internal struggle over the role of women in medicine.
- One side argued that the ravages of the Second World War demanded that America produce a steady flow of physicians, thus necessitating the admission of women.
- Traditionalists said that despite the war, the economy or the interests of women, society should protect the role of women as child bearers and keepers of the home.
- Following the debate closely, Mary felt torn by the arguments, especially since she was engaged to a man who proudly stated that his wife would "never work if I can help it, by God."
- She struggled with what was to be her role in a country at war, and the fact that she was about to become a Mrs.
- It was a question quickly answered when she became pregnant on her honeymoon, then saw her new husband shipped off to fight the Japanese in the Pacific theater.
- Her role as mother was all-consuming.
- Two years later, when her husband returned, he didn't recognize his two-year-old son or his new, independent wife, and the couple divorced in 1948.

Life at Work: Teacher

- Mary's first attempts to find a teaching job was a disaster.
- Despite a degree from one of the finest schools in America, she had no education courses, and therefore was not qualified for a teaching job in the New York system.
- She took a position at a private school, which was not as strict about teaching certificates.
- The challenges of raising a son alone and teaching school were immense, and fellow teachers were not supportive of her divorce or her decision to take back her maiden name.
- After five years of struggle and tears, she realized that teaching wasn't the problem—it was New York.
- Within days she made the decision to move to Miami, Florida, where the climate was good for her son's asthma, confident that a job would be available.
- The Cold War was creating opportunity, as America was willing to spend money on defense to stop the spread of communism.
- Homestead Air Force Base, just south of Miami, was reopened, and Mary found her place immediately, teaching fifth grade at Tangerine Elementary School, a collection of 14 detached, surplus Quonset huts donated by the military.
- The huts were located in neat rows in a flat, treeless field; pour a few sidewalks and a school was born.
- Most of the long, rounded, metal Quonset hut classrooms had windows down both sides to bring in light, all had fans to push the Florida air around, and a few had air conditioning.
- Because of the Cold War, the new military base and the resulting influx of workers, everything was happening so quickly there literally was no rule book for the school.
- In this atmosphere, Mary began to blossom.
- Her first quest was to get to know her students, many of whom were children of construction workers imported to Southeast Florida to build this overnight air base, or military kids who are so used to moving they rarely remember each other's last name.
- In New York and across the nation, teachers were taught that chatting with students or meeting with them during breaks instead of taking coffee in the teacher's lounge would contribute to the breakdown of discipline in the classroom.
- In Florida, she ignored that tradition of teaching.

- One of her first challenges was to assist a young girl who needed help in reading.
- A product of the deep South, the child had been in seven different schools because her migrant family moved so often.
- Because of Mary's heavy New York accent, using phonics to teach reading was difficult; she and the young Southerner simply did not pronounce their vowels the same way.
- Yet, the meaning of sentences and the content of stories made communication possible.
- So everyday she talked about books and discussed the stories that have been read; then she listened.
- The more Mary and the students talked about books, the more they read.
- One night she realized that the children could teach themselves if given the right opportunity

Mary's diverse students missed typical American recreation, but enjoyed learning each others' customs.

to learn; every child should be both student and teacher if the process is to work.
- Mary also found that the more she immersed herself in the life of her students, the more ready they were to learn—and the more she loved being a teacher.
- From her Cuban students she learned to properly cook rice and beans; from the military kids, she got a picture of life in Germany, England and the Philippines; and from the Floridian children she learned how to throw a cast net and spot motionless black crown night herons in the Everglades.
- She met Florida's environment at its best and worst.
- Recently, thousands of migrating fiddler crabs invaded the base and the land around the school, covering every inch of space and causing dozens of automobile accidents when car tires slid on thousands of slick, crushed crab bodies.
- She has also experienced the informality of south Florida, where wearing shorts after school is accepted and no one cared about one's past.
- It was the perfect place for a divorced woman who loved her son, her students and the uniqueness of Florida in the midst of change.
- The standard dress for her students was dresses every day for girls, blue jeans and collared shirts for boys.
- Because the school was so new, it had no cafeteria, so the children rode their bikes home at lunch and often returned with locally grown oranges for an afternoon snack.
- Often in the afternoons, Mary took the children outside to play music, which gave everyone a break from the Florida heat that built in the classrooms.
- After work she went home, changed clothes and toured in her blue 1947 Plymouth through the Everglades, where alligators and herons await.
- Twice she has even gotten to the nearly deserted place called Key West.

Life in the Community: Homestead Air Force Base, Florida
- Mary lived with the Cold War every day because of the school's location near Homestead Air Force Base in southern Dade County, Florida, approximately 25 miles southwest of Miami.
- The base was seven miles northeast of the town of Homestead and five miles east of the Everglades.
- Because of the military, Mary saws the composition of her class change often as children transferred to other bases with their families.

Mary's music lessons were not as structured as those up north, and often taught outdoors.

- Since arriving in Florida, she attended the funerals of three men whose planes crashed on take-off or failed to come back from a mission.
- Most parent-teacher conferences only involved mothers; the fathers rarely were seen at school except at the annual Christmas pageant.
- Last year, one fifth-grade boy was in tears before the Christmas play; his father had sent word from Morocco that he would not be home for Christmas.
- It was the fourth straight Christmas he had missed because of an overseas assignment.
- The international flavor of the base also created interesting classroom assignments.
- When Mary assigned a scrapbook on an African country, three children brought in pictures their Air Force pilot fathers had taken on recent trips to Egypt, the Gold Coast and South Africa.
- One set of boy-girl twins even showed up at school in authentic Moroccan costumes complete with a tall fez for the boy and lacy veils for the girl.
- The community was sensitive to the needs of the base; Spanish-language classes were taught beginning in the first grade on new television sets placed in every classroom.
- The School Board proudly said that the worker of tomorrow must be bilingual, and that teaching could be delivered in different ways, like a television instructor.
- Mary had two children in her class for whom English was a second language; their fathers both came to Homestead to do construction on the rapidly expanding military base.

Typical American Teenager—from Poland

Kira Leszczow left Poland with her family in the middle of a snowy night to escape Communist rule. After years in Germany, an American family sponsored them and they traveled to Missouri, then moved to Chicago, then finally settled in Benton Harbor, Michigan. In 1957, Kira enjoyed being a typical American teenager.

Life at Home

- When her family abandoned their Polish home in the middle of the night in January 1945, Kira Leszczow barely understood how her life was about to change.
- Her father, Afanasy, woke her up, put her favorite doll in her hands, and carried her into the living room.
- Kira's mother, Emilia, threw food and clothing into a rucksack, and small valuables into her beltpouch.
- Kira may have felt like this was an exciting adventure, but it was a life-or-death situation.
- The Second World War had recently come to a close in the European theater, and the Soviet Communists were advancing in on their Polish village of Bydgoszcz.
- Kira's father was a Russian officer during WWI and a Czarist supporter, and would be killed if caught by the communists. He fled Russia once to escape the communists, and now must abandon Poland if he wanted to live long enough to complete his religious studies.
- Emilia was not worried for herself because whe was born in Poland.
- With the bare essentials in hand, the family walked outside into the freezing night.
- Snow covered the streets, as a large open-bed truck waited with huddled families in the back.
- Kira's father spoke to a man in German, and Kira recognized him as a German Army officer whom her father had befriended, though he was not wearing his uniform.
- Kira and Emilia were helped into the back of the truck and were soon joined by Afanasy.
- At the outskirts of town, they met up with other trucks that were also packed full of people.
- A caravan formed heading west away from the advancing Soviet army and towards Germany.
- After a couple of hours of travel, the caravan stopped and a couple climbed out of a truck with a small bundle, and walked into the forest beside the road.

Kira Leszczow left Poland at 5, eventually settling in as an American teenager in Michigan.

119

Kira left Poland on a dark, snowy night.

- A few minutes later, they trudged solemnly out of the forest, having buried their child who froze to death.
- Early the next morning, the caravan stopped and everyone took shelter in a school to sleep having successfully crossed the border into Germany.
- They were both exhilarated at having escaped the Soviets and saddened at leaving their homes behind, perhaps forever.
- Later that day, a local farmer arrived in a horse-drawn sled and arrangements were made for Kira and her parents to stay with the farmer for a little while.
- They said good-bye bye to their fellow refugees, settled into the sled, and slid farther away from their old lives.
- After a stay at the farmer's home, the family journeyed with other refugees to Bitterfeld, Germany.
- They stayed until Germany was split by the treaty in 1949 into the Federal Republic of Germany and the German Democratic Republic.
- Afanasy knew that it was time to get out of the Soviet zone, so they moved to southern Germany, which was occupied by the Americans, and stayed in a DP, or displaced persons, camp.
- While in the DP camp, Afanasy became ordained as a Russian Orthodox priest, with dreams of going to America.
- They scraped by and eventually, when Kira was 11 years old, they were sponsored by the Logan family in the United States, who lived on a large farm in Colony, Missouri.
- The Leszczows left Germany on an American troop ship and traveled first to Venezuela to drop off other refugees, then to New Orleans, Louisiana.
- From there, the Leszczows traveled by train to Colony, Missouri, where lived for one year in a converted chicken coop on the Logan farm.
- Afanasy milked cows, delivered calves, took care of the animals, and mended fences.
- Emilia cleaned house for the Logans.
- Kira went to school and played with the local children, quickly picking up English, although with a distinct Russian accent.
- She continued to wear her European clothes and her hair in braids down the middle of her back.
- Neighborhood families spoiled the exotic visitors with ice cream and chocolate, so much so that Kira eventually began to loose her sweet tooth.
- In August of 1951, Afanasy was assigned to a Russian Orthodox church in Chicago.
- The Leszczows quickly decamped to Chicago, where Kira's parents were more comfortable away from the farm and close to other other Russian immigrants.

American sweets were overwhelming to Kira.

Life at Work: Russian Orthodox Priest

- Afanasy Leszczow was very proud to be the priest of the local Russian Orthodox church in Chicago, at last to be performing his life's calling.

- The church provided lodging for the family and paid their utility bills.
- After two years, he received a new assignment, and the family moved to Benton Harbor, Michigan.
- The Russian Orthodox church, on Thresher Avenue in Benton Harbor, was a two-story, square, cement-block building.
- The street level was the church and the top level was the Leszczows' apartment.
- At first, Kira was ashamed that her house was so unlike those of the other children in her school.

Kira's family quickly learned about American food.

- Secretly she was most upset that they didn't have a white picket fence like she saw in American movies.
- Her father's church was small and paid little, so he also worked at the Twin Cities Container Corporation factory.
- "He went every day in the morning with his lunch bucket to catch a ride with a neighbor, and came home in the evenings, sweaty and tired," Kira remembers.
- The family put a small amount into a savings account each week, only to have it embezzled by a high-level administrator at the bank.
- They were devastated.
- Afanasy was 62, and the factory work was strenuous, especially with the weight of a congregation on his shoulders.
- Kira's mother, Emilia, kept their apartment in order, bought groceries daily, cooked and cleaned, and occupied herself with church meetings.
- Kira worked at Wilder's Drug Store after school and on Saturdays.
- Wilder's employed three pharmacists and several older women who worked the jewelry and cosmetics counters.
- Kira worked the cash register and took great pride in always proving to the penny.
- When the store wasn't busy, Kira looked at the newspaper advertisements, seeing how to best spend her next paycheck.
- As a high school senior, her world revolved around friends and family, and she was rarely distracted by the tumult of civil rights demonstrations or the Russian invasion of Hungary.
- This insular world was emphasized by her parents' continued reliance on conversing mainly in Russian.
- When her family would get together with other Russian immigrants, they sang Russian songs, ate Russian food and cried over bittersweet memories.
- Kira wanted nothing to do with this.
- She wanted to be an American and, on occasion, would refuse to speak Russian to her parents.
- She did everything she could to make herself look more American; she had a ponytail, a felt skirt with a poodle on it, saddle shoes, and went to sock hops and football games.
- As a teen in Benton Harbor she learned all about spending the night at friends' houses, talking about boys half the night, going to the beach in the summer with her friends, as well as eating pizza and hamburgers.
- At school, she took English, composition, literature, history, French, math, choir, and gym.
- Kira excelled especially in French, with her extensive language background and fluency in Russian, German, Polish, and English.

Michigan schools were non-segregated prior to the 1954 Supreme Court decision.

- She felt special when her teachers asked her for help in pronunciation of foreign names, cities, and countries.
- Kira realized that, despite her best efforts, she would never be one of the popular kids.
- The classmates who were popular were the ones who had gone to school together since kindergarten, with the same hairstyles and clothes.
- Kira had a wide circle of friends—Americans, fellow immigrants, whites, browns and blacks.
- Michigan was one of the 17 states that prohibited the separation of races in educational settings before the landmark decision by the United States Supreme Court in 1954, *Brown v. Board of Education of Topeka*.
- While much of the country was embroiled in the civil rights movement Benton Harbor remained relatively insulated from it all.
- Even the growing tension wrought by Cold War conflicts between Russia and the United States did not intrude on Kira's American world.
- Here life revolved around friends, American music and American films.
- After school, she and her friends often stopped at soda shops and sipped malts, cokes, and played records on the juke box, including *The Four Freshmen, Nat King Cole,* and *Elvis Presley*.
- She went to movies to see stars like Pat Boone, Rita Hayworth, John Wayne, Doris Day, Gregory Peck, and Elizabeth Taylor.
- When she went to see the movie *Miss Sadie Thompson*, in which Rita Hayworth played a tongue-in-cheek ex-prostitute, Kira asked the lady in the next seat, "What is a prostitute?"
- The woman replied that she did not know either, and promptly moved several rows away.
- Kira's family didn't own a television set, but she watched *Howdy Doody, The Ed Sullivan Show, The Hit Parade,* and *Dragnet* at a friend's house.
- Kira and her friends were in the school choir and always took part in the musicals and plays that Benton Harbor High School produced.
- Her senior year, she was student director of the play *Oklahoma*.
- She loved bossing the popular kids around.
- In the summer, Kira went to the beaches of Lake Michigan with her friends.
- Although her parents didn't have a car, Kira's friends almost always had access to one, so they rarely rode the city bus.
- Her parents made adjustments as well, and simplified their last name to Leschoff.
- Afanasy and Emilia considered the name change a gesture of gratefulness to the United States, which they always called their "blessed land."

Life in the Community: Benton Harbor, Michigan

- Benton Harbor was in the southwest edge of Michigan, on Lake Michigan; its sister town, St. Joseph, was just across the St. Joseph River.
- Both were resort towns, due to their locations on Lake Michigan.
- However, Benton Harbor had more industry than its sister, and a bit less affluence.
- The Heath Corporation and Voice of Music both had factories in Benton Harbor.
- Both of these companies made electronic and audio equipment.
- They also had the Twin Cities Container Corporation, where Afanasy worked.
- The surrounding areas boasted fruit and vegetable farms and Benton Harbor was home to a large fruit market located in the "flats" area of town.

- Emilia shopped there for fresh cherries, blueberries, peaches, apples, and strawberries; after the family's days in displaced persons camps, nothing tasted quite so good to them as fresh fruit.

Kira spent time at Lake Michigan with her American friends.

- The Russian Orthodox community was small compared to other ethnic communities.
- Most of Afanasy's congregation had just recently immigrated and spoke little English.
- The majority of them worked at either farms or factories.
- English was learned mostly by the children of these families, since they were in American schools.
- The parents stayed home on the farms, spoke only Russian, and went to a Russian church where they communicated with other Russians.
- Their children would interpret for them when it was necessary to deal with Americans.

- Afanasy had an especially difficult time learning the new language; at his factory job he had little chance to converse with English speakers, and in his position as Russian Orthodox pastor, he dealt with parishioners that could, in most cases, only speak Russian.

Russian Immigration Timeline

1784: The Aleutian island of Kodiak became the first Russian settlement in North America.

1864: Congress legalized the importation of contract laborers.

1867: The Russian czar sold the Alaskan territory to the U.S.; Russian cultural influences persisted long afterward.

1880-1900: A great wave of emigration from the Russian Empire erupted including Ukrainians, Belarusians, Lithuanians, and Poles who moved to the United States in the hundreds of thousands; ethnic Russians were barred from leaving the country.

1881: The assassination of Czar Alexander II prompted civil unrest and economic instability throughout Russia.

1882: Russia's May Laws severely restricted the ability of Jewish citizens to live and work in Russia.

1885: Congress banned the admission of contract laborers.

1917: The imperial government of Russia was overthrown by socialist revolutionaries called Bolsheviks.

During four years of civil war more than two million fled the communist Soviet Union; around 30,000 made their way to the United States. These immigrants were called "white" Russians because of their opposition to the "red" communist Bolsheviks.

1917-1920: During the "Red Scare," the American government cracked down on political and labor organizations, especially those involved with Russian nationals; thousands of Russians were deported without a formal trial.

1929: Congress made annual immigration quotas permanent.

1930-1940: Thousands of Russians fled the Soviet Union in the fear of another world war.

1945: Once World War II was over in Europe, refugees from across Europe fled the chaos and depression of postwar Russia. More than 20,000 Russian refugees known as DPs, or displaced persons, successfully reached the United States.

1947-1957: The Second Red Scare occurred in the United States; anyone suspected of having communist sympathies was blacklisted, jailed, or deported.

1948: The United States admitted 205,000 refugees fleeing persecution in their native lands to enter.

1952: The Immigration and Nationality Act made individuals of all races eligible for naturalization; reaffirmed the national origins quota system; limited immigration from the Eastern Hemisphere; established preferences for skilled workers and relatives of U.S. citizens and permanent resident aliens; and tightened security and screening standards and procedures.

The Soviet government slowed the rate at which its artists and scientists were decamping to America, and established strict controls over emigration; Russian immigration to the U.S. became a rare and risky undertaking.

1953: Congress amended its 1948 refugee policy to allow for the admission of 200,000 more refugees.

Television Fanatics

Evelyn Marsh and her family were addicted to television, as were many folks were in 1957 in America. They made sure Sunday dinner was done in time to watch The Ed Sullivan Show and Evelyn and her siblings wanted the toys advertised during Howdy Doody and Captain Kangeroo, like Silly Putty and Mr. Potato Head.

Life at Home

- For the Marsh family, television dictated schedules, created conversations and stopped activities.
- Evelyn and her siblings planned their days around their favorite television programs, carefully instructing their mother to call them in when certain shows, especially *The Mickey Mouse Club* or *Howdy Doody*, come on the air.
- This obsession did not end with the children, as their parents used the handy *TV Guide* to organize their week.
- Sunday nights at 8 p.m. were reserved for *The Ed Sullivan Show*.
- By that time, dinner was done, baths taken and the whole family took their places in front of the TV.
- Evelyn thought variety show host Ed Sullivan looked like a cross between her father and the Frankenstein monster.
- She loved the puppets and the circus acts and the singers.
- The fan magazines reported that Ed Sullivan made over $250,000 a year.
- One evening, when there was no school the next day, she got to stay up and see *The Tonight Show* with Steve Allen, featuring the Muppets.
- While the family watched television, her father often roamed the house looking for lights that were left on, and loved to announce that he turned out a light in one of the home's six bathrooms or 14 closets.
- Evelyn was the fourth child and the second girl.
- Thanks to the Silly Putty she got for her birthday, she and her baby sister spent hours lifting comics off the funny pages, stretching the putty to make the faces change, making Evelyn's little sister giggle.
- To boost sales, Silly Putty commercials aired on *Howdy Doody* and *Captain Kangaroo*.

Evelyn Marsh and her family watched a lot of television.

Evelyn was christened in her grandmother's gown.

- Evelyn wanted a Mr. Potato Head kit as advertised on television, but she wanted a Hula Hoop more.
- The past spring, after a baptism at church, her mother showed Evelyn the gown she and her sisters were christened in.
- Made with Mechlin lace inserts, trim around the bottom, and three tiny mother-of-pearl buttons at the back, the dress was originally worn by her grandmother, when she was christened in 1890.
- When she was not playing with her baby sister or watching television, she went to her cousin Betsy's house to play with dolls.
- Betsy had a room full of dolls, doll clothing and furniture—much of it made by her parents.
- Often, the two girls sewed a dress themselves to make sure their dolls look right for every occasion.
- Evelyn loved knowing everything that went on in the house, like when the Grand Rapids Police Department brought her older brother home—drunk.
- He was caught drinking whiskey at a friend's house when their parents were out at their usual Wednesday night bridge game.
- She heard her mother say, "At this rate, he may be 90 before he gets his driver's license."
- Nothing was said the next morning, but Evelyn made sure her brother knew that she knew he was in trouble, even though the incident was never discussed in front of her.
- The next day, her brother and his classmates went to a special movie at school, sitting in chairs made to look like automobiles and watched a short movie about drinking, sex and cars.
- The children went to the doctor, even though they were not sick, to be vaccinated against polio.

Evelyn played dolls with her cousin, Betsy.

- She did not understand that "vaccinated" meant getting a shot until they arrived there, and was not pleased when she found out.
- To ward off polio, Evelyn's mother insisted that the children take afternoon naps when the heat exceeds 90 degrees, because hot days were believed to encourage the outbreak of the debilitating disease.
- On Friday nights her father often took all the children to a favorite hamburger place called McDonald's—where kids were welcomed and advertised, "Give Mom a Night Out."

American children weren't happy about polio shots.

- Wednesday night bridge club was often hosted at Evelyn's house, when five couples gathered at 6:00 for cocktails, played bridge at 7:00, and left by 10:00.
- Her mother always dressed up for bridge club, and Evelyn loved sitting in her mother's room while she dressed, combed her hair and applied makeup.
- Sometimes Evelyn was allowed to use lipstick and rosewater perfume, as long as Daddy didn't know.

Classes were expanding across the country.

- During these times, her mother described her dream that her boys would grow up to work in the family business, and her girls would grow up pretty and make good wives.
- The Marsh family loved Grand Rapids, and strived to buy products made in their city, including a Bissell carpet sweeper, Hekman Biscuits, an American Motors car and Hush Puppies shoes, all made in Grand Rapids.
- Their neighbor was CFO of Wolverine Shoe and Tanning Corporation, the parent company of Hush Puppies, which were wildly popular due to a special pig-skinning process, allowing the shoes to breathe.

Life at School and Summer Vacation

- Evelyn loved to read, but she and her teacher did not always agree on what to read.
- She liked mysteries, but not math.
- *Jack and Jill* magazine was a must-read, no matter how much homework she had.
- Her mother also loved to read, especially articles on child improvement and how to be a better parent.
- She sometimes found that a small tranquilizer pill and a short nap were a better solution to a well-run household than parenting articles.
- Evelyn's class took a field trip to the John Ball Zoological Park, where her favorite site was Monkey Island, where the monkeys scampered about as though just for her benefit.
- The city was known for partnerships that linked schools and parks, and planned for a park or playground with every school site.
- The park at her new school included restrooms, swings and recreational facilities, as well as programs built around summer vacations.
- She wanted to spend more time at the parks this summer, but her father loved to drive the family around to pick out sites for his new Holiday Inn motels.
- The only way the trips were even bearable was to bring lots of comic books—five for each child.
- Her older brother, the mean one, was not allowed to touch her comics without her permission or she told her mother.
- After 20 years in commercial construction, her father began building and operating Holiday Inns across the Midwest.
- He built 31 motels as part of the company's nationwide march across the country.
- Prior to the creation of the Holiday Inn chain, most travelers stopped at small mom-and-pop motels where the service, cleanliness and amenities varied widely.
- Mr. Marsh's motel-building career began because Kemmons Wilson, a successful home-builder in Memphis,

127

Evelyn's father was a Holiday Inn franchise holder.

Tennessee, decided to take his five children to see the nation's capital in Washington, DC.

- Based on his experience with expensive hotel rooms that were small and without air-conditioning Wilson decided to go into the motel business and offered the same opportunity to fellow contractors across America, including Evelyn's father.
- He named his company after a television show special, *Bing Crosby's Holiday Inn*.
- In the beginning, Wilson only charged fellow members of the National Homebuilders' Association $500 for the right to own a Holiday Inn in their city, plus a user fee of $0.05 a night per room.
- Only a few builders joined Marsh and took Wilson up on his offer; many said they didn't want to be in the travel business, while most claimed they didn't see much future in building motels because not enough people took vacations.
- Even though Congress passed a $76 billion federal highway building program, few saw the potential.
- Marsh, like Wilson, had grown wealthy building residential homes, generally erecting houses for $10 a square foot.
- Along a city highway, he built the first motel comprising 120 rooms, plus a restaurant, at a cost of $280,000; it took him 90 days to complete the project.
- The newer Holiday Inns had a gift shop and a swimming pool, and included an air conditioner and free television set in each room.
- The room rates were $4 a night for a single and $6 for a double, and letting children stay free attracted traveling families in search of a bargain.
- For the Marsh family, summers were spent traveling around picking sites for future motels and helping other franchise operators get started.
- Although Evelyn loved to travel, she hated being in the car because her big brother put his feet on her dress and made ugly faces at her when no one was looking.
- While on a recent scouting trip, her little brother swallowed too much water swimming in the Holiday Inn pool, threw up in front of everybody, and the pool had to be closed and drained.
- Her father was furious, but Evelyn thought it was funny.
- Her father copied the work habits of Ray Kroc of McDonald's—every executive's desk must be free of paper at the end of the day, every executive answered his own phone and neatness was an obsession.
- The only typewriters, cash registers and adding machines he allowed in his office were the R.C. Allens, made in Grand Rapids, and he often played golf with the Allen company owner at the country club.
- "Be good to those who have been good to you," he said as often as he can.

Life in the Community: Grand Rapids, Michigan

- Grand Rapids' earliest suburbs began around the turn of the century, arranged along the streetcar routes, making it possible for homes and businesses to spread outward from the city center.
- By the early 1950s, the automobile had clearly established the pattern of city migration, freeing residents from the necessity of living near public transportation.
- Struggling farms, which once ringed the city, became valuable housing developments for people eager to be on the move and part of a modern America.
- The area was a center for Dutch life in America, beginning before the American Civil War.

- Grand Rapids was attractive because of ample job opportunities, the availability of Dutch-language worship services and an existing, accepting Dutch community in the area.
- A second wave of Dutch immigrants arrived in the 1870s, attracted by the city's reputation as the furniture capital of America, welcoming skilled European woodworkers seeking opportunity.
- By 1900 persons of Dutch birth or ancestry made up 40 percent of the city's population—the largest proportion of Dutch in any large American city.
- As a result, Grand Rapids was the headquarters of the Christian Reformed Church, which arose from the beliefs of the first Dutch settlers, who preferred their Dutch-language brand of Calvinism to the Americanized practices of the Reformed Church of America.
- Membership in the Christian Reformed Church and the Reformed Church of America made up 40 percent of the city's population, while Catholics comprised another 40 percent.
- Grand Rapids retained its distinction as America's furniture manufacturing capital; $100 million in furniture and fixtures were produced in the city for export nationwide.
- The trademark "made in Grand Rapids" affixed to furniture carried a special significance for superiority in design and craft, and was protected by a court ruling.
- Since the end of World War II, the furniture business boomed as consumers continued their nationwide shopping spree after hard times and the war.
- Grand Rapids was battling a movement of mass-market furniture manufacturers to factories in the South, where labor was cheaper, particularly in North Carolina.
- As a result, many furniture factories expanded their lines to include furniture for the thousands of new offices and skyscrapers that were constructed across America.
- To survive in the traditional, home-based furniture market, many local companies specialized in limited-production, expensive, handcrafted furniture in a range of classic and modern styles.
- General Motors was the largest employer in Grand Rapids, with thousands employed at a metal-stamping plant built in the Depression, or at the GM Diesel Equipment Plant constructed during the Second World War.
- In addition, the Fisher Body Trim Fabrication Plant, which formerly made fuselages for the F-84 Thunderbird jet fighter, turned out interior trim for Chevrolets.

Young Carpenter

Tom Lakey married his high school sweetheart right after graduation. With a baby on the way, he got a job as a carpenter and the couple rented a small apartment from Tom's uncle, who was also a carpenter. Tom made $3.10 an hour in 1957, with no benefits. No work, due to weather or illness, meant no pay.

Life at Home

- Tom Lakey and Laura Baldwin were married on his graduation night, and he immediately went to work as a carpenter to work to support his wife and soon-to-be-born baby.
- They rented a small apartment from his uncle, who was also a carpenter, and were looking for a larger place.
- Tom and Laura looked at several of the suburbs where he was building houses, but didn't have the down payment for a house.
- Through the United Brotherhood of Carpenters and Joiners of America, he had health insurance to cover their anticipated medical expenses.
- She read a lot about healthy babies, and learned that a boy had a life expectancy of 66.64 years, and a girl had a life expectancy of 72.65 years.
- They enjoyed reading the Sears catalog, like their parents did, but unlike their parents, they purchased tools and furniture from the local Sears store instead of ordering through the catalog, a trend across America.
- Laura was a frugal homemaker, but as drawing and art were her passion, she spent .10 admission to visit the Walker Art Galleries and .25 admission to visit the Institute of Arts.
- Tom's passion was cars, and he owned a 1951 two-door Mercury, which he modified using ideas from *Hot Rod* and *Car and Custom*.
- They talked about selling his car and buying a new Nash Rambler Wagon, after the baby came, at a cost of about $2,400.
- Most nights, Tom and Laura watched *I Love Lucy* and *Gunsmoke* and ate off TV trays. During the day she watched *As the World Turns* and *The Edge of Night* which were called soap operas because their sponsors were often the makers of soaps and detergents.

Tom Lakey became a carpenter right out of high school.

131

Life at Work: Carpenter

Tom started out installing floors and constructing walls.

- Always good with his hands, Tom liked carpentry because of the chance to work out-of-doors.
- He worked for the same contractor for several years, and moved from job to job with this boss.
- He was paid by the hour, with no benefits.
- Tom received time-and-a-half when he worked over 40 hours and double-time for Sunday work, but if there was no work, there was no pay.
- He became a member of the carpenter's union and made $3.10 an hour, often working 50 hours a week and about 39 weeks a year, depending on the weather.
- Tom started out doing mostly rough carpentry work, installing flooring and erecting walls, and then switched to finished carpentry, installing molding around floors and ceilings, wood paneling, cabinets, door frames, and hardware.
- He was sturdy and well-coordinated, and accustomed to standing for an entire day while installing molding or building a form.
- Tom looked for opportunities to install hardwood floors or hang ceiling molding, as these required good skills and often paid better.
- His needed to be extremely accurate, because this kind of work, including mistakes, were highly visible.
- He never had a major injury on the job, although cuts and bruises were an everyday hazard on the job site.
- He worked mostly on houses in the rapidly expanding suburbs of the city, as well as on multistory apartments and small office buildings.
- The mid-1950s were a bonanza for builders as new suburban houses were built at an astonishing rate.
- *House and Garden Magazine* reported that suburbia was "the national way of life."

Life in the Community: Minneapolis, Minnesota

- Minneapolis boasted a population of 521,718 in 1950, and was the 17th largest city in America.
- The Twin Cities of Minneapolis and St. Paul were near the geographical center of North America, and together formed the nation's eighth largest city and stood at the headwaters of the Mississippi River.
- The two cities had different appearances; St. Paul's loop streets were narrow and concentrated and the city was hilly, while Minneapolis' center of activity extended many blocks along the broad shopping avenues and the city was level.
- The early history of both cities was dominated by French Canadians and Scandinavians.
- French Canadian whisky salesman Pierre Parrant was the first actual settler within the present limits of St. Paul, leading to the popular quip that "while

Lake Minneapolis in Minnesota.

Minneapolis had more than 52,00 acres of parkland.

Minneapolis was concerned about water power, St. Paul was born in whisky."
- Thanks to early visionary leadership, thousands of acres of land within Minneapolis was set aside for parks so that in 1957, the city boasted 144 parks, embracing 5,253 acres, or one park acre for every 92 people.
- Minnesota farms produced oats, butter, eggs, milk, corn, wheat, and potatoes; the state boasted 11,000 lakes and great fishing, hunting, and trapping.

Actress in West Side Story

Carol Lawrence was an Italian from Chicago whose parents reluctantly supported her dream of being an actress. They drove her to New York City, and encouraged her to change her name, so TV announcers could pronounce it when she made it big. In 1957, after years of small parts, she landed the leading role in West Side Story.

Life at Home

- *West Side Story* was first told 350 years ago, as *Romeo and Juliet*, a tale of star-crossed lovers by William Shakespeare.
- It was reframed as a New York-based gang rivalry between Jews and Catholics, and originally called East Side Story.
- But when this American musical finally arrived on the Broadway stage in 1957, the story pitted Puerto Rican immigrants against native-born Americans on the west side on Manhattan.
- Carol Lawrence, born Carolina Maria Laraia on September 5, 1932, was cast in the center of the love and violence as Maria.
- Carol grew up in Melrose Park, Illinois, near Chicago where her father was village clerk, and she was born to dance.
- By the age of 12, her tap class lessons were dominated by professionals already working in the Chicago theaters, and at 13, she lied about her age to get a theater work permit.
- As a teenager, Carol was active in local theatrical productions and worked in a number of Chicago-based television productions.
- At her strict Italian father's suggestion, she changed her last name to Lawrence from Laraia.
- "Laraia is really beautiful in Italian" Carol said, "but the poor TV announcers nearly went mad trying to get their tongues around it."
- Carol entered Northwestern University, but after her freshman year persuaded her parents that her future was on New York's Broadway stage.
- So mother, father and daughter journeyed to New York City to visit Broadway and, as Carol said, "They must have decided it was no worse than Chicago. Anyway, they let me stay, though they've always been a little nervous about the whole thing."
- Carol supported herself with a chorus job here, a small feature part there, a few television spots— anything that would keep the dream alive.

Carol Lawrence starred in West Side Story.

Young Carol started tap lessons at an early age.

- Her first Broadway play was in the chorus line of *Borsch Capades*, for which she was paid $25 a week.
- When New York slowed down in the summertime, she gained singing and dancing experience doing summer stock that demanded a different show each week, from *Guys and Dolls* to *Oklahoma!* to *Anything Goes*.
- Her mother lamented that she had not taken a secretarial course, and her father wanted to know whether she was supporting herself as a streetwalker.
- She fell in love with a puppet-master named Cosmo Allegretti, 11 years her senior, who worked on an experimental TV program called *Captain Kangaroo* that featured grown people singing children's songs and acting crazy in a gentle manner.
- They married in 1956 and settled into an apartment near Gramercy Park, where she helped Cosmo create puppets and repair lost eyes and whiskers.
- When Carol heard talk of a new musical set in the slums of the city's West Side, the Juliet part sounded beautiful, and she wanted the role more than anything in the world.
- *West Side Story* featured a script by Arthur Laurents, music by Leonard Bernstein, lyrics by Stephen Sondheim, and choreography by Jerome Robbins.
- "So I marched to the first informal audition with my heart in my mouth, and praise be, they asked me to come back."
- After the second audition, they asked her to come back again to work on a real stage, "and I began to dream."
- Her third tryout was on the stage of the 46th St. Theater and "Leonard Bernstein, the composer, was sitting out front, and I was afraid he'd know right away that I hadn't much voice training."
- Bernstein loved her voice because it wasn't "schooled."
- "We had to look for charm rather than perfection, because the audience might not believe in our "Juliet" if she sang like a full-blown opera star," the legendary composer said.
- She was asked back for one additional audition when someone asked her for her age.
- "I was afraid to answer for a second," Carol said. "I knew the girl was supposed to be 17, and I was 23."
- That's when the show's author, Arthur Laurents, shouted "She's exactly seventeen" and the issue was dropped.
- Laurents already knew that he wanted Carol in the role of Maria and "wouldn't have cared whether she was 70."
- During the final audition, Carol said, "...they asked me to take my hair down. I had a hair do that I'd spent two hours on, and when it all fell in ruins, I was sure I'd look like a real mess."
- It was exactly the look that Jerome Robbins was seeking.

- Set in New York City in the mid-1950s, *West Side Story* explored the rivalry between the Puerto Rican Jets and the white American Sharks, two teenage street gangs of different ethnic backgrounds.
- The young protagonist, Tony, one of the Jets, fell in love with Maria, the sister of Bernardo, the leader of the Sharks.
- The dark theme, sophisticated music, extended dance scenes, and focus on social problems marked a turning point in American musical theater.
- Bernstein's score for the musical included "Something's Coming," "Maria," "America," "Somewhere," "Tonight," "Jet Song," "I Feel Pretty," "A Boy Like That," "One Hand, One Heart," "Gee, Officer Krupke," and "Cool."

Life at Work: Broadway Actress

- *West Side Story* began the birthing process in 1949, when Jerome Robbins approached Leonard Bernstein and Arthur Laurents about collaborating on a contemporary musical adaptation of Romeo and Juliet.
- He proposed that the plot focus on the conflict between an Italian American Roman Catholic family and a Jewish family living on the lower East Side of Manhattan during the Easter-Passover season.
- Eager to write his first musical, Laurents immediately agreed.
- Bernstein wanted to present the material in operatic form, but Robbins and Laurents resisted the suggestion.

Leonard Bernstein loved Carol's voice.

- Laurents wrote a first draft he called East Side Story, but the three men went their separate ways and the piece was shelved for almost five years.
- When it was resurrected, the atmosphere surrounding *West Side Story* had been transformed by recent headlines detailing the brutal murder of two young teenagers in a Hell's Kitchen park by gang members.
- Even then, the creative team was told that *West Side Story* was an impossible project.
- No one would was going to be able to sing augmented fourths (Maria's role), and no one would want to see a show in which the first-act curtain comes down on two dead bodies lying on the stage.
- Also, they had the tough task of casting because the characters had to be able not only to sing but dance, act and be taken for teenagers.
- Numerous producers had turned down the show, deeming it too dark and depressing, when Sondheim convinced his friend Hal Prince to read the script.
- He liked it enough to fly to New York to hear the score, and Prince recalled, "Sondheim and Bernstein sat at the piano playing through the music, and soon I was singing along with them."
- Carol was confronted with newspaper stories describing the violent gang murders posted on the theater's bulletin board with the words, "This is your life."
- In rehearsal, the director told the two rival gangs they were not allowed to eat together or socialize, and demanded that the actors address each other using only their character's names, wanting to cultivate the tension and endemic hatred into every line of the play.
- The intensity of the atmosphere helped foster friendship between Carol and Chita Rivera, who played Anita, the sister she had always wanted.
- Carol said, "That was a new experience for me; it's almost impossible for women in the theater to form friendships because we're all competing for the same roles."

Carol's marriage fell as her career rose.

- In the play, Maria worked in a bridal shop with Anita, the girlfriend of Maria's brother, Bernardo.
- The musical was painted with an urban-tinted score accented by surly street attitudes, slanguage and snapping fingers, and language posed a problem.
- Cursing was uncommon in the theater at the time, and slang expressions were avoided for fear of dating the work.
- Ultimately, a new language was invented that sounded like real street talk but actually wasn't: "Cut the frabba-jabba," for example.
- As rapidly as Carol's singing career was cresting, so too was her marriage crashing.
- Her husband's equally successful career as a puppeteer on a popular TV program begin to appear pale compared to that of a Broadway actress starring in the most talked-about musical of the year.
- Despite being the voice behind Mr. Moose, Grandfather Clock, and the Bunny Rabbit, her husband was called Mr. Lawrence at public functions, and he fully understood that they got the finest table at a classy restaurant because of her fame, not his.

Life in the Community: New York City

- Throughout the 1950s, Broadway musicals were a major part of American popular culture evidenced by the number of hit records created each year from the newest stage musicals.
- Public demand, a booming economy and abundant creative talent kept Broadway fresh because it refused to stand still.
- As the Civil War came to a close, New York City slowly became the center of theatrical activity in America.
- By the mid-1880s, Union Square on 14th Street and Broadway became a gathering spot for producers to assemble touring companies, managers to book tours, and actors and singers to acquire new material.
- Soon a handful of theaters congregated around Union Square and Broadway began to develop its reputation.
- By the turn of the twentieth century, the theater district stretched from West 37th Street along Broadway to 40th Street, culminating at the Metropolitan Opera House.
- About the same time, a half-block on West 28th Street between Broadway and Sixth Avenue, began to hold tremendous sway over the burgeoning entertainment industry.
- This was the home of Tin Pan Alley, where an ever-changing collection of songwriters had gathered to support the booming song sheet industry.
- And the two learned to live in creative synergy.
- The theater district provided the publishers with a natural outlet for their material.
- By 1910, at least two billion copies of song sheets were purchased annually by the American music-loving public.
- The pioneer architect within the theater district was Prussian immigrant, inventor of cigar machines and successful businessman, Oscar Hammerstein, grandfather of the famous lyricist.

Songwriters in Tin Pan Alley: Gene Buck, Victor Herbert, John Philip Sousa, Harry B. Smith, Jerome Kern, Irving Berlin, George W. Meyer, Irving Bibo, Otto Harbach

- He developed several parcels of land from 43rd Street to 45th Street on the east side of Broadway, which became the anchor of the theater district.
- In 1899, he opened the Victoria Theater on the corner of 42nd and Seventh Avenue.
- By 1904, the city's new subway system was delivering thousands of theatergoers nightly, each eager for the Broadway experience, even though most of the theaters were not actually on Broadway itself.
- By 1910, there were 34 theaters north of or near 42nd Street, all focused on the tourist dollar and the opportunity to have their production advertised as "Direct from New York," which was understood nationwide to represent the gold standard in entertainment.
- There, the beautiful sets and girls of Ziegfeld Follies unashamedly sold the American dream, comedienne Fanny Brice spoofed the grand pretensions of middle-class art, and Will Rogers and W.C. Fields built their reputations.
- The outbreak of World War I spawned hundreds of patriotic songs and dozens of Broadway plays symbolizing America's devotion to its fighting men.
- During the 1920s, when the nation officially went dry thanks to prohibition, Broadway stayed wet.
- Following an evening at the theater, after the curtain went up at 8:45 most evenings, patrons completed their Broadway experience at a speakeasy or supper club nearby.
- By the late 1920s, 20 new theaters were constructed and as many as 264 plays and musicals were performed.
- The play, *Shuffle Along*, for example, introduced a variety of new dance styles, pioneered by America's finest emerging black talent.
- Broadway theaters prided themselves that, despite the showiness outside, the greatest glamour was inside where the gold gilt and dramatic décor might feature Victorian, art deco, or glitz galore.
- The 1930s arrived with a thunderous bang; tourists stopped traveling, producers shut down shows, and ushers had no one to usher.

- An estimated 25,000 theater people, the majority in New York, were displaced by the effects of the Great Depression.
- In some theaters, prices were dropped to a $0.25 minimum, with $1.00 being the top price.
- Actors and producers experimented with repertory productions to keep as many working as often as possible, and to keep as many productions as active as they could.
- The 1929-1930 season produced 233 productions, whereas the 1930-1931 season was reduced to 187 productions; new productions on Broadway dipped to 98 shows in 1939.
- Yet this period featured the work of Eugene O'Neill's *Ah, Wilderness!*, Ethel Merman, who opened in George and Ira Gershwin's *Girl Crazy*, and plays by Moss Hart such as *Once in a Lifetime, Merrily We Roll Along, You Can't Take It With You*, and *The Man Who Came to Dinner*.
- Comedy of the 1940s was rich with farces including *George Washington Slept Here*, a collaboration between George Kaufman and Moss Hart, and Irving Berlin's, *This Is the Army*.
- *On the Town* marked the Broadway debut of composer Leonard Bernstein and choreographer Jerome Robbins; songs included "New York, New York (It's a Helluva Town)."
- Then, breakout hit *Oklahoma!* spawned the first-ever original cast album to be released; the songs "People Will Say We're in Love," "Oh, What a Beautiful Mornin'" topped the charts.
- As the decade came to an end, Cole Porter's *Kiss Me, Kate* debuted; Carol Channing starred in *Gentlemen Prefer Blondes*, and *South Pacific* by Rodgers and Hammerstein won a Pulitzer Prize.
- The 1950s opened with the hit show *Guys and Dolls*, whose songs included "If I Were a Bell" and "Luck, Be a Lady," and the show *The King and I* starring Yul Brynner.
- By 1955, *Damn Yankees* became the second big hit for the songwriting team of Richard Adler and Jerry Ross, and the press began to call the era the Golden Age of Broadway.
- Monster hit *My Fair Lady* opened on Broadway and launched the careers of Julie Andrews and Rex Harrison.
- In 1957, all of Broadway's talk was devoted to *West Side Story* and *The Music Man*, which won the Tony for Best Musical.

Cotton Broker

Wilton Hayslett's family had been in the cotton business for five generations when he found himself a successful cotton broker making an annual $75,000 in 1957. He and his wife, who owned thousands of acres of farmland, were devoted to the Baptist Church and Billy Graham, who was at the height of his success.

Life at Home

- Veteran cotton broker Wilton Hayslett knew that little is predictable about the cotton business, especially the fluctuating price of cotton.
- Perhaps to compensate for the inability to control his business, he maintained consistency at home.
- Every morning he rose at 5:00, as did his farmer father and grandfather, took a walk, and returned to breakfast and the newspaper.
- His wife Bonnie typically made eggs, bacon, juice, fresh fruit, biscuits and grits, the only meal of the day she prepared.
- The family cook was in charge of the big afternoon meal and assisted with the evening meal before she left each night.
- After breakfast, Wilton dressed in a white shirt, black suit, black tie, black shoes and a hat, whether he went to work, church or a funeral.
- Wilton and Bonnie ate together at 1:00 p.m. whenever he was in town, after which he took a 20-minute nap.
- He was home by 6:00 p.m., unless he was ushering at church or helping raise money for the Boy Scouts, remembering his Eagle Scout days.
- Their only child, a 30-year-old son, was severely mentally handicapped, and was institutionalized when was 12 years old.
- Because Wilton was born and raised on a cotton farm near Gulf Port, Mississippi, going into the cotton business seemed only natural.
- Bonnie's family, also in the cotton business, owned thousands of acres of land, some of it acquired around 1815.
- Through the years, Wilton and Bonnie sold off pieces of property as the Gulf Port community grew.
- Today, the country club's golf course clubhouse stood on the exact spot where her grandfather built his first cabin 100 years ago.
- In addition to their cook, the Haysletts employed a gardener and two maids.

Wilton Hayslett was a successful cotton broker.

- One of the maids, a black woman named Etta, was raised with Bonnie on her family farm after both Etta's parents were killed in a farming accident, and worked for Bonnie ever since.
- Wilton believed that something must be done to help the Negro, seeing that his black laborers and servants had little more money or status than they did two decades ago.
- He believed that education, not integration, was the solution, although he knew it was inevitable.
- He and his wife quietly paid for three of his gardener's children to attend Morehouse College in Atlanta, and helped Etta's only daughter go through secretarial school.
- A member of the downtown Baptist Church, Wilton believed that too many young people strayed from religion to chase money and good times, and not enough people wanted to work hard anymore.
- He and his wife were proud that they gave 10 percent of their income to the church, and were delighted that the west window of the church was dedicated to Wilton's mother, who passed away a dozen years ago.
- When not worrying about the changing price of cotton, he focused on supporting his other passion, the Billy Graham crusade.
- He served as a volunteer during the Madison Square Garden event, and volunteered five times as a counselor.

Excerpted from God in the Garden, *Time*, May 27, 1957

'Hear the word of the Lord, ye rulers of New York; give ear unto the law of our God, ye people of New York.' The words were the prophet Isaiah's—about Sodom and Gomorrah— but the voice was the Southern smoothness of Billy Graham coming over the 18 loudspeakers in Manhattan's Madison Square Garden. The voice beat upon more than 18,000 people- seekers and servers of the Lord as well as the merely curious—and it etched itself upon the sliding ribbons of the tape recorders set up by radiomen. The evangelist of the mid-century set out last week on his toughest 'crusade'—to bring salvation to New York's eight million sinners.

If the heart of the crusade is Madison Square Garden, its head is a seven-room suite in Times Square where 35 permanent staff members, 30 temporary employees and more than 200 volunteer clerical workers control a hectic, complex organism. Automatic typewriters clack out letters appealing for prayer; duplicating machines roll our instructions and memorandums. On wall maps of New York, the U.S. and the world, red, blue and green pins and tape spot churches (1,510 in Greater New York) and prayer groups supporting the campaign. Staff members: 1) channel the activities of 108,415 'prayer partners' in the U.S.; 2) keep tabs on 158,817 'prayer partners' in 48 other countries; 3) ride herd on 'active' cooperating ministers, the 'partial supporting' ministers and the 'undecided' ministers; 4) process applications for blocks of seats.

• • •

Long before the crusade began, the personal counseling staff signed up 4,000 applicants in 11 centers throughout the city for a nine-week course in Scripture, how to apply Bible lessons, and how to handle people's problems. (Among the carefully drawn-up list of traits that disqualify applicants for counseling posts: inability to communicate, argumentative or surly attitude, unkempt appearance, and halitosis.) Of the 4,000 applicants, 3,800 stuck the course to the end, 2,143 qualified as counselors, and 350 were held in reserve. The counselors are evangelist Graham's shock troops.

• • •

The most critical and moving part of every evening's preaching is the 'invitation'—when Graham calls for those moved to commit their lives to Christ and come forward to the platform. The moment is carefully planned: 'When asked to bow our heads and close our eyes, do so,' say the mimeographed instructions to counselors. 'Then open your eyes and watch as unnoticeably as possible...watch for those of your own sex and age who are responding, and accompany them to the front...DO NOT BLOCK THE AISLE AT ANY TIME.' Graham's words now vary little, from evening to evening, and he delivers them hunched forward over the lectern—tensely, urgently, often a trifle hoarsely:

'I'm going to ask you to do something that I've seen people do all over world. I've seen the Congressman, the Governor, the film star. I've seen lords and ladies. I've seen professors. I'm going to ask every one of you tonight to say: "Billy, I will give myself to Christ, as Savior and Lord. I want to be born again. I want a new life in Christ. I want to be a new creation in Christ tonight. I'm willing come to the Cross in repentance." If you say that, I'm going to ask you to do a hard thing. Nothing easy. The appeal of Communism today partially is because it's a hard thing. They demand great things. Jesus demanded no less.

I'm going to ask every one of you to get up out of your seat—over here, in the balcony, everywhere, and come quietly and reverently. I don't want one person to leave the Garden, not one person. I'm not asking you to join a church tonight. I am not asking to come to some particular denomination. I am asking that you need Christ, your heart is hungry for Christ.

You may be a deacon or an elder. I don't know. You may be a Sunday school teacher. You may be a choir member. You may be an usher, but you need Christ tonight. Young man, young woman, father, mother, whoever you are, come right now. Just get up our of your seat and come now. Quickly right now. From everywhere you come, from up in the balconies all around, up here, back there. All of you that are coming, come right now now, we're going to wait. You come on now.

Cotton was important to Gulf Port's history.

- Proud to be a part of bringing salvation to New York's eight million sinners, Wilton was especially pleased to accompany a called Christian to the front when it was time for the altar call.
- He was angry that the press seemed so cynical about this great crusader's efforts to bring Christ to the world.

Life at Work: Cotton Broker

- The cotton industry was in the doldrums since 1954, and it was difficult for cotton brokers to turn a profit.
- To create more incentives for success, Weil Brothers Cotton issued company stock to its top managers, who previously shared in the profits of the company through a bonus pool.

- Weil Brothers also demanded that managers stay in constant touch with the head office to ensure a perpetual give-and-take of business intelligence and advice.
- Wilton joined the cotton industry as an accountant in the late 1920s, discovering early on that the office manager was juggling the books for his own personal benefit.
- The manager took a heavy position in low-grade cotton, but kept the sale off the company books.
- Had the weather lived up to its wet and miserable expectations, he would have made a bundle, but when the

Southern cotton brokers from an earlier time.

skies brightened and low-grade cotton became scarce, he was unable to deliver what he had contracted for.

- When impatient textile mill managers immediately began calling the home office demanding the promised cotton, Weil Brothers launched an investigation with Wilton's help.
- His honesty and cooperation catapulted his career, and he was named manager of the office the next year, not needing to spend time as a "classer" of cotton, normally a critical requirement for any cotton broker.
- He believed in volume and took calculated risks when he bought cotton if the volume was high enough to justify a quality return.
- Although casual about many issues, he believed that temperance was important, and did not trust anyone who regularly had a drink after work.
- He also thought that idleness was demoralizing, so during long summer days before the cotton harvest was in, he invented jobs for his office personnel so they would not play checkers.

Brokers on Wall Street.

Challenge to Cotton, *Time*, June 10, 1957

How much does the cotton support program cost taxpayers? Last week Lamar Fleming, Jr., board chairman of Anderson, Clayton and Co., the world's largest private cotton dealer, dug into Government figures and came up with the staggering total of $1.156 billion as the cost for this year. In a speech to the American Cotton Congress in Dallas, Fleming, a crusader for sound farm policies, pointed out that this equals more than $1,000 for each of the 850,000 farms on which cotton is grown. Fleming's figures are underlined in a press conference in Washington where Agriculture Secretary Ezra Taft Benson took pride in the fact that his department this fiscal year is selling 7.5 million bales of surplus cotton abroad v. total U.S. cotton exports last year of 2.2 million bales. But Benson conceded that the Government will lose $530 million by selling cotton for an average $115 a bale v. the Government cost of $186.

- Simply to keep his staff busy, he occasionally sent them to visit farmers.
- No one questioned his orders or his leadership, since his successful track record spoke for itself.
- In one hour, he typically put in a straddle order, bemoaned the imminent collapse of western civilization, gave a buy order to his stockbroker in New York, solicited donations for the Gulf Port United Way, made arrangements to testify in a court case and read a Bible reflection from a monthly publication sent to him by his church.
- Wilton also spent considerable time in the sample room where cotton samples, cut from bales in warehouses, were examined for color, trash content, staple (length) and character of fiber—the criteria that determined the cotton's eventual use and relative worth.
- Cotton that was examined piled up ankle-deep on the floor until it was swept away at the end of the day for resale as cotton waste

Machines have improved profitability of the cotton crop.

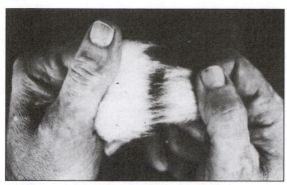
Learning to "class" cotton is an art.

and during the peak season, from September to March, visitors remarked that they felt like they were walking on clouds.

- The company was created by brothers Isidor and Herman Weil, Jewish immigrants from Germany who settled in Opelika, Mississippi.
- At that time the United States not only grew more cotton than any nation on earth, but also spun most of it.
- Although important, length was not the only consideration when buying cotton, which came in many variations of color, brightness, purity, resilience, tensile strength—all qualities that depended on the seed, vagaries of the weather, type of soil, and how the cotton was cultivated, harvested and ginned.
- Because the economics of the cotton business were firmly based on supply and demand, brokers like Wilton make money by estimating the demand for the various grades of cotton in relation to their probable availability—educated guesswork that determined what price to pay, based on what he could sell it for.
- The price of cotton often varied greatly from day to day, so Wilton reduced his risk by hedging his transactions on the futures exchange.
- Typically, he bought 10,000 bales of spot cotton if he thought he could sell 100 contracts (of 100 bales each) on the futures market the same day at a profit.

Life in the Community: Gulf Port, Mississippi

- This city of 40,000 on the Mississippi Sound and the Gulf of Mexico tied its fortune to transportation and shipping, especially of cotton.
- Laid out in 1887 as the terminus for the Gulf and Ship Island Railroad, Gulf Port became the center for timber distribution.
- By the 1920s, the community was focusing on cotton—building warehouses, compresses and mills—eventually becoming a major seaport with deep-water access to the Gulf, capable of bringing in lumber, bananas, cotton and seafood.
- It also served as a major port for sport fishermen seeking speckled trout, pompano, tarpon, redfish and shrimp.
- Like many men who grew up in Gulf Port, Wilton hunted extensively as a child, waiting especially for the months when migratory waterfowl such as teal, wood ducks, mallards and canvasbacks were in season.

Textile mills dominate the labor force of the South.

Mother and Phonics Advocate

Martha Gardner decided that her third grade son, Scott, would be a better reader if his teacher used the phonics—instead of the whole language—approach. She read and reread "Why Johnny Can't Read," which was a best seller in 1958, and made her case to Scott's teacher.

Life at Home

- Everyone Martha Gardner met commented—with only a little prompting—on what a bright boy her third grader, Scott, was.
- In school, however, his grades didn't reflect his brightness and Martha discovered that the reason was phonics.
- Martha suspected that Scott's problems were the school's fault, and Rudolf Flesch's best-selling book, *Why Johnny Can't Read* was the proof.
- She believed that America was in crisis due to the threat of communism and nuclear war, and that if America's schools properly taught children to read, the country would be a safer place.
- Martha grew up in rural Georgia near Macon, and married a military officer she met at the USO club at Warner Robins Air Force Base.
- He was tall, soft spoken and almost exotic with his Yankee background and mysterious way of smiling rather than talking.
- Not that anyone had a real opportunity to say anything when Martha was around, who spoke in gusts of 60 miles per hour with sustained winds of 50 mph.
- Scott was their second child and into everything—excess energy was his middle name.
- His older sister, Sally, mostly ignored her little brother, except when she wanted something, knowing that Scott could ask for anything, and get it.
- Sally worked hard, paid attention to the teacher and did her homework, while Scott only took his brain to school a few days a week and rarely did his homework.
- Now everyone was in a lather over his grades when it was entirely his own fault, Sally was convinced.
- Sally knew that Scott was capable of learning, and memorizing, anything he wanted, no matter how complex, if he slowed down long enough to pay attention.

Martha Gardner took her son's reading troubles into her own hands.

Sally worked hard in school, while brother Scott had trouble paying attention.

- Dating back to the colonial period, the alphabet was the focal point of reading instruction.
- Noah Webster's *Blue Backed Speller*, the first true reading textbook, sold 24 million copies, second only to the Bible, and served as the foundation for phonics.
- This was followed by the work of Favell Lee Mortimer, who employed phonics in the early flashcard set, *Reading Disentangled* in 1834, and *Reading Without Tears* in 1857.
- Then, in the middle of the nineteenth century, innovator Horace Mann criticized the repetitive drills in reading education and advocated that phonics not be taught at all, igniting the reading wars.
- John Dewey, the father of progressive education, noted the "drudgery" of the phonics method.
- What evolved was the whole-language "look-say" approach ensconced in the Dick and Jane readers popular in the mid-twentieth century, which dominated the field of early reading education.
- In 1955, Rudolf Flesch re-awakened the debate over phonics instruction and the prevailing preference for whole language teaching with his book *Why Johnny Can't Read*. "Reading," he wrote, "means getting meaning from certain combinations of letters. Teach the child what each letter stands for and he can read."
- The "whole language" approach to reading used in schools across America was predicated on the principle that children could learn to read given proper motivation, access to good literature, focus on meaning, and instruction to help them use meaning clues to determine the pronunciation of unknown words.
- The whole language method emphasized using words in context and focusing only a little on the sounds.
- All Martha knew was that she had been reading to her son since he was three, and couldn't understand why he had so much trouble reading new material, why he wasn't he able to read like his father did.

Life at Work: Phonics Advocate

- As the wife of an Air Force pilot, Martha Gardner endured long periods during which her husband was away when she raised the two children alone.
- Their current assignment was Homestead Air Force Base in Homestead, Florida, which housed a fleet of B-52 bombers under the control of the Strategic Air Command.
- After she read, *Why Johnny Can't Read*, she was eager to discuss her conclusions with her husband, and was enormously frustrated that he was overseas on assignment.
- So she read parts of the book a second time, especially the letter to parents that opened the book, and Martha decided she must talk to Scott's teacher and convince her that he could be her best student if only she changed her method.

- Mrs. Mildred Greene had been teaching for 17 years to both town children and military kids who flowed through the city for a year or two, never to return.
- She had been trained in both whole language and phonics, and preferred phonics, but the school district endorsed the whole language, look-say methodology.
- Mrs. Greene knew from experience that education theories swing in and out of favor on a regular basis, and that phonics would have its day again.
- She blended phonics and whole language-based reading in her class, but officially she followed the curriculum laid out by the district.
- She even owned a vintage collection of early McGuffey Readers, some of the first textbooks developed to teach reading.
- The McGuffey Readers included stories that emphasized the sounds of letters in words and contained stories that emphasized values like the rich helping the poor and being kind to animals.
- At the beginning of the twentieth century, the Progressive Education Movement pushed for instruction that focused more on the interests of students, using a more scientific approach to learning.

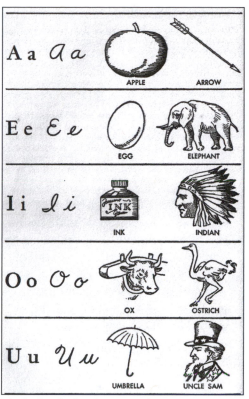

Martha thought that phonics was the answer.

- In the 1950s, the Dick and Jane Readers published by Scott Foresman used a "whole word" approach to teaching reading, where words were repeated on each page enough times that students could remember them.
- Phonics advocates charged that the whole word approach fell apart when students began reading children's stories that did not have carefully controlled vocabularies.
- Phonics, they said, gave the reader the necessary tools to sound out words based on how they were spelled, and allowed students—especially those with large vocabularies—to read a wide variety of children's literature.
- The history of reading instruction resembled a pendulum swinging between the two approaches.
- When Flesch's book came out in 1955, it was serialized in newspapers across the country, igniting significant debate.
- As soon as Martha came through the door, Mrs. Greene knew it was going to be a contentious meeting; Scott was a delightful young man when he settled down and paid attention—which wasn't often.
- Martha began politely enough, by first thanking Mrs. Greene for her skills and patience with Scott, then she pulled out a copy of *Why Johnny Can't Read.*
- According to Flesch's book, when confronted with an unknown word, the learner became confused, and the only logical conclusion was a revival of the phonics method, the teaching of reading by teaching learners to sound out words.
- Mrs. Greene was patient and worked hard to wait Martha out.
- The phonics model drew heavily from behaviorist learning theory associated with the work of the Harvard psychologist B.F. Skinner, while the whole language emphasis drew from constructivist learning theory and the work of the Russian psychologist Lev Vygotsky.
- Behaviorist learning theory was based on extrinsic rewards like money, grades, and gold stars rather than intrinsic rewards like feeling good about successfully accomplishing a difficult task.

- Constructivist learning theory was based on the idea that children learn by connecting new knowledge to previously learned knowledge.
- If children cannot connect new knowledge to old knowledge in a meaningful way, they may with difficulty memorize it (rote learning), but they will not have a real understanding of what they are learning.
- Mrs. Greene began quietly, "Learning to read is not a natural process," only to be interrupted by, "Scott started reading when he was three."
- Mrs. Greene began again, "Young children can memorize words rapidly in a way that gives the illusion of reading."
- Like many teachers, her approach was a systemic decoding of words blended with a literature-rich environment, a key aspect of the whole language approach.
- Martha listened carefully before asking again, "Why isn't Scott your best student? If only he could sound out the words, he would improve overnight. This book proves it."
- Mrs. Greene smiled, "Scott will learn to read the day he decides to settle down and pay attention. Not before. Phonics is not the problem, he is."
- Martha was unprepared for such a raw rendition of the problem and began to weep.
- Scott's older sister was an enthusiastic reader, his father was a dedicated and consistent reader, so why wasn't her son following that path?
- Mrs. Greene listened patiently and then suggested that Martha use a phonics book to help Scott, and she would reinforce those lessons in the classroom.
- "In my experience," Mrs. Greene said, "you can't force feed children to learn; all you can do is create the right environment and opportunity."

Life in the Community: Homestead, Florida

- Homestead, Florida, located 35 miles south of Miami, was nestled between Biscayne National Park to the east and Everglades National Park to the west.
- It was incorporated in 1913 as the second-oldest city in Miami-Dade County, after the city of Miami, and its name originates from when the Florida East Coast Railway extension to Key West was being built.
- On September 15, 1945, three years to the day after the base's founding, a massive hurricane roared ashore, sending winds of up to 145 mph tearing through the Air Field's buildings.
- Enlisted housing facilities, the nurses' dormitory and the Base Exchange were all destroyed.
- The roof was ripped from what would later become building 741, the "Big Hangar."
- The base laundry and fire station were both declared total losses, and the few remaining aircraft were tossed about like leaves.

Martha's husband was in the Air Force.

- Following an evaluation of the damage, officials announced on October 25, 1945, that Homestead AAF would be shut down, with a target date for complete closure of December 1, 1945.
- When the Air Force was created as a separate service on September 18, 1947, the old Homestead Army Air Field lay in ruins.
- In June of 1948, when the Soviets began the total land blockade of Berlin, the Air Force responded with an unprecedented airlift effort known as Operation Vittles.

- Twenty-four hours a day, seven days a week, for 16 months, Air Force C-54 "Sky Masters," many of them piloted by Homestead graduates, flew in and out of Berlin, keeping one of the world's great cities alive.
- In the early 1950s, as the Korean conflict was winding down, defense officials once again looked toward Homestead with an eye to making the site an integral part of the U.S. continental defense.
- In mid-1954, an advance party arrived at the old base to begin the cleanup effort, and on February 8, 1955, the installation was reactivated as Homestead Air Force Base.
- The base quickly became home to the 823rd Air Division, and by the end of the decade, Homestead housed more than 6,000 permanently assigned members, twice the size of its busiest World War II days, and a fleet of B-47 "Stratojet" bombers.

Two Years Wasted, Rudolph Flesch, *Why Johnny Can't Read*, 1955

If you are a mother of a child in the second or third grade who can't read and spell, you'll sooner or later go to the school and complain that your child isn't taught the letters and sounds. You will then be told, one way or the other, that phonics is utterly out of date; just wait, your boy or girl will suddenly catch on.

But if your child is in first grade, the answer you'll get will be considerably shorter, strongly resembling a brush-off. The teacher will tell you, with a rather indulgent smile: "He isn't ready, you know."

When you get to the subject of "readiness," you approach the holy of holies, the inner sanctum of the whole "science" of reading. In each of the fat tomes on how to teach reading, pages and pages are filled with profound discussions of what makes a child ready for reading, when does he get ready, how to tell whether he is or not, how to speed him up or slow him down, what to do with him before he gets ready, how to instill readiness, how to make it grow, how to use it, treat it, protect it, diagnose it, improve it, ripen it, and direct it. Deep mystery covers this whole recondite subject, and work has been going on for decades to explore its recesses.

One of the "authorities," in fact, went so far as to devote a whole book to the subject of "reading readiness." I went through that whole book in search of the definition of "readiness," being sincerely curious to know what was meant by the word. But there was no definition that could be found. So, since the experts didn't seem to help us, I'll offer my own definition. "Reading readiness" means the readiness of the teacher to let the child start reading.

If ever there was an example of reasoning in a vicious cycle, this is it. You take a six-year old child and start to teach him something. The child, as often happens, doesn't take to it at once. If you use a common-sense approach, you try again and again, exert a little patience, and after some time the child begins to learn. But if you are a twentieth-century American educator, equipped with the theory of "readiness," you drop the whole matter instantly and wait until the child, on his own, asks to be taught. Let's wait until he's seven, until he's eight, until he's nine. We've all the time in the world; it would be a crime to teach a child who wasn't "ready."

Hungarian Student Refugee

Jozef Kertesz was studying forestry in Hungary when he fled his country during the Hungarian Uprising. From Austria to Germany to New York, Jozef eventually made his way to distant relatives in the heavily Hungarian community in Cleveland, Ohio. In 1958, he worked in a sawmill to buy his parent's passage to America, putting his education on hold.

Life at Home

- In late October 1956, two separate crises captured the attention of the world: the Battle for the Suez Canal and the spontaneous Hungarian Uprising.
- Jozsef Kertész was transformed by the latter event, during which a group of engineering students in the Hungarian capital of Budapest demonstrated their support for the oppressed people of neighboring Poland.
- Word quickly spread throughout the city and people poured out of their shops, factories and homes to join the demonstration, which turned into an anti-government, anti-Soviet revolt.
- Jozsef felt liberated by the protest, like a dream after a long coma.
- Thousands of protesters toppled a huge statue of former Soviet leader Joseph Stalin, as Hungarian flags were displayed with holes replacing the hammer and sickle insignia.
- Jozsef told his friends they were witnessing a historic moment in Hungarian history.
- The euphoria was short-lived, however, for within weeks the Soviet army retook the city and initiated an unapologetic open season on demonstrators.
- Hundreds of buildings were damaged or destroyed, more than 2,500 Hungarians were killed, and thousands were arrested or disappeared.
- As the Soviets moved to suppress the revolt, thousands fled, some to Austria, some to Yugoslavia, benefiting from the worldwide media attention the Hungarian Uprising was attracting.
- Many in the West believed the Hungarians had risen up in response to encouragement from messages delivered by Radio Free Europe, the BBC and the Voice of America, and felt an obligation to come to the aid of the avalanche of Hungarian refugees.
- Jozsef and a friend headed to the Austrian border by oxcart, dodging police checkpoints and buying directions from a smuggler along the way.

Jozsef Kertesz fled Soviet oppression in Hungary.

- Jozsef was petrified, knowing that capture meant certain death or imprisonment and escape meant leaving behind everything he had known.
- He crossed the Austrian border with two layers of clothing, his school briefcase and approximately $20, feeling safe only when he heard the villagers speak German.
- Like many Hungarian refugees, he was transported to a center to be registered, then transferred to a refugee camp, built from the barracks of an abandoned military base.
- There he realized how closely the world was watching the events unfold and began to comprehend the size of the rescue effort.
- A train from Switzerland transported 400 refugees at a time to various cities, and buses from Sweden and trains from Belgium and the Netherlands carried Hungarians to those countries.
- By December 31, a phenomenal 91,900 people had been transported out of Austria into nearly a dozen countries.
- In all, a total of 180,000 refugees were distributed by trains, ships, planes and buses to 37 different countries.
- Canada accepted 38,000 Hungarians with minimal screening, and the U.S. passed a law that allowed it to take people on a temporary basis, bypassing the formal, lengthy process.
- Jozsef was taken by train to Germany, then sent to the United States sponsored by the International Rescue Committee, one of several major American charities working on resettlement.
- Only after he boarded an old troop carrier and sailed past the famous White Cliffs of Dover did the momentousness of his actions hit him—Hungary was his past and America was his future.
- After a rough journey on the Atlantic, he arrived in New York in January 1957 to a hero's welcome, as he and his fellow refugees symbolized freedom against the Communists.

Life at Work: Hungarian Refugee

- When Jozsef Kertész arrived in New York, Hungarian translators and immigration officials helped him establish his refugee status.
- Amid a dizzying welcome, news photographers snapped his picture, while newfound friends described a glowing future in America.
- When asked his goals, he replied that he wanted to complete his education in forestry and find his parents, who were still in Hungary.
- He was given a place to live at Camp Kilmer in New Jersey, in a converted U.S. Army base where newcomers were sponsored by different resettlement agencies representing a variety of religious, political, ethnic, and social groups.
- These sponsors helped coordinate the huge outpouring of support from American communities, including academia.
- Numerous universities contacted the Institute of International Education in the World University Service, tasked with coordinating scholarship offers, collect and distribute donations, and screen potential students.

At first, Jozsef lived in a converted Army camp in New Jersey.

- Of the 28,000 refugees admitted to the U.S. in the six months following Soviet incursion, approximately 1,200 were university students, most were males 19 to 21 years old, with a few, like Jozsef, graduate students in their late twenties or early thirties.

- Despite their anxiousness to continue their education, most did not possess sufficient English-language skills for university-level study, and college administrators wanted the new refugees to become more acclimated to U.S. academic life before entering school.
- Jozsef, along with 325 other Hungarian students, began his education in America at Bard College, with a nine-week course in English.
- Even though he could scarcely stop chatting in Hungarian, he learned enough English to manage.
- When his coursework was completed, he was give a train ticket to Cleveland, Ohio, where distant relatives were waiting, having secured for him both an apartment and a job.
- Cleveland was a center of Hungarian culture and prosperity in America, and many there viewed the Hungarian Uprising with enormous excitement and as an opportunity to give back to their homeland.
- Along the way to Ohio, he saw forests running to the horizon, manicured farms, busy cities and more cars than he could have imagined.
- In the rural sections of Hungary, oxcarts were still much in evidence, telephones rare and television unknown.

Speaking English was a requirement of American universities.

- Once he settled in Cleveland, he became memorized by television, singing TV theme songs in English and laughing at jokes he did not understand.
- His host family was distantly related to him on his mother's side and had been in America for two generations.
- They loved talking about Hungary and the ways of the old country, but Jozsef wanted only to talk about the future.

Jozsef moved in with distant relatives in Cleveland.

- His first job was in a prosperous sawmill and he enjoyed the feel of sawdust and sweat, along with hard work.
- When school began in the fall, he was offered a scholarship to cover tuition and a job at the university to cover expenses.
- He turned down these offers, deciding that he needed to earn the money to buy his parents' way into the United States.
- Completing his degree and managing the woodlands of America would have to wait.

Life in the Community: Cleveland, Ohio

- The Hungarian community of Cleveland, Ohio viewed the Hungarian Uprising as an opportunity to pull down the Iron Curtain built by the Soviets following WWII.
- When the Uprising collapsed in the face of Soviet aggression, Cleveland began organizing its support and sent a planeload of clothing, valued

Jozsef's first job was in a saw mill, where he worked hard and was paid well.

at $100,000, to the Austrian refugee camps filled with frightened Hungarians, and then they opened their homes.

- Following the Hungarian Uprising, about 3,000 students journeyed to Cleveland to start a new life.
- For more than 50 years, Cleveland had been home to a Hungarian community large enough to support two Hungarian newspapers: *Magyar Katolikus Vasarnapia* (The Catholic Hungarian's Sunday)and *Szabadsaq* (Liberty).
- Most Hungarians who moved to Ohio in the 1800s settled along Lake Erie, especially in Cleveland, where they found jobs in the factories or as day laborers and clustered in Hungarian communities.
- By the late 1800s, Cleveland claimed six distinct Hungarian communities spread across the city, with businesses that supplied fellow migrants with traditional Hungarian products.
- By 1900, the Hungarian communities had established their own Catholic and Protestant churches and formed the Hungarian Self-Culture Society, which allowed Hungarians to gather together and read newspapers in their home language and practice traditional beliefs.
- Some native-born residents believed that foreigners corrupted the morals of United States citizens and stole jobs from Americans, and they discussed laws that would limit or ban the cultural practices of recently arrived immigrants.

Hungarian Immigration Timeline

1848: Immigration to the U.S. was sparked by the Hungarian Revolution of 1848-1849.

1873: Pest, Buda and Obuda were unified: Budapest became a European metropolis.

1880: Hungarian immigration accelerated; between 1880 and 1898 about 200,000 Hungarians traveled to America.

1918: Germany and its allies, including Austro-Hungarian monarchy, surrendered in WWI.

1920: The Trianon Treaty reduced Hungary's land area by two-thirds.

During the previous 100 years, over 3.7 million people emigrated from the Austrian-Hungarian Empire to the United States; only Germany, Ireland and Italy recorded higher figures.

1924: New laws in Hungary limited the number of Jewish students allowed to pursue higher education in Hungary to 6 percent, sparking emigration.

1933: Hungary formed an alliance with Germany; both regimes shared an interest in revising the Trianon Peace Treaty.

1938-1940: Germany concluded treaties in Munich and Vienna, under which Southern Slovakia and Northern Transylvania were returned to Hungary.

1944: The Nazis occupied their ally Hungary; Hungarian soldiers suffered extensive losses on the Soviet front.

1945: The Soviet Army first liberated, then occupied, Hungary.

1947: The last, relatively free election was followed by Communist control; major emigration to America ensued.

1956: The Hungarian Uprising occurred; several hundred thousand Hungarians emigrated to 37 countries.

The Firm Start of a New Life, *Life,* January 7, 1957

With nothing in the world but their lives, their clothes and each other, the Csillags came to the U.S. in the first planeload of Hungarian refugees. Bedraggled, bewildered and more than a little afraid, they shivered at the chilling New Jersey airport. Behind them, as with those in the plane landings that followed, lay the harrowing days of their escapes to the Austrian border by truck and motorbike, then the soup kitchens, questions, refugee camps and papers. Ahead lay hope, a chance to make a place in the free world and to be what Vice President Nixon called "the kind of people who make good Americans."

For the Pal Csillag family, help came quickly and beyond believing. In Indianapolis a prosperous uncle, Joseph Singer, who had left Hungary as a boy 48 years before, offered them a new start. A brother-in-law, Alex Star (the English word for Csillag) promised to help look out for them. Two days later, dazzled and still incredulous, the Csillags found themselves rolling west aboard a fast train.

But they could not envision the new life that awaited them. They were used to a little food and less fuel. In their hometown of Csorna (population 8,957), they had known no one with

flush toilets or refrigerators. Of the family only Pal, 35, had seen a telephone and that from a distance. They could only wonder if the tales they had heard would come true....

Settled at last in a house, among friends, the Csillags immediately got down to the most vital business: a job for Pal and school for the girls. Both turned out to be remarkably easy. With Mrs. Star, Rose went down to see Mr. Stiebaugh, principal of P.S. 76. He told them the girls were welcome. "They're not the first to come here, strangers to the country and to English, and soon will be at home," he said.

Bill Hinkel, district manager of Anheuser-Busch, which sells baker's yeast as well as beer, read in the papers that Pal had been a baker. "I know a lot of bakers," he said. He called one. "These refugee people need help. How about giving him a job?" Pal went down to the Roselyn Bakeries and was soon at work. "Down there," Pal said, "you can drink all the coffee you want. They give it to you. It's real coffee. You can eat all the food you want free. And I am paid more than $75 a week. In Csorna I earned about $77 a month and it cost $34 for a pair of shoes." And after a week of work, Pal got another pleasant surprise. His sister and brother-in-law from Hungary, the Klopfers, were coming from the Camp Kilmer refugee center. He met them and proudly took them for a ride on the first escalator the Klopfers had ever seen.

President Urges Wide Law Change to Aid Immigrants, by Anthony Lewis, *The New York Times*, February 9, 1956

President Eisenhower today called for sweeping changes in the immigration laws.

In a special message to Congress he proposed a drastic revision of the quota system that has regulated immigration law the last 30 years. The effect would be to double the number of quota immigrants admitted in an average year and to increase sharply the proportion from Italy, Greece and other countries of southern and eastern Europe.

A private calculation showed that countries in these areas would be able to send a combined total of up to 125,000 immigrants a year to the United States under the President's proposal. They had been limited to 24,502 by the present quota.

General Eisenhower also asked Congress to do the following:

Permit a waiver of the requirement that aliens coming for temporary visits be finger-printed before they get United States visas.

Give the Attorney General discretion to grant relief in the thousands of alien hardship cases now handled by Congress each year in private bills.

Make several administrative changes in the law to eliminate "unnecessary restrictions upon travel" and "hardships."

The message fulfills promises made by President Eisenhower in the 1952 campaign to amend the McCarran-Walter Immigration Act, which was adopted that year. The act was sponsored by the late Senator Pat McCarran, Democrat of Nevada, and Representative Francis D. Walter, Democrat of Pennsylvania. It was passed over President Truman's veto.

Although General Eisenhower had criticized the act occasionally since 1952, these were his first specific proposals for amending it. They went further than critics of the act had expected.

"The recommendations are better and more comprehensive than I expected," Senator Herbert H. Lehman, Democrat of New York and a leading proponent of more liberal immigration laws, said. "He has come a considerable way down the road I and others have been pointing out the last four years."

A statement issued for Mr. Walters, who is a power in Congress on immigration affairs, criticized the president's message. Mr. Walter had read parts of the message before leaving on a Far Eastern tour.

"The President's proposals cast a threatening shadow over the basic immigration policies established by the McCarran-Walter Act," Mr. Walters said. "If, indeed, there are reasons for amending the immigration laws, they do not appear in the president's proposal, nor in the parade of politically inspired measures which had preceded them."

The far-reaching changes proposed in the quota evoked the most surprise. The present system, virtually unchanged since 1924, allots 154,657 quota numbers annually for would-be immigrants from outside the Western Hemisphere. There are no quota restrictions on immigration from countries in this hemisphere.

The quota total is divided according to the percentages of foreign-born persons in the United States under the 1920 census. The effect is to give most of the quota numbers, 125,165, to northern and western Europe and countries where there is little desire to emigrate.

In recent years such countries as Britain and Ireland have used only fractions of their quotas, while there have been long waiting lists for quota numbers in the poor, overpopulated lands of southern Europe. In 1954, the most recent year for which figures are available, only 94,000 quota immigrants arrived. About 60,000 quota numbers went unused.

President Eisenhower said the whole concept of national origins as the method of admitting aliens "needs to be re-examined" by Congress. He proposed broad "interim measures" during the study.

First, he suggested that the quota total be raised to 220,000 a year. He said "economic growth over the next 30 years" justified the increase. He proposed that the additional 65,000 numbers be distributed according to actual sources of immigration since 1924, thus giving more weight to southern Europe.

Second, he asked that unused quota numbers be pooled and made available to aliens having special skills or relatives in the United States. Under the first suggestion the southern European quota would rise to 45,000 and northern Europe's to 157,000. But chances are that the northern countries would use little more than their present average of about 70,000. This would leave as many as 80,000 unused numbers to be pooled each year and made available to southern Europe, raising the total immigration from that area to 125,000 a year.

The president asked that 5,000 quota numbers be set aside for admission of aliens "with special skills and cultural or technical qualifications," regardless of their national origin.

He urged the end of quota "mortgages" under the Displaced Persons Act of 1948.

This provision charged off immigrant refugees against future quotas. Fifty percent of the Greek quota had just been eliminated until the year 2017.

On the fingerprinting requirement, which has brought frequent protests from abroad, the president said experience had shown that it "does not significantly contribute to our national safety and security." He suggested the Attorney General and the Secretary of State be permitted to waive the regulation on a reciprocal basis with other countries.

Other recommended amendments would eliminate visa requirements for foreign travelers passing to the United States en route somewhere else; end immigration inspection of aliens coming from Hawaii or Alaska; and liberalize restrictions on obtaining citizenship by marriage or service in the Armed Forces.

You could use a haircut, young man," she said. "You're getting to look like one of these crazy Hungarians or something....

—J.D. Salinger, Franny and Zooey, 1955

> Solution of the problem of refugees from communism and overpopulation has become a permanent part of the foreign-policy program of the Democratic Party. We pledge continued cooperation with other free nations to solve it. We pledge continued aid to refugees from communism and the enactment of President Truman's proposals for legislation in this field. In this way we can give hope and courage to the victims of Soviet brutality and can carry on a humanitarian tradition of the Displaced Persons Act.
>
> —*The immigration plank of the 1952 Democratic Party's platform*

Grape Juice Company Sales Manager

Gordon Young was the national sales manager for Welch's Grape Juice in 1958. He made a significant contribution to the company's success, improving distribution, brand recognition and overall sales. His annual salary was $44,500, and he and his family lived a comfortable life in New York's grape growing region near Lake Erie.

Life at Home

- The Youngs lived in the former home of Paul Welch, one of the sons of the founder of Welch's Grape Juice, in Westfield, New York.
- They put considerable effort converting the yard into an elaborate English garden, giving townspeople, already suspicious of New Yorkers, more reason to be standoffish.
- A private man by nature, Gordon did not enjoy socializing, especially because he spent so much time on the road, and was cautious about forming close relations at work.
- His three children all graduated from good Eastern colleges and were married with children.
- When Gordon was away on business, Donna sometimes visited the grandchildren, most of whom lived in Manhattan where they were raised.
- On a recent trip, she, her daughter, and granddaughter all watched *Old Yeller* and cried together at the end.
- In Westfield, Donna attended a Tupperware party at a friend's house, advertised as the "answer to the Housewife's demand for efficiency-economy...the woman's demand for beauty."
- A dapper dresser, Gordon was proud of his trim figure, high position, and knowledge, taking care to be cordial to all.
- Rarely did he show emotion at work or at home, and believed that a temper was the sign of low-class people unable to control themselves.
- He loved his big, black cigars, which he smoked with tremendous flair, and was especially proud of the 1957 Corvette that he bought—in cash— as his reward for a great year.

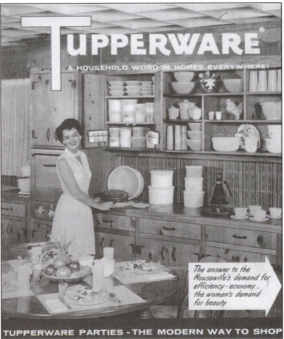

Gordon's wife hosted Tupperware parties.

Life at Work: National Sales Manager

- Gordon spent much of his time on the road overseeing brokers and promoting Welch's products, and was known for getting the job done without anyone's advice.

A 1957 Corvette was Gordon's present to himself.

- Welch's had more than 70 percent of the national grape juice and frozen grape juice concentrate market.
- Net sales reached $40 million, $4 million more than last year and gross profits topped $10.8 million, up $2 million over the previous year.
- Most of the competition came from private label and regional brands that lacked the history or sales expertise of Welch's.
- Welch's also sold grape spreads, cranberry cocktail, and tomato juice, placing them in direct competition with Smucker's, Kraft, Ocean Spray, and Libby's.
- Welch's was acquired through a planned buyout program, which shifted control from Jack Kaplan, who bought the company in 1945, to a cooperative of grape growers who supplied the Concord grapes critical to the quality of the product.
- The sale was engineered through an ingenious plan: Welch's Company would accept the growers' Concord grapes, process the fruit, manufacture and sell the products, and give the farmers the full net proceeds that would accrue for five years—which allowed them to buy the company without paying any cash from their own pockets.
- The five-year plan helped Welch's by guaranteeing a flow of quality grapes sufficient to the meet the demands of a growing company and demonstrate the mutual profitability of associating with Welch's.
- The National Grape Cooperative Association took control of Welch's in 1956, and Gordon's duties changed little since.
- Changes in the food industry forced him to pay more attention to marketing, demographic changes, and other modern sales approaches, though he was reluctant to rely on "marketing gimmicks."

Jack Kaplan bought Welch's in 1945.

- He kept Welch's product line limited and simple to make sales and distribution easy.
- Gordon focused on selling quality products at a quality price, and he felt that frequent sales promotions would erode the profitability of Welch's Grape Juice.
- He was under considerable pressure to promote additional grape-related products, such as Welch's "Fruit-of-the-Vine," a preserve of whole Concord grapes that gained rapid acceptance.
- One of his decisions was to move his advertising dollars from the popular *Howdy-Doody* television show to *Walt Disney's Mickey Mouse Club*.

The shores of Lake Erie grew great grapes.

- He also agreed to establish a grape juice concession in the Disneyland Amusement Center at Anaheim, California.
- Under his direction, Welch's spent a smaller average percentage of its budget for research and development than did other food companies.
- Competitors were amazed that he created the image of Welch's being a national brand without spending vast amounts of money on advertising.

- Instead of marketing with big advertising, Gordon moved in and out of different mediums, keeping people convinced that Welch's was a consistently advertised brand.
- He worked for Standard Brands, a major food company, for 25 years before joining the Welch's family in 1949.
- His first job with Welch's was as vice president in charge of sales and advertising, and his first assignment was to take a month and travel the United States, making a study of Welch's sales techniques.
- In 1953, he was named an executive president in the company, and reported only to the president, Jack Kaplan.
- He was disappointed that he was not named President of the company when the cooperative was created.
- When making a decision, Gordon deliberately and cautiously gathered information and rendered an opinion, and always assumed the final decision was his.
- The growers, who now owned the company, respected his cautious process, believing that sales were in good hands.
- Despite his strengths as a decision maker, he found it difficult to fire employees and often relegated the duty to others.
- At Welch's, he created a strong sales team who believed they were responsible for the product's success.
- Sales and production often blamed each other when a promotion was so successful that the company ran out of product.

"The lips that touch Welch's are all that touch mine"

Life in the Community: Westfield, New York

- The small farming community of Westfield was located on the western edge of New York state near Lake Erie.
- Westfield's largely white, homogeneous population of Methodists was known for its clannish, suspicious, hardworking ways, and change was not always welcome in this community dominated by grape growers and the Welch's Grape Juice Company.
- At the turn of the century, viticulture, or the growing of grapes, was limited to 12 states, including California, New York, Ohio, and Pennsylvania.
- In New York, grape growing was concentrated in four districts: Chautauqua, the Finger Lakes, the Hudson, and Niagara.

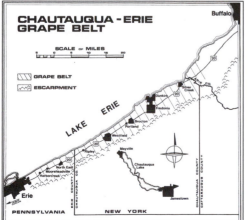

- Nationwide, good grape soils were numerous, though the perfect grape climate was rare, but the Chautauqua-Erie area, where Westfield was located, was nearly perfect.
- In the spring, the waters of Lake Erie were cool, which held back blooming until the threat of winter frost has passed, while in the fall, the warm waters of the lake extended the growing season.
- In 1898, the *Westfield Republican* advertised the community as being the "largest grape producing town in the grape belt."
- Only the sprawling state of California grew more grapes than did New York.

Welch's Grape Juice

- Welch's Grape Juice founder Dr. Charles E. Welch was driven by his disappointment at not joining the missionary movement to Africa, turning his energy into creating a grape juice devoid of alcohol.
- His grape juice company satisfied his need to serve his Methodist temperance devotion while creating a profitable business that allowed him to make large donations to Methodist-oriented causes.

Charles E. Welch was an inventor and master promoter.

- Dr. Welch established his company in Westfield, New York, in 1897 and it became one of the nation's first national brands with nationwide distribution outlets before the First World War.
- A want ad in 1911 reflected his beliefs: "Office Help, Young Man. No Tobacco. Methodist preferred, with business acumen, experience in dictating letters or similar work, with or without stenography; may find it of interest to write Dr. C.E. Welch, Westfield, New York."
- Dr. Welch's success was built on high-grade fruit for processing grape juice, a national network of selling through brokers, involvement in the international market, and a strong advertising program.
- The workday started at seven in the morning and ended at six in the evening but, even when the factory was overloaded with ripe, perishable grapes during the pressing season, the company never operated on Sunday.
- To court the grape farmers, Dr. Welch sponsored Grower's Dinners, gave tours of the processing plant, and invented uniform "Welch's crates" that were stackable, portable, and reusable for delivering grapes.
- Area farmers were loyal and Welch had a reputation for paying well for quality.
- A master promoter, Welch invented many ways to introduce Welch's Grape Juice to the public, including promoting temperance through drinking Dr. Welch's Unfermented Wine.
- During the Pan-American Exposition in 1901, cards were distributed reading, "good for a glass of Grape Juice" and he offered $10.00 in gold to anyone who could produce 1,366 words from the phrase "Welch's Grape Juice."
- Welch promoted his product to churches with an offer of free Welch's Unfermented Wine along with an essay written by his father entitled, "What Wine Shall We Use at the Lord's Supper" which offered nine objections to using intoxicating wine in church.
- When teetotaler Secretary of State William Jennings Bryan refused to serve wine during state dinners, the decision, which received generous press, came to be called Bryan's "grape juice diplomacy."
- Welch and his product received further publicity when Secretary of the Navy Josephus Daniels issued a "No Alcohol aboard Naval Vessels" order, and parodies were published reading, "Josephus Daniels is a goose/If he thinks he can induce/us to drink his damn grape juice."
- Dr. Welch's campaign to substitute grape juice for alcohol coincided with the popular groundswell for prohibition that culminated in the passage of the Eighteenth Amendment.

- The advertising budgets for Welch's Grape Juice Company averaged $575,000 a year from 1912 to 1926 and Charles E. Welch promoted his produce at state fairs, county fairs, medical conventions, and expositions.
- In 1924, $102,000 was spent on ads in magazines with national circulation such as *Ladies Home Journal, Woman's Home Companion, Good Housekeeping, Literary Digest, Harpers, Scribners,* and *Atlantic Monthly,* making Welch's product the only nationally known grape juice.
- In the 1920s, the company shifted from using pine boxes to ship its produce to cardboard boxes, allowing Welch's to double its dividend from $1.00 to $2.00 a share.
- To help create the feeling of a big, happy family, Charles Welch held annual picnics for the employees at his camp overlooking Chautauqua Lake, and salesmen for the company were known as Welch's Associates.
- Following Dr. Charles Welch's death in 1926, his sons sold The Welch's Grape Juice Company to the American National Company, a syndicate from Nashville, Tennessee.
- As part of the sale, the sons distributed 5,000 shares of Welch's Grape Juice stock to employees valued at $400,000, and the average gift per employee in 1928 was $1,400.
- The syndicate continued many of the practices begun by Welch and operated the company until 1945.
- One of the few changes was the use of radio, which captured half of the advertising dollars of the company.
- The focus of advertising in the 1930s was away from temperance themes and toward controlling your weight, and Welch's Grape Juice was widely advertised as a "get thin" drink.
- By the 1940s, the company was producing grape juice, tomato juice, grapeade, six kinds of preserves and eight types of jellies.
- Within the Chautauqua-Erie Grape Belt, the dependence on Welch's was nearly complete, and in 1941, 98 percent of the grapes grown in the area were used for grape juice.
- By 1945, the syndicate had earned substantial profits, invested little in plant upkeep, and sold to New York-based, Jewish businessman Jack Kaplan, who merged Welch's and the National Grape Company to create a national powerhouse.
- Sales from 1945 to 1956 jumped from $10 million to $36 million.

JAZZ

Jazz Musician

Gil Evans overcame the odds of growing up without a father and moving a lot with his mother. Introduced to hillbilly music at the age of 10, and Louis Armstrong at 15, Gil discovered his musical ear and talent for orchestration. He worked with many great musicians, but collaborating in 1958 with Miles Davis on Porgy and Bess *put Gil Evans on the map.*

Life at Home

- Miles Davis described Gil Evans as "the greatest musician in the world," even while Gil was invisible to most of the music establishment.
- Gil's mother Julia was 45 years old and on her third of five husbands when he was born in Canada in 1912.
- His father, a doctor and a committed gambler, died penniless a few months after Gil's birth.
- As a child, Gil traveled extensively with his mother as she moved from job to job, state to state, and boardinghouse to boardinghouse.
- When he was four years old, they lived in Florida, where his mother ran a hotel near Lake Worth amid alligators, rattlesnakes and wild horses.
- From Florida they moved to British Columbia, and then back to the United States, making stops in Spokane, Seattle, and Odessa, Washington.
- His mother once worked as a housekeeper and cook in the lumber camps of the northwest, leaving he house at 3 a.m. and not returning before 6 p.m.
- Gil, whose friends called him Buster, essentially raised himself in the midst of miners and lumberjacks, learning to be flexible, resourceful, and tough.
- At 10 years old, he was settled in Stockton, California, where his musical influences were a Victrola, a few records and "hillbilly" music.
- In 1922, Julia married a miner and Gil, whose full name was Ian Ernest Gilmore Green, took his stepfather's last name to become Gil Evans.
- In 1927, 15-year-old Gil bought his first Louis Armstrong record, *No One Else But You*, and traveled to San Francisco to see Duke Ellington play at the Orpheum, which set a new direction in his life.
- Gil plunged headlong into music, immersing himself in Red Nichols and His Five Pennies, the

Gil Evans teamed up with Miles Davis for huge success.

Wolverines, Fletcher Henderson, McKinney's Cotton Pickers, and, of course, Armstrong and Ellington.
- Gil was blessed with a remarkable ear and a fascination with sound, identifying the make of a car just from the sound of its motor.
- In a similar fashion, Gil taught himself to pick out the notes from every record he played, and he could transcribe a song straight from a live radio broadcast.
- By 1933, Gil was the leader of an orchestra performing the latest dance hits, jazz dance music, and the sound of the Casa Loma Orchestra, which was regularly heard on a coast-to-coast radio broadcast.
- They predominantly played one-night stands at country clubs and fraternity houses around Stockton, and the musicians each earned between $2.00 and $5.00 a night.
- In 1934, they were hired to play at Lake Tahoe in the summer—their first steady, out-of-town gig—and were paid $12 a week plus room and board.
- "We got our meals, which consisted of creamed turkey necks and turkey wings every night. And we slept up in this sort of an attic room above the ballroom. Most of us put our beds up in the rafters, because of the rats."

Miles Davis, the mysterious, trumpet-playing Prince of Darkness.

- This led to a steady five-nights-a-week job at the Stockton Dreamland Ballroom, where each musician was paid $25.
- On off days, members took a music lesson in the afternoon and then gathered to hear the latest jazz offered at the Palomar Ballroom in Los Angeles, featuring Jimmy and Tommy Dorsey, the Casa Loma Orchestra, and the biggest attraction of the day—Benny Goodman.
- Benny Goodman effectively launched the swing era from the Palomar starting in 1935, promulgating a sound that would change the face of pop music.
- Gil and his orchestra enthusiastically grabbed hold of swing music and achieved success, only to have Goodman hire away the band's best musicians.
- Gil's goal was perfection, and his standards were high when it came to music, but his casual attitude toward finances, promotion, and bookings caused the band to be less than successful.

Life at Work: Musician
- The assent of swing music reflected America's love of bigness, while still enjoying "hot" sounds.
- Now that Prohibition had ended, jazz emerged from the shadows of the speakeasy and dance to the rhythms of a nation desperately tired of the Depression.
- In 1938, Gil Evans was linked up with Claude Thornhill—pianist, arranger and composer—in a union of true respect.
- Gil was impressed with Thornhill's writing, and Thornhill was taken by Gil's distinctive arrangements and orchestrations.
- The collaboration set the stage for Gil's extensive work with Miles Davis.
- Thornhill, with backing from his friend Glenn Miller, landed a major East Coast assignment at the Glen Island Casino, on the northern shore of Long Island Sound, considered the most popular dance hall on the East Coast.

- Thornhill's light, "cloudlike" swing band sound was achieved using an unorthodox mixture of instruments, including six clarinets, several French horns and three trumpets for rhythm.
- Gil arrived in 1941 as an arranger, and he experimented freely with new musical ideas.
- This partnership lasted until 1948, during which Gil's apartment behind a New York City Chinese laundry became a meeting place for musicians looking to develop new musical styles outside of the bebop beat of the day, and often included leading bebop performer Charlie Parker.
- The unique sound created by Gil Evans and Claude Thornhill, whose moods and colorings thrilled live dance audiences, quickly became caught up in two wars—World War II, and the American Society of Composers, Authors and Publishers (ASCAP) war over publishing rights.
- In 1941, unable to agree on fee schedules between songwriters and publishers, and performing rights on copyrighted material controlled by the ASCAP network, the radio networks boycotted ASCAP.
- For 10 months, ASCAP-affiliated musicians received no radio airplay at all, and bands performing at dances were prevented from performing ASCAP material on their live radio broadcasts, including major hits the public came to demand during live performances.
- In 1942, another dispute arose between the major record companies and the American Federation of Musicians (AFM), over the establishment of a trust fund for unemployed musicians, which lasted two years, retarding recording and music once again.
- The union struggle to win compensation for its members meant musicians failed to have their newest music recorded during the strike and, because singers were not part of the American Federation of Musicians, record companies turned away from Big Bands.
- The strike, the shift to vocal talent, and the military draft hastened the demise of Big Bands.
- But a war-imposed 20 percent entertainment tax on music played for dancing, caused musical promoters and entrepreneurs to seek out instrumental groups willing to play small locations unsuitable for dancing.
- In many venues, particularly in Harlem, New York, a premium was placed on performances where virtuoso work was prized.
- In 1945, when Gil returned from military service his reputation as an orchestrator gained him immediate entry into the new music scene at 52nd Street.
- The military experience had mixed blacks and whites together, and it was impossible to separate them once the war ended—especially if they were musicians.
- Fifty-second Street became a center for "new" innovation, talent and technique.
- Marx Roach said, "Gil was always interested in the improvisational things we were doing. He was really fascinated with the lines of what Charlie Parker played."
- Those melodic lines—more than the rhythmic innovations of bebop—were central to Gil's musical education.
- When Claude Thornhill reformed his orchestra after the war in April 1946, the days of the Big Bands were over.
- Jazz was not considered serious music, needing a figurehead in much the same way that Pablo Picasso symbolized modern art.
- Miles Davis, the mysterious, trumpet-playing Prince of Darkness, filled that role with the help of Gil Evans.
- Handsome and debonair, Davis dressed well, drove exotic sports cars, and enjoyed the company of glamorous women.
- On the bandstand, he did not engage in idle chatter, but cultivated the image of a brooding, darkly romantic figure intent on perfection.

Unlike the Jim Crow south, black and white musicians lived and played together in New York City.

Porgy and Bess brought success to both Davis and Evans.

- He was the musician who led the charge to shift the sound of jazz from bebop to cool, from chord-based to scale-based, from acoustic instrumentation to electric.
- *Miles Ahead,* released in 1957, was the first album that Davis recorded with Gil Evans, and the team went on to release albums such as *Porgy and Bess* and *Sketches of Spain.*
- In *Miles Ahead,* Gil combined the 10 pieces that made up the album in a kind of suite, each following the preceding one without interruption.
- The album was designed to showcase Davis, who was back in the jazz scene after a six-year disappearance during which he wrestled with heroin addiction.
- The album was pronounced a "quiet masterpiece."
- The musical, commercial and critical success of *Miles Ahead* helped make future Miles Davis/Gil Evans ventures possible.
- Columbia Records gave them artistic control of the Samuel Goldwyn film adaptation of the George Gershwin/DuBose Heyward/Ira Gershwin opera *Porgy and Bess,* in production and set for release in June 1959.
- The pair then teamed up on *Porgy and Bess* in 1958 based on the book by DuBose Heyward and George Gershwin's opera *Porgy and Bess.*
- The album was recorded in four sessions at Columbia's 30th Street Studio in New York City, one more than the three-session standard, as Gil's style demanded more time.
- Within the structure of the album, Gil and Davis expressed their dissatisfaction with bebop and its increasingly complex chord changes.
- *Porgy and Bess* gave both men more room for experimentation, and the collaboration became one of Davis's bestselling albums, bringing prosperity to both artists.

Life in the Community: New York City

- In New York City, 52nd Street between Fifth Avenue and Seventh Avenue was the the center for musicians playing on Broadway, "legitimate" nightclubs, and the site of a CBS studio.
- Musicians who played for others around the city played for themselves on 52nd Street which, from 1930 through the 1950s, hosted such jazz legends as Charlie Parker, Billie Holiday, Miles Davis, Louis Prima, Dizzy Gillespie, Art Tatum, Thelonious Monk, Fats Waller, Harry Gibson, Marian McPartland, and Nat Jaffe.
- After Minton's Playhouse in uptown Harlem, 52nd Street was the second most important place for bebop.
- A tune called "52nd Street Theme" by Thelonious Monk became a bebop anthem and jazz standard.
- Virtually every jazz great of the era performed at clubs such as The Onyx, The Downbeat, The Three Deuces, The Yacht Club, Jimmy Ryan's, and The Famous Door.

The CBS studio was in the heart of New York's theater district.

- Jazz disc jockey Symphony Sid frequently did live broadcasts from the street, marking 52nd Street as the place to be across the country.

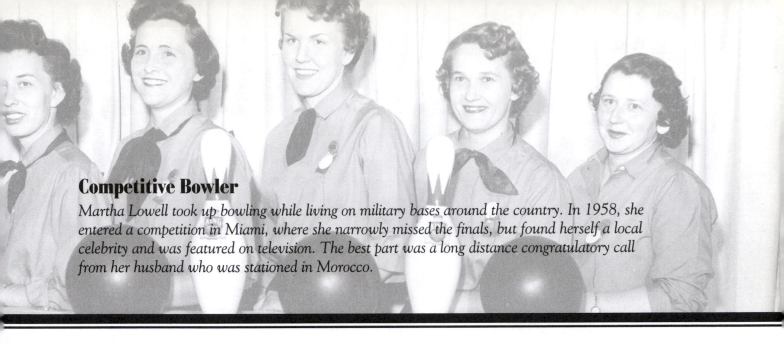

Competitive Bowler

Martha Lowell took up bowling while living on military bases around the country. In 1958, she entered a competition in Miami, where she narrowly missed the finals, but found herself a local celebrity and was featured on television. The best part was a long distance congratulatory call from her husband who was stationed in Morocco.

Life at Home

- Martha Lovell loved and hated the pressure of bowling competition, feeling alive and energized, but self-conscious too.
- Raised in the rural South, Martha was taught that a respectable woman's name only appeared in the newspaper when she married and when she died.
- Martha was raised by her mother after her father died in a bar fight when she was 12.
- They sold the family farm and moved into town where her mother Edna worked as a seamstress at a dry cleaner.
- As a child Martha competed to survive, first against her younger brother, who was the apple of everyone's eye, then against the town kids who had more money, and finally for her mother's attention, when money troubles, work or loneliness sent Edna to her bed for days at a time.
- Martha took up the slack, helped to raise her little brother, nurse her mother, and make good grades.
- Her grades were so good, in fact, that she was admitted to Winthrop College in Rock Hill, South Carolina, on a scholarship in 1943.
- There she met the love of her life—a Yankee who'd been assigned to the all-girl's campus for officer training school.
- Marrying a career military man took her to places she had only read about—Hawaii, California, Japan, Colorado and New York, where the couple lived in military base housing, drinking whiskey sours at the officers' club on Friday nights and where Martha always joined the bowling league.
- Every military base in America was outfitted with a bowling alley, where Martha competed without losing her Southern poise or appearing too aggressive.
- She especially enjoyed the mixed leagues when she and her husband bowled, and celebrated victory, together.
- Her husband was a captain and pilot for the Strategic Air Command of the United States Air Forces, and they lived in Homestead, Florida.
- Their children were 10 and seven, a girl and a boy, both as energetic as their mother and as athletic as their father.

Martha Lowell was a competitive bowler.

- Prior to meeting her husband Gordon, Martha had never seen a bowling alley, and preferred an air-conditioned movie theater.
- She first discovered bowling during her and Gordon's first overseas assignment in Hawaii in 1947 and, although shy at first, Martha quickly discovered that she had a natural lift that allowed a properly thrown bowling ball to curve perfectly into the pocket.

Martha loved the feel of the bowling ball.

- When she broke 100, she was hooked and when she broke 200, she became a true addict.

Life at Work: Competitive Bowler

- Martha Lovell's goal in the spring of 1958 was to bowl well enough to impress her husband, Gordon.
- Rising tensions around the world kept the Air Forces, particularly the Strategic Air Command, on constant alert and the Lovell household was disrupted every time Gordon left in the middle of the night to board his B-47 bomber.
- Martha believed that winning the state bowling championship would capture Gordon's attention, not to mention dethroning Sarah Middleton from her championship perch.
- Martha planned for the Miami tournament weeks in advance—babysitters for the children, the perfect outfit, and a hairstyle that would keep during the entire tournament.
- She had been to Miami twice, which was 25 miles away, the last time to practice at the bowling lanes where the tournament was to be held, leaving nothing to chance.
- She was named city champion, which earned her the right to battle for the state championship and a trip to nationals.
- Martha was so nervous she could not admit she was nervous.
- Gordon was on regular rotation in Morocco the entire month the tournament was to be held, and unless she caught someone on a direct duty mission to Sidi Slimane, letters took more than a week.
- A total of 178 bowling teams, a new record, was scheduled to compete, which required an elimination round and a chance to test the lanes.
- That first day Martha found the lanes to be fast and predictable, and her confidence was as high as her scores: 201-216-231.
- Her combined score of 648 was not only good enough to secure a return spot, but also designated her as "an up-and-coming star," according to the *Miami Herald*.
- Martha was thrilled and desperately wanted to tell Gordon, knowing that her children, although excited by her success were not terribly interested.
- Her daughter was more entwined in the drama surrounding the invitation list for an upcoming birthday swim party and her son was obsessed with *Leave It to Beaver*.
- For the second round of the competition, Martha dressed carefully, packed carefully and drove carefully to Miami.

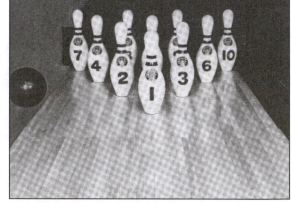

When Martha's score broke 200, she became a true addict.

- She was paired with a woman from Tallahassee who made it clear that military wives should not be allowed to compete in a Florida-sponsored tournament and asked her repeatedly, "Where again are you from, dear?"
- Once again, Martha rolled a combined score in excess of 615 and quieted the shrill questioner from Tallahassee.
- By the third round, the TV news camera that had been assigned to the event discovered Martha.
- In the first game she rolled a 261 with six strikes, in the second game she finished with 227, and after she opened the third game with four strikes that the camera moved in and the lights were turned on.

Bowling was a popular activity across America.

- With the chance to move to the finals in the balance, Martha made her five-step approach to the line thinking about her hair, her body and who might see her back home on television.
- The ball never broke, and instead of sliding gracefully into the pocket, rolled listlessly into the right corner picking up only two pins.
- She desperately wanted to cry and send the cameraman away, but instead, she picked up the returned ball in both hands, cradled it as she had been taught, inserted her fingers, set herself up for the approach and picked up the spare with a thunderous clatter.
- Realizing how close she came to ruining her chances, she rejoiced that the cameraman had stopped filming, only to discover he was waiting for her to bowl again.
- This time, even though she consciously ignored the interruption, she threw too hard and ended with a 7-10 split, and a pin in each corner—an extremely difficult spare to make.
- With the camera humming in the background and the lights slightly blinding her vision, Martha rolled cross-alley to the 10, which ricocheted back across the lane for a spare.

Martha converted the 7–10 split.

- The surrounding lanes broke into thunderous applause, and Martha's impossible spare was shown by the Miami television station that night, which noted that she had missed the finals by six pins.
- At home, Martha and her friends celebrated—appearing on television was a victory beyond the championship.
- Her children called her a movie star and ostentatiously bowed when she walked into a room but, best of all, Gordon called long-distance to congratulate her.

The History of Bowling

- The history of bowling can be traced back to the Stone Age.
- The first evidence of the game was discovered by the British anthropologist Sir Flinders Petrie and his team of archaeologists in Egypt in the 1930s.
- He unearthed a collection of objects from a small child's grave that appeared to have been a primitive form of the game.

- German historians counter-claimed that the game of bowling originated around 300 AD, originating as a religious ceremony for determining absence of sin.
- In England, several variations of bowling, such as half-bowls, skittles and ninepins, existed during the mid-1300s.
- The first written mention of the game was made by King Edward III in the year 1366, when he imposed a ban on playing the game because it was distracting the troops from archery practice.
- During the seventeenth century, English, Dutch and German settlers imported their own version of bowling to America, and it was regularly played in an area of New York City known as "Bowling Green," and it consisted of nine pins.
- Connecticut banned ninepins in 1841 because of its gambling implications.
- The American Bowling Congress was formed in 1895 and standardized bowling in the United States and organized official competitions.
- The Women's Bowling League followed in 1917, under the encouragement of Dennis Sweeny.
- In 1951 American Machine and Foundry Company (AMF, then a maker of machinery for the bakery, tobacco and apparel industries) purchased the patents to Gottfried Schmidt's automatic pinspotter, and by late 1952 production model pinspotters were introduced.
- Television embraced bowling in the 1950s, and the game's popularity grew exponentially.
- NBC's broadcast of *Championship Bowling* was the first network coverage of bowling, followed by shows like *Make That Spare, Celebrity Bowling,* and *Bowling For Dollars.*

Language of the Lanes, compiled by American Bowling Congress, 1958

Apple: The ball Bedposts: The 7-10 split
Benchwork: Conversation intended to upset or disconcert opponents
Big ears: The 4-6-7-10 split
Cheese cakes: Lanes where strikes are easy to get
Cherry: Ball that chops off the front pin of a spare and leaves the pin behind and/or to the right or left standing
Cincinnati: The 8-10 split
Crow hopper: Clawlike, loose grip on ball noticeable just at release over the foul line
Dead ball: An ineffective ball
Double wood: One pin directly behind another
Dutch 200: 200 game made by alternate strikes and spares
Foundation: A strike in the ninth frame
Go the route: To finish the game with three or more consecutive strikes
Holding alley: A lane that resists hook action
Honey: A good ball
Kindling wood: Light pins
Lift: Giving the ball an upward motion with fingers at point of release
Mother-in-law: The number 7 pin
Mule ears: The 7-10 split
Poison ivy: The 3-6-10 setup
Poodle: To roll the ball in the gutter
Rat club: A team that shoots unusually low scores for one game
Short pin: A pin that is rolling on the alley and fails to hit the standing pin
Snow plow: A wide hook that sweeps the pins off the lane
Steal: To get more pins than deserved on a hit
Throwing rocks: Throwing a lot of good strike balls
Turkey: Three strikes in a row
Woolworth: The 5-10 split

The Woman's Bowling Guide, Sylvia Wene, 1959

When I was 17 years of age and only 4 feet, 11 inches tall my brother and sister took me on my first visit to a bowling establishment. "You," my brother stated, "are too small to bowl so you have to sit there and keep score."

The game looked like great fun and I wanted to try my hand. But, as ordered, I sat there and tried to keep score while they bowled. But the next day I went back to those lanes with my mother to see how I would do. I wasn't very successful. As a matter of fact, I didn't come anywhere near 100. My mother did and, I suppose, that piqued me somewhat. Anyhow, I decided I was going to roll 100. It took me quite a while. And, by that time, I decided I wouldn't quit till I had rolled 200. Then, by the time I was able to accomplish 200, I was so crazy about the game, I was not able to give it up.

Now I am still only 4 feet, 11 inches tall. Yet I am proud of my record: First woman to bowl a perfect 300 game in a sanctioned East Coast play. A 206 national recorded average for three straight seasons. The world record of 11 700 series in one year. National individual match

champion in 1955. I am making it a point to accent these accomplishments to illustrate to you that stature has little to do with making you a better-than-average bowler. Consider that there are 25 million bowlers and the national average, for both men and women, is below 150.

There is one major reason for this pin topping deficiency: a scarcity of expert instructors to give individual instruction. The result is that most bowlers start by simply walking out on the lane with a few words of advice from a friend and roll away. If they approach their friend's peak efficiency, as low as it may be, they are satisfied thereafter to stay in a low-scoring rut from force of copied habit. I am not trying to tell you that championship bowling is easy. It takes long hours of hard work. But bowling well, which means scoring higher than the national average, isn't at all difficult if you master the basic principles. And, believe me, it is just as easy to learn the correct basic principles as it is to adopt improper ones.

Bowling Beauty Tips,
The Woman's Bowling Guide, Sylvia Wene, 1959

A woman is known by the aura of femininity that surrounds her. Her perfume, feminine daintiness, and makeup help to make her even more lovely. Sometimes, in the rush of daily living, we forget some of the details we should remember. But an afternoon or evening of bowling should be something special. So take those few extra seconds to double check. Wear a light, appealing fragrance, one that whispers and one that definitely doesn't shout. Work out a special makeup, one that is easy to apply, keeps you looking your loveliest, and is natural looking. Use a double amount of deodorant, since activity does speed up body process. All of which will make you feel better, look better, and thus possibly bowl better.

DEODORANTS: nothing spoils the illusion of feminine daintiness and, in a sport such as bowling, makes you feel more conspicuous than unsightly perspiration stains. Therefore, a good antiperspirant and deodorant should be used. And not only under the arms, but the same antiperspirant should be placed at the bend of the knee and the crook of the arm. There are any number of good antiperspirant deodorants in roll-on, spray, lotion, or cream form.

EYE MAKEUP: apply your eye makeup wisely. Use the eyebrow pencil but keep your eye shadow, if you wish to use it, extremely light. I would also suggest that you use mascara very sparingly. There are roll-on mascaras which are easily applied and which, being waterproof, resist perspiration.

HANDS AND NAILS: Even if your nails are strong, still be sure to reinforce them with extra coats of nail enamel. A sturdy manicure consists of a base coat, two coats of enamel, and a top coat. To this you may add an additional coat of enamel and a top coat. This builds up a shiny protective coat of armor.

Single Young Hairdresser

Ronnie Pettigrew was 26 years old in 1959. She made $2,855 a year as a hairdresser, a vocation she discovered as a teenager volunteering at her local hospital. She loved her job, but was so stressed at not having a steady boyfriend, that she took up smoking, trying not to focus on the fact that half of American women were married by the age of 20.

Life at Home

- Ronnie Pettigrew became a hairdresser when she graduated from high school.
- Before graduation, Ronnie worried sick about what she was going to do for a living and it didn't help that her parents constantly lectured her about potential and lack of ambition.
- She couldn't continue living at home, that was for sure and she didn't even suggest it to her father.
- With no steady boyfriend, marriage was an unlikely possibility and she was painfully aware that half of all American women were married by age 20.
- Most of the kids who went to the state university returned after one year with tales of wild parties, little money and less chance of returning to school, often winding up working at Boeing.
- Lots of Ronnie's friends, and her Boeing-mechanic father, had a love-hate relationship with the city's largest employer.
- "Boeing's like the benevolent kings of Europe," he repeated after two drinks. "They have the power to make or break you based on their whim. The workers are simply well-paid serfs."
- Ronnie did temporary work at the hospital, where she discovered she hated blood, sick people, and bossy doctors, but loved helping ladies prepare their hair when it was time to return home.
- Washing and styling the hair of new mothers was particularly satisfying as she was able to give these mothers some attention for a change, a welcomed shift from the babies being the center of attraction.
- Her mother encouraged Ronnie's decision to attend cosmetology school, and secretly supplied most of the tuition.
- Her father was happy to have his daughter out of the house, but felt that doing other ladies' hair wasn't a career, but a stopover on the road to marriage.
- When Ronnie got her first paycheck, her dad even suggested that part of it be set aside for her wedding.
- Ronnie bought clothes instead.

Life at Work: Hairdresser

- Every morning, Ronnie Pettigrew woke up knowing she was going to make someone's day.
- She loved getting paid to make people look and feel beautiful.

Ronnie Pettigrew became a hairdresser right out of high school.

- Working her magic with scissors and gel, Ronnie shaped limp strands of hair into well-styled coifs.
- When simple styling was not enough, she sharpened her creativity through formal up-dos and inspired color treatments, making clients feel important.
- "I love to see them leave smiling," she said when people asked how she managed in the competitive world of hairdressing.
- The work hours were long, normally eight to 10 hours on her feet, six days a week.
- Saturdays, when all her friends were at the lake having a good time, Ronnie worked.
- She especially enjoyed doing weddings, and often worked magic on brides and bridesmaids.

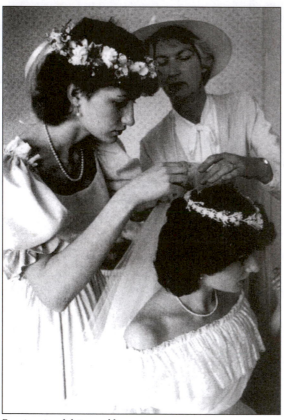

Ronnie enjoyed doing weddings.

- The work was fun, though sometimes demanding: Mrs. Mildred Johnson acted as though Ronnie caused the bald patch on the top of her head and Mrs. J. P. Holland was indifferent one week, and a tiger the next!
- Mrs. A. G. Wahl talked endlessly about how she spent her husband's newfound fortune in the real estate business, thanks to the booming economy of Seattle.
- Most of all, the ladies liked to talk about when Ronnie would get married.
- They arranged blind dates for her with their sons, nephews or friends, all of which were disasters.
- It was bad enough to hate your date, but was simply awful to explain yourself to his mother while she sat in your beauty parlor chair.
- The pressure to find a mate upset Ronnie so much that she secretly started to smoke cigarettes to calm herself down.
- Day after day, she kept her young mouth shut while she learned about life from a steady stream of talking heads, knowing that no one wanted to hear about her aching feet or tired back.
- Thursdays were long days, as the shop was open from 8 a.m. to 8 p.m.
- The money was good particularly the tips from evening appointments, but it hardly helped her social life.
- For slow and methodical Ronnie, hairdressing was sometimes stressful, especially when clients came in every half hour.
- It was important to pay attention to clients' comments, in case the customer picked up the conversation at her next appoiintment.
- After eight years, Ronnie predicted the conversation of many of the ladies—from children to country club parties to gossip, nothing was sacred.
- Ronnie read the local newspaper to keep up with the people under discussion in her chair: much of the talk was about Boeing, its future, and what it meant for Seattle.
- At work, Ronnie felt confident and in control because she knew how to make her clients happy but once she left the shop, she became shy and awkward.
- Ronnie saw herself as a professional with a real career and was always looking at people's hair, both on the streets or on television.
- The top style-setters were Jacqueline Kennedy, Marilyn Monroe, Audrey Hepburn and Sophia Loren.

Manufacturing Boeing airplanes was the major industry in Seattle.

Life in the Community: Seattle, Washington

- After some post-World War II readjustments, the United States hit its economic stride in the 1950s, and rolled up a 50 percent increase in the gross national product.
- Nationwide, real wages and employment rose.
- Consumers were on a spending spree, eager to buy television sets, power mowers, decorator telephones, poodle skirts, flashy cars and the ubiquitous barbecue grill.
- For Seattle, Boeing was the real success story.
- Boeing's payroll pumped $8.5 million into the local economy every two weeks.
- About 35,000 men and women worked for The Big B, slightly more than half of all manufacturing employees in the metropolitan area.
- Some fretted about Seattle being a one-company city, but most were proud of their role in growing the industry giant from its modest beginnings in 1916.
- As a result, the newspaper was always eager to provide coverage of Boeing's resurgence as a Cold War military contractor for the B-47 Stratojet and the B-52 Stratofortress jet bombers, and as a developer of jetliners for the commercial airlines.
- President Dwight Eisenhower's proposed defense budget was also big news.
- 1.5 million air travelers passed through Seattle-Tacoma Airport, dispelling fears that air travel was a luxury and the airport would be an empty failure.
- Instead, commercial jet flight was a raging success.
- In 1959, Boeing booked orders for nearly two hundred 707 airplanes.
- In Seattle, local retail sales nearly doubled, and the average family income increased from $5,255 to $7,042, a 34 percent jump during the boom between 1951 and 1960.

Airplane travel was catching on with the average traveller.

- By all indications, Seattle arrived: its streets and shops were bustling, and its theaters, restaurants and cultural institutions were more sophisticated than ever.
- The Alaskan Way viaduct was completed along the waterfront, and the Washington, Logan and Norton buildings changed the city's skyline.

Science Teacher in the Age of Sputnik

Carl Hyder's career as a science teacher—and science education in America—turned a corner when the Russians launched Sputnik. Despite American nerves about the Russian accomplishment, Carl noticed, in 1959, that American education was getting more attention—and money—and his students were more likely to enter science-related fields.

Life at Home

- Carl Hyder was a hometown hero, a savior, and definitely someone to talk to at the grocery store.
- As a science teacher in the age of Sputnik, Carl symbolized the man destined to educate the next generation of scientists and help America win the space race against mighty Russia.
- The event that changed his life occurred on the evening of October 4, 1957, when a Soviet R-7 intercontinental ballistic missile lifted off from the Baikonur Cosmodrome, on the steppes of Kazakhstan, carrying a 23-inch polished steel sphere called Sputnik.
- About 100 minutes later, the 184-pound Sputnik, trailing four metal antennas, passed the launch site, confirming that a human-made moon was orbiting the Earth; the new "Space Age" had begun in the midst of the Cold War.
- As news of the Soviet accomplishment spread by radio and television reports, millions climbed onto rooftops or clustered in backyards to scan the heavens for a brief glimpse of a rapidly moving star.
- Carl's students appeared at his front door, asking questions and hinting that they wanted to be on the back deck scanning the sky with his telescope.
- It was a communal experience that would later become known simply as "Sputnik Night."
- Much of America's immediate official response to Sputnik bordered on panic.
- *The Chicago Daily News* declared that if the Soviets "could deliver a 184-pound 'moon' into a predetermined pattern 560 miles out into space, the day is not far distant when they could deliver a death-dealing warhead onto a predetermined target almost anywhere on the earth's surface."
- *Newsweek* speculated that several dozen Sputniks equipped with nuclear bombs could "spew their lethal fallout over the U.S. and Europe."
- Senator Lyndon Johnson envisioned a day when the Soviets would be "dropping bombs on us from space like kids dropping rocks onto cars from freeway overpasses."

Carl Hyder's science students were inspired by the Sputnik launch.

Several of Carl's students were committed to scientific endeavors.

- "What is at stake is nothing less than our survival," Senator Mike Mansfield said.
- President Dwight D. Eisenhower referred to it as the "Sputnik Crisis," even though Sputnik itself was harmless.
- Shortwave radio operators picked up a persistent "beep ... beep ... beep" signal broadcast from the satellite as it passed overhead, traveling at 17,400 miles per hour.
- Rep. Clare Boothe Luce referred to Sputnik's beeps as "an intercontinental outer-space raspberry to a decade of American pretensions that the American way of life was a gilt-edged guarantee of our national superiority."
- For Carl, the orbiting capsule was a gift from God that would finally encourage the nation to focus its energies on creating talented scientists capable of winning the space race to the moon and beyond.
- Sputnik Night meant hamburgers at Carl's home and a night of stargazing, and with the entire class was present, they spotted the tiny satellite streaking across the night sky.
- Carl was thrilled as three students pledged to become space engineers.
- The class held political debates concerning America's failure to enter space first, and whether or not American schools were lagging behind the rest of the world.
- At the request of students, a "Parent's Sputnik Night" was created, put together by Carl, his wife, three students and another science teacher.
- The auditorium was filled with adults whose knowledge of space travel ranged from Buck Rogers fantasy tales to a religious fervor that demanded God's Heaven not be violated by man-made objects.
- Carl's family were all teachers—parents, grandparents, wife, and sisters, and all in math or science except his wife, whose specialty was history.
- Carl's family immigrated to America in 1834, eventually finding their way via Philadelphia and St. Louis to Oklahoma City in 1903.

Carl's mother, sister and wife were teachers.

- The family name was Heider, but when the First World War erupted, anti-German sentiment and a handful of rocks crashed through his windows, so Karl Heider changed his name to Carl Hyder.
- Ironically, in 1959, Oklahoma City looked to the Hyder family for protection from Russia.

Life at Work: Science Teacher

- Two years after the excitement surrounding Sputnik had faded, Carl Hyder was still walking on air.
- A dozen of his students entered science-related fields in college, inspired, they said, by the way he responded to Sputnik.
- The school district increased its funding for science laboratory equipment, and superb films were being created and distributed nationally, exploring the unknowns of space, the intellectual challenges of physics, and the opportunities offered by space exploration.

The NACA was created in 1958 to conducts America's civilian space efforts.

- Sputnik made his class relevant and alive, and Carl sensed his students were more engaged and that he was a better teacher for it.
- Nationwide, the response to Sputnik was multi-faceted.
- School curricula with an emphasis on science and mathematics were quickly established to prepare students for the challenges ahead.
- The National Defense Education Act provided $887 million over four years in student loans, scholarships, fellowships, and the purchase of scientific equipment for schools.
- The federal government displayed a willingness to finance education that could support national security goals—especially the training of scientists.
- Support was expanded for the National Science Foundation, and the Advanced Research Projects Agency was created.
- Sputnik was also largely responsible for the establishment of the National Aeronautics and Space Administration (NASA) in 1958 to conduct the country's civilian space efforts.
- For the first time in the decade, the president recommended deferring plans for school construction in favor of support for the sciences.
- Congress also increased the National Science Foundation (NSF) appropriation to $134 million, almost $100 million higher than that of the prior year.
- Fearing federal intervention, critics quickly pointed out that the U.S. Constitution did not give the federal government any role in education.
- Just as quickly, supporters demonstrated that the federal government had been funding and supporting schools dating back to the Land Ordinance Act of 1785 that set aside land for the establishment of schools in the new territories between the Appalachian Mountains and the Mississippi River.
- The National Defense Education Act was signed on September 2, 1958, by President Eisenhower, who felt it was essential to strengthen the American education system.
- Ultimately, legislation was also implemented to meet the basics of an elevated national security, the bill revolving around student loans and fellowships targeted for prospective college teachers.
- States received funding for students and equipment in the science, math, and foreign language fields, ranging from $1,000 to $5,000, to be repaid within 10 years after the student had graduated.
- Carl felt that Sputnik brought to the surface many of the issues raging within the education community, such as: 1) Should education be progressive, child-centered, or basic, discipline-centered? 2) Should priority be given to building the nation's scientific capability or to creating nationwide science literacy? 3) Who should decide what students were supposed to learn—teachers, school administrators and trustees, parents, or university scholars? 4) What should the balance be between the stability that comes with maintaining traditional content and the confusion and inefficiency that accompanied the introduction of major changes?
- Most scientists knew little about pre-college education, and few educators had a firm grasp of practical science.

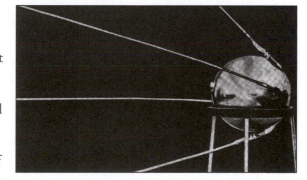

- The greatest result of Sputnik, Carl believed, was the way it stimulated additional science-oriented activities.
- Prior to Sputnik, little science was taught in the lower grades but since Sputnik, children were exposed to the fundamentals at an earlier age, allowing Carl to push them further when they reached his class.

Life in the Community: Oklahoma City, Oklahoma

- Oklahoma City, the capital and the largest city in Oklahoma, was founded during the Land Run of 1889, and grew to a population of over 10,000 within what seemed like hours.
- As the town continued to grow, the population doubled between 1890 and 1900.
- During the opening decades of the twentieth century, Oklahoma City developed one of the largest livestock markets in the world, attracting jobs and revenue from Chicago and Omaha.
- Oklahoma was admitted to the Union in 1907.
- Oklahoma City was a major stop on Route 66 during the early part of the twentieth century.

Oklahoma City was a center for oil production.

- With the 1928 discovery of oil within the city limits, it became a center of oil production.
- Natural gas, petroleum products and related industries became the largest sector of the local economy; oil derricks dotted the city, including the capitol grounds.
- Bisected by the North Canadian River, Oklahoma City experienced flooding every year until the 1940s, when a dam was built on the river to control the water.

Spudnik's [sic] Beeps Continue But Tones Varying,
Hamilton Journal **(Ohio), October 10, 1957**

Fog over the U.S. northeast coast today blanked out a major effort to get a visual fix on the Soviet Earth satellite hurtling through the skies.

Scientists and moon watchers of a Cambridge team man the telescopes atop the Harvard College Observatory as the moonlet sped on a southeasterly course above Nova Scotia, northeast of Boston, at 6:40 AM. But the fog hit the target, as clouds had done when the Cambridge observers made their first effort Wednesday.

Monitoring stations in the Western Hemisphere and Europe reported signals from the speeding sphere were coming in strong, although with varying tones.

There was some difference of opinion among scientists whether the satellite is maintaining its rate of speed and its altitude.

But broadcasts from Moscow said the man-made moon will stay aloft for a long time. Canada's Dominion Observatory at Ottawa said Wednesday night the Russian moonlet, launched last Friday, was photographed over Alberta. Earlier, it was reported that the photograph had been taken at Auckland, New Zealand....

The signals emitted by the sphere were reported by listening posts in various places to have changed from the original beep-beep sound. The U.S. Naval Research Laboratory said it was receiving a hum interspersed with an occasional beep. Radio operators in Mazatlan, Mexico, told of hearing a signal that sounded like "psst, psst, psst."

A spokesman for the Naval Research Laboratory said the difference in signals might be explained by a variation in receiving equipment, or perhaps the location of the sets in relation to the path of the satellite.

Two Moscow radio broadcasts, both for home listeners, gave conflicting views on the moonlet's speed. One said it was speeding up. The other said it was slowing down. There was no attempt to explain the conflict.

Political and Military Implications of Sputnik Throw Screen Around Scientific Value of Moon, *Hamilton Journal* (Ohio), October 10, 1957

The political and military implications of Sputnik are throwing a smokescreen around the scientific value of the man-made, man-controlled Earth satellite.

While the West mourns a race lost, Sputnik spins merrily on, its stuttering beeps apparently transmitting scientific data to its earthbound makers.

What information is Sputnik transmitting?

The Soviets have said it is counting meteor hits and collecting data on the South Magnetic Pole. One Russian scientist has hinted it also is measuring temperatures in space. That's only one part of what Earth satellites—Russian and American—were expected to do this International geophysical year. Six to 10 planned by the United States will study meteors, magnetism, and temperature as well as cosmic and sun rays, air density, space pressure, even the shape and composition of the earth.

These things have been studied before but never outside the atmosphere, the dense layer of air that envelops the earth and obscures the secrets of space.

Data gathered by the prying satellites probably will not have immediate practical value. But it will provide a foundation on which future practical results may be built.

A half-century ago, Albert Einstein formulated a basic theory that matter can be converted into energy. It was 40 years before practical atom energy grew up on that platform. The satellite reports can answer questions like these:

What effect do temperatures in the line of severe electric current have upon wind velocities on the surface of the earth? What does this mean for weather forecasters?

What is the connection between sunspots, those vast, turbulent storms on the face of the sun, and the auroras that frequently rob an earthly radio communication? What does this hold for the future of radio?

What is the source of cosmic rays, powerful and penetrating electromagnetic radiation, which create energy as they pass to the atmosphere? Can they be harnessed to serve mankind?

Satellites, of course, are man's first tentative steps toward space travel.

The artificial moons reach a balance at 18,000 miles an hour between the possessive pull of the earth's gravity and centrifugal force tending to hurl them into outer space. A relatively not much faster push would allow them to break out of this hold and possibly reach the moon, and they hope to hit within the next decade.

Federal Legislation Supporting Education

1787 and 1788: Land Ordinance Act and Northwest Ordinance: These ordinances provided for the establishment of public education first in the territory between the Appalachian Mountains and the Mississippi River, requiring that one square mile of every 36 be reserved for support of public education and then in new states be encouraged to establish "schools and the means for education."

1862 and 1890: Morrill Land Grant College Acts: These acts established 69 institutions of higher education in various states.

1917: Smith-Hughes Act: This act provided funds for teacher training and program development in vocational education at the high school level.

1944: Servicemen's Readjustment Act: This Act paid veterans' tuition and living expenses for a specific number of months.

1958: National Defense Education Act: In response to Sputnik, funds were allocated for student loans, the education of school counselors, and the strengthening of instructional programs in science, mathematics and foreign languages.

Rock 'n' Roll Career from Prison

Johnny Bragg was a rock 'n' roll pioneer who was discovered while in Tennessee State Prison for crimes he did not commit. He formed the Prisonaires, a group of talented prisoners that caught the attention of Governor Clement. When Johnny was paroled in 1959, he stepped from prison into a successful musical career.

Life at Home

- Singer-songwriter Johnny Bragg's mother Maybelle died in childbirth and the baby she left behind in 1926 was blind, black and poor in segregated Nashville, Tennessee, and needed constant care.
- It was not a propitious beginning for the rock and roll pioneer discovered while in prison serving 594 years for rapes he did not commit.
- Johnny's father, Wade, was a railway man who worked 12 hours a day, six days a week; he earned $6 weekly for his 72 hours of labor.
- Unable to care for the motherless flock, Wade Bragg farmed out Johnny and his three siblings to the children's grandmother and later their uncle, who was a minister and a lover of gospel music.
- At an early age Johnny learned to sing songs that reflected his life: "My Blue Heaven," and "What You Goin' to Do When the Rent Come 'Round?"
- The three boys, who saw their father only on Sundays, shared one room and one bed.
- At the age of six, Johnny inexplicably regained his sight, was able to enter school and immediately discovered he had no interest in an education.
- Johnny was a wild kid who relished fighting chickens for sport and when he was 14, served a month's confinement for riding in a stolen car.
- His life changed forever in 1943 when he caught his girlfriend, Jenny, having sex with his best friend.
- The girl angrily attacked Johnny and later, to explain her bruises, she accused Johnny of raping her.
- Her mother phoned the police, who beat Johnny until he signed a confession.
- While he was in his jail cell, the police paraded a dozen rape victims in front of Johnny, six of whom claimed that the 16-year-old had raped them.
- Even after Johnny's former girlfriend retracted her story and told the truth, Johnny was tried for the other crimes and given six 99-year sentences.

Johnny Bragg's musical talent was developed while he was in prison.

Johnny formed the Prisonaires *with other prisoners.*

- He was sent to the notorious Tennessee State Penitentiary and, on his seventeenth birthday, Johnny Bragg began his 594-year sentence, assigned to making prison clothes.
- Prison was where he became reacquainted with the gospel music of his youth.
- When Bragg heard a group of prisoners singing spirituals, he quickly moved into the role of lead tenor and encouraged the singers to be as disciplined as the groups he heard in church.
- He began to write songs, even though he could barely read and write.
- "I'd pick up an old piece of paper off the ground. If the song had the word 'heart' in it, all I would put in it was maybe a T or an H. If there was a girl I'd put G. I wrote a lot of songs that way."
- He formed the *Prisonaires* vocal group with Ed Thurman, tenor (who had killed the man who had killed his dog), William Stewart, baritone (charged with bludgeoning a white man to death, even though someone else had confessed to the killing), Marcell Sanders, bass (who stabbed the man who stabbed his girlfriend), and John Drue Jr., tenor (serving time for car theft).
- Their first performances were serenading prisoners before their state-sponsored execution in the electric chair.
- After the singing and the disturbing sight of a man's death by electrocution, Johnny would stay behind to loosen the straps on the condemned and clean up the mess.
- At the beginning of the decade, Big Bands had dominated popular music, especially those led by Glenn Miller, Tommy Dorsey, Duke Ellington, and Benny Goodman.
- Bing Crosby's smooth voice made him extremely popular, vying with Frank Sinatra, Dinah Shore, Kate Smith, and Perry Como for the public's attention.
- By the end of the decade, bebop and rhythm and blues were merging with distinctly black sounds, epitomized by Charlie Parker, Dizzy Gillespie, while Thelonious Monk, Billie Holiday, Ella Fitzgerald, and Woody Herman forged new avenues in blues and jazz.
- Radio was the lifeline for Americans in the 1940s, providing news, music and entertainment; programming included soap operas, quiz shows, children's hours, mystery stories, fine drama, and sports.
- Within the Tennessee State Prison, the radios, all of which were owned or controlled by the guards, blared blues, gospel, country-western, and some pop music all day long.
- Nashville stars would sometimes perform at the prison and, when Johnny met Hank Williams, he asked, "Do you ever sing songs written by other people?" "Depends," said Williams, "Are you one of those other people?"
- Johnny sang Williams a song which Williams bought for $5.
- Johnny always insisted that the song eventually became "Your Cheatin' Heart," a country standard.

Life at Work: Prisoner and Musician

- Johnny Bragg's music career outside the walls of the Tennessee State Penitentiary began with the election of Frank Clement—a politician whose style was a cross between the Rev. Billy Graham and President "Give 'em Hell" Harry Truman.
- Interested in being Tennessee's governor since he was 16, Clement became the nation's youngest governor at age 32 in 1953.
- To please his wife, Clement transformed the Governor's mansion into a showcase for music makers and music lovers and to please himself, he tackled the thorny issues of Prison reform.

Tennessee Governor Frank Clement.

- Johnny Bragg and the *Prisonaires* were the benefactors of both.
- In an unprecedented move, the *Prisonaires* were allowed to perform under armed guard at churches and civic functions, and then on local radio.
- For their first performance at the Governor's mansion, a 1929 Georgian brick estate boasting 22 rooms, the prisoners were driven and escorted by the warden's petite wife when the assigned prison guard failed to show up on time.
- They wore suits fashioned by Johnny in the prison laundry, were allowed to enter through the front door of the Governor's mansion, were introduced personally by the governor by name, and then sang for an élite group of guests that included future president Texas Senator Lyndon Johnson and U.S. Senator Albert Gore of Tennessee.
- The evening was a grand success, and within weeks the *Prisonaires* became regulars on local white radio stations, at churches and services organizations.
- "The *Prisonaires* represent the hopes of tomorrow rather than the mistakes of yesterday," Governor Clement announced the same week the men performed briefly on radio Station WSM, home of the Grand Ole Opry, a musical institution since 1926.
- Their next big break came when Johnny was walking across the courtyard to his duties in the laundry with habitual housebreaker and thief, Robert Riley.
- As the rain beat down, Johnny said, "Here we are just walking in the rain and wondering what the girls are doing," Riley said. "That's a song."
- Within a few minutes, Johnny had composed two verses and was convinced it was a hit: "Just walkin' in the rain, gettin' soakin' wet, torturin' my heart, tryin' to forget."
- Unable to read and write, he asked Riley to write it down in exchange for a writing credit.
- When the group recorded their first record for Sam Phillips of Sun Records, "Just Walkin' in the Rain" was on the A side-the song most likely to become popular.
- Johnny heard his song for the first time on WSOK, one of two stations that gave them their start.
- "We was coming in from dinner. Some of the guys were already in their cells. I passed Ed's headbolter desk where a radio was playing. I get within earshot and I keep moving closer to a familiar sound. The radio's playing 'Just Walkin.' Ed, he walked in behind me and sat at his desk. I said, 'Ed you hear that? That's us,' and he said, 'Yeah, it is. Sounds all right.'"
- By that time, the cellblock came alive with voices yelling with excitement.
- "The guards, they were looking us up and down, but they let it go."

The Prisonaires *wore prison-made suits when performing.*

The Prisonaires *frequently entertained at the Governor's mansion.*

- Soon after its June 1953 release, "Just Walkin'," with its elegant but simple arrangement, made the nation's R&B Top 10 and quickly sold 50,000 copies.
- The record was produced by Sun Studios, the same studio where Elvis Presley, Johnny Cash, and Carl Perkins had their starts.
- According to Johnny, he and Elvis Presley often traded musical ideas.
- The *Prisonaires* then received national publicity when the country star Roy Acuff presented them with a Gibson guitar.
- Their privileges were such that when bass singer Marcell Sanders was offered parole, he refused, saying that he wanted to stay with the group.
- In August 1953, they recorded a raucous "Softly and Tenderly" with Ike Turner on piano; their third single, the plaintive "A Prisoner's Prayer," was printed with stripes on the label, and their next, "There Is Love in You," was recorded at the penitentiary itself.
- The whole prison caught the magic of performing and writing songs; producer Sam Phillips picked up two songs from white inmates, "Without You" and "Casual Love Affair," that he was to rehearse with Elvis Presley.
- Eventually, Sanders was told that he would have to leave the prison, and tenor John Drue was also given parole.
- Not eligible for parole, Bragg reconstituted the group even though the mood at the prison began to change.
- Other prisoners became resentful of Johnny's freedom to leave the prison to perform, fights were started, and four white inmates threatened to cut out his vocal cords.
- Also, to meet the demands of the new rock 'n' roll era, the *Prisonaires* began recording more upbeat material and decided to change their name.
- They first chose the name *Sunbeams,* then switched to the *Marigolds* to record the song "Rocking Horse," which quickly topped the R&B chart; it was outsold by a cover version for the pop market by the *Fontane Sisters.*
- Songs originated by black groups but covered by white singers were becoming increasingly common.
- In 1956, Johnnie Ray's record producer, Mitch Miller, rediscovered "Just Walkin' in the Rain" and realized it was perfect for the popular singer nicknamed the "Cry Guy."
- Ray's performing style included rock 'n' roll theatrics, including beating up his piano, writhing on the floor and crying, earning the Oregon-born white singer the nicknames "Mr. Emotion," "The Nabob of Sob," and "The Prince of Wails."

To change their image, the Prisonaires *became the* Marigolds.

Lunch counters were popular—and segregated—in Nashville.

- Ray's fully orchestrated and highly histrionic performance went to No. 2 in the U.S. and topped the U.K. chart.
- The No. 1 American song was Elvis's "Don't Be Cruel."
- Johnny Bragg's songwriting royalties topped $8,700 for the year—the most money he ever made—that was put into a trust fund for him.
- He was even invited to the Broadcast Music Inc. black tie banquet because of the level of radio play that "Just Walkin'" had received.
- The warden did not allow him to attend.
- When Governor Clement asked the *Marigolds* to perform at an event at the Governor's mansion honoring Elvis Presley, he told them to perform "Jailhouse Rock."
- Presley had a wonderful time harmonizing with the inmates and suggested that they record together, but his manager Colonel Parker did not consider this a good career move.
- In March 1956, the *Marigolds* went to Nashville to record "Foolish Me" and "Beyond the Clouds," while "Heartbreak Hotel" by Elvis Presley was enjoying an eight-week run at the top of the charts.
- Thanks to the efforts of the Governor, Johnny Bragg was released on parole in January 1959 as one the last acts of Governor Clements.
- He was 32 years old and had spent 15 years in prison for crimes he did not commit and he was ready to begin again.

Life in the Community: Nashville, Tennessee

- When Johnny Bragg was growing up, Nashville, Tennessee, was considered to be the "Athens of the South," even though a pattern of racial exclusiveness prevailed in Nashville's schools and public facilities.
- In 1958, local black leaders founded the Nashville Christian Leadership Conference (NCLC), an affiliate of Martin Luther King, Jr.'s Southern Christian Leadership Conference.
- Early in 1959, the NCLC began a movement to desegregate downtown Nashville.
- The policy of segregation was tested at Harvey's and Cain-Sloan's department stores, where the Reverends Smith and James M. Lawson, Jr.'s students John Lewis, Diane Nash, James Bevel, Marion Barry, and others bought goods and then attempted to desegregate the lunch counters.
- Before the end of 1959, students from Nashville's black colleges, including Fisk University, Tennessee A&I State University, Meharry Medical College, and American Baptist Theological Seminary, were being trained to participate in the non-violent protests.
- Opened in 1898, the Tennessee State Prison was located near downtown Nashville, Tennessee.
- The Tennessee Prison contained 800 small cells, each designed to house a single inmate.
- The prison's 800 cells were opened to receive prisoners on February 12, 1898, and that day

Tennessee State Prison held 800 cells.

admitted 1,403 prisoners, creating immediate overcrowding which persisted throughout the next century.

- It was the advent of the Grand Ole Opry in 1925, combined with an already thriving publishing industry, that positioned Nashville to become "Music City USA."
- Beginning in the mid-1950s, the Nashville sound turned country music into a multimillion-dollar industry.
- Under the direction of producers such as Chet Atkins, Owen Bradley, and later Billy Sherrill, the sound brought country music to a diverse audience and expanded its appeal.
- The sound borrowed from 1950s pop stylings: a prominent and smooth vocal, backed by a string section and vocal chorus.
- Leading artists in this genre included Patsy Cline, Jim Reeves, and Eddy Arnold.
- The "slip note" piano style of session musician Floyd Cramer was an important component of this style.

Recorded Popular Songs

1950s
1. The Fat Man-Fats Domino
2. Please Send Me Someone to Love-Percy Mayfield
3. Teardrops From My Eyes-Ruth Brown
4. Mona Lisa-Nat "King" Cole
5. Tennessee Waltz-Patti Page
6. Long Gone Lonesome Blues-Hank Williams
7. Mardi Gras In New Orleans-Professor Longhair
8. I'm Movin' On-Hank Snow
9. Rollin' Stone-Muddy Waters
10. Double Crossing Blues-Johnny Otis (Little Esther & the Robins)

1951
1. Sixty Minute Man-Dominoes
2. Rocket 88-Jackie Brenston
3. Dust My Broom-Elmore James
4. Cry-Johnnie Ray
5. Too Young-Nat "King" Cole
6. Cold Cold Heart-Hank Williams
7. Glory of Love-Five Keys
8. Three O'Clock Blues-B.B. King
9. Hey Good Lookin'-Hank Williams
10. How High The Moon-Les Paul & Mary Ford

1952
1. Lawdy Miss Clawdy-Lloyd Price
2. Jambalaya (On The Bayou)-Hank Williams
3. Have Mercy Baby-Dominoes
4. One Mint Julep-Clovers
5. Night Train-Jimmy Forrest
6. My Song-Johnny Ace
7. Goin' Home-Fats Domino
8. Moody Mood For Love-King Pleasure
9. Juke-Little Walter
10. Baby, Don't Do It-"5" Royales

1953

1. Money Honey-Drifters featuring Clyde McPhatter
2. Your Cheatin' Heart-Hank Williams
3. Crying In The Chapel-Orioles
4. Gee-Crows
5. Shake a Hand-Faye Adams
6. Honey Hush-Joe Turner
7. Mama, He Treats Your Daughter Mean-Ruth Brown
8. Hound Dog-Willie Mae "Big Mama" Thornton
9. Kaw-Liga-Hank Williams
10. The Things That I Used To Do-Guitar Slim

1954

1. Rock Around The Clock-Bill Haley & His Comets
2. Shake, Rattle and Roll-Joe Turner/Bill Haley & His Comets
3. Earth Angel-Penguins
4. Sh-Boom-Chords
5. That's All Right-Elvis Presley with Scotty and Bill
6. Pledging My Love-Johnny Ace
7. Goodnite Sweetheart Goodnite-Spaniels
8. I've Got a Woman-Ray Charles
9. White Christmas-Drifters featuring Clyde McPhatter
10. Work With Me Annie-Royals/Midnighters

1955

1. Tutti Frutti-Little Richard
2. Maybellene-Chuck Berry
3. Bo Diddley-Bo Diddley
4. Why Do Fools Fall in Love?-Teenagers
5. The Great Pretender-Platters
6. Ain't That a Shame-Fats Domino
7. Folsom Prison Blues-Johnny Cash and the Tennessee Two
8. Speedo-Cadillacs
9. Story Untold-Nutmegs
10. My Babe-Little Walter

1956

1. Hound Dog-Elvis Presley
2. Long Tall Sally-Little Richard
3. Blue Suede Shoes-Carl Perkins/Elvis Presley
4. Don't Be Cruel-Elvis Presley
5. Be-Bop-a-Lula-Gene Vincent & the Bluecaps
6. Roll Over Beethoven-Chuck Berry
7. In the Still of the Night-Five Satins
8. Blueberry Hill-Fats Domino
9. Please, Please, Please-James Brown & the Famous Flames
10. I Walk The Line-Johnny Cash and the Tennessee Two

1957

1. Jailhouse Rock-Elvis Presley
2. Whole Lotta Shakin' Going On-Jerry Lee Lewis
3. That'll Be the Day-Crickets
4. Bye Bye Love-Everly Brothers

5. Great Balls of Fire-Jerry Lee Lewis
6. School Day-Chuck Berry
7. Rock and Roll Music-Chuck Berry
8. Peggy Sue-Buddy Holly
9. Lucille-Little Richard
10. Rocking Pneumonia & the Boogie Woogie Flu-Huey "Piano" Smith & the Clowns

1958

1. Johnny B. Goode-Chuck Berry
2. Summertime Blues-Eddie Cochran
3. Good Golly Miss Molly-Little Richard
4. For Your Precious Love-Jerry Butler & the Impressions
5. Sweet Little Sixteen-Chuck Berry
6. Yakety Yak-Coasters
7. La Bamba-Ritchie Valens
8. Since I Don't Have You-Skyliners
9. Rumble-Link Wray
10. Lonely Teardrops-Jackie Wilson

1959

1. What'd I Say-Ray Charles
2. I Only Have Eyes for You-Flamingos
3. Mack the Knife-Bobby Darin
4. There Goes My Baby-Drifters
5. Shout-Isley Brothers
6. Kansas City-Wilbert Harrison
7. Poison Ivy-Coasters
8. Money-Barrett Strong
9. Love Potion No. 9-Clovers
10. You're So Fine-Falcons

Music Trivia

- Little Richard's song "Tutti Frutti" originally contained the lyrics "Tutti Frutti, good booty," but in 1955, Specialty Records had songwriter Dorothy LaBostrie tame it down to "Tutti Frutti, oh Rudy."
- Ray Charles's 1959 release "What'd I Say" was created on the spot when he ran out of songs during a marathon dance show in Pittsburgh; concerning the sexy vocal bridge that made the song famous, Charles said, "Hell, let's face it, everybody knows about the ummmmh, unnnh. That's how we all got here."
- The rock 'n' roll song "Johnny B. Goode" by Chuck Berry, which was released in 1958, originally contained the words "That little colored boy could play," but was changed to "country boy" so the record could get airtime on the radio.
- Elvis Presley's release of "Hound Dog" in 1956 went through 31 takes at the RCA studios in New York. "I don't care what you say," he told a reporter. "It ain't nasty."
- The title of the Buddy Holly and the Crickets song "That'll Be the Day" came from a recurring line in the John Wayne Western movie *The Searchers*.
- Fats Domino's biggest hit "Blueberry Hill," released in 1956, was originally recorded by Gene Autry in 1940.

Inventor of the Microchip

As Americans continued to be obsessed with catching up with the Russians after their successful Sputnik launch, Jack Kirby, electrical engineer at Texas Instruments, was charged with creating a smaller, better, faster computer. Competition was stiff, and in 1959, Jack Kirby and another inventor filed for patents for the microchip.

Life at Home

- Jack Kilby was one of several dozen scientists struggling with the complexities of the integrated circuit.
- Already vales, relays and wires had given way to transistors, diodes and interconnects, dramatically improving reliability, but the challenge that loomed was how to use solid block materials such as silicon to connect all the key components needed for electronic systems.
- Jack was well prepared for the challenge.
- Born in 1923, Jack grew up in Great Bend, Kansas, where his father ran a small electric company that provided power to customers scattered across the rural western part of Kansas.
- During the summers, Jack accompanied his father on trips, often crawling through generating stations looking for faulty equipment, and got an education in the power of electricity to transform rural America.
- While Jack was in high school, a huge ice storm knocked down most of the poles that carried the telephone and electric power lines, so his father worked with amateur radio operators to communicate with customers who had lost their electricity and phone service.
- That experience with amateur radio sparked Jack's interest in electronics, and "that's when I decided that this field was something I wanted to pursue," he said years later.
- After high school, Jack planned to attend MIT but failed to get a passing mark on the entrance exam so instead entered the University of Illinois, where most of his classes were in electrical power.
- Four months after he entered college, the Japanese attack on Pearl Harbor compelled Jack to enlist and he spent part of his service in India, where he was assigned to radio repair.
- When he returned home from the war, he re-entered college and took some vacuum tube engineering and physics classes.

Jack Kilby invented the microchip.

- He graduated in 1947, just one year before Bell Labs announced the invention of the transistor, an innovation that rendered vacuum tubes obsolete.
- His first job was with an electronics manufacturer in Milwaukee, Wisconsin, that made parts for radios, televisions and hearing aids.
- There he worked on silk-screening techniques for printing a substrate onto which germanium transistors could be soldered—an important introduction into the integration of circuits.
- While still working in Milwaukee, Jack took evening classes at the University of Wisconsin towards a master's degree in electrical engineering.
- In 1958, he and his wife moved to Dallas, Texas, where Jack took a job with Texas Instruments, the only company willing to let him work full-time on electronic component miniaturization.
- Texas Instruments (TI) was founded to manufacture the newly invented transistor, but its roots stretched back to 1930 when Dr. J. Clarence Karcher and Eugene McDermott founded Geophysical Service, a pioneering provider of seismic exploration services to the petroleum industry.
- In 1939, the company reorganized as Coronado Corporation, with Geophysical Service Inc. (GSI) as a subsidiary.
- Two years later, on the day before the attack on Pearl Harbor, McDermott along with three other GSI employees purchased GSI and built submarine detection equipment for the U.S. Navy, discovering that the rugged nature of the equipment they built for the oil industry was similar to the military's equipment needs.
- In 1951, the company changed its name to Texas Instruments.
- Early in 1952, Texas Instruments purchased a patent license to produce germanium transistors from Western Electric Company, the manufacturing arm of AT&T, for $25,000 and hired Gordon K. Teal away from Bell Labs as research director.
- Teal brought expertise in semiconductor crystals that attracted talented scientists and engineers who were fascinated by the new and rapidly expanding semiconductor industry.

Life at Work: Electrical Engineer and Inventor

- During his first summer at Texas Instruments, Jack Kilby, as a new employee, had no vacation time coming and was left alone to work in the lab.
- The problem was simple: cut the distance that electrical impulses traveled so that computers could be smaller, more reliable, and faster.
- The solution, however, was complicated.
- After the launch of the Sputnik satellite in 1957, Americans became obsessed with "catching up" with the Russians and Jack was on the front lines of the technological battle.
- Slow-talking Jack considered himself an engineer, not a scientist.
- Engineers, he believed, were practical-minded people who made things work better, cheaper and more easily, compared to scientists who thought big thoughts that never went anywhere.
- Since no school in America taught one how to be an inventor, Jack felt that creating something new simply needed hard work.
- His job that summer was getting to the core of the problem as quickly as possible, searching for the unexpected and ignoring the obvious, even when doing so violated scientific convention.
- He also needed an affordable solution, because the more expensive a product was the less useful it would be.
- Jack knew it was possible to make diodes and transistors out of silicon if properly doped with the right impurities to conduct an electrical charge.
- He wrote in his lab notebook, "The following circuit elements could be made on a single slice: resisters, capacitors, distributed capacitors and transistors."

- Designing a complex electronic machine normally increased the number of components involved in order to make technical advances, unless there was a way to form a monolithic, single-crystal integrated circuit.
- When his new boss, Willis Adcock, returned from vacation, Jack explained his concept and requested funds to construct a model around his idea.
- That's when a deal was struck.
- If Jack could construct a working capacitor and a working transistor on separate pieces of silicon, funds would be found for an integrated circuit on a chip.
- The commercial race to financial success was also underway.
- In January 1954, Bell Labs created the first workable silicon transistor; working independently, TI unveiled the first commercial silicon transistor four months later.
- The breakthrough that began the "Silicon Age" occurred in early 1955, when Bell Labs invented the diffused-base silicon transistor created by solid-state diffusion of impurities—work critical to Jack's later discoveries.
- To increase the consumer demand for transistors, TI manufactured the first transistor radio using germanium transistors because silicon transistors were so expensive.
- Even though Texas Instruments had invested millions to develop equipment capable of purifying silicon and to build silicon transistors, few were suggesting that components be manufactured out of semiconductor material—before Jack went to work for TI.
- Jack created a circuit known as a phase-shift oscillator to complete his part of the deal and get his funding.
- Working with borrowed and improvised equipment, Jack then built the first electronic circuit in which all of the components, both active and passive, were fabricated in a single piece of semiconductor material half the size of a paper clip.
- Though the device he showed colleagues was relatively simple—only a transistor and other components on a slice of germanium—few realized that he was about to revolutionize the electronics industry.
- "Humankind eventually would have solved the matter, but I had the fortunate experience of being the first person with the right idea and the right resources available at the right time in history," Jack said.
- "What we didn't realize then was that the integrated circuit would reduce the cost of electronic functions by a factor of a million to one; nothing had ever done that for anything before."

Love Field, Dallas, Texas

- Six months later, Robert Noyce of Fairchild Semiconductor independently developed the integrated circuit with integrated interconnect.
- Both men filed for patents in 1959, igniting a battle that would last another decade.

Life in the Community: Dallas, Texas
- Dallas prided itself on being a city that liked to do business.

- In 1949, *Fortune* magazine remarked that Dallas was "a monument to sheer determination."
- City fathers bragged that "people do not come to Dallas looking for history but for progress."
- Located in North Texas, Dallas lacked the port facilities that defined most major cities, but sustained its growth as a center for the oil and cotton industries, thanks to its numerous railroad lines.
- Founded in 1841 and formally incorporated as a city in February 1856, Dallas primarily based its early economy on railroad transportation, publishing, lumbering and saddle manufacturing.
- By the turn of the twentieth century, Dallas was the leading drug, book, jewelry, and wholesale liquor market in the Southwestern United States.
- As the century progressed, Dallas transformed from an agricultural center to a center of banking, insurance, fashion retailing and other businesses, including the founding of Neiman Marcus.
- In 1911, Dallas became the location of the Eleventh Regional Branch of the Federal Reserve Bank, and millionaire Dr. William Worthington Samuell purchased the first ambulance for the city.
- In 1915, the Southern Methodist University opened.
- Aviation became a major industry in the city in World War I, when Love Field was established as an aviation training ground.
- Despite the onset of the Great Depression for most of the nation, construction flourished in Dallas in 1930, and Columbus Marion "Dad" Joiner struck oil 100 miles east of Dallas in Kilgore, spawning the East Texas oil boom.
- Dallas quickly assumed the role of financial center for the oil industry in Texas and Oklahoma, and its banks made loans to develop the oil fields.
- In 1936, Texas chose Dallas as the site of the Texas Centennial Exposition, attracting 10 million visitors.
- During World War II, Dallas served as a manufacturing center for the war effort; the Ford Motor plant in Dallas converted to wartime production.
- In 1957, developers Trammell Crow and John M. Stemmons opened a Home Furnishings Mart that grew into the Dallas Market Center, the largest wholesale trade complex in the world.
- The integrated circuit invented by Jack Kilby of Texas Instruments punctuated the Dallas area's development as a center for high-technology manufacturing.
- The city soon became the nation's third-largest technology center, with the growth of such companies as LTV Corporation and Texas Instruments.

Transistorized Sets Are Economical, Too,
The Brownsville Herald (Texas), August 5, 1958

A Texas company has perfected the television receiver that all but does away with vacuum tubes, the main source of trouble in TV set breakdowns.

The company is Texas Instruments, which makes transistors. It has substituted transistors for vacuum tubes. The only tubes in a transistorized Texas Instruments receiver are the picture and a high-voltage rectifier.

"The only reason we haven't got a transistor where we used the high-voltage rectifier is because the cost would be prohibitive," Cecil Lightfoot of Texas Instruments said. "We have the transistor."

Texas Instruments' transistor TV set was shown last week at the Texas Electronic Association meeting in Dallas. It has a nine-inch picture tube and weighs a total of 39 pounds, including battery.

The transistors require so little current—a little over eight watts, in this case, as opposed to 90 watts for an ordinary television set—that a battery will operate the set. The battery will operate the set for about four hours and it can be recharged by attaching it to the house current.

The set receives stations on a par with a vacuum tube set. Lightfoot said the difference in cost between it and the vacuum tube set is about the same as it is between a radio receiver with vacuum tubes and one with a transistorized circuit, if the set were in production.

Transistorized radios cost about three times more. Actually, Texas Instruments' TV is not for sale. It was built by the company's engineers to show TV manufacturers that it can be done. The set will not be put into production by Texas Instruments.

Transistorized television receivers should reduce television repair cost dramatically, since transistors last 20 to 25 years.

Inventions: 1950 to 1959

1950: Ralph Schneider invented the credit card.

1951: Super Glue was invented.

Francis W. Davis invented power steering.

Charles Ginsburg invented the first video tape recorder (VTR).

1952: Mr. Potato Head was patented.

The first patent for bar code was issued to inventors Joseph Woodland and Bernard Silver.

The first diet soft drink, a sugar-free ginger ale intended for diabetics, was sold.

Edward Teller and his team built the hydrogen bomb.

1953: Radial tires were invented.

RCA invented the first musical synthesizer.

David Warren invented the black box flight recorder.

Texas Instruments invented the transistor radio.

1954: An oral contraceptive for women (the "pill") was invented.

The first nonstick Teflon pan was produced.

Chaplin, Fuller and Pearson invented the solar cell.

1955: Tetracycline was invented.

Optical fiber was invented.

1956: The first computer hard disk was used.

Christopher Cockerell invented the hovercraft.

Bette Nesmith Graham invented "Mistake Out," later renamed Liquid Paper, to paint over mistakes made with a typewriter.

1957: The Fortran computer language was invented.

1958: The computer modem was invented.

Gordon Gould invented the laser.

Richard Knerr and Arthur "Spud" Melin invented the Hula Hoop.

Jack Kilby and Robert Noyce invented the integrated circuit.

1959: Wilson Greatbatch invented the internal pacemaker.

Ruth Handler (the co-founder of Mattel) invented the Barbie Doll, named after her own daughter Barbara.

Jack Kilby and Robert Noyce both invented the microchip.

SHOULD YOU BUY A FOREIGN CAR?

POPULAR MECHANICS

WRITTEN SO YOU CAN UNDERSTAND IT

AUGUST 1959

35 CENTS

RACE TO THE MOON
Are the Russians Ahead?

Hospital Worker and Union Organizer

Nidia Fernandez dropped out of high school to help her single mother, and learned the value of labor unions from her father. She was asked to join a new hospital workers union when she was a nursing assistant at Mount Sinai Hospital in New York City. When they voted to strike, she proudly joined the picket line, an action that resulted in improved wages and working conditions.

Life at Home

- Nidia Fernandez was born in 1930 in Paterson, New Jersey.
- She was the second child and only daughter of Juan Fernandez and Alicia Juarez.
- Her mother's parents were born in New Jersey and her father's parents immigrated to America from Puerto Rico.
- When Nidia was a toddler, her parents divorced and she moved to New York City with her mother and two brothers.
- As a single parent during the Great Depression, her mother struggled, working at a cannery at night and as a waitress during the day while her father helped watch the children.
- Nidia enjoyed a close relationship with her grandfather, who called her "seven tongues" because she always talked so much.
- During the 1940s and the onset of the war economy, her family's financial situation improved.
- Nidia's mother remarried and became the owner of a restaurant and hotel visited by Japanese, Chinese, Jews, Filipinos, and Puerto Ricans.
- At age 16, Nidia dropped out of school to work.
- She and her mother were often at odds, mostly about the boys with whom Nidia associated.
- Nidia began spending more time with her biological father, who taught her about the role unions played in helping workers gain their rights.
- In 1913 Paterson was the site of a major labor strike initiated by 800 broad silk weavers who were soon joined by ribbon weavers and dry house workers.
- The strike affected 300 mill and dye houses and 24,000 workers.
- Their demands included wage increases, the establishment of an eight-hour workday, and abolition of the four-loom system in broad cloth that required workers to service multiple looms.
- More than 2,000 workers allowed themselves to be arrested, flooding the jails and disrupting the courts.

Nidia Fernandez led her hospital co-workers to better working conditions.

- After several months of bitter picketing, the English-speaking and better-paid workers returned to work, breaking the back of the strike.
- This story taught Nidia that well-organized unions were the only way workers could gain the strength to demand a fair share.
- She was shocked that most unions were reluctant to accept women workers, but gender restrictions fell quickly under the pace of World War II production demands.
- Both the government and women workers applied pressure to open the doors of the unions.
- The International Association of Machinists; the Molders and Foundry Workers; the Iron Shipbuilders and Helpers; and the Carpenters and Joiners admitted women soon after the attack on Pearl Harbor.
- In the fall of 1942, the intransigent International Brotherhood of Boilermakers admitted women to its membership for the first time in its 62-year history.
- By 1944, 11 national unions reported more than 40,000 women members.
- By the war's end, nearly all AFL and CIO unions had accepted women, although many local unions remained opposed to their admission and many still remained closed to women of color.
- In 1948, Nidia took a job in a New York cafeteria, convinced that worker solidarity and clear demands would win the day.
- The prosperous economy of post-World War II America was creating many new jobs, but most of the best-paying jobs were going to men.
- After three months on her first job, Nidia demanded equal pay with men and bathroom break privileges and was promptly fired as a troublemaker.

Life at Work: Hospital Worker and Union Organizer

- In the winter of 1958, when Nidia Fernandez was approached about her participation in a new hospital worker's union, she asked a lot of questions.
- Twenty-nine, divorced and the mother of two, she was cautious about where she spoke out.
- She was a nursing assistant for three years at Mount Sinai Hospital in New York City where the work was steady and predictable, but the pay was poor.
- Nonprofit or voluntary hospitals claimed that they generated so few revenues, they should not be expected to pay competitive wages.
- "A hospital is not an economic, industrial unit," declared Dr. Martin Steinberg, director of Mount Sinai. "It is a social unit.... Human life should not be a pawn in jousting for economic gain or power."
- Most of the larger unions already had passed on proposals to organize legions of hospital workers, most of whom were black and Puerto Rican women.
- But Union Local 1199 had a long history of uniting diverse groups.
- Founded in 1932 by progressive pharmacists and clerks, 1199 and its leaders were guided by the slogan "An injury to one is an injury to all."
- In 1958, when 1199 undertook a campaign to organize New York City's voluntary hospital workers, most traditional labor leaders marked it for failure.
- The modest 5,000-member 1199 accepted the challenge almost by accident, when a black porter at the Montefiore Hospital happened to compare his wages and conditions with those of a relative who worked as a porter in a Bronx pharmacy.
- The unrepresented hospital porter was being paid $36.00 for a 44-hour week, while the drugstore porter, who worked for a 1199-unionized pharmacy, was earning $72.00 for 40 hours.
- In addition, the unionized employee was covered by an employer-financed pension plan and health and welfare protection.
- Disturbed by the difference, the Montefiore porter assembled a group of co-workers and went to the 1199 for support.

- The union assigned Elliott Godoff, who was formerly with the teamsters, to organize the workers; Theodore Mitchell, a black drugstore porter, was named to assist.
- Their goal was to organize bedpan emptiers, dietary aides and laundry room workers, most of whom were underrepresented Latin American, black or Puerto Rican women, in New York City's hospitals.
- Within three months, 600 of the 800 workers joined the union.
- The average wages were $34.00 to $38.00 a week for most and $50.00 to $55.00 for laboratory technicians.
- The union invited the hospital to negotiate wages, benefits and union representation.
- The hospital declined, stating clearly and accurately that employees of voluntary hospitals were excluded from labor legislation protection.
- Petitions, telegrams and several meetings failed to move the hospital trustees.

Hospital workers met with union leaders

- Even a much-sought-after union endorsement in *The New York Times* failed to persuade hospital administrators.
- The dam broke when, in December 1958, Montefiore workers voted overwhelmingly for 1199.
- Mount Sinai workers got into the act on March 6, 1959, when 800 workers boycotted the cafeteria in a lunch-hour demonstration.
- The workers, including Nidia, demanded that the hospital recognize the union.
- In all, 3,500 workers, including elevator operators, orderlies, nursing aides, kitchen workers and other housekeeping employees, exchanged their jobs for the picket line.
- When the New York hospital workers strike began, Nidia had no savings, but was living paycheck to paycheck since her divorce five years earlier.
- Every morning of the strike she dressed carefully and joined her fellow strikers on the picket line.
- She was proud to walk the line every morning and yell at the strike-breaking scabs who had picked a pitiful paycheck over union solidarity.
- Nidia's sign declared, "Mount Sinai workers can't live on $32.00 a week. ON STRIKE. Please help us win."
- She was proud that the newspapers described the picketers as "a bedraggled army" and invigorated when the same newspapers pointed out that the strikes made New York City's hospital workers the first employees in private, nonprofit hospitals in the nation to unionize.
- She never dreamed that the strike would last so long and attract national attention.
- For its part, the union leadership decried the "shameful working conditions" that "threaten the health of the infants and children of these workers...and breed juvenile delinquency, crime and violence."
- The Greater New York Hospital Association countered, "This is not a strike, but revolution against law and order."
- As far as Nidia was concerned, the secret weapon was the national attention the strike was attracting, thanks to its links with the civil rights movement.
- Starting in 1956, the union had solicited membership funds to support the Montgomery, Alabama bus boycott.
- As a result the union established a friendship with Dr. Martin Luther King, Jr., leader of the boycott.
- To rally public support, Local 1199 lined up backing from civil rights leaders like Dr. King, Bayard Rustin, A. Philip Randolph, and many elected officials and editorial writers.

- Dr. King, who described 1199 as his "favorite union," called the fight to raise wages for the $30.00-a-week workers a civil rights struggle.
- But links to Dr. King were only one of the workers' strengths.
- The hospital workers' strike also captured the attention of traditional labor leaders like NYC Central Labor Council President Harry Van Arsdale who saw the strike as a means of uniting the labor movement in the city.

Martin Luther King's family supported his alliance with the hospital workers' union.

- First, he participated in the marathon negotiating sessions with the hospital, then, he led 700 unionists in joining the picketers at Beth Israel Hospital.
- Nidia had been told repeatedly that the labor leaders themselves never walked the line so now she knew this strike would be successful.
- The bitter fight for recognition lasted 46 days during which the poor, undereducated workers had not been broken as the men downtown on both sides of the issue had predicted.
- But in the end the union was not recognized, despite a New York judge's accusation that the hospital management's refusal to recognize the union was an "echo of the nineteenth century."
- Management only agreed to arbitration.
- The final agreement guaranteed "no discrimination against any employee because he joins a union"; a minimum wage of $1.00 an hour; wage increases of $5.00 a week; a 40-hour week; time and a half for overtime; seniority rules; job grades; and rate changes.

Labor Timeline

1910: A bomb destroyed a portion of the Llewellyn Ironworks in Los Angeles, where a bitter strike was in progress.

1911: The Supreme Court ordered the AFL to cease its promotion of a boycott against the Bucks Stove and Range Company.

The Triangle Shirtwaist Company fire in New York City resulted in the death of 147 people, mostly women and young girls working in sweatshop conditions.

1912: Women and children were beaten by police during a textile strike in Lawrence, Massachusetts.

The National Guard was called out against striking West Virginia coal miners.

1913: Police shot three maritime workers during a strike against the United Fruit Company in New Orleans.

1914: The Ford Motor Company raised its basic wage from $2.40 for a nine-hour day to $5.00 for an eight-hour day.

Five men, two women and 12 children died in the "Ludlow Massacre" when company guards attempted to break a strike at Colorado's Ludlow Mine Field.

A Western Federation of Miners strike was crushed by the militia in Butte, Montana.

1915: Labor leader Joe Hill was arrested in Salt Lake City on murder charges and executed 21 months later despite worldwide protests and two attempts to intervene by President Woodrow Wilson.

Twenty rioting strikers were shot by factory guards in Roosevelt, New Jersey.

The Supreme Court upheld "yellow dog" contracts, which forbade membership in labor unions.

1916: A bomb set off during a "Preparedness Day" parade in San Francisco killed 10 and resulted in the conviction of Thomas J. Mooney, a labor organizer, and Warren K. Billings, a shoe worker.

Riots erupted during a strike at Everett Mills, Everett, Washington; local police watched and refused to intervene, resulting in the death of seven workers.

Federal employees won the right to receive worker's compensation insurance.

1917: Vigilantes forced 1,185 striking copper miners in Bisbee, Arizona, into manure-laden boxcars and "deported" them to the New Mexico desert.

The Supreme Court approved the Eight-Hour Act under the threat of a national railway strike.

Industrial Workers of the World (IWW) organizer Frank Little was lynched in Butte, Montana.

Federal agents raided the IWW headquarters in 48 cities.

1919: United Mine Worker organizer Fannie Sellins was gunned down by company guards in Brackenridge, Pennsylvania.

Looting and violence erupted in Boston after 1,117 Boston policemen declared a work stoppage to gain union representation.

Three hundred fifty thousand steel workers walked off their jobs to demand union recognition.

IWW organizer Wesley Everest was lynched after a Centralia, Washington IWW hall was attacked by Legionnaires.

Approximately 250 "anarchists," "communists," and "labor agitators" were deported to Russia, marking the beginning of the so-called "Red Scare."

1920: The U.S. Bureau of Investigation began carrying out the nationwide Palmer Raids, seizing labor leaders and literature to discourage labor activity.

Seven management detectives and two coal miners were killed in the Battle of Matewan in West Virginia.

1922: Violence resulted in the deaths of 36 people during a coal miners' strike in Herrin, Illinois.

1924: Congress approved a child labor amendment to the U.S. Constitution; only 28 of the necessary 36 states ratified it.

1925: Two company houses occupied by non-union coal miners were blown up by labor "racketeers" during a strike against the Glendale Gas and Coal Company in Wheeling, West Virginia.

1926: Textile workers fought with police in Passaic, New Jersey, during a year-long strike.

1930: Labor racketeers shot and killed contractor William Healy, with whom the Chicago Marble Setters Union had been having difficulties.

One hundred farm workers were arrested for their unionizing activities in Imperial Valley, California.

1931: Vigilantes attacked striking miners in Harlan County, Kentucky.

1932: Police killed striking workers at Ford's Dearborn, Michigan plant.

1933: Eighteen thousand cotton workers went on strike in Pixley, California.

1934: During the Electric Auto-Lite Strike in Toledo, Ohio, two strikers were killed and over 200 wounded by National Guardsmen.

Police stormed striking truck drivers in Minneapolis who were attempting to prevent truck movement in the market area.

A strike in Woonsocket, Rhode Island, directed at obtaining a minimum wage for textile workers, resulted in over 420,000 workers striking nationwide.

1935: The Committee for Industrial Organization (CIO) was formed to expand industrial unionism.

1937: General Motors recognized the United Auto Workers Union following a sit-down strike.

Police killed 10 and wounded 30 during the "Memorial Day Massacre" at the Republic Steel plant in Chicago.

1938: The Wages and Hours Act was passed, banning child labor and setting the 40-hour work week.

1939: The Supreme Court ruled that sit-down strikes were illegal.

1941: Henry Ford recognized the United Auto Workers.

The AFL agreed that there would be no strikes in defense-related industry plants for the duration of the war.

1944: President Franklin D. Roosevelt ordered the army to seize the executive offices of Montgomery Ward and Company after the corporation failed to comply with a National War Labor Board directive regarding union shops.

1946: Packinghouse workers nationwide went on strike.

Four hundred thousand mine workers struck.

The U.S. Navy seized oil refineries to break a 20-state postwar strike.

1947: The Taft-Hartley Labor Act, curbing strikes, was vetoed by President Harry Truman but overridden by Congress.

1948: Labor leader Walter Reuther was shot and seriously wounded by would-be assassins.

1950: President Truman ordered the U.S. Army to seize all the nation's railroads to prevent a general strike.

1952: President Truman ordered the U.S. Army to seize the nation's steel mills to avert a strike; the order was later ruled to be illegal by the Supreme Court.

1955: The two largest labor organizations in the U.S. merged to form the AFL-CIO, with a membership estimated at 15 million.

1956: Columnist Victor Riesel, a crusader against labor racketeers, was blinded when a hired assailant threw sulfuric acid in his face.

1959: The Landrum-Griffin Act passed, restricting union activity.

The Taft-Hartley Act was invoked by the Supreme Court to break a steel strike.

> Men make history and not the other way around. In periods where there is no leadership, society stands still. Progress occurs when courageous, skillful leaders seize the opportunity to change things for the better.
>
> —*Former President Harry S. Truman, 1959*

Victims of Charity, Dan Wakefield, *Nation*, March 14, 1959

A Negro lady from the nurses' aides' department spoke up to say: "We're doing pretty good in our department, but a lotta people are afraid-they think they're gonna be fired. And some of the nurses told the girls they shouldn't join a union because then the hospital would be like a 'business.' "

The others hooted, and one voice raised above the rest to say, "It's all right for the nurses to talk; they get plenty and they don't want us to get it."

A lady from the kitchen staff raised her hand and reported that "the ladies in the cafeteria say they get paid mostly by tips and the union can't help them. One of the supervisors said the union can't help us, we'll still have to work no matter what the union does. Well, all I know is when I see those people making $32.00 a week, I'm ready to join anything."

A.H. Raskin, *The New York Times*, May 29, 1959

They seem determined to carry on indefinitely. THEY say they are tired of being "philanthropists" subsidizing the hospitals with their labor. One girl picketer said: "Whenever we feel disheartened, we can always take out the stub of our last paycheck and get new heart for picketing." She pulled out her own and showed that it came to $27.00 in weekly take-home....

Financial hardship has been a part of their life so long that the prospect of higher pay is less of a goal for many than the pivotal issue of union recognition. They feel for the first time that they "belong" and this groping for human dignity through group recognition is more important than more cash.

6-Hospital Strike Delayed 2 Weeks, Union Bars Walkout Today After Hospitals Agree to Consider Fact Finding, Ralph Katz, *The New York Times*, April 22, 1959

A strike of nonprofessional employees at six voluntary hospitals, scheduled for 6 a.m. today, was deferred last night for two weeks. The union agreed to put off action while the hospital boards of trustees considered a fact-finding formula.

The development was announced by Mayor Wagner at 11 p.m. after a series of conferences at City Hall with union and management representatives. Earlier it appeared the strike was inevitable.

Talks had begun at 10 a.m. yesterday. By 8 p.m. it appeared that Local 1199 of the Retail Drug Employees Union would proceed with plans to call out its membership among the hospitals' 4,550 nonprofessional employees. The union claims 3,450 of the workers as members.

At issue is the union demand for recognition as collective-bargaining agent. The two-week delay was offered, the Mayor said, because five of the six hospitals are Jewish institutions. The Jewish High Holy Days of Passover begin at sundown tonight.

SECTION TWO: HISTORICAL SNAPSHOT

The 1950s in America was a happy time. Opportunity and optimism was everywhere and Americans were enjoying life. Inventions made life easier, from TV dinners to the BankAmericard credit card, to birth control pills. Music changed direction with the Motown sound, and theater productions combined classic genres like opera and ballet with contemporary beats. The melting pot got a little bigger, and Americans fought to keep Communism off our shores. These **Historical Snapshots** *highlight significant firsts and milestones as we ate instant mashed potatoes in front of The Ed Sullivan Show.*

Early 1950s

- Auto registrations showed one car for every 3.7 Americans
- Blue Cross insurance programs covered 3.7 million Americans
- Five million homes had television sets and 45 million had radios
- President Harry Truman ordered the Atomic Energy Committee to develop the hydrogen bomb
- Boston Red Sox Ted Williams became baseball's highest paid player at $125,000
- Senator Joseph McCarthy announced that he had a list of 205 known Communists in the State Department
- Otis Elevator installed the first passenger elevator with self-opening doors
- Coca-Cola's share of the U.S. cola market was 69 percent vs. Pepsi-Cola's 15 percent
- The FBI issued its first list of the Ten Most Wanted Criminals
- The first human kidney transplant was performed on a 49-year old woman in Chicago
- Charles M. Schultz's comic strip, *Peanuts*, debuted in eight newspapers
- Smokey the Bear, an orphaned cub found after a forest fire in New Mexico, became the living symbol of the U.S. Forestry Service
- *Betty Crocker's Picture Cookbook* was published
- Miss Clairol hair coloring and Minute Rice were marketed for the first time
- M&M candy, created in 1940, was stamped with an "M" to assure customers of the real thing
- The first Xerox copy machine was introduced
- The average cost of four years of college was $1,800, up 400 percent since 1900
- The 22nd Amendment to the Constitution, limiting the U.S. president to two terms, was adopted

- Univak, the first general-purpose electronic computer, was dedicated in Philadelphia
- CBS introduced color television in a program hosted by Ed Sullivan and Arthur Godfrey
- Lacoste tennis shirts with an alligator symbol were introduced in the U.S. by French manufacturer Izod
- Earl Tupper created the home sale party to market his plastic storage containers
- *Jet* news magazine was launched
- Chrysler Corporation introduced power steering in cars
- More than 75 percent of all U.S. farms were now electrified
- Harvard Law School admitted its first woman student
- H&R Block began offering tax preparation when the IRS stopped this service
- Margaret Sanger urged the development of an oral contraceptive
- Massive flooding covered more than a million acres of land in Oklahoma, Kansas, Missouri and Illinois
- The latest census reported that eight percent of the population was more than 65 years old, up from four percent in 1900
- For the first time in history, women outnumbered men in the United States
- Julius and Ethel Rosenberg were sentenced to death for espionage against the U.S.
- When Sioux City (Iowa) Memorial Park refused to bury Native American John Rice, who died in combat, President Truman dispatched an air force plane to retrieve his remains which were interred in Arlington National Cemetery
- Sugarless chewing gum, dacron suits, and telephone company answering service all made their first appearance
- Charles F. Blair flew solo over the North Pole
- Entertainer Milton Berle signed a 30-year, million-dollar-plus contract with NBC
- New York and other major cities increased the cost of a phone call from $0.05 to $0.10
- Women comprised 28.9 percent of the American workforce outside the home, up from 14.7 percent in 1880 and 21.4 percent in 1920
- The Topps Chewing Gum Company added statistics and biographic information to its colorful baseball cards

- Metropolitan Life Insurance Company reported a link between obesity and early mortality
- The median age at first marriage was 23 years for men and 19.8 years for women
- The Screen Actors Guild adopted by-laws banning communists from membership
- New York subway fares rose $0.05 to $0.15
- 30 million Americans attended classical music performances and 7.2 million children took music lessons
- The Dow-Jones Industrial Average reached a high of 293 and a low of 255
- Per-capita state taxes averaged $68.04
- An airmail stamp cost $0.07 per ounce, and a postcard, $0.02
- All-black military units had nearly disappeared as 90 percent of the military was integrated

- Leland Kirdel wrote in *Coronet* magazine: "The smart woman will keep herself desirable. It is her duty to be feminine and desirable at all times in the eyes of the opposite sex."
- In the wave of McCarthyism, libraries were ordered to remove books by "communists, fellow travelers and the like"
- Lucille Ball and Desi Arnaz signed an $8 million contract to continue *I Love Lucy* for 30 months
- *TV Guide* and *Playboy* began publication
- The number of comic books surged, comprising about 650 titles
- Twenty-five percent of young Americans were attending college, thanks to the GI Bill—an increase of 65 percent from before the Second World War
- During his inaugural address, President Dwight D. Eisenhower called on Americans to make whatever sacrifices may be necessary to meet the threat of Soviet aggression, and defined the Cold War as freedom against slavery
- General Motors introduced the Chevrolet Corvette, the first plastic laminated fiberglass sports car costing $3,250
- Elvis Presley paid $4.00 to cut *My Happiness* in Memphis for his mother's birthday
- Bell Aircraft Corporation landed a $35 million contract to make a guided missile
- Four out of five men's shirts sold in America were white
- The DC-7 propeller plane, Sugar Smacks, and 3-D cartoons all made their first appearance

Mid 1950s

- RCA sold the first color TV sets, priced at $1,000 each
- Felt skirts with poodle appliques swept the teenage fashion world
- Panty raids, roller-skating marathons and ducktail haircuts gained popularity
- Disney's TV program *Davy Crockett* ignited a national demand for coonskin hats
- A Gallup poll reported that a family of four could live on $60 a week
- Newspaper vending machines, breath-inhaled alcohol detectors, and Levi's faded blue jeans all made their first appearance
- Unemployment rose to 5.5 percent

- *On the Waterfront* with Marlon Brando won the Academy Award for Best Picture and *The Teahouse of the August Moon* by John Patrick captured the Pulitzer Prize for best play
- Disk jockey Alan Freed introduced the "rock 'n' roll" format on radio station WINS
- The American thermonuclear tests at Bikini Atoll wounded 31 Americans, 236 natives and 23 Japanese fishermen
- Wladziu Valentino Liberace became a TV music sensation with his candelabras, soft lights, wide smiles and outrageous clothes
- "Beat girls" sported heavy eye makeup known as the raccoon look
- Matisse's painting *Odalisque* sold for $75,000
- New words and phrases that entered the language included "do-it-yourself," "greaser," "hip," "bread" (for money) and "windfall profit"
- The Supreme Court ruled that the doctrine of "separate but equal" had no place in public education and that separate facilities were "inherently unequal."
- Millions of children across America watched *Howdy Doody* and *Buffalo Bob Smith*
- Ernest Hemingway won the Nobel Prize for literature
- Medical student Roger Bannister broke the four-minute mile with a 3.54-minute finish in Oxford, England
- The musical play *The Pajama Game* opened on Broadway
- The Supreme Court unanimously ruled for school integration in *Brown vs. Board of Education of Topeka, Kansas*
- President Eisenhower signed an order adding the words "under God" to the Pledge of Allegiance
- Elvis Presley's first commercial recording session, performing *That's All Right (Mama)*, took place at Sun Records in Memphis, Tennessee
- The first mass inoculation of children against polio with the Salk vaccine began
- Howard Hughes paid $23.5 million for the RKO motion picture company
- The Miss America pageant made its network TV debut on ABC

- Ellis Island closed after processing more than 20 million immigrants
- Popular movies included *White Christmas*, and *Rear Window*
- The Iwo Jima Memorial was dedicated in Arlington, Virginia
- Chevrolet introduced the V8 engine
- The film *Godzilla, King of the Monsters* was released
- The FORTRAN computer program was used for the first time
- Puerto Rican nationalists fired gunshots from the gallery of the House of Representatives, wounding five congressmen
- First Lady Mamie Eisenhower christened *Nautilus*, the nation's first atomic-powered submarine
- Boeing unveiled the "707," the first commercially successful jet aircraft

- The National Negro Network was established with 40 charter member radio stations
- President Dwight Eisenhower warned against United States' intervention in Vietnam
- Boxer Joey Giardello knocked out Willie Tory at Madison Square Garden, in the first televised boxing prize fight to be shown in color
- Congress authorized the United States Air Force Academy in Colorado
- Fifty-four percent of Americans owned a television set
- The first issue of *Sports Illustrated* magazine was published in the U.S.
- The last new episode of *The Lone Ranger* was aired on radio, after 2,956 episodes and 21 years
- The transistor radio was developed
- The U.S. Supreme Court decided the landmark case *Berman v. Parker*, upholding the federal slum clearance and urban renewal program
- For the first time, the Dow surpassed its 1929 peak level reached just before that year's crash
- The U.S. Senate voted 67-22 to condemn Joseph McCarthy for "conduct that tends to bring the Senate into dishonor and disrepute"
- The first Burger King opened in Miami, Florida
- The TV dinner was introduced by the American entrepreneur Gerry Thomas
- Gasoline averaged $0.29 per gallon
- Taxpayers with incomes of more than $100,000 paid more than $67,000 each in taxes
- Open-heart surgery was introduced by Minneapolis physician C. Walton Lillehe
- Births remained above four million per year
- The United States boasted 1,768 million newspapers, publishing 59 million copies daily
- Marian Anderson was the first Black soloist of the Metropolitan Opera
- Rosa Parks was arrested for refusing to give up the only seat available, which was in the front of the bus
- The federal minimum wage rose from $0.75 to $1.00 per hour
- AF of L and CIO labor unions merged
- *National Review* and *Village Voice* began publication
- Crest was introduced by Proctor and Gamble
- The number of millionaires in the United States was reported at 154
- New television shows included *The Adventures of Rin Tin Tin, Father Knows Best, Lassie,* and *Tonight with Steve Allen*
- The Ford Foundation gave $50 million to private colleges to raise faculty salaries

- Racial segregation on interstate buses and trains was ordered to end
- The Whirlpool Corporation merged with Seeger Refrigerator Company and began producing refrigerators, air conditioners and cooking ranges
- National City Bank merged with First National Bank, both of New York, to form the third largest bank in America
- The Salk vaccine was successful in preventing polio and received full approval by the Food and Drug Administration
- The United Automobile Workers union forced Ford and General Motors to pay workers a modest weekly sum during layoffs
- Noel Coward reportedly earned $40,000 a week to entertain in Las Vegas
- The United Nations celebrated its tenth anniversary
- Former President Harry Truman was paid $600,000 for his memoirs
- The Pentagon announced a plan to develop ICBMs (intercontinental ballistic missiles) armed with nuclear weapons
- President Eisenhower sent the first U.S. advisors to South Vietnam
- Evan Hunter's movie adaptation of the novel *Blackboard Jungle* premiered, featuring the single *Rock Around the Clock* by Bill Haley and His Comets
- The TV quiz program *The $64,000 Question* premiered on CBS-TV
- *The Lady and the Tramp*, the Walt Disney Company's fifteenth animated film, premiered in Chicago
- The first edition of *The Guinness Book of Records* was published in London
- *Gunsmoke, Alfred Hitchcock Presents and The Mickey Mouse Club* all debuted on television
- The Brooklyn Dodgers won the World Series, defeating the New York Yankees
- American cytogeneticist Joe Hin Tjio discovered that there are 46 human chromosomes
- General Motors Corporation became the first American company to make an annual profit of over $1 billion
- The game Scrabble debuted
- Ray Kroc opened the ninth McDonald's restaurant and oversaw its worldwide expansion
- KXTV of Stockton, California, signed on the air to become the 100th commercial television station in the country
- The nation boasted 7,000 drive-in theaters
- The DNA molecule was photographed for the first time
- Teen fashions for boys included crew cut haircuts known as "flaptops"
- Procter and Gamble created Pampers disposable diapers
- Ford Motor Company went public and issued over 10 million shares which were sold to 250,000 investors
- A survey showed that 77 percent of college-educated women married and 41 percent worked part-time
- Boston religious leaders urged the banning of rock 'n' roll
- Eleven percent of all cars sold were station wagons
- For the first time airlines carried as many passengers as did trains
- Broadway openings included *Waiting for Godot, Long Day's Journey into Night*, and *My Fair Lady*
- After vowing never to allow Elvis Presley's vulgarity on his TV show, Ed Sullivan changed his mind and paid Presley $50,000 for three appearances
- Midas Muffler Shops, La Leche League, and women ministers in the Presbyterian Church all made their first appearance
- Don Larsen of the New York Yankees pitched the first perfect game in the World Series

- John F. Kennedy won the Pulitzer Prize for his book *Profiles in Courage*
- Television premieres included *As the World Turns*, *The Edge of Night* and *The Huntley-Brinkley Report*
- American colleges began actively recruiting students from the middle classes
- Martin Luther King, Jr. said, "Nonviolence is the most potent technique for oppressed people. Unearned suffering is redemptive."
- European autos gained in popularity In the U.S.
- Dynamite exploded on the porch of Martin Luther King's home
- Elvis Presley's *Hound Dog/Don't Be Cruel* was the number one single for a record 11 weeks
- The U.S. banned the launching of weather balloons because of Soviet complaints
- The Montgomery, Alabama bus boycott sparked hundreds of arrests, including that of Martin Luther King
- Union workers struck the Westinghouse Electric Corporation for 156 days
- Ampex Corporation introduced a commercial videotape recorder
- Popular music ranged from *(You've Got) The Magic Touch* by the Platters to Harry Belafonte's album *Calypso*
- President Dwight Eisenhower signed the Agriculture Act that created a "soil bank" plan to reduce surpluses
- Jerry Lewis and Dean Martin stopped working together after 16 movies
- The United States Federal Highway Act authorized a 42,500-mile network, largely financed by the federal government, linking major urban centers
- America established a Middle-East Emergency Committee to assure Western Europe of oil supplies if the Suez crisis interrupted shipments
- Adlai E. Stevenson was nominated for president at the Democratic National Convention
- The Tennessee National Guardsmen halted rioters protesting the admission of 12 African Americans to schools in Clinton
- The first prefrontal lobotomy was performed
- Dr. Albert Sabin created the oral polio vaccine
- *The Wizard of Oz* was first televised
- The Eisenhower-Nixon Republican ticket won the presidential election

Late 1950s

- The FCC approved AT&T's plan to send U.S. programming to Cuba
- A record 4.3 million babies were born in the U.S.
- Per capita margarine consumption exceeded butter for the first time
- *Sputnik I*, the world's first manmade earth satellite, was launched by the Soviet Union in 1957 and orbited until it fell to Earth in 1958
- Allen Ginsberg's book *Howl* was seized by the police for being obscene
- The Everly Brothers' song *Wake Up, Little Susie* was banned in Boston
- On the third anniversary of the U.S. Supreme Court's *Brown v. Board of Education* decision, Bobby Lynn Cain graduated from Clinton High School (Tennessee), the first black in the state ever to graduate from an integrated school
- A University of Wisconsin study showed that 20 percent of Americans lived in poverty
- The first civil rights legislation since 1872 passed despite South Carolina Senator Strom Thurmond's record 24-hour, 18-minute filibuster

- The painkiller Darvon was introduced by Eli Lilly
- The terms "Asian flu," "meter maid" and "funky" all entered the language
- *Fortune* named Paul Getty the richest American, estimating his worth at more than $1 billion
- Volkswagen sold 200,000 Beetles
- Massachusetts governor reversed the 1692 witchcraft convictions of six Salem women
- Ford Motor Company's introduction of the Edsel, named after Henry Ford's son, was a major manufacturing and marketing failure
- *The Bridge on the River Kwai, And God Created Woman* and *12 Angry Men* all had their movie premieres
- An intensive study of birth control in pill form was begun in Puerto Rico
- Tennessee Williams's *Orpheus Descending* and Noel Coward's *Nude with Violin* both opened on Broadway
- *Perry Mason, To Tell the Truth*, and *American Bandstand* all premiered on television
- Leonard Bernstein became the musical director of the New York Philharmonic
- Anticoagulants were shown to aid stroke victims and reduce permanent damage
- James Agee's *A Death in the Family* won the Pulitzer Prize for fiction
- The average wage for a factory production worker was $2.08 an hour, or $82 a week
- The Mad Bomber of New York City was arrested after a 16-year search and the planting of 32 homemade bombs
- Due to new medications, the number of long-term patients in psychiatric hospitals decreased
- Bestselling books included *Peyton Place* by Grace Metalious, *Atlas Shrugged* by Ayn Rand, and *Kids Say the Darndest Things* by Art Linkletter
- Hits songs included *All Shook Up, All the Way, A White Sport Coat and a Pink Carnation*, and *Chances Are*
- The UN Emergency Force was the first multinational peacekeeping force in history
- Painter Mark Rothko completed *Red, White and Brown* and sculptor Alexander Calder's *125,1957* was installed in Idlewild Airport, New York
- The San Francisco and Los Angeles stock exchanges merged to form the Pacific Coast Stock Exchange
- Hamilton Watch Company introduced the first electric watch
- Wham-O Company produced the first Frisbee
- Ku Klux Klan members forced truck driver Willie Edwards to jump off a bridge to his death into the Alabama River

- The FBI arrested union leader Jimmy Hoffa and charged him with bribery
- Elvis Presley bought Graceland in Memphis, Tennessee, for $100,000
- Rodgers and Hammerstein's *Cinderella*, the team's only musical written especially for television, was telecast live and in color by CBS, starring Julie Andrews
- IBM sold the first compiler for the FORTRAN scientific programming language
- Brooklyn Dodgers owner Walter O'Malley agreed to move the baseball team to Los Angeles
- Oklahoma celebrated its semi-centennial statehood by burying a brand-new Plymouth Belvedere in a time capsule, to be opened 50 years later

- John Lennon and Paul McCartney met for the first time, three years before forming the Beatles
- Marine Major John Glenn flew an F8U supersonic jet from California to New York in three hours, 23 minutes and eight seconds, setting a new transcontinental speed record
- The International Atomic Energy Agency was established
- *American Bandstand,* a local dance show produced by WFIL-TV in Philadelphia, joined the ABC Television Network
- President Eisenhower announced a two-year suspension of nuclear testing
- *West Side Story* premiered on Broadway and ran for 732 performances
- Toyota began exporting vehicles to the U.S.
- Gordon Gould invented the laser
- The first U.S. attempt to launch a satellite failed when the rocket blew up on the launch pad
- The Boeing 707 airliner was introduced
- "Beat" and "beatnik" took hold as new words to describe the "Beat Generation"
- Unemployment in the U.S. reached 5.2 million, a post-war high

- Martin Luther King, Jr., helped organize the Southern Christian Leadership Conference (SCLC) and became its first president
- Evangelist Billy Graham held a five-month-long revival at Madison Square Garden in New York that attracted more than 500,000 people
- After 38 years, *Collier's Magazine* published its final issue
- Tennis player Althea Gibson became the first Black athlete to win at Wimbledon
- New York's first trolley car was retired
- Frisbee was introduced by Wham-O Manufacturing
- Gasoline cost $0.304 cents per gallon
- BankAmericard credit card was introduced
- First-class postal rates climbed to $0.04 per ounce
- Sweet'n' Low sugarless sweetener was introduced
- Eleanor Roosevelt was first on the "Most Admired Women" list for the 11th time
- The paperback edition of *Lolita* sold a million copies
- College tuition had doubled since 1940 and now topped $1,300 a year
- Elvis Presley was inducted into the Army
- The Grammy award, the Chevrolet Impala, and cocoa puffs all made their first appearance
- At the movies, *Cat on a Hot Tin Roof* and *Gigi* were all major hits
- A round-trip ticket on Air France from New York to Paris cost $489.60, while round trip from New York to Houston cost $66.65
- Television premieres included *The Donna Reed Show, 77 Sun-set Strip* and *Wanted: Dead or Alive*
- Stan Musial of the St. Louis Cardinals connected on his 3,000th hit

- Arnold Palmer was the PGA's top money winner with $42,607
- Van Gogh's *Public Gardens at Arles* sold for $369,600 and Renoir's *La Pensée* for $201,600
- The construction of a nuclear power plant in California was stopped by court action initiated by environmental groups
- NASA was organized to unify and develop U.S. nonmilitary space efforts
- The first regular domestic jet service from New York to Miami began
- *Breakfast at Tiffany's* by Truman Capote and *Dr. Zhivago* by Boris Pasternak were published
- Fourteen-year-old Bobby Fischer won the U.S. Chess Championship
- The first successful American satellite, *Explorer 1*, was launched into orbit
- Ruth Carol Taylor became the first African-American flight attendant
- Pope Pius XII declared Saint Clare the patron saint of television
- The peace symbol was designed by Gerald Holtom and commissioned by the Campaign for Nuclear Disarmament to protest the Atomic Weapons Research Establishment

- The *USS Wisconsin* was decommissioned, leaving the United States Navy without an active battleship for the first time since 1896
- A U.S. B-47 bomber accidentally dropped an atomic bomb on Mars Bluff, South Carolina, but no nuclear fission occurred
- Unemployment in Detroit reached 20 percent at the height of the 1958 recession
- Van Cliburn won the Tchaikovsky International Competition for pianists in Moscow
- The bodies of unidentified soldiers killed during World War II and the Korean War were buried at the Tomb of the Unknowns in Arlington National Cemetery
- The first International House of Pancakes (IHOP) opened in Toluca Lake, California
- Congress formally created the National Aeronautics and Space Administration (NASA)
- The nuclear-powered submarine *USS Nautilus* became the first vessel to cross the North Pole under water
- *Have Gun, Will Travel* debuted on radio
- The conservative John Birch Society was founded in the U.S. by Robert Welch, a retired candy manufacturer
- To offset the rising cost of tinplate, Coors beer adopted the use of the aluminum can
- Movie premieres included *Ben-Hur* starring Charlton Heston, and *Some Like It Hot* with Tony Curtis, Marilyn Monroe and Jack Lemmon
- Mary Leakey discovered the skull of the 1.78 million-year-old Australopithecus in the Olduvai Gorge, Tanganyika
- The Soviet *Lunik II* became the first manmade object to strike the moon

- Rock 'n' roll stars Buddy Holly, Ritchie Valens and the Big Bopper were killed in an airplane crash
- A new law declared modern art to be duty-free
- Weather stations made their first appearance
- The U.S. Navy successfully orbited a Vanguard satellite, the forerunner of the first weather station in space
- A *Raisin in the Sun, The Miracle Worker,* and *Mark Twain Tonight* all premiered on Broadway
- Disc jockeys came under investigation for accepting "payola"
- NASA selected the Mercury Seven astronauts: John Glenn, Scott Carpenter, Virgil Grissom, Gordon Cooper, Walter Schirra, Donald Slayton and Alan Shepard
- Perry Como signed a $25 million contract with Kraft Foods
- Alaska and Hawaii were admitted to the Union as the forty-ninth and fiftieth states
- American Airlines entered the jet age with the first scheduled transcontinental flight of a Boeing 707 from Los Angeles to New York for $301.00
- Arlington and Norfolk, Virginia, peacefully desegregated their public schools
- The United States successfully test-fired a Titan intercontinental ballistic missile from Cape Canaveral
- The FCC applied the equal time rule to TV newscasts of political candidates
- Miles Davis recorded the album *Kind of Blue* with John Coltrane, Cannonball Adderly, Philley Joe Jones, Paul Chambers and Bill Evans
- The Barbie doll was unveiled at the American Toy Fair in New York City by the Mattel Toy Company for $3.00
- The *USS Skate* became the first submarine to surface at the North Pole
- *The Battle Of New Orleans* by Johnny Horton peaked at number one on the pop singles chart and stayed there for six weeks
- Congress authorized food stamps for poor Americans
- The first telephone cable linking Europe and the United States was laid
- Television's *The Twilight Zone* and *Bonanza* all premiered
- The Guggenheim Museum, designed by Frank Lloyd Wright, opened in New York City
- The Rodgers and Hammerstein musical *The Sound of Music* opened on Broadway
- The film *Ben-Hur*, starring Charlton Heston, had its world premiere in New York
- The first color photograph of Earth was received from outer space
- Motown Records was founded by Berry Gordy, Jr.
- Walt Disney released his sixteenth animated film, *Sleeping Beauty*
- The *USS George Washington* was launched as the first submarine to carry ballistic missiles
- The United States recognized the new Cuban government of Fidel Castro
- Racecar driver Lee Petty won the first Daytona 500
- The Marx Brothers made their last TV appearance in *The Incredible Jewel Robbery*
- Busch Gardens in Tampa, Florida, was dedicated and opened its gates
- The St. Lawrence Seaway linking the North American Great Lakes and the Atlantic Ocean officially opened to shipping
- Charles Ovnand and Dale R. Buis became the first Americans killed in action in Vietnam
- The Henney Kilowatt went on sale in the United States, becoming the first mass-produced electric car in almost three decades

SECTION THREE: ECONOMY OF THE TIMES

More opportunities for Americans in the 1950s meant the chance to earn more money.
Economy of the Times *illustrates three economic elements: Consumer Expenditures; Annual Income of Standard Jobs; and Selected Prices. We highlighted three specific years for each category—1953, 1955, and 1958—for easy comparison. For example, telephone and telegraph service cost Americans 15% more from 1953 to 1958, but income for workers in that industry rose 26% over those same years. The cost of transportation went down .57 but income for transportation workers rose $762.*

Consumer Expenditures

The numbers below are average per capita consumer expenditures in the years 1953, 1955, and 1958, for all workers nationwide.

Category	1953	1955	1958
Auto Parts	$9.40	$9.68	$10.91
Auto Usage	$164.19	$193.01	$183.76
Clothing	$117.19	$118.59	$118.87
Dentists	$7.52	$9.08	$10.91
Food	$409.86	$414.46	$447.34
Furniture	$23.19	$26.62	$29.29
Gas and Oil	$46.38	$52.03	$60.87
Health Insurance	$8.15	$8.47	$8.61
Housing	$187.38	$208.14	$241.18
Intercity Transport	$6.89	$6.66	$6.32
Local Transport	$12.53	$11.49	$10.91
New Auto Purchase	$69.56	$83.49	$55.70
Per Capita Consumption	$1,457.71	$1,560.43	$1,691.73
Personal Business	$50.76	$58.69	$70.06
Personal Care	$19.43	$22.39	$28.14
Physicians	$20.68	$22.99	$29.29
Private Education and Research	$13.79	$15.13	$19.54
Recreation	$81.47	$87.73	$93.03
Religion/Welfare Activities	$19.43	$21.18	$25.27
Telephone and Telegraph	$16.92	$18.76	$22.39
Tobacco	$31.96	$30.86	$34.45
Utilities	$54.52	$61.72	$70.63

Annual Income, Standard Jobs

The numbers below are annual income for standard jobs across America in the years 1953, 1955, and 1958.

Category	1953	1955	1958
Average of All Industries, Excluding Farm Labor	$3,927	$4,224	$4,818
Average of All Industries, Including Farm Labor	$3,852	$4,128	$4,707
Bituminous Coal Mining	$4,061	$4,470	$4,809
Building Trades	$4,354	$4,607	$5,305
Domestics	$1,805	$1,874	$2,131
Farm Labor	$1,464	$1,498	$1,690
Federal Civilian	$4,411	$4,801	$5,781
Federal Employees, Executive Departments	$3,410	$3,774	$4,462
Federal Military	$2,927	$3,237	$3,697
Finance, Insurance, and Real Estate	$3,663	$4,005	$4,523
Gas and Electricity Workers	$4,404	$4,757	$5,543
Manufacturing, Durable Goods	$4,383	$4,737	$5,478
Manufacturing, Nondurable Goods	$3,784	$4,134	$4,725
Medical/Health Services Workers	$2,365	$2,488	$2,751
Miscellaneous Manufacturing	$3,560	$3,789	$4,408
Motion Picture Services	$3,326	$4,330	$4,940
Nonprofit Organization Workers	$3,041	$3,291	$3,672
Passenger Transportation Workers, Local and Highway	$3,809	$4,142	$4,571
Personal Services	$2,573	$2,766	$3,140
Public School Teachers	$3,314	$3,608	$4,343
Radio Broadcasting and Television Workers	$5,734	$6,250	$7,051
Railroad Workers	$4,418	$4,701	$5,836
State and Local Government Workers	$3,140	$3,447	$3,958
Telephone and Telegraph Workers	$3,720	$4,153	$4,707
Wholesale and Retail Trade Workers	$3,446	$4,616	$5,294

Selected Prices

1953

Aspirin, Bayer, 30 Tablets................$0.30
Automobile, Chassis Lubrication..........$1.25
Bedspread, Cotton Jacquard $6.35
Blender, Waring.......................$44.50
Cake Mix, Betty Crocker, 20 oz...........$0.35
Carbon Paper.........................$1.19
Chord Organ, Hammond..............$975.00
Clock................................$3.98
Curling Iron...........................$1.79
Diamond, DeBeers, per Caret..........$857.50
Doll, Goldberger in Party Dress..........$3.98
Hair Dryer, Ann Barton................$21.50
Lawnmower..........................$88.00
Lighter Fluid, Zippo....................$0.25
Motor Oil, Quart.......................$0.32
Mouse Seed, Reardon Laboratories........$0.25
Nylon Hose, per Pair...................$0.95
Peanut Butter, Hollob's Supreme, 12 oz.....$0.33
Radio, Table Model....................$21.70
Razor, Gillette.........................$1.00
Record, *Kiss Me Kate*..................$4.85
Refrigerator, Admiral..................$189.95
Roller Skates..........................$2.45
Rug, Axminster, All Wool...............$93.50
Sheet, Dan River, Bordered.............$10.50
Sleeping Bag..........................$4.88
Stationery, 48-Piece Set.................$0.49
Toilet Tissue, per Roll...................$0.09
Tooth Extraction.......................$5.50
Vacuum Cleaner, Upright...............$86.70
Wallet, Kerrybrooke....................$3.50
Water Heater, Gas, 30 Gallons..........$151.90
Wieners, Oscar Mayer, per Pound.........$0.49

1955

Acne Cream..........................$0.59
Air Freshener.........................$0.49
Antiseptic, Listerine...................$0.79
Automobile, Chrysler New Yorker........$4,243
Baby Doll, Gerber.....................$2.00
Baby Food, Gerber, Four Three-Ounce Jars..$0.87
Baseball Glove.........................$9.95
Bath Towel...........................$0.95
Boy Scout Uniform....................$8.97
Brassiere, Playtex......................$3.95

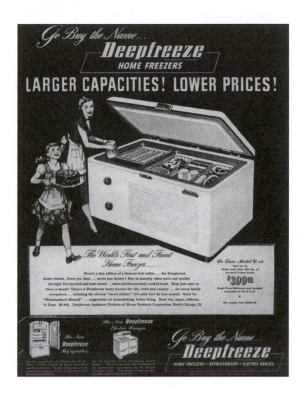

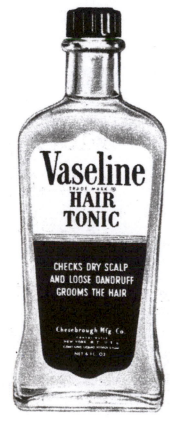

Cake Mix.............................$1.00
Candy, Tootsie Roll $0.05
Cat Food, Puss 'n' Boots $0.39
Chandelier, Crystal $425.00
Chocolate Covered Cherries, Brach's, 13 oz. . $0.55
Clearasil Lotion.......................$0.59
Coca-Cola $0.05
Cooker, Presto......................$12.95
Dance Lessons......................$25.00
Drink Powder, Nestle's Quik..............$0.66
Eyelash Curler, Maybelline $1.00
Eyeliner, Max Factor $1.50
Face Powder.........................$1.38
Flashlight Battery $0.14
Gin, Gordon's, per Fifth $4.47
Girdle, Playtex.......................$4.95
Girdle, Warner's LeGant $4.95
Grill, Capri Roto-Broil 400 ....$79.95
Guitar, Washburn $27.50
Hotel Room, Ritz Carlton, Boston $9.00
License Plate $1.00
Lighter, Zippo........................$4.75
Mattress, Serta, King Size $79.50
Nylons, Kotex Miracle Brand $1.00
Outboard Motor, Johnson..............$430.00
Paint, Sherwin-Williams Kem-Tone,
    per Gallon $5.59
Paneling.............................$47.00
Pocket Radio $75.00
Pork and Beans, Van Camp's $0.25
Potato Chips, Pound $0.49
Potatoes, Burbank Russet, 20 Pounds.......$0.49
Race Car Kit $2.75
Radio, Transistor Pocket $75.00
Railroad Fare, Chicago to San Francisco ... $63.12
Razor Blades, 20 ....$0.79
Rit Dye..............................$0.25
Shirt, Tam o' Shanter Beau Brummel,
    Three-Piece Set......................$4.98
Shoes, Child's Buster Brown..............$6.99
Sofabed $69.95
Soup, Campbell's, Can $0.16
Suit, Man's Botany 500 ....$59.50
Television, Zenith $550.00
Tootsie Roll $0.05
Typewriter, Smith Corona..............$164.50
Vacuum Cleaner, Eureka
    Super Roto-Matic $69.95
Watch, Timex Boy Scout $9.95

Whiskey, Seagram's, per Fifth $4.89
Wool Rug Cleaner, Glamorene,
    Half-Gallon $2.29

1958

Automobile, Chrysler Simca DeLuxe . . . $1,698.00
Candygram, Western Union, Pound $2.95
Clearasil $0.59
Coffee Maker, Cory $39.95
Cough Syrup, Troutman's $0.49
Exercise Bike, Home Riding $71.50
Facial Treatment, Royal $5.50
Food Processor $12.98
Fruit Cocktail $0.93
Hamburger, Burger King Whopper $0.37
Home Barber Set, Craftsman $14.95
Home Permanent $1.50
Hosiery, Roy Garter, Top $0.97
Hotel Room, Ritz-Carlton, Boston $9.00
Hotel, Harbor View, Single Room,
    per Night $6.00
House, Four Bedrooms,
    Chicago Area $34,000.00
Lawn Sprinkler, Sunbeam Rain King,
    Automatic $9.95
Life Magazine, Weekly $0.25
Lighter, Zippo, Chrome Finish $4.75
Loudspeakers, Acoustic Research AR-2,
    per Pair $89.00
Magazine, Life $0.25
Makeup, Pressed Powder/Foundation $1.35
Man's Shirt, Arrow $5.00
Mattress, Serta Perfect Sleeper $79.50
Milk, per Quart $0.60
Movie Projector $89.95
Orange Juice, per Glass $0.40
Photoflash Lamp $0.10
Photostat, Each $0.20
Pillows, Goose Down , Extra Large $14.97
Raincoat, Ballerina $5.74
Scotch, Fifth $8.00
Shirt, Hercules Snap-Front Model $2.34
Shoes, Kerrybroke Soft Leather $3.77
Theatre Ticket, New York $3.85
Typewriter, Smith-Corona
    Portable Electric $164.50
Vodka, Smirnoff, Fifth $5.23
Woman's Suit $17.95

Value of a Dollar Index 1860-2010
2010=$1.00

Year	Amount	Year	Amount	Year	Amount	Year	Amount
1860	$26.32	1898	$26.32	1936	$15.69	1974	$4.42
1861	$25.00	1899	$26.32	1937	$15.15	1975	$4.05
1862	$21.74	1900	$25.64	1938	$15.47	1976	$3.83
1863	$17.24	1901	$25.64	1939	$15.69	1977	$3.60
1864	$13.89	1902	$25.64	1940	$15.58	1978	$3.35
1865	$13.33	1903	$25.00	1941	$14.84	1979	$3.00
1866	$13.70	1904	$24.39	1942	$13.38	1980	$2.65
1867	$14.71	1905	$25.00	1943	$12.61	1981	$2.40
1868	$15.38	1906	$24.39	1944	$12.39	1982	$2.26
1869	$16.13	1907	$23.26	1945	$12.12	1983	$2.19
1870	$16.67	1908	$23.81	1946	$11.18	1984	$2.10
1871	$17.86	1909	$23.81	1947	$9.78	1985	$2.03
1872	$17.86	1910	$22.73	1948	$9.09	1986	$1.99
1873	$18.18	1911	$22.73	1949	$9.16	1987	$1.92
1874	$19.23	1912	$22.73	1950	$9.05	1988	$1.84
1875	$20.00	1913	$22.03	1951	$8.39	1989	$1.76
1876	$20.41	1914	$21.81	1952	$8.20	1990	$1.67
1877	$20.83	1915	$21.59	1953	$8.14	1991	$1.60
1878	$21.74	1916	$20.01	1954	$8.11	1992	$1.55
1879	$21.74	1917	$17.04	1955	$8.14	1993	$1.51
1880	$21.28	1918	$14.54	1956	$8.02	1994	$1.47
1881	$21.28	1919	$12.61	1957	$7.76	1995	$1.43
1882	$21.28	1920	$10.91	1958	$7.55	1996	$1.39
1883	$21.74	1921	$12.18	1959	$7.47	1997	$1.34
1884	$22.22	1922	$12.98	1960	$7.37	1998	$1.31
1885	$22.73	1923	$12.75	1961	$7.29	1999	$1.27
1886	$23.26	1924	$12.75	1962	$7.20	2000	$1.27
1887	$22.73	1925	$12.46	1963	$7.13	2001	$1.23
1888	$22.73	1926	$12.32	1964	$7.04	2002	$1.21
1889	$23.81	1927	$12.53	1965	$6.92	2003	$1.19
1890	$23.81	1928	$12.68	1966	$6.71	2004	$1.15
1891	$23.81	1929	$12.68	1967	$6.53	2005	$1.12
1892	$23.81	1930	$13.06	1968	$6.27	2006	$1.08
1893	$24.39	1931	$14.35	1969	$5.94	2007	$1.05
1894	$25.64	1932	$16.04	1970	$5.62	2008	$1.01
1895	$25.64	1933	$16.91	1971	$5.39	2009	$1.02
1896	$25.64	1934	$16.28	1972	$5.22	2010	$1.00
1897	$26.32	1935	$15.92	1973	$4.91		

SECTION FOUR: ALL AROUND US

This section offers a ring side seat to the issues and attitudes that were 1950s America. Reminiscent of the "current events" homework assignment, these 33 documents are exact reprints from popular 1950s magazines, local and national newspapers, and political speeches. Labeled the decade of optimism, confidence was high as Americans in the 1950s dealt with how best to educate their children, controversy over desegregation, how to answer the threat of communism, and how to deal with increased automation in the work force. These documents also remind us that, while details have changed, education, racism, foreign threats and the economy have been on the minds of Americans throughout history, a fact that is not likely to change.

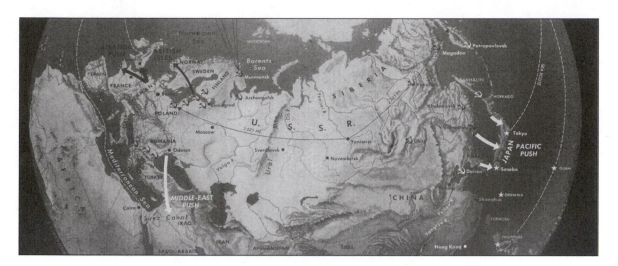

The Nature of the Enemy
Editorial, *Life*, February 27, 1950
The Elemental Fact of 1950

This is the age of obliteration. Formal war between the possessors of nuclear weapons means the obliteration of society as most of humankind—Communist and non-Communist—now knows it. Therefore it is necessary to avoid war, to control nuclear weapons and to fashion a formula for permanent peace.

Opposed to these necessities is the elemental fact of 1950: The enemy of the free world is implacably determined to destroy the free world.

This enemy cannot surrender and cannot make peace. The makers and leaders of Stalinist thought have said again and again and again that the object of Soviet Communism is "the victory of Communism throughout the world." They have also said that this victory is essential to the safety and welfare of the Soviet Union itself. Their own system is so grounded upon this objective that is has become a driving necessity; to abandon it would be to invite the collapse of their system and the destruction of themselves.

There can be no compromise and no agreement with Soviet Communism. It is not merely that Soviet Communists refuse to fulfill agreements. It is that they use compromise and agreement to destroy those with whom they compromise and agree. Any compromise, any agreement can only be, so far as the Communists are concerned, a further stage in the war which they continually wage.

Every relevant act and attitude of Soviet Communism during the first years of the atomic age compels the conclusion that any atomic agreement acceptable to the Communists would be used by them as every agreement has been used—to further "the victory of Communism throughout the world."

When and in what situations Soviet Communism will proceed from informal war to shooting war is unpredictable. It is conceivable that the Soviet Communists will not choose shooting war as the method of final decision. Stalin himself has often expressed contempt for war ("imperialist war" of course) as a solution. But the military power of the Soviet Union is a vaunted instrument of world Communism. Its propagandists continually boast of the Soviet Union's military might. What they studiously avoid is any predefinition of the situation in which Soviet Communism would resort to shooting war (except attack upon the Soviet homeland). Therefore, the strategists of the free world cannot calculate with certainty that this or that choice, decision, situation will make for shooting war or avoid shooting war. All-out war is never predictable. But it is always possible.

This week *Life* appraises the military defenses of the U.S. in the light of the military capacity of the Soviet Union. This appraisal is undertaken in awareness that the problem of U.S. defense is not entirely a military problem. The American people could make no worse mistake than to assume that there is safely in military defense alone, however massive and costly the defense may become.

Then why undertake such an appraisal?

First, although there is no sure safety in military defense alone, there is sure ruin in any miscalculation or neglect of military defense.

Second, the wisdom and adequacy with which the officials who are in charge of he U.S. policy calculate the defense necessities of the time provide a measure of the wisdom and adequacy with which they calculate the total necessities of the time.

The net showing of our report is that the defense necessities of the U.S. have been avoidably underestimated by the President, by his Secretary of Defense and (to the extent that they have participated in final policy decisions) by the chiefs of the military services. Not in extenuation of these officials but to indicate the scale of the turnabout in attitudes and policies now required, this must be added:

The official estimate of U.S. defense necessities has on the whole been welcomed by the U.S. Congress, the public and the press. The dominate desire has been to let the postwar economy run its course toward full civilian abundance. Most everybody had come to realize that the U.S. was in something called "the world conflict," that the conflict might even be called a kind of war and that a certain amount of dollars and goods had to be put up for the fight against Communism, which most everybody had come to detest. But hardly anybody really thought that the U.S. was really in a real war, a war for survival that might cut into the civilian economy and take more out of it than the U.S. has as yet been willing to pony up.

Now, chunk by chunk, the walls of illusion are falling away…

The Supreme Question: How Strong is Freedom?
We have said, the free wold must know its enemy. But knowing the enemy is not enough.

The free world must know itself. It must know-it must never forget-that its freedom and its strength are one. Without freedom it cannot have strength. Without strength it cannot preserve freedom. Without the will for freedom it cannot have the strength of freedom.

At this hour of this age these are not empty words. They have a very present meaning for free men, and especially for free Americans who guard the source and center of the free world's strength.

The danger and the power of obliteration on a nuclear scale are new to mankind. Only now, five years after Hiroshima, is the prospect coming home in its full meaning to Americans. As it must for all men, it will affect the lives, the ways and the standards of America. The supreme question-and the sooner it is spelled out the better-is whether it will alter the American idea and the American love of freedom.

The national habit, the good habit, is to say as a matter of course that freedom is something to enjoy, to defend, if need be to die for (though preferably not in person). The habit and the idea of freedom have been stronger than any force yet arrayed against them. Are they stronger, will they be stronger than the prospect and power of obliteration? The accustomed "what is life without freedom?" takes on an unaccustomed meaning when there is the prospect of no life. What price the free life in the free society, free men will ask, if to defend freedom is to risk all life and all society?

These are the questions, this is the risk that America will be living with until further notice.

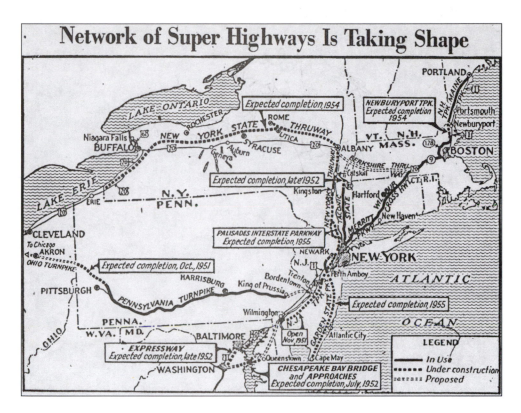

U.S. Will Base Road Building on War Needs
***New York Herald Tribune*, November 11, 1950**

Plans for a sweeping revision of the federal-state road construction program to meet the nation's military needs are rapidly shaping up. The new program follows President Truman's request that all government agencies coordinate their activities, insofar as possible, with the military preparedness program.

Federal Bureau of Roads officials say a state-by-state survey shows that half of the projects scheduled for construction on the 400,000-mile secondary system can be eliminated.

However, officials said plans for reconstruction and expansion of the 40,000-mile interstate system will go ahead as originally scheduled. The substituted projects in the secondary system will include highways to hitherto untapped mineral and agricultural resources vital to the nation's military needs.

TOPS Take off Pounds
***Life Magazine*, 1951**

During the war, when she had a job in a Milwaukee brewery, it was the sensible custom of Mrs. Esther Manz to wear slacks. It was also the pleasant habit of her employer to call a short halt in the mid-morning and mid-afternoon and serve each employee a glass of the company product. Mrs. Manz had always been a bit overweight, and this kind of treatment soon betrayed her. She found she was too fat to get into her slacks.

Then, unlike most U.S. adults who are overweight—as 25 percent of them are—Mrs. Manz did something about it. She quit her job and started TOPS (Take Off Pounds Sensibly). Today, three years later, there are TOPS clubs for some 2,500 overweight women in Wisconsin,

Michigan, California, Massachusetts, Illinois, and South Dakota, and Mrs. Manz is kept busy answering pone calls (she has 5,000) and letters (40 a week) and visiting the 43 clubs in Milwaukee.

TOPS, which has no dues and gives Mrs. Manz no salary, is neither fad nor cult. In some ways, it is modeled after Alcoholics Anonymous, bur unlike AA it does not operate in privacy; excess weight, being what it is, is hard to keep secret. At weekly meetings, TOPS members gather to weight in, sing songs("every mealtime check your eats, count the calories, dodge the sweets") and dance and play games and plan low-calorie meals which are the basis of their reducing method.

࿐࿐࿐࿐࿐࿐࿐

Marriage Is a Way of Life,
by Amy A. McGregor, *Nautilus Magazine*, March 1951

"I wish I weren't married; then I'd be able to afford a car."

The young man who made this statement is not at all dissatisfied with his wife; he is more than ordinarily proud of his little girl. But the fetters of married life chafe him. So does the constant sacrifice—the doing without something he would like to have, and could afford if he were single. In truth, he is dissatisfied with marriage itself.

The squabble over sex education has distorted and overemphasized the physical side of marriage. Some preparation for the responsibilities of marriage is given to our young girls, but that also is physical. It is important to learn to budget one's earnings, to learn to care for a house, to look after the welfare of a small baby, to sew, to cook and to do the various things which promote physical well-being. But of what use is a spic-and-span house, a healthy, happy baby, a well-balanced budget, or a well-cooked meal, if the husband always refers to things he would like to have but cannot because he is married? Would anyone in his right mind call that a happy marriage?

If it is important that a girl be taught such details appertaining to the physical side of marriage, how much more important is it that both boys and girls should be taught the one most obvious lesson they will need for marriage: the art of living together?

The family group, on which our present civilization is based, is supposed to teach this lesson. But our modern news items, particularly those concerned with juvenile delinquency and divorce, testify that I does not. From the other members of his family, the child is supposed to receive his first true impressions of the world, and his first contacts with it. From that group, he should learn the fine art of living with others, and be made aware that the universe does not center directly about him.

Instead, what happens? The child is born, and immediately becomes the pivot around which the household revolves. The parents can deny him nothing, and the whole routine of the household is disrupted to fit his pleasure, instead of gradually fitting the child into the already established routine.

As he grows older, there is an eager rush to keep him from realizing the world of reality. He is fed with fairy stories and tales of the world as his parents imagine it should be. Each idle wish is fulfilled as if by magic, even though the parents have to go without necessary comforts for themselves.

When he enters adolescence, he is thoroughly self-centered. He really knows nothing of the world. His ideas of his playmates are based on the world of make-believe in which he has lived all those years Physically, he is becoming aware of himself as never before, and this tends to make him even more self-centered. At the same time, he feels the need of companionship from those of his own age, and is unable to meet them on an equal footing. Is it any wonder that the process of growing up is so difficult? Is it any wonder that the divorce rate sours to even higher levels each year?

ळ-ळ-ळ-ळ-ळ-ळ-ळ

The World of Children
by Peter Cardozo, *Good Housekeeping*, February 1951

Want to be a fairy princess? Small fry in Oakland, California, have discovered an exciting land of make-believe. The magic passwords? Oakland Costume Loan Service. Sponsored by the city's Recreation Department, this unique community service stocks over 10,000 costumes for holiday festivals, school pageants, amateur theatricals and any make-believe in which a girl becomes a fairy princess or a boy an Indian chief. Schools, church groups, playgrounds and other nonprofit organizations can rent costumes; a small fee covers the cost of laundering. Through the magic of colorful fabrics, needles, and thread, youngsters can be transformed into Puritan maidens, elves, Dutch folk with wooden shoes, gypsies, even knights in armor. Seven thousand costumes loaned each year!

Let's make ice cream. With miniature dairy plants set up right in the classroom, three million children will soon be "pasteurizing" milk and churning make-believe scoops of ice cream. Dairy-class Workit, a new teaching aid, includes cutout sheets of trucks and machinery the children can fold, paste together and assemble on a lithographed dairy layout. By adding the full-color background picture of the farm, a three-dimensional model of the dairy plant can actually be operated. A "textbook" tells youngsters how bottles of milk get to their doorsteps. Sponsored by the National Dairy Council, these Class Workits supplement field trips to farms, giving a realistic picture of the dairy industry at work.

Like a diamond in the sky. Twinkle, twinkle, Little Star! How I wonder what you are..." This year in New York, children are learning the scientific answer. They attend a series of heavenly talks now being given in the Theater of the Stars, at the Hayden Planetarium. Especially adapted for eight- to 14-year-olds, the Young People's astronomy course covers such topics as the sun, the planets, the moon, and the constellations. The purpose of the course: To acquaint junior astronomers with the wonders of the heavens and make them feel at home under the night sky. Each child who sits under the Planetarium's magic domed ceiling becomes a superman. He sees in seven seconds how the sky picture changes in a whole year; he can even take a trip to the moon and back!

Paper Pianos. Without leaving their desks, children in Public School 119 in New York City are learning to play the piano. Sounds impossible, but it isn't. Taking part in a "class piano" experiment, youngsters from eight to 12 spend 40 minutes a week learning to play the piano. Each child spreads out a three-octave piano keyboard. (These are made of paper, cost only $0.25.) While the teacher plays a simple melody on a real piano, the children will "play" it on their paper keyboard, following the notes and chords written on the blackboard. They sing the melody as they play, take turns at the real piano, give a recital at the end of the year. Teachers and students find group teaching (10 pupils at the same time) as satisfactory as private lessons; the children like to learn together.

ର୍ଯ୍ୟକ୍ଷକ୍ଷକ୍ଷକ୍ଷକ

The Grass Roots of Opera in America, Colleges and Universities Set the Pace in Creating Opera Centers Throughout the U.S. by H. W. Hinesheimer, *The Etude*, December 1951

It was only yesterday—or was it the day before?—when it was a commonly accepted fact, never doubted and scarcely questioned by anyone, that this country would never give a hoot about opera. Opera—why, it was always considered an Un-American Activity. Foreign singers, conductors and managers presenting foreign works in foreign languages (although for domestic dollars) to an audience which stepped out of their Rolls Royce just before the first intermission, displayed their ermine capes, jewels and queen-like necklines and left as soon as the lights dimmed for the beginning of the last act. Opera, many a wise man told me when I first came here, full of enthusiasm after years of operatic adventures in Europe and expecting the same experiences over here, opera will never catch on in America. Unless it has a horse or at least soap to its name, it won't go. Forget it.

But this is a strange and wonderful country. The unexpected happens all the time, and when it happens, it happens big. Having saturated its musical air with the creation of some 150

symphony orchestras within the short period of one human generation-something unheard of in musical history-America is now beginning to open its door to opera. Strangely enough-it's the backdoor that admits the merry procession of unexpected guests: singers, stage managers, conductors, composers, colorful costumes, whirling dancers, the wonderful make-believe world of opera that has nothing like it in all the world of arts.

It's a spectacle, scarcely to believe and unique again, as have been so many facets of American cultural progress, in the annals of musical history, something that, in its freshness, spontaneity and scope, could only happen here. Professors, economists and scholars have bemoaned and are still bemoaning the lack of operatic activity in America. Here's the world's richest country, they point out-and look what we have: Two big professional companies, the Metropolitan and San Francisco, both drawing from the same roster of international stars, a few smaller ones, a few traveling companies of questionable artistic competence—no Stadttheater, no state support here—nothing. Compare this with impoverished countries like Austria and Germany or almost any European country and their flourishing operatic life, many independent opera houses, public support, regular seasons of eight or even 10 months.

All this, of course, is true. America, that just began to build its first roads through the wilderness and organize a continent of staggering dimensions, when Europe was already dotted with opera houses, has never caught up with the intricate organization of operatic life that is part of 300 years of European history, a firm and established heritage of its greater past, carried on into its smaller present.

But look what is happening now. Cities or states do not pay lavish subsidies to American operatic groups. Yet they are spreading rapidly all over the country. There are at present more than 200 different organizations producing opera in America. Most of them did not exist only a few years ago...

The driving force behind it is the university. One can almost say that the American university is now taking the place of the archbishops and princes that supported opera in its European beginnings. That is exactly what is happening here. The opera departments of such diversified places as Drake University in Des Moines, Indiana University in Bloomington, Minnesota in Minneapolis, University of Washington in Seattle, Louisiana State in Baton Rouge, University of Southern California in Los Angeles, University of Colorado at Denver—to mention just a few that come to mind-have taken over active leadership in a new, modern, aggressive, and very American approach toward opera.

The response is tremendous. Denver, for example, produced, last summer, Menotti's difficult opera *The Consul*, complete with singers, scenery and orchestra. The success with the students and townspeople was so outspoken, a whole series of additional performances had to be scheduled. The theaters of the University of Minnesota, which, only recently, added opera to its repertory, report of similar striking and most unexpected response. Drake in Des Moines, after they gave their first college performance of *The Consul*, wired the composer to say this was "the most important and most exciting event in the history of the University."

Many of these operatic centers—and that is what they swiftly grow into—started out simply as part of the school activities. In Urbana, for instance, the school of music had no opera department until 1947. The students themselves approached the faculty with a request to add operatic activities to the curriculum. The Opera Workshop at the University of Illinois now presents regularly at least one complete opera at the University of Illinois Theater, usually on four consecutive nights…

Just as active as are the universities in living up to the demands of this new, sweeping movement are the workshops that have developed everywhere during the past few years. I have seen many of them, and believe with all my heart in their mission and eventual success. Take Cincinnati, for instance, where the Music Drama Guild, for several years already, is presenting a most unusual fare—contemporary works as well as off-the-beaten-path classical operas—ith continued and ever-increasing success. They have rapidly become a set feature in the cultural life of their town—and if such sustained, ambitious and well-patronized activities are not the closest to a successful, decentralized operatic life along the lines of the European Stadttheater that can be expected, I'd like to know what is.

The fact that this group, to whom it is all a labor of love and certainly not a business, have done so successfully what they have done, has perhaps greater significance for the musical presence and future of America than still another lavishly endowed *Fledermaus* or even *Don Carlo* at the Metropolitan Opera.

Teenomania
by Marion Walker, *Alcaro*, September 1952

I want to make it perfectly plain that I have nothing whatsoever against teenagers. Some of my favorite people are teenagers, including my oldest son. But I can't help wondering if there isn't currently much too much commotion about them.

I wonder if the teens haven't come to be considered too much an age apart, an age completely different from any other. I wonder if the teenager isn't too continually in both the public and the family limelights. And, at the risk of being put summarily in my place by the experts, I wonder if parents, those long-suffering clay pigeons in How-To-Bring-Up-Your-Children propaganda, haven't been given a good deal of slightly hysterical and extremely unsound advice about how to cope with this particular stage in their offspring's development.

The teenager is a fairly recent discovery. Twenty years or so ago, if you were between 12 and 17, you were referred to rather vaguely as being "at that age" or "in between." There were no clothes designed especially for you; you wore little girl dresses until the waistlines were under your armpits. And then you graduated abruptly into your mother's kind of clothes. If you were a boy, you were promoted to pants when your legs got long enough. No one considered your patois amusing. No one considered your antics diverting. And no one considered your problems important. You were low man on the social totem pole.

This was a deplorable state of affairs and clearly needed improvement. But now the pendulum seems to have swung as far the other way. Today the teenager, also known as teenster, the teener, the subdeb, the prep, and the junior miss-is a national celebrity. He, or she, is society's most publicized and pampered pet. Newspapers headline his doing. Magazines feature his problem. Novels, plays, comic strips, movies, radio serials, and television programs are based on his escapades and his wit. Fashion experts vie to design his clothes. And the general public views him with the flattering mixture of affection and alarm that used to be reserved for collegians in raccoon coats.

At home, the teenager used to be treated like an ordinary member of the family. Today it is considered de rigueur to treat him like visiting royalty. The family kitchen and the family living room should be at his instant disposal, the experts tell us. Some authorities suggest that we remodel an entire section of the family residence for his exclusive use. According to the experts, it is a teenager's privilege to monopolize the family radio and the family telephone. It is considered his privilege to monopolize practically all his parents' time, effort, patience, energy and attention…

This vogue of lionizing the teenager is based on good intentions. Its purpose is to give him a fair share of social prominence, to help him avoid some well-known pitfalls, and help him solve the problems of growing up. But does it really accomplish what it sets out to? In my opinion, it is being carried to such extremes that it creates new problems instead of solving old ones. In my opinion, it is unfair to everyone concerned.

Let's try a novel experiment. Let's take a look at the parent's side of the question. For parents are people, too, a fact that often seems to escape the experts. Parents, a well as growing boys and girls, have emotional difficulties to overcome, romances to keep alive and glowing, friendships to maintain, and personal enthusiasms to pursue. Can they accomplish any of these feats of balanced and successful living if they are required quite literally to knock themselves out for their teenage children?…

Few teenagers grow up to find society quick to make allowances for them. Instead, they are expected to be adult, mature, responsible, cooperative. Is it fair to expect them to develop these qualities if we make them the lodestar of their parents' whole existence?

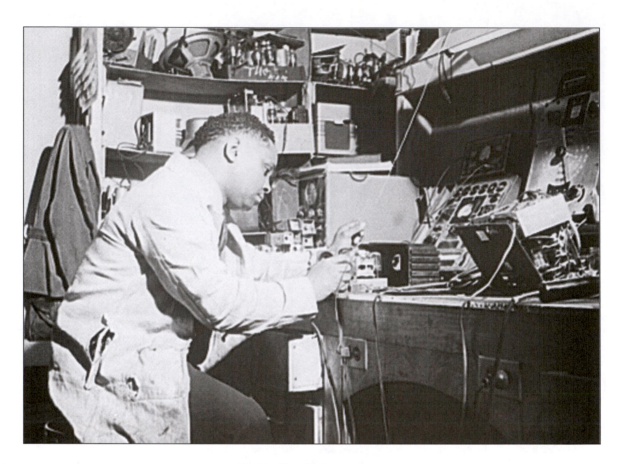

Radio Aids Enforcement
Troy Tribune (Illinois), February 14, 1952

Modernization of the Illinois State Police radio system by installation of frequency modulation for all transmitting and receiving stations has been completed. The change to FM on all 50 permanent stations, 400 squad cars and three airplanes understates police supervision.

Radio first became an adjunct of the Illinois State Police in 1936 with the establishment of seven stations which could transmit to squad cars within a 25-mile radius. The vehicles could not return calls in those early days. Five years later, a two-way system was installed and the distance for reception was more than doubled by construction of booster stations.

In January 1950, the Federal Communications Commission granted its first police experimental FM license to Illinois. Two years of testing equipment and methods and waiting for completely satisfactory equipment followed before adoption of the static-free system.

The new state police network consists of 11 5,000-watt stations for the radius of 85 miles, 22 transmitters at 50 watts installed in truck weighing stations, three 250-watt stations and 14 booster stations. This system enables radio voice coverage of the entire state.

The present network permits three-way conversation. Each squad car now is equipped to talk with the permanent stations and other cars in its area. Each vehicle is a moving radio transmitting and receiving station.

America's Speed Classic
by Wieand Bowman, *Auto Sport Review*, April, 1952

This year will mark the 36th running of the International Sweepstakes at Indianapolis. In an area 13 times as large as the famous Circus Maximus of Rome, 33 cars will try to make 200 circuits of the rectangle track surface at near peak speed. That probably no more than a dozen will complete the entire distance is a foregone conclusion.

Few of the 175,000 or more fans expected to attend this year's go will remember the first "500" run back in 1911 or the number 32 Marmon which carried ex-ribbon clerk Ray Harroun the distance at 74.59 mph average. Ray won a $14,250 b.t. purse for his efforts. And before taxes 14 grand plus with the best steak in town at four bits wasn't just so much mown grass.

Since 1911 a limited few racers have been paid altogether more than two and a half-million dollars in purse and lap monies for their attempts to win the big one. Even with taxes, that ain't hay.

Few spectators on Memorial Day, 1952, would know many of the makes of cars that were entered in the three-day race back on August 19, 1911, when the track was surfaced with oiled dirt. Bob Burman won that first main event, a 250-miler, in slightly more than four and a half hours. His winning car was a Buick pitted against a field comprising three Buicks, a Knox, two Nationals, a Jackson and two Stoddard-Daytons. But the first race ever run at the Speedway was a five-miler earlier that same day, and the winning car was a Stoddard-Dayton.

During the inaugural meet-curtailed after accidents had taken a death toll of a driver, two mechanics and two spectators-Barney Oldfield in a German Benz smashed world records for five-, 10-, 15-, 20-, and 25-mile distances and proved the circuit was fast, if unsafe.

The track was resurfaced with 3,200,000 pressed paving bricks and four more race meets were held before the first annual Memorial Day Classic was conducted in 1911.

In 1925 Peter DePaolo, with Norm Batten as relief driver, was the first race car racer to break the magical 100 mph average mark, winning with a 101.13 mph pace for the distance. DePaolo's mount was an eight cylinder Duesenberg of 121.5 c.i. piston displacement and equipped with a 5-1 ratio centrifugal blower...

A radical increase in cubic inch allowance in 1930 brought in a tremendous array of equipment with representative engines of four, six, eight and 16 cylinders and a top piston displacement limit 366 c.i.s. imposed with superchargers barred on four cycle engines. The 100.448 mph mark of Billy Arnold in the front-drive Miller-Hartz still fell short of DePaolo's 1925 record. Miller's once again outshone the other designs with the first four spots going to Harry Miller's designing genius...

The trend for '52 will be toward lighter chassis weight with increased use of dural and magnesium frame components. Fuel injection systems will largely replace conventional carbureton. Those in the know insist that the 140 mph qualifying mark will be topped and the current combination of the 138.122 mph record holding driver, Walt Faulkner and car owner J.C. Agajanian, may again be the record-shattering combination. It is generally thought that averages of under 132 mph won't make the 33-car starting field and the possibility of 128 mph mark plus average for the distance is high.

How to explain the Santa Claus story to younger children.

Careful planning makes champions in any sport.

Strengthen any weak link in a child's character.

A happy child is a healthy child.

Don't Push Children Toward Success, by Amy Selwyn, *Coronet*, April 1952

If you are like most parents, you are not content to sit back and daydream of your child's success. You want to do everything possible to improve his chances of attaining it. Before you try harder, however, there is a vital fact you should know: from a certain point on, the harder you strive to insure a fortunate future for your child, the poorer are his chances of achieving it. Recently, a 22-year-old youth sobbed a pathetic tale to an interviewer at a Philadelphia employment agency. "During the past two years,' he said morosely, "I have held eight jobs and have been fired from all. The longest I have held any job is four months. I'm desperate for money now, but I don't dare ask my family for help. Ever since I was a child, my parents have drummed it into me that I'd be a big success when I grew up. I have been so scared of disappointing them that I make a mess of everything I do…"

Such examples are all too common. As Dr. Nina Ridenour, educational director of the National Association for Mental Health, points out: "Probably far more problems are created by parents out of their desire to improve their children than from negligence, indifference, or just pure cussedness. There are six principal ways to which well-intentioned parents unknowingly push their children toward frustration and failure: they urge them to outshine others; they burden them with too many responsibilities; they praise them too much; they pick their pastimes; they demand perfection; and they decide their vocation."

How to develop good sportsmanship.

Keep your child from growing into a "Hot-head."

Don't let your child burden his happiness with grudges.

World's Future Lies in Hands of GOP
Newsweek, **January 26, 1953**

After 20 years of impatient waiting, the Republicans have had their celebration. The era of the Deals, New and Fair, is ended. General Dwight D. Eisenhower has taken the oath making him President Dwight D. Eisenhower. The triumphant inaugural parade has flashed its color along Pennsylvania Avenue. The confetti has been swept up and the stands are coming down.

Today, the United States Government is operating under new management. This management stands pledged to clean up corruption in Washington, restore some of the American freedoms which have been curtailed in recent years, and bring new blood and new methods into the Washington councils. Yet, the new managers must deal with old problems.

These problems can't be swept away or torn down. They constitute a challenge of unprecedented proportions to the determination and ingenuity of American statesmanship. Nothing less than the world's future hangs on the new administration's success.

The basic problems confronting President Eisenhower are these:

- To organize the free world in such a way that it can and will resist the continuous spread of Russian communism, make itself strong, and keep itself free.

- To achieve this without allowing the clash between the free world and the communist world to degenerate into a third world war, which, fought as it would be with atomic weapons, would be unspeakably destructive to both sides.

- To guard the immediate prosperity and opportunity for happiness of 160 million Americans at home while protecting their long-range interests abroad.

Whereas the Democrats throughout the Roosevelt and Truman administrations relied primarily upon academic advisers and trained politicians to make policy, the incoming Republicans will rely most heavily upon a professional soldier and a group of trained business executives. Therefore, the government's approach to the old problems will be essentially different.

Cover Photo, Frankie Albertson
Coach and Athlete, April 1953

Track fans who witness Tennessee's track meets this spring will be privileged to see one of the smoothest "picture runners" in the country.

He is Frank Albertson, wiry 130-pound Southeastern conference record holder and senior at the University of Tennessee, who will be competing against the nation's best in the half-mile run. Albertson's easy, relaxed running style has caused more than one critic to exclaim in delight. More important, it has been a prime factor in his becoming the greatest half-miler in Dixie history.

Frankie's diminutive size is probably responsible for his being somewhat limited in running strength, compared to the six-footers he regularly chops down to size. Moreover, he is not exceptionally blessed with speed, although he has gotten down to 50 seconds in the quarter. His saving grace, most observers agree, is the complete efficiency of his form. There just isn't any wasted motion when the black-haired little speedster of Atlantan takes off around the oval.

Handicapped most of last season with a bronchial condition, Albertson rounded into top form late in the season. He broke Alf Holberg's Tennessee state meet record in the half-mile, then took on the best 880-yard field that the SEC has ever seen in its annual meet. In that race, defending champion John Paris of Mississippi led most of the way. With Albertson close on his heels, Paris passed the quarter-mile post in 54 seconds. This was the order as they went into the home stretch. Here the contest ended. Albertson barreled ahead to win by nine yards, feeling, as he put it, "like new money." His time of 1:52.8 knocked more than a second off the old SEC record set 15 years earlier by Dave Rogan of Kentucky.

☙❧☙❧☙❧☙❧

The Week's Mail, Think Machines
Letter to the Editor, *Collier's*, May 16, 1953

John Lear's article, "Can a Mechanical Brain Replace You?" (April 4) is an excellent presentation of a very difficult subject. Being a computer-systems engineer, I feel that he has done much to enlighten an otherwise uninformed public.

I would, however, like to comment on two points. Mr. Lear stated that a deterrent to the application of digital computer…"is no longer one of learning how to fit numbers to facts, but how to get enough facts to make the equation foolproof." It has been my experience that most repetitive operations, the type most suitable for a mechanical brain to perform, are impossible to make entirely foolproof.

Equations can be readily designed to handle 99 per cent of the problems to be solved by a mechanical brain. The mechanical brain is told to refer the remaining 1 per cent to a human operator who is no longer burdened down by 100 per cent of the operation and can devote his entire time to the remaining 1 per cent.

The second point is the question of where do we go from here? As Mr. Lear indicates, all mechanical brains thus far developed have been designed primarily for the solution of scientific problems. But these represent a relatively small investment in time and money compared to the millions of repetitive clerical operations that must be performed each day by humans.

These jobs will soon start to be replaced by digital computers, not in 10 to 20 years, but commencing within two to five years.

Signed Jerome Svigals, Haddonfield, New Jersey

---

48 States of Mind, by Walter Davenport, *Collier's*, May 16, 1953: Mr. L. F. Wheeler reports that to discourage speeding, Houston, Texas, police cars have been equipped with radar. *The Houston Chronicle* discovered that local traffic cops average a mere fraction of more than one violation arrest a day. *The Chronicle* suggested abandoning radar and equipping traffic officers with Seeing Eye dogs.

Desegregation's Hot Spots
Time, October 25, 1954

Pudgy Ed Turner, Democratic candidate for Congress from Maryland's First District, paused for an instant in his speech to an audience one day last week. Then he got off a remark that, on the surface, seemed singularly unexciting. Said Turner: "You know how I stand on our traditional way of life here on the Shore." His listeners immediately began stomping the floor, broke into wild whoops and hollers of approval. For the Eastern Shoremen did know how Ed Turner stands; he stands foursquare for the continued segregation of whites and Negroes in Maryland schools.

In this year's campaign the segregation issue burns mostly beneath the surface, but it nevertheless burns hot. In its desegregation decision last May, the Supreme Court decreed a social change that cannot fail to leave its mark on the nation's politics for years to come…

In Maryland and Delaware the segregation issue may have decisive statewide effects. Just a few weeks ago, before Maryland schools opened, Republican Gov. Theodore Roosevelt McKeldin was an odds-on favorite for re-election over Democrat H. C. (Curley) Byrd. Then came trouble in the newly segregated schools, and by last week the race was a toss-up.

Curley Byrd has been working hard, for the most part privately, on the segregation issue. Example: with a newsman within earshot, a farmer sidled up to Byrd and asked: "What're you going to do about the shines?" Said Curley: "Keep 'em out!" When the nearby reporter said he was going to include the exchange in his story, Byrd blew up and flatly denied having made the remark.

Now Byrd is handling the issue more openly. Said he, in a speech in Snow Hill on the Eastern shore: "You will want members of the School Board appointed who will be able to feel and act in accordance with the age-old customs and traditions that have been part of our way of life." As with Ed Turner, they were stomping, whooping and hollering. Gov. McKeldin's reply to this veiled demagoguery is: "I stand for the law."

಄ಀ಄ಀ಄ಀ಄ಀ

Now the Dark Streets Shineth
by Marilyn Parks Davis, *American Home*, December 1954

Back in the spring of 1951, in Evanston, Illinois, housewife Alice Hamm reflected upon the forthcoming Christmas. She was not pondering about her own projects, but upon the problem of how a community could recapture the spiritual significance of this holy day.

What could she herself do? Could one busy mother recruit enough help to make a dent in the overly commercialized observance of Christ's birthday? Not long afterward, in a meeting at the Hamm home, a room full of young married couples organized the Christian Family Christmas Committee. Their aim the first year was encouragement of public displays portraying the season's deeper meaning; their slogan: "Put Christ Back into Christmas."

They set to work immediately. By November, volunteers had given 30 talks to various groups, and 100 citizens attended the public meeting at Northwestern University. After that, all Evanston pitched in-judges businessman, housewives, churchmen, teachers, civic leaders. "Practically no one turned us down," recalls an early booster, and young people joined their elders enthusiastically in building life-size Nativity figures for outdoor displays. Lumbermen offered patterns to home craftsmen, an art studio offered free instructions in the making of creches. Pastors and priests wrote Christmastide editorials, and the local press published them. A bank ran a full-page Christ-in-Christmas ad. Buses carried slogan on cards; radio and TV joined in.

Before Christmas Eve, 60 public Nativity scenes cast their spell of love and tenderness and hope upon all who had eyes to see and hearts to receive. It was apparent to townspeople that their community had arisen to show love for Christ and his birthday. Upon out-of-towners, the impact was startling. "First," reported one woman visitor, "we stopped at the electric company to admire the beautiful creche in the window. Strains of Handel's *Messiah* quickened the air; we were thrilled to see the manger depicted in the windows of jewelers, bakers, and florists. Then we passed an insurance building in which a Nativity soared six stories high. Later, passing a theater we were confronted with giant letters on the marquee: 'Put Christ Back in Christmas.' The cumulative impact was impressive. We went home feeling that amid the feverish hustle of shopping, we had been warmed and nurtured by the deep, inner core of Christmas."

കൎൟൎൟൎൟൎൟൎൟൎൟ

Youth Forum: Youth Is Not Silent
by Irene Dunne, *Life Today*, April-May 1954

Silent? No. Confused? Yes. Doomed? Far from it. I sensed in most of the letters an awareness of what the difficulties are, and an inspiring degree of courage and reliance on spiritual values.

The question: "What is your greatest fear for your future and what are you going to do to combat it?" gave writers the option of emphasis on the negative or the positive. With a small percentage of exceptions, youth seemed determined to adjust to the present and hope for the future.

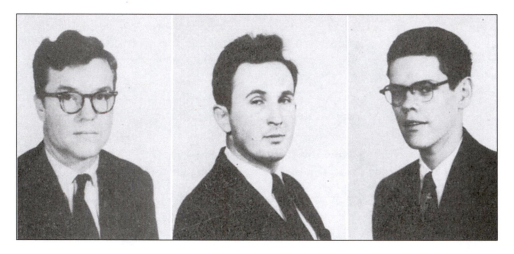

A silent generation! A bunch of crazy mixed-up kids, they say. Sure there are those of us who make the unfavorable headlines, but think of the many more who are ruled by level-headedness. We're individuals-not like boxes that must be packed together and given an over-all-label.

The silent generation! What human being wouldn't be silent in finding he had inherited a world of corruption and turmoil? It's up to him to find a solution. He makes his way through the hullabaloo in order to stand back and think. When you of the older generation choose to call us lost, immoral or doomed, think of what you have left for us to finish.

Shirley Haynes
Detroit, Michigan

•••

I was pleased to learn that letters such as the one that follows are in the minority. The editors tell me that the whole idea of the Youth Forum is to provide an opportunity for young people to speak their minds. Naturally, the ideas expressed are the writers', not necessarily those of the editors. In selecting letters for publication, the editors have chosen those which are representative of classified groups.

Although I never went to high school, I feel that I have as much brains as the average young man of my age. What do the youngsters of today want out of life, and what do they fear most? Young men are confused. What are they confused about? First, they are confused about their future. Will I get drafted? How long will I be in the service? Should I quit school? Should I marry? Will I see action? Why not have fun today and forget tomorrow? All over the United States, young people are so confused and upset that they don't dare have any hope for tomorrow. As a young man myself, I believe that the U.S. people will live in fear forever and ever because they have never seen the worst times like other nations and they fear war with the Russians. We Americans will live in fear for as long as we live no matter even if we have the best war material.

Today, young American boys of 18 to 24 are confused in mind because of war fear. They don't want any part of war, nor any part of politics, and no part of responsibility outside of the home. What they want are love, friends, games, dancing, school, music, and a job. Not a job to be rich, but just to live. We young people will never be able to be rich. Today's prices are up to the sky and wages are down to the ground. Young people get into crime because of the fear of going in the service-and sex-crimes, too, and doing things years ago never heard of. They cannot overcome fear.

Peter Di Biase
Portland, Maine

•••

Somewhat along the same line as the foregoing, but with a calm, almost grim determination to arrive at the "best solution" is this letter-typical of many.

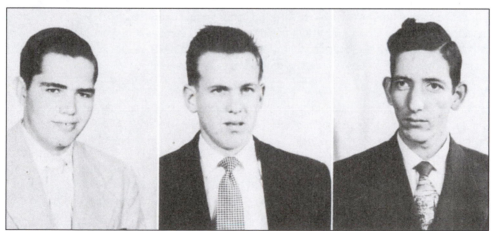

Whether or not military service will interrupt my college education is my greatest fear for the future. I am a high school senior and want to enter college upon my graduation. If I should finish several years and then be drafted, those years might be wasted. The insecurity of our age and the animosity existing between nations are serious problems facing every adult, but especially youth, for it is youth that leave their homes and schools and may have to fight on foreign soil. I think the best solution is to attend college anyway, and pray for the best.

William G. Poole
Covington, Kentucky

•••

About 30 percent of the letters indicated what to some will seem to be a surprising amount of interest in social, political and economic affairs on community, national and international levels. In all truth, from these letters I have gained the impression that today's youth are better informed and more thoughtful than the younger generation of which I was a part.

My greatest fear is complacency. American youth does not seem disturbed by the anxieties which are so puzzling to the leaders of the world, being preoccupied with atomic weapons. They tell us that they want to preserve peace through armed strength. Since when has peace ever been accomplished by warlike preparation? Is it any concern of mine? Very much so. I must face the fact that it is.

Another threat to our future, as I see it, is our materialistic outlook on life. Everybody seems to pursue happiness in nerve-tingling thrills, in sensual indulgence and material success. This has become the prime concern of our life.

I see, also, danger in the fact that all the vital affairs affecting our life are left in the hands of professional politicians.

I do not believe that all woes and ills of the world can be solved by governments, no matter what social system they represent. I think every individual should accept a responsible share in the task of making the world better…

The potential power of an individual to influence the thinking of our country is much greater than is generally realized.

Herman Mahlerman
Winnipeg, Manitoba

•••

A surprising number of the letters show insight, reflecting conditions to which their elders should see through the eyes of youth. All of the letter writers expressed fears, which is to be expected because of the topic. Most of the letters indicated that the young people could identify their fears with the draft, the threat of war, economic stress, results of youthful errors, but some-this one in particular-indicated that fear is a contagion.

What is my greatest fear? I don't know. Maybe I ought to say—everything. I'm just afraid. The funny thing is, I'm not afraid of anything that's now, like football, or doing a tough job, or girls, or a fight if I have to fight. I guess what I'm afraid of is what comes next. I don't think I'd be afraid to die, but the idea of the draft scares me. We fellows sit around sometimes and bellyache about things. Everyone has got a beef. Girls, too.

I used to think it was just me, but now I know that everybody else is scared too. It isn't just us kids, either. I remember my grandfather was afraid all the time, always saying something was liable to happen. I've heard my father tell my mother lots of times how scared he was he would lose his job, and then what would they do? My mother was always afraid for me to go out if it was cold, or wet, and if it was too hot, too. She didn't want me to play games because I might get hurt.

Politicians are trying to make us scared of communists and the scientists want us to be scared of the atom bomb and the H-bomb. Even the preacher at my church, where I don't go much, tries to scare us all into religion by talking about hell. I don't know what I fear most so I don't know what to do to combat it except to sit tight and see what happens.

B.J.S.
Chicago, Illinois

Computers in Business, The Large Electronic Machines, Heretofore Found Only in the Computation Laboratory, Are Now Being Applied to the Automatic Handling of Entire Office Procedures
Scientific American, January 1954

When the first giant, all-electric digital computer went into operation in 1945, fantastic predictions about its capacity were heard. Such "giant brains," it was said, would speedily take over all the paper functions of business and the running of entire automatic factories. Actually, these impressive monsters have proven harder to tame and put to work than was first thought. But their domestication is underway, and it is possible to report how some of them have begun to function in everyday business tasks.

The machines are a different genus from the smaller electronic computers or data processing machines that evolved out of them in some profusion after 1945. The small case scale electronic computers that are widely used in business are employed only for limited routine tasks for special purposes; for example, one electronic computer handles all seat reservations at New York for a major airline, and another collates flight schedules for the Civil Aeronautics Authority. The jobs to be given to the new giants are of a higher order of magnitude: increased inventory control, general accounting, factory management and even the human equation.

Essentially, these machines operate in the same way as the smaller ones: they add, subtract, multiply and divide, and they work with "bits" of information represented by pulsed electrical signals based on the binary number system. They have the same basic organs as any electronic computer: an arithmetical unit for computation, a control unit to direct the sequence of operations, a memory unit to store numbers and instructions, and several input-output devices for putting data and instructions into the machine and getting answers out. But they have many more of them, and the greater complexity enables them to work on very large problems, or groups of problems, without human intervention.

The giant computers still inspire the same awe that the first of the genus, ENIAC, did when its thousands of vacuum tubes began winking eerily in the basement of the Moore School of Engineering at the University of Pennsylvania nine years ago. There is something a bit frightening about them. An operator demonstrates their incredible speed in a problem involving some 780 arithmetical steps: before he has lifted his finger from the starting button, the machine is typing out the answer. Another machine reads and translates Russian documents at the rate of 100 words a minute. Another takes in masses of personal data on college freshmen and predicts with better than 90 percent accuracy which students will flunk out of a college course. (The same technique can be applied to the hiring of employees.)

ENIAC was designed to calculate ballistic tables and work on other complex equations in science and engineering. Scientific problems are still the main occupation of these machines, of which there are now more than 30 in the U.S. The reason their adaptation to business problems has been slow is not merely their cost ($1 million for a machine installed), but the fact that the kind of operation required for a business task is very different. A scientific problem usually involves a great deal of computation on relatively small amounts of data within a few fixed rules. Most business problems, on the other hand, are characterized by masses of data, relatively little computation, and multitudes of variables. Attempts to translate these problems into large programs are just beginning.

The business possibilities are well illustrated, on a limited scale, by an inventory control machine called Distribution, which was built by the Chicago mail-order house of John Plain & Co. by Engineering Research Associates, a division of Remington Rand. While the machine is by no means a "giant brain," it is the first major application of its kind and a simple approach to the larger type of problem. It is so simple that one of its designers says depreciatingly: "This machine does practically nothing, but it does nothing extremely well." Its first successful work out came in the Christmas rush just ended.

The problem was this. John Plain sells some 8,000 gift and houseware items by catalogue through about 1,000 retail merchants, mostly rural. Its business is highly seasonal, ranging from less than 2,000 orders per day in the off-season to more than 15,000 per day in the Christmas period. The company must follow inventories closely and ship items fast when they are needed. For checking inventories, it employed a battery of women clerks, who recorded each order with a checkmark against the catalogue number on a tally card and registered the totals from hundreds of these cards each week in a master tally. Since the work was tedious and seasonal, it did not attract a high grade of workers. During the rush season, the reports fell a week or two behind, and there were many errors.

Last season, the company replaced the 60 tally clerks with the Distribution machine and 10 operators. The machine is about the size of an office locker. It contains a magnetic drum memory and a small arithmetical control unit for simple addition and subtraction, to which are attached 10 input units like small desk adding machines. The orders are recorded on the revolving magnetic drum, whose sensitized surface is divided into 130 invisible tracks capable of holding 39,000 digits or "bits" of information. The quantity of each item in stock is imprinted as tiny magnetized spots at a place designating the catalogue number, and the spots already at intervals on the tracks. When an order is received for a dozen, say, of some item, the operator taps out the quantity and the catalogue number on her keyboard. If she types a wrong catalogue number, the machine flashes a signal and tells her to try again. The machine then searches the drum surface, traveling at 100 mph, finds the catalogue number, plucks off the stock total or the day's sales total, transmits it to holding relays, subtracts 12 from one total or adds 12 to the other and returns a new total to the proper place in the drum-all in 2/5 of a second.

The machine can handle 90,000 tallies a day. To get out the sales total on any one item, an operator simply types out O plus the catalogue number; the total instantly appears in illuminated numbers on the panel above her keyboard. For sales embracing more than one item, the machine has a separate output unit to which is punched the required catalogue numbers and causes it to type out those numbers in their store sales totals on a paper strip. Each night, the machine is set up to run off automatically a complete report on all of the 8,000 items in the catalogue. To compile a daily stock report by the old tally card method would have required some 150 clerks. Moreover, the Distribution does its work far more accurately than tally clerks could.

With modifications in size and in the type of input-output, the same machine can handle many other kinds of inventory problems, materials scheduling and so on. It belongs to a class of moderately fast magnetic drum machines which are now offered by a number of manufacturers. A neat, medium-sized model capable of a large variety of office jobs has reached quantity production by the Computer Research Corporation of California, recently acquired by the National Cash Register Company. The latest is the International Business Machines Corporations Magnetic Drum Calculator. Somewhat more versatile than others, it stores up to 20,000 digits and up to 2,000 separate operating instructions. It can hold entire rate tables for calculating insurance policies, freight invoices, inventory bills and the like, or entire production programs for scheduling the flow of parts and materials. The price range of the magnetic drum machines is $50,000-$100,000, or if they are rented, from $500-$1,000 a month. On a small scale, they introduce into the business machine field the important principle of the internal stored program…

The Monsanto Chemical Company recently took to IBM's computer center a problem in cost distribution. The task was to figure out how overhead charges, such as utility services, steam and the like, should be apportioned to calculate the cost of producing a certain chemical product. In multi-product industries, such as chemicals and oil, cost distribution becomes exceedingly complicated, and in many simpler industries they are so obscured that managers never get to know the actual cost per product in time for the information to have any significance. The problem that Monsanto presented to the 701 computer involved a large set of simultaneous equations and about 400,000 arithmetic operations. The machine worked out a cost sheet for the product in a few hours. Monsanto has ordered an advanced version of the 701 to prepare such cost sheets on about 1,200 items and to compute quarterly reports and do other accounting jobs which it has been doing for two years on much smaller IBM electronic computers.

The School Bus: What Happens in That Period between Home and School?
This Week, September 17, 1955

On the other side of the bus there was some talk about television. "The bus is always quiet on Thursdays," Leo (the bus driver) told me. "They are tired out from staying up for Disneyland. The quietest trip I ever made was the day after Peter Pan!"

At one stop, three little girls got on the bus. Their dog, a brown and white spaniel, got on with them. He ran to the rear and crawled under the seat. The children dragged him out, rushed him back down the aisle and pushed him to the ground.

"That dog tries to come to school every morning," Tommy told me. The dog started to bark and chase the bus. The children all rose to their feet and barked back at him.

"Sit down!" yelled the Safety Patrols. The next stop brought another small boy with an enormous bag of marbles. As the bus lurched, the bag struck against a seat and burst open. A shower of marbles hurtled in all directions. Good-naturedly, the rest of the children helped pick them up. "That happens nearly every day, too," Leo said, rubbing a marble-sized bruise on the back of his head.

We heard a loud horn honking. A smart brown coupe pulled up in front of us. A lady leaped out, flagged the bus to a halt and jumped aboard, carrying a bundle. "You forgot your lunch and your arithmetic book and your hat!" she said breathlessly to a child in one of the front seats. As the mother drove off, the boy opened the lunch box and peered inside. He pulled out a sandwich and ate it. Then he ate an apple. I wondered what he would do at noon.

Some of the children were singing softly, "My Bonnie Lies over the Ocean." "You should hear the carol-singing on the bus at Christmastime," Leo said. "It brings tears to my eyes."

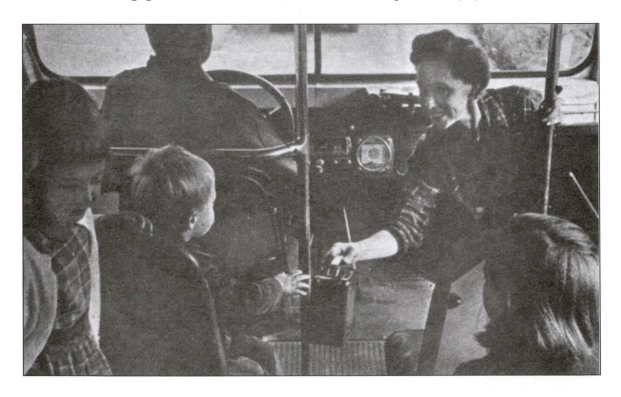

Teen-agers' Biggest Problems in 1956
Woman's Home Companion, January 1956

Last year the *Companion* started the first magazine column ever conducted for teen-agers, by teen-agers—we present here our new Talk of the Teens Panel and their questions for 1956.

- What is the ethical thing to do when you do not approve of the behavior of the rest of the crowd? Should you let a boy kiss you on the first date?

- Just how can I get that "certain someone" interested in me?

- Future careers and work seem most important to me at the moment…most teen-agers have many ideas but aren't quite sure which to choose.

MARGERY MICHEL-MORE, 17, *senior Foxboro High School Foxboro, Massachusetts* "I would like to know what going to college or getting a job after high school will be *really* like."

- I would like to see discussed the ideas, amusements and activities which keep teen-agers from border to border in continual motion.

- Teen Tact or Teen-plomacy—What do you do when he insists on sounding his horn in front of the house, when your parents insist that he come inside to see you?

- For many parties the country boy or girl is excluded unless he or she has ready transportation. If country teen-agers want jobs, the transportation problem again must be solved.

- Going steady is a problem with which almost every teen-ager comes in contact at least once during high school life.

- Let's have a column to discuss the wallflower-one of the most painful experiences for a

- boy or girl is to attend a dance and remain in the background because of shyness.

- I would like to know what going to college or getting a job after high school is really like.

- Popularity—just how important is it? Is the popular teen-ager automatically a happy, well-adjusted teen-ager?

- Ever since the days of Cleopatra the problem of the "other girl" has plagued women's minds. Today's teen-age girl would like to know how to cope with the dilemma.

MARY ELLEN CLARK, 16, *senior Lakin Rural High School Lakin, Kansas* "For many parties the country boy or girl is excluded unless he or she has ready transportation. If country teen-agers want jobs, the transportation problem again must be solved."

- I know what the teen-agers in Fair Lawn [New Jersey] think of going steady, but I would like to know the opinion of other teen-agers.

- I would like to see discussed boys' and girls' schools versus coeducation, and the value of college fraternities and sororities.

- We wonder what's right and what's wrong, and we wonder about religion.

- About the age of 15, the girls in Cincinnati get very excited over clothes. I believe articles on fads in other cities and ways to dress for different occasions would be very helpful.

- Jobs are on many teen-age minds right now. A breakdown of the main kinds of jobs would be helpful.

- Let's discuss the art of getting along well with other people and of meeting and making new friends.

MARIANNE FANALE, 16, *junior* *Sacred Heart Academy* *Springfield, Illinois* "Teen Tact or Teenplomacy—What do you do when he insists on sounding his horn in front of the house, when your parents insist that he come inside to see you?"

- How can teen-agers and their parents become better friends?

- All teen-agers are confronted with a serious problem in this day: How can they gain self-confidence?

- What can I do about the fact that my parents and I often disagree on money, clothes and what I should or shouldn't be allowed to do?

- I would very much like to see the problem of interracial dating discussed. ...I believe that an unprejudiced opinion is needed in discussing both sides.

- There are advantages and disadvantages to going steady. Just what is the general opinion of high school students throughout the country?

SALLY DAKEN, 15, *junior* *Withrow High School* *Cincinnati, Ohio* "About the age of 15, girls in Cincinnati get very excited over clothes. I believe articles on fads in other cities and ways to dress for different occasions would be very helpful."

- What about manners? Do all teen-agers know which fork to pick up first or how to make proper introductions?

- I would like to see discussed in your column the problem of younger brothers and sisters.

- Should a girl who plans on getting married and does not intend to pursue a career attend college? Is it worth all the time and expense?

- Most teen-agers take greater note of world events, religion and planning their futures than adults often realize. I would like to hear the opinions of teens throughout the nation.

Everyone Gets into the Act
Sports Illustrated, November 26, 1956

When the curtain goes up on the TV game of the week between USC and UCLA this Saturday, everyone—even the fan in the highest seat on the tall concrete rim of vast Los Angeles Memorial Coliseum to the patient reserves warming the bench—will be a performer in the biggest, brashest, loudest, greatest show on earth. That adds up to a cast somewhere close to 100,000, a fittingly grandiose spectacle for a production taking place on the outskirts of Hollywood. This will be football western-style—a pageant that is as different from the restrained enthusiasm of the Ivy League as the high-pitched call of the carnival barker from the well-modulated tones to be heard at a literary tea. It is the spontaneous outburst of a city where no service station is christened without a battery of searchlights to sweep the sky...

The football game itself, of course, is much the same as football everywhere. But in the window dressing the influence of neighboring Hollywood has rubbed off on the students who stage the performance, and the TV screens will reflect a good deal of this at halftime. The unique part of the spectacle-the contribution of the West Coast is added to the football extravaganza-is in the meticulously drilled rooting sections which will demonstrate their ingenious animated card tricks while the football teams are resting...

The mechanics of card sections are fairly simple, but first of all they require a warm climate so the rooter can shed his jacket to provide a solid background of white shirts. To begin with, the designs are drawn on graph paper by student managers. Each student in this section is then provided with five cards, colored on each side, his instructions are fastened to the back seat of the seat in front of him. At a signal from a cheerleader the cards are flipped. In the more elaborate productions, they are flipped in sequence to provide motion.

All of this started, oddly enough, in Corvallis, Oregon. Back in 1924, a postgraduate Oregon State student named Linsley Bothwell equipped his 500-man rooting section with cards, and the first animated stunt in history showed a beaver (the OSC mascot) with a big tail standing over a huge lemon yellow O (symbolizing the Beavers' opponent that day, the University of Oregon). At a signal the beaver brought his tail down on the O, demolishing it and providing a source of fun and entertainment which has survived the years. Bothwell, as one might suspect, hailed from Southern California.

Bothwell's pioneering did not go unnoticed and, in 1925, the University of Southern California took a try when their Burdette Henney devised a stunt in which the USC's mascot, the Trojan horse, winked its eye and bucked. By 1931, UCLA was using card stunts, and the following year the Uclans animated their pictures in the growing vogue. UCLA moved a step ahead of the art and science of card pictography in 1935 when Yell Leader Maury Crossman directed 1,000 students in electric displays during the night game against the University of Hawaii. The lights formed a hula girl swaying her hips amid palm trees to the accompaniment of some music from a Walt Disney movie. At the 1954 Rose Bowl game UCLA took cognizance of technical improvements and unveiled what it called a "widescreen UCLArama," in which a total of 3,456 students were card holders. This was the biggest card stunt on record at the time. And next Saturday the UCLA and USC cheering sections will be the largest yet.

Reprinted courtesy of *Sports Illustrated:* "Everyone Gets Into the Act" by Tex Maule, November 26, 1956. Copyright @1956 Time Inc. All rights reserved.

Desegregation Will Fail
Speech by the Rev. Leon C. Burns of Columbia, Tennessee,
February 19, 1956

In discussing this subject tonight it is not our purpose to add to the already high state of unrest and fear existing here in the South over the segregation problem. We simply wish to study this problem in the light of all that has developed in the 21 months since the Supreme Court handed down its decision on desegregation in the schools of the South.

I have no desire to favor either the White or the Colored race in this discussion, but I do sincerely desire to look at this question with common sense and reason in the hope that I will be able to help both races do all they can to preserve America. Few people seem to realize that the trouble caused over this question is undoubtedly the effort of alien powers to divide and destroy America.

Let it be understood that I am appealing to the honest, sincere, and patriotic American of both races, not the radical fringe of either race. I am convinced that the majority of the colored people, especially in the South, want what is best for America. They know, as we all know, that if the American way of life is not preserved, the last vestige of human freedom and liberty will perish from the earth.

Since, in 1933, Franklin Roosevelt forced us to recognize Soviet Russia, the Communist Party has tried with ever increasing zeal to create strife between the Negroes and Whites of the South; not because they cared about the freedoms of the Negro, but simply because they saw an opportunity to stir racial hatred in America. In 1935, the Communist

Party published a pamphlet called "The Negroes in a Soviet America." This pamphlet was reviewed and exposed in a full-length article which appeared in the *Nashville Banner* on July 31, 1945. The Communist plan, as revealed by a carefully drawn map, was to take over the South and create what they called a "Black Belt" which swung across the South from Texas to Maryland to Virginia. The idea was to form in this "Black Belt" a "Soviet Negro Republic," which was to form a federation with the Soviet Union. This plan was accepted by the Southern Conference for Human Welfare, a Communist-front organization. The Negroes of the South were too intelligent and too patriotic to fall for such a scheme.

The Communists, however, have not ceased in their efforts to destroy America by creating race hatred in the South. They have done this by poisoning the minds of Northern Negroes and sending them into the South to stir hatred in the hearts of their own people.

A few isolated events have been seized upon by Northern newspapers, played up and twisted out of all proportions, in an effort to make the rest of the country believe that the honest and sincere Negro of the South is in revolt, but those of us in the South know this is not the case. It is my sincere prayer that the Southern Negro is still too intelligent and too patriotic to fall for this effort of a foreign power to destroy America.

It is now a matter of record that the so-called race riot which occurred here in Columbia several years ago was seized upon by every Communist and Communist-front organization in the country in an effort to create trouble in the South.

The most successful effort of the Communist has been to encourage the creation of the National Association for the Advancement of Colored People (NAACP). This organization denies that it is Communist, but it has followed the Communist Party Line in every detail. It is no accident that the *Daily Worker*, the official Communist paper in America, has often announced the plans of the NAACP before these plans were announced by the Association itself. Walter White, Executive Secretary of the NAACP, has repeatedly stated that it was his organization that finally forced the Supreme Court decision of May 17, 1954…

The Negro in the South has made greater progress in the past 50 years than any race of people since the beginning of time. This desegregation decision will not just temporarily halt this progress, but will set it back 100 years. In my lifetime I have seen the Southern Negro grow in the respect and admiration of the White people. When I came to Columbia just 15 years ago, you would never see a Negro mentioned in the daily paper unless he happened to get caught stealing a chicken, but long before the Supreme Court decision, news reports of civic and social activities of Negroes of our community, along with their pictures, were appearing in the paper. Negroes were taking part in Red Cross drives and in other civic movements. This has been going on allover the South for many years. Every Negro that has shown talent and the desire to get ahead has been given every possible encouragement and opportunity, opportunities seldom granted even to White people. Negro musicians, writers, doctors, statesmen, and athletes or businessmen have never gone unpraised or unrespected, but now that we are forced by un-American influences to bow before a decision that we know was not made in the interest of the Negro, the progress made by the Negro of the South in the past 50 years will be lost.

Common sense and a little knowledge of human nature should teach us that forced desegregation is wrong, and is not in the interest of either the White or Colored race. We should remember that all racial problems are deep-seated. They are not born in a day, but are the result of customs, characteristics, and environments that have accumulated through hundreds of years. You do not change such customs by handing down a decree.

You do not unite the hearts and minds of a people by simply passing a law which says they shall be united. Neither can you make people equal by simply passing a law which says they shall be equal. Equality is a thing which must take place in the minds and souls of men, and can never be forced upon any man; it must be the growth of mutual understanding, respect and confidence. When this takes place among men, no law is needed to make them equal, and until this does take place, there can be no equality.

It is human nature to seek the companionship of those of our own race and class. The Negro is happy among his own people, and to try to force him into a society that is not prepared to receive him is the most inhuman thing you could do. To force a Negro child to attend school where Whites greatly outnumber Negroes is the most unkind deed you

could practice on the child. Can you realize what may happen to the mind and heart of a Negro child when he's forced into a group where he may not be wanted and may constantly be reminded of this fact? It is grossly inhuman to make children the victim of such cruel circumstances. It will not be surprising if these children turn into criminals of the worst sort in their rebellion against a society that was not ready to accept them.

There is not the slightest doubt in my mind that the Negro would have gradually worked his way into the life and economy of the South, and hence would have brought a gradual end to segregation if he had been allowed to do so, but under forced desegregation it is extremely doubtful that he ever will. It is impossible to visualize the economic

pressure, social injustices, suffering and misery that may be brought upon the Negro of the South, not by honest God-fearing people, but by those who care nothing for a human soul-White or Negro. It is sad indeed when the honest and sincere people of two races are made to suffer, and the peace and harmony of America threatened, by a small group of Communistically influenced individuals. It is sadder still when this same group-bent upon the destruction of America-is allowed to interpret our Constitution and make our laws. The present members of the Supreme Court of the United States should dress themselves in sackcloth and ashes, and bow their heads in shame.

If we are able to avoid conflict, you may rest assured that there will develop a sort of passive resistance to the Negro in the South, as there is already in the North. This sort of thing can

become more permanently detrimental to the Negro than open war. However it turns out, the Negro will be the one to suffer most; there is no way to escape it.

Before closing this talk, let me try to answer one question about the South. People of the North seem unable to understand the attitude of the Southerner toward the Negro. They are constantly asking, "Why do you Southerners feel as you do?" They fail to understand that the feeling of the Southerner toward the Negro is not one of hate or of superiority. The Southerner's feeling is a part of his heritage, born of many things, over many years. The worship of a cow by the people of India is to us a foolish thing, but to the people of India it is something very real, and very powerful. Who would think of trying to convert the people of India by suddenly killing all of their cows? The same is true with regard to the Southerner. His attitude toward the Negro may seem foolish to the rest

of the world, but to him it is very real, and very important. Is anyone so foolish as to think the federal government can convert the Southerner from his way of thinking by simply handing down a decree which demands that he make this change within a few months? The Supreme Court seems to think this can be done. How could any sane person be so thoughtless?

Having been reared in the South, I have worked with Negroes all of my life. I know their problems and sincerely believe I am as well qualified to speak for them as any White man should be. The honest and sincere Negro of the South is a peace-loving soul. He wants no trouble with White people, nor does he wish to impose himself upon anybody. He simply wants the right to live and be happy, and to make a place for himself in the world, not as a White man, nor as a cross-breed, but as a Negro.

In closing, let me sound a solemn warning to those of you who are members of the Negro race. Those groups in America now claiming to fight your battle of freedom are Communistic. They care no more for you than they would for a dog trotting down the street. They see in you a chance to foster the godless doctrine of Communism and the destruction of America. I would appeal to you not to be carried away by these sowers of discord and strife, but to think soberly and prayerfully on any question that involves your relationship with other races.

To the White people of the South, may I urge that you not allow prejudice and hatred to rule your thinking, but remember that God will solve our every problem if we but give Him a chance. I would be unworthy of the patience with which you have listened to me if I did not offer some solution to our racial problem. In this respect I have but four suggestions to make. They are:

1. Reverse by act of Congress the Supreme Court decision of May 17, 1954.

2. Allow the Southern States to work out their own racial problems to the best interest of both races, thus allowing each State to maintain the dignity of self-government, and each individual-Black or White, to maintain the dignity of free men.

3. An intensified program of education among the Negroes of the South, supplying them with educational advantages second to none.

4. A thorough investigation of the NAACP by the Federal Bureau of Investigation.

Forecasting of Weather Tough Task
Denton Record-Chronicle (Texas), July 26, 1957

The weatherman, even with modern electronic computers, cannot accurately forecast day-by-day variations in the weather more than one week in advance, University of Texas meteorologist K. H. John says.

"Many people tend to believe that the computer is the final achievement in weather forecasting. They think the present weather conditions can be fit into the computer, which would then produce a perfect forecast," John says. That is not the case. Computers may be expected to be more professional, but they are not necessarily more accurate than man," John explains.

Detailed weather forecasts are possible for two or three days in advance, but the reliability of the prediction decreases progressively after the first day, John says in explaining just what the public might expect from a professional meteorologist.

"Forecasts of the weather expected three to seven days in advance must be issued in less specific terms than the shorter range of projections and are ordinarily restricted to a statement that the temperature will be higher or lower than general for that time of year."

Lyndon Pledges Satellite Probe
The Paris News (Texas), October 18, 1957

Sen. Lyndon Johnson said yesterday the only reason the successful Earth satellite was labeled "made in Moscow" was lack of intelligent, united effort in the United States. He promised to lead efforts in Congress to find out why and what can be done about this "man-made object whizzing through the air over our heads."

The Senate majority leader spoke at the Tyler Rose Festival.

"We have got to admit frankly without evasion the Soviets have beaten us at our own game: daring scientific advances in the atomic age," Johnson said.

"This is obviously a situation which requires a careful study by Congress. The reports are conflicting. Official sources are long on warm optimism, short on cold facts…"

Johnson said his subcommittee's preliminary work would try to get answers to such questions as: "Could we have matched Soviet achievement? Would it have been worthwhile to match the Soviet achievement? Does the Soviet satellite indicate that this country has slipped behind in the development of its defense? If so, what do we have to do to catch up?"

"We may discover that the alarms are false; that there is no great cause for concern," Johnson said. "But we may also find out that our whole defense structure needs a thorough overhaul top to bottom."

The Age of Psychology in the U.S. Less Than a Century Old
Life Magazine, January 7, 1957

"After getting up the other day, John Jones, America, shaved with a razor he had bought on the strength of a magazine ad approved by the head psychologist of an advertising agency. At his breakfast table, in his morning newspaper, letter writer that her errant husband probably he read two columns of psychological fact and advice. One told him that women were absolutely not more intuitive than men, all popular opinions to the contrary notwithstanding. The invited him to find his 'happiness quotient' by answering a series of 10 questions. He then drove to work, guided by road signs painted yellow and black because a psychologist once discovered that these colors make for easier reading. At the plant he walked past the office of the company psychiatrist, where he would have been free to go in and seek counsel had he felt especially disturbed about anything that morning, and got right to work at his job, to which he had been promoted after taking a series of psychological tests.

Among his other duties this particular morning was a conference with an industrial psychologist who had been retained to advise on the company's spending contract negotiations with union. At noon, over his lunch, he read two more psychological columns in his afternoon paper, one telling him how to improve his relations with his mother-in-law, the other advising a letter writer that her errant husband probably had a mother fixation. He also read in his favorite gossip column that one of his pet movie actresses, about to go on location in Africa, was taking along her personal psychoanalyst lest she lapse into another of her spells of melancholy…

All these things might have happened to any American last week. They could not have happened to any previous generation and they could not have happened even last week in any other country, for widespread use of psychology as an applied science of everyday living is brand-new and strictly American. The birth of modern psychology took place less than 100 years ago, of psychoanalysis scarcely more than 50. In many parts of the world al knowledge of them is still restricted to the college classroom or the doctor's office. But in the U.S. for better or worse, this is the age of psychology and psychoanalysis as much as it is the age of chemistry or the atom bomb.

Message to the Wives of McDonald's Employees, by Ray Kroc, McDonald's President, 1957: When beef, steak and chops are extremely high, it certainly seems logical to use more fish, fowl, casserole dishes, and things of that sort that really have more flavor and save a lot of money. The same is true of baked goods. I had some pumpkin bread that Virginia Lea baked that was made with canned pumpkin, orange juice, flour, dates, and nuts that was out of this world. At one time you could bake a month's supply. The same might be said for chicken pot pie when stewing chickens are on sale. One day could be spent processing this and putting it in the freezer. So what I am saying is that the smarter you are, the further your money will go.

Blows against Segregation
Life Magazine, January 1957

The edifce of segregation shook last week and the chips are flying in several southern areas. Montgomery, Alabama, offices have received the U.S. Supreme Court order to let Negroes sit in buses wherever they liked, thus bringing at least a temporary end to the almost total boycott of the city buses which Negroes had maintained for an incredible 381 days. And now, because of the Court's firm stand, new bus desegregation campaigns are gathering momentum in other cities in Alabama, Louisiana, and Florida.

In Montgomery itself the legal triumph still had far to go before it became an accepted fact. Though most Whites adjusted to the new situation and Negroes diligently practiced good manners, sporadic violence flared. Several buses were shot up. In one a Negro woman was wounded in both legs, an incident which caused the jittery city government to halt bus service temporarily.

In Birmingham, Alabama, Negroes defied segregation ordinances and mingled with Whites on city buses after the house of one Negro leader was dynamited. As a result, 22 were arrested. But they obtained a test case to bring before the U.S. District Court.

In Tallahassee, Florida, Negroes, who had been boycotting buses since the end of May, began riding in forbidden seats. When the bus line did not stop it the city council furiously suspended its franchise and drivers were arrested. But the action was unlikely to stand up in court. Said Federal Judge Dozier Devane, as he granted the bus line a temporary injunction, "Every segregation act…is dead as a doornail.'"

Washington Outlook
Business Week, August 23, 1958

Eisenhower is much worried about inflation, according to associates. The result may be a cut in spending plans during the winter and spring months. The summer step-up in defense and public works spending can't be slowed quickly…

Spending will be sharply up—In January, President Eisenhower thought the cash outlay would approach $74 billion, or about $2 billion more than was spent in the year ended June 30. Prospects now are that spending will be near $79 billion. Part of this is for defense-the race with Russia in outer space. Part is for recession cures—[spending on] public works.

Agriculture Secy. Benson's farm victory will be costly—Benson forced Congress to come around to his position—less control of acreage and lower government price props. Nearly everyone agrees this was a major victory, in the economic sense. But it does have its drawbacks. The GOP, thinned out in the Midwest farm belt in 1954 and 1956, will be pressed harder than ever to hold on to House and Senate seats. And there will be no relief for the taxpayer. With fewer price controls, plantings will rise. And given good weather, Benson's policy may produce the biggest farm glut ever next year. That's when politics may take over again, with a return to high price supports at a heavy cost to taxpayers.

School integration will influence the fall voting—The issue isn't confined to the Southern and border sates, where it has been dramatized in the past two years. Racial tensions will be high in all major cities, often centering around schools. Eisenhower has threatened to put troops back in Little Rock [Arkansas]. And across the Potomac from the White House, there's the threat in Virginia to close the public schools, rather than accept court-ordered integration.

Eisenhower's role in the fall campaign is still uncertain—The President will make at least one major swing, perhaps two, before the Congressional elections in November. The President is dissatisfied with his party. He has never backed it across the board. Many party workers feel that's the chief reason Eisenhower, since his fist landslide in 1952, has had a Democratic Congress since 1954. Local bosses consider their party as permanent and Eisenhower as temporary. This has made cooperation, based on compromise, difficult.

French Car of the Future Needs No Gasoline Tank, *Popular Mechanics*, June 1958: Tomorrow's car will be driven by electricity and will need no gasoline tank, if the dreams of French designers materialize. The dream car, called the Arbel, generates its own electricity with an engine mounted in the rear. Four separate electric motors, one at each wheel, do the driving and eliminate the need for a transmission or differential. The chassis is made of rugged tubing which, being hollow, is used as the fuel tank. Still only a dream, the car is said to be easily adaptable to nuclear power.

≈≈≈≈≈≈≈≈

Marketing: Big Appetite for Gourmet Foods
Business Week, August 23, 1958

"Next week, the National Fancy Food & Confection Show will hold its fourth annual exhibit for buyers in New York. They expect at least 20 percent more than last year's 14,000. Four years ago only 7,000 buyers showed.

A clue to the trend was the entry of General Foods, giant in the mass distribution food field, into the market just a year ago. The fancy food industry doesn't ever expect to be a billion-dollar industry. But the fact that a company of the size of General Foods is sticking its toe into this relatively small pool epitomizes what is happening. The mass market that itches for something new percent of fancy foods are imported. In.ation and better has reached far beyond its old economic and social boundaries. To a man, the industry agrees the recession has passed them by.

To be sure, General Foods is a special case. Its prime concern is to keep customers hungry for its mass-distribution foods. In setting up Gourmet Foods, it had a sharp eye on the potential prestige value of such a line to the staple lines that are its mainstay.

Old-timers in the fancy food field have no such double objective. They have flourished simply by catering to today's more demanding palates.

"This is a small industry, but a growth industry," says Harry Lesser, president of Cresca Co. Inc., conceded to be one of the biggest companies in the field. The National Association for the Specialty Food Trade estimates wholesale volume has jumped from $39 million in 1931 to

$70 million this year. Specialty food outlets have doubled since 1950, to 6,000 today. Add in the other outlets that carry some specialty foods and the total is around 15,000, Lesser figures. He estimates 1958's wholesale volume at around $100 million…

How to account for surging appetites for Danish ham, pickled water chestnuts, wild oar, Euphrates bread, innumerable cheese concoctions, marinated mushrooms-not to mention the "spooky foods," such as chocolate-covered ants and fried grasshoppers?

Economic Factors-the pervading uptrend of income explains much, of course. Another economic factor, say Harold Roth, head of the agent-importer firm of Roth & Liebmann, Inc., and now trade association president, is that the rising cost of food staples is narrowing the gap between them and the fancy foods. Some 65 to 70 percent of fancy foods are imported. Inflation has hit many foreign countries is less severely than the U.S. and the growing volume of imports tends to bring prices down, too.

But economics isn't the whole story. Travel has given the industry a tremendous push. Whether consumers go to Europe or the Orient or to a new section of the U.S., they come back home with appetites whetted for new tastes.

Home Entertainment-The home-centered trend of postwar decades puts new stress on home entertaining. Even the humblest hostess wants at least one special goody for such occasions. The recession, which makes dining out costly, may have built up this trend. John G. Martin, president of Heublein, Inc. has some ideas for consumer tastes. His company's No. 1 product by far is Smirnoff Vodka, but it also imports gourmet foods and makes specialty foods.

Tired Palates-Martin is convinced that the U.S. consumer-at any economic level-finds the foods on his table rather dull. This partly explains the small, steady growth of such Heublein gourmet items such as Edouard Artzner Pate de Foie Gras, Grey Poupon Mustard, James Robertson & Sons Preserves, and Huntley & Palmer Biscuits.

ૐ᱖ᱚ᱖ᱚ᱖ᱚ᱖ᱚ᱖ᱚ

Eight Mistakes Parents Make and How to Avoid Them
Exerpt, *Parents Association*, 1958

MISTAKE No. 5: There's a Secret Trick about the Use of Praise. It's a big mistake not to learn it.

The biggest objection of all to overemphasizing the punishment idea is that it generally means looking into the past with a spirit of fault-finding. This, according to a law of human nature, tends to rub the fur the wrong way. It is far better to use a system that looks forward instead of backward. Then, when a child does something which requires training to avoid a repetition in the future, the matter is put on an EDUCATIONAL basis and the spirit of both parent and child is FRIENDLY, which is the way you want it. When the details of this system come into your hands, you will never even want to try getting along without it.

Did you ever stop to think of this? A young child gives very little thought to whether his habits are good or bad. He simply reacts in a natural way to whatever methods his parents happened to use in his training. If the methods are such as to call forth desirable actions, we say the child is "good." But if the methods are not good, we too often think of the child as being "bad."

The first time this thought impressed itself on my mind was when I was riding on a train. My attention was called to a worried mother who was trying desperately to manage two small children. They kept running back and forth from one end to the other of the Pullman car-annoying everyone as they passed. The mother was upset almost to the point of distraction. The children themselves were far from happy because of the mother's continual attempts at correction and punishment

A Child Reflects His Parental Training—Or LACK of It

It was that incident-perhaps more than any other single one-that led me to devote my life to the study of child training. After watching those untrained children and that untrained mother struggle through unpleasant hours that should have been very happy hours, I had a vision of the happiness I might bring to children and parents all over the world.

Straight across the aisle from me on that same Pullman car was a mother with two nice-looking and well-mannered children. I could not help but admire the quiet way in which this mother talked with her children. I noticed them in the dining car, too. They were all kind and courteous, one to another. It was pleasing to observe such harmony and fine culture. Without any attempt to attract undue attention to themselves, it was evident from their friendly smiles and occasional laughter that they were all really enjoying their trip to the fullest.

Now, since you are to picture clearly in your mind these two mothers I have mentioned with such a wide contrast between their method and corresponding result, let's do a little analyzing. Let's see why one mother failed miserably and why the other succeeded so well.

Why One Parent Fails and Another Succeeds

Of course, for a quick analysis in just a sentence or two, we would say that the mother whose children ran away from her control and were all over the place, disturbing others with their unwelcome noise and antics, had no correction system to help her at all. She was totally lacking in any definite plan, while the other mother was at least doing wonderfully well in practicing ONE of the five basic principles taught in my course—namely, the Principle of Friendship.

But now, let's go a step further in the analysis. The mother whose children gave her such a rough time was constantly scolding them and telling them they were "naughty." That error on her part was in violation of the Principle of Suggestion, and if she had the Course to which you are looking forward, she would know for sure that she cannot violate that principle without suffering a penalty for her violation.

Many parents who are more enlightened than the mother just referred to would know that it is wrong to tell any child that he is naughty. It is the wrong approach entirely. But their is a finer point that is not practiced by most parents until after it is specifically called to their attention.

You Will Soon Learn an Important Secret and How to Apply It

Every parent who thinks clearly has doubtlessly discovered for himself how praise can be used to encourage a child.

After a child has already completed some praiseworthy act, it is common knowledge that to praise him for the act will have the effect of inclining the child toward repeating the act to get further desired praise. But the secret of how to use praise in situations where the child does nothing at all to deserve and justify praise is not common knowledge.

Some of the most outstanding results I ever secured in clinic work were achieved by praising a child for conduct which was the exact opposite of that which he usually displayed. You will be amazed at the simple was in which you can do this yourself.

Questionnaire Writer Stirs Up Trouble
by George E. Sokolski, *The Appleton Post-Crescent* (Wisconsin), March 16, 1959

The questionnaire writer is still busy stirring up trouble for innocent parents. I have before me a questionnaire used in an American university. The one I have asks only 35 questions but it appears that there is a longer one that has 140 questions. Here are eight samples of the questions asked:

- Have you been embarrassed because of the type of work your father does in order to support the family?

- Has either of your parents insisted on your obeying him or her regardless of whether or not the request was reasonable?

- Do you think your parents fail to recognize that you are a mature person and hence treat you as if you were still a child?

- Have your parents frequently objected to the type of companions that you go around with?

- Is either of your parents easily irritated?

- Have you disagreed with your parents about your life work?

- Was your father what you would consider your ideal of manhood?

- Do you occasionally have conflicting moods of love and hate for members of your family?

I picked these eight questions out of 35 because nearly every child can answer them affirmatively at some stage. Sure, mother dominates the home! Who else? Otherwise, children would be young anarchists.

In a full family, there is a mother, a father and children. Of course, mother and father sometimes disagree and all children believe that their parents are at times unreasonable. That is part of the process of growing up.

When kids turn on the radio to blare horrible rock-n-roll music, which is an insult to anyone's intelligence, naturally a father or a mother or both will, after a while, complain. Are they unreasonable? The first thing a child must learn, and it is something that is extremely hard to learn, is that when there is more than one person in the house, consideration for others is very important. And that sense of consideration, if lacking, makes of the unfortunate creature a boor whom others avoid.

It has been the good fortune in the United States that it has had no hereditary aristocracy, no landed gentry, no elite by birth. At the beginning of this century, some feared that rich families would combine like fraternity brothers in campus politics, to dominate both the economic and political life in the country. This has not happened.

No aristocracy, not even a monied one, forms itself in this country. New York, and to a degree Palm Beach, Miami, Los Angeles and Beverly Hills, have become playgrounds for the defrocked and evil aristocracy of Europe, some of whom marry Americans for a respite from poverty. Others travel about this country more or less on the cuff, serving as shills for various mercantile enterprises.

Question one in the above questionnaire is therefore not only an irritant in the household but offensive. Before child labor laws put a ceiling on juvenile ingenuity, children who were dissatisfied with family earnings could be newsboys or bootblacks or do a hundred and one odd jobs to show their independence. In this socialistic era, they are required to be idle, listen to rock-n-roll, hang around the soda counter and call themselves beatniks to prove that they hate themselves and the world. Dissatisfied kids should be given an opportunity to work off their beefs.

Don't Smash the Profit Machinery
by Malcolm S. Forbes, *Forbes*, May 14, 1959

At the turn of the eighteenth century in Great Britain, the social upheaval we now call 'technological unemployment' raised an exceedingly ugly head. Cartwright's and Arkwright's new steam-driven spinning looms could turn out cloth far faster than the old hand-operated looms. The result was that tens of thousands of people were thrown out of jobs.

The workers' reply was a senseless and violent movement known as Luddism. Masked men would raid Midland textile mills in the dead of night, smash the frames, and sometimes burn the very buildings, acting in the name of a probably mythical 'General Ludd.' They thought they were protecting their jobs against the dreaded machines.

Luddism did the workers themselves no good and certainly helped not at all the cause of human progress. It is merely a footnote to history. But there is a moral in all this which Mr. David McDonald, Mr. Walter Reuther and some like-minded labor leaders would do well to ponder at this time. Once again we are facing technological unemployment. Currently, our Gross National Product is running nine percent ahead of a year ago, but unemployment is up only 2.4 percent. Unemployment is shrinking, but at 4.3 million it is still far higher than we would like to see it at a time when the GNP is at a record level.

Part of this is due to the growth of the labor force. But in part, it is technological unemployment, pure and simple, caused by the tremendous strides of automation. Five years ago U.S. manufacturing plants had 17.2 million workers; today we produce more goods with only 15.4 million workers.

What do some of our labor leaders suggest we do about it? "The U.S. Government," says Walter Reuther, "should take measures to raise consumer buying power…there should be a progressive reduction of the work week…The government should also create new jobs." On other occasions, Mr. Reuther has suggested that the trouble was profits were claiming too large a portion of what the industry produced. In his preliminary broadside for the forthcoming steel industry talks, United Steel Workers' President David J. McDonald has said much the same thing. He made it very clear that he thinks the steel industry can and should pay higher wages without raising prices.

The only way it can do so, of course, is by dipping into profits. I am afraid these two labor leaders do not quite realize what they are proposing. Mr. McDonald and Mr. Reuther are making the same mistakes the Luddites made. They misunderstand the nature of technological unemployment. For if one man can operate a machine where two men toiled, then the way to give the misplaced man a job is to build another machine for him to produce with.

This, of course, means that we have to find someone willing and able to pay for the machine. For this we must have profits. Profits supply today much of the savings with which we build new capital equipment. They also provide the incentive without which no one will invest his dollars and cents in machinery and plants.

SECTION FIVE: CENSUS DATA

This section begins with 16 state-by-state comparative tables that rank data from the 1950, 1960, and 2010 census, designed to help define the times during with the families profiled in Section One lived. Table topics are listed below. Following the state-by-state tables is Demographic Trends in the 20th Century-a study by the U.S. Census of four topics-population, age, race, and housing. Results are portrayed by charts, graphs and maps, making it easy to visualize the environment that shaped the 1950s, as well as how the "decade of opportunity" affected the years that followed.

Total Population

Area	Population 1950	Population 1960	Population 2010	1950 Area	1950 Rank	1960 Area	1960 Rank	2010 Area	2010 Rank
Alabama	3,061,743	3,266,740	4,779,736	New York	1	New York	1	California	1
Alaska	128,643	226,167	710,231	California	2	California	2	Texas	2
Arizona	749,587	1,302,161	6,392,017	Pennsylvania	3	Pennsylvania	3	New York	3
Arkansas	1,909,511	1,786,272	2,915,918	Illinois	4	Illinois	4	Florida	4
California	10,586,223	15,717,204	37,253,956	Ohio	5	Ohio	5	Illinois	5
Colorado	1,325,089	1,753,947	5,029,196	Texas	6	Texas	6	Pennsylvania	6
Connecticut	2,007,280	2,535,234	3,574,097	Michigan	7	Michigan	7	Ohio	7
Delaware	318,085	446,292	897,934	New Jersey	8	New Jersey	8	Michigan	8
DC	802,178	763,956	601,723	Massachusetts	9	Massachusetts	9	Georgia	9
Florida	2,771,305	4,951,560	18,801,310	North Carolina	10	Florida	10	North Carolina	10
Georgia	3,444,578	3,943,116	9,687,653	Missouri	11	Indiana	11	New Jersey	11
Hawaii	499,794	632,772	1,360,301	Indiana	12	North Carolina	12	Virginia	12
Idaho	588,637	667,191	1,567,582	Georgia	13	Missouri	13	Washington	13
Illinois	8,712,176	10,081,158	12,830,632	Wisconsin	14	Virginia	14	Massachusetts	14
Indiana	3,934,224	4,662,498	6,483,802	Virginia	15	Wisconsin	15	Indiana	15
Iowa	2,621,073	2,757,537	3,046,355	Tennessee	16	Georgia	16	Arizona	16
Kansas	1,905,299	2,178,611	2,853,118	Alabama	17	Tennessee	17	Tennessee	17
Kentucky	2,944,806	3,038,156	4,339,367	Minnesota	18	Minnesota	18	Missouri	18
Louisiana	2,683,516	3,257,022	4,533,372	Kentucky	19	Alabama	19	Maryland	19
Maine	913,774	969,265	1,328,361	Florida	20	Louisiana	20	Wisconsin	20
Maryland	2,343,001	3,100,689	5,773,552	Louisiana	21	Maryland	21	Minnesota	21
Massachusetts	4,690,514	5,148,578	6,547,629	Iowa	22	Kentucky	22	Colorado	22
Michigan	6,371,766	7,823,194	9,883,640	Washington	23	Washington	23	Alabama	23
Minnesota	2,982,483	3,413,864	5,303,925	Maryland	24	Iowa	24	South Carolina	24
Mississippi	2,178,914	2,178,141	2,967,297	Oklahoma	25	Connecticut	25	Louisiana	25
Missouri	3,954,653	4,319,813	5,988,927	Mississippi	26	South Carolina	26	Kentucky	26
Montana	591,024	674,767	989,415	South Carolina	27	Oklahoma	27	Oregon	27
Nebraska	1,325,510	1,411,330	1,826,341	Connecticut	28	Kansas	28	Oklahoma	28
Nevada	160,083	285,278	2,700,551	West Virginia	29	Mississippi	29	Connecticut	29
New Hampshire	533,242	606,921	1,316,470	Arkansas	30	West Virginia	30	Iowa	30
New Jersey	4,835,329	6,066,782	8,791,894	Kansas	31	Arkansas	31	Mississippi	31
New Mexico	681,187	951,023	2,059,179	Oregon	32	Oregon	32	Arkansas	32
New York	14,830,192	16,782,304	19,378,102	Nebraska	33	Colorado	33	Kansas	33
North Carolina	4,061,929	4,556,155	9,535,483	Colorado	34	Nebraska	34	Utah	34
North Dakota	619,636	632,446	672,591	Maine	35	Arizona	35	Nevada	35
Ohio	7,946,627	9,706,397	11,536,504	DC	36	Maine	36	New Mexico	36
Oklahoma	2,233,351	2,328,284	3,751,351	Rhode Island	37	New Mexico	37	West Virginia	37
Oregon	1,521,341	1,768,687	3,831,074	Arizona	38	Utah	38	Nebraska	38
Pennsylvania	10,498,012	11,319,366	12,702,379	Utah	39	Rhode Island	39	Idaho	39
Rhode Island	791,896	859,488	1,052,567	New Mexico	40	DC	40	Hawaii	40
South Carolina	2,117,027	2,382,594	4,625,364	South Dakota	41	South Dakota	41	Maine	41
South Dakota	652,740	680,514	814,180	North Dakota	42	Montana	42	New Hampshire	42
Tennessee	3,291,718	3,567,089	6,346,105	Montana	43	Idaho	43	Rhode Island	43
Texas	7,711,194	9,579,677	25,145,561	Idaho	44	Hawaii	44	Montana	44
Utah	688,862	890,627	2,763,885	New Hampshire	45	North Dakota	45	Delaware	45
Vermont	377,747	389,881	625,741	Hawaii	46	New Hampshire	46	South Dakota	46
Virginia	3,318,680	3,966,949	8,001,024	Vermont	47	Delaware	47	Alaska	47
Washington	2,378,963	2,853,214	6,724,540	Delaware	48	Vermont	48	North Dakota	48
West Virginia	2,005,552	1,860,421	1,852,994	Wyoming	49	Wyoming	49	Vermont	49
Wisconsin	3,434,575	3,951,777	5,686,986	Nevada	50	Nevada	50	DC	50
Wyoming	290,529	330,066	563,626	Alaska	51	Alaska	51	Wyoming	51
United States	151,325,798	179,323,175	308,745,538	United States	–	United States	–	United States	–

Source: U.S. Census Bureau, 1950 Census of Population; U.S. Census Bureau, 1960 Census of Population; U.S. Census Bureau, Census 2010

White Population

Area	Percent of Population 1950	1960	2010	1950 Area	Rank	1960 Area	Rank	2010 Area	Rank
Alabama	67.9	69.9	68.5	Vermont	1	Vermont	1	Vermont	1
Alaska	n/a	77.2	66.7	New Hampshire	2	New Hampshire	2	Maine	2
Arizona	87.3	89.8	73.0	Maine	3	Maine	3	New Hampshire	3
Arkansas	77.6	78.1	77.0	Iowa	4	Iowa	4	West Virginia	3
California	93.7	92.0	57.6	Minnesota	5	Minnesota	5	Iowa	5
Colorado	97.9	97.0	81.3	Wisconsin	6	Idaho	6	Wyoming	6
Connecticut	97.3	95.6	77.6	Idaho	6	Utah	7	North Dakota	7
Delaware	86.1	86.1	68.9	Oregon	8	North Dakota	8	Montana	8
DC	64.6	45.2	38.5	Massachusetts	9	Oregon	9	Idaho	9
Florida	78.2	82.1	75.0	Utah	9	Wyoming	10	Kentucky	10
Georgia	69.1	71.4	59.7	North Dakota	11	Massachusetts	11	Wisconsin	11
Hawaii	n/a	32.0	24.7	Nebraska	11	Rhode Island	11	Utah	12
Idaho	98.8	98.5	89.1	Rhode Island	13	Wisconsin	11	Nebraska	12
Illinois	92.4	89.4	71.5	Colorado	14	Nebraska	14	South Dakota	14
Indiana	95.5	94.1	84.3	Wyoming	15	Colorado	15	Minnesota	15
Iowa	99.2	99.0	91.3	Washington	16	Washington	16	Indiana	16
Kansas	96.0	95.4	83.8	Connecticut	17	Montana	16	Kansas	17
Kentucky	93.1	92.8	87.8	Montana	18	South Dakota	18	Oregon	18
Louisiana	67.0	67.9	62.6	South Dakota	19	Connecticut	19	Missouri	19
Maine	99.7	99.4	95.2	Kansas	20	Kansas	20	Ohio	20
Maryland	83.4	83.0	58.2	Indiana	21	West Virginia	21	Pennsylvania	21
Massachusetts	98.3	97.6	80.4	West Virginia	22	Indiana	22	Rhode Island	22
Michigan	92.9	90.6	78.9	Pennsylvania	23	Kentucky	23	Colorado	23
Minnesota	99.0	98.8	85.3	California	24	Pennsylvania	24	Massachusetts	24
Mississippi	54.6	57.7	59.1	Nevada	25	Nevada	25	Michigan	25
Missouri	92.4	90.8	82.8	New York	26	New Mexico	26	Connecticut	26
Montana	96.8	96.4	89.4	Ohio	26	California	27	Tennessee	26
Nebraska	98.2	97.4	86.1	New Jersey	28	Ohio	28	Washington	28
Nevada	93.6	92.3	66.2	Kentucky	29	New Jersey	29	Arkansas	29
New Hampshire	99.8	99.6	93.9	Michigan	30	New York	30	Florida	30
New Jersey	93.3	91.3	68.6	New Mexico	31	Missouri	31	Arizona	31
New Mexico	92.5	92.1	68.4	Illinois	32	Michigan	32	Oklahoma	32
New York	93.5	91.1	65.7	Missouri	32	Oklahoma	33	Illinois	33
North Carolina	73.4	74.6	68.5	Oklahoma	34	Arizona	34	Texas	34
North Dakota	98.2	98.0	90.0	Arizona	35	Illinois	35	Delaware	35
Ohio	93.5	91.8	82.7	Texas	36	Texas	36	New Jersey	36
Oklahoma	91.0	90.5	72.2	Delaware	37	Delaware	37	Virginia	36
Oregon	98.4	97.9	83.6	Tennessee	38	Tennessee	38	North Carolina	38
Pennsylvania	93.9	92.4	81.9	Maryland	39	Maryland	39	Alabama	38
Rhode Island	98.1	97.6	81.4	Florida	40	Florida	40	New Mexico	40
South Carolina	61.1	65.1	66.2	Virginia	41	Virginia	41	Alaska	41
South Dakota	96.3	96.0	85.9	Arkansas	42	Arkansas	42	Nevada	42
Tennessee	83.9	83.5	77.6	North Carolina	43	Alaska	43	South Carolina	42
Texas	87.2	87.4	70.4	Georgia	44	North Carolina	44	New York	44
Utah	98.3	98.1	86.1	Alabama	45	Georgia	45	Louisiana	45
Vermont	99.9	99.8	95.3	Louisiana	46	Alabama	46	Georgia	46
Virginia	77.8	79.2	68.6	DC	47	Louisiana	47	Mississippi	47
Washington	97.4	96.4	77.3	South Carolina	48	South Carolina	48	Maryland	48
West Virginia	94.3	95.1	93.9	Mississippi	49	Mississippi	49	California	49
Wisconsin	98.8	97.6	86.2	Alaska	n/a	DC	50	DC	50
Wyoming	97.8	97.8	90.7	Hawaii	n/a	Hawaii	51	Hawaii	51
United States	89.1	88.5	72.4	United States	–	United States	–	United States	–

Source: U.S. Census Bureau, 1950 Census of Population; U.S. Census Bureau, 1960 Census of Population; U.S. Census Bureau, Census 2010

Black Population

Area	Percent of Population			1950		1960		2010	
	1950	1960	2010	Area	Rank	Area	Rank	Area	Rank
Alabama	32.0	30.0	26.2	Mississippi	1	DC	1	DC	1
Alaska	n/a	3.0	3.3	South Carolina	2	Mississippi	2	Mississippi	2
Arizona	3.5	3.3	4.1	DC	3	South Carolina	3	Louisiana	3
Arkansas	22.3	21.8	15.4	Louisiana	4	Louisiana	4	Georgia	4
California	4.4	5.6	6.2	Alabama	5	Alabama	5	Maryland	5
Colorado	1.5	2.3	4.0	Georgia	6	Georgia	6	South Carolina	6
Connecticut	2.7	4.2	10.1	North Carolina	7	North Carolina	7	Alabama	7
Delaware	13.7	13.6	21.4	Arkansas	8	Arkansas	8	North Carolina	8
DC	35.0	53.9	50.7	Virginia	9	Virginia	9	Delaware	9
Florida	21.8	17.8	16.0	Florida	10	Florida	10	Virginia	10
Georgia	30.9	28.5	30.5	Maryland	11	Maryland	11	Tennessee	11
Hawaii	n/a	0.8	1.6	Tennessee	12	Tennessee	12	Florida	12
Idaho	0.2	0.2	0.6	Delaware	13	Delaware	13	New York	13
Illinois	7.4	10.3	14.5	Texas	14	Texas	14	Arkansas	14
Indiana	4.4	5.8	9.1	Missouri	15	Illinois	15	Illinois	15
Iowa	0.8	0.9	2.9	Illinois	16	Michigan	16	Michigan	16
Kansas	3.8	4.2	5.9	Michigan	17	Missouri	17	New Jersey	17
Kentucky	6.9	7.1	7.8	Kentucky	17	New Jersey	18	Ohio	18
Louisiana	32.9	31.9	32.0	New Jersey	19	New York	19	Texas	19
Maine	0.1	0.3	1.2	Ohio	20	Ohio	20	Missouri	20
Maryland	16.5	16.7	29.4	Oklahoma	20	Pennsylvania	21	Pennsylvania	21
Massachusetts	1.6	2.2	6.6	New York	22	Kentucky	22	Connecticut	22
Michigan	6.9	9.2	14.2	Pennsylvania	23	Oklahoma	23	Indiana	23
Minnesota	0.5	0.7	5.2	West Virginia	24	Indiana	24	Nevada	24
Mississippi	45.3	42.0	37.0	California	25	California	25	Kentucky	25
Missouri	7.5	9.0	11.6	Indiana	25	West Virginia	26	Oklahoma	26
Montana	0.2	0.2	0.4	Kansas	27	Nevada	27	Massachusetts	27
Nebraska	1.5	2.1	4.5	Arizona	28	Connecticut	28	Wisconsin	28
Nevada	2.7	4.7	8.1	Connecticut	29	Kansas	28	California	29
New Hampshire	0.1	0.3	1.1	Nevada	29	Arizona	30	Kansas	30
New Jersey	6.6	8.5	13.7	Rhode Island	31	Alaska	31	Rhode Island	31
New Mexico	1.2	1.8	2.1	Massachusetts	32	Colorado	32	Minnesota	32
New York	6.2	8.4	15.9	Colorado	33	Massachusetts	33	Nebraska	33
North Carolina	25.8	24.5	21.5	Nebraska	33	Rhode Island	34	Arizona	34
North Dakota	<0.1	0.1	1.2	Washington	35	Nebraska	34	Colorado	35
Ohio	6.5	8.1	12.2	New Mexico	36	Wisconsin	36	Washington	36
Oklahoma	6.5	6.6	7.4	Wyoming	37	New Mexico	37	West Virginia	37
Oregon	0.8	1.0	1.8	Wisconsin	38	Washington	38	Alaska	38
Pennsylvania	6.1	7.5	10.8	Oregon	38	Oregon	39	Iowa	39
Rhode Island	1.8	2.1	5.7	Iowa	38	Iowa	40	New Mexico	40
South Carolina	38.8	34.8	27.9	Minnesota	41	Hawaii	41	Oregon	41
South Dakota	0.1	0.2	1.3	Utah	42	Minnesota	42	Hawaii	42
Tennessee	16.1	16.5	16.7	Montana	43	Wyoming	42	South Dakota	43
Texas	12.7	12.4	11.8	Idaho	43	Utah	44	Maine	44
Utah	0.4	0.5	1.1	New Hampshire	45	New Hampshire	45	North Dakota	44
Vermont	0.1	0.1	1.0	Maine	45	Maine	45	Utah	46
Virginia	22.1	20.6	19.4	Vermont	45	Montana	47	New Hampshire	46
Washington	1.3	1.7	3.6	South Dakota	45	South Dakota	47	Vermont	48
West Virginia	5.7	4.8	3.4	North Dakota	49	Idaho	47	Wyoming	49
Wisconsin	0.8	1.9	6.3	Alaska	n/a	Vermont	50	Idaho	50
Wyoming	0.9	0.7	0.8	Hawaii	n/a	North Dakota	50	Montana	51
United States	9.9	10.5	12.6	United States	–	United States	–	United States	–

Source: U.S. Census Bureau, 1950 Census of Population; U.S. Census Bureau, 1960 Census of Population; U.S. Census Bureau, Census 2010.

American Indian/Alaska Native Population

Area	Percent of Population			1950		1960		2010	
	1950	1960	2010	Area	Rank	Area	Rank	Area	Rank
Alabama	<0.1	<0.1	0.6	Arizona	1	Arizona	1	Alaska	1
Alaska	n/a	6.4	14.8	New Mexico	2	Alaska	1	New Mexico	2
Arizona	8.8	6.4	4.6	South Dakota	3	New Mexico	3	South Dakota	3
Arkansas	<0.1	<0.1	0.8	Nevada	4	South Dakota	4	Oklahoma	4
California	0.2	0.2	1.0	Montana	5	Montana	5	Montana	5
Colorado	0.1	0.2	1.1	Oklahoma	6	Oklahoma	6	North Dakota	6
Connecticut	<0.1	<0.1	0.3	North Dakota	7	Nevada	7	Arizona	7
Delaware	0.0	0.1	0.5	Wyoming	8	North Dakota	8	Wyoming	8
DC	<0.1	0.1	0.3	Washington	9	Wyoming	9	Washington	9
Florida	<0.1	0.1	0.4	Utah	9	Utah	10	Oregon	10
Georgia	<0.1	<0.1	0.3	Idaho	9	Idaho	10	Idaho	10
Hawaii	n/a	0.1	0.3	Minnesota	12	North Carolina	10	North Carolina	12
Idaho	0.6	0.8	1.4	Wisconsin	12	Washington	13	Nevada	13
Illinois	<0.1	<0.1	0.3	Oregon	12	Minnesota	14	Utah	13
Indiana	<0.1	<0.1	0.3	Nebraska	15	Oregon	14	Colorado	15
Iowa	<0.1	0.1	0.4	California	16	Wisconsin	16	Minnesota	15
Kansas	0.1	0.2	1.0	Maine	16	Nebraska	16	California	17
Kentucky	<0.1	<0.1	0.2	New York	18	California	18	Kansas	17
Louisiana	<0.1	0.1	0.7	Michigan	18	Maine	18	Nebraska	17
Maine	0.2	0.2	0.6	Colorado	18	Colorado	18	Wisconsin	17
Maryland	<0.1	<0.1	0.4	Kansas	18	Kansas	18	Arkansas	21
Massachusetts	<0.1	<0.1	0.3	Mississippi	18	New York	22	Texas	22
Michigan	0.1	0.1	0.6	North Carolina	18	Hawaii	22	Louisiana	22
Minnesota	0.4	0.5	1.1	Massachusetts	24	Rhode Island	22	New York	24
Mississippi	0.1	0.1	0.5	Connecticut	24	Michigan	22	Rhode Island	24
Missouri	<0.1	<0.1	0.5	Rhode Island	24	Florida	22	Michigan	24
Montana	2.8	3.1	6.3	New Jersey	24	DC	22	Alabama	24
Nebraska	0.3	0.4	1.0	New Hampshire	24	Delaware	22	Maine	24
Nevada	3.1	2.3	1.2	Illinois	24	Texas	22	Delaware	29
New Hampshire	<0.1	<0.1	0.2	Vermont	24	Iowa	22	Missouri	29
New Jersey	<0.1	<0.1	0.3	Pennsylvania	24	Virginia	22	Mississippi	29
New Mexico	6.2	5.9	9.4	Ohio	24	Louisiana	22	Florida	32
New York	0.1	0.1	0.6	DC	24	Mississippi	22	Maryland	32
North Carolina	0.1	0.8	1.3	Florida	24	Massachusetts	34	Virginia	32
North Dakota	1.7	1.9	5.4	South Carolina	24	Connecticut	34	South Carolina	32
Ohio	<0.1	<0.1	0.2	Maryland	24	New Jersey	34	Iowa	32
Oklahoma	2.4	2.8	8.6	Texas	24	New Hampshire	34	Vermont	32
Oregon	0.4	0.5	1.4	Iowa	24	Illinois	34	New Jersey	38
Pennsylvania	<0.1	<0.1	0.2	Indiana	24	Vermont	34	Hawaii	38
Rhode Island	<0.1	0.1	0.6	Missouri	24	Pennsylvania	34	Massachusetts	38
South Carolina	<0.1	<0.1	0.4	West Virginia	24	Ohio	34	Illinois	38
South Dakota	3.6	3.8	8.8	Louisiana	24	Maryland	34	Connecticut	38
Tennessee	<0.1	<0.1	0.3	Virginia	24	Indiana	34	DC	38
Texas	<0.1	0.1	0.7	Kentucky	24	Missouri	34	Georgia	38
Utah	0.6	0.8	1.2	Georgia	24	West Virginia	34	Tennessee	38
Vermont	<0.1	<0.1	0.4	Arkansas	24	Georgia	34	Indiana	38
Virginia	<0.1	0.1	0.4	Tennessee	24	Kentucky	34	Pennsylvania	47
Washington	0.6	0.7	1.5	Alabama	24	South Carolina	34	New Hampshire	47
West Virginia	<0.1	<0.1	0.2	Delaware	49	Alabama	34	Ohio	47
Wisconsin	0.4	0.4	1.0	Alaska	n/a	Arkansas	34	Kentucky	47
Wyoming	1.1	1.2	2.4	Hawaii	n/a	Tennessee	34	West Virginia	47
United States	0.2	0.2	0.9	United States	–	United States	–	United States	–

Source: U.S. Census Bureau, 1950 Census of Population; U.S. Census Bureau, 1960 Census of Population; U.S. Census Bureau, Census 2010

Asian Population

Area	Percent of Population 1950	1960	2010	1950 Area	Rank	1960 Area	Rank	2010 Area	Rank
Alabama	<0.1	<0.1	1.1	California	1	Hawaii	1	Hawaii	1
Alaska	n/a	0.8	5.4	Washington	2	California	2	California	2
Arizona	0.4	0.4	2.8	Utah	2	Washington	3	New Jersey	3
Arkansas	<0.1	0.1	1.2	Nevada	4	Alaska	4	New York	4
California	1.7	2.0	13.0	Colorado	4	DC	5	Nevada	5
Colorado	0.5	0.5	2.8	Arizona	6	Utah	5	Washington	5
Connecticut	0.1	0.1	3.8	Oregon	6	Nevada	7	Maryland	7
Delaware	<0.1	0.1	3.2	DC	6	Oregon	7	Virginia	7
DC	0.4	0.6	3.5	Idaho	6	Colorado	7	Alaska	9
Florida	<0.1	0.1	2.4	New York	10	Arizona	10	Massachusetts	10
Georgia	<0.1	0.1	3.2	Illinois	10	Idaho	10	Illinois	11
Hawaii	n/a	65.3	38.6	Montana	10	New York	12	Minnesota	12
Idaho	0.4	0.4	1.2	Wyoming	10	Massachusetts	13	Texas	13
Illinois	0.2	0.2	4.6	Massachusetts	14	Illinois	13	Connecticut	13
Indiana	<0.1	0.1	1.6	Connecticut	14	Montana	13	Oregon	15
Iowa	<0.1	<0.1	1.7	Rhode Island	14	Maryland	13	DC	16
Kansas	<0.1	0.1	2.4	New Jersey	14	Wyoming	13	Georgia	17
Kentucky	<0.1	<0.1	1.1	Michigan	14	New Mexico	13	Delaware	17
Louisiana	<0.1	0.1	1.5	Minnesota	14	Connecticut	19	Rhode Island	19
Maine	<0.1	0.1	1.0	Nebraska	14	New Jersey	19	Arizona	20
Maryland	0.1	0.2	5.5	Maryland	14	Rhode Island	19	Colorado	20
Massachusetts	0.1	0.2	5.3	Texas	14	New Hampshire	19	Pennsylvania	22
Michigan	0.1	0.1	2.4	New Mexico	14	Michigan	19	Florida	23
Minnesota	0.1	0.1	4.0	Mississippi	14	Maine	19	Kansas	23
Mississippi	0.1	0.1	0.9	New Hampshire	25	Florida	19	Michigan	23
Missouri	<0.1	0.1	1.6	Maine	25	Pennsylvania	19	Wisconsin	26
Montana	0.2	0.2	0.6	North Dakota	25	Wisconsin	19	North Carolina	27
Nebraska	0.1	0.1	1.8	Vermont	25	Minnesota	19	New Hampshire	27
Nevada	0.5	0.5	7.2	Pennsylvania	25	Ohio	19	Utah	29
New Hampshire	<0.1	0.1	2.2	Wisconsin	25	Delaware	19	Nebraska	30
New Jersey	0.1	0.1	8.3	Ohio	25	Texas	19	Oklahoma	31
New Mexico	0.1	0.2	1.4	Florida	25	Nebraska	19	Iowa	31
New York	0.2	0.3	7.3	South Dakota	25	Indiana	19	Ohio	31
North Carolina	<0.1	<0.1	2.2	Delaware	25	Missouri	19	Indiana	34
North Dakota	<0.1	<0.1	1.0	Iowa	25	Kansas	19	Missouri	34
Ohio	<0.1	0.1	1.7	Indiana	25	Virginia	19	Louisiana	36
Oklahoma	<0.1	0.1	1.7	Missouri	25	Louisiana	19	New Mexico	37
Oregon	0.4	0.5	3.7	Kansas	25	Oklahoma	19	Tennessee	37
Pennsylvania	<0.1	0.1	2.7	West Virginia	25	Georgia	19	South Carolina	39
Rhode Island	0.1	0.1	2.9	Louisiana	25	Mississippi	19	Vermont	39
South Carolina	<0.1	<0.1	1.3	Virginia	25	Arkansas	19	Idaho	41
South Dakota	<0.1	<0.1	0.9	Oklahoma	25	Vermont	42	Arkansas	41
Tennessee	<0.1	<0.1	1.4	Kentucky	25	North Dakota	42	Alabama	43
Texas	0.1	0.1	3.8	Georgia	25	South Dakota	42	Kentucky	43
Utah	0.7	0.6	2.0	Arkansas	25	Iowa	42	Maine	45
Vermont	<0.1	<0.1	1.3	North Carolina	25	West Virginia	42	North Dakota	45
Virginia	<0.1	0.1	5.5	Tennessee	25	Kentucky	42	South Dakota	47
Washington	0.7	1.0	7.2	Alabama	25	South Carolina	42	Mississippi	47
West Virginia	<0.1	<0.1	0.7	South Carolina	25	North Carolina	42	Wyoming	49
Wisconsin	<0.1	0.1	2.3	Alaska	n/a	Alabama	42	West Virginia	50
Wyoming	0.2	0.2	0.8	Hawaii	n/a	Tennessee	42	Montana	51
United States	0.2	0.5	4.8	United States	–	United States	–	United States	–

Source: U.S. Census Bureau, 1950 Census of Population; U.S. Census Bureau, 1960 Census of Population; U.S. Census Bureau, Census 2010

281

Foreign-Born Population

Area	Percent of Population 1950	Percent of Population 1960	Percent of Population 2010	1950 Area	1950 Rank	1960 Area	1960 Rank	2010 Area	2010 Rank
Alabama	0.4	0.5	3.4	New York	1	New York	1	California	1
Alaska	n/a	3.6	7.2	Massachusetts	2	Massachusetts	2	New York	2
Arizona	6.3	5.4	14.2	Connecticut	3	Hawaii	3	New Jersey	3
Arkansas	0.5	0.4	4.3	Rhode Island	4	Connecticut	3	Nevada	4
California	10.0	8.5	27.2	New Jersey	5	New Jersey	5	Florida	5
Colorado	4.6	3.4	9.8	New Hampshire	6	Rhode Island	6	Hawaii	6
Connecticut	14.8	10.9	13.2	California	7	California	7	Texas	7
Delaware	4.1	3.3	8.2	Michigan	8	New Hampshire	8	Massachusetts	8
DC	5.3	5.1	13.0	Illinois	9	Michigan	9	Arizona	9
Florida	4.7	5.5	19.2	Washington	10	Illinois	9	Illinois	10
Georgia	0.5	0.6	9.6	Maine	11	Washington	11	Maryland	11
Hawaii	n/a	10.9	17.7	North Dakota	12	Maine	12	Connecticut	11
Idaho	3.4	2.3	5.9	Vermont	13	Vermont	13	DC	13
Illinois	9.1	6.8	13.6	Pennsylvania	14	Florida	14	Washington	14
Indiana	2.5	2.0	4.4	Montana	15	Arizona	15	Rhode Island	15
Iowa	3.2	2.0	4.1	Minnesota	16	Pennsylvania	16	Virginia	16
Kansas	2.0	1.5	6.3	Nevada	17	DC	17	Colorado	17
Kentucky	0.5	0.6	3.1	Arizona	18	North Dakota	18	New Mexico	18
Louisiana	1.1	0.9	3.6	Wisconsin	18	Nevada	19	Oregon	18
Maine	8.2	6.2	3.3	Oregon	20	Montana	20	Georgia	20
Maryland	3.7	3.0	13.2	Ohio	20	Wisconsin	21	Utah	21
Massachusetts	15.4	11.2	14.5	DC	22	Minnesota	22	Delaware	21
Michigan	9.5	6.8	5.9	Florida	23	Ohio	23	North Carolina	23
Minnesota	7.1	4.2	7.0	South Dakota	23	Oregon	24	Alaska	24
Mississippi	0.4	0.4	2.2	Wyoming	25	Utah	25	Minnesota	25
Missouri	2.3	1.8	3.7	Colorado	25	Alaska	25	Kansas	26
Montana	7.4	4.5	2.0	Utah	27	Colorado	27	Michigan	27
Nebraska	4.4	2.9	5.9	Nebraska	28	Delaware	28	Idaho	27
Nevada	6.7	4.6	19.3	Delaware	29	Texas	29	Nebraska	27
New Hampshire	10.9	7.4	5.3	Maryland	30	Maryland	30	Pennsylvania	30
New Jersey	13.2	10.1	20.3	Texas	31	Nebraska	31	New Hampshire	31
New Mexico	2.6	2.3	9.7	Idaho	32	Wyoming	31	Oklahoma	32
New York	17.4	13.6	21.7	Iowa	33	South Dakota	33	South Carolina	33
North Carolina	0.4	0.5	7.4	New Mexico	34	New Mexico	34	Wisconsin	34
North Dakota	7.8	4.7	2.4	Indiana	35	Idaho	34	Tennessee	35
Ohio	5.6	4.1	3.8	Missouri	36	Iowa	36	Indiana	35
Oklahoma	0.8	0.9	5.2	Kansas	37	Indiana	36	Arkansas	37
Oregon	5.6	4.0	9.7	West Virginia	38	Missouri	38	Iowa	38
Pennsylvania	7.5	5.3	5.6	Louisiana	39	Kansas	39	Vermont	39
Rhode Island	14.4	10.0	12.6	Virginia	39	West Virginia	40	Ohio	40
South Carolina	0.3	0.5	4.7	Oklahoma	41	Virginia	41	Missouri	41
South Dakota	4.7	2.7	2.3	Kentucky	42	Louisiana	42	Louisiana	42
Tennessee	0.4	0.4	4.4	Georgia	42	Oklahoma	42	Alabama	43
Texas	3.6	3.1	16.1	Arkansas	42	Georgia	44	Maine	44
Utah	4.5	3.6	8.2	Mississippi	45	Kentucky	44	Wyoming	45
Vermont	7.6	6.0	4.0	North Carolina	45	South Carolina	46	Kentucky	45
Virginia	1.1	1.2	10.8	Tennessee	45	North Carolina	46	North Dakota	47
Washington	8.3	6.3	12.7	Alabama	45	Alabama	46	South Dakota	48
West Virginia	1.7	1.3	1.3	South Carolina	49	Mississippi	49	Mississippi	49
Wisconsin	6.3	4.3	4.6	Alaska	n/a	Arkansas	49	Montana	50
Wyoming	4.6	2.9	3.1	Hawaii	n/a	Tennessee	49	West Virginia	51
United States	6.9	5.4	12.7	United States	–	United States	–	United States	–

Source: U.S. Census Bureau, 1950 Census of Population; U.S. Census Bureau, 1960 Census of Population; U.S. Census Bureau, American Community Survey, 2006-2010 Five-Year Estimate

Urban Population

Area	Percent of Population			1950		1960		2010	
	1950	1960	2010	Area	Rank	Area	Rank	Area	Rank
Alabama	43.8	54.8	55.0	DC	1	DC	1	DC	1
Alaska	26.6	37.9	60.5	New Jersey	2	New Jersey	2	New Jersey	2
Arizona	55.5	74.5	86.7	New York	3	Rhode Island	3	California	3
Arkansas	33.0	42.8	52.0	Massachusetts	4	California	3	Massachusetts	4
California	80.7	86.4	93.2	Rhode Island	5	New York	5	Rhode Island	5
Colorado	62.7	73.7	82.0	California	6	Massachusetts	6	Nevada	6
Connecticut	77.6	78.3	87.9	Connecticut	7	Illinois	7	Hawaii	7
Delaware	62.6	65.6	80.1	Illinois	7	Connecticut	8	Florida	8
DC	100.0	100.0	100.0	Michigan	9	Hawaii	9	Connecticut	9
Florida	65.5	73.9	89.3	Pennsylvania	10	Texas	10	Illinois	10
Georgia	45.3	55.3	70.7	Ohio	11	Utah	11	Arizona	11
Hawaii	69.0	76.5	90.0	Maryland	12	Arizona	12	Maryland	12
Idaho	42.9	47.5	63.8	Hawaii	12	Florida	13	New York	13
Illinois	77.6	80.7	87.3	Florida	14	Colorado	14	Utah	14
Indiana	59.9	62.4	72.1	Utah	15	Michigan	15	Colorado	15
Iowa	47.7	53.0	61.4	Washington	16	Ohio	15	Washington	16
Kansas	52.1	61.0	71.1	Colorado	17	Maryland	17	Texas	17
Kentucky	36.8	44.5	55.9	Texas	17	Pennsylvania	18	Delaware	18
Louisiana	54.8	63.3	72.1	Delaware	19	Nevada	19	Ohio	19
Maine	51.7	51.3	36.6	Missouri	20	Washington	20	Oregon	20
Maryland	69.0	72.7	86.4	Indiana	21	Missouri	21	Pennsylvania	21
Massachusetts	84.4	83.6	91.1	Wisconsin	22	New Mexico	22	New Mexico	22
Michigan	70.7	73.4	72.2	New Hampshire	23	Delaware	23	Michigan	23
Minnesota	54.5	62.2	68.3	Nevada	24	Wisconsin	24	Indiana	24
Mississippi	27.9	37.7	48.7	Arizona	25	Louisiana	25	Louisiana	24
Missouri	61.5	66.6	68.3	Louisiana	26	Oklahoma	26	Virginia	26
Montana	43.7	50.2	52.0	Minnesota	27	Indiana	27	Kansas	27
Nebraska	46.9	54.3	68.4	Oregon	28	Minnesota	28	Georgia	28
Nevada	57.2	70.4	90.6	Kansas	29	Oregon	28	Nebraska	29
New Hampshire	57.5	58.3	55.6	Maine	30	Kansas	30	Minnesota	30
New Jersey	86.6	88.6	94.7	Oklahoma	31	New Hampshire	31	Missouri	30
New Mexico	50.2	65.9	73.7	New Mexico	32	Wyoming	32	Wisconsin	32
New York	85.5	85.4	85.6	Wyoming	33	Virginia	33	Oklahoma	33
North Carolina	33.7	39.5	59.1	Iowa	34	Georgia	34	Idaho	34
North Dakota	26.6	35.2	54.0	Virginia	35	Alabama	35	Tennessee	35
Ohio	70.2	73.4	78.9	Nebraska	36	Nebraska	36	Wyoming	36
Oklahoma	51.0	62.9	65.1	Georgia	37	Iowa	37	Iowa	37
Oregon	53.9	62.2	77.9	Tennessee	38	Tennessee	38	South Carolina	38
Pennsylvania	70.5	71.6	76.4	Alabama	39	Maine	39	Alaska	39
Rhode Island	84.3	86.4	90.9	Montana	40	Montana	40	North Carolina	40
South Carolina	36.7	41.2	61.2	Idaho	41	Idaho	41	Kentucky	41
South Dakota	33.2	39.3	51.6	Kentucky	42	Kentucky	42	New Hampshire	42
Tennessee	44.1	52.3	63.6	South Carolina	43	Arkansas	43	Alabama	43
Texas	62.7	75.0	80.7	Vermont	44	South Carolina	44	North Dakota	44
Utah	65.3	74.9	85.4	West Virginia	45	North Carolina	45	Arkansas	45
Vermont	36.4	38.5	33.6	North Carolina	46	South Dakota	46	Montana	45
Virginia	47.0	55.6	71.4	South Dakota	47	Vermont	47	South Dakota	47
Washington	63.2	68.1	81.3	Arkansas	48	West Virginia	48	Mississippi	48
West Virginia	34.6	38.2	46.4	Mississippi	49	Alaska	49	West Virginia	49
Wisconsin	57.9	63.8	65.8	North Dakota	50	Mississippi	50	Maine	50
Wyoming	49.8	56.8	62.4	Alaska	50	North Dakota	51	Vermont	51
United States	64.0	69.9	77.6	United States	–	United States	–	United States	–

Source: U.S. Census Bureau, 1950 Census of Housing; U.S. Census Bureau, 1960 Census of Housing; U.S. Census Bureau, Census 2010

Rural Population

Area	Percent of Population			1950		1960		2010	
	1950	1960	2010	Area	Rank	Area	Rank	Area	Rank
Alabama	56.2	45.2	45.0	North Dakota	1	North Dakota	1	Vermont	1
Alaska	73.4	62.1	39.5	Alaska	1	Mississippi	2	Maine	2
Arizona	44.5	25.5	13.3	Mississippi	3	Alaska	3	West Virginia	3
Arkansas	67.0	57.2	48.0	Arkansas	4	West Virginia	4	Mississippi	4
California	19.3	13.6	6.8	South Dakota	5	Vermont	5	South Dakota	5
Colorado	37.3	26.3	18.0	North Carolina	6	South Dakota	6	Arkansas	6
Connecticut	22.4	21.7	12.1	West Virginia	7	North Carolina	7	Montana	6
Delaware	37.4	34.4	19.9	Vermont	8	South Carolina	8	North Dakota	8
DC	0.0	0.0	0.0	South Carolina	9	Arkansas	9	Alabama	9
Florida	34.5	26.1	10.7	Kentucky	10	Kentucky	10	New Hampshire	10
Georgia	54.7	44.7	29.3	Idaho	11	Idaho	11	Kentucky	11
Hawaii	31.0	23.5	10.0	Montana	12	Montana	12	North Carolina	12
Idaho	57.1	52.5	36.2	Alabama	13	Maine	13	Alaska	13
Illinois	22.4	19.3	12.7	Tennessee	14	Tennessee	14	South Carolina	14
Indiana	40.1	37.6	27.9	Georgia	15	Iowa	15	Iowa	15
Iowa	52.3	47.0	38.6	Nebraska	16	Nebraska	16	Wyoming	16
Kansas	47.9	39.0	28.9	Virginia	17	Alabama	17	Tennessee	17
Kentucky	63.2	55.5	44.1	Iowa	18	Georgia	18	Idaho	18
Louisiana	45.2	36.7	27.9	Wyoming	19	Virginia	19	Oklahoma	19
Maine	48.3	48.7	63.4	New Mexico	20	Wyoming	20	Wisconsin	20
Maryland	31.0	27.3	13.6	Oklahoma	21	New Hampshire	21	Minnesota	21
Massachusetts	15.6	16.4	8.9	Maine	22	Kansas	22	Missouri	21
Michigan	29.3	26.6	27.8	Kansas	23	Minnesota	23	Nebraska	23
Minnesota	45.5	37.8	31.7	Oregon	24	Oregon	23	Georgia	24
Mississippi	72.1	62.3	51.3	Minnesota	25	Indiana	25	Kansas	25
Missouri	38.5	33.4	31.7	Louisiana	26	Oklahoma	26	Virginia	26
Montana	56.3	49.8	48.0	Arizona	27	Louisiana	27	Indiana	27
Nebraska	53.1	45.7	31.6	Nevada	28	Wisconsin	28	Louisiana	27
Nevada	42.8	29.6	9.4	New Hampshire	29	Delaware	29	Michigan	29
New Hampshire	42.5	41.7	44.4	Wisconsin	30	New Mexico	30	New Mexico	30
New Jersey	13.4	11.4	5.3	Indiana	31	Missouri	31	Pennsylvania	31
New Mexico	49.8	34.1	26.3	Missouri	32	Washington	32	Oregon	32
New York	14.5	14.6	14.4	Delaware	33	Nevada	33	Ohio	33
North Carolina	66.3	60.5	40.9	Colorado	34	Pennsylvania	34	Delaware	34
North Dakota	73.4	64.8	46.0	Texas	34	Maryland	35	Texas	35
Ohio	29.8	26.6	21.1	Washington	36	Michigan	36	Washington	36
Oklahoma	49.0	37.1	34.9	Utah	37	Ohio	36	Colorado	37
Oregon	46.1	37.8	22.1	Florida	38	Colorado	38	Utah	38
Pennsylvania	29.5	28.4	23.6	Maryland	39	Florida	39	New York	39
Rhode Island	15.7	13.6	9.1	Hawaii	39	Arizona	40	Maryland	40
South Carolina	63.3	58.8	38.8	Ohio	41	Utah	41	Arizona	41
South Dakota	66.8	60.7	48.4	Pennsylvania	42	Texas	42	Illinois	42
Tennessee	55.9	47.7	36.4	Michigan	43	Hawaii	43	Connecticut	43
Texas	37.3	25.0	19.3	Connecticut	44	Connecticut	44	Florida	44
Utah	34.7	25.1	14.6	Illinois	44	Illinois	45	Hawaii	45
Vermont	63.6	61.5	66.4	California	46	Massachusetts	46	Nevada	46
Virginia	53.0	44.4	28.6	Rhode Island	47	New York	47	Rhode Island	47
Washington	36.8	31.9	18.7	Massachusetts	48	Rhode Island	48	Massachusetts	48
West Virginia	65.4	61.8	53.6	New York	49	California	48	California	49
Wisconsin	42.1	36.2	34.2	New Jersey	50	New Jersey	50	New Jersey	50
Wyoming	50.2	43.2	37.6	DC	51	DC	51	DC	51
United States	36.0	30.1	22.4	United States	–	United States	–	United States	–

Source: U.S. Census Bureau, 1950 Census of Housing; U.S. Census Bureau, 1960 Census of Housing; U.S. Census Bureau, Census 2010

Males per 100 Females

Area	Males per 100 Females			1950		1960		2010	
	1950	1960	2010	Area	Rank	Area	Rank	Area	Rank
Alabama	96.4	95.0	94.3	Wyoming	1	Alaska	1	Alaska	1
Alaska	n/a	132.3	108.5	Nevada	2	Hawaii	2	Wyoming	2
Arizona	102.3	101.2	98.7	Montana	3	Nevada	3	North Dakota	3
Arkansas	99.3	96.9	96.5	North Dakota	4	Wyoming	4	Nevada	4
California	100.1	99.4	98.8	South Dakota	5	North Dakota	5	Utah	5
Colorado	100.8	98.5	100.5	Idaho	6	Montana	6	Montana	6
Connecticut	97.0	96.4	94.8	Washington	7	Idaho	7	Colorado	7
Delaware	97.9	98.2	93.9	New Mexico	8	South Dakota	8	Idaho	8
DC	89.1	88.3	89.5	Oregon	9	New Mexico	9	Hawaii	9
Florida	97.3	96.9	95.6	Arizona	10	Washington	10	South Dakota	10
Georgia	96.2	95.5	95.4	Utah	11	Arizona	10	Washington	11
Hawaii	n/a	114.8	100.3	Virginia	11	Utah	12	California	12
Idaho	106.2	102.9	100.4	Michigan	13	Virginia	13	Arizona	13
Illinois	98.3	96.6	96.2	Nebraska	14	California	14	Minnesota	14
Indiana	99.1	97.2	96.8	Minnesota	15	Oregon	15	Nebraska	14
Iowa	100.0	97.2	98.1	Wisconsin	16	Wisconsin	16	Wisconsin	14
Kansas	100.2	98.6	98.4	Colorado	17	Kansas	17	Texas	17
Kentucky	100.4	98.6	96.8	West Virginia	18	Kentucky	17	Kansas	17
Louisiana	96.7	95.6	95.9	Texas	19	Michigan	19	Iowa	19
Maine	98.8	97.7	95.8	Kentucky	19	Colorado	19	Oregon	20
Maryland	99.2	97.8	93.6	Kansas	21	Minnesota	21	Oklahoma	20
Massachusetts	93.8	93.4	93.7	California	22	Nebraska	21	New Mexico	22
Michigan	101.7	98.5	96.3	Iowa	23	Delaware	23	New Hampshire	23
Minnesota	101.3	98.4	98.5	Oklahoma	24	Texas	24	West Virginia	23
Mississippi	97.7	96.2	94.4	Arkansas	25	Maryland	25	Vermont	25
Missouri	96.4	95.3	96.0	Maryland	26	Maine	26	Indiana	26
Montana	109.9	103.8	100.8	Indiana	27	South Carolina	27	Kentucky	26
Nebraska	101.4	98.4	98.5	Maine	28	North Carolina	28	Arkansas	28
Nevada	113.3	107.1	102.0	Vermont	28	Iowa	29	Virginia	29
New Hampshire	96.9	96.5	97.3	North Carolina	30	Indiana	29	Michigan	29
New Jersey	97.2	96.0	94.8	Illinois	31	Oklahoma	29	Illinois	31
New Mexico	104.2	101.8	97.7	Delaware	32	Florida	32	Missouri	32
New York	95.4	93.8	93.8	Ohio	33	Arkansas	32	Louisiana	33
North Carolina	98.6	97.3	95.0	Mississippi	34	Vermont	34	Maine	34
North Dakota	108.8	104.5	102.1	Rhode Island	35	West Virginia	34	Florida	35
Ohio	97.8	96.4	95.4	Florida	35	Illinois	36	Georgia	36
Oklahoma	99.8	97.2	98.0	Tennessee	35	New Hampshire	37	Ohio	36
Oregon	103.2	99.0	98.0	New Jersey	38	Connecticut	38	Pennsylvania	38
Pennsylvania	97.0	94.8	95.1	Connecticut	39	Rhode Island	38	Tennessee	38
Rhode Island	97.3	96.4	93.4	Pennsylvania	39	Ohio	38	North Carolina	40
South Carolina	96.7	97.4	94.7	New Hampshire	41	Mississippi	41	New Jersey	41
South Dakota	106.9	102.4	100.1	Louisiana	42	New Jersey	42	Connecticut	41
Tennessee	97.3	95.3	95.1	South Carolina	42	Louisiana	43	South Carolina	43
Texas	100.4	98.1	98.4	Missouri	44	Georgia	44	Mississippi	44
Utah	101.9	99.8	100.9	Alabama	44	Missouri	45	Alabama	45
Vermont	98.8	96.8	97.1	Georgia	46	Tennessee	45	Delaware	46
Virginia	101.9	99.6	96.3	New York	47	Alabama	47	New York	47
Washington	106.0	101.2	99.3	Massachusetts	48	Pennsylvania	48	Massachusetts	48
West Virginia	100.7	96.8	97.3	DC	49	New York	49	Maryland	49
Wisconsin	101.1	98.9	98.5	Alaska	n/a	Massachusetts	50	Rhode Island	50
Wyoming	114.1	104.9	104.1	Hawaii	n/a	DC	51	DC	51
United States	98.6	97.1	96.7	United States	–	United States	–	United States	–

Source: U.S. Census Bureau, 1950 Census of Population; U.S. Census Bureau, 1960 Census of Population; U.S. Census Bureau, Census 2010.

High School Graduates

Area	Percent of Population			1950		1960		2010	
	1950	1960	2010	Area	Rank	Area	Rank	Area	Rank
Alabama	21.9	30.3	82.1	DC	1	Utah	1	Wyoming	1
Alaska	n/a	54.7	91.0	Utah	2	Alaska	2	Minnesota	2
Arizona	38.5	45.7	85.6	California	3	Nevada	3	Montana	3
Arkansas	21.5	28.9	82.9	Nevada	4	Colorado	4	New Hampshire	4
California	47.6	51.5	80.7	Washington	5	Wyoming	4	Alaska	5
Colorado	43.7	52.0	89.7	Wyoming	6	California	6	Vermont	5
Connecticut	37.3	43.8	88.6	Colorado	7	Washington	6	Utah	7
Delaware	34.8	43.3	87.7	Oregon	8	Idaho	8	Iowa	7
DC	50.2	47.8	87.4	Massachusetts	9	Oregon	9	Nebraska	9
Florida	35.8	42.6	85.5	Idaho	10	Kansas	10	Maine	10
Georgia	20.8	32.0	84.3	Kansas	11	DC	11	North Dakota	10
Hawaii	n/a	46.1	89.9	Montana	12	Montana	11	Wisconsin	12
Idaho	40.7	48.6	88.3	Nebraska	13	Nebraska	13	Hawaii	13
Illinois	35.1	40.4	86.9	Iowa	14	Massachusetts	14	Washington	14
Indiana	35.9	41.8	87.0	Arizona	15	Iowa	15	Colorado	15
Iowa	38.9	46.3	90.6	Maine	16	Hawaii	16	South Dakota	16
Kansas	40.3	48.2	89.2	Connecticut	17	Arizona	17	Kansas	17
Kentucky	22.3	27.6	81.9	New Hampshire	18	New Mexico	18	Massachusetts	18
Louisiana	22.5	32.3	81.9	Vermont	19	Minnesota	19	Oregon	19
Maine	37.6	43.2	90.3	Ohio	20	Connecticut	20	Michigan	20
Maryland	32.1	40.0	88.1	New York	21	Delaware	21	Connecticut	21
Massachusetts	42.7	47.0	89.1	Indiana	22	Maine	22	Pennsylvania	22
Michigan	34.9	40.9	88.7	Florida	23	New Hampshire	23	Idaho	23
Minnesota	35.6	43.9	91.8	Minnesota	24	Vermont	23	Maryland	24
Mississippi	22.0	29.8	81.0	New Mexico	24	Florida	25	Ohio	24
Missouri	30.8	36.6	86.9	Illinois	26	South Dakota	26	New Jersey	26
Montana	40.0	47.8	91.7	Michigan	27	Ohio	27	Delaware	27
Nebraska	39.4	47.7	90.4	New Jersey	28	Indiana	28	DC	28
Nevada	46.5	53.3	84.7	Delaware	28	Wisconsin	29	Indiana	29
New Hampshire	37.2	42.9	91.5	South Dakota	30	New York	30	Illinois	30
New Jersey	34.8	40.7	88.0	Oklahoma	31	Michigan	30	Missouri	30
New Mexico	35.6	45.5	83.3	Wisconsin	32	New Jersey	32	Virginia	32
New York	36.1	40.9	84.9	Maryland	33	Oklahoma	33	Oklahoma	33
North Carolina	20.9	32.3	84.7	Pennsylvania	34	Illinois	34	Arizona	34
North Dakota	30.7	38.9	90.3	Rhode Island	35	Maryland	35	Florida	35
Ohio	36.5	41.9	88.1	Missouri	36	Texas	36	New York	36
Oklahoma	33.8	40.5	86.2	North Dakota	37	North Dakota	37	Nevada	37
Oregon	43.1	48.4	88.8	Texas	37	Pennsylvania	38	North Carolina	37
Pennsylvania	32.0	38.1	88.4	Virginia	39	Virginia	39	Georgia	39
Rhode Island	31.6	35.0	83.5	West Virginia	40	Missouri	40	South Carolina	40
South Carolina	19.0	30.4	84.1	Tennessee	41	Rhode Island	41	Tennessee	41
South Dakota	34.5	42.2	89.6	Louisiana	42	Louisiana	42	Rhode Island	42
Tennessee	24.6	30.4	83.6	Kentucky	43	North Carolina	42	New Mexico	43
Texas	30.7	39.5	80.7	Mississippi	44	Georgia	44	West Virginia	44
Utah	49.9	55.8	90.6	Alabama	45	West Virginia	45	Arkansas	45
Vermont	37.1	42.9	91.0	Arkansas	46	South Carolina	46	Alabama	46
Virginia	29.4	37.9	86.5	North Carolina	47	Tennessee	46	Louisiana	47
Washington	45.0	51.5	89.8	Georgia	48	Alabama	48	Kentucky	47
West Virginia	24.9	30.6	83.2	South Carolina	49	Mississippi	49	Mississippi	49
Wisconsin	33.6	41.5	90.1	Alaska	n/a	Arkansas	50	California	50
Wyoming	44.4	52.0	92.3	Hawaii	n/a	Kentucky	51	Texas	50
United States	34.3	41.1	85.6	United States	–	United States	–	United States	–

Note: Figures cover the population 25 years old and over.

Source: U.S. Census Bureau, 1950 Census of Population; U.S. Census Bureau, 1960 Census of Population; U.S. Census Bureau, American Community Survey, 2010 One-Year Estimate

College Graduates

Area	Percent of Population			1950		1960		2010	
	1950	1960	2010	Area	Rank	Area	Rank	Area	Rank
Alabama	3.9	5.7	21.9	DC	1	DC	1	DC	1
Alaska	n/a	9.5	27.9	California	2	Colorado	2	Massachusetts	2
Arizona	7.7	9.1	25.9	Colorado	2	Utah	3	Colorado	3
Arkansas	3.2	4.8	19.5	Utah	4	Delaware	4	Maryland	4
California	8.4	9.8	30.1	New York	5	California	5	Connecticut	5
Colorado	8.4	10.7	36.4	Arizona	5	New Mexico	5	New Jersey	6
Connecticut	7.2	9.5	35.5	Nevada	7	Connecticut	7	Virginia	7
Delaware	7.5	10.1	27.8	Delaware	8	Alaska	7	Vermont	8
DC	13.6	14.3	50.1	Massachusetts	9	Washington	9	New Hampshire	9
Florida	6.5	7.8	25.8	Washington	9	Maryland	9	New York	10
Georgia	4.5	6.2	27.3	Wyoming	11	Arizona	11	Minnesota	11
Hawaii	n/a	9.0	29.5	Connecticut	12	Hawaii	12	Washington	12
Idaho	5.6	7.2	24.4	Maryland	12	New York	13	Illinois	13
Illinois	6.1	7.3	30.8	New Mexico	14	Massachusetts	14	Rhode Island	14
Indiana	5.3	6.3	22.7	New Jersey	15	Wyoming	15	California	15
Iowa	5.3	6.4	24.9	Oregon	16	Oregon	16	Kansas	16
Kansas	6.1	8.2	29.8	Virginia	17	New Jersey	17	Hawaii	17
Kentucky	3.9	4.9	20.5	Florida	18	Virginia	17	Utah	18
Louisiana	5.0	6.7	21.4	Oklahoma	19	Nevada	19	Oregon	19
Maine	4.9	5.5	26.8	Montana	20	Kansas	20	Montana	19
Maryland	7.2	9.3	36.1	Texas	21	Texas	21	Nebraska	21
Massachusetts	7.4	8.8	39.0	New Hampshire	22	Oklahoma	22	Alaska	22
Michigan	5.4	6.8	25.2	Illinois	22	Florida	23	Delaware	23
Minnesota	5.8	7.5	31.8	Kansas	22	Montana	24	North Dakota	24
Mississippi	3.9	5.6	19.5	Rhode Island	25	Minnesota	24	Georgia	25
Missouri	5.1	6.2	25.6	Vermont	26	Illinois	26	Pennsylvania	26
Montana	6.3	7.5	28.8	Minnesota	27	Vermont	26	Maine	27
Nebraska	5.2	6.8	28.6	Ohio	27	Idaho	28	North Carolina	28
Nevada	7.6	8.3	21.7	Idaho	29	New Hampshire	29	Wisconsin	29
New Hampshire	6.1	7.1	32.8	Pennsylvania	30	Ohio	30	South Dakota	29
New Jersey	6.9	8.4	35.4	Wisconsin	30	South Carolina	31	Texas	31
New Mexico	7.1	9.8	25.0	South Carolina	30	Michigan	32	Arizona	31
New York	7.7	8.9	32.5	Michigan	33	Nebraska	32	Florida	33
North Carolina	5.1	6.3	26.5	Iowa	34	Wisconsin	34	Missouri	34
North Dakota	4.6	5.6	27.6	Indiana	34	Louisiana	34	Michigan	35
Ohio	5.8	7.0	24.6	Nebraska	36	Rhode Island	36	New Mexico	36
Oklahoma	6.4	7.9	22.9	Missouri	37	Pennsylvania	37	Iowa	37
Oregon	6.8	8.5	28.8	North Carolina	37	Iowa	37	Ohio	38
Pennsylvania	5.5	6.4	27.1	South Dakota	39	Indiana	39	South Carolina	39
Rhode Island	6.0	6.6	30.2	Louisiana	39	North Carolina	39	Idaho	40
South Carolina	5.5	6.9	24.5	Maine	41	Missouri	41	Wyoming	41
South Dakota	5.0	5.7	26.3	North Dakota	42	Georgia	41	Tennessee	42
Tennessee	4.1	5.5	23.1	Georgia	43	South Dakota	43	Oklahoma	43
Texas	6.2	8.0	25.9	West Virginia	44	Alabama	43	Indiana	44
Utah	7.8	10.2	29.3	Tennessee	45	North Dakota	45	Alabama	45
Vermont	5.9	7.3	33.6	Kentucky	46	Mississippi	45	Nevada	46
Virginia	6.7	8.4	34.2	Mississippi	46	Maine	47	Louisiana	47
Washington	7.4	9.3	31.1	Alabama	46	Tennessee	47	Kentucky	48
West Virginia	4.4	5.2	17.5	Arkansas	49	West Virginia	49	Arkansas	49
Wisconsin	5.5	6.7	26.3	Alaska	n/a	Kentucky	50	Mississippi	49
Wyoming	7.3	8.7	24.1	Hawaii	n/a	Arkansas	51	West Virginia	51
United States	6.2	7.7	28.2	United States	–	United States	–	United States	–

Note: Figures cover the population 25 years old and over.
Source: U.S. Census Bureau, 1950 Census of Population; U.S. Census Bureau, 1960 Census of Population; U.S. Census Bureau, American Community Survey, 2010 One-Year Estimate

One-Person Households

Area	Percent of Population			1950		1960		2010	
	1950	1960	2010	Area	Rank	Area	Rank	Area	Rank
Alabama	6.7	9.5	27.4	Alaska	1	DC	1	DC	1
Alaska	17.6	16.2	25.6	Nevada	2	Nevada	2	North Dakota	2
Arizona	12.2	13.6	26.1	Montana	3	California	3	Montana	3
Arkansas	8.7	12.6	27.1	DC	4	Washington	4	Rhode Island	4
California	14.0	17.9	23.3	Washington	5	Montana	5	South Dakota	5
Colorado	12.5	15.5	27.9	California	6	Oregon	6	New York	6
Connecticut	7.3	11.6	27.3	Oregon	7	Alaska	6	Ohio	7
Delaware	8.5	10.9	25.6	Colorado	8	New York	8	Massachusetts	8
DC	14.3	27.0	44.0	Wyoming	9	Colorado	8	Nebraska	8
Florida	11.0	14.5	27.2	Arizona	10	Oklahoma	8	Pennsylvania	10
Georgia	6.9	10.1	25.4	Kansas	11	Missouri	11	Maine	10
Hawaii	10.5	12.1	23.3	Florida	12	Florida	12	Iowa	12
Idaho	10.9	13.3	23.8	Idaho	13	Illinois	13	West Virginia	12
Illinois	9.8	14.4	27.8	Missouri	13	Wyoming	14	Missouri	14
Indiana	9.2	12.3	26.9	New Hampshire	15	Massachusetts	15	Wisconsin	15
Iowa	10.2	13.8	28.4	Oklahoma	15	Nebraska	15	Vermont	15
Kansas	11.3	14.0	27.8	Nebraska	17	Kansas	17	New Mexico	17
Kentucky	7.3	10.6	27.5	Hawaii	17	Iowa	18	Minnesota	17
Louisiana	9.2	12.3	26.9	Iowa	19	Rhode Island	19	Wyoming	17
Maine	9.8	12.6	28.6	Minnesota	20	Minnesota	19	Colorado	20
Maryland	7.4	10.1	26.1	South Dakota	21	Arizona	21	Michigan	20
Massachusetts	8.8	14.2	28.7	Illinois	22	Idaho	22	Illinois	22
Michigan	8.1	11.6	27.9	Maine	22	New Hampshire	23	Kansas	22
Minnesota	10.0	13.7	28.0	New York	24	South Dakota	24	Oklahoma	24
Mississippi	7.7	10.7	26.3	Vermont	25	Maine	25	Kentucky	24
Missouri	10.9	15.2	28.3	Indiana	26	Texas	25	Oregon	26
Montana	14.4	16.8	29.7	Louisiana	26	Arkansas	25	Alabama	26
Nebraska	10.5	14.2	28.7	North Dakota	28	Vermont	28	Connecticut	28
Nevada	16.0	18.9	25.7	Utah	28	Indiana	29	Florida	29
New Hampshire	10.7	13.1	25.6	New Mexico	28	Louisiana	29	Washington	29
New Jersey	7.1	11.3	25.2	Rhode Island	31	Wisconsin	31	Arkansas	31
New Mexico	9.1	10.7	28.0	Texas	31	Hawaii	32	North Carolina	32
New York	9.6	15.5	29.1	Massachusetts	33	Ohio	32	Tennessee	33
North Carolina	5.4	8.3	27.0	Arkansas	34	Utah	34	Indiana	33
North Dakota	9.1	11.9	31.5	Ohio	35	Pennsylvania	35	Louisiana	33
Ohio	8.5	12.1	28.9	Delaware	35	North Dakota	35	South Carolina	36
Oklahoma	10.7	15.5	27.5	Wisconsin	37	Connecticut	37	Mississippi	37
Oregon	12.9	16.2	27.4	Michigan	38	Michigan	37	Arizona	38
Pennsylvania	7.9	11.9	28.6	Pennsylvania	39	New Jersey	39	Maryland	38
Rhode Island	8.9	13.7	29.6	Mississippi	40	Delaware	40	Virginia	40
South Carolina	6.8	9.4	26.5	Maryland	41	New Mexico	41	Nevada	41
South Dakota	9.9	12.8	29.4	Connecticut	42	Mississippi	41	Delaware	42
Tennessee	6.4	9.7	26.9	Kentucky	42	Kentucky	43	Alaska	42
Texas	8.9	12.6	24.2	New Jersey	44	Maryland	44	New Hampshire	42
Utah	9.1	12.0	18.7	Georgia	45	West Virginia	44	Georgia	45
Vermont	9.4	12.5	28.2	West Virginia	46	Georgia	44	New Jersey	46
Virginia	6.6	9.4	26.0	South Carolina	46	Tennessee	47	Texas	47
Washington	14.1	17.6	27.2	Alabama	48	Alabama	48	Idaho	48
West Virginia	6.8	10.1	28.4	Virginia	49	Virginia	49	California	49
Wisconsin	8.2	12.2	28.2	Tennessee	50	South Carolina	49	Hawaii	49
Wyoming	12.3	14.3	28.0	North Carolina	51	North Carolina	51	Utah	51
United States	9.3	13.3	26.7	United States	–	United States	–	United States	–

Source: U.S. Census Bureau, 1950 Census of Housing; U.S. Census Bureau, 1960 Census of Housing; U.S. Census Bureau, Census 2010

Homeownership

Area	Percent of Population			1950		1960		2010	
	1950	1960	2010	Area	Rank	Area	Rank	Area	Rank
Alabama	49.4	59.7	69.7	Michigan	1	Michigan	1	West Virginia	1
Alaska	54.5	48.3	63.1	Minnesota	2	Minnesota	2	Minnesota	2
Arizona	56.4	63.9	66.0	North Dakota	3	Utah	3	Michigan	3
Arkansas	54.5	61.4	66.9	Idaho	4	Indiana	4	Iowa	3
California	54.3	58.4	56.0	Indiana	4	Idaho	5	Delaware	5
Colorado	58.1	63.8	65.5	Oregon	6	Oregon	6	Maine	6
Connecticut	51.1	61.9	67.5	Utah	6	Iowa	7	New Hampshire	7
Delaware	58.9	66.9	72.0	Washington	8	Kansas	8	Vermont	8
DC	32.3	30.0	42.0	Kansas	9	Wisconsin	9	Utah	9
Florida	57.6	67.5	67.3	Wisconsin	10	Washington	10	Idaho	10
Georgia	46.5	56.2	65.7	Iowa	11	North Dakota	11	Indiana	11
Hawaii	33.0	41.1	57.7	Maine	12	Pennsylvania	12	Alabama	12
Idaho	65.5	70.5	69.9	South Dakota	13	Florida	13	Pennsylvania	13
Illinois	50.1	57.8	67.4	Vermont	14	Ohio	14	Mississippi	13
Indiana	65.5	71.1	69.8	Ohio	15	South Dakota	15	South Carolina	15
Iowa	63.4	69.1	72.1	Nebraska	16	Oklahoma	16	Wyoming	15
Kansas	63.9	68.9	67.7	Montana	17	Delaware	17	Missouri	17
Kentucky	58.7	64.3	68.7	Oklahoma	18	Maine	18	Kentucky	18
Louisiana	50.3	59.0	67.3	Pennsylvania	19	Vermont	19	New Mexico	19
Maine	62.8	66.5	71.3	Delaware	20	New Mexico	20	Tennessee	20
Maryland	56.3	64.5	67.5	New Mexico	21	New Hampshire	21	Wisconsin	21
Massachusetts	47.9	55.9	62.3	Kentucky	22	Texas	22	South Dakota	21
Michigan	67.5	74.4	72.1	New Hampshire	23	Nebraska	22	Montana	23
Minnesota	66.4	72.1	73.1	Colorado	23	Maryland	24	Kansas	24
Mississippi	47.8	57.7	69.6	Missouri	25	Missouri	25	Ohio	25
Missouri	57.7	64.3	68.8	Florida	26	West Virginia	25	Maryland	26
Montana	60.3	64.0	68.0	Texas	27	Kentucky	25	Connecticut	26
Nebraska	60.6	64.8	67.2	Tennessee	28	Montana	28	Illinois	28
Nevada	48.7	56.3	58.8	Arizona	29	Arizona	29	Florida	29
New Hampshire	58.1	65.1	70.9	Maryland	30	Colorado	30	Oklahoma	29
New Jersey	53.1	61.3	65.4	Virginia	31	Tennessee	31	Louisiana	29
New Mexico	58.8	65.3	68.5	West Virginia	32	Wyoming	32	Virginia	32
New York	37.9	44.8	53.3	Arkansas	33	Connecticut	33	Nebraska	32
North Carolina	53.3	60.1	66.7	Alaska	33	Arkansas	34	Arkansas	34
North Dakota	66.2	68.4	65.4	California	35	New Jersey	35	North Carolina	35
Ohio	61.1	67.4	67.6	Wyoming	36	Virginia	35	Arizona	36
Oklahoma	60.0	67.0	67.3	North Carolina	37	North Carolina	37	Georgia	37
Oregon	65.3	69.3	62.1	New Jersey	38	Alabama	38	Colorado	38
Pennsylvania	59.7	68.3	69.6	Connecticut	39	Louisiana	39	New Jersey	39
Rhode Island	45.3	54.5	60.7	Louisiana	40	California	40	North Dakota	39
South Carolina	45.1	57.3	69.3	Illinois	41	Illinois	41	Washington	41
South Dakota	62.2	67.2	68.1	Alabama	42	Mississippi	42	Texas	42
Tennessee	56.5	63.7	68.2	Nevada	43	South Carolina	43	Alaska	43
Texas	56.7	64.8	63.7	Massachusetts	44	Nevada	44	Massachusetts	44
Utah	65.3	71.7	70.5	Mississippi	45	Georgia	45	Oregon	45
Vermont	61.3	66.0	70.7	Georgia	46	Massachusetts	46	Rhode Island	46
Virginia	55.1	61.3	67.2	Rhode Island	47	Rhode Island	47	Nevada	47
Washington	65.0	68.5	63.9	South Carolina	48	Alaska	48	Hawaii	48
West Virginia	55.0	64.3	73.4	New York	49	New York	49	California	49
Wisconsin	63.5	68.6	68.1	Hawaii	50	Hawaii	50	New York	50
Wyoming	54.0	62.2	69.3	DC	51	DC	51	DC	51
United States	55.0	61.9	65.1	United States	–	United States	–	United States	–

Source: U.S. Census Bureau, 1950 Census of Housing; U.S. Census Bureau, 1960 Census of Housing; U.S. Census Bureau, Census 2010

Median Home Value

Area	Median Home Value ($)			1950		1960		2010	
	1950	1960	2010	Area	Rank	Area	Rank	Area	Rank
Alabama	4,473	8,600	123,900	DC	1	Hawaii	1	Hawaii	1
Alaska	3,477	9,100	241,400	Hawaii	2	Connecticut	2	DC	2
Arizona	5,935	11,100	168,800	Connecticut	3	New Jersey	3	California	3
Arkansas	4,087	6,700	106,300	New Jersey	4	DC	4	New Jersey	4
California	9,564	15,100	370,900	New York	5	New York	5	Massachusetts	5
Colorado	7,151	12,300	236,600	Rhode Island	6	Nevada	6	Maryland	6
Connecticut	11,862	16,700	288,800	California	7	California	7	New York	7
Delaware	9,079	12,400	243,600	Massachusetts	8	Illinois	8	Connecticut	8
DC	14,498	15,400	426,900	Delaware	9	Massachusetts	9	Washington	9
Florida	6,612	11,800	164,200	Nevada	10	Ohio	10	Rhode Island	10
Georgia	5,235	9,500	156,200	Illinois	11	Minnesota	11	Virginia	11
Hawaii	12,283	20,900	525,400	Ohio	12	Wisconsin	12	Oregon	12
Idaho	5,852	10,600	165,100	Maryland	13	Utah	12	Delaware	13
Illinois	8,646	14,700	191,800	Wisconsin	14	Delaware	14	New Hampshire	14
Indiana	6,226	10,200	123,300	Minnesota	15	Rhode Island	15	Alaska	15
Iowa	6,320	9,900	123,400	Michigan	16	Colorado	15	Colorado	16
Kansas	5,462	9,300	127,300	Utah	17	Wyoming	15	Utah	17
Kentucky	5,283	8,800	121,600	Washington	18	Michigan	18	Vermont	18
Louisiana	5,141	10,700	137,500	Colorado	19	Maryland	19	Minnesota	19
Maine	4,856	8,800	179,100	Pennsylvania	20	Florida	20	Illinois	20
Maryland	8,033	11,900	301,400	Oregon	21	Washington	21	Montana	21
Massachusetts	9,144	13,800	334,100	Wyoming	22	Arizona	22	Wyoming	22
Michigan	7,496	12,000	123,300	Florida	23	Montana	23	Maine	23
Minnesota	7,806	12,800	194,300	Virginia	24	Missouri	23	Nevada	24
Mississippi	4,159	7,900	100,100	Missouri	25	Virginia	25	Wisconsin	25
Missouri	6,399	10,900	139,000	Iowa	26	New Hampshire	26	Arizona	26
Montana	5,797	10,900	181,200	Vermont	27	New Mexico	26	Pennsylvania	27
Nebraska	5,918	9,400	127,600	Indiana	28	Louisiana	26	Idaho	28
Nevada	8,859	15,200	174,800	New Hampshire	29	Idaho	29	Florida	29
New Hampshire	6,199	10,700	243,000	Arizona	30	Oregon	30	New Mexico	30
New Jersey	10,408	15,600	339,200	Nebraska	31	Pennsylvania	31	Georgia	31
New Mexico	5,697	10,700	161,200	Idaho	32	Indiana	31	North Carolina	32
New York	10,152	15,300	296,500	Texas	33	Iowa	33	Tennessee	33
North Carolina	4,901	8,000	154,200	Montana	34	North Dakota	34	Missouri	33
North Dakota	5,396	9,800	123,000	New Mexico	35	Vermont	35	South Carolina	35
Ohio	8,304	13,400	134,400	West Virginia	36	Georgia	36	Louisiana	36
Oklahoma	5,228	7,900	111,400	Kansas	37	Nebraska	37	Ohio	37
Oregon	6,846	10,500	244,500	South Dakota	38	Kansas	38	South Dakota	38
Pennsylvania	6,992	10,200	165,500	North Dakota	39	Alaska	39	Texas	39
Rhode Island	9,767	12,300	254,500	Kentucky	40	Maine	40	Nebraska	40
South Carolina	5,112	7,500	138,100	Tennessee	41	Texas	40	Kansas	41
South Dakota	5,410	8,800	129,700	Georgia	42	South Dakota	40	Alabama	42
Tennessee	5,268	8,300	139,000	Oklahoma	43	Kentucky	40	Iowa	43
Texas	5,805	8,800	128,100	Louisiana	44	Alabama	44	Michigan	44
Utah	7,409	12,600	217,200	South Carolina	45	Tennessee	45	Indiana	44
Vermont	6,277	9,700	216,800	North Carolina	46	North Carolina	46	North Carolina	46
Virginia	6,581	10,800	249,100	Maine	47	Oklahoma	47	Kentucky	47
Washington	7,169	11,700	271,800	Alabama	48	Mississippi	47	Oklahoma	48
West Virginia	5,473	7,600	95,100	Mississippi	49	West Virginia	49	Arkansas	49
Wisconsin	7,927	12,600	169,400	Arkansas	50	South Carolina	50	Mississippi	50
Wyoming	6,811	12,300	180,100	Alaska	51	Arkansas	51	West Virginia	51
United States	7,354	11,900	179,900	United States	–	United States	–	United States	–

Source: U.S. Census Bureau, 1950 Census of Housing; U.S. Census Bureau, 1960 Census of Housing; U.S. Census Bureau, American Community Survey, 2010 One-Year Estimate

Median Gross Rent

Area	Median Gross Rent ($/month)			1950		1960		2010	
	1950	1960	2010	Area	Rank	Area	Rank	Area	Rank
Alabama	25	45	667	DC	1	Alaska	1	Hawaii	1
Alaska	n/a	126	981	New Jersey	2	Nevada	2	DC	2
Arizona	37	69	844	Wisconsin	2	Illinois	3	California	3
Arkansas	28	47	638	New York	4	DC	4	Maryland	4
California	42	79	1,163	Massachusetts	5	New Jersey	5	New Jersey	5
Colorado	39	72	863	Michigan	5	California	6	New York	6
Connecticut	45	77	992	Illinois	5	Wisconsin	6	Virginia	7
Delaware	46	77	952	Nevada	5	Maryland	8	Massachusetts	8
DC	57	81	1,198	Delaware	9	Connecticut	9	Connecticut	9
Florida	39	71	947	Maryland	9	Michigan	9	Alaska	10
Georgia	27	51	819	Connecticut	11	Delaware	9	Nevada	11
Hawaii	n/a	72	1,291	Oregon	12	Massachusetts	12	Delaware	11
Idaho	44	65	683	Idaho	12	Ohio	12	New Hampshire	13
Illinois	47	85	848	Washington	14	New York	14	Florida	14
Indiana	42	70	683	North Dakota	14	Hawaii	15	Washington	15
Iowa	43	68	629	Minnesota	14	Minnesota	15	Rhode Island	16
Kansas	38	66	682	Nebraska	14	Colorado	15	Colorado	17
Kentucky	31	55	613	Iowa	14	Washington	18	Illinois	18
Louisiana	27	53	736	California	19	Florida	18	Arizona	19
Maine	41	64	707	Ohio	19	North Dakota	18	Vermont	20
Maryland	46	78	1,131	South Dakota	19	New Mexico	18	Georgia	21
Massachusetts	47	75	1,009	Indiana	19	Virginia	18	Oregon	22
Michigan	47	77	730	New Hampshire	23	Oregon	23	Texas	23
Minnesota	43	72	764	Maine	23	Indiana	23	Utah	24
Mississippi	25	43	672	Vermont	23	Arizona	25	Minnesota	25
Missouri	36	65	682	Montana	23	Iowa	26	Pennsylvania	26
Montana	41	66	642	Wyoming	23	Nebraska	27	Louisiana	27
Nebraska	43	67	669	New Mexico	23	Wyoming	27	North Carolina	28
Nevada	47	91	952	Rhode Island	29	South Dakota	27	Michigan	29
New Hampshire	41	65	951	Pennsylvania	29	Montana	30	South Carolina	30
New Jersey	49	80	1,114	Utah	29	Utah	30	Wisconsin	31
New Mexico	41	71	699	Florida	32	Kansas	30	Maine	32
New York	48	74	1,020	Colorado	32	New Hampshire	33	New Mexico	33
North Carolina	30	55	731	Virginia	32	Idaho	33	Tennessee	34
North Dakota	43	71	583	Kansas	35	Missouri	33	Wyoming	35
Ohio	42	75	685	Arizona	36	Maine	36	Ohio	36
Oklahoma	34	57	659	Texas	36	Pennsylvania	36	Idaho	37
Oregon	44	70	816	Missouri	38	Rhode Island	38	Indiana	37
Pennsylvania	40	64	763	Oklahoma	39	Vermont	38	Kansas	39
Rhode Island	40	62	868	Kentucky	40	Texas	40	Missouri	39
South Carolina	26	49	728	Tennessee	40	Oklahoma	41	Mississippi	41
South Dakota	42	67	591	North Carolina	42	Kentucky	42	Nebraska	42
Tennessee	31	52	697	West Virginia	43	North Carolina	42	Alabama	43
Texas	37	60	801	Arkansas	43	West Virginia	44	Oklahoma	44
Utah	40	66	796	Louisiana	45	Louisiana	44	Montana	45
Vermont	41	62	823	Georgia	45	Tennessee	46	Arkansas	46
Virginia	39	71	1,019	South Carolina	47	Georgia	47	Iowa	47
Washington	43	71	908	Mississippi	48	South Carolina	48	Kentucky	48
West Virginia	28	53	571	Alabama	48	Arkansas	49	South Dakota	49
Wisconsin	49	79	715	Alaska	n/a	Alabama	50	North Dakota	50
Wyoming	41	67	693	Hawaii	n/a	Mississippi	51	West Virginia	51
United States	42	71	855	United States	–	United States	–	United States	–

Source: U.S. Census Bureau, 1950 Census of Housing; U.S. Census Bureau, 1960 Census of Housing; U.S. Census Bureau, American Community Survey, 2010 One-Year Estimate

Households Lacking Complete Plumbing

Area	Percent of Households			1950		1960		2010	
	1950	1960	2010	Area	Rank	Area	Rank	Area	Rank
Alabama	67.8	38.5	3.6	Mississippi	1	Mississippi	1	Alaska	1
Alaska	47.5	29.4	11.9	Arkansas	2	Arkansas	2	West Virginia	2
Arizona	34.8	13.4	2.3	Alabama	3	Kentucky	3	Maine	3
Arkansas	70.5	43.2	4.3	North Dakota	4	South Carolina	4	New Mexico	4
California	11.8	5.1	1.1	South Carolina	5	Alabama	4	Arkansas	5
Colorado	37.7	14.1	1.3	North Carolina	6	North Carolina	6	Mississippi	5
Connecticut	16.8	7.3	1.1	Kentucky	7	Tennessee	7	Montana	7
Delaware	29.5	12.4	1.6	Georgia	8	Georgia	8	Louisiana	8
DC	11.4	7.7	2.2	Tennessee	9	North Dakota	9	Alabama	9
Florida	39.0	15.0	1.4	South Dakota	10	West Virginia	10	Kentucky	10
Georgia	63.4	33.7	2.2	Louisiana	11	Maine	11	Oklahoma	11
Hawaii	38.8	16.8	1.5	West Virginia	12	South Dakota	12	Michigan	12
Idaho	36.7	14.7	1.6	Missouri	13	Louisiana	13	Indiana	12
Illinois	31.7	13.4	2.1	Virginia	14	Alaska	14	Missouri	12
Indiana	42.8	17.3	3.1	Iowa	15	Virginia	15	South Dakota	12
Iowa	48.0	19.8	1.7	New Mexico	16	Missouri	16	Pennsylvania	16
Kansas	41.2	15.9	2.3	Alaska	16	Minnesota	17	Texas	17
Kentucky	63.7	39.7	3.5	Oklahoma	18	Oklahoma	18	South Carolina	17
Louisiana	58.3	29.5	3.9	Maine	19	Montana	19	Vermont	17
Maine	46.6	30.5	4.7	Minnesota	19	New Mexico	19	North Carolina	20
Maryland	27.5	10.5	1.5	Texas	21	Texas	21	Tennessee	21
Massachusetts	19.1	9.6	1.0	Indiana	22	Iowa	22	North Dakota	21
Michigan	28.0	11.7	3.1	Nebraska	23	Vermont	23	Arizona	23
Minnesota	46.6	22.1	2.1	Montana	24	Nebraska	24	Kansas	23
Mississippi	74.0	47.8	4.3	Kansas	25	Indiana	25	Ohio	23
Missouri	50.7	25.9	3.1	Wisconsin	26	Wisconsin	26	DC	26
Montana	42.1	20.4	4.1	Florida	27	Hawaii	27	Georgia	26
Nebraska	42.7	17.5	2.2	Hawaii	28	New Hampshire	28	Nebraska	26
Nevada	23.2	9.8	1.2	Wyoming	29	Kansas	29	Illinois	29
New Hampshire	34.2	16.7	1.6	Colorado	30	Wyoming	30	Minnesota	29
New Jersey	14.9	6.5	1.2	Rhode Island	31	Florida	31	Virginia	31
New Mexico	47.5	20.4	4.6	Idaho	32	Idaho	32	Rhode Island	32
New York	14.0	8.0	1.6	Arizona	33	Colorado	33	Wyoming	32
North Carolina	64.8	35.6	2.5	New Hampshire	34	Rhode Island	34	Wisconsin	34
North Dakota	65.9	33.1	2.4	Vermont	35	Illinois	35	Iowa	35
Ohio	28.9	12.8	2.3	Illinois	36	Arizona	35	New York	36
Oklahoma	47.0	20.8	3.2	Delaware	37	Ohio	37	Delaware	36
Oregon	23.9	9.9	1.3	Ohio	38	Delaware	38	Idaho	36
Pennsylvania	26.9	11.3	2.7	Michigan	39	Michigan	39	New Hampshire	36
Rhode Island	37.1	13.6	1.9	Maryland	40	Pennsylvania	40	Hawaii	40
South Carolina	65.1	38.5	2.6	Pennsylvania	41	Maryland	41	Maryland	40
South Dakota	61.3	30.3	3.1	Oregon	42	Oregon	42	Washington	40
Tennessee	63.3	34.9	2.4	Nevada	43	Washington	43	Florida	43
Texas	45.4	19.9	2.6	Massachusetts	44	Nevada	43	Colorado	44
Utah	18.4	6.1	1.2	Washington	44	Massachusetts	45	Oregon	44
Vermont	33.1	18.7	2.6	Utah	46	New York	46	New Jersey	46
Virginia	49.6	27.4	2.0	Connecticut	47	DC	47	Nevada	46
Washington	19.1	9.8	1.5	New Jersey	48	Connecticut	48	Utah	46
West Virginia	53.9	32.3	5.2	New York	49	New Jersey	49	California	49
Wisconsin	40.8	17.2	1.8	California	50	Utah	50	Connecticut	49
Wyoming	38.1	15.8	1.9	DC	51	California	51	Massachusetts	51
United States	35.5	16.8	2.2	United States	–	United States	–	United States	–

Note: Complete plumbing facilities are defined as hot and cold piped water, a bath- tub or shower, and a flush toilet. In earlier censuses, these facilities must have been for exclusive use of a housing unit's inhabitants; this requirement was dropped in 1990.
Source: U.S. Census Bureau, 1950 Census of Housing; U.S. Census Bureau, 1960 Census of Housing; U.S. Census Bureau, American Community Survey, 2010 One-Year Estimate

Chapter Highlights
POPULATION SIZE AND GEOGRAPHIC DISTRIBUTION

National Trends

The United States population more than tripled from 76 million people in 1900 to 281 million people in 2000.

The United States ranked as the fourth most populous country in the world from the start of the century until the breakup of the Soviet Union in 1991, and as the world's third most populous country since then, after China and India.

The population growth of 32.7 million people in the 1990s was the largest numerical increase of any decade in U.S. history.

U.S. population density increased twofold during the period 1900 to 2000, but the level in 2000 (an average of 80 people per square mile) remained low in comparison with the density in most countries, and lower than the world population density of 120 people per square mile.

Between 1900 and 2000, the center of population shifted 324 miles west and 101 miles south, moving from Bartholomew County, Indiana, to Phelps County, Missouri.

The U.S. population grew increasingly metropolitan each decade, from 28 percent in 1910 to 80 percent in 2000.

The suburban portion of metropolitan areas, rather than central cities, accounted for most metropolitan growth during the century. By 2000, half of the U.S. population lived in suburban areas.

Nearly one-third of Americans lived in a metropolitan area with 5 million or more residents by the close of the century.

Regional Trends

In 1900, the majority (62 percent) of the U.S. population lived in either the Northeast or the Midwest. However, by the end of the century, the majority (58 percent) of the population resided in either the South or West.

The population of the West grew faster than the population in each of the other three regions of the country in every decade of the 20th century.

The population density of the Northeast far exceeded the densities of the other regions from 1900 to 2000.

The Northeast also had the highest percentage of its population living in metropolitan areas for the entire 20th century.

State Trends

In 1900, New York's population of 7.3 million exceeded that of any other state. In 2000, California had the largest population (33.9 million), and 10 other states (including New York) had populations larger than New York's population at the beginning of the century.

The 1990s was the first decade when none of the 50 states lost population, although the District of Columbia's population declined for the fifth consecutive decade.

From 1900 to 2000, Florida's ranking in population size increased more than any other state, from 33rd to 4th, followed by Arizona's, from 48th to 20th. Iowa's ranking declined the most, from 10th in 1900 to 30th in 2000.

Among the 50 states, Rhode Island had the highest population density from 1900 to 1960, and New Jersey had the highest population density from 1970 to 2000.

Alaska had the lowest population density of all states throughout the century. Excluding Alaska prior to its statehood in 1959, Nevada had the lowest population density every decade.

The percentage of population living in metropolitan areas increased for every state from 1910 to 2000. By 2000, the majority of the population in 37 of the 50 states lived in a metropolitan area.

Chapter 1
POPULATION SIZE AND GEOGRAPHIC DISTRIBUTION

The trends in the size and geographic distribution of the United States population reflect the country's historical trends in fertility, mortality, and internal and international migration. Over the course of the 20th century, the United States population experienced several major changes. Overall growth was substantial in both numerical and in percentage terms, although it varied from decade to decade. Although U.S. population growth was remarkable compared with other industrialized countries, the U.S. share of the world's population declined as less developed countries grew more rapidly. Population growth resulted in the country becoming increasingly more densely populated, but the large land area of the United States kept overall population density at a comparatively moderate level in global terms.

Regionally, the distribution of the U.S. population generally experienced a shift toward the South and the West. These regions dominated the 20th century's population growth, especially in the latter half of the century. The gains in total population share of the South and the West occurred at the expense of corresponding losses in population share of the Northeast and the Midwest.

State trends in population size, percentage growth, and rankings varied considerably. California accounted for one-sixth of national population growth during the 100-year period. Just eight states—California, Texas, New York, Florida, Illinois, Michigan, Ohio, and New Jersey—were responsible for more than half of the total population gain from 1900 to 2000. Not all states gained population in every decade. While several states in the South and the West stood out as clear

leaders in population growth trends during the century, states in the Northeast consistently ranked among the most densely populated.

"Metropolitanization" particularly characterized the demographic change of the United States in the 20th century. Prior to World War II, the majority of Americans lived outside of metropolitan territory. By the end of the century, 4 out of every 5 people in the United States resided in a metropolitan area. The growth of metropolitan areas in the 20th century was essentially a growth of the suburban population (defined here as the metropolitan population living outside of central cities), especially in the latter half of the century. In 2000, the central city population represented a smaller share of the U.S. population than it did in 1950. By the end of the century, the percentage metropolitan in the regions ranged from 74 percent in the Midwest to 90 percent in the Northeast. Eight states—California, Connecticut, Florida, Maryland, Massachusetts, New Jersey, New York, and Rhode Island—had all reached at least 90 percent metropolitan population by 2000.

The graphics and text in this chapter portray the decade-to-decade trends in the U.S. population. State trends often are covered graphically through the use of thematic maps showing data for the beginning, middle, and end of the century. Trends in population density and metropolitan population are also discussed. Detailed data for each decade for the United States, regions, and states on total population size, population density, and metropolitan classification are provided in Appendix Tables 1, 2, and 3. State trends and rankings based on total population size include Alaska and Hawaii.

The U.S. population more than tripled from 76 million in 1900 to 281 million in 2000.

The United States population more than tripled, growing from 76 million people in 1900 to 281 million people in 2000 (see Figure 1-1). From the start of the century until the breakup of the Soviet Union in 1991, the United States ranked as the fourth most populous country in the world, and since 1991 as the world's third most populous country. The net addition of more than 200 million people to the U.S. population over the course of the 20th century represents more than the current population of every country in the world, except China, India, and Indonesia.

Net change in the U.S. population results from adding births, subtracting deaths, adding people who migrated to the United States, and subtracting people who left the country. During the past 100 years, net immigration to the United States was roughly 40 million people. In the same period, about 330 million babies were born, and nearly 165 million people died. The subtraction of total births minus total deaths yields a natural increase of about 165 million people, which includes the natural increase contribution resulting from births and deaths to migrants.

Many social and demographic factors contributed to the huge growth of the U.S. population in the 20th century. Declining mortality was one such factor. As public sanitation, personal hygiene, and scientific and medical technology improved, life expectancy improved. Average life expectancy at birth increased by about 30 years over the course of the 20th century, from about 47 years in 1900 to about 77 years in 2000. Infants, in particular, benefited from 20th century advances in health and medicine. The infant mortality rate (the number of deaths to infants less than 1 year of age per 1,000 births) decreased sharply over the century, from a rate well in excess of 100 per 1,000 births at the start of the century, to a rate less than 10 per 1,000 births by the century's end.

Figure 1-1.
Total Population: 1900 to 2000
(Millions)

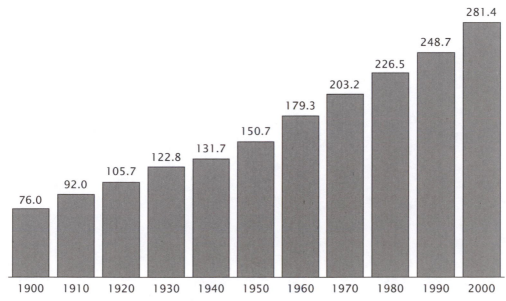

Source: U.S. Census Bureau, decennial census of population, 1900 to 2000.

The 1990 to 2000 population increase was the largest in U.S. history.

Population growth in the United States varied greatly throughout the century, both numerically and in percentage terms. The population growth of 32.7 million in the 1990s was the largest numerical increase in U.S. history (see Figure 1-2).[1] The previous record increase was in the 1950s, a gain fueled primarily by the post-World War II baby boom (1946 to 1964).

Population growth in the 1930s was the smallest of any decade during the period 1900 to 2000. The low growth in this Depression-era decade was due to low levels of fertility and negligible net international migration.

The decade-to-decade pattern of the percentage change in population followed the same up-and-down course as the numerical population change. However, while the maximum numerical population increase occurred in the last decade of the century, the highest percentage increase in the total U.S. population took place at the start of the century, 1900-1910.[2] During this period, the country experienced relatively high birth rates and, most significantly, the arrival of an exceptionally large number of immigrants. Immigration and high fertility levels also contributed to the high growth of the following two decades, 1910-1920 and 1920-1930.

The 1930s, which was the decade with the lowest numerical increase in population, also was the decade with the lowest percentage increase (7.2 percent). After this low point, the population growth rate increased in the 1940s and 1950s.

While the first period of rapid population growth was due primarily to immigration, the second period, from 1950 to 1960, was due primarily to the post World War II baby boom. The 1950s represented the second highest decade of population increase during the century in both numerical (28.6 million) and percentage (19.0 percent) terms.

After the high growth rate in the 1950s, the percentage increase in population declined over the next three decades. The U.S. population continued to grow, but at an increasingly slower rate. However, the rate of population growth increased during the 1990s for the first decade since the 1950s, exceeding the growth rate of the 1970s and 1980s, but still less than in the first three decades of the century.

---

[1] See U.S. Census Bureau, 2001g, *Population Change and Distribution: 1990 to 2000*, by Marc J. Perry and Paul J. Mackun. Population change in any decade may result from changes in census coverage, as well as from births, deaths, and net international migration.

[2] The higher percentage increase results because the total population base in 1900 (76.0 million) is much smaller than the population base in 1990 (248.7 million).

Figure 1-2.
Population Increase by Decade: 1900 to 2000

Numerical increase in millions

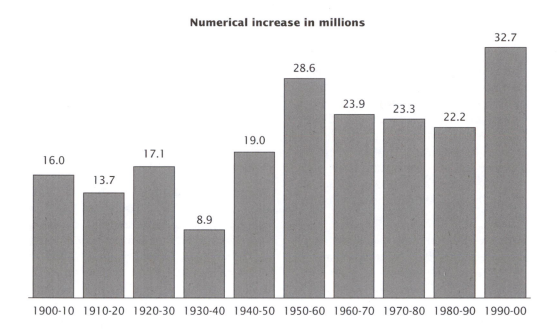

Percent increase

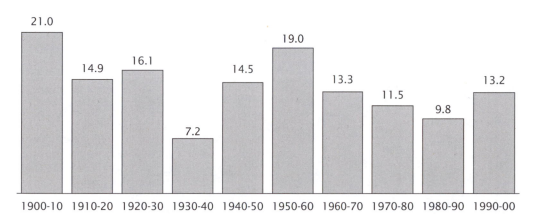

Source: U.S. Census Bureau, decennial census of population, 1900 to 2000.

From 1950 to 2000, the United States and the rest of the developed world comprised a declining share of the world's population.

Population estimates prepared by the U.S. Census Bureau for all countries of the world provide an opportunity to view the trend in U.S. population growth in a global context.[3] As noted earlier, the United States ranked as the fourth most populous country in the world from 1900 until the breakup of the Soviet Union in 1991 and has ranked as the world's third most populous country since then. China and India ranked 1st and 2nd, respectively, in total population size throughout the 20th century.

In 1950, using present-day boundaries, the ten most populous countries were (in order): China, India, the United States, Russia, Japan, Indonesia, Germany, Brazil, the United Kingdom, and Italy. By 2000, the ten most populous countries were: China, India, the United States, Indonesia, Brazil, Russia, Pakistan, Bangladesh, Japan, and Nigeria.

Over the 50-year period, seven countries stayed among the ten most populous countries. The countries that dropped out of the top ten (Germany, the United Kingdom, and Italy) were among the world's more developed countries (MDCs), and were replaced by Pakistan, Bangladesh, and Nigeria, all less developed countries (LDCs).[4] Furthermore, Russia and Japan (both MDCs) dropped in rank, while the ranks of Indonesia and Brazil (both LDCs) increased.

China constituted about one-fifth of the world's population throughout the latter half of the century (see Figure 1-3). More than one-third of the world's population lived in either China or India. The U.S. share of the world's population declined each decade, from 6.0 percent in 1950 to 4.5 percent in 2000. Due to faster growth rates of LDCs than of MDCs, the combined share of the United States and all other MDCs fell from about one-third (32 percent) of the world's population in 1950 to about one-fifth (19 percent) in 2000. In contrast, the share of world population increased in each of the less developed regions.

---

[3] See U.S. Census Bureau, the International Data Base at *www.census.gov/ipc/www/idbnew.html.*

[4] For the definition of more developed countries and less developed countries, see the Glossary.

Figure 1-3.
World Population Distribution: 1950 to 2000
(Percent)

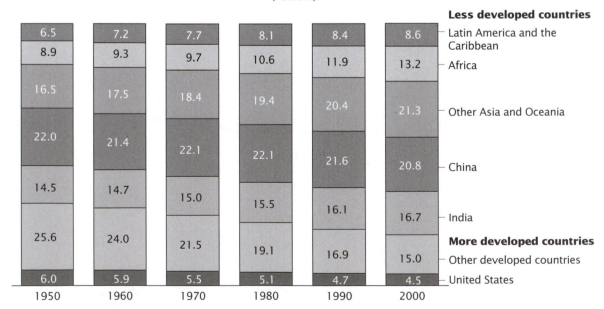

Note: Estimates are for July 1.
Source: U.S. Census Bureau, International Data Base, *www.census.gov/ipc/www/idbnew.html.*

U.S. population density tripled between 1900 and 2000, but remained relatively low compared to most countries.

Given a fixed land area, any increase or decrease in population is accompanied by a corresponding increase (or decrease) in population density.[5] Over the course of the century, the population density of the United States tripled from 26 people per square mile of land area in 1900 to 80 people per square mile in 2000 (see Figure 1-4).

In 1959, Alaska and Hawaii became the 49th and 50th states, respectively. The addition of Alaska, the largest U.S. state in terms of land area, had a major impact on population density. In interpreting the historical trend, population density actually declined slightly from 1950 (not including Alaska and Hawaii prior to statehood) to 1960 (including Alaska and Hawaii). The effect of including Alaska and Hawaii on the trend in population density for the period 1900 to 1950 is shown in Figure 1-4.

Although population density tripled during the period 1900 to 2000, the U.S. density level in 2000 remained relatively low in comparison with most countries of the world, and lower than the overall world population density of 120 people per square mile.

Density levels vary considerably among the countries of the world. Among countries with 5 million or more people in 2000, Australia, Canada, and Libya each had population densities less than 10 people per square mile, while the Netherlands and South Korea had densities of over 1,200 people per square mile, and Bangladesh a density of nearly 2,500. Of the world's ten most populous countries in 2000, Russia, Brazil, and the United States all had relatively low density levels (less than 100), followed by Indonesia, Nigeria, China, and Pakistan (in the 300 to 500 range), Japan and India (829 and 883, respectively), and then Bangladesh.[6]

[5] Density represents the average number of people per unit of land area (such as square miles, square kilometers). All density calculations for the United States, regions, and states in this report are based on land area measurement used for Census 2000.

[6] See U.S. Census Bureau, 2000, *Statistical Abstract of the United States: 2000* (120th edition), Washington, DC.

Figure 1-4.
Population Density: 1900 to 2000
(People per square mile of land area)

—— Density levels if Alaska and Hawaii are included from 1900 to 1960

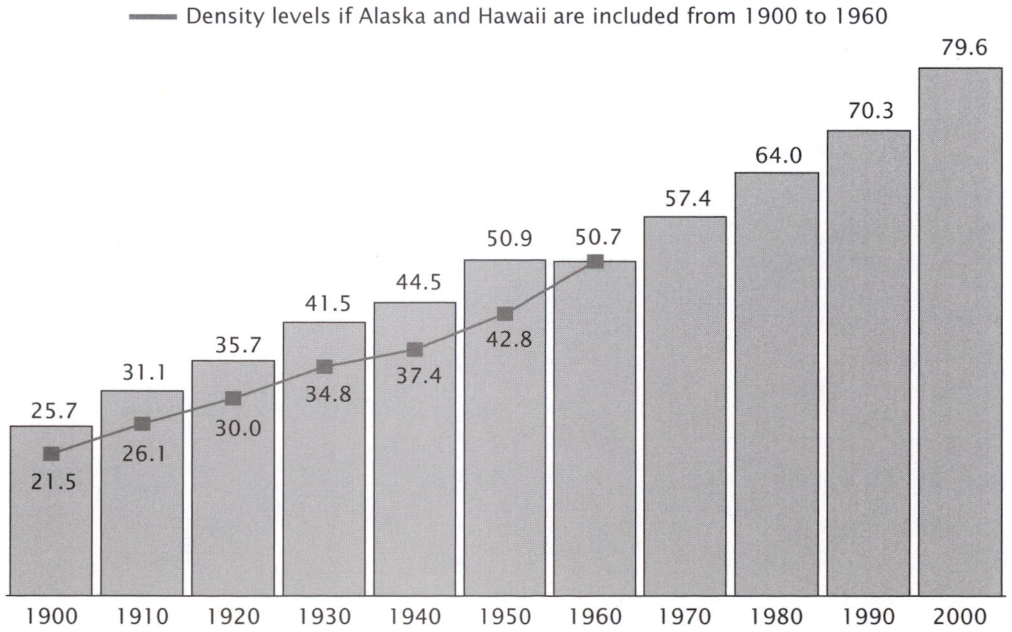

Source: U.S. Census Bureau, decennial census of population, 1900 to 2000.

Between 1900 and 2000, the mean center of the U.S. population moved about 324 miles west and 101 miles south.

Each decade, after tabulating the results of the decennial census, the Census Bureau calculates the mean and median centers of population. The "mean center of population" refers to the point at which an imaginary, flat, weightless, and rigid map of the United States would balance perfectly if weights of identical value were placed on it so that each weight represented the location of one person on the date of the census.

Historically, the mean center of population has followed a trail that reflects the movement of the country's population across America. The trend follows a path indicating the settling of the frontier, waves of immigration, and internal migration west and south.

Over the course of the 20th century, the mean center of population continually moved westward, starting from Bartholomew County, Indiana, in 1900, progressing through Indiana, crossing Illinois, and by 2000 stopping in Phelps County, Missouri (see Figure 1-5). This represents a shift of 324 miles west and 101 miles south from its location at the start of the century.

From 1900 through 1940, the mean center of population was in the southern part of Indiana. From 1950 through 1970, it was in Illinois, and from 1980 through 2000, it was in Missouri.

During the second half of the century, the mean center continued to shift westward, and during the last five decades, began also to move in an increasingly southerly direction. Of the 101 miles the mean moved southward from 1900 to 2000, 22 miles were moved between 1900 and 1950, but 79 miles between 1950 and 2000.[7]

---

[7] The calculation of the mean center of population for 1900 through 1950 is based on the population of the conterminous United States and for 1960 through 2000 includes the populations of Alaska and Hawaii. Including Alaska and Hawaii in 1960 had the effect of shifting the mean center about 2 miles farther south and about 10 miles farther west.

Another measure of the geographic center of population is the "median center of population." The median center is located at the intersection of two median lines, a north-south line constructed so that half of the country's population lives east and half lives west of it, and an east-west line selected so that half of the country's population lives north and half lives south of it. The median center of population is less sensitive to population shifts than the mean center, since it is only affected by population movements that cross the north-south or the east-west median lines.

In every decade of the 20th century, the median center of population was located in either Indiana or Ohio. In 1900 and 1910, the median was in Randolph County, Indiana. At the next three censuses, 1920, 1930, and 1940, the median was located farther east in Darke County, Ohio, a southwestern county in Ohio bordering Indiana. The eastward trend of the median in 1920, 1930, and 1940 compared with 1900 and 1910 may be attributed in part to the impact of migration to industrial urban areas in the Northeast.

The relatively strong westward and southerly shift of the mean center of population in the latter half of the 20th century is paralleled by movement of the median center during the same period. In 1950, the median center had returned to Indiana in a county (Wayne county) adjacent to and south of its location in 1900 and 1910 (Randolph county). Over the next five decades, the median center moved much farther south and west within the state of Indiana, reaching Daviess County at the close of the century. The largest shifts in the median center of population occurred during the 1970s and 1980s.

Figure 1-5.
Mean and Median Centers of Population: 1900 to 2000

Source: U.S. Census Bureau, Geography Division.

The South and West accounted for nearly two-thirds of the U.S. population increase from 1900 to 2000.

While all four regions[8] of the United States grew considerably in the 20th century, the South and the West experienced the largest increases in population, 76 million and 59 million, respectively. Combined, these two regions increased by 471 percent during the century, compared with the combined increase of 149 percent for the Northeast and Midwest. Between 1900 and 2000, the combined increase of 135 million people in the South and the West represented 66 percent of the U.S. population increase of 205 million people.

From 1900 to 2000, the population more than doubled in the Northeast (21 million to 54 million) and in the Midwest (26 million to 64 million). The South's population during this period quadrupled from 25 million to 100 million, while the West's population was more than fifteen times larger in 2000, increasing from 4 million in 1900 to 63 million at the end of the century (see Figure 1-6).

From 1900 to 1930, the Midwest was the most populous region of the country. From 1940 onward, the South had the largest population of all the regions. By 2000, the West's population (63 million) had nearly reached the Midwest's population (64 million). The Northeast (by far the smallest in land area) became the country's least populous region by 1990 and remained the least populous in 2000.

Despite the West's phenomenal growth in population, it remained the region with the smallest proportion of the U.S. population as recently as 1980 (see Figure 1-7). As recently as 1950, the West's proportion (13 percent) of the total U.S. population was just half of the next largest region (Northeast, 26 percent). Yet by 1990, the West's population had become a larger proportion of the total

U.S. population than the Northeast's, and appears likely to overtake the Midwest as the country's second most populous region in the near future.

One of the most significant demographic trends of the 20th century has been the steady shifting of the population west and south. (See the earlier discussion of the mean and median centers of population, Figure 1-5.) In 1900, the majority (62 percent) of the population lived in either the Northeast or the Midwest. This combined proportion declined each decade during the century. By 1980, the majority (52 percent) of the country's population resided in either the South or the West. This trend continued to the end of the century, with the combined South and West regional populations representing 58 percent of the total population of the United States in 2000.

More than one-third of the U.S. population lived in the South in 2000, and about one-third (between 31 to 36 percent) lived in this region over the entire century. The Northeast represented about one-fourth of the U.S. population for most of the century (ranging between 24 percent to 28 percent during the period 1900 to 1970), but its share declined every decade since 1910, to about one-fifth of the U.S. population in 2000. The Midwest's share of the country's total population declined every decade throughout the century, and its percentage-point decline was even more than the Northeast's. The Midwest's share fell by 12 percentage points, from more than one-third (35 percent) of the total population in 1900 to just under one-fourth (23 percent) in 2000. The West represented just 5 percent of the country's population in 1900, but its share increased every decade of the century and reached 22 percent in 2000. As a result of the changing regional distribution of population over the course of the century, the West, Midwest, and Northeast each represented similar fractions (around one-fifth) of the total U.S. population in 2000.

---

[8] Since the 1950 census, the U.S. Census Bureau has classified all states and the District of Columbia into one of four regions—Northeast, Midwest, South, and West. For the definition of each region by state, see the Glossary.

Figure 1-6.
Total Population by Region: 1900 to 2000

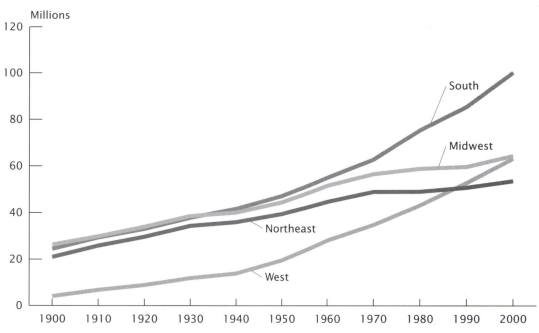

Source: U.S. Census Bureau, decennial census of population, 1900 to 2000.

Figure 1-7.
Population Distribution by Region: 1900 to 2000

(Percent)

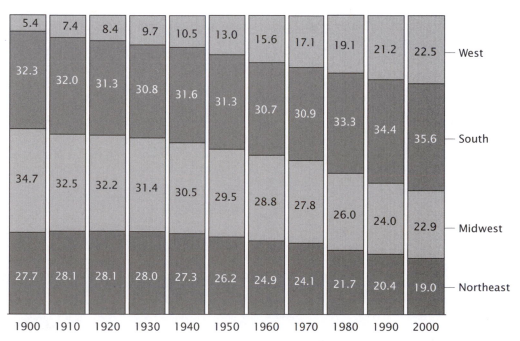

Source: U.S. Census Bureau, decennial census of population, 1900 to 2000.

The West grew faster every decade than all other U.S. regions.

The population of the West grew faster than the other three regions of the country in every decade of the 20th century (see Figure 1-8). In fact, with the exception of the 1930s, the rate of growth in the West was at least double the rate of the other regions for the decades from 1900 to 1960.

For most of the century, the West and the South experienced relatively higher growth rates than the Northeast and the Midwest. The Northeast and the Midwest both had relatively lower growth rates in the 1930s and each decade from the 1960s through the 1990s. The Northeast also had a growth rate below 10 percent in the 1940s. Every region had growth rates above 10 percent during the century's first three decades, when net immigration and fertility rates were generally higher, and again in the 1950s during the peak baby boom years.

In the first third of the century (i.e., 1900 to 1930), the Northeast had the second highest growth rate among the regions. The South replaced the Northeast as the second fastest growing region in the country in the 1930s and remained so for the rest of the century.

The Northeast and Midwest experienced similar growth rate trends every decade since the 1910 to 1920 period. Either the Northeast or the Midwest was the slowest-growing region during every decade of the century, with the exception of 1910 to 1920, when the South had a slightly lower growth rate than the other regions.

The growth of the population peaked in the decade 1900 to 1910 for both the Northeast (23 percent) and the West (67 percent). The 1950s represented the peak decade for the growth of the population in the Midwest (16 percent), and the 1970s was the fastest-growing decade in the South (20 percent).

The growth of the population reached its lowest point for both the South (10 percent) and the West (17 percent) in the 1930s Depression-era decade, which was the period with the lowest growth rate for the United States as a whole. The West's lowest percentage growth during the century (in the 1930s) exceeded the Midwest's highest percentage growth (in the 1950s). The lowest growth decade for the Northeast was the 1970s, with an increase of just 0.2 percent, and the Midwest's lowest growth decade was the 1980s (1.4 percent).

Figure 1-8.
Percent Change in Population per Decade by Region: 1900 to 2000

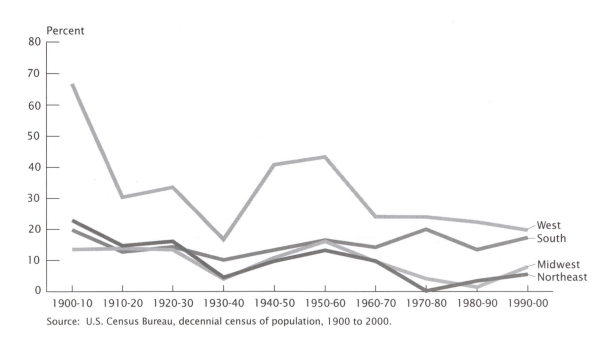

Source: U.S. Census Bureau, decennial census of population, 1900 to 2000.

The Northeast was the most densely populated region throughout the 20th century.

While the Midwest (until 1930) and the South (since 1940) had the largest populations among the regions, and the West grew the fastest each decade, the population density of the Northeast far exceeded the densities of the other regions from 1900 to 2000 (see Figure 1-9). The West's land area, which constitutes nearly half of the total U.S. land area, had the fewest people per square mile of the regions.

The Midwest and the South had similar density levels and trends over the period 1900 to 1970, with the Midwest's density slightly higher than the South's. Since 1980, the South's density level has exceeded the Midwest's level, making the South the second most densely populated region, and the gap between these two regions widened between 1980 and 2000.

Population density levels reflect a combination of population and land area. Although the Northeast represented the smallest share (19 percent) of the U.S. population in 2000, it represented an even smaller share (about 5 percent) of the U.S. land area. Thus, the Northeast had about one-fifth of the U.S. population living in just one-twentieth of the country's land area.

In contrast, while the West also represented about one-fifth (22 percent) of the U.S population in 2000, this population lived in 50 percent of the U.S. land area, resulting in low population density. In 2000, the Midwest's shares of population and land area were similar, 23 and 21 percent, respectively, while the South's population share (36 percent) was greater than its share (25 percent) of the U.S. land area.

Density levels, along with total population, increased every decade for each region of the country, except for the West, where a slight decline occurred from 1950 to 1960, due to the addition to the region of Alaska, a large-area, low-density state (see Appendix Table 2). Even after 100 years of population growth and high rates of growth in the West and, in recent decades, the South, density levels in the Midwest, South, and West in 2000 were still less than the Northeast's population density at the start of the century. Between 1900 and 2000, the average number of people per square mile increased from 130 to 330 in the Northeast, from 35 to 86 in the Midwest, from 28 to 115 in the South, and from 3 to 36 in the West.

Figure 1-9.
Population Density by Region: 1900 to 2000

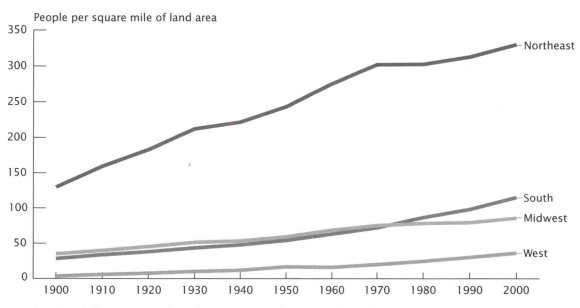

Source: U.S. Census Bureau, decennial census of population, 1900 to 2000.

In 1900, nearly half of the states had fewer than 1 million people. By 2000, only 7 states (and the District of Columbia) had a population under 1 million.

At the beginning of the century, no state had 10 million or more people. In 1900, state population totals ranged from a low of 42,000 in Nevada to 7.3 million in New York (see Appendix Table 1). By 1950, three states, New York, Pennsylvania, and California had passed the 10-million mark. At the end of the century, 7 states had reached a population of at least 10 million—California, Texas, New York, Florida, Illinois, Pennsylvania, and Ohio. The state with the most people in 2000 was California, with a population of 33.9 million.

In 1900, New York and Pennsylvania were the only states with populations of at least 5 million (see Figure 1-10). By 1950, four states—Illinois, Michigan, Ohio, and Texas had between 5 and 10 million people. (As noted above, after the first five decades of the century, New York and Pennsylvania had crossed the threshold of 10 million.) By 2000, a total of 13 states had a population size between 5 and 10 million, comprised of 12 new states, plus 1 holdover, Michigan, from 1950.

Twenty-three states had fewer than 1 million residents in 1900, and 12 of these states were in the West.[9] By 1950, the number of states with fewer than 1 million residents had fallen to 16, and 9 of these were western states. Only 7 states had populations of less than 1 million throughout the century. In 2000, Wyoming had the fewest people, with a population of 494,000, followed by Vermont, Alaska, North Dakota, South Dakota, Delaware, and Montana.[10]

Florida was the only state to grow from a population of less than 1 million at the start of the century to a population of over 10 million by the century's end.

Only 4 states—California, Illinois, Ohio, and Texas—grew from between 1 and 5 million in 1900 to join the 10-million-and-over club by the end of the century. California had already grown to a population of over 10 million by midcentury, increasing greatly from just 1.5 million people in 1900 to 10.6 million people in 1950. Illinois reached 10 million by 1960 and Ohio and Texas by 1970.

Arizona and Washington were the only states to increase from less than 1 million population in 1900 to between 5 million and 10 million (5.1 and 5.9 million, respectively) in 2000.

In 2000, California was the only state with a population of more than 30 million. Texas (with a population of 20.9 million in 2000) was the only other state to have crossed the 20-million threshold.

As mentioned above, New York's total population of 7.3 million in 1900 was greater than any other state. By 2000, the populations of 11 states exceeded this figure: in addition to the 7 states with 10 million or more population listed above, Michigan (9.9 million), Georgia (8.2 million), New Jersey (8.4 million), and North Carolina (8.0 million) had populations that were larger than New York's had been at the start of the 20th century.

[9] The District of Columbia, considered a state equivalent for statistical purposes, had less than 1 million residents for the entire century.

[10] The District of Columbia, with 572,059 residents in 2000, had a smaller population than every state, except Wyoming.

Figure 1-10.
Total Population by State: 1900, 1950, and 2000

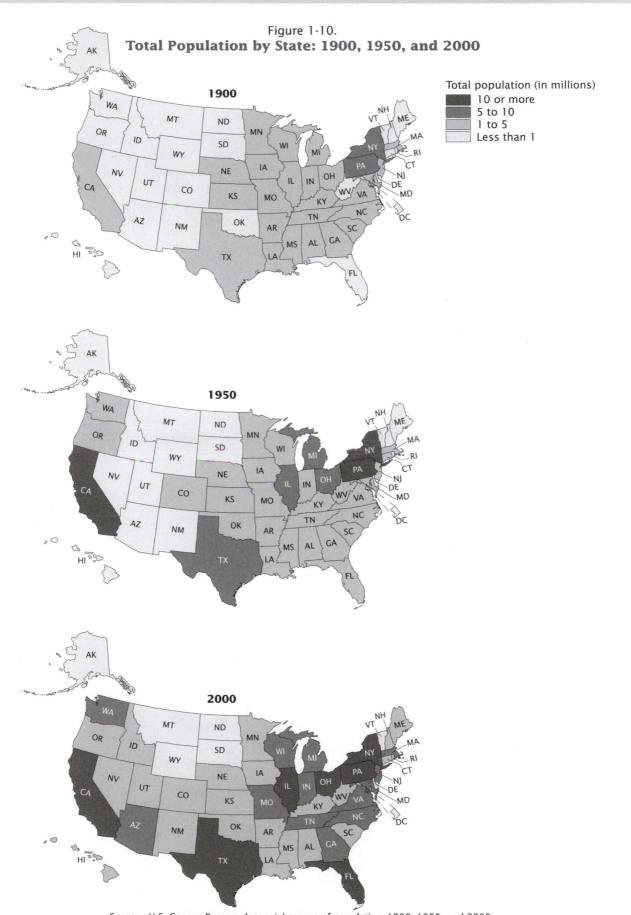

Total population (in millions)

- 10 or more
- 5 to 10
- 1 to 5
- Less than 1

1900

1950

2000

Source: U.S. Census Bureau, decennial census of population, 1900, 1950, and 2000.

California, Texas, Florida, and New York accounted for more than one-third (38 percent) of the U.S. population increase in the 20th century.

The U.S. population increased by more than 200 million people between 1900 and 2000. The population increases in the 4 most populous states at the end of the century—California (32.4 million), Texas (17.8 million), Florida (15.5 million), and New York (11.7 million)—together represented 38 percent of the total growth in the United States over the past 100 years. These were also the only states that increased by more than 10 million people over this period (see Figure 1-11).

California's increase alone accounted for nearly one-sixth of the total U.S. increase and was more than the combined increase of 27 states. In 1900, California's population was about the same as the population of Kansas (1.5 million) but, over the next 10 decades, California increased by 32.4 million while Kansas grew by an additional 1.2 million people.

Over one-half of the U.S. population increase in the 20th century occurred in just eight states. They included Illinois, Michigan, Ohio, and New Jersey, in addition to California, Texas, New York, and Florida. The population increase in ten additional states represented another 25 percent of the total U.S. increase. Thus, over three-fourths of the population increase in the United States from 1900 to 2000 took place in just 18 states.

The population of 10 states increased between 5 million and 10 million during the period from 1900 to 2000. With the exception of Arizona, all of these states are "coastal" states, meaning states bordering either the Atlantic or Pacific Oceans, the Gulf of Mexico, or the Great Lakes.

Thirteen states (and the District of Columbia) gained fewer than 1 million people during the 20th century. Several of these states are geographically contiguous, such as Maine, New Hampshire, and Vermont in New England, and the northern interior states of Montana, Wyoming, North Dakota, South Dakota, Nebraska, and Iowa.

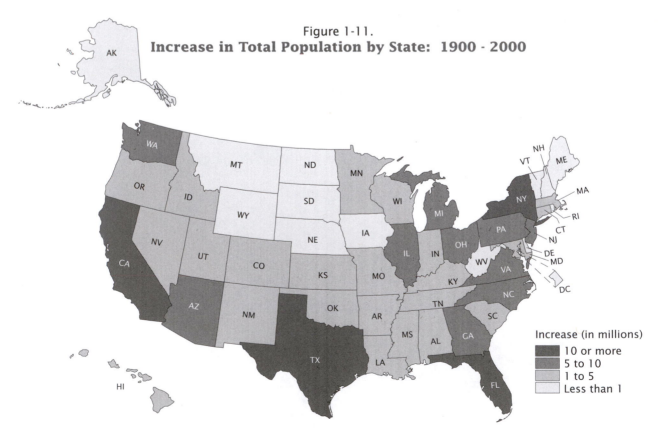

Figure 1-11.
Increase in Total Population by State: 1900 - 2000

Increase (in millions)
- 10 or more
- 5 to 10
- 1 to 5
- Less than 1

Source: U.S. Census Bureau, decennial census of population, 1900 and 2000.

The population declined in more states in the 1930s than during any other 20th century decade, and the 1990s was the first decade when no state's population declined.

Although every state's population was larger at the century's end than at the start, the population of every state did not grow in each individual decade. During the century, a decline in population from one census to the next in either a state or the District of Columbia occurred 32 times (see Table 1-1).

The 32 instances of population decline during the ten decades of the century took place in just 15 states (and the District of Columbia). The District of Columbia's population declined most often during the period, losing population every decade since the 1950s. North Dakota's population fell four times between censuses; Mississippi's and West Virginia's populations fell three times; and Arkansas's, Iowa's, Oklahoma's, South Dakota's, and Vermont's populations each fell twice. Seven states experienced one decade of population decline during the century: Alaska, Kansas, Montana, Nebraska, New York, Nevada, and Wyoming. By region, the group represents five states in the Midwest, four (and the District of Columbia) in the South, four in the West, and two in the Northeast.

Of the 32 instances of population decline, southern states (and the District of Columbia) accounted for 15, midwestern states for 10, western states for 4, and northeastern states for 3 declines.

More states declined in population in the 1930s than in any other decade of the 20th century. Nearly all the state population declines in this period occurred in Great Plains states, extending northward from Oklahoma to Kansas, Nebraska, South Dakota, and North Dakota.

Only states in the South and Midwest lost population between censuses during the period 1940 to 1970. In the 1950s, only southern states lost population. The only states outside the South and the Midwest to lose population since 1930 were New York (1970s), Vermont (1930s), and Wyoming (1980s). New York's population decline (679,000) was by far the largest of any decade: no other state level decline exceeded 200,000.

The 1990s was the first decade when none of the 50 states lost population, although the District of Columbia's population declined for the fifth consecutive decade.

Table 1-1.
States Experiencing Intercensal Population Decline: 1900-1910 to 1990-2000

Decade and state	Region	Change	Decade and state	Region	Change
1900-1910			**1950-1960**		
Iowa	Midwest	-7,082	Arkansas	South	-123,239
			District of Columbia	South	-38,222
1910-1920			Mississippi	South	-773
Vermont	Northeast	-3,528	West Virginia	South	-145,131
Mississippi	South	-6,496	**1960-1970**		
Alaska	West	-9,320	North Dakota	Midwest	-14,685
Nevada	West	-4,468	South Dakota	Midwest	-15,007
			District of Columbia	South	-7,446
1920-1930			West Virginia	South	-116,184
Montana	West	-11,283			
			1970-1980		
1930-1940			New York	Northeast	-678,895
Vermont	Northeast	-380	District of Columbia	South	-118,177
Kansas	Midwest	-79,971	**1980-1990**		
Nebraska	Midwest	-62,129	Iowa	Midwest	-137,053
North Dakota	Midwest	-38,910	North Dakota	Midwest	-13,917
South Dakota	Midwest	-49,888	District of Columbia	South	-31,433
Oklahoma	South	-59,606	West Virginia	South	-156,167
			Wyoming	West	-15,969
1940-1950					
North Dakota	Midwest	-22,299	**1990-2000**		
Arkansas	South	-39,876	District of Columbia	South	-34,841
Mississippi	South	-4,882			
Oklahoma	South	-103,083			

Note: The District of Columbia is considered a state equivalent for statistical purposes.

Source: U.S. Census Bureau, decennial census of population, 1900 to 2000.

309

Nine western states and Florida accounted for the ten fastest-growing states from 1900 to 1950 and eight western states plus Florida and Texas were the fastest growing from 1950 to 2000.

At the state level, patterns of percentage change in population portray a different picture than patterns of numerical population change. In any period, a state with a small base population may not grow a large amount in terms of population numbers, but may increase by a large proportion of its original population size.

From 1900 to 2000, Nevada's population grew faster (4,620 percent) than the population of any other state. Arizona ranked second, with an increase of 4,074 percent. Western states accounted for 9 of the 10 fastest-growing states during this period. The southern state of Florida ranked third, with an increase of 2,924 percent.

In contrast, no western state ranked among the ten slowest-growing states during the century, while states in each of the other regions did. Iowa had the lowest percentage increase (31 percent) from 1900 to 2000, followed by Nebraska (60 percent).

During the first half of the century, states in the West also accounted for 9 of the 10 states with the highest percentage growth in population (see Figure 1-12). The top five states from 1900 to 1950 were (in rank order): California, Arizona, Florida, Washington, and Nevada. During this period, California grew by more than 600 percent. The populations of the ten fastest-growing states at least tripled (increased by 200 percent or more). The populations of an additional 12 states (and the District of Columbia) more than doubled in size.

From 1900 to 1950, the ten slowest-growing states all grew by less than 50 percent. Vermont grew the slowest (10 percent), followed by Iowa, Nebraska, Missouri, and New Hampshire.

Western states also accounted for 8 of the 10 fastest-growing states in the 1950 to 2000 period. From 1950 to 2000, the five fastest-growing states (in rank order) were: Nevada, Arizona, Florida, Alaska, and Colorado. Nevada's population increased by more than 1,100 percent during this period.

During the second half of the century, the populations of 7 states at least tripled, while the populations of 11 additional states more than doubled.

From 1950 to 2000, the ten states or state equivalent with the lowest percentage changes were: the District of Columbia, West Virginia, North Dakota, Iowa, South Dakota, Pennsylvania, New York, Nebraska, Mississippi, and Rhode Island. During this period, the populations of the District of Columbia and West Virginia declined by 29 percent and 10 percent, respectively.

Comparing population change in the first and second halves of the century, California grew fastest in the first part and Nevada in the second half. Nevada, Arizona, and Florida ranked among the five fastest-growing states in both periods. In addition, California, New Mexico, and Washington ranked among the ten fastest-growing states for each 50-year period.

Iowa was the only state to appear among the five slowest-growing states in population for both halves of the century, while Nebraska and Mississippi were among the ten slowest-growing states.

The population of 11 western states, Florida, and Texas at least doubled in size during both 50-year periods.

Figure 1-12.
Percent Change in Total Population by State:
1900 - 1950 and 1950 - 2000

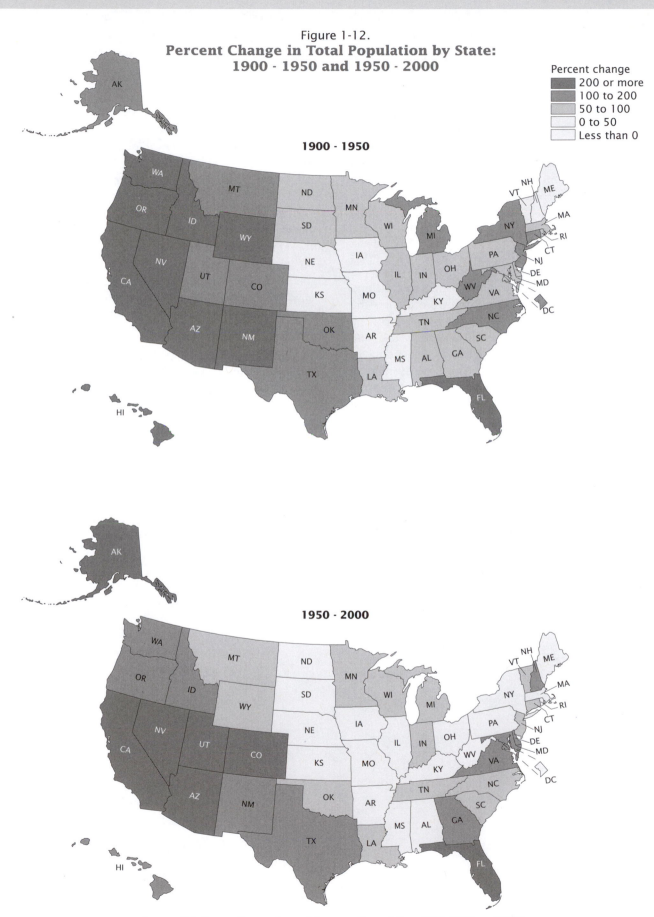

Source: U.S. Census Bureau, decennial census of population, 1900, 1950, and 2000.

Florida's rank by population size jumped the most, while Iowa's fell the most from 1900 to 2000.

The numeric and percentage change in population size for the 50 states and the District of Columbia varied widely over the century. These differences produced marked shifts in the relative ranking of states in terms of population size (see Table 1-2).

Between 1900 and 2000, 15 states ranked among the 10 most populous at least once. Six of them were among the ten largest throughout the century—Illinois, Michigan, New York, Ohio, Pennsylvania, and Texas. Of the remaining nine, four were among the ten largest in 1900 but then dropped below this rank and never re-entered—Indiana, Iowa, Missouri, and Massachusetts; three entered the ten largest and never left—California, Florida, and New Jersey; North Carolina was the tenth largest in 1950; and Georgia was the tenth largest state in 1910 and in 2000 (see Appendix Table 1).

New York had the largest state population from 1900 through the 1960 census. California became the largest state by the 1970 census and has remained the most populous. Texas became the second largest state by 2000, dropping New York to third.

State rankings fluctuate from census to census depending on population growth. However, some state rankings progressively increased during the century, while others progressively declined. In 2000,

15 states were ranked at their highest level of the century. All of these states were either in the West (ten states or the South (five states). In contrast, 11 states ranked at their highest point during the century in 1900. Most of these are in the Northeast (Maine, New Hampshire, Rhode Island, and Vermont) and the Midwest (Indiana, Iowa, Missouri, and Nebraska). None of these states is in the West. Although five states in the South were at their peak rank in 2000 (Delaware, Florida, Georgia, Texas, and Virginia), three states in the South had their highest population rank in 1900—Kentucky, Mississippi, and Tennessee.

While population changes altered the state ranking order, most state ranks did not vary by more than ten positions during the 100-year period. Five states increased their ranking by more than ten places: four states in the West (Arizona, California, Nevada, and Washington), plus Florida, which increased in rank more than any other state, from 33rd to 4th. (Arizona's rank increased nearly as much, from 48th in 1900 to 20th in 2000.)

Seven states and the District of Columbia dropped by more than ten places in their ranking over the century, all of them either in the Midwest or the South. Iowa's ranking declined the most, from 10th in 1900 to 30th in 2000.

Table 1-2.
States Ranked by Population Size: 1900, 1950, and 2000

State	1900	1950	2000
Alabama	18	17	23
Alaska	50	51	48
Arizona	48	38	20
Arkansas	25	30	33
California	21	2	1
Colorado	32	34	24
Connecticut	29	28	29
Delaware	45	48	45
District of Columbia	41	36	50
Florida	33	20	4
Georgia	11	13	10
Hawaii	47	46	42
Idaho	46	44	39
Illinois	3	4	5
Indiana	8	12	14
Iowa	10	22	30
Kansas	22	31	32
Kentucky	12	19	25
Louisiana	23	21	22
Maine	31	35	40
Maryland	26	24	19
Massachusetts	7	9	13
Michigan	9	7	8
Minnesota	19	18	21
Mississippi	20	26	31
Missouri	5	11	17
Montana	43	43	44
Nebraska	27	33	38
Nevada	51	50	35
New Hampshire	37	45	41
New Jersey	16	8	9
New Mexico	44	40	36
New York	1	1	3
North Carolina	15	10	11
North Dakota	40	42	47
Ohio	4	5	7
Oklahoma	30	25	27
Oregon	36	32	28
Pennsylvania	2	3	6
Rhode Island	35	37	43
South Carolina	24	27	26
South Dakota	38	41	46
Tennessee	14	16	16
Texas	6	6	2
Utah	42	39	34
Vermont	39	47	49
Virginia	17	15	12
Washington	34	23	15
West Virginia	28	29	37
Wisconsin	13	14	18
Wyoming	49	49	51

Note: States in color are or have ranked in the top ten most populous states.

Source: U.S. Census Bureau, decennial census of population, 1900, 1950, and 2000.

Among the 50 states, New Jersey, Rhode Island, Massachusetts, and Connecticut had the highest population densities throughout the century.

Since population density is determined both by population size and by land area, relatively less-populated states can have a high population density, and relatively more-populated states can have a low population density. For example, Rhode Island ranked first among the 50 states in population density in each census from 1900 through 1960, even though it ranked among the smaller states in population size.[11] Conversely, Texas, which became the second-most populated state in 2000, still ranked 28th in terms of population density at the end of the century.

At the beginning of the century, all the more densely populated states were in the eastern half of the country (see Figure 1-13). State densities generally increased over time as the population increased, since the changes in the land area of states during the period were minimal.[12] Even in 2000, the eastern half of the country remained more densely populated than the western half.

Most of the states with a high population density have a relatively small total land area. As noted above, Rhode Island had the highest population density among the 50 states from 1900 to 1960. By 1970, New Jersey had become the country's most densely populated state and has remained so since then. At the end of the century, both of these states had population densities of more than 1,000 people per square mile (see Appendix Table 2). Massachusetts had the second or third highest density level throughout the century, and Connecticut ranked fourth every decade from 1900 to 2000.

Throughout the 20th century, all of the least densely populated states were relatively large-area states in the West and Midwest regions. Maine was the Northeast region's least densely populated state throughout the century. From 1900 to 1950, the least densely populated state in the South was either Florida or Texas. From 1960 to 2000, Oklahoma and Arkansas had the lowest population densities in the South. For the West region and for the United States, Alaska (with just over one person per square mile in 2000) had the lowest population density of all the states, a result of the combination of a relatively small population size and a very large land area. Prior to Alaska's statehood in 1960, the state with the lowest population density every decade was Nevada.

The number of states with more than 200 people per square mile increased from 3 (New Jersey, Rhode Island, and Massachusetts) in 1900 to 12 in 2000. The nine additional states, ranked by density in 2000, are: Connecticut, Maryland, New York, Delaware, Florida, Ohio, Pennsylvania, Illinois, and California.

In 1900, 14 states (and Alaska) had densities of fewer than 10 people per square mile. They included Florida and California, which, as noted above, had increased to more than 200 people per square mile by the end of the century. Five states—South Dakota, North Dakota, Montana, Wyoming, and Alaska—still had fewer than ten people per square mile in 2000.

---

[11] The District of Columbia is usually considered a state equivalent for statistical purposes, and its density was higher by far than all 50 states throughout the century. However, it is excluded from the general discussion of state population density due to its lesser comparability attributable to a relatively small land area and its greater comparability to other cities, rather than states.

[12] State population density calculations in this report are based on land area measurement used for Census 2000.

Figure 1-13.
Population Density by State: 1900, 1950, and 2000

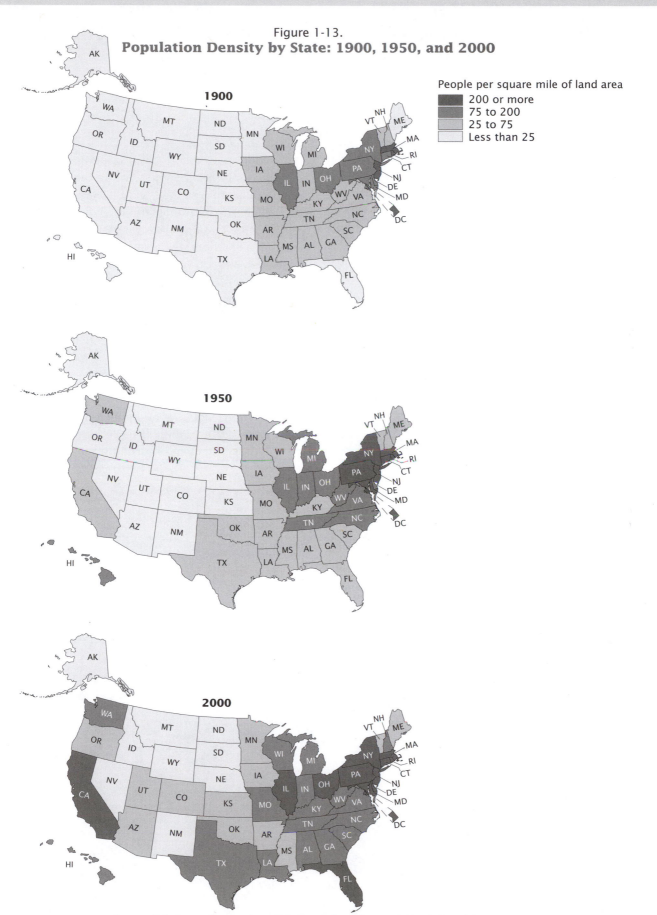

People per square mile of land area
- 200 or more
- 75 to 200
- 25 to 75
- Less than 25

Source: U.S. Census Bureau, decennial census of population, 1900, 1950, and 2000.

In 1950, the U.S. population became predominantly metropolitan and became increasingly more metropolitan in each subsequent decade.

The U.S. Census Bureau defined metropolitan population concentrations[13] for the first time in 1910. At that time, 26.1 million people lived in 19 metropolitan districts of 200,000 or more population and cities of 100,000 to 200,000 and their adjacent territory, leaving 65.9 million who lived in nonmetropolitan territory. With each passing decade, the metropolitan population increased, while the nonmetropolitan population generally decreased (see Figure 1-14).

While metropolitan concentrations certainly grew as a result of births and migration, they also grew as a result of territorial expansion. Over the course of the century, the changing definition of "metropolitan" caused new areas to achieve metropolitan status and existing metropolitan areas to acquire more territory.

---

[13] The 1910 forerunner of a metropolitan area was the "metropolitan district." Metropolitan districts/areas were redefined at each census. The definition of metropolitan areas was based on county boundaries for the first time in 1950 (see the Glossary). Data presented in Figures 1-14 through 1-19 are based on the definition of metropolitan at the time of each census.

During the early part of the century, the metropolitan population grew quickly, due in part to the influx of immigrants into large cities, while the nonmetropolitan population changed very little. The smallest increase in the metropolitan population occurred during the 1930s (8.2 million people). This was also the last decade when the nonmetropolitan population increased, although it remained larger than the metropolitan population into the 1940s.

By 1950, the U.S. population had become predominantly metropolitan for the first time, and the metropolitan population exceeded the nonmetropolitan population by 18.3 million people. By 2000, the metropolitan population (226 million) was four times the size of the nonmetropolitan population (55 million).

From 1910 to 2000, the metropolitan population grew by nearly 200 million people, with the largest increase, 33.3 million, occurring from 1990 to 2000.

Figure 1-14.
Total Population by Metropolitan Status: 1910 to 2000

(Millions)

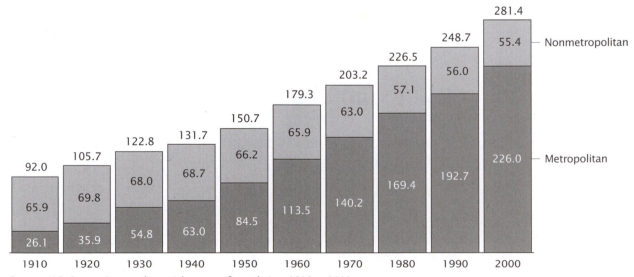

Source: U.S. Census Bureau, decennial census of population, 1910 to 2000.

While the metropolitan population grew rapidly during the century, most of that growth occurred in the suburbs, with little change in the percentage of population living in central cities.

Metropolitan areas accounted for a growing proportion of the U.S. population over the course of the century. In 1910, less than a third (28 percent) of the total population lived in metropolitan areas, but by 1950, more than half of the U.S. population lived in metropolitan areas. In 2000, the metropolitan population represented 80 percent of the U.S. resident total of 281.4 million people (see Figure 1-15).

The highest percentage increase in metropolitan population growth occurred from 1920 to 1930, when metropolitan areas grew by 52 percent. The lowest metropolitan percentage growth occurred from 1980 to 1990, when metropolitan areas grew by 14 percent.

Metropolitan areas include two parts: central cities and suburbs.[14] From 1910 to 2000, suburbs accounted for most of the growth of metropolitan areas.

[14] For the definitions of metropolitan, central city, and suburb, see the Glossary.

From 1910 to 1960, the population of central cities accounted for a larger proportion of the total population than the population living in suburbs. For example, in 1910, 21 percent of the total U.S. population lived in central cities, while only 7 percent of the population lived in suburbs.

From 1910 to 1930, both central cities and suburbs grew rapidly. Growth in the 1930s continued, but at a slower pace. From 1940 onward, suburbs accounted for more population growth than central cities and, by 1960, the proportion of the total U.S. population living in the suburbs (31 percent) was almost equal to the proportion of the population living in the central cities (32 percent).

From 1940 to 2000, the proportion of the population living in central cities remained relatively stable, while the suburbs continued to grow substantially. By 2000, half of the entire U.S. population lived in the suburbs of metropolitan areas.

Figure 1-15.
Percent of Total Population Living in Metropolitan Areas and in Their Central Cities and Suburbs: 1910 to 2000

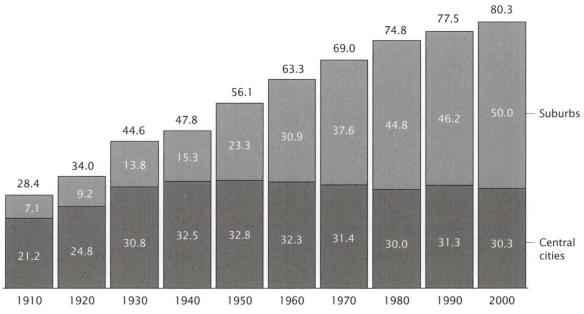

Source: U.S. Census Bureau, decennial census of population, 1910 to 2000.

Since 1990, more than half of the U.S. population has lived in metropolitan areas of at least 1 million people.

Most of the metropolitan population lives in relatively large concentrations (see Figure 1-16). In 1950, only 14 metropolitan areas had populations of at least 1 million people, which constituted less than a third (29 percent) of the total U.S. population. By 2000, 50 metropolitan areas had populations of at least 1 million people, which accounted for over half (57 percent) of the total U.S. population.[15]

From 1950 to 2000, the population living in metropolitan areas of at least 1 million people increased by 117.1 million and accounted for 83 percent of the total metropolitan growth and 90 percent of the total U.S. population growth. It is important to note that the growth of the different size categories of metropolitan areas is directly affected by the addition of new metropolitan areas, the movement of existing metropolitan areas into larger size categories due to population increase, and the territorial growth of metropolitan areas due to changing metropolitan boundaries, which often adds counties to existing metropolitan areas.

Between 1950 and 2000, the share of the population living in metropolitan areas with 1 million up to 5 million people and with 5 million or more people increased greatly (by 10.2 and 17.7 percentage points, respectively), while the share of the population living in the other two size categories stayed within a narrow range. Although the share of the population living in metropolitan areas of 250,000 up to 1 million, and less than 250,000 increased in two decades during the 50-year period, a smaller share of the U.S. population lived in these areas in 2000 than in 1950. For the two larger size classes, the lowest population share occurred in 1950, while for the two smaller size classes, the lowest population share occurred in 2000.

---

[15] Metropolitan trends have been limited in most figures to censuses since 1950, when metropolitan areas based on county units were first defined.

Figure 1-16.
Percent of Total Population Living in Metropolitan Areas by
Size of Metropolitan Area Population: 1950 to 2000

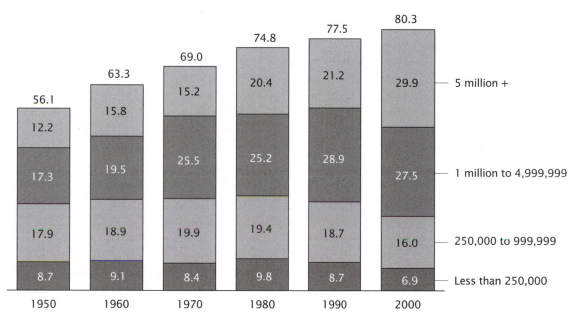

Source: U.S. Census Bureau, decennial census of population, 1950 to 2000.

From 1950 to 2000, New York was the most populous metropolitan area.

Since 1950, the ten largest metropolitan areas have always had populations of 1 million or more. In 1950, Cleveland, Ohio, the 10th largest metropolitan area had nearly 1.5 million people. By 2000, the 10th largest metropolitan area, Houston-Galveston-Brazoria, Texas, had a population of 4.7 million (see Table 1-3).

In 1950, New York and Chicago were the only metropolitan areas with populations of 5 million or more. Their combined population in 1950 (18.4 million) accounted for 12.2 percent of the total U.S. population.[16] By 2000, they had been joined by 7 other metropolitan areas,[17] creating a combined population of 84.1 million, or 29.9 percent of the U.S. total. By 2000, nearly 1 in 3 Americans lived in a metropolitan area with 5 million or more residents.

While metropolitan areas grew significantly from 1950 to 2000, some relatively slower-growing metropolitan areas in the Northeast and the Midwest dropped out of the category of the ten largest metropolitan areas. For example, the tenth largest metropolitan area in 1950, Cleveland, Ohio, was no longer in the top ten by 1960.

St. Louis, Missouri, and Pittsburgh, Pennsylvania, dropped out of the top ten by 1980, when Houston-Galveston, Texas, and Dallas-Fort Worth, Texas, were added for the first time.

From 1950 to 2000, New York was the largest metropolitan area in the United States, with a population ranging from 12.9 million people in 1950 to 21.2 million people in 2000.[18] In 2000, New York accounted for 7.5 percent of the total U.S. population. From 1950 to 1970, Chicago and Los Angeles were the second and third largest metropolitan areas in the United States, respectively. However, from 1980 to 2000, they switched ranks and Los Angeles was the second most populous metropolitan area.

While New York remained by far the largest metropolitan area in the United States from 1950 to 2000, its proportional lead over the second largest metropolitan area slowly closed from 1950 to 1990 and then slightly increased from 1990 to 2000. In 1950, New York was more than twice the size of Chicago, the second largest metropolitan area. However, by 2000, New York was about 1.3 times the size of Los Angeles, the next largest metropolitan area.

---

[16] See U.S. Census Bureau. 1991. *Metropolitan Areas and Cities.* 1990 Census Profile, Number 3.

[17] Los Angeles-Riverside-Orange County, Washington-Baltimore, San Francisco-Oakland-San Jose, Philadelphia-Wilmington-Atlantic City, Boston-Worcester-Lawrence, Detroit-Ann Arbor-Flint, and Dallas-Fort Worth.

---

[18] Although metropolitan areas were first classified as such in 1950, clearly New York ranked first in metropolitan population throughout the entire century.

Table 1-3.
Ten Most Populous Metropolitan Areas: 1950 to 2000

Year and area	Region	Population
1950		
New York, N.Y.-Northeastern New Jersey SMA.....................	Northeast	12,911,994
Chicago, Ill. SMA...	Midwest	5,495,364
Los Angeles, Calif. SMA......................................	West	4,367,911
Philadelphia, Pa. SMA	Northeast	3,671,048
Detroit, Mich. SMA..	Midwest	3,016,197
Boston, Mass. SMA..	Northeast	2,369,986
San Francisco-Oakland, Calif. SMA............................	West	2,240,767
Pittsburgh, Pa. SMA	Northeast	2,213,236
St. Louis, Mo. SMA	Midwest	1,681,281
Cleveland, Ohio SMA	Midwest	1,465,511
1960		
New York, N.Y.-Northeastern New Jersey SCA	Northeast	14,759,429
Chicago, Ill.-Northwestern Indiana SCA.......................	Midwest	6,794,461
Los Angeles-Long Beach, Calif. SMSA	West	6,742,696
Philadelphia, Pa.-N.J. SMSA.................................	Northeast	4,342,897
Detroit, Mich. SMSA	Midwest	3,762,360
San Francisco-Oakland, Calif. SMSA..........................	West	2,783,359
Boston, Mass. SMSA	Northeast	2,589,301
Pittsburgh, Pa. SMSA	Northeast	2,405,435
St. Louis, Mo.-Ill. SMSA	Midwest	2,060,103
Washington, D.C.-Md.-Va. SMSA	South	2,001,897
1970		
New York, N.Y.-Northeastern New Jersey SCA	Northeast	16,178,700
Chicago, Ill.-Northwestern Indiana SCA.......................	Midwest	7,612,314
Los Angeles-Long Beach, Calif. SMSA	West	7,032,075
Philadelphia, Pa.-N.J. SMSA.................................	Northeast	4,817,914
Detroit, Mich. SMSA	Midwest	4,199,931
San Francisco-Oakland, Calif. SMSA..........................	West	3,109,519
Washington, D.C.-Md.-Va. SMSA	South	2,861,123
Boston, Mass. SMSA	Northeast	2,753,700
Pittsburgh, Pa. SMSA	Northeast	2,401,245
St. Louis, Mo.-Ill. SMSA	Midwest	2,363,017
1980		
New York-Newark-Jersey City, N.Y.- N.J.-Conn. SCSA	Northeast	16,121,297
Los Angeles-Long Beach-Anaheim, Calif. SCSA....................	West	11,497,568
Chicago-Gary-Kenosha, Ill.-Ind.-Wis. SCSA	Midwest	7,869,542
Philadelphia-Wilmington-Trenton, Pa.-Del.-N.J.-Md. SCSA [1]..........	Northeast	5,547,902
San Francisco-Oakland-San Jose, Calif. SCSA....................	West	5,179,784
Detroit-Ann Arbor, Mich.SCSA...............................	Midwest	4,618,161
Boston-Lawrence-Lowell, Mass.-N.H. SCSA	Northeast	3,448,122
Houston-Galveston, Tex. SCSA	South	3,101,293
Washington, D.C.-Md.-Va. SMSA	South	3,060,922
Dallas-Fort Worth, Tex. SMSA................................	South	2,974,805
1990		
New York-Northern New Jersey-Long Island, NY-NJ-CT CMSA........	Northeast	18,087,251
Los Angeles-Anaheim-Riverside, CA CMSA......................	West	14,531,529
Chicago-Gary-Lake County, IL-IN-WI CMSA	Midwest	8,065,633
San Francisco-Oakland-San Jose, CA CMSA.....................	West	6,253,311
Philadelphia-Wilmington-Trenton, PA-NJ-DE-MD CMSA [1].............	Northeast	5,899,345
Detroit-Ann Arbor, MI CMSA	Midwest	4,665,236
Boston-Lawrence-Salem, MA-NH CMSA.........................	Northeast	4,171,643
Washington, DC-MD-VA MSA	South	3,923,574
Dallas-Fort Worth, TX CMSA.................................	South	3,885,415
Houston-Galveston-Brazoria, TX CMSA	South	3,711,043
2000		
New York-Northern New Jersey-Long Island, NY-NJ-CT-PA CMSA	Northeast	21,199,865
Los Angeles-Riverside-Orange County, CA CMSA	West	16,373,645
Chicago-Gary-Kenosha, IL-IN-WI CMSA.........................	Midwest	9,157,540
Washington-Baltimore, DC-MD-VA-WV CMSA.....................	South	7,608,070
San Francisco-Oakland-San Jose, CA CMSA	West	7,039,362
Philadelphia-Wilmington-Atlantic City, PA-NJ-DE-MD CMSA [1]	Northeast	6,188,463
Boston-Worcester-Lawrence, MA-NH-ME-CT CMSA	Northeast	5,819,100
Detroit-Ann Arbor-Flint, MI CMSA..............................	Midwest	5,456,428
Dallas-Fort Worth, TX CMSA.................................	South	5,221,801
Houston-Galveston-Brazoria, TX CMSA	South	4,669,571

[1]A small portion of the Philadelphia SCSA (1980) and CMSA (1990 and 2000) includes population in states of the South region (Delaware and Maryland).

Source: U.S. Census Bureau, decennial census of population, 1950 to 2000.

The density of central cities declined during the second half of the century, yet remained far higher than the densities of suburban areas, which increased, and the densities of nonmetropolitan areas, which were steady during the period.

Metropolitan population density levels remained higher than nonmetropolitan density (see Figure 1-17) since 1950, when metropolitan areas were first defined. From 1950 to 2000, the density of metropolitan areas ranged from 299 to 407 people per square mile, and the density of nonmetropolitan territory ranged from 19 to 24 people per square mile.

While the density of nonmetropolitan areas remained relatively stable from 1950 to 2000, the density of metropolitan areas fluctuated.[19] The peak of metropolitan population density in the last half of the century occurred in 1950. Then, it declined steadily from 1950 to 1980, driven primarily by the steep decline in the population of central cities, one of the components of metropolitan areas. As Figure 1-17 shows, the density of central cities was substantially higher than the density of suburban and nonmetropolitan areas throughout the second half of the century, although it declined every decade during this period, from a peak of 7,517 people per square mile in 1950 to a low of 2,716 people per square mile in 2000.

The decline of central city populations was partly offset by the movement of population into the suburbs, the other component of metropolitan areas. The density of suburban areas steadily increased from 1950 to 1970, however, this increase had little effect on the overall density of metropolitan areas. To some extent, this phenomenon reflects the addition of land area (usually relatively lower density suburban counties) to metropolitan areas as a whole with each passing census.[20] Increased land area, coupled with population declines of many central cities, resulted in an overall decline in metropolitan density between 1950 and 2000.

In the 1980s, metropolitan area density increased slightly, then decreased slightly in the 1990s. Similarly, the density of the suburban areas increased slightly from 1980 to 1990, then leveled off from 1990 to 2000. Although the density of central cities continued to decline in both the 1980s and 1990s, the rate of the decline slowed considerably during this period.

---

[19] The relative stability of nonmetropolitan density occurred even though the nonmetropolitan population was smaller in 2000 than in 1950. A corresponding decline in the total area of nonmetropolitan territory partially offset the drop in population.

[20] The density levels for suburban areas shown in Figure 1-17 should be interpreted with caution. Suburban population as used in this report refers to the population living in metropolitan areas, outside central cities. Using this definition includes a nontrivial portion of county land area that is predominantly rural. This produces lower density levels than would result if suburban were defined by using the population living in the "urban fringe" of urbanized areas.

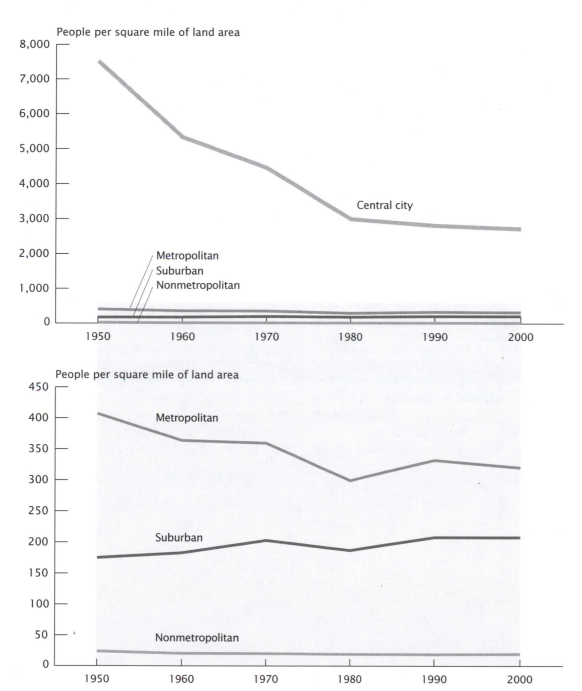

Figure 1-17.
**Population Density by Metropolitan Area
Status: 1950 to 2000**

Source: U.S. Census Bureau, decennial census of population, 1950 to 2000.

The Northeast had the highest percentage of people living in metropolitan areas of all four regions for the entire century.

The percentage of people living in metropolitan areas increased in every decade for every region. In 1910, more than half of the Northeast's population, about a quarter of the Midwest's and the West's, and about a tenth of the South's population was metropolitan. By 2000, at least three quarters of the populations in the Northeast, the South, and the West were metropolitan and nearly three quarters (73.8 percent) of the population in the Midwest lived in metropolitan areas (see Figure 1-18).

The proportions of the populations that lived in metropolitan areas grew relatively faster in the South and the West than in the Northeast and the Midwest. In the South, the metropolitan population increased from 9 percent in 1910 to 75 percent in 2000, and in the West it grew from 28 percent in 1910 to 87 percent in 2000.

The ranking of the regions in terms of percentage metropolitan remained fairly stable over the century. The Northeast had the highest percentage of people living in metropolitan areas for the entire century. From 1910 to 1990, the Northeast was followed by the West, the Midwest, and then the South. However, the South passed the Midwest for the first time in 2000, making the Midwest the least metropolitan of the regions.

Comparing the regions to the national average in terms of percentage of metropolitan population, the Northeast remained above the national average throughout the century and the West stayed above the national average from 1930 to 2000. However, the percentage metropolitan in the South and Midwest remained below the national average for the whole century.

As all four regions increased their metropolitan populations, the difference in the proportion living in metropolitan areas between the regions converged. The largest differential (54 percentage points) between the regions in the percentage metropolitan was in 1930 (74 percent in the Northeast compared with 20 percent in the South). By 2000, the difference between the regions had narrowed to 16 percentage points (90 percent in the Northeast compared with 74 percent in the Midwest).

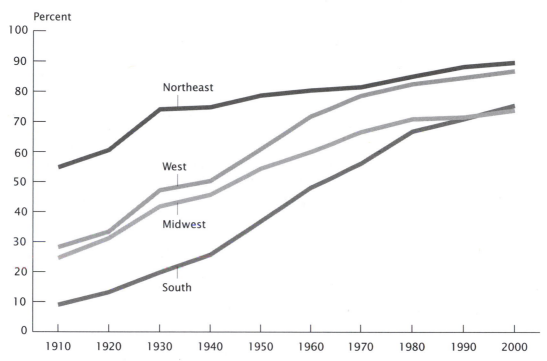

Figure 1-18.
**Percent of Population Living in Metropolitan
Areas by Region: 1910 to 2000**

Source: U.S. Census Bureau, decennial census of population, 1910 to 2000.

In 1910, no state had 75 percent or more of its population living in metropolitan areas. In 2000, more than one-third of the states had 75 percent or more of their populations living in metropolitan areas.

The percentage of population living in metropolitan areas increased for every state from 1910 to 2000. In 1910, only five states (Maryland, Massachusetts, New Jersey, New York, and Rhode Island), concentrated primarily along the northeastern seaboard, had a majority of their populations living in metropolitan areas and no state had 75 percent or more of its population living in metropolitan areas.[21] Thirty-three states had less than a quarter of their populations living in metropolitan areas, of which 19 states had no metropolitan population.

By 1950, the number of states with a majority metropolitan population had tripled to 15, and these states were more dispersed throughout the country, spreading into parts of the Midwest and West. By 2000, at least 50 percent of the population in 37 states lived in metropolitan areas, and no states had less than 25 percent metropolitan. As Figure 1-19 shows, by 2000, more than one-third (21) of the states had 75 percent or more of their populations living in metropolitan areas and they were distributed among every region. Some clustering of these states occurred along the Atlantic coast from Massachusetts to

Virginia and into the large midwestern states (Ohio, Michigan, and Illinois). Still another cluster extended inland from California including Nevada, Utah, Arizona, and Colorado.

While increasing numbers of states were becoming mostly metropolitan, as late as 1970, three states (Alaska, Vermont, and Wyoming) had no metropolitan population at all. By 1980, all 50 states had a portion of their populations living in metropolitan areas.

The top ten states with the highest percentage metropolitan remained fairly stable from 1910 to 2000. Seven states (California, Connecticut, Maryland, Massachusetts, New Jersey, New York, and Rhode Island) were consistently among the top ten. By 2000, all seven of these states, plus Florida, were at least 90 percent metropolitan. Illinois and Pennsylvania were also among the states with the highest proportions of metropolitan population for large portions of the century (1910 to 1970 for Illinois, and 1910, 1930 to 1960, and 1990 for Pennsylvania).

On the other hand, five states (Idaho, North Dakota, South Dakota, Vermont, and Wyoming) remained among the ten states with the lowest percentage metropolitan and, by 2000, none of these states had a majority metropolitan population. Three more states, Maine, Mississippi, and Montana, each ranked among the ten states with the lowest percentage metropolitan for all but one census during the period 1910 to 2000.

---

[21] The District of Columbia is usually considered a state equivalent for statistical purposes, and its percentage metropolitan was 100 percent in every census from 1910 to 2000. However, it is excluded from the general discussion of the percentage metropolitan by state due to its particularly greater comparability to other cities, rather than states, on this population measure.

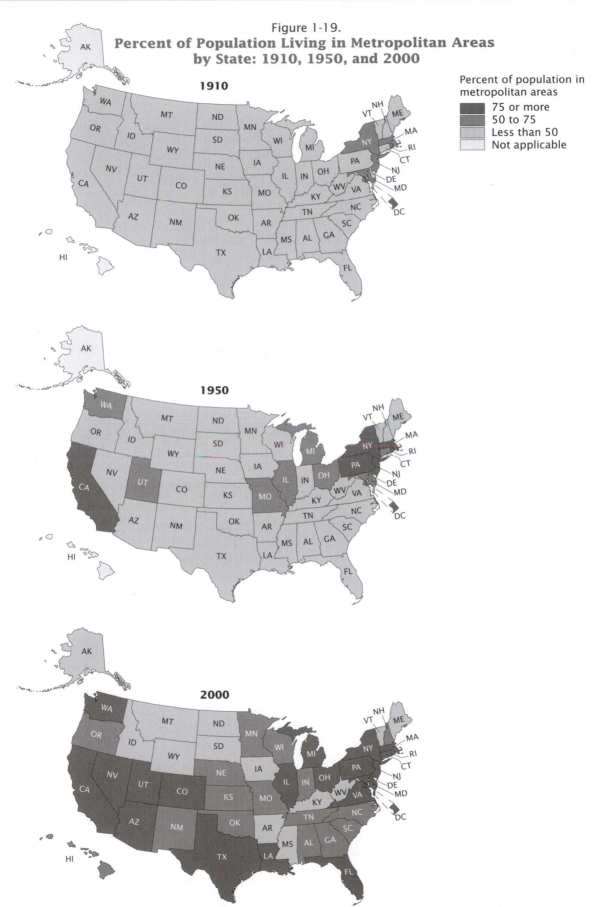

Figure 1-19.
**Percent of Population Living in Metropolitan Areas
by State: 1910, 1950, and 2000**

Percent of population in
metropolitan areas

- 75 or more
- 50 to 75
- Less than 50
- Not applicable

1910

1950

2000

Source: U.S. Census Bureau, decennial census of population, 1910, 1950, and 2000.

The percentage of the U.S. population living in the ten largest cities increased to a peak in 1930, then declined every following decade of the century.

Despite the significant growth of metropolitan areas in the United States, the percentage of the population living in the ten largest cities grew steadily in the first three decades of the 20th century, but declined appreciably over the next seven decades. The percentage of the population living in the ten largest cities peaked in 1930 (15.5 percent) and fell every decade thereafter, reaching its lowest point in 2000 (8.5 percent, see Figure 1-20).

The growth of the ten largest cities from 1900 to 1930 and their subsequent decline as a proportion of the U.S. population mirrors the growth and decline of the total central city population in the United States in the 20th century. During the first part of the century, immigrants as well as natives poured into the cities. In the second half of the century, the growth of cities slowed and in some cases even declined as the proportion of the population living in the suburbs increased.

In 1900, 8 of the 10 largest cities were northeastern or midwestern cities. Among the largest cities, San Francisco was the only western city, and Baltimore was the only southern city (see Appendix Table 4). New York, Chicago, and Philadelphia, the only cities with 1 million or more population in 1900, also were the only cities to rank among the 10 largest throughout the century.

Los Angeles and Detroit grew rapidly, and by 1930 had crossed the 1-million-or-more population threshold. By mid-century, Buffalo, San Francisco, and Cincinnati had dropped out of the group of the ten largest cities, and had been replaced by Los Angeles (ranked 4th), Detroit (5th), and Washington, DC (9th). (Pittsburgh ranked among the ten largest cities from 1910 to 1940.)

Over the last half of the century, the growth and change in the ten largest cities reflected the growth of the U.S. population in the Sunbelt. During this period, St. Louis, Boston, Baltimore, Cleveland, and Washington, DC, dropped out of the ten largest cities. They were either replaced by cities in Texas (Houston, Dallas, and San Antonio) or in the West (Phoenix and San Diego). None of the cities that fell from the list of the 10 largest ever reached 1 million population, while all the cities that replaced them passed the 1 million mark. In 2000, for the first time in U.S. history, a city (Detroit) declined from a population above 1 million to a population below 1 million.

Throughout the century, New York's population far exceeded the population of any other city, ranging from 3.4 million to 8.0 million. From 1900 to 2000, its population was always at least double the population of the second largest city.

Figure 1-20.
**Percent of Total Population Living in the
Ten Largest Cities: 1900 to 2000**

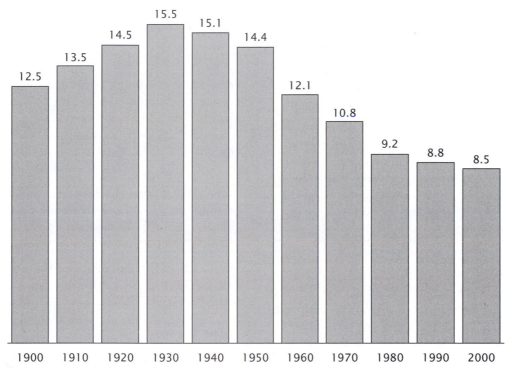

Source: U.S. Census Bureau, decennial census of population, 1900 to 2000.

Chapter Highlights
AGE AND SEX COMPOSITION

National Trends

Past fertility trends exerted the strongest influence on the U.S. age structure in the 20th century. Relatively high fertility at the start of the century, lower fertility in the late 1920s and during the 1930s, higher fertility of the baby-boom period, followed by lower fertility of the baby-bust period, all affected the country's age composition.

At the beginning of the century, half of the U.S. population was less than 22.9 years old. At the century's end, half of the population was less than 35.3 years old, the country's highest median age ever.

Children under age 5 represented the largest 5-year age group in 1900 and again in 1950. By 2000, the largest 5-year age groups were ages 35 to 39 years and 40 to 44 years, a large segment of the baby-boom generation.

During the last half of the century, the baby-boom generation's entry into an age group had a major impact on the growth of that age group. This effect on the age distribution will continue into the 21st century. For example, rapid growth of the population age 65 and over will begin in 2011, when the first of the baby-boom generation reaches age 65, and will continue for many years.

The population age 65 and over increased tenfold during the century, from 3.1 million in 1900 to 35.0 million in 2000, compared with a twofold increase for the total population.

The proportion of the population age 65 and over declined for the first time in the 1990s, due partly to the relatively low number of births in the late 1920s and early 1930s.

Prior to 1950, the male population outnumbered the female population. From 1950 to 2000, the female population outnumbered the male population.

The sex ratio (males per 100 females) declined every decade from 1910 to 1980, then increased in the 1980s and the 1990s.

Central cities had lower sex ratios than suburban and nonmetropolitan areas.

Throughout the century, women represented most of the population age 85 and over, and their predominance in this age group greatly increased between 1900 and 2000.

Regional Trends

From 1900 to 1960, the South had the highest proportion of children under age 15 and the lowest proportion of people 65 and over, making it the "youngest" region. The West had the highest percentage under age 15 in 1990 and 2000, and the lowest percentage 65 and over from 1970 to 2000.

Among the regions, the Northeast had the highest proportion age 65 and over for each census of the 20th century, except from 1910 to 1950, when the Midwest's proportion age 65 and over ranked highest.

The West had the highest sex ratio, and the Northeast had the lowest sex ratio among the regions for the entire century.

State Trends

From 1900 to 2000, only Mississippi and Utah ranked among the ten states with the highest percentage of the population under age 15 in every decade.

Florida's rank in terms of percentage of the population 65 and over jumped from 42nd in 1900 to 1st by 1970, and remained 1st through 2000, while its rank on percentage under age 15 fell from 14th in 1900 to 49th in 2000.

In 1900, Arkansas ranked as the 4th youngest state, but by the end of the century ranked as the 9th oldest. California changed in the opposite direction, moving from the 6th oldest state in 1900 to the 6th youngest state in 2000.

In 2000, only seven western states—Alaska, Colorado, Hawaii, Idaho, Nevada, Utah, and Wyoming—had a larger male population than female population.

Chapter 2
AGE AND SEX COMPOSITION

The age and sex composition of the United States population changed considerably during the 20th century, as a consequence of fluctuations in births, deaths, and migration. Marriage patterns and changes in contraceptive use are among many factors affecting birth trends. Medical advances affecting mortality rates, especially infant mortality in the first part of the century and old age mortality in recent decades, also shaped the country's age structure. Laws and policies influencing international migration further contributed to U.S. age and sex composition in the past and continue to have an impact today.

In 1900, the U.S. population had an age and sex composition similar to many of today's developing countries. That is, the country was characterized by its "youngness." The median age (half of the population younger and half older) was about 23 years. Although the U.S. population aged during the century, with a median age of about 35 years in 2000, the extended length of the baby-boom period (1946 to 1964), plus the continued infusion of migrants kept the country's age structure younger than that of most developed countries of the world. Although the population in each 5-year age group increased numerically, younger age groups fell as a proportion of the total population, while the proportion in older age groups rose. Apart from these general trends, changes in age and sex structure varied from one decade to the next. Past U.S. fertility trends exerted the strongest influence on age composition. Low fertility from the late 1920s through the early 1940s, the post World War II baby boom, and a subsequent return to low fertility altered the composition of the U.S. population by age. The effect of the baby boom on the age and sex structure of the United States will extend several decades into the 21st century as the baby boomers age through the life cycle.

Between 1900 and 2000, overall regional and state trends followed the basic U.S. trend. Regionally, the title of the "youngest" region shifted from the South to the West during the century, while that of the "oldest" region shifted from the Midwest to the Northeast. States in the South and the West consistently ranked among the youngest and those from the Midwest and the Northeast among the oldest throughout the century. The relative changes in age structure were more pronounced in some states. In terms of percentage of population age 65 and over, Florida ranked 42nd in 1900, but has ranked 1st since 1970. Arkansas transformed from one of the ten youngest states in 1900 to one of the ten oldest in 2000. Conversely, California ranked among the ten oldest states at the beginning of the century, but ranked among the ten youngest states in 2000.

The United States gender composition shifted from a majority male population to a majority female population around midcentury. Larger gains for women than men in life expectancy and attrition of the large number of immigrants in decades prior to World War I (who were predominantly male) accounted for this shift. The West had the highest regional proportion of male population and the Northeast the highest proportion of female population during every decade of the 20th century. Only seven states, all in the West, still had a larger male than female population at the end of the century.

The graphics and text in this chapter depict the evolution of the number and proportional distribution of people in the United States by age and sex. These changes are described for the total population, regions, and states. Age trends focus on broad age groups, with particular emphasis on the population under age 15 and on the population age 65 and over. Trends in sex composition are discussed with the age distribution and separately by examining the trends in the relative numbers of the male and female populations at each age by region, state, and metropolitan status. Detailed data for each decade for the United States for 5-year age groups by sex are provided in Appendix Table 5. Detailed data for the United States, regions, and states for the male and female population and for broad age groups are provided in Appendix Tables 6 and 7, respectively.

At the beginning and the middle of the century, the most populous 5-year age group was under age 5. In 2000, people age 35 to 39 years outnumbered all other age groups.

The number of people in each age group grew during the course of the 20th century, but some age groups grew much more than others. The growth and the changing age and sex composition of the U.S. population can be portrayed through the use of population pyramids. The overall shape of the pyramid and the size of the bars for each age group depict the changes.

Both the male and female populations increased between 1900 and 1950 and again between 1950 and 2000 for every 5-year age group. This is shown in the superimposed population pyramids in Figure 2-1.

Under age 5 represented the largest 5-year age group in 1900, with a population of 9.2 million (4.6 million males and 4.5 million females). As Figure 2-1 shows, each successive age group in 1900 was smaller than the preceding age group, creating the traditional pyramid shape or "broad-based" population.

In 1920, the largest 5-year age group was still children under age 5, with a population of 11.6 million (see Appendix Table 5). The sizable decline in fertility starting in the 1920s and continuing through the Depression changed the age composition. By 1940,

the 15-to-19 year age group (corresponding essentially to people born from 1920 to 1924) was the largest (12.3 million).

In 1950, as a result of the post-World War II baby boom (1946 to 1964), the group under age 5 was again the largest, with a population of 16.2 million. With each passing decade since 1950, the largest 5-year age group has fallen in the range of ages that included the baby boomers. In 2000, the largest age groups were the 35-to-39 and 40-to-44 age groups (corresponding essentially to people born from 1960 to 1964 and 1955 to 1959, respectively).[22]

Further evidence of the impact of the baby boom on the U.S. age structure is seen in the measure of total population growth by age group from 1900 to 2000. The age groups 35-to-39 years, 40-to-44 years, and 45-to-49 years experienced the largest increases in population of any age group from the beginning to the end of the century (17.7 million, 18.2 million, and 16.6 million, respectively).

---

[22] See U.S. Census Bureau. 2001a. *Age: 2000*, by Julie Meyer.

Figure 2-1.
**Total Population by Age and Sex:
1900, 1950, and 2000**

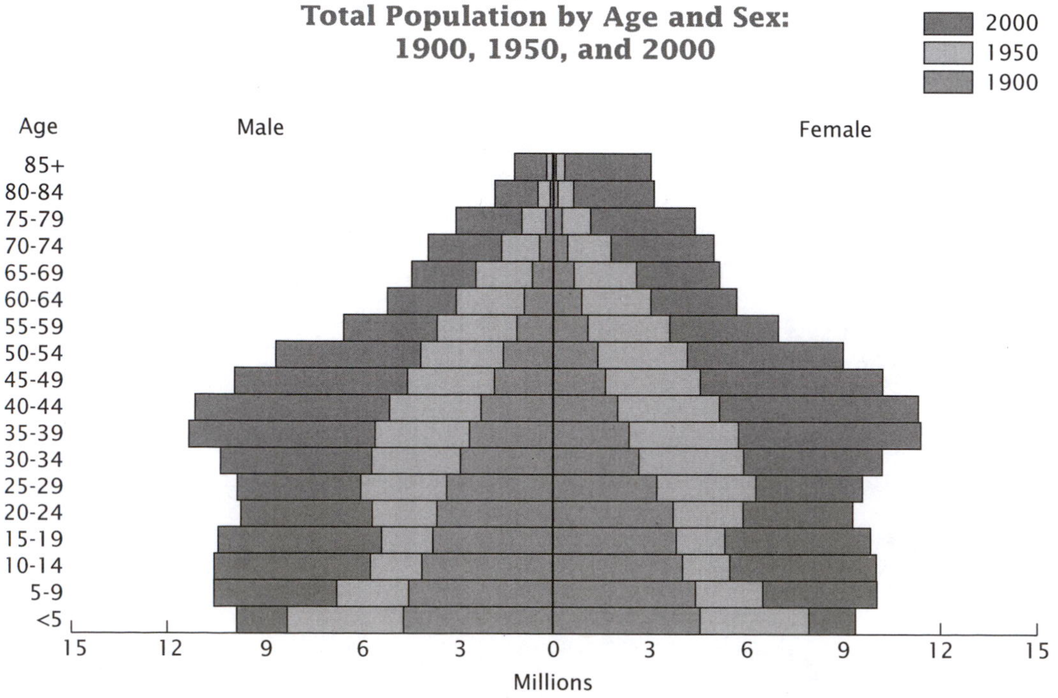

Source: U.S. Census Bureau, decennial census of population, 1900, 1950, and 2000.

Over the century, the age distribution of the U.S. population changed from relatively young to relatively old.

Changes in the U.S. age structure over the century may be illustrated by population pyramids where each bar represents the percentage of the total population in each age-sex group.[23]

The distribution of the population by age and sex in 1900 exhibits the classic pyramid shape, wider at the bottom and narrower at the top (see Figure 2-2). This broad-based shape characterizes a young, relatively high fertility population. In 1900, children under age 5 accounted for 12 percent of the U.S. population.

The general shape of the pyramid remained essentially the same into the 1920s, although declining fertility rates led to smaller proportions of the total population in the youngest age groups. By 1940, the base of the pyramid had taken on a more rectangular look. Younger age groups (under 5 through 29 years) still comprised a relatively large proportion of the population, but each 5-year age group was roughly equal in size at 8 or 9 percent of the population, rather than exhibiting the steadily declining proportions by age of the 1900 pyramid.

[23] This method standardizes (to 100 percent) the total area of each pyramid. In this representation, the shape of the pyramid is more useful than the length of each bar when making pyramid-to-pyramid comparisons.

By 1950, the onset of the baby boom altered the bottom of the pyramid, as 11 percent of the population was under age 5. Once again, the age-sex pyramid had a large base of very young people. The low fertility of the Depression years is evidenced by the "pinch" in the age structure, as people born during the 1930s were 10 to 19 years old.

The aging of the U.S. population in the second half of the 20th century is shown by the more rectangular shape of the Census 2000 age-sex pyramid. The proportions do not begin to decline with each successive age group until after ages 35 to 39 years. Some variability in the pyramid's shape occurs in the 20-to-29 age group, where the slight "pinch" in the pyramid results from a relatively low number of births during the 1970s. Also, the baby-boom bulge appears in the 2000 pyramid in the 35-to-54-age range.

Another feature of the 2000 age-sex pyramid is the less "cone-like" shape at the top of the pyramid compared with the 1900 and 1950 pyramids. The larger proportions of the population in older age groups in part result from sustained low fertility levels and from relatively larger declines in mortality at older ages in the latter part of the century.

Figure 2-2.
Age and Sex Distribution of the Total Population: 1900, 1950, and 2000

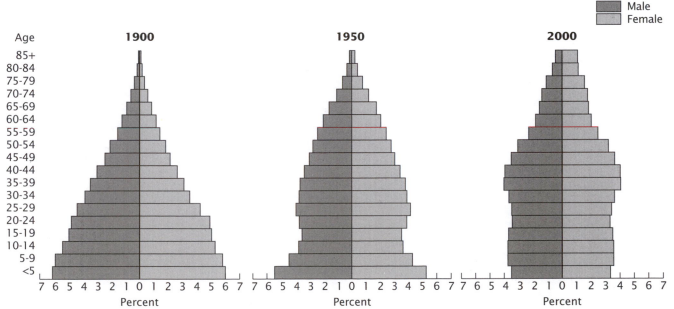

Source: U.S. Census Bureau, decennial census of population, 1900, 1950, and 2000.

Population growth in broad age groups varied throughout the century, with major fluctuations due to changing fertility.

The U.S. population in every age group at the end of the 20th century was much larger than at the start of the century. The decadal trends in specific broad age groups show that for some groups, such as ages 25 to 44 years, 45 to 64 years, and 65 and over, population increases occurred during every 10-year period (see Figure 2-3). In contrast, the under-15 age group and the 15-to-24-year age group experienced some population declines between censuses.

The population declines for people under age 15 from 1930 to 1940 and for people age 15 to 24 from 1940 to 1950 reflect the drop in fertility starting in the 1920s. Similarly, the population declines for those under age 15 from 1970 to 1980 and for those 15 to 24 from 1980 to 1990 result from the drop in fertility after the baby boom.

Large population increases from one decade to the next also are closely related to these fluctuations in fertility. This is especially evident in the rapid increases in the population under age 15 in the 1950s, 15 to 24 years in the 1960s, 25 to 44 years in the 1970s and 1980s, and 45 to 64 in the 1990s (see Appendix Table 5). The entry of the baby-boom generation into each of these age groups yielded rapid population growth. The population age 65 years and over will begin to increase rapidly starting in 2011, when the first of the baby-boom generation reaches age 65, and the rapid growth of this age group will continue for two decades.

In 1900, the youngest broad age group (under 15 years) had the most members, and the oldest group (65 years and over) had the least. In 2000, the oldest group was still the smallest, but people age 25 to 44 and those age 45 to 64 outnumbered the population under age 15 years.

Figure 2-3.
Total Population by Broad Age Group: 1900 to 2000

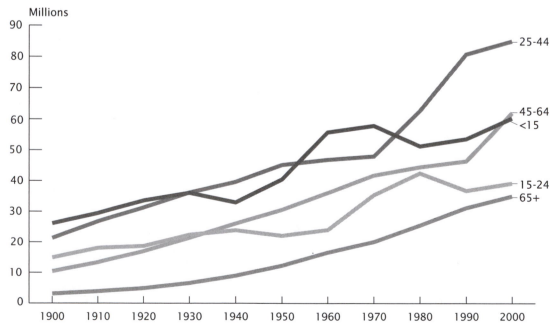

Source: U.S. Census Bureau, decennial census of population, 1900 to 2000.

The share of the population under age 15 declined more than the share of any other broad age group.

Although the populations in the five broad age groups all increased in size over the course of the century, their proportional shares of the total population changed in different directions as a result of the different rates of growth for each group. In general, the shares of the population of the older age groups increased, while those of the younger age groups declined (see Figure 2-4).

The proportion of the U.S. population that was under age 15 declined more than the proportion of any other broad age group. At the beginning of the century, 1 out of every 3 people was under age 15 years. By 2000, only 1 of every 5 people was under age 15.

The total population share represented by 15-to-24 year olds generally declined from 1900 onward, reaching a low of 13 percent in 1960. This was followed by increases in the 1960s and 1970s, as the baby-boom cohort passed through this age group, and by declines as the baby-boom cohort moved out of the age group.

The share of the U.S. population represented by the age group 25 to 44 reached its lowest level of any census during the 20th century in 1970, and then increased over the next two decades to its maximum level in 1990. As with many of the changes in age structure experienced in the second half of the century, this trend largely reflects the entrance of the baby-boom cohort into this age group.

Both the population age 45 to 64 years and the population age 65 years and over were at their lowest proportional levels of the U.S. total population at the beginning of the century. Their shares of the total population increased each decade until 1950 and 1990, respectively. After some fluctuation and decline, the proportion age 45 to 64 increased sharply in the 1990s, largely fueled by people born during the first half of the baby boom, and reached its highest level (22 percent) of the century in 2000. The decade of the 1990s was the first to show a decline in the proportion of the population age 65 and over, reflecting the relatively low number of births during the late 1920s and early 1930s.

Figure 2-4.
Percent Distribution of the Total Population by Age: 1900 to 2000

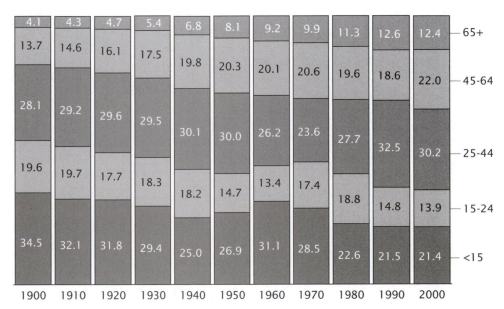

Source: U.S. Census Bureau, decennial census of population, 1900 to 2000.

The median age rose from 23 in 1900 to 35 in 2000 but declined between 1950 and 1970.

The median age[24] of a population often is used to describe a population as "young" or "old." Populations with a median age under 20 years may be classified as relatively young, and those with a median age of 30 years or more as relatively old. The United States population aged over the course of the century, although not in each decade.

_____

[24] The median age is the age that divides the population into two equal-size groups. Half of the population is older than the median age and the other half is younger. See the Glossary.

The median age rose gradually from 23 in 1900 to 26 in 1930 and then rose more rapidly to 29 in 1940 with the relatively small number of births during the 1930s (see Figure 2-5). After increasing to 30 in 1950, the median age fell, as a result of the baby boom, to 28 in 1970.

Beginning in the 1970s, lower fertility combined with the aging of the baby boom generation (the oldest turned age 30 in 1976), pushed the median age sharply higher. It reached 30 in 1980—the same median age as in 1950—and continued to increase to a record high of 35 in 2000.

Figure 2-5.
Median Age: 1900 to 2000
(Years)

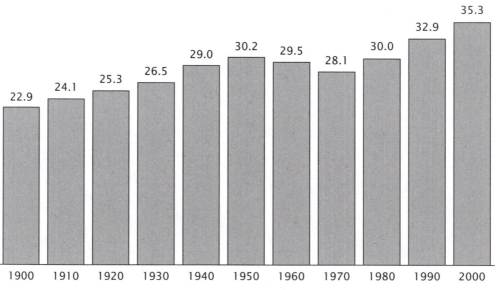

Source: U.S. Census Bureau, decennial census of population, 1900 to 2000.

The population age 65 years and older increased more than tenfold between 1900 and 2000.

As discussed earlier, the United States population aged during the 20th century as the growth rate of the elderly[25] population far exceeded the growth rate of the total population. In this century, the total population more than tripled, while the 65 years and over population grew more than tenfold, from 3.1 million in 1900 to 35.0 million in 2000 (see Figure 2-6).

The faster rate of growth of the elderly population increased its share of the U.S. population from 4.1 percent in 1900 to 12.6 percent in 1990 (see Figure 2-7). The 65-to-74 age group made up the majority of the 65 and over population throughout the century. In most decades, this age group also accounted for the largest share of the growth of the 65 and over population (see Appendix Table 5).

From 1900 to 1990, the elderly population grew faster than the total population in each decade, but between 1990 and 2000, for the first time in the history of the census, the 65 years and over population grew slower than the total population.[26] During the 1990s, the total population increased by 13.2 percent, while the population 65 years and over increased by only 12.0 percent. As a result, people age 65 and over represented a slightly smaller share of the U.S. population in 2000 (12.4 percent) than in 1990 (12.6 percent).

The declining proportion of the 65 and over population from 1990 to 2000 is directly related to the low fertility of the late 1920s and early 1930s. (People born during this period entered the 65 and over age group during the 1990s.) In particular, the population 65 to 69 years dropped from 10.1 million in 1990 to 9.5 million in 2000. The decline in the proportion of elderly in the population is expected to reverse as the baby boomers (born from 1946 to 1964) reach age 65, starting in 2011.

Among the elderly population, growth of the population 85 years and over is particularly notable, increasing from 122,000 in 1900 to 4.2 million in 2000. From 1940 to 2000, the 85 and over population increased at a more rapid rate than 65-to-74 year olds and 75-to-84 year olds in every decade.

The 85 and over age group also increased as a proportion of the elderly population, from 4 percent in 1900 to 12 percent in 2000, although they represented just 1.5 percent of the total U.S. population at the end of the 20th century.

---

[25] In this report, the term elderly refers to individuals aged 65 years and over.

[26] See U.S. Census Bureau. 2001h. *The 65 Years and Over Population*, by Lisa Hetzel and Annetta Smith.

Figure 2-6.
Population Age 65 and Over: 1900 to 2000
(Millions)

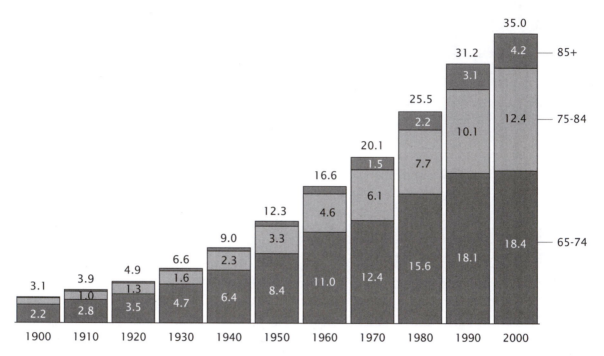

Source: U.S. Census Bureau, decennial census of population, 1900 to 2000.

Figure 2-7.
Percent of Total Population Age 65 and Over:
1900 to 2000

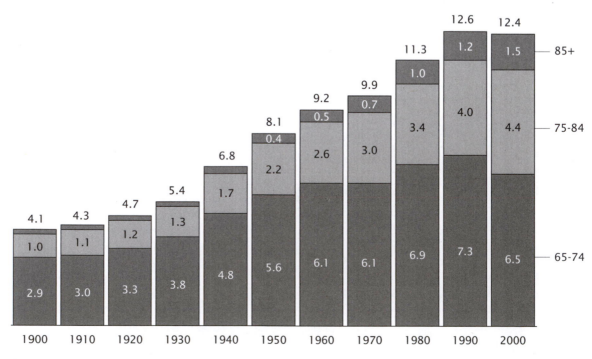

Source: U.S. Census Bureau, decennial census of population, 1900 to 2000.

The South had the youngest regional age structure in the first half of the century but was replaced by the West by the end of the century. The Midwest generally had the oldest population during the first half of the century, and the Northeast had the oldest during the latter half.

The trends in the proportions of people under 15 years old and those age 65 and over generally moved in opposite directions during the century. Every region's proportion of people under age 15 in 2000 declined substantially from its level in 1900, while the proportion of people 65 years and over increased (see Figure 2-8).

The proportion under 15 years fell from regional highs (in the Northeast, Midwest, and South) in the range of 30 percent to 40 percent in 1900 to lows of 20 percent to 23 percent in 1990 and 2000. However, the highest percentage under age 15 in the West occurred in 1960 rather than in 1900. The lowest regional percentage under age 15 occurred in 1990 or 2000 in every region.

Regional lows in the percentage 65 years and over occurred in 1910 in the Northeast and in 1900 for the other regions, and ranged from 3 percent in the South to 5 percent in the Northeast. Regional highs occurred in 2000 in the West and in 1990 for the other regions, and ranged from 11 percent in the West to 14 percent in the Northeast.

From 1900 through 1960, the South had the highest proportion of people under age 15 and the lowest proportion of people age 65 and over, making it the "youngest" region (see Appendix Table 7). The highest percentage under age 15 resided in the Midwest in 1970, the South in 1980, and the West since 1990. The West had the lowest percentage 65 years and over from 1970 to 2000. The relative "youngness" of the South in the first half of the century was in part due to relatively higher fertility among Blacks, who represented a larger proportion of the South's population. Similarly, the relative "youngness" of the West's population in the latter part of the century is in part due to relatively higher fertility among Hispanics, who constituted a larger share of the region's population. Although the West had the highest percentage under age 15 since 1990, it had the lowest proportion of people in this age group from 1910 to 1930.

The Northeast had the highest regional proportion in the elderly group in 1900 but was replaced by the Midwest from 1910 to 1940. The Northeast returned to having the highest proportion age 65 and over in 1950 and remained the "oldest" region throughout the rest of the century.

Figure 2-8.
Percent Under Age 15 and Percent Age 65 and Over by Region: 1900 to 2000

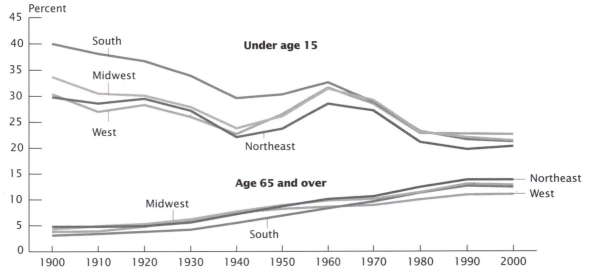

Source: U.S. Census Bureau, decennial census of population, 1900 to 2000.

Mississippi's and Utah's populations ranked among the ten youngest in every decade of the 20th century.

While the U.S. population as a whole aged over the 20th century, many states remained relatively "younger" or "older" during the period. Still, every state and the District of Columbia had a lower percentage under age 15 in 2000 than in 1900. Similarly, every state had a much higher percentage age 65 and over in 2000 than 100 years earlier.

All ten states with the highest percentage under age 15 in 1900, 1950, and 2000 were in the South and the West. The regional composition of these youngest states shifted from nine in the South and one in the West in 1900 to four in the South and six in the West in 2000.

From 1900 to 2000, only Mississippi and Utah ranked among the ten states with the highest percentage of people under age 15 every decade (see Appendix Table 7). In 1900, 42 percent of Mississippi's population and 41 percent of Utah's population were under age 15, ranking them second and ninth, respectively (see Table 2-1). By 2000, the percentage under age 15 in Mississippi had declined to 22 percent and in Utah to 27 percent. Even so, Utah had become the youngest state. South Carolina also ranked among the ten youngest states in the country for most of the century (1900 to 1980).

States in the Northeast and the Midwest tended to have relatively higher proportions of elderly[27] people over the period 1900 to 2000. These regions accounted for eight of the ten oldest states in 1900, all ten in 1950, and seven of the ten oldest in 2000. Three northeastern states, Maine, New Hampshire and Vermont and one midwestern state, Iowa, ranked among the ten states with the highest percentage elderly for much of the century.

Florida's ranking in terms of percentage 65 and over jumped from 42nd in 1900 to 1st since 1970. Correspondingly, Florida's ranking of percentage under age 15 fell from 14th in 1900 to 49th in 2000. Arkansas and California also experienced marked changes in their relative "youngness" or "oldness." At the beginning of the century, Arkansas ranked as the fourth youngest state, but by the end of the century ranked as the ninth oldest. California changed in the opposite direction, moving from the sixth oldest state in 1900 to the sixth youngest state in 2000.

---

[27] For the purposes of this report, elderly refers to the population 65 years and over.

Table 2-1.
Ten States With the Highest Percents Under Age 15 and Age 65 and Over: 1900, 1950, and 2000

Rank	1900		1950		2000	
	State	Percent	State	Percent	State	Percent
	Percent under age 15 years					
1	South Carolina	42.8	New Mexico	34.8	Utah	26.6
2	Mississippi	42.0	South Carolina	34.8	Alaska	25.2
3	Texas	41.8	Mississippi	34.0	Texas	23.5
4	Arkansas	41.6	Utah	33.5	Idaho	23.4
5	Oklahoma	41.5	Alabama	32.7	New Mexico	23.0
6	Georgia	41.5	North Carolina	32.3	California	23.0
7	North Carolina	41.4	Arkansas	31.9	Mississippi	22.5
8	Alabama	41.3	Arizona	31.9	Arizona	22.4
9	Utah	41.1	West Virginia	31.7	Louisiana	22.4
10	Louisiana	40.7	Idaho	31.7	Georgia	22.2
	Percent age 65 years and over					
1	Vermont	8.1	New Hampshire	10.8	Florida	17.6
2	Maine	8.0	Vermont	10.5	Pennsylvania	15.6
3	New Hampshire	7.9	Iowa	10.4	West Virginia	15.3
4	Connecticut	5.6	Missouri	10.3	Iowa	14.9
5	Nevada	5.4	Maine	10.2	North Dakota	14.7
6	California	5.2	Kansas	10.2	Rhode Island	14.5
7	Massachusetts	5.1	Massachusetts	10.0	Maine	14.4
8	Ohio	5.0	Nebraska	9.8	South Dakota	14.3
9	Michigan	5.0	Indiana	9.2	Arkansas	14.0
10	Wisconsin	5.0	Minnesota	9.0	Connecticut	13.8

Source: U.S. Census Bureau, decennial census of population, 1900, 1950, and 2000.

Prior to 1950, the male population outnumbered the female population. Since then, the female population has outnumbered the male population.

A frequently used measure to summarize the balance between the male and female population is known as the sex ratio.[28] A sex ratio of 100 indicates a balance between the male and female populations, ratios above 100 indicate a larger male population, and ratios below 100 indicate a larger female population. Figure 2-9 shows the trend in the sex ratio for the United States for every decade since 1900.

For each census from 1900 to 1940, the sex ratio was above 100. Males outnumbered females by a high of 2.7 million in 1910 but by only about 0.5 million in 1940 (see Appendix Table 6).

Several demographic factors contributed to the excess of males in the early part of the century. First, the influx of male immigrants to the United States at the turn of the century exceeded the influx of female immigrants. Also, younger populations tend to have higher sex ratios than older populations and the

United States, as discussed earlier, had a much younger population in the early part of the century.[29]

By the 1950 census, the sex ratio had dropped below 100. Over the next several decades, the numeric difference between the sexes continued to grow. The excess of the female population in the second half of the century ranged from 1.0 million in 1950 to 6.4 million in 1980 (see Appendix Table 6).

The sex ratio declined during every decade from 1910 to 1980. However, after declining to a low of 94.5 in 1980, the sex ratio increased in the following two decades to 96.3 in 2000. This is due to the fact that the male population increased at a more rapid rate than the female population during both the 1980s and 1990s. Higher net male than female immigration and relatively greater declines in male mortality rates contributed to this reversal of the downward trend in the sex ratio.

[29] Differences in census coverage also affect the sex ratio. In the United States, men generally have been less completely counted than women. This implies that the census-based sex ratio is slightly lower than if all people had been completely counted (see J. Gregory Robinson, "Accuracy and Coverage Evaluation: Demographic Analysis Results," March 12, 2001.)

[28] Calculated as the male population divided by the female population, times 100. See the Glossary.

Figure 2-9.
Sex Ratio: 1900 to 2000

(Males per 100 females)

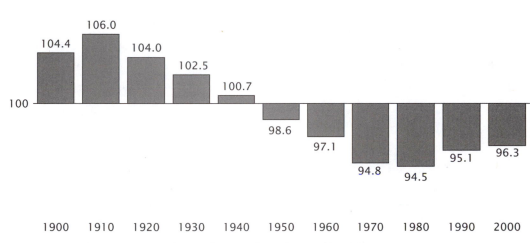

Source: U.S. Census Bureau, decennial census of population, 1900 to 2000.

While the shift to a larger female than male population occurred in every region, the West maintained the highest sex ratio of all U.S. regions throughout the century.

While all four regions had similar trends in the sex ratio to that of the United States, they differed in the degree to which their male and female populations counterbalanced throughout the century (see Figure 2-10). The peak sex ratio for every region occurred in 1910, and the lowest ratio occurred in 1970 in the West, 1980 in the Northeast and the South, and 1990 in the Midwest.

Every region had relatively higher sex ratios during the first half of the century. The sex ratio in the Northeast and the South dropped below 100 during the 1930s, followed by the Midwest during the 1940s. The West, which did not have a larger female population until the 1960s, had the highest sex ratio among the regions for the entire century.

The sex ratios in the West in 1900 (128.1) and 1910 (128.9) were the highest of the 100-year period. In general, the high ratios in the West during the first several decades of the century reflect the "frontier" character of this region and both international and internal migration starting in the late 19th century of men who were attracted in part by employment opportunities in male-dominated industries, including mining and railroad construction.

During the entire century, the Midwest consistently had the second highest sex ratio (except for 1990), followed by the South, with the third highest sex ratio. The Northeast consistently had the lowest sex ratio of all U.S. regions.

The widest regional difference in the sex ratio occurred in 1900, when the sex ratio ranged from 100.0 in the Northeast to 128.1 in the West. The regional differences narrowed each decade, until 1970, when the sex ratio ranged from 92.5 in the Northeast to 97.7 in the West. In 2000, the sex ratio ranged from 93.5 in the Northeast to 99.6 in the West.

Figure 2-10.
Sex Ratio by Region: 1900 to 2000

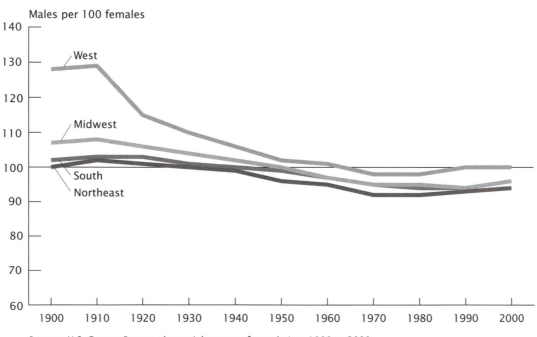

Source: U.S. Census Bureau, decennial census of population, 1900 to 2000.

The number of states with a larger female than male population quadrupled from 11 in 1900 to 44 in 2000.

As the century progressed, an increasing number of states had a larger female population than male population. In 1900, the female population exceeded the male population in only 11 states (including the District of Columbia), all in the Northeast or the South (see Figure 2-11).

By 1950, 27 states (including the District of Columbia) had a sex ratio below 100. The trend had spread into the Midwest as well as into more states in the Northeast and the South. All states in the West still had a sex ratio above 100.

Between 1900 and 2000, the number of states with a larger female than male population quadrupled to 44 (including the District of Columbia). In 2000, only seven western states (Alaska, Colorado, Hawaii, Idaho, Nevada, Utah, and Wyoming) remained with a larger male population.[30]

The sex ratio of every state was lower in 2000 than in 1900. In other words, the female population had increased relatively more than the male population over the 100-year period. Despite this shift among all states toward a proportionately larger female population, Nevada and Wyoming maintained a sex ratio above 100 throughout the century (see Appendix Table 6). In addition, both Alaska and Hawaii have had an excess of males in every decade since their inclusion as states in the census of 1960. Massachusetts, North Carolina, Rhode Island, South Carolina, and the District of Columbia had larger female populations throughout the century.

Throughout the century, several states remained among the highest or lowest ranking in terms of their sex ratio. States consistently ranking among the highest included Idaho, Montana, Nevada, and Wyoming. Since the overwhelming majority of states had larger female than male populations by 2000, even some of the states with the highest-ranking sex ratios had proportionally larger female populations. Montana, for example, had a sex ratio of 99.3 in 2000. Only Massachusetts and the District of the Columbia remained among the ten states (or equivalent) with the lowest sex ratios for the entire century.

Prior to Alaska's statehood, either Nevada or Wyoming had the country's highest sex ratio every decade from 1900 to 1950. Once Alaska became a state, it had the highest sex ratio from 1960 through 2000. The sex ratio in Alaska steadily declined from 132.3 in 1960 to 107.0 in 2000.

Among the 50 states, Massachusetts had the lowest sex ratio every decade from 1900 through 1960.[31] In 1970 and 1980, New York held this distinction. The state with the lowest sex ratio changed to Mississippi in 1990 and then to Rhode Island in 2000.

The gap between the highest and the lowest state sex ratios generally narrowed during the century. After 1910, the difference became smaller each decade until 1960, when the gap widened because Alaska was included as a state. The gap then continued to narrow each decade, reaching the smallest gap in the century in 2000, when the sex ratio ranged from a low of 92.5 in Rhode Island (89.0 in the District of Columbia) to 107.0 in Alaska.

---

[30] See U.S. Census Bureau. 2001b. *Gender: 2000*, by Denise I. Smith and Reneé E. Spraggins.

[31] The District of Columbia, a state equivalent for statistical purposes, had the lowest sex ratio for every decade throughout the century.

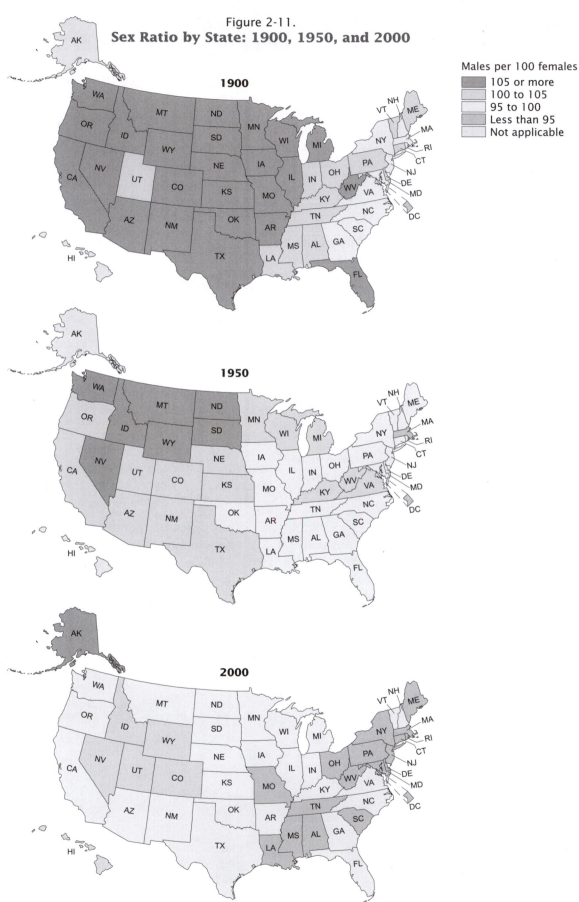

Figure 2-11.
Sex Ratio by State: 1900, 1950, and 2000

Source: U.S. Census Bureau, decennial census of population, 1900, 1950, and 2000.

Central cities had relatively larger female than male populations compared with suburban and nonmetropolitan areas.

Decennial data available by sex for metropolitan areas from 1950 to 2000 indicate that the sex ratio trend for metropolitan and nonmetropolitan areas followed a path similar to that of the United States as a whole.[32] The sex ratio in both metropolitan and nonmetropolitan areas declined steadily from 1950 to 1980 (see Figure 2-12). The nonmetropolitan sex ratio remained stable from 1980 to 1990, whereas the metropolitan sex ratio followed the U.S. pattern of increasing sex ratios from 1980 to 1990 and again from 1990 to 2000.

The nonmetropolitan sex ratio exceeded the metropolitan sex ratio for the entire period from 1950 to 2000, indicating a greater predominance of the female population in metropolitan areas than in the nonmetropolitan population. In fact, in 1950 the male population in nonmetropolitan areas still outnumbered the female population, although the sex ratio in

the United States had already fallen below 100. Over the latter half of the century, the nonmetropolitan sex ratio ranged from 96.0 to 101.6 (in 1990 and 1950, respectively), and the metropolitan sex ratio ranged from 93.9 to 96.4 (in 1980 and 1950, respectively, see Appendix Table 16).

In 1950, there was a relatively large gap between the metropolitan and nonmetropolitan sex ratios, which steadily narrowed from 1950 to 1990. However, in the 1990s, the sex ratio in nonmetropolitan areas increased more than in metropolitan areas, widening the gap again.

Within metropolitan areas, sex ratios were much lower in central cities than they were in the suburbs. In the central cities, the sex ratio ranged from 90.7 in 1970 to 94.6 in 2000, which was its highest point in 40 years. In the suburbs, the sex ratio stayed within a narrow range during the period, from a low of 96.0 in 1980 to a high of 98.6 in 1960.

---

[32] Metropolitan areas were formally defined beginning with the 1950 census.

Figure 2-12.
Sex Ratio by Metropolitan Area Status: 1950 to 2000

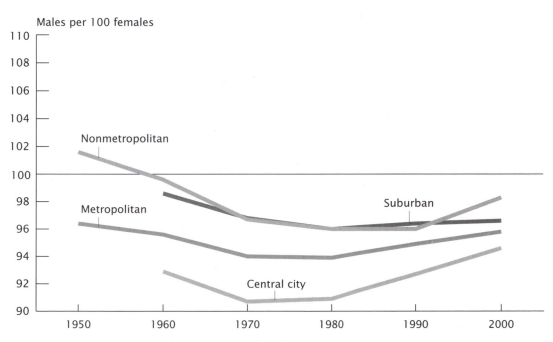

Source: U.S. Census Bureau, decennial census of population, 1950 to 2000.

Throughout the century, women represented most of the population age 85 and over, and the predominance of women greatly increased between 1900 and 2000.

In the absence of migration, sex ratios tend to decrease with age due to higher male mortality rates at each age.[33] The sex ratio at birth is about 105. Higher male mortality decreases the sex ratio, and the age at which the sex ratio drops below 100 (i.e., the female population exceeds the male population) depends on both the level of mortality and differences in age-specific mortality rates by sex. The predominance of women is most pronounced among the elderly and especially among the population 85 years and over.

While sex ratios in the United States for broad age groups largely reflect the typical pattern (see Figure 2-13), prior to 1960, U.S. sex ratios did not consistently decrease with age. In the early part of the century, the highest sex ratios occurred for the 45-to-64 age group, reflecting the predominantly male,

large-scale immigration in preceding decades. This age group had the century's highest sex ratio (115.2 in 1920). Since 1960, sex ratios by age have followed the expected pattern, with the highest sex ratio in the under 15 age group and steadily decreasing ratios for each subsequently older age group.

From 1920 to 1980, the sex ratios of the 45 to 64, 65 to 84, and 85 and over age groups all steadily declined. Generally, the declining sex ratios over time resulted from greater improvements in female mortality rates than in male mortality rates during these decades. The sex ratio for the under 15 age group remained fairly stable during the century, although slight, steady increases occurred during most decades.

From 1980 to 2000, the sex ratio increased for most age groups, except the 85-and-over group, which had a declining sex ratio in the 1980s. In 1990, this group had the century's lowest sex ratio: 38.6, and during both decades women outnumbered men by more than 2-to-1.

---

[33] In 1999, average life expectancy at birth (based on age-specific mortality rates in 1999) was 73.9 years for males and 79.4 years for females. See U.S. National Center for Health Statistics, 2002, *United States Life Tables, 1999*, Table A.

Figure 2-13.
Sex Ratio by Broad Age Group: 1900 to 2000

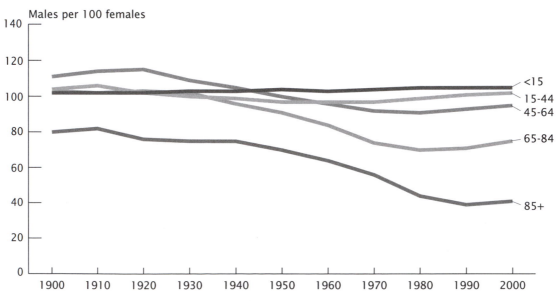

Source: U.S. Census Bureau, decennial census of population, 1900 to 2000.

Chapter Highlights
RACE AND HISPANIC ORIGIN

RACE

National Trends

The United States population was much more racially diverse in 2000 than in 1900. At the beginning of the century, 1 out of 8 Americans was of a race other than White; at the end of the century, the ratio was 1 out of 4.

The increased diversity in the United States was largely a phenomenon of the latter part of the century. Both the White population and the Black population represented a slightly smaller share of the U.S. total population in 1970 than they did in 1900.

From 1970 to 2000, the population of races other than White or Black grew considerably and, by 2000, was comparable in size to the Black population.

Among the races, the American Indian and Alaska Native population had the highest percentage under age 15 for most of the 20th century (peaking at 42 percent in 1960). In 2000, the Two or more races population (identified in Census 2000 for the first time) had the highest proportion (36 percent).

Regional Trends

The Black population was concentrated in the South and the Asian and Pacific Islander population in the West from 1900 to 2000. However, these regional concentrations declined during the century.

The American Indian and Alaska Native population also was heavily concentrated in the West, and this concentration remained relatively stable throughout the century.

The South had the highest percentage of races other than White in every census from 1900 to 1980. The West had the highest percentage of races other than White in 1990 and 2000.

In the Northeast, the Midwest, and the South, Blacks constituted the largest share of the population of races other than White in every decade of the 20th century, while in the West, each of the races other than White represented the largest share during the century.

State Trends

Increased racial diversity characterized most states during the 20th century. By 2000, 40 states and the District of Columbia had populations with at least 10 percent races other than White. The 10 states with 90 percent or more White in 2000 were: Idaho, Iowa, Kentucky, Maine, Montana, New Hampshire, North Dakota, Vermont, West Virginia, and Wyoming.

Only five states—Alabama, Arkansas, Mississippi, South Carolina, and West Virginia—had a lower percentage of races other than White in 2000 than in 1950.

HISPANIC ORIGIN

National, Regional, and State Trends

From 1980 to 2000, the Hispanic population (of any race) more than doubled.

More than 40 percent of the Hispanic population lived in the West from 1980 to 2000.

In every region, the percentage of Hispanics increased during the 1980s and again during the 1990s.

New Mexico had the highest proportion of Hispanics in its population of any state in 1980, 1990, and 2000. By 2000, 42 percent of New Mexico's population was Hispanic.

MINORITY AND WHITE NON-HISPANIC

National, Regional, and State Trends

The aggregated Minority population (people of races other than White or of Hispanic origin) increased by 88 percent between 1980 and 2000, while the White non-Hispanic population grew by only 7.9 percent during the 20-year period.

Younger age groups had a higher percentage of Minority population than did older age groups. By 2000, the percentage of Minority population ranged from 16 percent for people age 65 and over to 39 percent for those under age 25.

In 1980, more than 50 percent of the population in Hawaii and the District of Columbia was Minority. By 2000, California and New Mexico had also become more than 50 percent Minority, and Texas was the only other state with at least 40 percent Minority (48 percent).

Chapter 3
RACE AND HISPANIC ORIGIN

Racial and ethnic diversity increasingly characterized the population of the United States during the last half of the 20th century, especially in the last three decades of the century. Race and ethnicity are separate concepts as defined by the federal government. People of a specific race may be of any ethnic origin, and people of a specific ethnic origin may be of any race. Large-scale immigration, primarily from Latin America and Asia, underlies both increased racial and ethnic diversity. In just the last two decades of the century, the Asian and Pacific Islander population tripled, and the Hispanic population more than doubled.

Every population census in the United States collected data on race, beginning with the first national enumeration in 1790. The number of specific groups identified in a census generally increased over time. Census 2000 was the first U.S. census to allow individuals to identify themselves as being of more than one race. The trends by race in this chapter cover the following five groups: White, Black, American Indian and Alaska Native, Asian and Pacific Islander, and Some other race. For additional detail on the data on race included in this report, see Appendix C, Sources and Quality of Data.

The population of Hispanic origin is defined as another group for federal statistical purposes and may be of any race. Prior to 1970, determinations of Hispanic origin were only made indirectly, such as through questions on Spanish surname, or tabulating people who reported Spanish as their "mother tongue." The 1970 census was the first to include a question on Hispanic origin, but it was asked only for a 5-percent sample of all households. Beginning with the 1980 census, information on Hispanic origin was collected on a 100-percent basis. The analysis of trends in the Hispanic population in this chapter covers the period from 1980 to 2000. For additional detail on the data on Hispanic origin included in this report, see Appendix C, Sources and Quality of Data.

In general, Blacks, Asians and Pacific Islanders, American Indians and Alaska Natives, and Hispanics have represented increasing shares of the national population and of each region's population. The Black share of the South's population, which declined from 32 percent in 1900 to 19 percent in 2000, is a notable exception. In 1900, only two non-Southern states (Nevada and Arizona) had populations with at least 10 percent races other than White but, by 2000, 26 non-Southern states had at least 10 percent races other than White, reflecting the spread of diversity across the country. By the end of the century, three states—California, Hawaii, and New Mexico—and the District of Columbia had more than 50 percent Minority populations (including Hispanics).

Data on age by race and Hispanic origin revealed increased "aging" of every population, but also important differences among the groups, showing Whites (and White non-Hispanics) and Asians and Pacific Islanders as relatively older groups and Blacks, Hispanics, and American Indians and Alaska Natives as relatively younger groups. Also, younger age groups consistently had higher levels of racial and ethnic diversity than older age groups.

The graphics and text in this chapter depict trends in the number and proportional distribution of the U.S. population by race from 1900 to 2000 and by Hispanic origin from 1980 to 2000. Changes in racial and ethnic composition are described for the total population, regions, and states. Trends in Hispanic origin, when discussed irrespective of race, are compared with the non-Hispanic population, and when discussed along with race, include the White non-Hispanic population trend for comparison. The chapter introduces data on changes in an aggregate Minority population, which pertains to the population of races other than White and people who are Hispanic, regardless of their race. In addition to examining trends in total size, proportional distribution, and geographic distribution by race and Hispanic origin, this chapter also examines age and sex composition trends and metropolitan concentration by race and Hispanic origin. Detailed data for each decade for the United States, regions, and states for individual race groups and for the population by Hispanic origin are provided in Appendix Tables 8, 9, and 10, and detailed data by age, race, and Hispanic origin for the United States are provided in Appendix Table 11.

Since 1970, the population of races other than White or Black has grown significantly; however, Whites remained the largest race group.

The White population continues to be the largest race group in the United States (see Figure 3-1). As recently as 1970, the U.S. population was nearly entirely classified as either White or Black, and the population of races other than White or Black was only 2.9 million, or 1.4 percent of the population. By 2000, the number of people in the United States who were of races other than White or Black had grown to 35 million, comparable in size to the Black population.

Numerically, the White population increased substantially in the 20th century. The White population grew from 66.8 million in 1900, exceeded 100 million by 1930, and passed the 200 million mark by 2000. The combined population of all races other than White in 2000 was comparable in size to the White population at the beginning of the 20th century.

The Black population increased steadily throughout the century from 8.8 million in 1900 to about 4 times larger in 2000 (34.7 million people reported Black alone and 36.4 million people reported Black alone or in combination with one or more other races). Compared with the combined population of races other than White or Black, the Black population in 1960 was more than 10 times larger, in 1980 was slightly more than double, and in 2000 was of comparable size, reflecting the rapid growth of these other races in the United States.

Races other than White and Black include American Indian and Alaska Native, Asian and Pacific Islander, and Some other race (see Figure 3-2).[34] For the first time, Census 2000 also included a count of the number of people reporting two or more races, which at 6.8 million exceeded the American Indian and Alaska Native population.

The Asian and Pacific Islander and the Some other race (who are primarily Hispanic) populations particularly increased during the period from 1970 to 2000. International migration and subsequent births to the immigrant population contributed to this rapid population increase.

Within the groups comprising the races other than White or Black, Some other race was the smallest in 1970, but has been the largest group since the 1980 census. The size of this race group is greatly influenced by the overwhelming number of Hispanics who answer the question on race by reporting themselves as a specific Hispanic-origin group that is categorized as Some other race.

Figure 3-1 and Figure 3-2 show two values for the population of each race in Census 2000. The smaller value represents the number of people who reported belonging to that race alone and no other race, while the larger value represents the number of people who reported the specified race only, plus those who reported the specified race and one or more other races. These numbers may be thought of as representing the minimum-maximum range for the number of people in the particular race group. The basic trends in population size by race over the 20th century shown in Figure 3-1 and Figure 3-2 hold up, regardless of which value is used from Census 2000.

---

[34] In Census 2000, the Asian and Pacific Islander group was split into "Asian" and "Native Hawaiian and Other Pacific Islander." For comparability throughout the century, this report combines these two groups. Separate data for each group from Census 2000 are provided in Appendix Table 9.

Figure 3-1.
Total Population by Race: 1900 to 2000

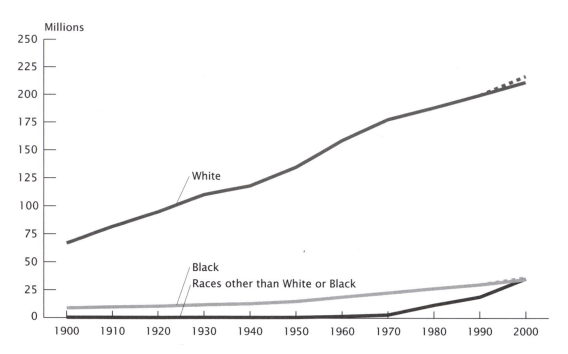

Note: For Census 2000, the lower value represents people reporting the specified race alone, while the higher value represents people reporting the specified race, whether or not they reported any other races.
Source: U.S. Census Bureau, decennial census of population, 1900 to 2000.

Figure 3-2.
Population of Races Other Than White or Black by Race: 1900 to 2000

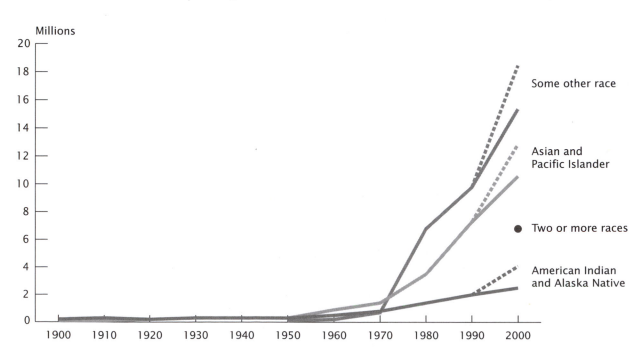

Note: For Census 2000, the lower value represents people reporting the specified race alone, while the higher value represents people reporting the specified race, whether or not they reported any other races.
Source: U.S. Census Bureau, decennial census of population, 1900 to 2000.

In 1900, about 1 out of 8 Americans was of a race other than White. By 2000, about 1 out of 4 Americans was of a race other than White.

While the White population grew in every decade throughout the 20th century, its share of the total U.S. population did not follow this same pattern (see Figure 3-3). Between 1900 and 1930, the percentage White of the U.S. population increased, while the percentage Black declined. Since then, the White share of the total population has decreased every decade, while the Black share has increased.[35]

People of races other than White or Black represented less than 1 percent of the U.S. population between 1900 and 1960. In recent decades, the share this group composed of the U.S. total increased greatly, from 1.4 percent in 1970 to 12.5 percent by 2000.

Figure 3-4 illustrates the details of the rapid growth in races other than White or Black over the course of the century. Prior to 1950, all people in this broad grouping were reported as either American Indians and Alaska Natives or as Asians and Pacific Islanders. Beginning in 1950 and continuing for the remainder of the century, people could also be identified as Some other race. In 2000, the category Two or more races was used for the first time.

The American Indian and Alaska Native population and its share of the U.S. total increased each decade in the second half of the century, although its share represented about 1 percent in 2000. In contrast, the growth of Asians and Pacific Islanders and people in the Some other race category primarily accounted for

the large increase in the share of the U.S. population comprised of people of races other than White or Black.

Comparing the beginning and the end of the century, the United States in 2000 is clearly much more racially diverse than in 1900. At the beginning of the century, just 1 out of 8 Americans was of a race other than White. At the end of the century, the proportion was 1 out of 4. The decade-to-decade trend shows that this increasing diversity is largely a phenomenon of the second half of the century. As recently as 1970, the White population's share of the U.S. total was slightly smaller than at the beginning of the century. The Black population also represented a slightly smaller share of the U.S. total population in 1970 than in 1900, and even at the century's close, its share was less than 1 percentage point higher than in 1900.

The significant decline since 1970 in the White share of the U.S. population mainly resulted from the much faster growth of the Asian and Pacific Islander and the Some other race populations. The decline of 12.3 percentage points in the White share between 1970 and 2000 may be attributed to the following percentage point increases: 5.1 for Some other race; 3.1 for Asian and Pacific Islander; 2.4 for Two or more races (who may be any combination of the individual races, including combinations with White); 1.2 for Black; and 0.5 for American Indian and Alaska Native.

As noted previously, the increased shares for Asians and Pacific Islanders and Some other race may largely be explained by large increases in international migration and subsequent births to the immigrants for these groups. (The high immigration of Hispanics, who frequently are categorized as Some other race, and changes in the reporting of race by Hispanics account for much of the increase in the Some other race share of the total population.)

---

[35] In Figure 3-3 and all following graphics including a percentage of the population for a specific race group, the percentage shown for Census 2000 is based on the number of people reporting the specified race *alone* rather than the number reporting the specified race *alone or in combination* with any other race. The use of the race *alone* concept does not imply that it is a preferred method of presenting or analyzing data. In general, either the *alone* population or the *alone or in combination* population can be used, depending on the purpose of the analysis. The Census Bureau uses both approaches. See U.S. Census Bureau, 2001f, *Overview of Race and Hispanic Origin*, by Elizabeth M. Grieco and Rachel C. Cassidy.

Figure 3-3.
Distribution of Total Population by Race:
1900 to 2000

(Percent)

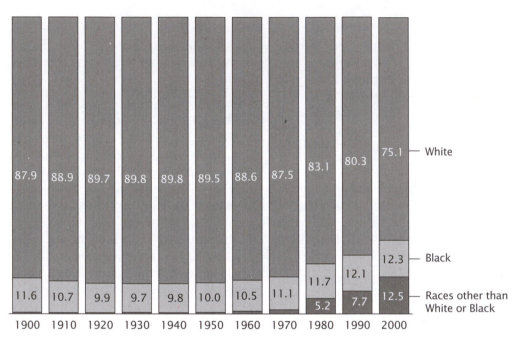

Note: In 2000, the percent distribution is based on the reporting of race alone for Whites and Blacks.
Source: U.S. Census Bureau, decennial census of population, 1900 to 2000.

Figure 3-4.
Percent Races Other Than White or Black
by Race: 1900 to 2000

(Percent of total population)

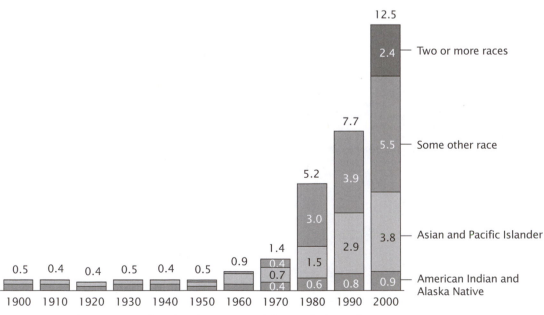

Note: In 2000, the percents are based on the reporting of the specified race alone.
Source: U.S. Census Bureau, decennial census of population, 1900 to 2000.

The Hispanic population more than doubled in size from 1980 to 2000.

The Hispanic population includes people who may be of any race.[36] As discussed earlier, the 1980 census was the first to include a separate question on Hispanic origin asked of every individual in the United States.[37]

The Hispanic population more than doubled in size from 1980 to 2000 (see Figure 3-5). In 1980, there were 14.6 million Hispanics in the United States. From 1980 to 1990, they grew by 7.7 million people, or 53 percent, to 22.4 million, and in the next decade the growth rate was even higher. During the 1990s, the Hispanic population increased by 13.0 million people,

[36] For a more detailed discussion about race and Hispanic origin, see the Sources and Quality of Data section.

[37] The 1970 census included a question on the Hispanic origin of individuals asked of a 5-percent sample. In this report, data on Hispanic origin are shown from 1980 to 2000.

or 58 percent, reaching a population of 35.3 million at the century's close.

Overall, the Hispanic population grew by 20.7 million people from 1980 to 2000. High levels of immigration contributed to this rapid growth, coupled with relatively high fertility levels.

The much more rapid growth of the Hispanic population relative to the non-Hispanic population increased the Hispanic share of the total population in both decades. In 1980, Hispanics constituted 6.4 percent of the total population. By 1990, their share had increased to 9.0 percent, and during the 1990s, their share increased by an additional 3.5 percentage points, so that by 2000, Hispanics represented 12.5 percent of the U.S. population, nearly twice the proportion than just 20 years earlier.

Figure 3-5.
Hispanic Population and Percent Hispanic of Total Population: 1980 to 2000

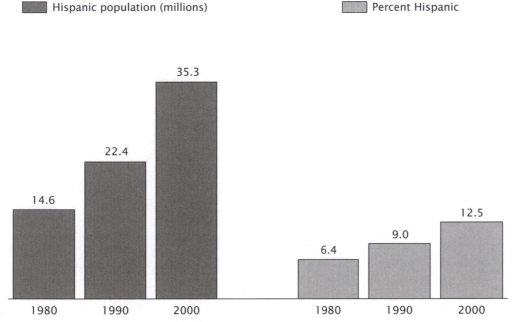

Source: U.S. Census Bureau, decennial census of population, 1980 to 2000.

The White population grew more slowly than every other race group in the second half of the 20th century and for the century as a whole.

By the end of the 20th century, the fact that the U.S. population had become increasingly diverse was generally well-known. However, when the century is split into halves, this conventional wisdom does not entirely hold true. The White population grew at a lower rate, on average, than each of the other race groups for the periods 1900-2000 and 1950-2000 (Figure 3-6), when some groups grew many times faster. However, during the first half of the century, the White population grew at a faster rate than either the Black population or the American Indian population.

The trend in the average annual growth rates by race moved in an opposite direction for Whites compared with every other race. That is, the White population had a higher average annual growth rate (1.4 percent) during the first half of the century than during the second half (0.9 percent), while the 50-year average annual growth rate for each of the other races was higher in the second half of the century.

Among races with available data throughout the century, Asians and Pacific Islanders grew faster than the other groups in both halves of the 100-year period. This high growth rate resulted from a combination of considerable immigration and a relatively small population

size. American Indians and Alaska Natives increased at the slowest rate of the groups in the first half of the century, but grew rapidly during the latter period, a statistical change that is partly due to changes in reporting. The growth rate of the Black population, which is much less influenced by immigration, increased from an average rate of 1.1 percent in the first half of the century to 1.7 percent in the second half.

The "other race" category (not shown) had the highest growth rate during the century: an average annual increase of 9.9 percent from 1950 to 2000. In part, this high rate of growth resulted from the fact that the Hispanic population increased rapidly during this period and a large proportion of the responses of Hispanics to the question on race were categorized as Some other race (beginning in 1980), since the number of Hispanics is determined from a separate question. Another contributing factor is the small population size of the "other race" category in 1950.[38]

---

[38] Since the write-in responses to race prior to 1950 were tabulated as specific races and were classifiable into one of the four specific race groups, no fifth other race category is applicable for these censuses. As a result, growth rates are not available for this classification for the 1900-1950 and 1900-2000 periods shown in Figure 3-6.

Figure 3-6.
Average Annual Growth Rate by Race: 1900-1950, 1950-2000, and 1900-2000

(Percent)

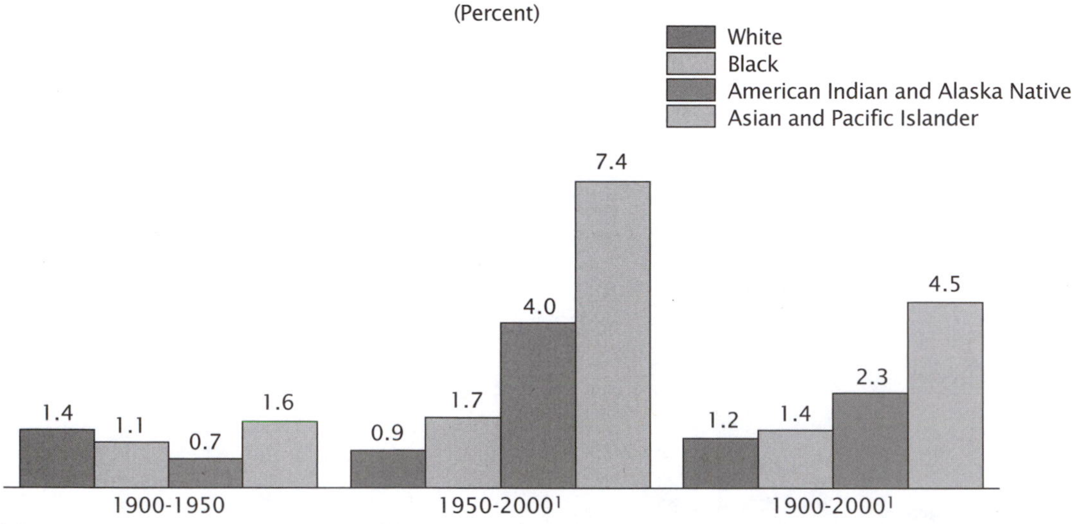

Legend:
- White
- Black
- American Indian and Alaska Native
- Asian and Pacific Islander

1900-1950: 1.4, 1.1, 0.7, 1.6
1950-2000[1]: 0.9, 1.7, 4.0, 7.4
1900-2000[1]: 1.2, 1.4, 2.3, 4.5

[1] The rate excludes Alaska and Hawaii at the beginning date and includes Alaska and Hawaii at the ending date. This has the effect of increasing the rate, particularly for American Indians and Alaska Natives and for Asians and Pacific Islanders.
Source: U.S. Census Bureau, decennial census of population, 1900, 1950, and 2000.

The Minority population grew 11 times
as rapidly as the White non-Hispanic population
between 1980 and 2000.

Immigration and subsequent births to the new arrivals during the last few decades of the century played a major role in changing the racial and ethnic composition of the U.S. population. These influences are indicated by the very high percentage increases in the Asian and Pacific Islander (204 percent) and the Hispanic (142 percent) populations from 1980 to 2000 (see Figure 3-7).

Considering race without regard to Hispanic origin, the White population grew slower than every other race. The rapid growth of the Some other race population was strongly influenced by the large number of people in this group who are Hispanic. (For example, Census 2000 results showed that 97 percent of the population who reported Some other race alone were Hispanic.)[39] The high percentage change of the American Indian and Alaska Native population in part may be attributed to a higher tendency among

respondents to report as this race in Census 2000 than in 1980, as well as changes in methodology and improvements in coverage of this population.

Considering Hispanic origin without regard to race, Hispanics grew much faster than non-Hispanics. Combining race and Hispanic origin, the White non-Hispanic population grew by only 7.9 percent between 1980 and 2000, while the aggregated Minority population (people of races other than White and people of every race who were of Hispanic origin) increased 11 times as fast (88 percent) during the 20-year period.

Among all the population groups shown in Figure 3-7, only the White, the non-Hispanic, and the White non-Hispanic populations grew more slowly than the total population. The higher percentage increases for each individual race other than White and for the Hispanic population produced a high percentage growth for the Minority population, resulting in an increase in the Minority share of the U.S. population from 20 percent in 1980 to 31 percent in 2000 and a corresponding decrease in the White non-Hispanic share.

---

[39] See U.S. Census Bureau. 2001f. *Overview of Race and Hispanic Origin*, by Elizabeth M. Grieco and Rachel C. Cassidy.

Figure 3-7.
**Percent Change in Population Size by Race and
Hispanic Origin: 1980-2000**

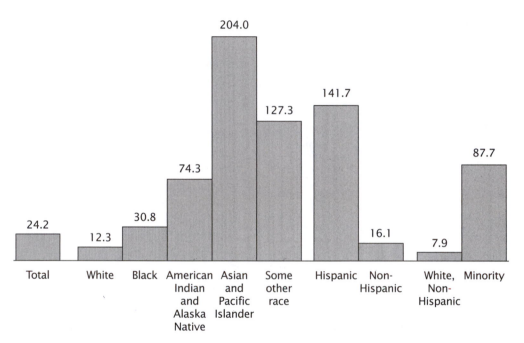

Source: U.S. Census Bureau, decennial census of population, 1980 and 2000.

Blacks, along with Asians and Pacific Islanders, have been the most regionally concentrated races. More than half of Blacks still live in the South and, until 2000, more than half of Asians and Pacific Islanders lived in the West.

The population of each race was not evenly distributed across the regions of the United States in the 20th century (see Figure 3-8). The trend in the distribution of the White population by region most closely mirrored the regional distribution of the total U.S. population. This, of course, reflects the fact that the White population represents such a large percentage of the U.S. population.

The Black, Asian and Pacific Islander, and American Indian and Alaska Native populations all exhibited strong regional concentrations. Each race also followed quite different decade-to-decade trends in their regional distributions.

The Black population was, and continues to be, concentrated in the South. However, the extent of this concentration diminished considerably during the 20th century. For the first two decades of the century, nearly 9 out of 10 Blacks lived in the South. In 1940, over three-fourths of the Black population lived in the South. After World War II, the percentage of the Black population in the South declined more rapidly, reflecting the effect of substantial Black migration, especially to large metropolitan areas in the Midwest and Northeast. This migration contributed to the corresponding rise in the proportion of the Black population in these regions through 1970. This trend generally reversed toward the end of the century. By 2000, the Northeast's and the Midwest's shares of the Black population had dropped below their shares in 1970, while the South's share had increased. Throughout the century, the West had the smallest share of the Black population Even though the West's share of the Black population increased every decade from 1900 to 1990, by the end of the century fewer than 10 percent of all Blacks lived in the West.

The Asian and Pacific Islander population also had a strong regional concentration, particularly in the first half of the century. During the period 1900 to 1940, about 4 out of 5 Asians and Pacific Islanders lived in the West. The proportion in the West dropped significantly between 1940 and 1950, primarily due to a decline in the Japanese population in California, Washington, and Oregon and a corresponding increase in the Japanese populations in Illinois (increasing the Midwest's share) and in New York, New Jersey, and Pennsylvania (increasing the Northeast's share). The sharp increase in the West's share from 1950 to 1960 resulted from the addition of Hawaii as the 50th state.

As with the Black population, the regional concentration of Asians and Pacific Islanders diminished during the century. The Northeast's and the South's shares of Asians and Pacific Islanders increased rapidly during this period, with the Northeast's share ranking 2nd among the regions and the South's share surpassing the Midwest's, although the Midwest's share also generally rose in the last half of the century.

The American Indian and Alaska Native population also was characterized by concentration in the West. In contrast to the trends of other races, however, their regional distribution remained fairly stable throughout the century. Of the total U.S. population of American Indians and Alaska Natives, the Northeast had the lowest proportion, and, with the exception of 1950, the South had the 2nd highest share.

Figure 3-8.
**Regional Distribution of Total Population
by Race: 1900 to 2000**

Northeast
Midwest
South
West

White
Percent

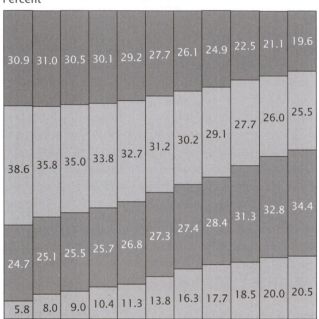

Asian and Pacific Islander
Percent

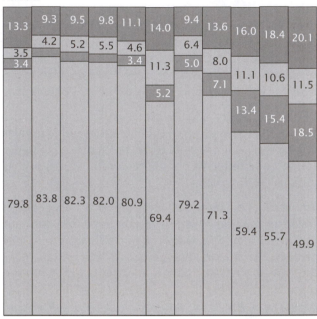

Black
Percent

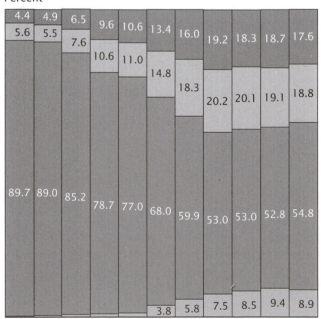

American Indian and Alaska Native
Percent

Source: U.S. Census Bureau, decennial census of population, 1900 to 2000.

The percentage of races other than White was highest in the South from 1900 to 1980 and highest in the West since 1990.

During the first half of the 20th century, the population of races other than White composed 5 percent or less of the total population in the Northeast, the Midwest, and the West (see Figure 3-9). In contrast, the South had much higher percentages of races other than White during this period, even though this percentage declined each decade, from a high of 33 percent in 1900 to 22 percent in 1950.

The South differed from the other regions in both the level and trend of the percentage of races other than White. In terms of the level, the South had the highest percentage of races other than White during every decade 1900 to 1980. During the second half of the century, the rapid growth of races other than White in the West made it the region with the highest percentage of races other than White in 1990 and 2000. The percentage of people other than White in the Northeast's population increased every decade, as it did in the Midwest (except from 1900 to 1910). The West experienced little change until 1940, but increased every decade thereafter. The South's share of its population represented by races other than White declined every decade from 1900 to 1970 and the percentage White increased. From 1970 to 2000, the percentage of races other than White increased in every region.

As the percentage of races other than White in the South declined, the corresponding percentages in other regions increased, narrowing the differences between the regions. The widest gap occurred in 1900, when the percentage of races other than White ranged from a low of 1.9 percent in the Northeast to 32.6 percent in the South. The gap narrowed each succeeding decade, reaching the smallest regional difference in 1980, when the percentage of races other than White ranged from 11.3 percent in the Midwest to 21.8 percent in the South. Since 1980 the gap widened, as the increase in the percentage of races other than White in the West exceeded the increase in the other regions.

The specific racial composition of the population of races other than White also differed by region. In the Northeast, the Midwest, and the South, Blacks constituted the largest share of races other than White in every decade of the 20th century. However, in the West, American Indians and Alaska Natives represented the largest share in 1900, Asians and Pacific Islanders the largest share from 1910 to 1940, Blacks the largest share from 1950 to 1970, and Some other race (which is nearly all Hispanic) represented the largest share from 1980 to 2000.

While Hispanics may be of any race, a sizable proportion are classified as Some other race. (The question on race is separate from the question on Hispanic or Latino origin). The high growth rate of the Hispanic population since 1980 is reflected by the relatively high share that the "Some other race" group represents of the total percentage of races other than White. Since 1980, the share of Some other race exceeded the shares of Asians and Pacific Islanders and American Indians and Alaska Natives in every region.

Census 2000 was the first to include the option for individuals to identify themselves as more than one race. Among the regions, the percentage of the population categorized as Two or more races ranged from 1.6 percent in the Midwest to 4.3 percent in the West. In Figure 3-9, the totals for the percentage in each specific race group for 2000 represent those people who reported that specific race alone. Those who reported any specific race in combination with any other race (including people who reported White as one of the races) are shown in the Two or more races category. In every region, the percentage of the population of Two or more races exceeded the percentage American Indian and Alaska Native.

Figure 3-9.
Percent Races Other Than White by Race and Region: 1900 to 2000
(Percent of region's population)

Two or more races
Some other race
Asian and Pacific Islander
American Indian and Alaska Native
Black

Northeast

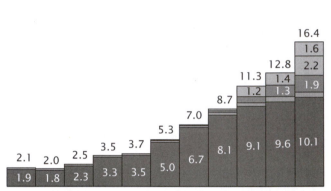

Midwest

South

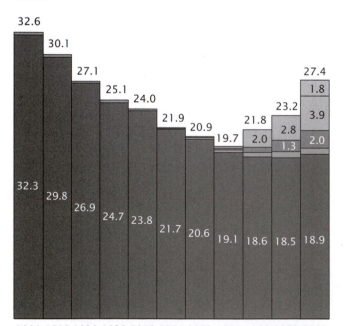

West

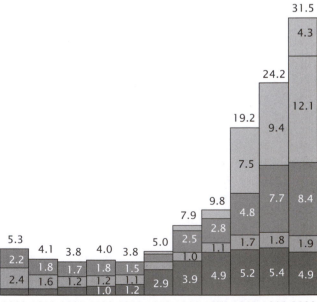

Source: U.S. Census Bureau, decennial census of population, 1900 to 2000.

While the Hispanic population was concentrated in the West, the percentage Hispanic increased in every region from 1980 to 2000.

The regional distribution of the Hispanic population remained relatively stable from 1980 to 2000. The majority of Hispanics lived in the South and the West, with smaller proportions living in the Northeast and the Midwest, respectively.

More than 40 percent of the Hispanic population lived in the West from 1980 to 2000 (see Figure 3-10). This reflects the fact that all the states along the U.S.-Mexico border (except Texas) are western states and most of the Hispanic population is Mexican in origin. From 1980 to 1990, the proportion of Hispanics living in the West increased from 43 percent to 45 percent and then declined to 43 percent in 2000.

A slightly higher proportion of Hispanics lived in the South in 2000 (33 percent) than in 1980 (31 percent). In 2000, more than three-quarters of the Hispanic population lived in the South or the West.[40]

The Northeast was the only region in the United States with a steadily declining share of Hispanics, dropping from 18 percent in 1980 to 15 percent in 2000.

Hispanics were least likely to live in the Midwest. Although their share increased from 1990 to 2000

[40] See U.S. Census Bureau, 2001c, *The Hispanic Population: 2000*, by Betsy Guzmán.

after dropping during the 1980s, fewer than 1 of 10 Hispanics lived in the Midwest at the century's close.

While the regional distribution of Hispanics did not change very much between 1980 and 2000, their total numbers and proportion of each region's population increased during both the 1980s and the 1990s in every region (see Figure 3-11).

The West had the highest proportion of Hispanics of any region from 1980 to 2000, rising rapidly from 14 percent of the region's population in 1980 to 24 percent in 2000. The West was the only region in which the proportion of Hispanics exceeded the national level (see Appendix Table 10).

The proportion of Hispanics in the South's population nearly doubled from 5.9 percent in 1980 to 11.6 percent in 2000. Although the South's proportion of Hispanics ranked 2nd among the regions, its proportion at the end of the century was less than half the proportion Hispanic in the West.

The Northeast and the Midwest had the smallest proportions of Hispanics in their populations, less than 10 percent and less than 5 percent, respectively, in 2000.

Figure 3-10.
Hispanic Population Distribution by Region: 1980 to 2000
(Percent)

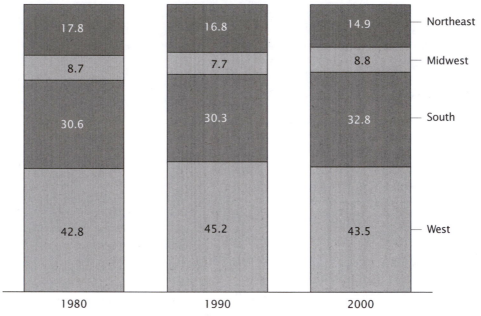

Source: U.S. Census Bureau, decennial census of population, 1980 to 2000.

Figure 3-11.
Percent Hispanic of Regional Population: 1980 to 2000

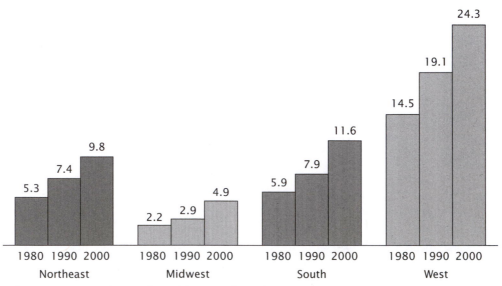

Source: U.S. Census Bureau, decennial census of population, 1980 to 2000.

The percentage Minority increased rapidly in every region since 1980, especially in the West.

The increasing racial and ethnic diversity of the U.S. population in the 20th century has largely been a post-1970 development, with regional patterns generally reflecting the trend of the United States as a whole. From 1980 to 2000, the percentage Minority[41] markedly increased in every region, and each region's percentage-point increase was larger in the 1990s than in the 1980s (see Figure 3-12).

Each region's rank according to its percentage of Minority population remained the same from 1980 to 2000. At each census, the West had the highest percentage Minority, followed by the South, the Northeast, and the Midwest.

In 1980, the percentage Minority in the West (27 percent) narrowly exceeded the percentage Minority in the South (26 percent). Since 1980, the West has experienced an especially rapid increase in its percentage

Minority, and the difference between the West and the other regions widened. In 2000, the Minority population represented 42 percent of the total population of the West and 34 percent of the population of the South.

The lack of data on Hispanic origin precludes calculating the percentage Minority for most of the century. However, since the Black population represented, by far, most of the Minority population during this period, the South would have ranked as the region with the highest percentage Minority during the first half of the century.

From 1980 to 2000, percentage-point increases in the percentage Minority in the Northeast exceeded those of the Midwest. By 2000, the Minority population in the Northeast had grown to 27 percent, comparable to the West and the South two decades earlier. Although the percentage Minority increased rapidly in the Midwest in the 1990s, it remained less than half that of the West in 2000 (19 percent and 42 percent, respectively).

---

[41] In this report, the Minority population refers to the aggregate number of people who are races other than White (and other than White alone for Census 2000) or who are Hispanic.

Figure 3-12.
Percent Minority by Region: 1980 to 2000

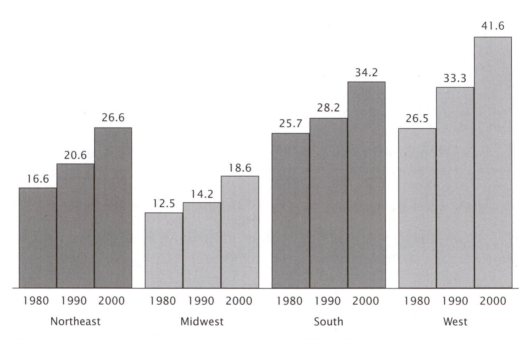

Source: U.S. Census Bureau, decennial census of population, 1980 to 2000.

From 1900 to 2000, the number of non-Southern states with populations of at least 10 percent races other than White increased from 2 to 26.

At the beginning of the century, less than 10 percent of the people in most states were of races other than White. Nevada and Arizona had the only populations outside of the South with at least 10 percent races other than White. In contrast, the population of every Southern state, except West Virginia, had at least 10 percent races other than White (see Figure 3-13). The percentage of races other than White in the Southern coastal states stretching from Virginia to Louisiana exceeded 30 percent. In two of these states, Mississippi and South Carolina, the majority of the population was races other than White in 1900.

By 1950, the state pattern of the percentage of races other than White had changed little. Arizona was the sole non-Southern state with more than 10 percent races other than White. The number of Southern states with less than 10 percent races other than White increased to include Kentucky and Oklahoma, in addition to West Virginia. While the percentages in 1950 were still relatively high in the South, they had declined in every Southern state except West Virginia.[42]

The increased diversity of the United States that occurred between 1950 and 2000 is evident from the state map for 2000 shown in Figure 3-13. By 2000, only 10 states had populations with less than 10 percent races other than White: Idaho, Iowa, Kentucky, Maine, Montana, New Hampshire, North Dakota, Vermont, West Virginia, and Wyoming. In the other 40 states, the percentage ranged from 10 percent in Nebraska to 76 percent in Hawaii. The District of Columbia's population had 69 percent races other than White.

At the end of the century, states with relatively higher percentages (20 percent or more) of races other than White were generally coastal and U.S-Mexican border states, extending south from New York and across the southern and southwestern states to California. States in the South still had relatively high percentages of races other than White at the century's close and were joined by several states outside the region. In 1900 and 1950, no state outside the South had at least 30 percent races other than White.[43] In 2000, five non-Southern states—Alaska, California, Hawaii, New Mexico, and New York—each had over 30 percent races other than White.

Across the country and in most states, the proportions of people other than White increased during the course of the century. Although all Southern states except West Virginia had a lower percentage of races other than White in 1950 than in 1900, their proportions remained at a high level. In nearly all states, the percentage of races other than White was higher in 2000 than in 1950. The five exceptions were: Alabama, Arkansas, Mississippi, South Carolina, and West Virginia, where the percentage of races other than White was lower in 2000 than in 1950, so, their percentage White was higher at the century's end than at midcentury.

---

[42] In addition to West Virginia, the percentage of races other than White was also higher in 1950 than in 1900 in the District of Columbia, considered a state equivalent for statistical purposes and also part of the U.S. Census Bureau's South region.

[43] Alaska and Hawaii were not included in the calculations prior to statehood. If included from 1900 to 1950, Hawaii would have had more than 30 percent races other than White in every census and Alaska in each census from 1900 through 1940.

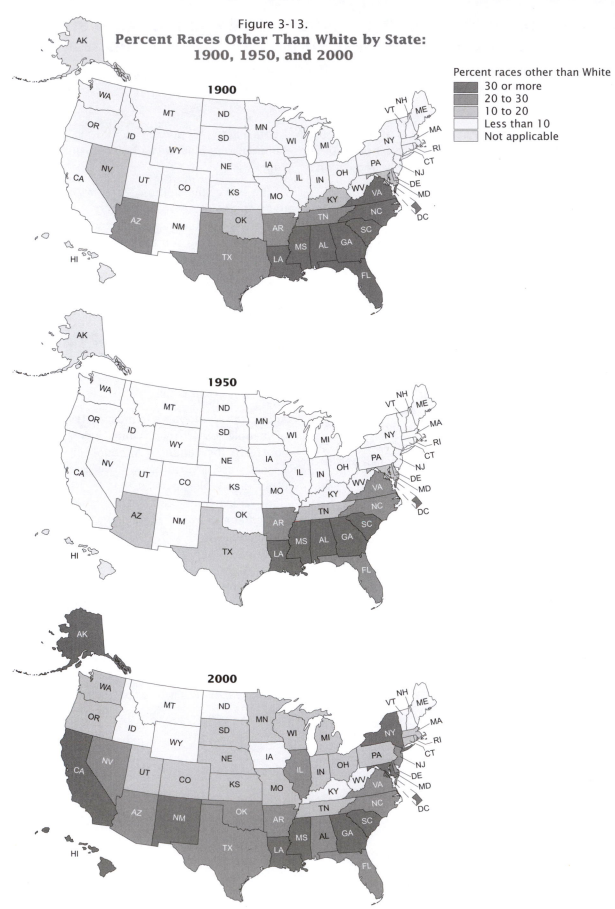

Figure 3-13.
**Percent Races Other Than White by State:
1900, 1950, and 2000**

Percent races other than White

- 30 or more
- 20 to 30
- 10 to 20
- Less than 10
- Not applicable

1900

1950

2000

Source: U.S. Census Bureau, decennial census of population, 1900, 1950, and 2000.

The ten states with the highest percentage Black were all in the South in 1900, 1950, and 2000; no state in the Northeast ranked among the ten highest in percentage American Indian and Alaska Native; and while the ten states with the highest percentage Asian and Pacific Islander were all in the West in 1900, every region was represented by 2000.

Previous discussion of the increased diversity of the U.S. population as measured by the percentage of people who are races other than White showed that this diversity is becoming widespread throughout the 50 states. At the same time, examination of the states with the highest percentages of their populations in specific race groups reveals that some groups remained concentrated in particular states throughout the century (see Table 3-1).

Among the 50 states, Mississippi had the highest percentage of Blacks in its population in every decade, 1900 to 2000. (The District of Columbia, treated as a state equivalent for statistical purposes, has ranked first in percentage Black since 1960.) In 1900, 1950, and 2000, all ten states (including the District of Columbia) with the highest percentages Black were in the South.

In 1900, Blacks constituted the majority in Mississippi and South Carolina and remained more than 50 percent of the population in these states until 1930 and 1920, respectively (see Appendix Table 8). The population in the District of Columbia has been 50 percent or more Black since 1960. The highest-ranking states in percentage Black in 1950 were the same as in 1900, although the ranking shifted among the states. In 2000, 8 of these 10 states were still among the top ten in percentage Black, and Maryland and Delaware had replaced Florida and Arkansas.

The states with the highest percentage of American Indians and Alaska Natives in their populations have also generally remained the same throughout the century. Eight of the ten states with the highest percentage American Indian and Alaska Native in 1900 were also among the ten highest in 1950 and in 2000.

Washington dropped out of the ten highest-ranked states by 1950, replaced by Utah. However, by 2000, Utah dropped out of the ten highest-ranked states, along with Nevada, and they were replaced by Washington, which reentered the ten highest-ranked states, and by Alaska, which was not ranked prior to statehood. (If Alaska were included, it would have ranked 1st among all states in the percentage of population American Indian and Alaska Native throughout the century.) The Northeast was the only region without a state ranked among the 10 highest percentages American Indian and Alaska Native during the century.

The changes in the rankings of states according to their percentage Asians and Pacific Islanders varied more than the changes in rankings for Blacks and American Indians and Alaska Natives. In 1900, the states with the ten highest percentages of Asians and Pacific Islanders were all in the West. Of these ten, only California, Nevada, and Washington also were among the ten highest in 1950 and 2000. In 1950, 9 of the 10 highest-ranking states were still in the West, with only the District of Columbia outside the region. However, by the end of the century, the number of Western states among the ten highest had fallen to five, which were joined by the southern states of Maryland and Virginia and by the northeastern states of Massachusetts, New Jersey, and New York. Alaska and Hawaii each ranked among the ten highest states in percentage Asian and Pacific Islander in 2000. (Neither state was ranked prior to 1960, the first census after they became the 49th and 50th states, respectively. However, Hawaii would have ranked 1st among all states in the percentage of population Asian and Pacific Islander if it had been included.)

Table 3-1.
Ten States With the Highest Percents Black, American Indian and Alaska Native, and Asian and Pacific Islander: 1900, 1950, and 2000

Rank	1900		1950		2000	
	State	Percent	State	Percent	State	Percent
	Black					
1	Mississippi	58.5	Mississippi	45.3	District of Columbia	60.0
2	South Carolina	58.4	South Carolina	38.8	Mississippi	36.3
3	Louisiana	47.1	District of Columbia	35.0	Louisiana	32.5
4	Georgia	46.7	Louisiana	32.9	South Carolina	29.5
5	Alabama	45.2	Alabama	32.0	Georgia	28.7
6	Florida	43.7	Georgia	30.9	Maryland	27.9
7	Virginia	35.6	North Carolina	25.8	Alabama	26.0
8	North Carolina	33.0	Arkansas	22.3	North Carolina	21.6
9	District of Columbia	31.1	Virginia	22.1	Virginia	19.6
10	Arkansas	28.0	Florida	21.8	Delaware	19.2
	American Indian and Alaska Native					
1	Arizona	21.5	Arizona	8.8	Alaska	15.6
2	Nevada	12.3	New Mexico	6.2	New Mexico	9.5
3	Oklahoma	8.2	South Dakota	3.6	South Dakota	8.3
4	New Mexico	6.7	Nevada	3.1	Oklahoma	7.9
5	South Dakota	5.0	Montana	2.8	Montana	6.2
6	Montana	4.7	Oklahoma	2.4	Arizona	5.0
7	Idaho	2.6	North Dakota	1.7	North Dakota	4.9
8	North Dakota	2.2	Wyoming	1.1	Wyoming	2.3
9	Washington	1.9	Idaho	0.6	Washington	1.6
10	Wyoming	1.8	Utah	0.6	Idaho	1.4
	Asian and Pacific Islander					
1	California	3.8	California	1.4	Hawaii	51.0
2	Nevada	3.7	Utah	0.7	California	11.3
3	Oregon	3.1	Washington	0.6	Washington	5.9
4	Washington	1.8	Colorado	0.4	New Jersey	5.7
5	Montana	1.7	Nevada	0.4	New York	5.6
6	Idaho	1.7	Oregon	0.4	Nevada	4.9
7	Arizona	1.4	Idaho	0.4	Alaska	4.5
8	Wyoming	0.9	Arizona	0.4	Maryland	4.0
9	Utah	0.4	District of Columbia	0.3	Massachusetts	3.8
10	New Mexico	0.2	Wyoming	0.2	Virginia	3.7

Source: U.S. Census Bureau, decennial census of population, 1900, 1950, and 2000.

Hawaii had the highest percentage (21 percent) of people who reported as more than one race in 2000.

Census 2000 was the first time individuals were allowed to identify themselves as more than one race in the history of census-taking in the United States. Of the total population (281.4 million) in 2000, 6.8 million people, or 2.4 percent, reported as more than one race. Regionally, the West had the highest number (2.7 million) and the highest proportion (4.3 percent) of people of two or more races.

Among the states, Hawaii had, by far, the largest percentage (21.4 percent) of its population reporting more than one race. Only three other states—Alaska (5.4 percent), California (4.7 percent) and Oklahoma (4.5 percent)—had 4.0 percent or more of their populations reporting more than one race (see Figure 3-14). In fourteen states, the percentage reporting more than one race exceeded the U.S. level of 2.43 percent.[44] In

---

[44] See U.S. Census Bureau. 2001i. *The Two or More Races Population: 2000*, by Nicholas A. Jones and Amy Symens Smith.

addition to the four states already named, the other ten were: Arizona, Colorado, Nevada, New Jersey, New Mexico, New York, Oregon, Rhode Island, Texas, and Washington.

Most states (36) and the District of Columbia had lower percentages reporting as more than one race than the overall United States percentage. Twenty-five of these states were in the 1 percent to 2 percent range, while 6 states and the District of Columbia ranged from 2 percent up to the U.S. level (2.43 percent). In five states (four of which are in the South), less than 1 percent of the population reported being more than one race: Alabama, Maine, Mississippi, South Carolina, and West Virginia.

The three states with the largest populations, California, Texas, and New York, were also the three states with the largest numbers of people reporting two or more races (1.6 million, 515,000 and 590,000, respectively, see Appendix Table 9).

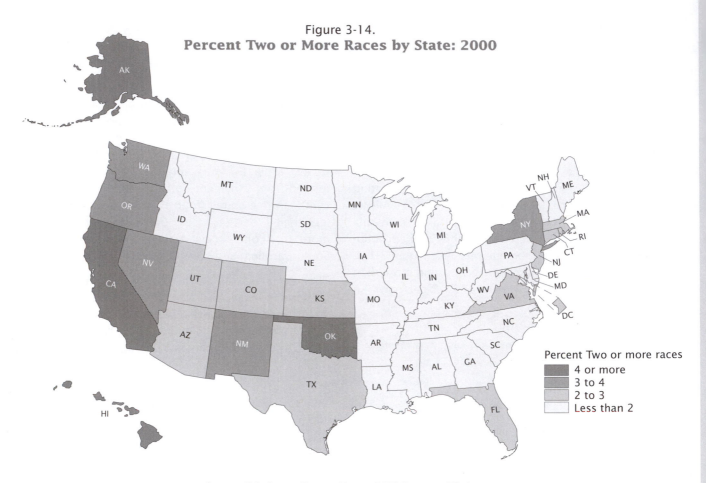

Figure 3-14.
Percent Two or More Races by State: 2000

Percent Two or more races
- 4 or more
- 3 to 4
- 2 to 3
- Less than 2

Source: U.S. Census Bureau, Census 2000 Summary File 1.

In 1980, Colorado was the only state not bordering Mexico which had an Hispanic population of at least 10 percent. By 2000, five more nonborder states had populations which were at least 10 percent Hispanic.

In every state except Hawaii, the percentage of the population that was Hispanic increased during the 20-year period from 1980 to 2000. The percentage Hispanic in Hawaii decreased by less than 1 percentage point and Hawaii was among the top 20 states in terms of its percentage of Hispanic population (see Appendix Table 10).

The number of states with populations of at least 10 percent Hispanic doubled from five to ten between 1980 and 2000. In 1980, only Arizona, California, Colorado, New Mexico, and Texas had populations that were at least 10 percent Hispanic (see Figure 3-15). By 1990, three more states, Florida, New York, and Nevada, were added to the list. In 2000, the number of states with populations that were at least 10 percent Hispanic increased to ten, with the addition of Illinois and New Jersey.

In 1980, New Mexico was the only state in which Hispanics represented at least one-fourth of its population. By 2000, Hispanics made up at least 25 percent of the population in three additional states (Arizona, California, and Texas). All four of these states are on the U.S.-Mexico border.

In 1980, Colorado was the only state with a 10 percent or greater Hispanic population that did not share a border with Mexico. By 2000, Hispanics represented at least 10 percent of the population in five additional nonborder states: Florida, Illinois, Nevada, New Jersey, and New York.

The states with the highest proportion of Hispanics were concentrated primarily in the West. In 1980, 7 of the 12 states that were at least 5 percent Hispanic were in the West. Nearly all of the states in the Midwest, the South, and the Northeast had less than 5 percent Hispanic in their populations. However, four states outside the West (Florida, New Jersey, New York, and Texas) ranked among the ten states with the highest percentages of Hispanics from 1980 to 2000. By 2000, the proportions of Hispanics among the midwestern states remained relatively low. Illinois was the only state in the Midwest with Hispanics representing at least 10 percent of its population.

New Mexico had the highest proportion of Hispanics in its population of any state in 1980, 1990, and 2000 (see Appendix Table 10). More than one-third of New Mexico's population was Hispanic in 1980. By 2000, 42 percent of its population was Hispanic.

Following New Mexico in terms of percentage Hispanic were Texas and California. In 1980, Hispanics represented 21 percent of Texas' population and 19 percent of California's. In 1990, California surpassed Texas with a slightly higher proportion of Hispanics. In 2000, California and Texas remained ranked second and third, respectively, in terms of percentage Hispanic, with Hispanics making up nearly a third of their populations.

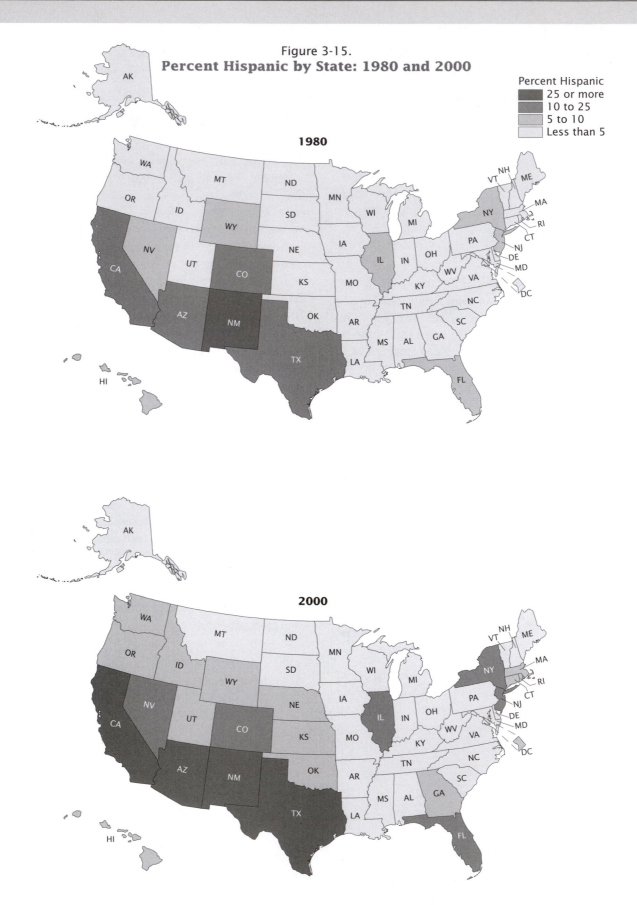

Figure 3-15.
Percent Hispanic by State: 1980 and 2000

Source: U.S. Census Bureau decennial census of population, 1980 and 2000.

Among the 50 states, Hawaii, New Mexico, Mississippi, Texas, and California had the 5 highest percentage Minority populations from 1980 to 2000.

As noted earlier, between 1980 and 2000 the White non-Hispanic population of the United States increased much less than the aggregated Minority (people of races other than White or of Hispanic origin) population (7.9 percent and 88 percent, respectively). The more rapid increase of the Minority population results in this collective group representing a larger share of the total population. The faster growth of the Minority population occurred in all 50 states. Thus, the percentage Minority increased in each of the 50 states between 1980 and 2000. (The percentage Minority in the District of Columbia declined from 74 percent in 1980 to 72 percent in 2000).

Figure 3-16 illustrates the widespread shift to higher proportions of Minority population throughout the United States during the 20-year period, 1980 to 2000. In 1980, 21 states had populations with less than 10 percent Minority. By 2000, the number of such states had dwindled to 6—Iowa, Maine, New Hampshire, North Dakota, Vermont, and West Virginia. The number of states with 30 percent or higher percentage Minority population doubled, from just 8 states (including the District of Columbia) in 1980 to 17 states in 2000. In 1980, all 8 states with 30 percent or more Minority populations were in the West or the South. These two regions also accounted for 6 of the 9 states added to this category in 2000, the remaining being Illinois, New Jersey, and New York.

Over time, several state populations became "majority Minority." In 1980, only Hawaii and the District of Columbia had populations with more than 50 percent Minority. By 2000, California and New Mexico had also become majority Minority. Texas, with 48 percent Minority in 2000, was the only other state with at least 40 percent Minority.

Among the 50 states, the percentage-point increases from 1980 to 2000 in the Minority population ranged from 1 percentage point in West Virginia to 20 percentage points in California.[45] The Minority population share rose by 10 percentage points or more in 14 states. After California, the next largest increases were in Nevada (18 percentage points), and Texas, New Jersey, and New York (13 percentage points each). The Minority population share in the remaining nine states with substantial percentage-point increases—Arizona, Connecticut, Florida, Illinois, Massachusetts, Maryland, Oklahoma, Rhode Island, and Washington—all increased by 10 to 12 percentage points.

The large increases in the percentage Minority during the period 1980 to 2000 occurred across all categories in states with relatively low, moderate, and high initial levels of percentage Minority in 1980. For example, the Minority population shares in Massachusetts, Rhode Island, and Washington each increased by at least 10 percentage points, yet all had less than 10 percent Minority in 1980. At the same time, California and Texas also had large increases in their Minority population shares, even though they already ranked among the states with the highest shares in 1980.

The District of Columbia had the highest percentage Minority in 1980. In 2000, Hawaii (77 percent) had the highest Minority population share. Among the 50 states, Hawaii, New Mexico, Mississippi, Texas, and California had the 5 highest percentages Minority in both 1980 and 2000. In 1980, the percentage Minority in these states ranged from 33 percent in California to 69 percent in Hawaii. At the end of the century, the Minority share in these states ranged from 39 percent in Mississippi to 77 percent in Hawaii. In 1980, Vermont had the lowest Minority share (1.5 percent). At the century's close, Maine had the lowest percentage Minority (3.5 percent).

---

[45] The percentage Minority is equivalent to 100 minus the percentage White non-Hispanic (see Appendix Table 10).

Figure 3-16.
Percent Minority by State: 1980 and 2000

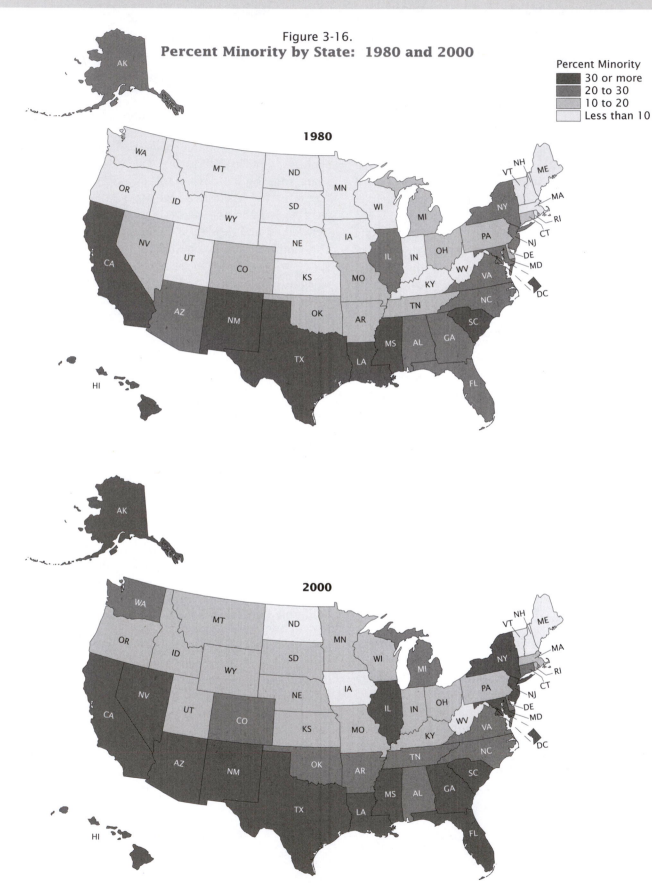

Source: U.S. Census Bureau, decennial census of population, 1980 and 2000.

From 1970 to 2000, Asians and Pacific Islanders were most likely, and American Indians and Alaska Natives were least likely, to live in metropolitan areas.

The percentage of each race and Hispanic origin group living in metropolitan areas increased every decade from 1960 to 2000 (see Figure 3-17). This trend follows the U.S. pattern of an increasing share of the total population living in metropolitan areas over the course of the century.

The percentage metropolitan for each group increased, and every race and ethnic group maintained its relative ranking every decade. For censuses with available data, Asians and Pacific Islanders have been most likely, and American Indians and Alaska Natives least likely, to live in metropolitan areas. By 2000, nearly 96 percent of all Asians and Pacific Islanders lived in a metropolitan area (see Appendix Table 16). In contrast, the American Indian and Alaska Native population lived primarily in nonmetropolitan areas before the 1990 census, when a majority (51 percent) lived in metropolitan areas for the first time.

After Asians and Pacific Islanders, Hispanics had the second highest proportion living in metropolitan areas. From 1980 to 2000, the percentage of Hispanics living in a metropolitan area increased from 88 to 91 percent.

In 1960, 65 percent of Blacks and 63 percent of Whites lived in metropolitan areas. The shares of the Black and the White populations living in metropolitan areas increased every decade, 1960 to 2000, but the gap grew wider every 10 years. By 2000, the difference widened to 8 percentage points, with 86 percent of Blacks and 78 percent of Whites living in a metropolitan area.

Although American Indians and Alaska Natives consistently had the least likelihood of living in a metropolitan area from 1970 to 2000, their percentage metropolitan increased more than every other group during the period. As a result, the range between the highest and lowest percentages metropolitan declined between 1970 and 2000.

Among people who reported being more than one race, a choice available for the first time in Census 2000, a relatively high percentage (88 percent) lived in metropolitan areas. They were slightly less likely than Asians and Pacific Islanders and Hispanics, but more likely than Blacks, Whites, and American Indians and Alaska Natives to live in a metropolitan area.

Figure 3-17.
**Percent Metropolitan by Race and Hispanic
Origin: 1960 to 2000**

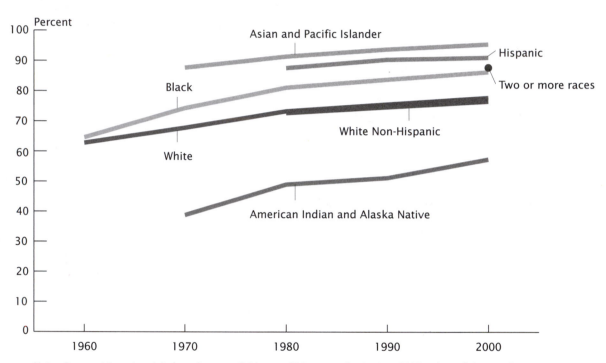

Note: Data on Hispanic origin have been available on a 100-percent basis since 1980 only, and data on the
population of Two or more races are available from Census 2000 only.
Source: U.S. Census Bureau, decennial census of population, 1960 to 2000.

The White, Black, and American Indian and Alaska Native populations all aged over the century.

As Figure 3-18 shows, every race group's age structure changed considerably from 1900 to 2000. The White and Black populations followed a somewhat similar pattern while the changes among the American Indian and Alaska Native population and the Asian and Pacific Islander population were more distinct. While fertility and mortality trends have influenced the age structure changes in all these populations, immigration trends have also been a major factor underlying changes in the age structure of the Asian and Pacific Islander population.

In 1900, the White, Black, and American Indian and Alaska Native populations were all relatively young, which can be seen by the pyramid shape of their age structures. The under 5 age group was the largest for all three races (see Appendix Table 11). On the other hand, the Asian and Pacific Islander population in 1900 consisted largely of working-age men, as a result of the heavy influx of Chinese and Japanese workers to the United States during the late 19th century. The largest 5-year age group was 35-to-39 year olds, who made up 15 percent of the Asian and Pacific Islander population. The absence of women in the population pyramid reflects the effects of various exclusionary immigration policies. As a result of the unique immigration patterns of the Asian and Pacific Islander population, its age pyramid in 1900 differed sharply from that of the other races and this marked difference continued for decades.

From 1900 to 1950, the White and Black populations became older as fertility declined, but somewhat large proportions of their populations were still under age 10. The largest 5-year age group for both Blacks and Whites in 1950 was children under age 5. This reflects the fertility during the start of the post World War II baby boom.

The American Indian and Alaska Native population remained a very young population in 1950, and the base of its age pyramid had not narrowed since 1900 as it did in the White and Black populations. This was due to the relatively high fertility of the American Indian and Alaska Native population. Graphically, the age structure generally remained in the classic pyramid shape of five decades earlier. The under 5 age group among American Indians and Alaska Natives was still proportionally larger (15 percent of the total) than the rest of the other 5-year age groups.

By 2000, the age structures of the White, Black, and American Indian and Alaska Native populations had taken on a more rectangular shape, characteristic of older populations. While all three groups had older populations, the White population was the oldest. In 2000, 7.0 percent of the White population was 75 years or older compared with only 2.1 percent of the American Indian and Alaska Native population and 3.5 percent of the Black population.

The age structure of the Asian and Pacific Islander population changed significantly during both halves of the century. From 1900 to 1950, it became much less unbalanced among the different age groups and also between the sexes. By 2000, the age structure of the Asian and Pacific Islander population more closely resembled the age structures of the White, Black, and American Indian and Alaska Native populations, with a more balanced sex ratio. However, the influence of international migration remained, as evidenced by the relatively high proportion in the young adult age groups.

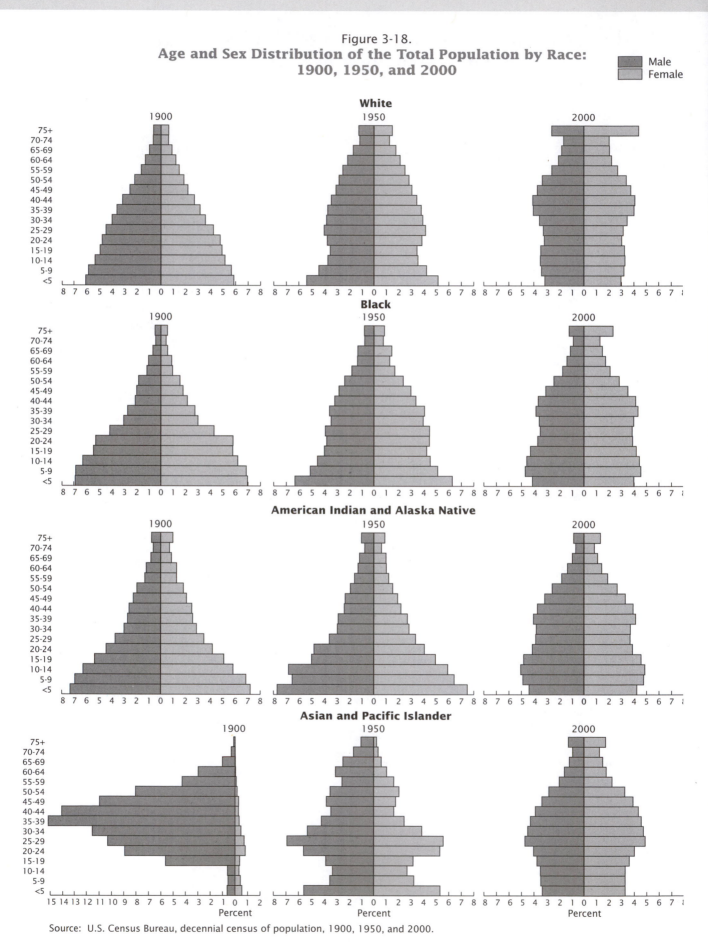

Figure 3-18.
**Age and Sex Distribution of the Total Population by Race:
1900, 1950, and 2000**

Male
Female

White

Black

American Indian and Alaska Native

Asian and Pacific Islander

Source: U.S. Census Bureau, decennial census of population, 1900, 1950, and 2000.

In 1980 and 2000, Hispanics were much younger than non-Hispanics.

The age and sex distributions for the Hispanic and non-Hispanic populations for 1980 and 2000 are shown by the population pyramids in Figure 3-19. The shapes of the pyramids reveal that Hispanics were much younger than non-Hispanics in 1980 and 2000, although both populations "aged" over the 20-year period.

The age and sex distributions of the Hispanic population in 1980 and 2000 show large proportions at young ages and progressively smaller proportions at older ages, indicating a relatively young population. The wider base of the pyramid reflects relatively high Hispanic fertility. Comparatively, the age and sex pyramid of the non-Hispanic population has a much more rectangular shape, indicative of an older population. The base of the non-Hispanic pyramid is narrower, and the proportion of the population in the older age groups is much higher.

In 1980, children under age 5 represented the largest 5-year age group (11 percent) of the Hispanic population, compared with non-Hispanics, who had only 7 percent of their population under age 5. In contrast to Hispanics, 20-to-24-year olds represented the largest 5-year age group for the non-Hispanic population in 1980 (see Appendix Table 11).

Two decades later, the Hispanic population had grown older, but remained relatively young. In 2000, the largest 5-year age group in the Hispanic population was still children under age 5. Among non-Hispanics, the largest 5-year age group in 2000 had shifted to the 40-to-44-year olds, reflecting the aging of the group

born during the peak years of the baby boom (1956 to 1960) over the period 1980 to 2000.

The Hispanic age and sex structure maintained a "bulge" around the broad age range of 15 to 29 years in both 1980 and 2000. While the individual 5-year age groups within that range did not exceed the proportion of the population in the under 5 age group, together they accounted for nearly one-third of the Hispanic population (31 percent). This bulge resulted primarily from the continued migration of Hispanics to the United States.

For non-Hispanics, the bulge in the 1980 age distribution was also concentrated around the younger age groups, extending roughly from the ages of 15 to 34 years. However, the bulge in the non-Hispanic population in these ages coincides with the presence of the baby-boom generation (roughly ages 16 to 34 in 1980). Unlike the Hispanic age distribution, the bulge in the non-Hispanic population shifted to the age range 35-to-54 years by 2000, again reflecting the aging of the baby-boom generation.

The youthfulness of the Hispanic population compared with the non-Hispanic population is also apparent from the proportions of their populations at older ages. While the age distributions of both populations become progressively smaller with age, non-Hispanics had much larger proportions in older age groups than Hispanics. About 5 percent of the Hispanic population was 65 years and over in both 1980 and 2000, whereas people age 65 and over represented 12 percent of non-Hispanics in 1980 and 14 percent in 2000.

Figure 3-19.
Age and Sex Distribution of the Total Population by Hispanic Origin: 1980 and 2000

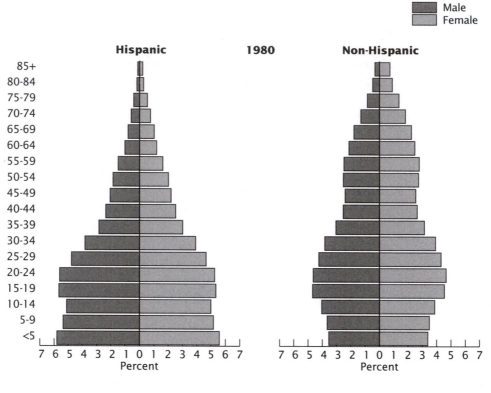

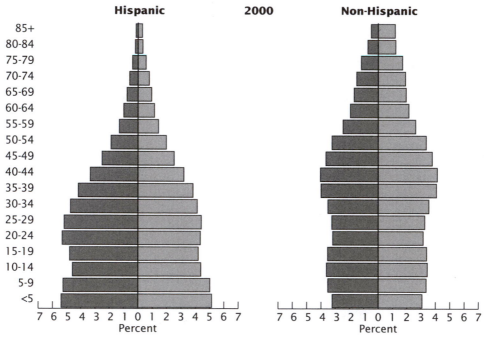

Source: U.S. Census Bureau, decennial census of population, 1980 and 2000.

The Black and the American Indian and Alaska Native populations were younger than the White and the Asian and Pacific Islander populations during the entire century.

The trends in median age by race and Hispanic origin over the course of the century reveal some similarities and some marked differences (see Figure 3-20). For example, the White and the Black populations followed similar patterns of change, with increasing median ages every decade during the first half of the century, declining median age in the 1950s and 1960s, and increasing median ages throughout the remainder of the century.

In contrast, the American Indian and Alaska Native and the Asian and Pacific Islander populations followed quite different trends. From 1900 and for most of the century, the median age for American Indians and Alaska Natives changed little, and more than half of this population was under 21 years old (see Appendix Table 11). Asians and Pacific Islanders, on the other hand, had their highest median age at the outset of the century, and it generally declined until 1980. The high median ages at the beginning of the century are a by-product of predominantly adult male migration.

Apart from the general trends of each group, there have been fairly consistent differences in the relative levels of median ages across race and Hispanic origin. Both Blacks and American Indians and Alaska Natives had younger median ages throughout the century than did other races. Hispanic origin data, first collected on a 100-percent basis in 1980, show that Hispanics also had a young median age. Furthermore, Census 2000 showed that people who reported more than one race are another very young population group. By comparison, the White and the Asian and Pacific Islander populations consistently had higher median ages. Between the race and Hispanic-origin groups, the White non-Hispanic population has had the "oldest" median age, increasing from 31.7 in 1980 to 38.6 in 2000.

Figure 3-20.
Median Age by Race and Hispanic Origin: 1900 to 2000

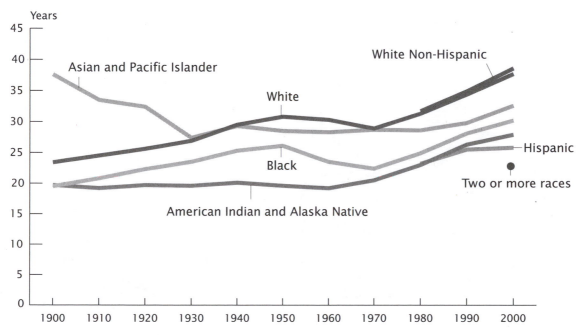

Note: Data on Hispanic origin have been available on a 100-percent basis since 1980 only, and data on the population of Two or more races are available from Census 2000 only.
Source: U.S. Census Bureau, decennial census of population, 1900 to 2000.

Younger age groups had the highest percentage Minority, and older age groups had the lowest.

The rapidly increasing diversity of the U.S. population in the last two decades of the 20th century is indicated by the trend in the age distribution of the aggregate Minority population (see Figure 3-21).[46] Each broad age group increased in a consistent pattern over the last 20 years of the century.

Figure 3-21 demonstrates that younger age groups have had a higher percentage Minority than older age groups. In 1980, the percentage Minority ranged from 12 percent for the population age 65 and over to 25 percent for people under age 25. By 2000, the percentage Minority ranged from 16 percent for the population age 65 and over to 39 percent for people under age 25.

[46] The aggregate Minority population as shown in this report represents people who are races other than White (and other than White alone for Census 2000) or who are Hispanic. For more details, see the Sources and Quality of Data section and the Glossary.

For every age group, the percentage-point increase in the 1990s for the Minority population exceeded the 1980s increase. In addition to an overall higher percentage Minority, younger age groups experienced greater percentage-point gains than older age groups in both the 1980s and the 1990s. As a result, the difference between the youngest and the oldest age groups in their percentage of Minority population widened over the 20-year period.

The trends in the percentage Minority for most age groups reflect the relatively high levels of international migration of Asians and Hispanics in recent decades. Since immigration is a less significant factor for the population age 65 years and over, the increase in the percentage Minority for this age group has been less pronounced.

Figure 3-21.
Percent Minority by Broad Age Group: 1980 to 2000

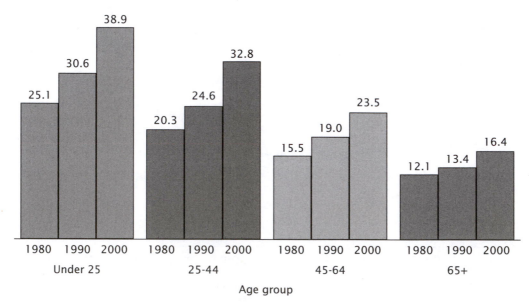

Source: U.S. Census Bureau, decennial census of population, 1980 to 2000.

American Indians and Alaska Natives had the highest percentage under age 15 and Blacks the second highest, for most of the 20th century.

During the 20th century, race groups in the United States had varying rates of fertility, the principal factor determining the proportion of young people in a population. Even so, nearly every race group experienced a general decline in their young populations.

The proportion under age 15 was lower in 1940 than in 1900 for every race group, with the exception of the Asian and Pacific Islander population (see Figure 3-22). Asians and Pacific Islanders experienced a large increase in their young population due to a combination of factors, including the increased immigration of families and their natural increase.

The only period of increase in the under age 15 population for every race group occurred from 1940 to 1960. This period coincides with the majority of the baby-boom years (1946 to 1964). However, from the 1960s onward, the proportion of young people in each race group's population continued to decline as fertility rates declined. Hispanics experienced a slight increase in the proportion under age 15 years during the 1990s.

The Black and the American Indian and Alaska Native populations had much higher proportions of people under 15 years of age compared with the White and the Asian and Pacific Islander populations. The American Indian and Alaska Native population had the highest percentage under age 15 for most of the 20th century, and in 1960 had a higher proportion (42 percent) than any race or ethnic group during the entire century (see Appendix Table 11).

In 1980, when data first became available for the Hispanic population at the 100-percent level, Hispanics had the highest percentage under age 15 (32 percent) among the groups considered, although just slightly higher than the American Indian and Alaska Native population. Relatively high fertility of the Hispanic population mainly accounts for this high proportion. On the other hand, White non-Hispanics had the lowest percentage under age 15 from 1980 to 2000. In 2000, the Two or more races population (available in Census 2000 for the first time) had the highest proportion of people under age 15 (36 percent).

Figure 3-22.
Percent Under Age 15 by Race and Hispanic Origin: 1900 to 2000

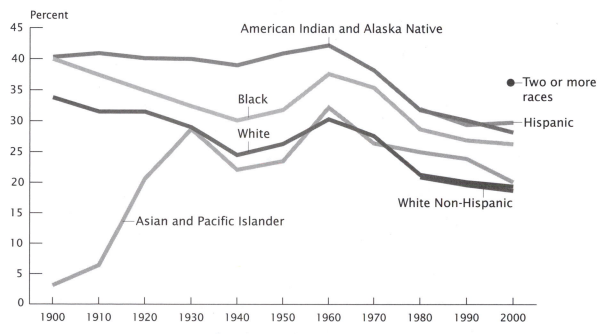

Note: Data on Hispanic origin have been available on a 100-percent basis since 1980 only, and data on the population of Two or more races are available from Census 2000 only.
Source: U.S. Census Bureau, decennial census of population, 1900 to 2000.

Since 1930, the White (and since 1980 the White non-Hispanic) population has had the highest percentage age 65 years and over.

The proportion of the population age 65 years and over was higher in 2000 than in 1900 for every race (see Figure 3-23), but different trends occurred among the groups. For the Black and White populations, the proportion elderly grew steadily, in contrast to the fluctuation in the proportion 65 years and over for the Asian and Pacific Islander population. The proportion elderly for American Indians and Alaska Natives fluctuated slightly, but remained relatively stable over the course of the century.

The White population experienced the largest increase in its proportion elderly, from 4 percent in 1900 to 14 percent in 2000. Conversely, the American Indian and Alaska Native population experienced the least change in its proportion elderly, varying from 4.6 percent in 1900 to 5.8 percent in 1990 (see Appendix Table 11).

The American Indian and Alaska Native population had the highest proportion elderly from 1900 to 1920, but then had one of the lowest proportions elderly by the end of the century. By 1930, the proportion of the White population that was 65 years and over had surpassed that of the American Indian and Alaska Native population. Since then, the White, and since 1980, the White non-Hispanic, populations have had, by far, the highest percentage elderly. In 2000, the White non-Hispanic population had the century's highest proportion age 65 years and over of any race or ethnic group (15 percent). This results primarily from the sustained lower fertility levels of this population group.

Over the decades, the group with the lowest proportion of elderly shifted across race and ethnic groups. Asians and Pacific Islanders had the lowest proportion elderly from 1900 to 1940 (and the lowest of the century—1.5 percent in 1900), followed by American Indians and Alaska Natives from 1950 to 1970. Since 1980, when data on the Hispanic population were first collected on a 100-percent basis, Hispanics have had the lowest proportion of elderly in each census. Relatively high levels of fertility combined with large-scale immigration of young adults have kept the proportion of elderly low among Hispanics. Census 2000, the first census to allow individuals to report themselves as more than one race, found that the Two or more races population also had a low proportion age 65 and over (5.0 percent), comparable to that of the Hispanic population (4.9 percent).

Figure 3-23.
Percent Age 65 and Over by Race and Hispanic Origin: 1900 to 2000

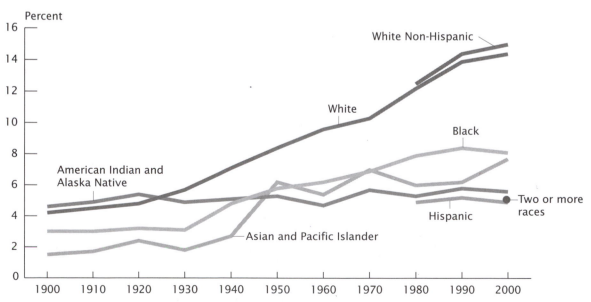

Note: Data on Hispanic origin have been available on a 100-percent basis since 1980 only, and data on the population of Two or more races are available from Census 2000 only.
Source: U.S. Census Bureau, decennial census of population, 1900 to 2000.

Black females outnumbered Black males in every decade of the century.

The sex ratio trends of the Black and the White populations have been similar during the century, while the Asian and Pacific Islander population and the American Indian and Alaska Native population have followed two distinct patterns (see Figure 3-24).

The sex ratios of the White and the Black populations increased early in the century, steadily declined to 1980, then increased to 2000. The arrival of relatively more male immigrants at the beginning of the century contributed to the initial sex ratio increase for Whites. Greater improvement in female than male mortality rates generally explains the declining sex ratios up to 1980 for the White and Black populations, while greater improvement in male than female mortality rates in part explains the 1980 to 2000 increase.

The sex ratio for Asians and Pacific Islanders varied much more than for other race groups. In 1900, Asian and Pacific Islanders had the highest sex ratio (1,974) of the century. This extreme excess of males originated because Asian and Pacific Islander immigrants in the late 19th century were almost exclusively men. As late as 1950, Asians and Pacific Islanders had a sex ratio of 145 (see Appendix Table 16). The sex ratio declined as family immigration and fertility among the immigrants increased the representation of women within the Asian and Pacific Islander population.

The sex ratio trend for the American Indian and Alaska Native population also followed a unique path. In general, the sex ratio rose from 1900 to 1950, declined to 1970, and increased slightly for the remainder of the century. Interpreting the factors contributing to this trend is problematic, as documentation of changes in the American Indian and Alaska Native population have been affected by changes in census procedures and changes in racial affiliation.[47]

Between the race and Hispanic-origin groups, Blacks had the lowest sex ratio throughout the century. Black females outnumbered Black males every decade, and the Black population had the century's lowest sex ratio (89.6) in 1980. Differences in the census coverage of Black males relative to Black females contributed to overall lower sex ratios for the Black population, as did a comparatively lower sex ratio at birth.

Asians and Pacific Islanders had the highest sex ratio of the race and ethnic groups from 1900 to 1970. Hispanics maintained the highest sex ratio of these groups from 1980 to 2000.

At the end of the century, the male population exceeded the female population among Hispanics and (slightly) for the Two or more races population. For all other race and ethnic groups, the female population outnumbered the male population.

---

[47] For further discussion of the history of population data on the American Indian and Alaska Native population, see C. Matthew Snipp, 2000, "American Indians and Alaska Natives," *Encyclopedia of the U.S. Census*, Margo J. Anderson (ed.).

Figure 3-24.
Sex Ratio by Race and Hispanic Origin: 1900 to 2000

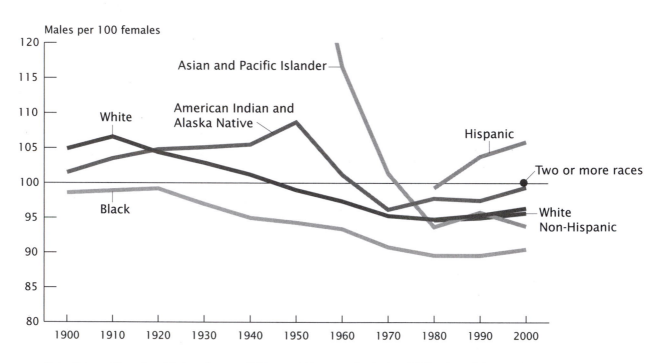

Note: Data on Hispanic origin have been available on a 100-percent basis since 1980 only, and data on the population of Two or more races are available from Census 2000 only. Data for the Asian and Pacific Islander population by sex are available prior to 1960 but the sex ratios are not shown since the values far exceed the highest level shown in Figure 3-24. The sex ratios for the Asian and Pacific Islander population declined from 1,974 in 1900 to 145 in 1950.
Source: U.S. Census Bureau, decennial census of population, 1900 to 2000.

Chapter Highlights
HOUSING

National Trends

From 1940 to 2000, the number of housing units in the United States more than tripled—from 37.3 million to 115.9 million.

From 1940 to 2000, the largest housing unit increase (19.7 million) occurred in the 1970s, and the smallest increase (8.7 million) took place in the 1940s.

The number of vacant housing units increased in every decade from 1940 to 2000, except for the 1960s, when they declined by 73,000. The lowest housing vacancy rate (6.6 percent) occurred in 1940, and the highest vacancy rate (10.1 percent) in 1990.

Prior to 1950, over half of all occupied housing units were rented. By 1950, homeownership became more prevalent than renting. The homeownership rate continued to increase until 1980, decreased slightly in the 1980s, and then increased in the 1990s, reaching the highest level of the century (66 percent) in Census 2000.

From 1960 to 2000, nonmetropolitan areas had higher homeownership rates than metropolitan areas. Within metropolitan areas, the homeownership rate was much higher in the suburbs than in central cities.

From 1960 to 2000, householders age 65 years and over were more likely to own their homes than householders under age 65.

At the end of the 20th century, householders who were Black, Hispanic, or of two or more races were more likely to rent than own their homes.

From 1940 to 2000, householders living alone were less likely to own their homes than householders living with other people.

Regional Trends

Every region experienced an increase in vacancy rates during the 1950s, 1970s, and 1980s and a decrease in vacancy rates during the 1960s and the 1990s.

From 1940 to 1960, the West had the highest vacancy rate, then from 1970 to 2000, the South had the highest vacancy rate.

The 1930s was the only decade when the proportion of owner-occupied housing units declined in every region. The largest increase in homeownership rates for each region then occurred in the following decade, the 1940s, as the economy recovered from the Depression and experienced post-World War II prosperity.

Each region's highest homeownership rate of the century was recorded in 2000.

The Midwest had the highest homeownership rate for every decade of the century, except in 1910, when the West ranked first.

State Trends

Ohio and Illinois ranked among the ten states with the lowest vacancy rates in every census from 1940 to 2000.

Maine, Montana, New Hampshire, and Vermont all ranked among the ten states with the highest vacancy rates every census from 1940 to 2000.

South Carolina's homeownership rate experienced the largest percentage point increase (42 percentage points) during the century, from 31 percent in 1900 to 72 percent in 2000. North Dakota experienced the largest percentage point drop (14 percentage points) in its homeownership rate, from 81 percent in 1900 to 67 percent in 2000.

Michigan and Minnesota were the only two states to be among the ten states with the highest homeownership rates for every census. States with consistently low homeownership rates included Alaska, Hawaii, Massachusetts, New York, and Rhode Island.

Chapter 4
HOUSING

Prior to 1940, the population census collected limited information on the number of occupied housing units in the United States. More detailed information on the characteristics of housing units became available when the first census of housing was conducted in 1940. Information on housing tenure (owner occupied or renter occupied) has been collected on a 100-percent basis since 1900 and information on occupancy status (occupied or vacant) since 1940. Many other characteristics of housing units were collected in Census 2000, but only on a sample-basis.

In the 20th century, a basic American dream of owning a home became a reality for the majority of U.S. households. In the censuses of 1900 to 1940, most Americans reported renting their homes. By 1950, most Americans owned their homes, and by 2000, homeownership in the United States had reached its highest level (66 percent) ever. Economic prosperity, changes in the mortgage financing system, and corresponding increases in the proportion of households that could afford to buy a home propelled these 20th century trends.

The number of housing units in the United States tripled from 37.3 million in 1940 to 115.9 million in 2000. During the same period, the number of vacant housing units increased from 2.5 million to 10.4 million, representing 9 percent of all U.S. housing units in 2000. Vacancy rates both nationally and in each region fluctuated over the years. From 1970 to 2000, the South had the highest proportion of vacant housing units. Most state vacancy rates were higher in 2000 than in 1940, and the 11 states whose vacancy rates decreased were in either the Northeast or the West. Only Ohio and Illinois consistently ranked among the ten states with the lowest vacancy rates from 1940 to 2000, while Maine, Montana, New Hampshire, and Vermont all consistently ranked among the ten states with the highest vacancy rates during this period. These high vacancy rate states have high proportions of "seasonal vacants."

While the homeownership rate in the United States reached its highest level ever in Census 2000, important geographic differences and differences by the characteristics of the householder remained. Regionally, the Midwest (except for 1910) had the highest rate of homeownership throughout the century. By the end of the century, homeowners represented the majority of householders in the 50 states. (In the District of Columbia, a state equivalent for statistical purposes, renters continued to outnumber homeowners.) Census data reveal that from 1960 to 2000, central city householders had lower levels of homeownership than suburban householders and non-metropolitan householders throughout the period. Considering householder characteristics, older householders, White and White non-Hispanic householders, and householders living with at least one other person were more likely to be homeowners than younger householders, Hispanic or race-other-than-White householders, or people living alone, respectively.

The graphics and text in this chapter depict the trends in the number and proportional distribution of total, occupied, and vacant housing units and in the numbers and proportions of owner-occupied and renter-occupied housing units. Trends are shown for different periods of time depending on the availability of data. Housing unit and homeownership trends are examined for the United States, regions, and states (and by metropolitan status for homeownership). Additionally, the chapter discusses homeownership trends by the age, race, and Hispanic origin of the householder and by the size of the household. Appendix Table 12 provides detailed data by occupancy and tenure.

Between 1940 and 2000, about 90 percent of all housing units were occupied.

In 1940, when the U.S. Census Bureau conducted the first census of housing, there were 37.3 million housing units (see Figure 4-1).[48]   By 2000, the number of housing units had more than tripled to 115.9 million. The largest numerical census-to-census increase in housing units (19.7 million) and the highest percentage increase (29 percent) occurred from 1970 to 1980. While the smallest numerical increase in housing units (8.7 million) took place in the 1940s, the lowest percentage increase (13 percent) occurred in the 1990s.

As Figure 4-1 shows, housing units are classified as either occupied or vacant. From 1940 to 2000, the number of occupied housing units increased every decade. In 1940, there were 34.9 million occupied housing units. By 2000, the number of occupied housing units had tripled to 105.5 million. As was true for total housing units, both the largest numerical and percentage increases in occupied units occurred in the 1970s (16.9 million and 27 percent, respectively). The smallest numerical increase in occupied housing units (8.0 million) occurred in the 1940s and the lowest percentage increase (14 percent) in the 1980s.

Vacant housing units increased every decade except for the 1960s, when they declined by 1.4 percent, or by 73,000 units (see Appendix Table 12). In 1940, there were 2.5 million vacant housing units. By 2000, there were 10.4 million vacant housing units. The largest increase in vacant housing units (2.8 million) coincided with the largest increase in occupied housing units from 1970 to 1980, while the highest percentage increase (68 percent) occurred in the 1950s.

From 1940 to 2000, the proportion of all housing units that were occupied remained fairly stable (see Figure 4-2). Vacant housing units exist for a number of reasons, such as local economic conditions, seasonal housing units, or the result of people moving from one residence to another.[49]

In 1940, only 6.6 percent of all housing units were vacant, the lowest vacancy rate from 1940 to 2000. Between 1940 and 1960, the proportion of vacant housing units increased slightly, while from 1960 onward the proportion of vacant housing units fluctuated. The highest vacancy rate was in 1990, when 10.1 percent of all housing units in the United States were vacant.

---

[48] See the Glossary for the definition of a housing unit.

[49] Census 2000 subdivided vacant housing units into six housing market classifications: for rent; for sale only; rented or sold, not occupied; for seasonal, recreational, or occasional use; for migrant workers; and other vacant.

Figure 4-1.
Total Housing Units by Occupancy Status: 1940 to 2000

(Millions)

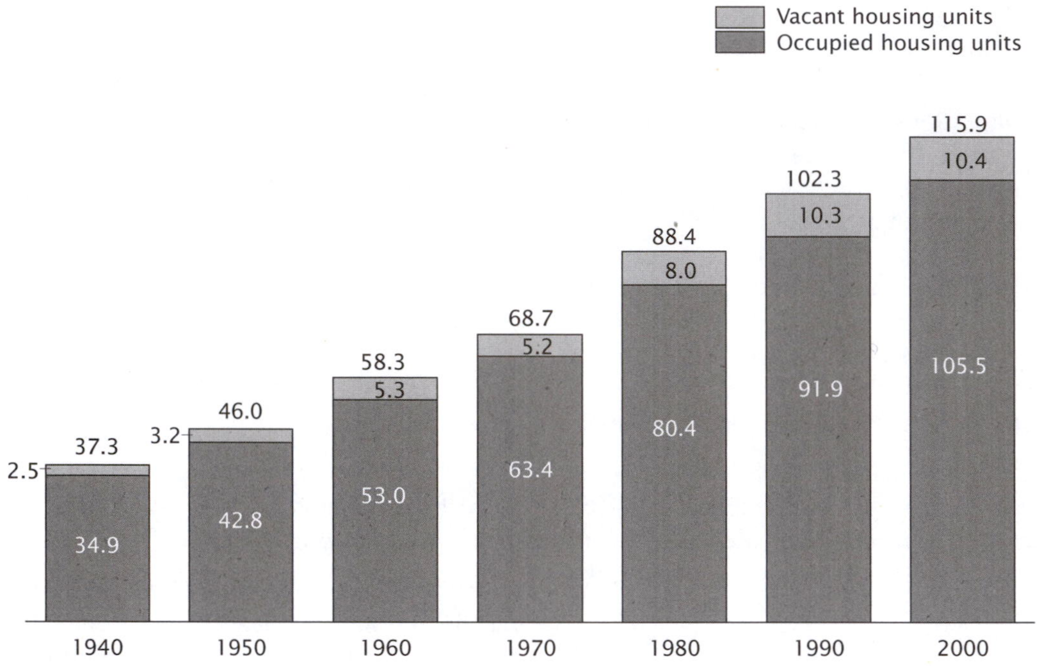

Vacant housing units
Occupied housing units

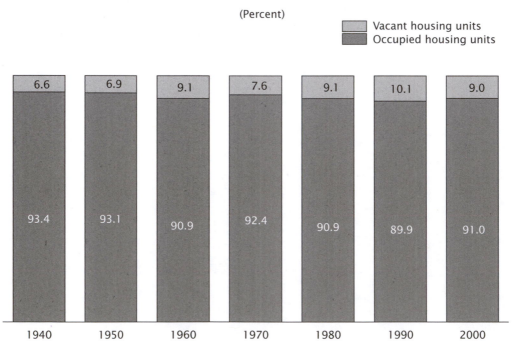

	1940	1950	1960	1970	1980	1990	2000
Total	37.3	46.0	58.3	68.7	88.4	102.3	115.9
Vacant	2.5	3.2	5.3	5.2	8.0	10.3	10.4
Occupied	34.9	42.8	53.0	63.4	80.4	91.9	105.5

Source: U.S. Census Bureau, decennial census of housing, 1940 to 2000.

Figure 4-2.
Distribution of Total Housing Units by Occupancy Status: 1940 to 2000

(Percent)

Vacant housing units
Occupied housing units

	1940	1950	1960	1970	1980	1990	2000
Vacant	6.6	6.9	9.1	7.6	9.1	10.1	9.0
Occupied	93.4	93.1	90.9	92.4	90.9	89.9	91.0

Source: U.S. Census Bureau, decennial census of housing, 1940 to 2000.

From 1970 to 2000, the South had the highest housing vacancy rate.

The regions generally followed similar patterns in the changes in their proportion of vacant housing units from 1940 to 2000 (see Figure 4-3). Every region experienced an increase in vacancy rates during the 1950s, 1970s, and 1980s and a decrease in vacancy rates during the 1960s and the 1990s.

The Northeast, the Midwest, and the South had their highest vacancy rate in 1990 (9.3 percent, 8.9 percent, and 11.8 percent, respectively). The lowest vacancy rate in the Midwest and the South occurred in 1940 (5.5 percent for both), and the Northeast's lowest vacancy rate occurred in 1950 (6.8 percent). The West differed from the other regions, as its highest vacancy rate was in 1960 (9.8 percent) and was followed by its lowest vacancy rate in 1970 (7.1 percent).

The regions experienced different ranges in their vacancy rates over the 1940 to 2000 period. The Northeast experienced the narrowest range (2.5 percentage points), and the South experienced the widest gap (6.3 percentage points).

From 1940 to 1960, the West had the highest vacancy rate among the regions. From 1970 to 2000, the South recorded the highest vacancy rates in the country, including the highest vacancy rate of any region during the period from 1940 to 2000 (11.8 percent in 1990). The Midwest or the Northeast had the lowest vacancy rate in every census from 1940 to 1990. The West had the lowest vacancy rate (7.9 percent) in 2000, becoming the only region to have had both the lowest and the highest (from 1940 to 1960) vacancy rates during the 1940 to 2000 period.

The difference in the vacancy rates between the region with the highest rate and the region with the lowest rate varied. The largest differential (3.5 percentage points) occurred in 1940, when the West had a vacancy rate of 8.9 percent and the Midwest a vacancy rate of 5.5 percent. By 1960, the difference in vacancy rates decreased to 1.4 percentage points, the smallest difference of the period. The difference increased to 2.9 percentage points in 1990 and then decreased to 2.4 percentage points in 2000.

Figure 4-3.
Vacancy Rate by Region: 1940 to 2000

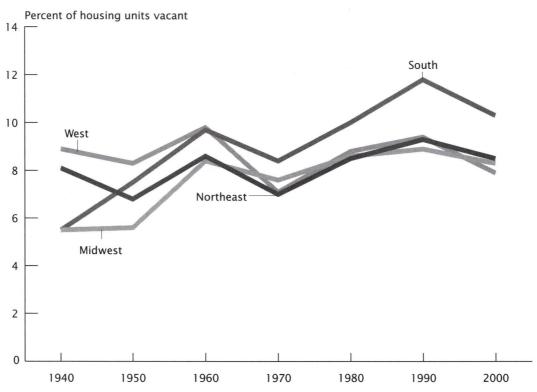

Source: U.S. Census Bureau, decennial census of housing, 1940 to 2000.

From 1940 through 2000, Maine, New Hampshire, Vermont, and Montana ranked among the ten states with the highest vacancy rates.

Most states had higher vacancy rates in 2000 than they did in 1940, but only 11 states in the Northeast or the West had lower rates: California, Colorado, Connecticut, Massachusetts, Nevada, New Hampshire, New Jersey, New York, Oregon, Rhode Island, and Washington.

From 1940 to 2000, an increasing number of states had a housing vacancy rate of 10 percent or more (see Figure 4-4). In 1940, eight states (Arizona, Colorado, Florida, Maine, New Hampshire, New Jersey, New Mexico, and Vermont) had vacancy rates of at least 10 percent. In some cases, particularly in Florida and Maine, higher vacancy rates result from a relatively high proportion of housing units classified as "Vacant for seasonal, recreational, and occasional use," also known as "vacation" homes.

By 2000, the number of states with a vacancy rate of 10 percent or more tripled to 24. Four states (Maine, New Hampshire, New Mexico, and Vermont) maintained a vacancy rate of 10 percent or higher from 1940 through 2000 (see Appendix Table 12).

Ohio and Illinois were the only states to be among the ten states with the lowest vacancy rates every decade from 1940 to 2000. The vacancy rate remained below 7 percent for the entire period in Illinois, and from 1940 to 1990 in Ohio.

The lowest vacancy rate during the period from 1940 to 2000 occurred in the District of Columbia in 1950, when only 2.4 percent of its housing units were vacant. Among the 50 states, West Virginia had the lowest vacancy rate during the period: 3.2 percent in 1940. However, by 2000, the vacancy rate in West Virginia had risen to 13 percent, a rate well above the national average of 9 percent.

Maine had the highest vacancy rate from 1940 to 2000, at 24 percent in 1970. Even at its lowest level of vacancy in 1940, 16 percent of the housing units in Maine were vacant. Maine, Montana, New Hampshire, and Vermont all ranked among the ten states with the highest vacancy rates every decade from 1940 to 2000.

The six states which were below the national vacancy rate every decade from 1940 to 2000 were Illinois, Indiana, Iowa, Ohio, Tennessee, and Virginia.

From 1940 to 2000, more states (25) experienced their lowest vacancy rate in 1940 than in any other census year. On the other hand, more states (22, including the District of Columbia) experienced their highest vacancy rate in 1990 than in any other census year.

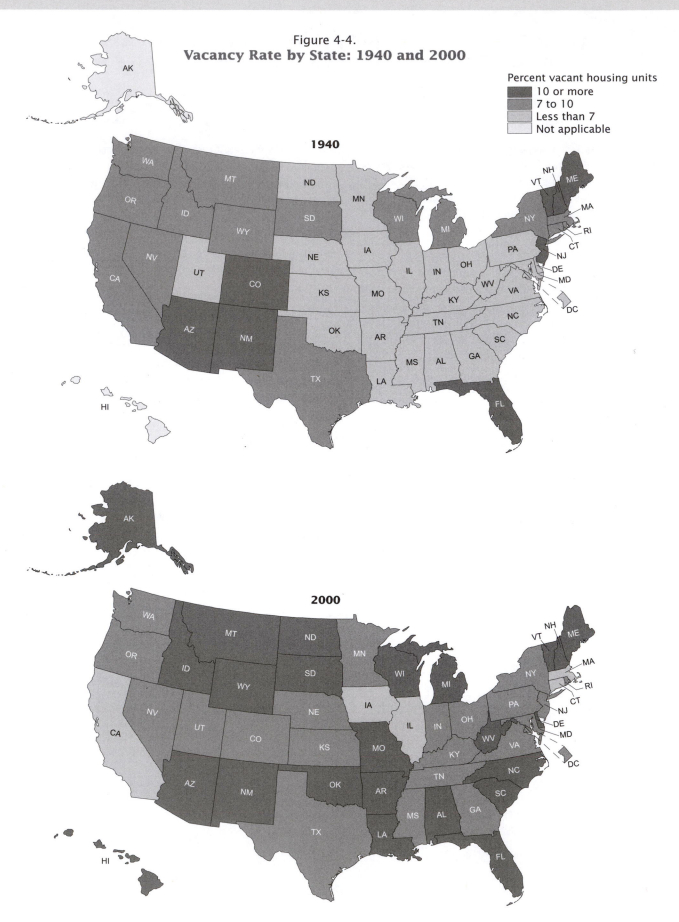

Figure 4-4.
Vacancy Rate by State: 1940 and 2000

Percent vacant housing units
- 10 or more
- 7 to 10
- Less than 7
- Not applicable

1940

2000

Source: U.S. Census Bureau, decennial census of housing, 1940 and 2000.

Since 1950, more than half of all occupied housing units have been owner occupied.

Occupied housing units are classified as either owned or rented. Renter-occupied housing units outnumbered owner-occupied housing units from 1900 to 1940 (see Figure 4-5). In 1900, there were 8.2 million renter-occupied housing units and 7.2 million owner-occupied housing units. Owner-occupied units increased by only 1.2 million from 1930 to 1940, while renter-occupied units increased by 4.3 million.

As the U.S. economy improved during the 1940s, so did the level of homeownership. From 1940 to 1950, owner-occupied units increased by 8.4 million while renter-occupied units decreased by about 400,000, the only decrease in either owner- or renter-occupied housing units to take place during the century.

From 1900 to 1950, the number of owner-occupied housing units tripled to 23.6 million. The number of renter-occupied units more than doubled to 19.3 million. By 1950, owner-occupied units outnumbered renter-occupied units and continued to do so for the remainder of the century.

From 1950 to 2000, the increase in owner-occupied units far outpaced the growth of renter-occupied units. Owner-occupied units grew by 46.3 million, to a total of 69.8 million in 2000, while renter-occupied units increased by only 16.4 million, to a total of 35.7 million in 2000.

In 1900, 47 percent of housing units were owner occupied (see Figure 4-6), a proportion that remained fairly stable until the 1930s, when the depression lowered homeownership rates. By 1940, only 44 percent of housing units were owner occupied, the lowest proportion of owners during the entire century.

By 1950, more than half of all occupied housing units were owned. Homeownership rates had surpassed rental rates and continued to increase until 1980, when 64 percent of housing units were owner occupied. The homeownership rate decreased slightly during the 1980s, but increased during the 1990s to reach the highest homeownership rate of the century in 2000 at 66 percent.

Figure 4-5.
Occupied Housing Units by Tenure: 1900 to 2000
(Millions)

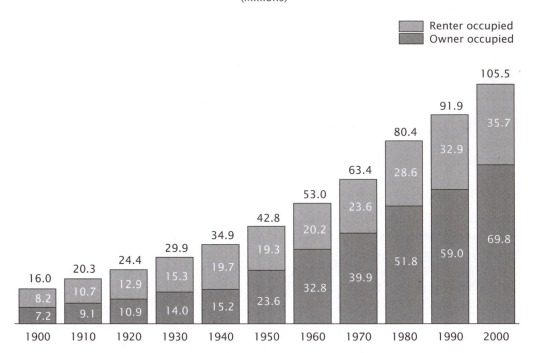

Note: Totals for 1900 to 1930 include occupied housing units with tenure unknown.
Source: U.S. Census Bureau, decennial census of population, 1900 to 1930, and decennial census of housing, 1940 to 2000.

Figure 4-6.
Distribution of Occupied Housing Units
by Tenure: 1900 to 2000
(Percent)

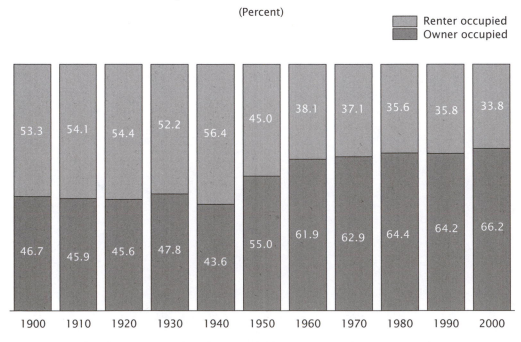

Note: Percents for 1900 to 1930 are based on occupied housing units with tenure reported.
Source: U.S. Census Bureau, decennial census of population, 1900 to 1930, and decennial census of housing, 1940 to 2000.

For every decade, except the 1910s, the Midwest had the highest homeownership rate.

Every region followed a relatively similar pattern in homeownership rates over the century and had a higher homeownership rate in 2000 than in 1900 (see Figure 4-7). Homeownership rates among the regions ranged from 37 percent in the Northeast in 1910 to 70 percent in the Midwest in 2000.

The period from 1930 to 1940 was the only decade in which the proportion of owner-occupied housing units declined in every region. Conversely, the largest percentage-point increase in homeownership rates for every region took place during the following decade, from 1940 to 1950, as the U.S. economy rebounded and home building expanded after World War II.

Homeownership rates continued to increase during the 1950s. By the 1960 census, the rate of homeownership was 50 percent or higher in every region for the first time, and it remained above 50 percent through the end of the century.

In 1940, the Midwest, the South, and the West recorded their lowest homeownership rates of any decennial census during the century, while the Northeast experienced its lowest rate in 1910. Each region's highest homeownership rate of the century occurred in 2000.

Among the regions, the Midwest had the highest homeownership rate for every decade of the century, except in 1910, when the West ranked first. More than half of all housing units in the Midwest and in the West were owner occupied at every census, except in 1940, when the homeownership rate declined to 49 percent. During the first half of the century, the West ranked behind the Midwest in terms of homeownership but was replaced by the South from 1960 to 2000. The Northeast had the lowest homeownership rate for most of the century, except for the South in 1930 and the West in 1990 and 2000.

Since 1910, the gap between the region with the highest homeownership rate and the region with the lowest homeownership rate narrowed each decade, except in the 1940s. The widest differential was 18.7 percentage points in 1910 (55 percent in the West and 37 percent in the Northeast). The smallest differential was 8.7 percentage points in 2000 (70 percent in the Midwest and 61 percent in the West).

Figure 4-7.
Percent Owner-Occupied Housing Units by Region: 1900 to 2000

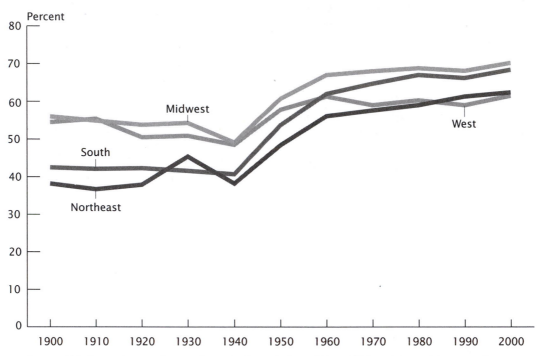

Source: U.S. Census Bureau, decennial census of population, 1900 to 1930, and decennial census of housing, 1940 to 2000.

Michigan and Minnesota were the only states to rank among the ten states with the highest homeownership rates throughout the century.

Overall, homeownership rates among the states and the District of Columbia were higher in 2000 than they were in 1900 (see Figure 4-8). Idaho, Nevada, North Dakota, and South Dakota were the only states with lower homeownership rates in 2000 than in 1900. The lowest and the highest homeownership rates of the century occurred in 1900 (24 percent in the District of Columbia and 81 percent in North Dakota).

In 1900, 26 states had homeownership rates of 50 percent or higher. Of those 26, only 3 states, Idaho, South Dakota, and North Dakota, had home-ownership rates of 70 percent or higher. By 2000, all 50 states had a homeownership rate of 50 percent or higher and the number of states with a homeowner-ship rate of 70 percent or more had increased to 17.

Several states experienced significant increases or decreases in their homeownership rates from 1900 to 2000. South Carolina experienced the largest percent-age-point increase, from 31 percent in 1900 to 72 per-cent in 2000 (an increase of 42 percentage points). Other states that experienced increases of 30 percent-age points or more were Alabama, Delaware, Georgia, Louisiana, Mississippi, New Jersey, and Rhode Island. North Dakota experienced the largest percentage-point drop (14 percentage points) in its homeownership rate, from 81 percent in 1900 to 67 percent in 2000.

Several states had consistently high (50 percent or more) homeownership rates over the century (see Appendix Table 12). These states are concentrated in the upper Midwest and the West. For example, Michigan and Minnesota were the only states that ranked among the ten states with the highest homeownership rates at every census. Idaho, Maine, and Utah were also among the top ten, with the exception of a decade or two. Utah was the only state in which the homeownership rate never dropped below 60 percent.

On the other hand, states with consistently lower homeownership rates included Alaska, Hawaii, Massachusetts, New York, and Rhode Island. In 1980, New York was the only state with more renters than homeowners, but by 1990, it reached a homeowner-ship rate exceeding 50 percent. The District of Columbia, a state equivalent for statistical purposes, had the lowest homeownership rate for every census but one (Georgia was lowest in 1930) and never reached a homeownership rate of 50 percent. In 2000, it reached its highest homeownership rate at 41 percent.

The ranking of the rate of homeownership by state changed significantly during the century. Comparing rankings in 1900 with those in 2000, Alabama, Delaware, Mississippi, and South Carolina experienced the largest increases, led by South Carolina's jump from 47th to 9th in 2000. Nevada, North Dakota, Oregon, and South Dakota experienced the largest decreases in their rank of homeownership, led by Nevada's drop from 6th in 1900 to 46th in 2000.

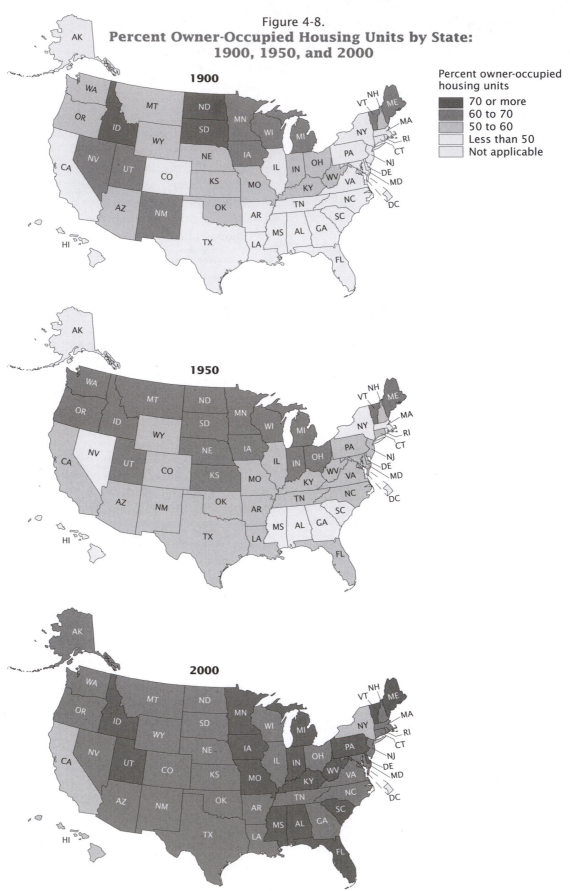

Figure 4-8.
**Percent Owner-Occupied Housing Units by State:
1900, 1950, and 2000**

Percent owner-occupied
housing units

- 70 or more
- 60 to 70
- 50 to 60
- Less than 50
- Not applicable

1900

1950

2000

Source: U.S. Census Bureau, decennial census of population, 1900, and decennial census of housing, 1950 and 2000.

Residents in central cities have been much less likely to own their homes.

From 1960 to 2000, nonmetropolitan[50] areas had higher homeownership rates than metropolitan areas (see Figure 4-9). Homeownership rates in nonmetropolitan areas ranged from 67 percent in 1960 to 74 percent in 2000. Homeownership rates in metropolitan areas ranged from 59 percent in 1960 to 64 percent in 2000. Even at its highest point, the homeownership rate in metropolitan areas was still below the lowest homeownership rate in nonmetropolitan areas (see Appendix Table 16).

Homeownership rates were higher in 2000 than in 1960 for both metropolitan and nonmetropolitan areas. The homeownership rate increased every decade from 1960 to 2000 for metropolitan areas, while the rate in nonmetropolitan areas increased

from 1960 to 1980, declined during the 1980s, and then increased again during the 1990s.

Within metropolitan areas, the homeownership rate in the suburbs was much higher than in central cities. During the period 1960 to 2000, the homeownership rate ranged from 70 percent to 73 percent in the suburbs but from 47 percent to 51 percent in central cities. In 1960, the homeownership rate in the suburbs was higher than in nonmetropolitan areas, but from 1970 onward, nonmetropolitan areas have had a higher homeownership rate than either suburban areas or central cities.

Less than half of occupied housing units in central cities were owner occupied from 1960 to 1990. Owner-occupied units exceeded renter-occupied units in central cities for the first time in Census 2000.

---

[50] See the Glossary for definitions of metropolitan areas, nonmetropolitan areas, suburbs, and central cities.

Figure 4-9.
Percent Owner-Occupied Housing Units by Metropolitan Status: 1960 to 2000

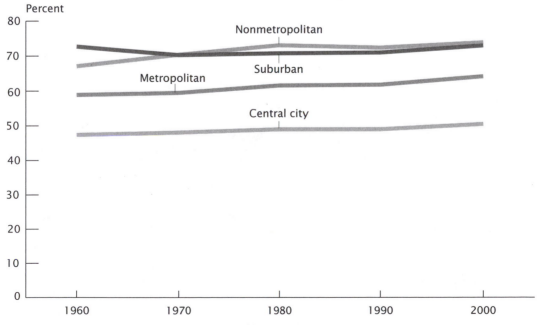

Source: U.S. Census Bureau, decennial census of housing, 1960 to 2000.

Householders age 65 years and over were more likely to own a home than householders under age 65.

As people age, they are more likely to have characteristics that make it easier to own a home, such as being married and having a higher income. In general, homeownership rates increase as age increases, peaking at 65-to-74 years of age and declining with age thereafter.[51] As Figure 4-10 shows, from 1960 to 2000, householders age 65 years and over were more likely to own their homes than householders under age 65.

The homeownership rate among householders age 65 and over declined between 1960 and 1970; among householders under age 65 it declined between 1980 and 1990, but both groups attained their highest homeownership rates in 2000, 78 percent and 63 percent, respectively.

In addition to having higher homeownership rates, elderly[52] homeowners experienced a larger percentage-point increase in their homeownership rate from 1960 to 2000, increasing by 6.2 percentage points, than householders under age 65, who increased by 4.7 percentage points.

The difference between the homeownership rates of householders age 65 and over and householders under age 65 converged to its lowest point in 1970, 5.8 percentage points. From 1970 to 2000, the difference in their homeownership rates steadily widened. The homeownership rate among householders age 65 and over steadily increased. The homeownership rate among householders under age 65 increased during the 1970s, decreased during the 1980s, and then increased again during the 1990s. In 2000, the differential between their homeownership rates was the largest in the 1960 to 2000 period: 15.1 percentage points.

---

[51] U.S. Census Bureau. 2001e. *Housing Characteristics: 2000*, by Jeanne Woodward and Bonnie Damon.

[52] In this report, "elderly" is defined as anyone 65 years old or older. See the Glossary.

Figure 4-10.
Homeownership Rate by Age of Householder: 1960 to 2000
(Percent)

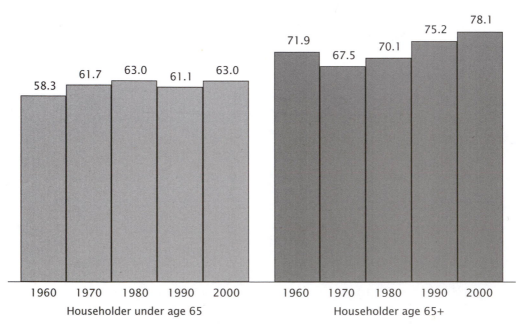

Source: U.S. Census Bureau, decennial census of housing, 1960 to 2000.

In 1980 and 2000, householders who were Black, Hispanic, or of two or more races were more likely to rent than to own their homes.

Homeownership rates were higher in 2000 than in 1980 for all race groups and for Hispanics, however, there were also distinct differences among these groups (see Figure 4-11).

White non-Hispanic householders had the highest homeownership rates in 1980 and 2000, 68 percent and 72 percent, respectively, and White householders[53] had only slightly lower rates. The homeownership rates of all other races and of Hispanics were much lower and below the national averages of 1980 and 2000 (64 percent and 66 percent, respectively).

Following White householders, American Indian and Alaska Native householders and Asian and Pacific Islander householders had the next highest home-ownership rates, respectively. Their homeownership

rates were in the 52 percent to 56 percent range in 1980 and 2000.

Blacks and Hispanics had similar homeownership rates in 1980 and 2000, below 50 percent. In 1980, the rate for Blacks was 44 percent and for Hispanics it was 43 percent. In 2000, the homeownership rate for both groups and for householders who reported them-selves as more than one race was 46 percent. At the end of the century, householders who were Black, Hispanic, or of two or more races were more likely to rent than to own their homes.

In addition to having the highest homeownership rate, White non-Hispanic householders also had the largest increase in their homeownership rate from 1980 to 2000 of any race group and Hispanics (4.0 percentage points). Asian and Pacific Islander householders had the smallest increase in their homeownership rate (0.7 percentage points).

---

[53] Including White Hispanic householders.

Figure 4-11.
Homeownership Rate by Race and Hispanic Origin of Householder: 1980 and 2000

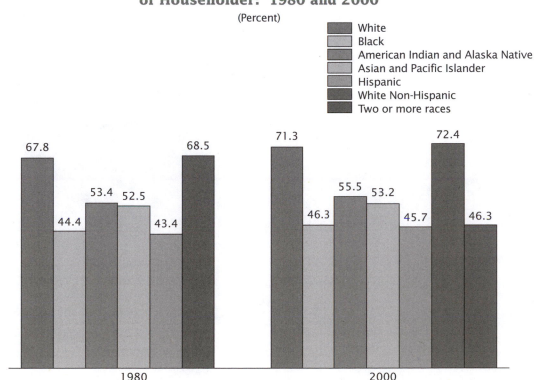

(Percent)

- White
- Black
- American Indian and Alaska Native
- Asian and Pacific Islander
- Hispanic
- White Non-Hispanic
- Two or more races

1980: 67.8, 44.4, 53.4, 52.5, 43.4, 68.5

2000: 71.3, 46.3, 55.5, 53.2, 45.7, 72.4, 46.3

Source: U.S. Census Bureau, decennial census of housing, 1980 and 2000.

People living alone were less likely to own their homes than householders living with other people.

From 1940 to 2000, householders living alone were less likely to own their homes than householders living with other people (see Figure 4-12). In part, this reflects higher mobility rates and the generally more limited economic resources available for one-person households. In addition, some one-person householders may prefer to rent, rather than own, their homes.

The homeownership rate of householders living with other people rose from 44 percent in 1940 to 71 percent in 2000. The homeownership rate for householders living alone ranged from 39 percent in 1940 to 52 percent in 2000, the first time people living alone became more likely to own, rather than rent, their homes. Both groups experienced their lowest homeownership rate in 1940 and their highest homeownership rate in 2000.

Both types of householders experienced one decade of decline in their homeownership rate, during the 1950s for one-person households and the 1980s for householders living with other people. The 1980s was also the decade in which householders living alone experienced the largest increase in their homeownership rate.

From 1940 to 1980, the differential between the homeownership rates of householders living alone and householders living with other people widened. The difference in their homeownership rates increased from 4.6 percentage points in 1940 to 27 percentage points in 1980. From 1980 to 2000, the differential converged.

Figure 4-12.
Homeownership Rate by Household Size: 1940 to 2000
(Percent)

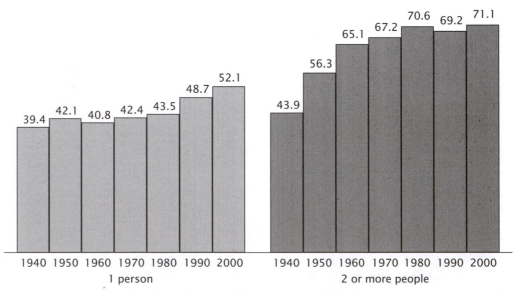

Source: U.S. Census Bureau, decennial census of housing, 1940 to 2000.

Chapter Highlights
HOUSEHOLDS

National Trends

In 1900, the most common household contained seven or more people. From 1940 to 2000, households with two people represented the most common household size.

Average household size declined from 4.60 in 1900 to 2.59 in 2000, or by 44 percent.

Householders age 45 and over represented the majority of all householders during the period 1950 to 2000.

Between 1950 and 2000, married-couple households declined from more than three-fourths of all households (78 percent) to just over one-half (52 percent) of all households.

The proportional share of one-person households increased more than any other size. In 1950, one-person households represented 1 of every 10 households (9.5 percent), but by 2000, they composed 1 of every 4 households (26 percent).

During the period 1960 to 2000, women age 65 and over accounted for 27 percent to 33 percent of one-person households, but just 5 percent to 8 percent of the total population.

In every census from 1970 to 2000, approximately three-fourths of all female householders age 65 and over lived alone.

The proportion of one-person households maintained by women decreased in each census, 1970 to 2000, although women still constituted the majority (57 percent) of one-person households in 2000.

In 1970, women represented about 1 of every 5 (21 percent) householders in the United States. By 2000, the proportion had grown to more than 1 of every 3 (36 percent) U.S. householders.

For total, married-couple, and other family households, the proportion of female householders among Black householders exceeded the proportion of female householders among householders of any other race or Hispanics.

In 1960, 3 of every 5 (59 percent) married-couple households included at least one of their own children under age 18. By 1990 (and in 2000), less than half (46 percent) of married-couple households had an own child under age 18.

In 1950, only 1 of every 5 (19 percent) male family households with no wife present had an own child under age 18. By 2000, half (50 percent) of all male family households with no wife present had at least one own child under age 18.

Regional Trends

The West's share of all U.S. households increased during every decade of the century, while the slow growth of households in the Midwest led to this region representing an ever-shrinking share of all households.

By 2000, one-person households represented about one-fourth of all households in each region.

The West had the highest proportion of one-person households for each census from 1940 to 1970. The Northeast had the highest regional proportion from 1980 to 2000.

State Trends

In 1940, fewer than 20 percent of the households in every state were one-person households. In 1970, only California, the District of Columbia, and New York had at least 20 percent one-person households. By 2000, every state, except Utah, had at least 20 percent one-person households.

Nevada, California, Arizona, and Idaho ranked among the 10 states with the highest percentage of one-person households in 1900 and 1940, but ranked among the 12 states with the lowest percentage of one-person households in 2000.

Chapter 5
HOUSEHOLDS

The number, size, types, and age, sex, and racial composition of households in the United States markedly changed in the 20th century, particularly in the later decades. Contributing factors included women having fewer children, changes in age at first marriage, increased mobility of the population, affordability of homes, and the overall increase in the racial and ethnic diversity of the U.S. population. A small proportion of the U.S. population lives in group quarters: of the 281.4 million people counted in Census 2000, 273.6 million people lived in households, while 7.8 million people lived in group quarters (such as correctional institutions, nursing homes, and college dormitories).

In 1900, nearly half of the U.S. population lived in households of six or more people. By 2000, more than half of the population lived in households of one, two, or three people. The trends in the number and proportion of householders by age through the last half of the century followed the movement of the baby-boom generation through the census years. Married-couple households fell from over three-fourths (78 percent) of all households in 1950 to just over one-half (52 percent) of all households in 2000. Other major household types increased, especially one-person households. In the last several decades of the century, the share of one-person households maintained by male householders increased and male householders with no wife present became increasingly likely to have children in their households.

Between 1900 and 2000, overall regional and state trends in the number and distribution of households followed the population trends for these areas. Regionally, the South's and the West's shares of all households increased during the century, while the Northeast's and the Midwest's shares decreased. The proportions of one-person households in all states and regions increased rapidly in the latter part of the century. Notably, in the first half of the century, most western states had much higher proportions of one-person households than states in other regions, but the ranking of some western states changed markedly during the century. For example, Arizona, California, Idaho, and Nevada ranked among the states with the highest proportions of one-person households in 1900, but the lowest proportions in 2000.

The graphics and text in this chapter depict the trends in the number and proportional distribution of households, sizes of households, and various household types by age, sex, race, and Hispanic origin of the householder. These changes are described for the United States, regions, and states. Age of householder trends focus on broad age groups, and trends in the gender of the householder are discussed for specific family types and by race and Hispanic origin. Detailed data by size and type of household are provided in Appendix Tables 13, 14, and 15.

The proportion of households with five or more people declined significantly from 1900 to 2000.

While the total U.S. population increased greatly during the 20th century, the percentage increase in the number of households was even greater, reflecting the trend of higher proportions of people living in smaller households. From 1900 to 2000, the total U.S. population increased from 76 million to 281 million, an increase of 270 percent. By comparison, the total number of U.S. households grew from 16 million in 1900 to 105 million in 2000, an increase of 561 percent (see Figure 5-1 and Appendix Table 13).

Available data on the number of households by size shows that, in absolute numbers, households with one, two, three, or four members increased every decade. Households with five or more people declined in the 1940s, then increased until 1970, declined again in the 1970s and 1980s, and increased again in the 1990s.

Most of the increase in the number of households from 1900 to 2000 (89.5 million) occurred among households having one or two members. These categories accounted for nearly two-thirds (65 percent) of the total U.S. increase in the number of households over the 100-year period, while households with 5 or more members represented just 5 percent of the total increase in U.S. households.

In 1900, households with seven or more people represented the most common household size (see Appendix Table 13), reflecting the high fertility in the United States at that time, plus a greater tendency for people to live in extended family households. Two-person households became the most common household size by 1940 and remained so for the rest of the century.

The proportion of households with five or more people declined significantly from 1900 to 2000, from 45 percent to just 11 percent (see Figure 5-2). The share of households with four people, while generally decreasing, remained in the range of 14 percent to 18 percent of all households during the century. Similarly, three-person households remained in the range of 17 percent to 23 percent over the period. Still, the shares of both three-person and four-person households were at their lowest levels at the end of the century.

The shares of both one-person and two-person households greatly increased during the 20th century.   In 1900, only 1 of every 5 (20 percent) U.S. households had one or two people. Since 1980, households of one or two people have represented an increasing majority of households in the United States, reaching a combined 58 percent of all households by 2000.   The shares of one-person and two-person households increased nearly every decade, and the share of each of these household sizes was at its highest level at the end of the century. In 2000, about 1 out of every 3 U.S. households (33 percent) had two people, and 1 out of every 4 households (26 percent) had one person.

The proportion of the household population living in large households has, by definition, always been much larger than the proportion of households that are large. In 1900, the 45 percent of households with five or more people accounted for 66 percent of the household population, and the 30 percent of households with six or more people accounted for 50 percent of the household population.   In 2000, the 11 percent of households with five or more people accounted for 24 percent of the household population, and the 4 percent of households with six or more people accounted for 11 percent of the household population (see Appendix Table 13).

Figure 5-1.
Households by Size: 1900 and 1940 to 2000
(Millions)

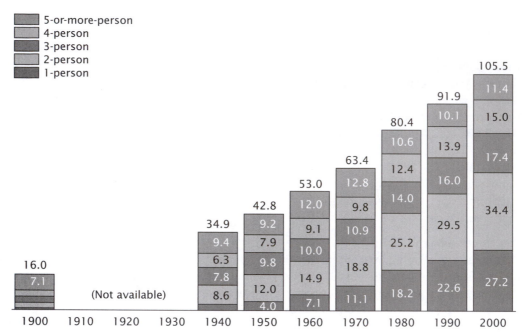

Source: U.S. Census Bureau, decennial census of population, 1900, and decennial census of housing, 1940 to 2000.

Figure 5-2.
Distribution of Households by Size: 1900 and 1940 to 2000
(Percent)

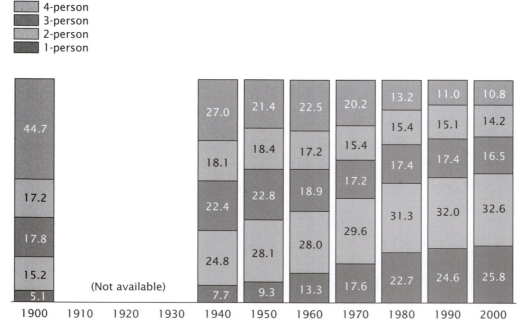

Source: U.S. Census Bureau, decennial census of population, 1900, and decennial census of housing, 1940 to 2000.

Average household size declined by 2 people per household during the century, from 4.6 people per household in 1900 to 2.6 in 2000.

The total population of the United States consists of people who live in households and those who live in group quarters.[54] Average household size is determined by dividing the total household population (or equivalently, the total population excluding the group quarters population) by the total number of households. In the United States, as the proportion of the population living in one-person and two-person households grew, the average number of people per household declined.

Available data for each census year indicates a continuous decline in average household size during the century (see Figure 5-3). Over the first four decades of the 20th century, average household size declined by an average of nearly 1 person, from 4.60 to 3.68 people per household. Then, over the next five decades, average household size again dropped by

another person, from 3.68 in 1940 to 2.63 in 1990. Average household size declined the least in the 1990s, from just 2.63 to 2.59 people per household. Over the century, average household size declined by 2 people per household, from 4.60 in 1900 to 2.59 in 2000.

Steep declines in average household size occurred in the 1930s and 1940s, in part reflecting the low fertility through the end of World War II. The baby-boom period (1946 to 1964) then had a leveling effect on average household size for the 1950 to 1970 period. The steepest decline in average household size occurred in the 1970s, a period coinciding with the baby-bust period, relatively low levels of immigration, and increasing proportions of people living alone.

As mentioned above, the smallest decline in average household size occurred in the 1990s. Relatively higher immigration levels and the tendency for immigrants to live in larger households may have kept average household size relatively unchanged from 1990 to 2000.

---

[54] See Appendix Table 13. For definitions of households and group quarters, see the Glossary. In Census 2000, 97.2 percent of the population lived in households and 2.8 percent in group quarters.

Figure 5-3.
Average Household Size: 1900 and 1930 to 2000
(People per household)

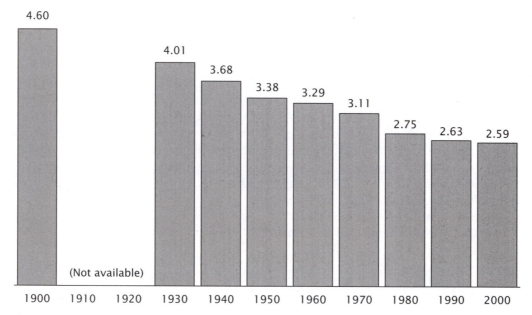

Source: U.S. Census Bureau, decennial census of population, 1900 and 1930 to 2000, and decennial census of housing, 1940.

From 1900 to 1970, the majority of U.S. households were in the Northeast and Midwest, but since 1980, the majority were in the South and West.

The pattern of change in the total number of households by region mirrors the pattern of change in total population size. The total number of households increased every decade in each region, growing rapidly in the West throughout the century and sharply in the South after 1960.

The Midwest had more households than any other region throughout the period 1900 to 1950 (see Figure 5-4). By 1960, the South had overtaken the Midwest, and the gap between these two regions widened with each decade. The West had far fewer households than any other region until 1990, when it surpassed the Northeast.

Among the regions, the Midwest and the Northeast had the most similar patterns of growth in their total number of households during the 100-year period. In the Midwest, the number of households was 4.4 times larger in 2000 compared with 1900, and in the Northeast it was 4.5 times larger. In contrast, in the South, the number of households in 2000 was 7.8 times larger (38.0 million) than in 1900 (4.9 million), and in the West, it was 25.3 times larger (see Appendix Table 14).

The growth of households differed by region, altering each region's proportional share of the total number of U.S. households. Rapid growth in the West increased its share of all households during every decade of the century to 21 percent by 2000 (see Figure 5-5). Conversely, the slow growth of households in the Midwest reduced its share of all households from 35 percent in 1900 to 23 percent in 2000. The proportional share of U.S. households in the Northeast also generally declined during the century, dropping from 29 percent in 1900 to 19 percent by 2000. The South's share of households followed a more distinctive pattern, declining during the first part of the century, increasing in the 1930s, followed by a period of stability from 1940 to 1960, and then greatly increasing from 1960 through the end of the century.

The Midwest's proportional share of U.S. households declined the most (12 percentage points) during the period 1900 to 2000, from 35 percent in 1900 to 23 percent in 2000. The Northeast experienced a 9-percentage-point loss in share during the century. The West experienced the greatest gain (16 percentage points) in share of all households over the 100-year period.

As noted above, the South's share of U.S. households declined during the first three decades of the century. From 1900 to 1930, its proportional share of all households fell by nearly 2 percentage points. After less than a percentage point increase in the 1930s, followed by a stable period from 1940 to 1960, the South's proportional share of all households rose by 7 percentage points from 1960 to 2000. Overall, the South had the most stable proportional share of all households, ranging from 29 percent to 36 percent.

Combined, the Northeast and Midwest regions represented the majority of all U.S. households during the period 1900 to 1970. However, this majority became smaller every decade, declining from 64 percent in 1900 to 52 percent in 1970. By 1980, the South and West represented the majority (52 percent) of all U.S. households. By 2000, the South and West together accounted for 57 percent of all households.

Throughout the century, the proportional shares of households remained highly correlated with population size, differing to the extent that the average number of people per household varied by region. For example, at the end of the century, the Northeast, the Midwest, and the South had slightly higher proportional shares of households than population, while the West held a higher proportion of the population than households. This occurs because the West had a relatively larger average household size (2.75 people per household) than the Northeast, the Midwest, and the South (2.56, 2.53, and 2.56 people per household, respectively).[55]

---

[55] See U.S. Census Bureau. 2001d. *Households and Families: 2000*, by Tavia Simmons and Grace O'Neill.

Figure 5-4.
Total Households by Region: 1900 to 2000

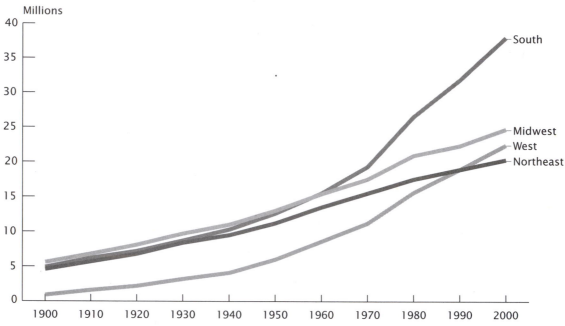

Source: U.S. Census Bureau, decennial census of population 1900 to 1930, and decennial census of housing, 1940 to 2000.

Figure 5-5.
Distribution of Households by Region:
1900 to 2000

(Percent)

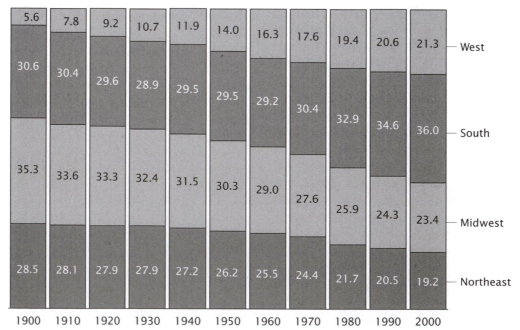

Source: U.S. Census Bureau, decennial census of population 1900 to 1930, and decennial census of housing, 1940 to 2000.

From 1950 to 2000, slightly more than half of all households were maintained by people age 45 years and over.

The census-to-census growth from 1950 to 2000 in the number of households in categories defined by the age of the householder reflects the changing population by age during this period. The number of householders age 25 to 44 years, 45 to 64 years, and 65 years and over increased every census (see Figure 5-6). Households maintained by a person under age 25 years increased until 1980, declined during the 1980s, then increased slightly in the 1990s. The decline of 1.7 million householders under age 25 in the 1980s coincides with a large decline (5.7 million people) in the population age 15 to 24 years, as the baby-boom generation moved out of this age group during the decade.

As the baby-boom cohort became householders and aged, it greatly affected the number of householders in particular age groups. For example, the relatively large increases in the number of households maintained by people under age 25 in the 1960s and 1970s, by people age 25 to 44 in the 1970s and 1980s, and by people age 45 to 64 in the 1990s all occurred as the baby-boom cohort moved into these age ranges during these decades.

The maximum increase in the number of householders in the second half of the 20th century occurred in the 1970s for the total number of households and for every broad age group, except householders age 45 to 64 years, who increased the most in the 1990s. The decade with the minimum census-to-census change in the number of households varied by age group. During the 50-year period, the only decline in the number of householders among the age groups considered occurred in the 1980s for householders under age 25.

Each of the four broad age groups had a decade in the period 1950 to 2000 when it was the fastest-growing group in terms of percentage change in the number of households. Three of the four groups (all except householders age 65 and over) also had at least one decade when it was the slowest-growing group. Householders age 25 to 44 years most often (in the 1950s, 1960s, and 1990s) grew by the least percentage.

The shares that each age group represented of the total number of households varied over the decades (see Figure 5-7). These fluctuations particularly occurred for householders age 25 to 44 years and 45 to 64 years. Householders under age 25 represented an increasing proportion of all households from 1950 to 1980, then declined in the 1980s and 1990s. Householders age 65 and over increased as a proportion of all householders from 1950 to 1990, then declined in the 1990s.

Householders age 45 and over represented the majority of all householders during the period 1950 to 2000. This group's share increased from 1950 to 1970, declined from 1970 to 1990, then increased again from 1990 to 2000. The share of all householders age 45 and over ranged from a low of 51 percent in 1990 to a high of 56 percent in 1970.

Figure 5-6.
**Total Households by Age of Householder:
1950 to 2000**
(Millions)

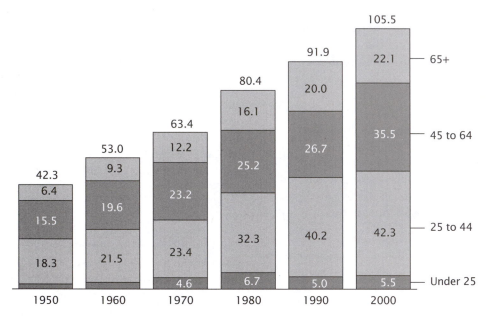

Source: U.S. Census Bureau, decennial census of population, 1950 to 2000.

Figure 5-7.
**Distribution of Households by Age
of Householder: 1950 to 2000**
(Percent)

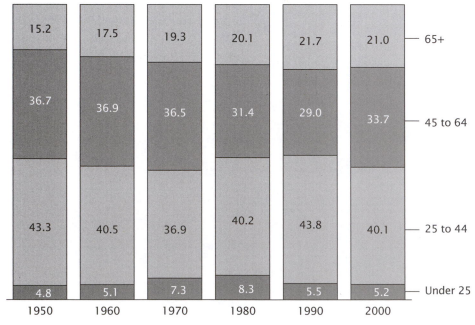

Source: U.S. Census Bureau, decennial census of population, 1950 to 2000.

Married-couple households declined from more than 3 out of every 4 households (78 percent) in 1950 to just over one-half (52 percent) in 2000.

Households may be classified as either family households or nonfamily households. Within family households, married-couple households represent the most common type. Within nonfamily households, one-person households (people living alone) represent the most common type.[56]

All types of households increased numerically between each census 1950 to 2000 (see Figure 5-8). The largest decadal increase in the number of households for 3 of the 4 major household types (all except married-couple households) occurred in the 1970s. The largest numerical increase of married-couple households occurred in the 1950s.

Although married-couple households remain the most common type of household, one-person households increased more than any other type during the 50-year period. Of the total increase of 63 million households, one-person households accounted for 23 million, married couples for 21 million, other family households for 13 million, and other nonfamily households for 6 million.

During each decade from 1950 to 2000, one of the nonfamily household types grew fastest. Other nonfamily households had the highest percentage increase every decade except for the 1960s, when one-person households grew fastest. Conversely, one of the family household types grew the slowest each decade. Married-couple households increased by the lowest percentage each decade except for the 1950s, when other family households grew the slowest.

While all household types increased numerically from decade to decade, the slower increase of married-couple households resulted in a continual shrinking of the proportion of all U.S. households represented by married-couple households (see Figure 5-9). Between 1950 and 2000, married-couple households declined from more than 3 out of every 4 households (78 percent) to just over one half (52 percent) of all households.

Other family households declined as a proportion of all households in the 1950s, but increased every decade thereafter. By 2000, other family households represented about 1 of every 6 U.S. households (16 percent).

The shares of all U.S. households represented by both types of nonfamily households increased every decade during the period 1950 to 2000. The proportional share of one-person households increased more than any other type. In 1950, one-person households represented about 1 of every 10 households (9.5 percent). By 2000, one-person households comprised 1 out of every 4 households (26 percent). The proportional share of other nonfamily households also increased every decade. In 1950, other nonfamily households represented only 1.1 percent of households in the United States. By 2000, this category still represented the smallest share of the major household types, but it had increased to 6.1 percent of all U.S. households.

---

[56] For definitions of households, householders, and various household types, see the Glossary.

Figure 5-8.
Households by Type: 1950 to 2000
(Millions)

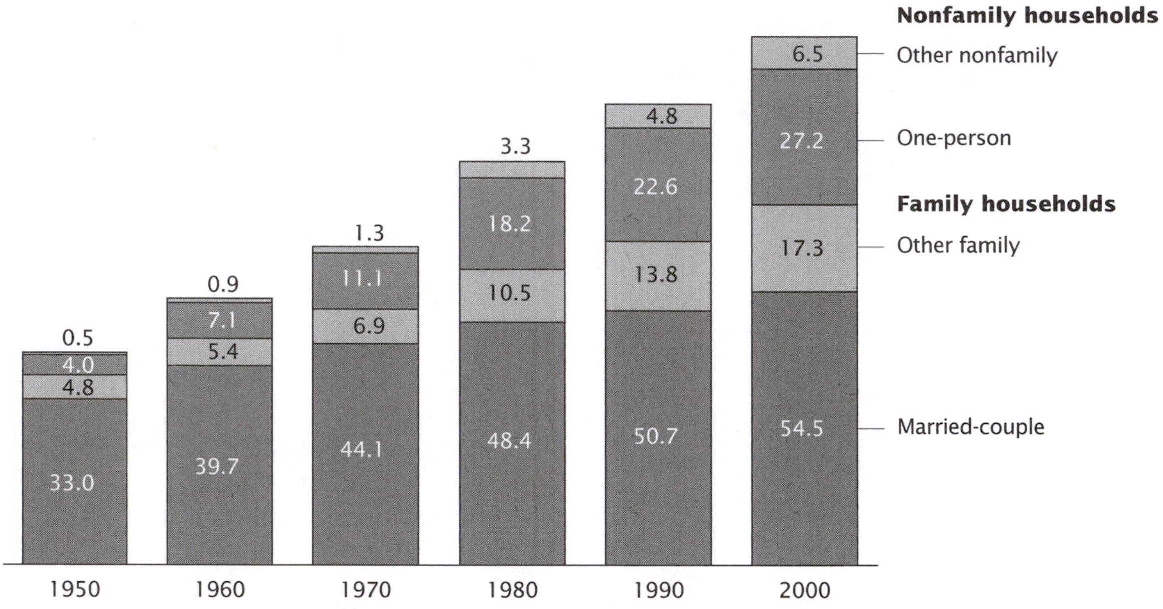

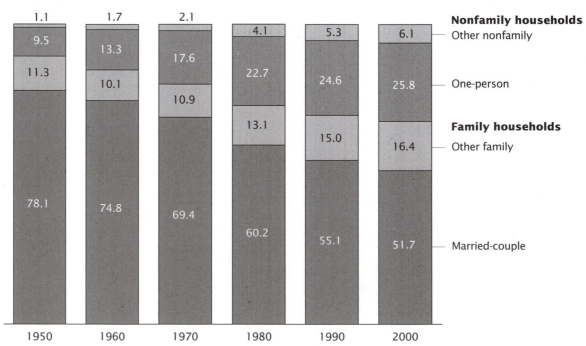

Nonfamily households
Other nonfamily
One-person
Family households
Other family
Married-couple

Source: U.S. Census Bureau, decennial census of population, 1950 to 2000, and decennial census of housing, 1950 and 1960.

Figure 5-9.
Distribution of Households by Type:
1950 to 2000
(Percent)

Nonfamily households
Other nonfamily
One-person
Family households
Other family
Married-couple

Source: U.S. Census Bureau, decennial census of population, 1950 to 2000, and decennial census of housing, 1950 and 1960.

All regions had increasing proportions of one-person households, reaching around one-fourth of all households in 2000.

As noted previously, the proportional share of all U.S. households represented by one-person households increased more than any other major household type, comprising one-fourth of all U.S. households (26 percent) by 2000. Similar regional trends occurred over the decades, with one-person households also representing about one-fourth of the households in each region by the end of the century (see Figure 5-10 and Appendix Table 14).

During the century, the Northeast, the Midwest, and the South all had similar proportions and patterns of growth of one-person households. The West also had an increasing proportion of one-person households 1900 to 2000, but its levels and pattern of change followed the most distinct trend of the regions.

In 1900, the West's proportion of one-person households (13 percent) far exceeded the proportions of the other regions, and it maintained the highest proportion of one-person households for each census, 1940 to 1970. Since 1980, the Northeast ranked 1st among the regions in the proportion of one-person households.

The gap between the regions with the highest and the lowest proportion of one-person households narrowed with each census from 1900 to 1990, then became slightly wider in the 1990s. Differences between the Northeast's, the Midwest's, and the South's proportions of one-person households remained within a narrow range throughout the century, from 0.9 percentage points in 1900 to a maximum of 2.4 percentage points in 1970.

Although the West held the highest regional proportion of one-person households through 1970, the gap narrowed as every other region's increase in their proportion of one-person households exceeded the West's increase. By 1990 and again in 2000, the West had the smallest proportion of one-person households among the regions.

Figure 5-10.
**Percent One-Person Households by Region:
1900 and 1940 to 2000**

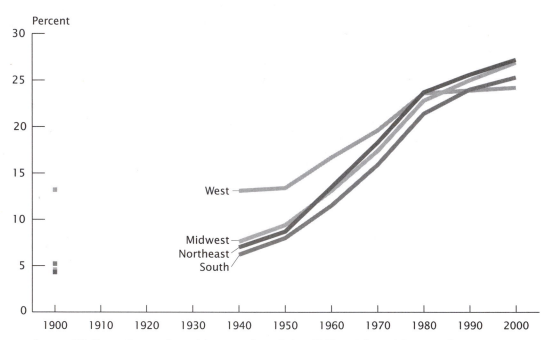

Source: U.S. Census Bureau, decennial census of population, 1900, and decennial census of housing, 1940 to 2000.

No state had at least 20 percent one-person households in 1940, but all states except Utah exceeded this level in 2000.

The major growth in the proportion of one-person households occurred in the second half of the century. Data available from the population census of 1900 show that one-person households constituted at least 10 percent of all households in only 11 states, 10 western states, plus North Dakota (see Appendix Table 14). Although data are not available from the 1910 through 1930 censuses, data from the first census of housing in 1940 show the number of states with at least 10 percent one-person households remained essentially unchanged: Nevada, Montana, Washington, California, Oregon, Wyoming, Arizona, Colorado, and Idaho (just nine states). All of them had been among the 11 with at least 10 percent one-person households in 1900, and all were in the West. Of the 11 states with at least 10 percent one-person households in 1900, New Mexico's and North Dakota's proportions declined below 10 percent by 1940 (to 8.4 percent and 7.9 percent, respectively). The proportion of one-person households increased in 34 states and the District of Columbia between 1900 and 1940 and declined in 14 states.

No state had at least 20 percent one-person households in 1940. The only states with at least 15 percent one-person households in 1940 were Nevada (18 percent) and Montana (15 percent, see Figure 5-11).

While little growth occurred in the proportions of one-person households in the first 40 years of the century, 30 years later, one-person households comprised at least 10 percent of the total number of households in all 50 states and the District of Columbia. Most states in 1970 had proportions of one-person households ranging between 15 percent and 20 percent of all households. Only California, the District of Columbia, and New York had at least 20 percent one-person households. All 11 states with less than 15 percent one-person households were either in the South or the West.

The proportion of one-person households was higher in every state in 1970 than in 1940. Of the 48 states in 1940, the proportions of one-person households in the states with the 10 highest proportions increased but did not double. However, in 35 of the remaining 38 states (all except New Hampshire, New Mexico, and Utah), the proportion of one-person households more than doubled from 1940 to 1970.

Between 1970 and 2000, the proportions of one-person households again increased in every state and the District of Columbia. While no state's proportion of one-person households doubled from 1970 to 2000, one-person households represented at least 20 percent of all households in 49 of the 50 states by the end of the century, when only Utah (18 percent) had less than 20 percent one-person households.

In 2000, one-person households represented at least 25 percent of all households in 36 of the 50 states, where the proportion ranged narrowly from 25.0 percent to 29.3 percent, led by North Dakota. The next highest-ranking states in percentage one-person households were all in the Northeast—Rhode Island, New York, Massachusetts, and Pennsylvania.[57]

Among the 14 states with the lowest percentage (less than 25 percent) one-person households in 2000, four of these states—Nevada, California, Arizona, and Idaho—had ranked among the 10 states with the highest percentage one-person households in 1900 and 1940. Nevada and California also had ranked among the states with the 10 highest percentage one-person households as recently as 1980.

---

[57] One-person households represented 44 percent of all households in the District of Columbia in 2000.

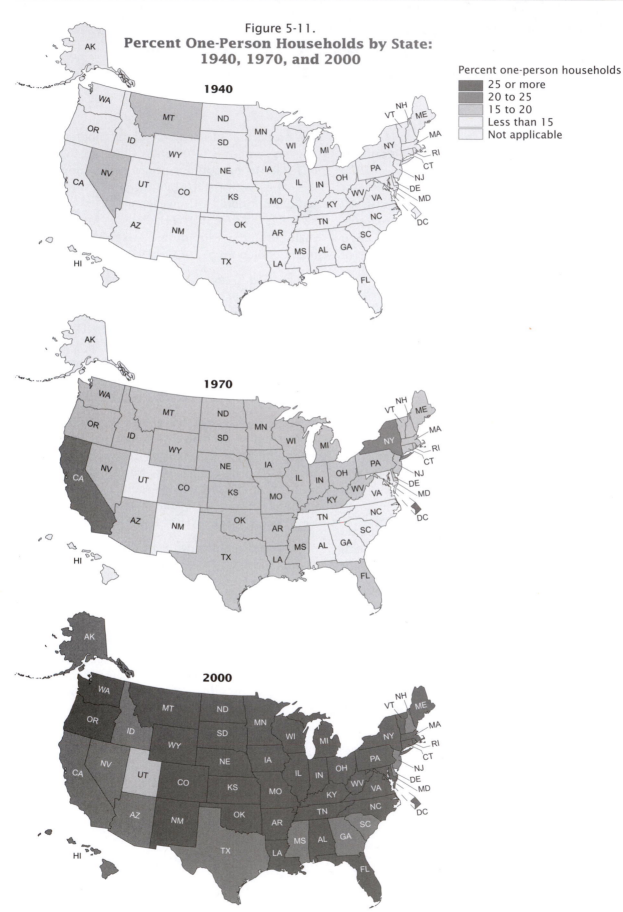

Figure 5-11.
**Percent One-Person Households by State:
1940, 1970, and 2000**

1940

1970

2000

Percent one-person households

25 or more
20 to 25
15 to 20
Less than 15
Not applicable

Source: U.S. Census Bureau, decennial census of housing, 1940, 1970, and 2000.

The number of one-person households increased every census, 1960 to 2000, for men, women, younger householders, and older householders.

From 1960 to 2000, the number of one-person households increased for both male and female householders and for householders both under age 65 and age 65 and over. Between 1960 and 2000, the number of men under age 65 living alone increased by 7.6 million, women under age 65 living alone by 5.7 million, men age 65 and over living alone by 1.5 million, and women age 65 and over living alone by 5.3 million (see Figure 5-12).

Of the four age-sex groups shown in Figure 5-12, the number of women age 65 and over living alone increased more than any other group in the 1960s, but the number of men under age 65 living alone increased the most for each decade thereafter.

The largest decadal increase in the number of one-person households for each group occurred in the 1970s, with the exception of men age 65 and over, who increased the most in the 1990s. The number of men under age 65 living alone more than doubled in the 1970s, the highest proportional increase in any decade during the period among the four groups considered. In part, the increases in one-person households in the 1970s coincide with the influx of the baby-boom generation into new households and increasing levels of divorce. Increases for women age 65 and over living alone throughout the period 1960 to 2000 suggest that growing numbers of women in this age group are living alone as a result of widowhood.

In 1960, more women under age 65 lived alone than did any of the other groups. In 1970, women age 65 and over living alone outnumbered people living alone in the other groups. In each census, 1980 to 2000, men under age 65 represented the age and sex group with the most one-person households. Men age 65 and over had both the fewest one-person households and the least increase in one-person households each census, 1960 to 2000.

From 1970 to 2000, men under age 65 living alone increased their share of the total number of one-person households (see Figure 5-13). From 1960 to 1990, the proportion of one-person households composed of women under age 65 decreased.

Over the period 1960 to 2000, women under age 65 and men age 65 and over had their largest proportional shares of one-person households in 1960; women 65 and over in 1970, and men under age 65 in 2000.

Although both men and women householders under age 65 represented sizable proportions of all one-person households, these proportions were much less than these age groups' share of the total population. For example, while men under age 65 represented a range of 25 percent to 34 percent of all one-person households over the years 1960 to 2000, this age group represented 44 percent to 45 percent of the population during this same period. Similarly, women under age 65 represented from 29 percent to 34 percent of one-person households, but 44 percent to 46 percent of the population.

In contrast, men, and especially women, age 65 and over represented proportionally larger shares of one-person households than they did of the total population. From 1960 to 2000, men age 65 and over represented just 4 percent to 5 percent of the total population, but a range of 8 percent to 12 percent of all one-person households. Women age 65 and over represented just 5 percent to 8 percent of the total population during this period, but a disproportionately higher range (27 percent to 33 percent) of the total number of one-person households.

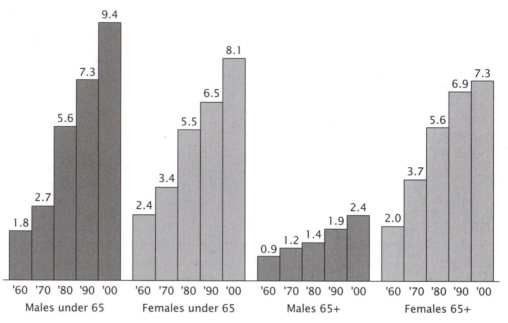

Figure 5-12.
**One-Person Households by Age and Sex
of Householder: 1960 to 2000**

(Millions)

Source: U.S. Census Bureau, decennial census of population, 1960 to 2000.

Figure 5-13.
**Distribution of One-Person Households by Age and Sex
of Householder: 1960 to 2000**

(Percent)

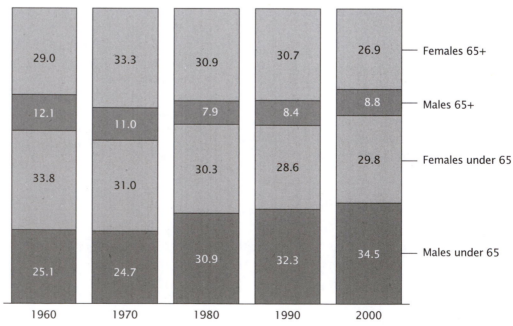

Source: U.S. Census Bureau, decennial census of population, 1960 to 2000.

Older female householders were far more likely to live alone than younger female householders and than younger and older male householders.

Older female householders had a much greater likelihood of living alone than did younger female householders or male householders, regardless of age (see Figure 5-14). In every census from 1970 to 2000, between 73 to 77 percent of all female householders age 65 and over lived alone.

Younger female householders were also more likely to live alone than both younger male householders and older male householders. In 1960 and 1970, 40 percent and 41 percent, respectively, of all female householders under age 65 lived alone, however, this proportion declined each census after 1970 to 29 percent in 2000.

From 1960 to 2000, the proportion of all male householders under age 65 living alone increased each census, from 4.7 percent to 16.9 percent, but this group was the least likely to be living alone. This fact derives from the very high proportion of men who are identified as the householder among married-couple households.[58]

The proportion of all male householders age 65 and over living alone also generally increased during the period 1960 to 2000, with a slight decline occurring in the 1970s. A higher proportion of male householders age 65 and over lived alone than male householders under age 65 at each census during the period, although the gap between these two groups reached its narrowest point at the end of the century. By 2000, 1 out of every 5 male householders age 65 and over lived alone.

The generally declining proportions of female householders under age 65 who lived alone, combined with increasing proportions of both under-65 and 65-and-over male householders who lived alone, reduced the gap between these three groups to its narrowest point by 2000. However, the gap between the proportion of women householders under age 65 and those age 65 and over who lived alone widened, except in the 1990s.

---

[58] Prior to 1980, men were identified as the householder for all married-couple households.

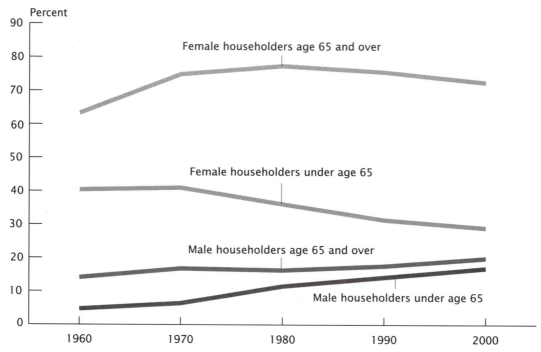

Figure 5-14.
**Percent One-Person Households Within Specific
Age-Sex Groups: 1960 to 2000**

Source: U.S. Census Bureau, decennial census of population, 1960 to 2000.

Female householders increased as a proportion of total householders.

Female-maintained households represented an increasing proportion of all U.S. households from 1970 to 2000 (see Figure 5-15). In 1970, women represented about 1 of every 5 (21 percent) householders in the United States; by 2000, the proportion was more than 1 of every 3 (36 percent). However, different trends occurred among the major household types during the last 30 years of the century.

As noted earlier, all households may be broadly classified as either family households or nonfamily households. Family households may be further broken down into married-couple households and other family households. Similarly, nonfamily households may be separated into one-person households and other nonfamily households.

Prior to 1980, every U.S. population census automatically designated the husband as the householder of all married-couple families. Since then, either the husband or the wife may be the householder, depending on which one lists himself or herself as the first person on the questionnaire. From 1980 to 2000, the proportion of female householders in married-couple households increased, from 3.7 percent in 1980 to 12.9 percent in 2000. In contrast, the proportion of female householders in each of the other major household types was lower in 2000 than in 1970.

Among the major household types, women represented the largest proportion of other family householders each census, 1970 to 2000. Female-maintained other family households declined as a proportion of all other family households, but still represented 75 percent of all such households in 2000. (This decline implies that male-maintained other family households increased as a percentage of all other family households.)

The proportion of one-person households maintained by women declined each census, 1970 to 2000, but remained the majority (57 percent) of all one-person households in 2000. Among other nonfamily households, women represented the majority of householders in 1970. However, this proportion fell substantially by 1980, then increased to the point that females maintained 42 percent of other nonfamily households in 2000.

The proportion of all family households with a female householder increased each census, from 11 percent in 1970 to 28 percent in 2000. In contrast, the proportion of female householders among all nonfamily households decreased each census, from 63 percent in 1970 to 54 percent in 2000. Furthermore, although the share of female householders among married-couple households increased, the share of female householders of all households other than married couples declined, from 69 percent in 1970 to 61 percent in 2000.

Figure 5-15.
**Percent of Households With a Female Householder
by Type of Household: 1970 to 2000**

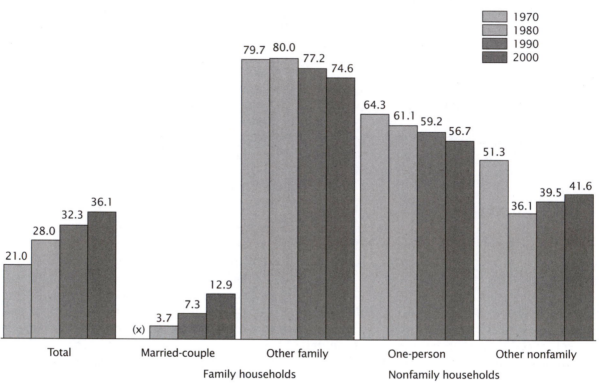

(x) Not applicable.
Source: U.S. Census Bureau, decennial census of population, 1970 to 2000.

For total, married-couple, and other family households, the proportion of female householders among Black householders exceeded the proportion of female householders among householders of any other race or of Hispanic householders.

Between 1980 and 2000, an increasing trend occurred in the proportion of householders who were women for every race and Hispanic-origin group (see Figure 5-16). However, while strong similarities occurred in the patterns of change from census to census, important differences among the groups in 1980 remained in 2000.

The proportion of all householders who were female increased for each race and Hispanic group from 1980 to 2000. Women consistently represented the highest proportion of householders among Blacks, followed by American Indians and Alaska Natives. Among all Black householders, women have been more likely than men to be identified as the householder since 1990. Throughout the 20-year period, the lowest proportion of female householders was found among Asian and Pacific Islander households.

Women also represented an increasing proportion of all married-couple householders for every race and Hispanic-origin group since 1980, when women first became eligible to be identified as the householder of a married-couple household. Black women householders accounted for a higher proportion of married-couple households than women of any other race or Hispanic origin for each census, 1980 to 2000. White (and White non-Hispanic) women and Asian and Pacific Islander women were least likely to be identified as the householder within married-couple households.

Women were listed as the householder in the vast majority of other-family households for every race and Hispanic-origin group between 1980 and 2000. In 1980, females represented at least three-fourths of all other-family householders for every race and Hispanic-origin group, except for Asians and Pacific Islanders. Although Asian and Pacific Islander other-family households had the lowest proportion of female householders throughout the period, they still represented around two-thirds of these households. Blacks had the highest proportion of female-maintained other-family households, with women maintaining 84 percent to 86 percent of Black other-family households throughout the period.

Among nonfamily households, the direction of change between 1980 and 2000 in the proportion of female householders varied by group. Female householders represented a slightly declining proportion of nonfamily householders between 1980 and 2000 among White, American Indian and Alaska Native, and Hispanic householders, and a slightly increasing proportion among Black and Asian and Pacific Islander householders.

In 1980 and 2000, White female householders and Black female householders (and in 2000, White non-Hispanic female householders) represented slightly over one-half of all nonfamily householders. In contrast, male householders represented the majority of nonfamily householders for every other group. Among the groups, Black female householders represented the highest proportion of married-couple householders and other-family householders, while White (and White non-Hispanic) female householders represented the highest proportion of nonfamily householders.

Figure 5-16.
Percent Female Householders of Total Householders by Type of Household and Race and Hispanic Origin of the Householder: 1980 and 2000

(Percent)

1980
2000

Total households

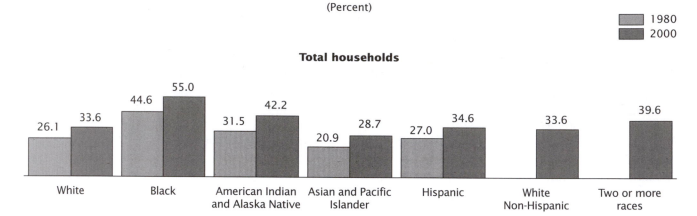

	White	Black	American Indian and Alaska Native	Asian and Pacific Islander	Hispanic	White Non-Hispanic	Two or more races
1980	26.1	44.6	31.5	20.9	27.0		
2000	33.6	55.0	42.2	28.7	34.6	33.6	39.6

Married-couple households

	White	Black	American Indian and Alaska Native	Asian and Pacific Islander	Hispanic	White Non-Hispanic	Two or more races
1980	3.4	7.1	4.9	3.2	3.9		
2000	11.9	22.1	20.1	12.2	15.0	11.8	18.1

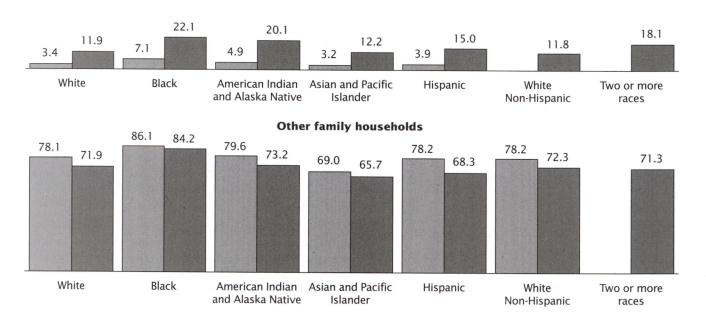

Other family households

	White	Black	American Indian and Alaska Native	Asian and Pacific Islander	Hispanic	White Non-Hispanic	Two or more races
1980	78.1	86.1	79.6	69.0	78.2	78.2	
2000	71.9	84.2	73.2	65.7	68.3	72.3	71.3

Nonfamily households

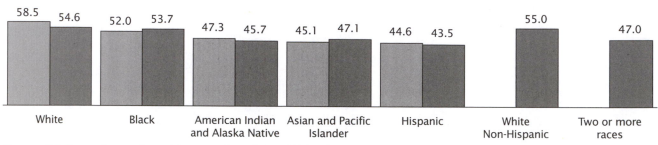

	White	Black	American Indian and Alaska Native	Asian and Pacific Islander	Hispanic	White Non-Hispanic	Two or more races
1980	58.5	52.0	47.3	45.1	44.6		
2000	54.6	53.7	45.7	47.1	43.5	55.0	47.0

Source: U.S. Census Bureau, decennial census of population, 1980 and 2000.

Each decade from 1960 to 2000, married-couple households were less likely to include children under age 18, while male family households with no wife present were more likely to include children under age 18.

Family households consist of married-couple households and other family households. Other family households include those maintained by a man with no wife present or by a woman with no husband present. Family households also may be characterized by the presence or absence of one or more of the householders' own children.[59] The trend in the proportion of family households with their own children under age 18 varied considerably by family type during the period 1950 to 2000 (see Figure 5-17 and Appendix Table 15).

Among married-couple households, the proportion with their own children under age 18 has declined since 1960. In 1960, 3 out of every 5 married-couple households (59 percent) had at least one own child under age 18. By 1990 (and in 2000), less than half (46 percent) of married-couple households had any own children under age 18.

Among female family households with no husband present, the proportion with their own children under age 18 increased from 1 out of every 3 (34 percent) households in 1950 to 3 out of every 5 households (60 percent) by 1980. This proportion declined slightly in the 1980s, then increased slightly in the 1990s, while remaining fairly stable.

Among male family households with no wife present, the proportion with their own children under age 18 increased in every decade from 1950 to 2000. In 1950, only 1 out of every 5 (19 percent) male family households with no wife present had own children under age 18. By 2000, half (50 percent) of these households had own children under age 18.

In addition to the overall differences among family types, the trends in the age composition of the children within each type also display some important differences. For example, among male family households with no wife present, the proportions of these house-

holds including their own children under age 6 (and no other own children) increased in every census from 1960 to 2000. In fact, by the end of the century, male family households with no wife present were more likely to have children under age 6 only than either married-couple households or female family households with no husband present. In contrast, the trend in the proportion of married-couple households with children under age 6 only went in the opposite direction, declining from 15 percent in 1960 to 11 percent in 2000.

The trends in the proportions of households with their own children only within the ages 6 to 17 years fluctuated for each family type. Among married-couple households, the proportion remained within a narrow range during the period 1960 to 2000, from 24 percent to 28 percent. For female family households with no husband present, the proportion with children only within the ages 6 to 17 increased to a peak of 39 percent in 1980, declined during the 1980s to 34 percent in 1990, then increased in the 1990s to 37 percent in 2000. Among the family types, female family households with no husband present were the most likely to have children ages 6 to 17 years only in the household. For male family households with no wife present, the proportion generally increased from 1960 to 2000, with one slight decline in the 1980s.

The proportion of married-couple households with children under age 6 and children age 6 to 17 generally declined, from about one-fifth (18 percent) of married-couple households in 1960 to just one-tenth (10 percent) in 2000. In comparison, the proportion of female family households with no husband present and with their own children under age 6 and age 6 to 17 remained steady at around one-tenth during the 40-year period. The percentage of male family households with no wife present and with children under age 6 and age 6 to 17 generally increased during the period, although they remained the family type least likely to have children of both age groups in the household.

[59] See the Glossary for a definition of own children.

Figure 5-17.
Figure 5-17.
Percent of Family Households With Own Children Under 18
by Family Type and Age of Children: 1950 to 2000

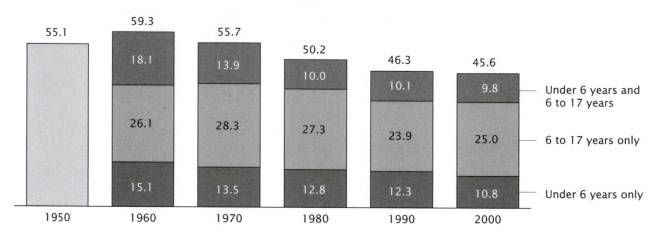

Married-couple

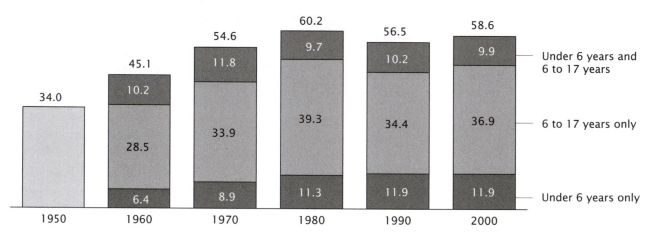

Female householder, no spouse present

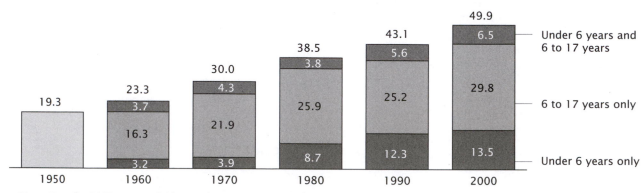

Male householder, no spouse present

Note: Data for 1950 on own children under 18 are not available in the detailed age categories shown.
Source: U.S. Census Bureau, decennial census of population, 1950 to 2000.

CITIZENSHIP	RESIDENCE, APRIL 1, 1935														PERSONS 14 YEARS OLD AND OV	OCCUPA

16	17	18	19	20	D	21	22	23	24	25	E	26	27	28
	Same House			No		Yes	—	—	—	—	1	40	—	Foreman
	Same House			No		No	No	No	No	H			—	
	Same House			No		No	No	No	No	S			—	
	Same House			No		Yes	—	—	—	—	1	—	—	Laborer

General

Carter, Paul A. *Another Part of the Fifties* (New York: Columbia University Press, 1983).

Chafe, William H. *The Unfinished Journey: America since World War II* (New York: Oxford University Press, 1986).

Chafe, William H., and Harvard Sitkoff, eds. *A History of Our Time: Readings on Postwar America*, 5th ed. (New York: Oxford University Press, 1999).

Cummins, D. Duane, et al., eds. *Combat and Consensus: The 1940's and 1950's* (Encino, CA: Glencoe, 1980).

Daniel, Pete. *Lost Revolutions: The South in the 1950s* (Chapel Hill: University of North Carolina Press for Smithsonian National Museum of American History, 2000).

Diggins, John Patrick. *The Proud Decades: America in War and Peace, 1941–1960* (New York: Norton, 1988).

Dunar, Andrew. *America in the Fifties* (Syracuse, NY: Syracuse University Press, 2006).

Foreman, Joel, ed. *Interrogating Midcentury American Icons* (Urbana: University of Illinois Press, 1997).

Galbraith, John Kenneth. *The Affluent Society* (Boston: Houghton Mifflin, 1958).

Gillman, Richard, ed. *Power in Postwar America* (Boston: Little, Brown, 1971).

Goldman, Eric. *The Crucial Decade: America 1945–1955* (New York: Knopf, 1956).

Halberstam, David. *The Fifties* (New York: Villard Books, 1993).

Hart, Jeffrey. *When the Going Was Good: American Life in the Fifties* (New York: Crown, 1982).

Harvey, Brett. *The Fifties: A Women's Oral History* (New York: Harper-Collins, 1973).

Hodgson, Godfrey. *America in Our Time: From World War II to Nixon; What Happened and Why* (New York: Vintage Books, 1976).

Jezer, Marty. *The Dark Ages: Life in the United States, 1945–1960* (Boston: South End Press, 1982).

Kallen, Stuart A. *The 1950s* (San Diego: Greenhaven Press, 2000).

Leuchtenberg, William E. *A Troubled Feast: American Society since 1945* (Boston: Little, Brown, 1983).

Lewis, Peter. *The Fifties* (New York: Lippincott, 1978).

Maclean's Magazine. *Canada in the Fifties: From the Archives of Maclean's* (Toronto and New York: Viking, 1999).

Mann, Jessica. *Fifties Mystique* (London: Quartet, 2012).

Marías, Julián, *America in the Fifties and Sixties: Julián Marías on the United States*, tr. by Blanch de Puy and Harold C. Raley, ed. by Michael Aaron Rockland (University Park: Pennsylvania State University Press, 1972).

Merritt, Jeffrey D. *Day by Day, The Fifties*, ed. by Steven L. Goulden (New York: Facts on File, 1979).

Meyerowitz, Joanne, ed. *Not June Cleaver: Women and Gender in Postwar America, 1945–1960* (Philadelphia: Temple University Press, 1994).

Miller, Douglas T., and Marion Nowak. *The Fifties: The Way We Really Were* (Garden City, NY: Doubleday, 1977).

Olson, James S. *Historical Dictionary of the 1950s* (Westport, CT: Greenwood Press, 2000).

O'Neill, William L. *American High: The Years of Confidence, 1945–1960* (New York: Free Press, 1986).

Paschen, Stephen H., and Leonard Schlup, comps. *Documents Depicting the 1950s: A Decade of Conformity and Dissent* (Lewiston, NY: Edwin Mellen Press, 2008).

Patterson, James T. *Grand Expectations: The United States, 1945–1974* (New York: Oxford University Press, 1996).

Pells, Richard H. *The Liberal Mind in a Conservative Age: American Intellectuals in the 1940s and 1950s* (Middletown, CT: Wesleyan University Press, 1989).

Perret, Geoffrey. *A Dream of Greatness: The American People, 1945–1963* (New York: Coward, McCann and Geoghegan, 1979).

Rogin, Michael Paul. *The Intellectuals and McCarthy* (Cambridge, MA: Harvard University Press, 1967).

Rose, Lisle. *The Cold War Comes to Main Street: America in 1950* (Lawrence: Kansas University Press 1999).

Samuelson, Robert J. *The Good Life and Its Discontents: The American Dream in the Age of Entitlement, 1945–1990* (New York: Times Books, 1995).

Schwartz, Richard A. *The 1950s* (New York: Facts on File, 2003).

Social Casework. Social Casework *in the Fifties; Selected Articles, 1951–1960* (New York: Family Service Association of America, 1962.)

Stone, I. F. *The Haunted Fifties, 1953–1963* (1963; reprint, Boston: Little, Brown, 1989). [Foreword by Arthur Miller.]

Super, John C., ed. *The Fifties in America*, 3 vols. (Pasadena, CA: Salem Press, 2005).

Time-Life Books, *The American Dream: The 50s* (Alexandria, VA, 1998).

Time-Life Books, *Shadow of the Atom, 1950–1960* (Alexandria, VA, 1991).

Wechsler, James. *The Age of Suspicion* (New York: Random House, 1953).

Weiss, Jessica, *To Have and to Hold: Marriage, the Baby Boom, and Social Change* (Chicago: University of Chicago Press, 2000).

Young, William H., with Nancy K. Young. *The 1950s* (Westport, CT: Greenwood Press, 2004).

Zinn, Howard. *Postwar America: 1945–1971* (1973; reprint, Cambridge, MA: South End Press, 2002).

Art and Design

Anfam, David. *Abstract Expressionism* (New York: Thames and Hudson 1990.)

Ashton, Dore. *American Art since 1945* (New York: Oxford University Press, 1982).

Belgrad, Daniel. *The Culture of Spontaneity: Improvisation and the Arts in Postwar America* (Chicago: University of Chicago Press, 1998).

Buettner, Stewart. *American Art Theory, 1945-1970* (Ann Arbor, MI: UMI Research Press, 1981).

Cox, Annette. *Art-as-politics: The Abstract Expressionist Avant-Garde and Society* (Ann Arbor, MI: UMI Research Press, 1982).

Craven, David. *Abstract Expressionism as Cultural Critique: Dissent during the McCarthy Period* (Cambridge, Eng.: Cambridge University Press, 1999).

De Kooning, Elaine. *The Spirit of Abstract Expressionism: Selected Writings,* with an essay by Rose Slivka (New York: George Braziller, 1994).

Doss, Erika. *Benton, Pollock, and the Politics of Modernism: From Regionalism to Abstract Expressionism* (Chicago: University of Chicago Press, 1991).

Frascina, Francis, ed. *Pollock and After: The Critical Debate,* 2nd ed. (London: Routledge, 2000).

Gibson, Ann Eden. *Abstract Expressionism: Other Politics* (New Haven: Yale University Press, 1997).

Guilbaut, Serge. *How New York Stole the Idea of Modern Art: Abstract Expressionism, Freedom, and the Cold War,* trans. by Arthur Goldhammer (Chicago: University of Chicago Press, 1983).

Hemingway, Andrew. *Artists on the Left: American Artists and the Communist Movement, 1926-1956* (New Haven: Yale University Press, 2002).

Johnson, Ellen H., ed. *American Artists on Art from 1940 to 1980* (New York: Harper and Row, 1982).

Johnson, Steven, ed. *The New York Schools of Music and Visual Art: John Cage, Morton Feldman, Edgard Varese, Willem De Kooning, Jasper Johns, Robert Rauschenberg* (New York: Routledge, 2002).

Leclerc, Denise. *The Crisis of Abstraction in Canada: The 1950s,* with a technical essay by Marion H. Barclay (Ottawa: National Gallery of Canada, 1992).

Polcari, Stephen. *Abstract Expressionism and the Modern Experience* (Cambridge, Eng.: Cambridge University Press, 1991).

Quinn, Bradley, *Mid-Century Modern: Interiors, Furniture, Design* (London: Conran Octopus, 2004).

Ross, Clifford, ed. *Abstract Expressionism: Creators and Critics: An Anthology* (New York: Harry N. Abrams, 1990).

Sawin, Martica. *Surrealism in Exile and the Beginning of the New York School* (Cambridge, MA: MIT Press, 1995).

Shapiro, David, and Cecile Shapiro, eds. *Abstract Expressionism: A Critical Record* (Cambridge, Eng.: Cambridge University Press, 1990).

Siegel, Katy. *Abstract Expressionism* (London: Phaidon Press, 2011).

Thistlewood, David, ed. *American Abstract Expressionism* (Liverpool: Liverpool University Press and Tate Gallery Liverpool, 1993).

Whitelaw, Anne, et al., eds. *The Visual Arts in Canada: The Twentieth Century* (Don Mills, Ont.: Oxford University Press, 2010).

Wood, Paul, et al. *Modernism in Dispute: Art since the Forties* (New Haven: Yale University Press, in association with the Open University, London, 1993).

Business and Economy

Blackwelder, Julia Kirk. *Now Hiring: The Feminization of Work in the United States, 1900-1995* (College Station: Texas A&M University Press, 1997).

Ezra, Michael, ed. *The Economic Civil Rights Movement: African Americans and the Struggle for Economic Power* (New York: Routledge, 2013).

Heald, Morrell. *The Social Responsibilities of Business: Company and Community, 1900-1960,* with a new introduction by the author (1988; reprint, New Brunswick, NJ: Transaction Publishers, 2005).

McQuaid, Kim. *Uneasy Partners: Big Business in American Politics, 1945-1990* (Baltimore: Johns Hopkins University Press, 1994).

Squires, Gregory D., ed. *Unequal Partnerships: The Political Economy of Urban Redevelopment in Postwar America* (New Brunswick: Rutgers University Press, 1989).

Steinmann, Marion, and the Women of the Cornell Class of 1950. *Women at Work: Demolishing a Myth of the 1950s* (Philadelphia: Xlibris, 2005).

United States Department of Labor. *Average Retail Prices, 1955; Bulletin No. 1197* (USGPO, 1956)

United States Department of Labor. *Family Income, Expenditures and Savings in 1950; Bulletin No. 1097* (USGPO, 1953)

Cold War Politics and McCarthyism

Bell, Daniel. *The End of Ideology: On the Exhaustion of Political Ideas in the Fifties* (New York: Macmillan, 1961).

Bernhart, Nancy. *US Television News and Cold War Propaganda, 1947–1960* (Cambridge, Eng.: Cambridge University Press, 1998).

Bogle, Lori Lyn. *The Pentagon's Battle for the American Mind: The Early Cold War* (College Station: Texas A&M University Press, 2004).

Borstelmann, Thomas. *The Cold War and the Color Line: American Race Relations in the Global Arena* (Cambridge, MA: Harvard University Press, 2001).

Campbell, Graig, and Fredrik Logevall. *America's Cold War: The Politics of Insecurity* (Cambridge, MA: Harvard University Press, 2009).

Chomsky, Noam et al. *The Cold War and the University: Towards an Intellectual History of the Postwar Years* (New York: New Press, 1997).

Craven David. *Abstract Expressionism as Cultural Critique: Dissent during the McCarthy Period* (Cambridge, Eng.: Cambridge University Press, 1999).

Doherty, Thomas Patrick. *Cold War, Cool Medium: Television, McCarthyism, and American Culture* (New York: Columbia University Press, 2003).

Fried, Albert, ed. *McCarthyism: The Great American Red Scare: A Documentary History* (Oxford, Eng.: Oxford University Press, 1997).

Fried, Richard. *Nightmare in Red: The McCarthy Era in Perspective* (New York: Oxford University Press, 1990).

Garber, Marjorie, and Rebecca Walkowitz, eds. *Secret Agents: Rosenberg Case, McCarthyism and Fifties America* (New York: Routledge, 1995).

Guilbaut, Serge. *How New York Stole the Idea of Modern Art: Abstract Expressionism, Freedom, and the Cold War,trans.by Arthur Goldhammer* (Chicago: University of Chicago Press, 1983).

May, Lary, ed. *Recasting America: Culture and Politics in the Age of the Cold War* (Chicago: University of Chicago Press, 1989).

McEnaney, Laura. *Civil Defense Begins at Home: Militarization Meets Everyday Life in the Fifties* (Princeton, NJ: Princeton University Press, 2000).

Morgan, Ted. *Reds: McCarthyism in America from Woodrow Wilson to George W. Bush* (New York: Random House, 2003).

Schrecker, Ellen *The Age of McCarthyism: A Brief History with Documents,* 2nd ed. (New York: Palgrave, 2002).

Schrecker, Ellen. *Many Are the Crimes: McCarthyism in America* (Boston: Little, Brown, 1998).

Schrecker, Ellen, ed. *Cold War Triumphalism: The Misuse of History after the Fall of Communism* (New York: New Press, 2004).

Film, Television, and Popular Culture

Abrams, Nathan, and Julie Hughes, eds. *Containing America: Cultural Production and Consumption in Fifties America* (Birmingham, Eng.: University of Birmingham Press, 2000).

Adler, Bill. *Do You Remember the 50s?* (New York: Avon Books, 1992).

Amidi, Amid. *Cartoon Modern: Style and Design in Fifties Animation* (San Francisco: Chronicle Books, 2006).

Anderson, Christopher. *Hollywood TV: The Studio System in the Fifties* (Austin: Texas University Press, 1994).

Arnold, Eve, et al. *The Fifties: Photographs of America* (New York: Pantheon Books, 1985). [Introduction by John Chancellor.]

Balio, Tino, ed. *Hollywood in the Age of Television* (Boston: Unwin Hyman, 1990).

Belfrage, Sally. *UnAmerican Activities: A Memoir of the Fifties* (New York: HarperCollins, 1994).

Berman, Jay. *The Fifties Book* (New York: Berkley, 1974).

Bernhart, Nancy. *US Television News and Cold War Propaganda, 1947–1960* (Cambridge, Eng.: Cambridge University Press, 1998).

Biskind, Peter. *Seeing Is Believing: How Hollywood Taught Us to Stop Worrying and Love the Fifties* (New York: Pantheon, 1983).

Boddy, William. *Fifties Television: The Industry and Its Critics.* (Urbana: Illinois University Press, 1990).

Boyer, Paul. *By the Bomb's Early Light: American Thought and Culture at the Dawn of the Atomic Age* (New York: Pantheon, 1961).

Breines, Wini. *Young, White and Miserable: Growing Up Female in the Fifties* (Boston: Beacon Press, 1992).

Brode, Douglas. *The Films of the Fifties:* Sunset Boulevard *to* On the Beach (Secaucus, NJ: Citadel Press, 1976).

Brode, Douglas. *Lost Films of the Fifties.* (New York: Citadel Press, 1991).

Burns, Eric. *Invasion of the Mind Snatchers: Television's Conquest of America in the Fifties* (Philadelphia: Temple University Press, 2010).

Byars, Jackie. *All That Hollywood Allows: ReReading Gender in 1950s Melodrama* (Chapel Hill: North Carolina University Press, 1991).

Caputi, Mary. *A Kinder, Gentler America: Melancholia and the Mythical 1950s* (Minneapolis: University of Minnesota Press, 2005).

Clarke, Alison. *Tupperware: The Promise of Plastic in 1950s America* (Washington, DC: Smithsonian Institution Press, 1999).

Cohan, Steven. *Masked Men: Masculinity and the Movies in the Fifties* (Bloomington: Indiana University Press, 1997).

Cohen, Lizabeth. *A Consumer's Republic: The Politics of Mass Consumption in Postwar America.* (New York: Knopf, 2003).

Connolly, Joseph. *All Shook Up: A Flash of the Fifties* (London: Cassell, 2000).

Corber, Robert J. *In the Name of National Security: Hitchcock, Homophobia, and the Political Construction of Gender in Postwar America* (Durham, NC: Duke University Press, 1993).

Costello, Mathew. *Secret Identity Crisis: Comic Books and the Unmasking of Cold War America* (London: Continuum, 2007).

Cripps, Thomas. *Making Movies Black: The Hollywood Message Movie from World War II to the Civil Rights Era* (New York: Oxford University Press, 1993).

Doherty, Thomas Patrick. *Cold War, Cool Medium: Television, McCarthyism, and American Culture* (New York: Columbia University Press, 2003).

Doherty, Thomas Patrick. *Teenagers and Teenpics: The Juvenilization of American Movies in the 1950s* (Boston: Unwin Hyman, 1988).

Dowdy, Andrew. *The Films of the Fifties: The American State of Mind* (New York: Morrow, 1973).

Dowdy, Andrew. *Movies Are Better than Ever: Wide Screen Memories of the Fifties* (New York: Morrow, 1973).

Drake, Nicholas. *The Fifties in Vogue* (New York: H. Holt, 1987). [Foreword by Audrey Hepburn.]

Field, Douglas, ed. *Cold War Culture* (Edinburgh: Edinburgh University Press, 2005).

Finch, Christopher. *Walt Disney's America* (New York: Abbeville, 1978).

Findlay, M. John. *Magic Lands: Western Cityscapes and American Culture after 1940s* (Berkeley: California University Press, 1997).

Freedland, Michael, and Barbara Paskin. *Hollywood on Trial: McCarthyism's War against the Movies* (London: Robson, 2007).

Gans, Herbert. *The Levittowners: Ways of Life and Politics in a New Suburban Community* (New York: Pantheon, 1967).

Gow, Gordon. *Hollywood in the 50's* (New York: Barnes, 1971).

Graham, Allison. *Framing the South: Hollywood, Television, and Race during the Civil Rights Struggle* (Baltimore: John Hopkins University Press, 2001).

Halliwell, Martin. *American Culture in the 1950s* (Edinburgh: Edinburgh University Press, 2007).

Hawes, William. *Live Television Drama, 1946–1951* (Jefferson, NC: McFarland, 2001).

Heimann, Jim, ed. *Mid-Century Ads: Advertising from the Mad Men Era*, 2 vols. (Köln: Taschen, 2012).

Hendershot, Cyndy. *AntiCommunism and Popular Culture in Midcentury America* (Jefferson, NC: McFarland, 2003).

Hendershot, Cyndy. *I Was a Cold War Monster: Horror Films, Eroticism, and the Cold War Imagination* (Bowling Green, OH: Bowling Green State University Popular Press, 2001).

Hendershot, Cyndy. *Paranoia, the Bomb, and 1950s Science Fiction Films* (Bowling Green, OH: Bowling Green State University Popular Press, 1999).

Henriksen, Margot. *Dr. Strangelove's America: Society and Culture in the Atomic Age* (Berkeley: California University Press, 1997).

Ikuta, Yasutoshi. *Cruise-o-matic: Automobile Advertising of the 1950s* (San Francisco: Chronicle Books, 2000).

Jancovich, Mark. *Rational Fears: American Horror in the 1950s* (Manchester, Eng.: Manchester University Press, 1996).

Jenness, David, and Don Velsey. *Classic American Popular Song: The Second Half-Century, 1950–2000* (New York: Routledge, 2006).

Jones, Darryl, et al., eds. *It Came from the 1950s: Popular Culture, Popular Anxieties* (Hampshire, Eng.: Macmillan, 2011).

Kashner, Sam, and Jennifer MacNair. *The Bad and the Beautiful: Hollywood in the Fifties* (London: Little, Brown, 2002).

Krutnik, Frank et al. *UnAmerican Hollywood: Politics and Film in the Blacklist Era* (New Brunswick, NJ: Rutgers University Press 2007).

Langman, Larry, and Daniel Finn. *A Guide to American Crime Films of the Forties and Fifties* (Westport, CT: Greenwood Press, 1995).

Lasch, Christopher. *The Culture of Narcissism: American Culture in the Age of Diminishing Expectations* (New York: Norton, 1978).

Lattin, Don. *The Harvard Psychedelic Club: How Timothy Leary, Ram Dass, Huston Smith, and Andrew Weil Killed the Fifties and Ushered in a New Age for America* (New York: HarperOne, 2010).

Leibman, Nina. *Living Room Lectures: The Fifties Family in Film and Television* (Austin: University of Texas Press, 1995.

Lewis, Mark. *Stars of the Fifties* (London: Octopus, 1986).

Lindop, Edmund, with Sarah Decapua. *America in the 1950s* (Minneapolis: Twenty-First Century Books, 2010).

Lipschutz, Ronnie. *Cold War Fantasies: Film, Fiction and Foreign Policy* (Lanham, MD: Rowman and Littlefield, 2001).

Lipsitz, George. *Class and Culture in Cold War America: A Rainbow at Midnight* (New York: Praeger, 1981).

Lucanio, Patrick. *Them or Us: Archetypical Interpretation of Fifties Alien Invasion Film* (Bloomington: Indiana University Press, 1987).

MacDonald, Fred. *Blacks and White TV: African Americans in Television since 1948,* 2nd ed. (Chicago: Nelson-Hall, 1992).

Marling, Karal Ann. *As Seen on TV: The Visual Culture of Everyday Life in the 1950s* (Cambridge, MA: Harvard University Press, 1996).

Marcus, Daniel. *Happy Days and Wonder Years: The Fifties and the Sixties in Contemporary Cultural Politics* (New Brunswick, NJ: Rutgers University Press, 2004).

Martinson, Tom. *America's Dreamscape: The Pursuit of Happiness in Postwar Suburbia* (New York: Carroll & Graf, 2000).

May, Lary, ed. *Recasting American Culture and Politics in the Age of the Cold War* (Chicago: Chicago University Press, 1989).

McEnaney, Laura. *Civil Defense Begins at Home: Militarization Meets Everyday Life in the Fifties* (Princeton, NJ: Princeton University Press, 2000).

Meeuf, Russell, *John Wayne's World: Transnational Masculinity in the Fifties* (Austin : University of Texas Press, 2013).

Meyerowitz, Joanne, ed. *Not June Cleaver: Women and Gender in Postwar America, 1945–1960* (Philadelphia: Temple University Press, 1994).

Noonan, Bonnie. *Women Scientists in Fifties Science Fiction Films* (Jefferson, NC: McFarland, 2005).

Nourmand, Tony, and Graham Marsh. *Film Posters of the 1950s* (London: Aurum, 2000).

Olian, Joanne, ed. *Everyday Fashions of the Fifties as Pictured in Sears Catalogs* (Mineola, NY: Dover Publications, 2002).

Palmer, R. Barton, ed. *Larger than Life: Movie Stars of the 1950s* (New Brunswick, NJ: Rutgers University Press, 2010).

Pomerance, Murray, ed. *American Cinema of the 1950s: Themes and Variations* (New Brunswick, NJ: Rutgers University Press, 2005).

Riesman, David. *The Lonely Crowd* (New Haven: Yale University Press, 1950).

Roffman, Peter. *The Hollywood Social Problem Film: Madness, Despair and Politics from the Depression to the Fifties* (Bloomington: Indiana University Press, 1981).

Sanjek, Russell, and David Sanjek. *American Popular Music Business in the Twentieth Century* (New York: Oxford University Press, 1991).

Saxton, Martha. *Jayne Mansfield and the American Fifties* (Boston: Houghton Mifflin,1975).

Sayre, Nora. *Running Time: Films of the Cold War* (New York: Dial Press, 1982).

Schatzberg, Jerry, with texts by Julia Morton and Gail Buckland. *Women Then: Photographs, 1954-1969* (New York: Rizzoli, 2010).

Seed, David. *American Science Fiction and the Cold War* (Edinburgh: Edinburgh University Press, 1999).

Seed, David. *Under the Shadow: The Atomic Bomb and Cold War Narratives* (Kent, OH: Kent State University Press 2012).

Shapiro, Laura. *Something from the Oven: Reinventing Dinner in 1950's America* (New York: Viking, 2004).

Sivok, Ed. *Laughing Hysterically: American Screen Comedy of the 1950s* (New York: Columbia University Press, 1994).

Spigel, Lynn. *Make Room for TV: Television and the Family Ideal in Postwar America* (Chicago: Chicago University Press, 1992).

Spigel, Lynn. *Welcome to the Dreamhouse: Popular Media and Postwar Suburbs* (Durham, NC: Duke University Press, 2001).

Sterritt, David. *Mad to Be Saved: The Beats, the 50s, and Film* (Carbondale: Southern Illinois University Press, 1998).

Taylor, Ella. *Prime Time Families: Television Culture in Postwar America* (Berkeley: University of California Press, 1989).

Thompson, Graham. *The Business of America: The Cultural Production of a Post-War Nation* (London: Pluto, 2004).

Vieth, Errol. *Screening Science: Contexts, Texts and Science in Fifties Science Fiction Films* (Lanham, MD: Scarecrow Press, 2001).

Wakefield, Dan. *New York in the Fifties* (Boston: Houghton Mifflin, 1992).

Whitfield, Stephen. *The Culture of the Cold War* (Baltimore: John Hopkins University Press, 1990).

Wills, Charles. *America in the 1950s* (New York: Facts on File, 2006).

Warren, Bill. *Keep Watching the Skies: American Science Fiction Movies of the Fifties* (Jefferson, NC: McFarland, 1997).

Warren, Carol. *Madwives: Schizophrenic Women in the 1950s* (New Brunswick, NJ: Rutgers University Press, 1991).

Weiss, Jessica. *To Have and to Hold: Marriage, the Baby Boom, and Social Change* (Chicago: University of Chicago Press, 2000).

Zinman, David. *50 from the 50s: Vintage Films from America's Midcentury* (New Rochelle, NY: Arlington House, 1979).

Literature and Performing Arts

Baker, Houston. *Blues, Ideology and Afro American Literature* (Chicago: University of Chicago Press, 1984).

Bartlett, Lee, ed. *The Beats: Essays in Criticism* (Jefferson, NC: McFarland, 1981).

Bell, Bernard W. *The Afro-American Novel and Its Tradition* (Amherst: University of Massachusetts Press, 2004).

Bell, Bernard W. *The Contemporary African American Novel: Its Folk Roots and Modern Literary Branches* (Amherst: University of Massachusetts Press, 2004).

Booker, Keith. *Monsters, Mushroom Clouds and the Cold War: American Science Fiction and the Roots of Postmodernism, 1946-1964* (Westport: Greenwood Press, 2001).

Bram, Christopher. *Eminent Outlaws: The Gay Writers Who Changed America* (New York: Twelve, 2012).

Brater, Enoch, ed. *Arthur Miller's America: Theater and Culture in a Time of Change* (Ann Arbor: University of Michigan Press, 2005).

Brier, Evan. *A Novel Marketplace: Mass Culture, the Book Trade, and Postwar American Fiction* (Philadelphia: University of Pennsylvania Press, 2010).

Brunner, Edward. *Cold War Poetry: The Social Text in the Fifties Poem* (Urbana: University of Illinois Press, 2001).

Campbell, James. *This Is the Beat Generation: New York, San Francisco, Paris* (London: Secker & Warburg, 1999).

Carr, Roy, et al. *The Hip: Hipsters, Jazz and the Beat Generation* (London: Faber, 1986).

Castronovo, David. *Beyond the Gray Flannel Suit: Books from the 1950s That Made American Culture* (New York: Continuum, 2004).

Caute, David. *The Dancer Defects: The Struggle for Cultural Supremacy during the Cold War* (Oxford, Eng.: Oxford University Press, 2003).

Charters, Ann, ed. *Beat Down to Your Soul: What Was the Beat Generation?* (New York: Penguin, 2001).

Charters, Ann, ed. *The Penguin Book of the Beats* (London: Penguin, 1992).

Ciuraru, Carmela. *Beat Poets* (New York: Knopf, 2002).

Cooper, Brendan. *Dark Airs: John Berryman and the Spiritual Politics of Cold War American Poetry* (Oxford, Eng., Peter Lang, 2009).

Darrah, Fred. *Beat Generation: Glory Days in Greenwich Village* (New York: Prentice Hall, 1996).

Dickstein, Morris. *Leopards in the Temple: The Transformation of American Fiction, 1945-1970* (Cambridge, MA: Harvard University Press, 2002).

Evans, Mike. *The Beats: From Kerouac to Kesey, an Illustrated Journey through the Beat Generation* (Philadelphia: Running Press, 2007).

Gair, Christopher. *The Beat Generation: A Beginner's Guide* (Oxford, Eng.: Oneworld, 2008).

Gold, Herbert. *Fiction of the Fifties: A Decade of American Writing* (New York: Doubleday, 1959).

Greenberg, Martin Harry, and Joseph Olander, eds. *Science Fiction of the Fifties* (New York: Avon, 1979).

Hammond, Andrew. *Cold War Literature: Writing the Global Conflict* (London, Routledge, 2006).

Hendin, Josephine. *A Concise Companion to Post War American Literature and Culture* (New York: Blackwell, 2004).

Johnson, Rob. *Encyclopaedia of Beat Literature* (New York: Facts on File, 2007).

Jumonville, Neil. *Critical Crossings: The New York Intellectuals in Postwar America* (Berkeley: University of California Press, 1991).

Keenan, Larry. *Postcards from the Underground: Portraits of the Beat Generation* (San Francisco: City Lights Books, 1999).

Knight, Brenda. *Women of the Beat Generation: The Writers, Artists and Muses at the Heart of a Revolution* (Berkeley: Conari Press, 1996).

Kostelanetz, Richard. *Politics in the African American Novel: James Weldon Johnson, W.E.B. Du Bois, Richard Wright, and Ralph Ellison* (New York: Greenwood Press, 1991).

Lardas, John. *The Bop Apocalypse: The Religious Visions of Kerouac, Ginsberg and Burroughs* (Urbana: University of Illinois Press, 2001).

Lukin, Josh, ed. *Invisible Suburbs: Recovering Protest Fiction in the 1950s United States* (Jackson: University of Mississippi Press, 2008).

McConachie, Bruce A. *American Theater in the Culture of the Cold War: Producing and Contesting Containment* (Iowa City: University of Iowa Press, 2003.

McNally, Dennis. *Desolate Angel: Jack Kerouac, the Beat Generation and America* (New York: Random House, 1979).

Miles, Barry. *Beat Hotel: Ginsberg, Burroughs and Corso in Paris* (New York: Grove, 2000).

Mordden, Ethan. *Coming Up Roses: The Broadway Musical in the 1950s* (New York: Oxford University Press, 1998).

Morgan, Bill. *The Beat Generation in San Francisco: A Literary Tour* (San Francisco: City Lights Books, 2003).

Morgen, Hickey. *The Bohemian Register: An Annotated Bibliography of the Beat Literary Movement* (Metuchen, NJ: Scarecrow Press, 1990).

Mortenson, Eric. *Capturing the Beat Moment: Cultural Politics and the Poetics of Presence* (Carbondale: Southern Illinois University Press, 2011).

Nadel, Alan. *Containment Culture: American Narratives, Postmodernism and the Atomic Age* (Durham: Duke University Press, 1995).

Newhouse, Thomas. *The Beat Generation and the Popular Novel in the United States, 1945-1970* (Jefferson, NC: McFarland, 2000).

Podhoretz, Norman. *Doings and Undoings: The Fifties and After in American Writing* (New York: Farrar, Straus, 1964).

Phillips, Lisa. *Beat Culture and the New America, 1950-1965* (New York: Whitney Museum, 1995).

Raskin, Johan. *American Scream: Allen Ginsberg's "Howl" and the Making of the Beat Generation* (Berkeley: University of California Press, 2005).

Robinson, Marc, *The Other American Drama* (Cambridge, Eng.: Cambridge University Press, 1994).

Schaub, Thomas. *American Fiction in the Cold War* (Madison: University of Wisconsin Press, 1991).

Stephenson, Gregory. *The Daybreak Boys: Essays on the Literature of the Beat Generation* (Carbondale: Southern Illinois University Press, 1990).

Sterritt, David. *Mad to Be Saved: The Beats, the 50s, and Film* (Carbondale: Southern Illinois University Press, 1998).

Tanner, Tony. *City of Words: American Fiction 1950-1970* (New York: Harper and Row, 1987).

Tytell, John. *Literary Outlaws: Remembering the Beats* (New York: Morrow, 1999).

Tytell, John. *Naked Angels: The Lives and Literature of the Beat Generation* (New York: McGraw Hill, 1976).

Waldman, Anne, ed. *The Beat Book: Writings from the Beat Generation* (Boston: Shambhala, 1996).

Watson, Steven. *The Birth of the Beat Generation: Visionaries, Rebels and Hipsters, 1944-1960* (New York: Pantheon Books, 1995).

Wilson, Edmund, *The Fifties: From Notebooks and Diaries of the Period*, ed. Leon Edel (New York: Farrar, Straus, 1986).

Music

Garrett, Charles H., *Struggling to Define a Nation: American Music and the Twentieth Century* (Berkeley: University of California Press: The Roth Family Foundation Music in American Endowment, 2008).

Heintze, James R., ed. *Perspectives on American Music since 1950* (New York: Garland, 1999).

Jenness, David, and Don Velsey. *Classic American Popular Song: The Second Half-Century, 1950–2000* (New York: Routledge, 2006).

Karolyi, Otto. *Modern American Music; From Charles Ives to the Minimalists* (London: Cygnus Arts; Madison, NJ: Fairleigh Dickinson University Press, 1996).

Kirkpatrick, John, et al., *New Grove Twentieth-Century Masters: Ives, Thomson, Sessions, Cowell, Gershwin, Copland, Carter, Barber, Cage, Bernstein* (New York: Norton, 1988).

Machlis, Joseph. *American Composers of Our Time* (1963; reprint, Westport, CT: Greenwood Press, 1990).

Peress, Maurice. *Dvořák to Duke Ellington: A Conductor Explores American Music and Its African American Roots* (Oxford, Eng.: Oxford University Press, 2004).

Rich, Alan: *American Pioneers: Ives to Cage and Beyond* (London: Phaidon, 2008).

Sanjek, Russell, and David Sanjek. *American Popular Music Business in the Twentieth Century* (Oxford, Eng.: Oxford University Press, 1991).

Simmons, Walter. *The Music of William Schuman, Vincent Persichetti, and Peter Mennin: Voices of Stone* (Lanham, MD: Scarecrow Press, 2011).

Simmons, Walter. *Voices in the Wilderness: Six Neo-Romantic Composers* (Lanham, MD: Scarecrow Press 2004).

Tawa, Nicholas E. *A Most Wonderous Babble: American Art Composers, Their Music, and the American Scene, 1950-1985* (New York: Greenwood Press, 1987).

Zak, Albin J., III. *I Don't Sound Like Nobody: Remaking Music in 1950s America* (Ann Arbor: University of Michigan Press, 2010.

Race and Ethnic Relations

Bartley, Numan. *The Rise of Massive Resistance: Race and Politics in the South during the 1950s* (Baton Rouge: Louisiana State University Press, 1969).

Biondi, Martha. *To Stand and Fight: The Struggle for Civil Rights in Postwar New York City* (Cambridge, MA: Harvard University Press, 2003).

Borstelmann, Thomas. *The Cold War and the Color Line: American Race Relations in the Global Arena* (Cambridge, MA: Harvard University Press, 2001).

Burns, Stewart. *To the Mountaintop: Martin Luther King Jr.'s Sacred Mission to Save America, 1955-1968* (San Francisco: HarperSanFrancisco, 2004).

Conyers, James L., Jr., ed. *Engines of the Black Power Movement: Essays on the Influence of Civil Rights Actions, Arts, and Islam* (Jefferson, NC: McFarland, 2007).

Davis, Thomas. *Race Relations in the United States: 1940-1960* (Westport, CT: Greenwood Press, 2008).

King, Richard. *Race, Culture and the Intellectuals, 1940-1970* (Baltimore: John Hopkins University Press, 2004).

Lewis, George. *The White South and the Red Menace: Segregationists, Anticommunism, and Massive Resistance, 1945-1965* (Gainesville: University Press of Florida, 2004).

Miller, Paul. *The Postwar Struggle for Civil Rights: African Americans in San Francisco, 1945-1975* (New York: Routledge, 2010).

Polenberg, Richard. *One Nation Divisible: Class, Race and Ethnicity in the United States since 1938.* (London: Penguin, 1980).

Robinson, Greg. *After Camp: Portraits in Midcentury Japanese American Life and Politics* (Berkeley: University of California Press, 2012).

Theoharis, Jeanne, and Komozi Woodard, eds. *Freedom North: Black Freedom Struggles outside the South, 1940-1980* (New York: Palgrave Macmillan, 2003).

Religion

Carroll, Jackson, et al. *Religion in America, 1950 to the Present* (San Francisco: Harper and Row, 1979).

Conyers, James L., Jr., ed. *Engines of the Black Power Movement: Essays on the Influence of Civil Rights Actions, Arts, and Islam* (Jefferson, NC: McFarland, 2007).

Ellwood, Robert. *The Fifties Spiritual Marketplace: American Religion in a Decade of Conflict* (New Brunswick, NJ: Rutgers University Press, 1997).

Ellwood, Robert. *1950, Crossroads of American Religious Life* (Louisville, KY: Westminster John Knox Press, 2000).

Hedstrom. Matthew S. *The Rise of Liberal Religion: Book Culture and American Spirituality in the Twentieth Century* (Oxford, Eng.: Oxford University Press, 2013).

Hudnut-Beumler , James. *Looking for God in the Suburbs: The Religion of the American Dream and Its Critics, 1945-1965* (New Brunswick, NJ: Rutgers University Press, 1994).

Marty, Martin E. *The Improper Opinion: Mass Media and the Christian Faith* (Philadelphia, Westminster Press 1961).

Neusner, Jacob. *Stranger at Home: "The Holocaust," Zionism, and American Judaism* (1981; reprint, Atlanta: Scholars Press, 1997).

Newman, William M., and Peter L. Halvorson. *Patterns in Pluralism: A Portrait of American Religion, 1952-1971* (Washington, DC: Glenmary Research Center, 1980).

Niebuhr, Reinhold. *Pious and Secular America* (New York: Scribner's, 1958).

Shapiro, Edward S. *A Time for Healing: American Jewry since World War II* (Baltimore: Johns Hopkins University Press, 1992).

Silk, Mark. *Spiritual Politics: Religion and America since World War II* (New York: Simon and Schuster, 1988).

Stevens, Jason W. *God-Fearing and Free: A Spiritual History of America's Cold War* (Cambridge, MA: Harvard University Press, 2010).

2013 Title List

Visit **www.greyhouse.com** for Product Information, Table of Contents and Sample Pages

General Reference
America's College Museums
American Environmental Leaders: From Colonial Times to the Present
An African Biographical Dictionary
An Encyclopedia of Human Rights in the United States
Constitutional Amendments
Encyclopedia of African-American Writing
Encyclopedia of the Continental Congress
Encyclopedia of Gun Control & Gun Rights
Encyclopedia of Invasions & Conquests
Encyclopedia of Prisoners of War & Internment
Encyclopedia of Religion & Law in America
Encyclopedia of Rural America
Encyclopedia of the United States Cabinet, 1789-2010
Encyclopedia of War Journalism
Encyclopedia of Warrior Peoples & Fighting Groups
From Suffrage to the Senate: America's Political Women
Nations of the World
Political Corruption in America
Speakers of the House of Representatives, 1789-2009
The Environmental Debate: A Documentary History
The Evolution Wars: A Guide to the Debates
The Religious Right: A Reference Handbook
The Value of a Dollar: 1860-2009
The Value of a Dollar: Colonial Era
This is Who We Were: A Companion to the 1940 Census
This is Who We Were: The 1910s
This is Who We Were: The 1950s
US Land & Natural Resource Policy
Weather America
Working Americans 1770-1869 Vol. IX: Revol. War to the Civil War
Working Americans 1880-1999 Vol. I: The Working Class
Working Americans 1880-1999 Vol. II: The Middle Class
Working Americans 1880-1999 Vol. III: The Upper Class
Working Americans 1880-1999 Vol. IV: Their Children
Working Americans 1880-2003 Vol. V: At War
Working Americans 1880-2005 Vol. VI: Women at Work
Working Americans 1880-2006 Vol. VII: Social Movements
Working Americans 1880-2007 Vol. VIII: Immigrants
Working Americans 1880-2009 Vol. X: Sports & Recreation
Working Americans 1880-2010 Vol. XI: Inventors & Entrepreneurs
Working Americans 1880-2011 Vol. XII: Our History through Music
Working Americans 1880-2012 Vol. XIII: Education & Educators
World Cultural Leaders of the 20th & 21st Centuries

Business Information
Complete Television, Radio & Cable Industry Directory
Directory of Business Information Resources
Directory of Mail Order Catalogs
Directory of Venture Capital & Private Equity Firms
Environmental Resource Handbook
Food & Beverage Market Place
Grey House Homeland Security Directory
Grey House Performing Arts Directory
Hudson's Washington News Media Contacts Directory
New York State Directory
Sports Market Place Directory
The Rauch Guides – Industry Market Research Reports
Sweets Directory by McGraw Hill Construction

Health Information
Comparative Guide to American Hospitals
Complete Directory for Pediatric Disorders
Complete Directory for People with Chronic Illness
Complete Directory for People with Disabilities
Complete Mental Health Directory

Diabetes in America: A Geographic & Demographic Analysis
Directory of Health Care Group Purchasing Organizations
Directory of Hospital Personnel
HMO/PPO Directory
Medical Device Register
Obesity in America: A Geographic & Demographic Analysis
Older Americans Information Directory
Pharmaceutical Industry Directory

Statistics & Demographics
America's Top-Rated Cities
America's Top-Rated Small Towns & Cities
America's Top-Rated Smaller Cities
American Tally
Ancestry & Ethnicity in America
Comparative Guide to American Hospitals
Comparative Guide to American Suburbs
Profiles of America
Profiles of... Series – State Handbooks
The Hispanic Databook

Education Information
Charter School Movement
Comparative Guide to American Elementary & Secondary Schools
Complete Learning Disabilities Directory
Educators Resource Directory
Special Education

Financial Ratings Series
TheStreet.com Ratings Guide to Bond & Money Market Mutual Funds
TheStreet.com Ratings Guide to Common Stocks
TheStreet.com Ratings Guide to Exchange-Traded Funds
TheStreet.com Ratings Guide to Stock Mutual Funds
TheStreet.com Ratings Ultimate Guided Tour of Stock Investing
Weiss Ratings Consumer Box Set
Weiss Ratings Guide to Banks & Thrifts
Weiss Ratings Guide to Credit Unions
Weiss Ratings Guide to Health Insurers
Weiss Ratings Guide to Life & Annuity Insurers
Weiss Ratings Guide to Property & Casualty Insurers

Bowker's Books In Print® Titles
Books In Print®
Books In Print® Supplement
American Book Publishing Record® Annual
American Book Publishing Record® Monthly
Books Out Loud™
Bowker's Complete Video Directory™
Children's Books In Print®
Complete Directory of Large Print Books & Serials™
El-Hi Textbooks & Serials In Print®
Forthcoming Books®
Law Books & Serials In Print™
Medical & Health Care Books In Print™
Publishers, Distributors & Wholesalers of the US™
Subject Guide to Books In Print®
Subject Guide to Children's Books In Print®

Canadian General Reference
Associations Canada
Canadian Almanac & Directory
Canadian Environmental Resource Guide
Canadian Parliamentary Guide
Financial Services Canada
Governments Canada
Libraries Canada
The History of Canada

Grey House Publishing

4919 Route 22, PO Box 56, Amenia NY 12501-0056 | (800) 562-2139 | www.greyhouse.com | books@greyhouse.com